Ecosystem Health and Sustainable Agriculture 3

Rural Development and Land Use

Editors:
Ingrid Karlsson and Lars Rydén

Editors:Ingrid Karlsson and Lars Rydén

Layout: Magnus Lehman
Cover Photo: Gary Scott
Print: Elanders
ISBN 978-91-86189-11-2

CONTENTS

Series Preface

The Baltic Sea and the North American Great Lakes are influenced by many different and similar problems affecting its environmental status. The Baltic Sea was classified by the United Nations International Maritime Organization (IMO) as a Particularly Sensitive Sea Area (PSSA) in April 2004. Both the Baltic Sea and the Great Lakes are of ecological, socioeconomic, cultural or scientifically importance. Discharge of nutrients from agriculture and waste-water treatment plants, as well as from industries, transportation and other human activities leads to eutrophication and other forms of pollution. The Ecosystem Health and Sustainable Agriculture project aims at updating knowledge in the field of rural development, sustainable agriculture and animal health pertaining to the Baltic Sea Region and to some degree also the Great Lakes region.

The agricultural activities are often based on individual producer´s decisions and on their attitudes, knowledge and level of technology. It is however also based on political and economic considerations, attitudes and opinions from the society. Thus, continuously updated scientifically based knowledge, both from an environmental, social and economic view, need to be disseminated and applied with a much increased ambition. Technological facts may be well known, but still strong social and economic reasons and pressure from outside to make short term profits hinders the appropriate application of relevant measures. This is the reason why we have all parts of the sustainability concept covered in our texts: the ecological, the social, the economical, and the institutional/juridical.

The books produced as part of this project include:

1. Sustainable Agriculture
2. Ecology and Animal Health
3. Rural Development and Land Use

These three books are based on experience from the Baltic Sea and Great Lakes Regions and written by prominent experts and scientists from the two regions. Two networks have been involved in the production of the books, The Baltic University Programme (BUP) and the Envirovet Baltic Networks. The BUP is a network of approximately 220 universities in the drainage basin to the Baltic Sea that cooperates on sustainable development, studies of the region, its environment and its political changes. The program, founded in 1991 at Uppsala University, Sweden, operates by producing courses, holding conferences and seminars. In 2010, the BUP network delivered courses at more than 100 universities serving nearly 9,500 undergraduate and graduate students. The Envirovet Baltic, a network of environmental health scientist/ educators from USA and the nine countries bordering the Baltic Sea, was founded in 2001 on an initiative of the College of Veterinary Medicine, University of Illinois and the Centre for Reproductive Biology in Uppsala,

Swedish University of Agricultural Sciences with scientists from universities in the Baltic Sea Region (BSR). Courses are delivered separately by each university in the networks in both cases. Preferably all the three books should be studied to give a comprehensive overview on actual experience and research findings. We have chosen to use the ecosystem health concept to understand and prevent problems for the future. It is our aim that the books will strengthen knowledge on ecosystems and its interaction with human activities in a wider sense. The texts presented in this book should deepen and update our knowledge on all aspects of rural development and sustainable agriculture. Our aim is furthermore to provide explanations of the problem complexity and examples of problem solving.

Target groups are students, teachers, experts and people working in government offices, ministries, municipalities and as agricultural advisors and managers of different natural resource based activities in rural areas.

The Baltic Sea Watershed with its population of more than 85 million people contributes to an ongoing environmental disaster. The disaster is well documented and can be summarized as:

1) Eutrophication from heavy contamination of excess Nitrogen and Phosphorus – sources are diffuse sources, point sources and atmospheric downfall
2) Excess fishing, distorting the marine ecosystem; diminishing cod population being the most drastic example
3) Contaminants other than nutrients, mainly PCB, heavy metals, oil spill, human and animal drugs, etc.
4) Distortions of the biodiversity of the sea, e.g extinction of many indigineous species, and introduction of alien species which distort the ecological balance drastically
5) Threats connected to climate change

Sustainable Agriculture and Sustainable Rural Development

"Sustainable agriculture" has become a popular way of expressing that what society wants is an environmentally sound, productive, economically viable, and socially desirable agriculture. However, the concept of agricultural sustainability does not lend itself to precise definition. Agriculture is practiced in so many climates and in different cultural contexts, so "sustainable agriculture" cannot possibly imply a special way of thinking or of using farming practices.

Sustainable agriculture is an approach to securing the necessary resources for safeguarding global food production, biodiversity reserves, recreation needs, water quality and well developed rural areas and wildlife areas. It can also be an effective means of poverty reduction and of achieving the Millennium Development Goals, as well as means of mitigating climate change. It is also about health, welfare, respect and ethics regarding animals and man, as well as quality of food and feed. In other words they are truly transdisciplinary and represent a new holistic outlook on ecosystem health and sustainable agriculture.

We have chosen to give agriculture a wider meaning than the traditional. It is common to understand agriculture as being the activity which is securing food supply. But as we shall see in the chapters on historical trends, activities on the countryside have always been complex and integrated with other activities in rural areas, such as small business, forestry, fishing, and other activities. Also several hundred years ago, the farmer combined biological and technical knowledge with economical and organisational skill, and very often he or she made money from different other jobs like carpentry, timber and coal production, horse- and oxen driving, cheese production, food conservation etc. Today the diversity in income generation is even higher and in fact, every farming enterprise has at least one or two side activities. Our definition of agriculture as main activity would today be: to produce and manage biomass. Some examples, explained in more detailed in our books, are (besides food production):

- public goods in the form of natural and cultural amenities to benefit the ecosystem (such as management national parks and of landscape for a certain type of desired biodiversity)
- fish production
- biomass for timber and fibre products
- biomass for energy production

- social caretaking of, for instance, sick people or people who needs rehabilitation from criminal or other lives
- tourism (including views, maintenance of tracks, camping sites, buildings, etc)
- recreation (such as horseback riding and horse racing, golf- and soccer fields, fishing sites, hunting etc)
- animal raising and caretaking (dog- and cat kennels etc)

A widespread definition of sustainability of agriculture, with which we sympathise, is the FAO (Food and Agricultural Organisation of the UN) statement:

> *"Overall objectives of technological interventions for sustainable agriculture can be summarized as food security and risk resilience, environmental compatibility, economic viability, and social acceptability."*

An addition to the FAO definition would need, as we see it, the following phrasing: *Sustainable agriculture is not linked to any particular technological practice. Sustainable agriculture should have adaptability and flexibility over time to respond to demands for biomass production but it should also have ability to protect the soil, the genetic resources and the waters.*

We also want to recall the definition done for the specific Baltic Sea Region, as expressed by the Baltic Agenda 21:

Sustainable agriculture is the production of high-quality food and other agricultural products and services in the long run, with consideration taken to economy and social structure in such a way that the resource base of non-renewable and renewable resources is maintained. Important sub goals are:

- *The farmers` income should be sufficient to provide a fair standard of living in the agricultural community;*
- *The farmers should practice production methods which do not threaten human or animal health or degrade the environment, including biodiversity, and a the same time minimise the environmental problems that future generations must assume responsibility for;*
- *Non-renewable resources gradually have to be replaced by renewable resources, and that re-circulation of non-renewable resources is maximized;*
- *Sustainable agriculture will meet the needs of food and recreation, and preserve the landscape, cultural values and historical heritage of rural areas, and contribute to the creation of stable, well-developed and secure rural communities;*
- *The ethical aspects of agricultural production are secured.*

It is our firm belief that agriculture and related activities can, if well managed, be positive for the ecosystems and for biodiversity. Contrary, agricultural activities can also give disastrous effects to the environment including humans living in the area. Often national goals are not only to sustain a food security of the country, but also to keep an open landscape and rural lifestyle. A sustainable rural development has its backbone in a sustainable agriculture.

The books were produced with the main financing from the Swedish International Development Authority, SIDA. Additional funding was received from the Swedish Environmental Protection Agency, the Swedish Institute, the University of Illinois, the Hewlett Foundation and some private donors, as well as within the networks of the Baltic University Programme and Envirovet Baltic.

Authors have to a great degree contributed with unpaid work. All these contributions are gratefully acknowledged.

Uppsala August 2011

Christine Jakobsson, Leif Norrgren, Ingrid Karlsson, and Jeffrey Levengood

Introduction

Ingrid Karlsson and Lars Rydén
Uppsala University
Kalev Sepp
Estonian University of Life Sciences, Tartu

A Perspective on Development

This book is about rural development and its main geographical focus is the Baltic Sea Region in Northern Europe (see Figure 1). Comparisons are made to other northern parts of the world when appropriate, (e.g. North America). Much of the information presented is relevant for development in general, and describes past and present problems and solutions with the aim of providing ideas and tools for future sustainable development in northern rural areas.

Development is often perceived as change for the better (for humans) in our societies – or at least positive change for the majority of the population. Certainly, during recent decades new technologies, economic investments and political reforms have improved the lives of many. Material standards have improved; we have more belongings, live better and travel more freely, health care has improved and communications are easier. Such development may have been slower in some countries than others, but in a global perspective all countries in the Baltic Sea region are perceived as 'rich'.

In the past few decades we have seen dramatic changes in the Baltic Sea region. However, this is a small part of a development process that has more or less increased material standards of living since the 17th century and the beginning of the modern scientific era. It is not always easy to see life in this long-term perspective, but films and books on historical times can help.

In general, 'development' in this sense is regarded as being an improvement. It is only recently that an understanding has emerged that such development has occurred at a cost. This insight comes from a new direction. In general reformers of our societies, politicians and economists have not included 'Nature' or 'the environment' in their calculations. The environment has instead been regarded as a background condition always available, always providing, limitless, robust and impervious to harm.

For example, in Marxist theory nature and natural resources were perceived as free assets and were not allocated a price. In capitalist economies natural resources were exploited and sold for a price, with the costs of the environmental consequences of extraction not included

Box 1. Development 1900-2000

Global population increased 4 times from 1.5 to 6 billion
Global economy increased 14 times
Industrial production increased 40 times
Energy use increased 16 times , almost entirely by fossil fuels
Carbon dioxide emissions increased 17 times
Sulphur dioxide emissions increased 13 times
Ocean fishing catches increased 9 times
Blue whales decreased by 99.75%
Number of pigs increased 9 times
Agricultural land increased 2 times
Deforestation was 20%

Source: McNeill, 2000

but termed 'externalities'. This was (and continues to be) a classical market failure. In both systems, the environmental conditions for running a society and for providing everything from space, food and shelter to beauty and wilderness were not taken care of properly and as a result things have gone very wrong. While the costs of environmental impacts and use of resources were not being paid, we also increased our use of resources.

At the end of the 1990s the USA historian John McNeill took on the task of writing a global environmental history (McNeill, 2000). His starting point was the conviction that the 'environmentalists' were complaining about the recent impact on the environment without understanding that the situation was normal, that 'there is nothing new under the sun'. However during his research he changed his mind. Our situation at the beginning of the 21st century is in fact unique and unparalleled in the history of Earth and of our societies. Some of his data are summarised above (Box 1).

Figure 1. The Baltic Sea region. The Baltic basin, i.e. the drainage area of the Baltic Sea including Kattegatt, is marked by the bold line. In this region all water flows towards the Baltic Sea. Source: UNEP, Grid Arendal.

Since 1900, the world population has increased over fourfold, from 1.5 to more than 7 billion people. On top of that, each individual today on average uses about four times more resources per capita than in 1900. As a result, during this period resource use has increased close to 16-fold, at different rates for different kinds of resources.

Much of this development was driven by the North. The average data disguise the fact that Northern Europe and the Europeans inhabiting North America use the lion's share of these resources, giving rise to an exceptional gap between rich and poor in the world: The 12% that live in North America and Western Europe today account for 60% of private consumption and the former colonies of Europe in Southern Asia and sub-Saharan Africa, where 33% of the global population lives, account for only 3.2%.

If we look more carefully at development over time, we see that the rate of growth has actually accelerated. There is close to exponential growth in resource use. In industrialized western societies this was typical for the period about 1955-1975. Since then resource use is increasing less rapidly, but still increasing. Of course, we cannot go on like this forever. There are limits to growth and these limits are set by our planet.

That is why we need a different type of development: We need to re-use and make smarter use of our only non-earth resource – solar energy. We need a form of development that does not lead to problems but that is sustainable.

A Note on the Regions

The regions dealt with in the book are the Baltic Sea Region (BSR) and the Great Lakes District (GLD) of North America, bridging the USA and Canada. These areas concerned are delineated here using a definition based on their drainage basin or watershed. Other definitions used are often based on political divisions, but in our case drainage basins are relevant since a common concern in the regions is the common water and lake systems, which is greatly influenced by agriculture and other rural practices.

The Baltic Sea region is defined as the watershed of the Baltic Sea and includes the whole or parts of 14 countries: Norway, Denmark, Sweden, Finland, The Federal Republic of Russia, Estonia, Latvia, Lithuania, Ukraine, Republic of Belarus, Slovak Republic, Czech Republic, Poland and Germany (See further Table 1).

There is much space and diversity in nature in these respective countries. The area within the Baltic Sea watershed is predominantly (>90%) rural, but people are rapidly becoming increasingly urbanised, especially in the more densely populated countries of Denmark and Germany. Thus the majority of the population is urban, but almost all land area is rural.

Table 1. Country Statistics. Source: CIA Factbook. https://www.cia.gov/library/publications/the-world-factbook/.

Country	Area (km²)	Population 2011[a]	GDP/capita ($ 2010)[a]	Arable land (% 2005)	Urban population (% 2010)	Agriculture share of GDP (% 2010)	Agriculture share of labor force (% year)
Belarus	207,600	9,577,552	13,600	26.77	75	9.4	14.0 (2003)
Czech Rep.	78,867	10,190,213	25,600	38.82	74	2.4	3.1 (2009)
Denmark	43,094	5,529,888	36,600	52.59	87	1.2	2.5 (2005)
Estonia	45,228	1,282,963	19,100	12.05	69	2.7	2.8 (2008)
Finland	338,145	5,259,250	35,400	6.54	85	2.9	4.9 (2009)
Germany	357,022	81,471,834	35,700	33.13	74	0.9	2.4 (2005)
Latvia	64,589	2,204,708	14,700	28.19	68	4.0	12.1 (2005)
Lithuania	65,300	3,535,547	16,000	44.81	67	3.4[b]	14.0 (2008)
Norway	323,802	4,691,849	54,600	2.7	79	2.5	2.9 (2008)
Poland	312,685	38,441,588	18,800	40.25	61	3.4	17.4 (2005)
Russia	17,098,242	138,739,892	15,900	7.17	73	4.0	10.0 (2008)
Slovak Rep.	49,035	5,477,038	22,000	29.23	55	3.9	3.5 (2009)
Sweden	450,295	9,088,728	39,100	5.93	85	1.9	1.1 (2008)
Ukraine	603,550	45,134,707	6,700	53.8	69	9.4	15.8 (2008)
USA	9,826,675	313,232,044	47,200	18.01	82	1.1	0.7 (2009)
Canada	9,984,670	34,030,589	39,400	4.57	81	2.2	2.0 (2006)

Please note data referer to national statistics. Source: CIA Factbook. https://www.cia.gov/library/publications/the-world-factbook/.
a estimation, b 2008 est.

What is Sustainable Development?

The sustainability discussion thus starts by recognising the mismatch between what exists (natural resources) and what we use. This needs to be changed. Sustainable development aims to lead to a society that provides for itself through long-term available resources. That is, it uses only renewable resources. However, this is not all. Sustainability also requires decent social and economic conditions for all citizens in society.

Sustainability can be most basically illustrated in a graph showing resource use and social and economic conditions for each country (or any other part of society). The best known example involves plotting the ecological footprint as a measure of resource use against Human Development Index (See Figure 2) as a measure of social and economic development. The resulting graph shows that no country is sustainable at present. The 'richer' countries (including all BSR countries) are using too many resources, while the 'poor' countries (especially in Africa) have too low HDI.

Sustainability refers to the long-term – even forever. Therefore it includes the requirement to preserve the long-term survival and wellbeing of society and the natural environment. A sustainable society is one that allows sufficient natural resources and decent conditions for the following generations, grandchildren and their grandchildren.

There are thus limited resources available. A very sensitive issue is how these resources should be divided between users. This is a particularly critical issue since it is obvious that resources are today divided very unevenly both between countries and within countries. Many politicians and scientists argue that this current uneven distribution of resources is the greatest threat to our societies

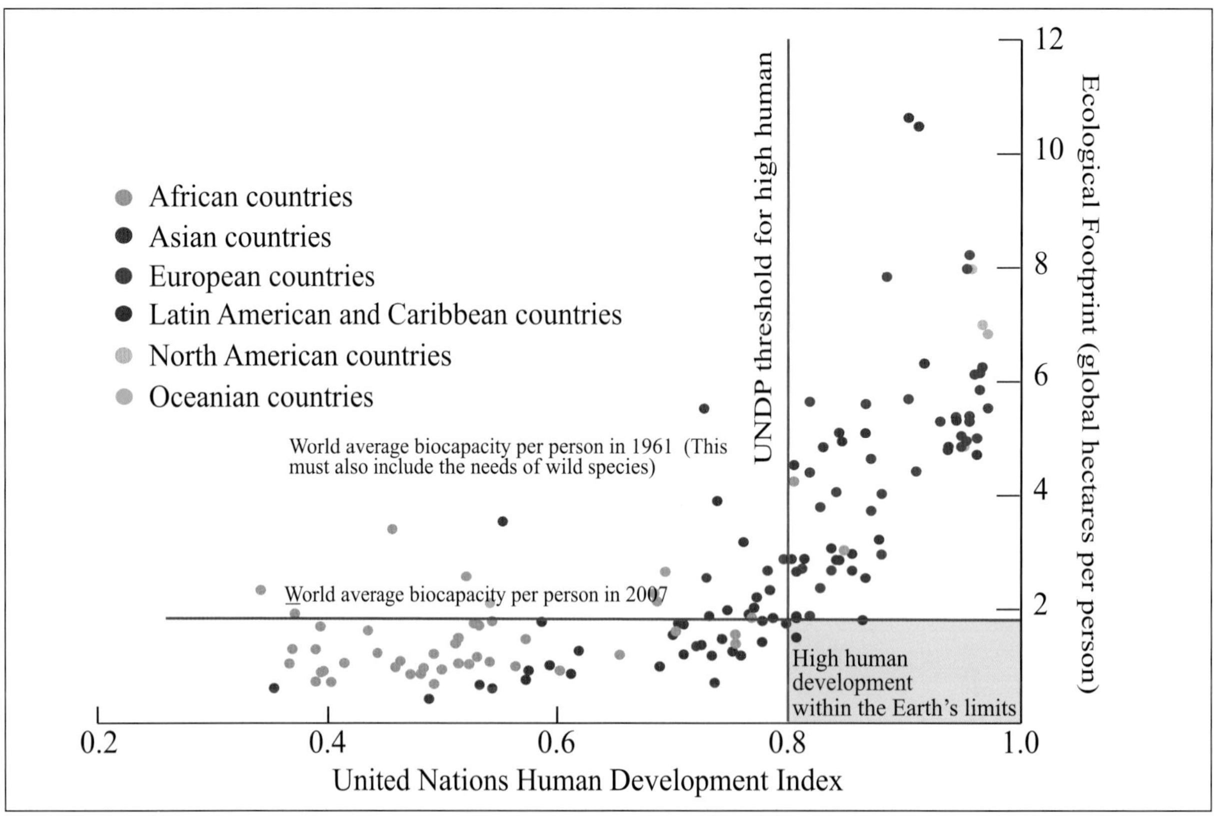

Figure 2. Ecological footprint in relation to United Nations Human Development Index, 2007. Ecological Footprint Atlas, 2010.

and their sustainability. Many NGOs and governments regard the even distribution of all resources between all people living on the planet as the basic starting point in the ongoing climate negotiations.

The Ethics of Sustainable Development

Sustainable development is a highly normative concept. The first clear statement on a value to be protected through sustainable development was included in the 1980 World Conservation Strategy, which was put forward in a joint effort by the International Union for the Conservation of Nature (IUCN), the United Nations Environmental Program (UNEP) and the World Wildlife Fund (WWF). This strategy very clearly pointed out that the extremely rapid large-scale destruction of biodiversity is highly unethical and a violation of man's duty to protect and conserve the planet. To achieve this the Conservation Strategy identified sustainable development as the solution (the beginning of a more public debate on sustainable development.) However, the motives listed for using the strategy are not just ethical, as scientific and objective circumstances are also referred to for the purpose of explaining and promoting the strategy.

In addition, sustainability includes our duty not to destroy the possibilities for future generations to lead a good life. This is also a normative statement. There is no scientific reason for this point of view but it was the main message from the Brundtland Commission in 1987, which used this normative platform to practically 'define' what it meant by sustainability. The chair of the Commission, Dr Brundtland, has since repeatedly stated that there will be no future if mankind does not accept the ethics of sustainable development and acknowledge its duty to future generations.

Sustainability also refers to the just distribution of resources between all people living here and now. This argument was very much a part of the statements from the United Nations Conference on Environment and Development (UNCED) in Rio de Janeiro in 1992.

All three values of sustainability can be most clearly formulated in terms of an ethics of justice. There are three types of justice:

- Justice between mankind and all other life forms (bioethics)
- Justice between us and future people (inter-generational justice)
- Justice between us living here and now (intra-generational justice)

It is clear that one can easily find other, non-normative, arguments for all three kinds of justice. This makes the normative dimension of sustainability even stronger.

Box 2. Definitions of Rural

Although policies for 'rural' areas have been discussed and analysed for hundreds of years, there is no single commonly internationally accepted definition. The three main reasons for this, according to a recent communication from EU (EU, 2009, pp. 2-3), are:

(1) There are various perceptions of what is (and what is not) rural and of the elements characterising 'rurality' (natural, economic, cultural, etc.)
(2) There is an inherent need to have a tailor-made definition of rurality according to the 'object' analysed or policy concerned.
(3) It is difficult to collect relevant data at the level of basic geographical units (administrative unit, grid cell, plot, etc.).

The Politics of Sustainable Development

Organisations that uphold sustainability have defined the concept in a variety of ways and have interpreted it according to their view of the environment and man's relation to the latter:

- The World Commission on Environment and Development (WCED, 1987) noted in the Brundtland report that 'Sustainable development is development that meets the needs of the present without compromising the ability of future generations to meet their own needs.'
- The International Union for the Conservation of Nature, UNEP and the World Wide Fund for Nature

(IUCN, and WWF, 1991) states that: 'Sustainable development means improving the quality of life while living within the carrying capacity of supporting ecosystems.'
- The International Council for Local Environment Initiative (ICLEI, 1994) states that: 'Sustainable development is development that delivers basic environmental, social and economic services to all residents of a community without threatening the viability of the natural, built and social systems upon which the delivery of these services depends.'

The Brundtland definition has the highest priority in official documents in Europe. The UN has adopted the Brundtland definition of sustainable development, which has given it a global dimension. The EU work has its standpoint in the report 'Our Common Future'. The combination of 'sustainable' and 'development' was referred to in the Brundtland report, but 'environment' and 'development' were introduced already in discussions back at the UN conference in Stockholm in 1972.

ICLEI (1994) to some extent introduced another definition. "*Sustainable development is development that delivers basic environmental, social and economic services to all,without threatening the viability of the natural, built and social systems upon which the delivery of these services depends*". This definition is based on a similar definition as the Brundtland Report but emphasises equal distribution between human beings today and does not meet the responsibility for coming generations. IUCN, UNEP and WWF (1991) defined the concept in a slightly different way: "*Sustainable development means improving the quality of life while living within the carrying capacity of supporting ecosystems*". Their definition is interpreted as a combination of an anthropocentric and ecocentric perspective.

What is Sustainable Rural Development?

This book also provides a short historical background to the current situation in rural areas. It appears that rural areas have never been completely sustainable anywhere; on the contrary, quite drastic changes have taken place in rural areas, especially during the past hundred years. However, rural people are more attached to their homestead, and they travel less frequently than urban people. This is often seen as the result of a conscious choice of lifestyle, but in many cases it is also the result of lower economic standards and fewer possibilities to have education and training leading to jobs in the city.

The very definition of 'rurality' is of course that it is a sparsely inhabited area, from which follows that it is further away from large urban areas (see Box 2 for a discussion on definitions of rurality).

In short, the EU definition is based on a definition initially introduced by the OECD that a rural area is an area with a population density of less than 150 inhabitants per square kilometre. A rural region is *predominantly* rural if more than 50% of the population of the region is living in rural communities with less than 150 inhabitants/km^2.

According to this standard definition, more than 91% of the territory of the EU is 'rural' or 'predominantly rural', and this area is home to more than 56% of the EU population (Figure 3). Human activities, mainly in agriculture and forestry, influence the rural landscape to a large extent. The types of farming and forest production practised in Europe today are largely governed by EU legislation and EU economic incentives, especially in EU countries. In addition, the development of other rural activities is stimulated by EU regional and rural development policies.

According to the same standard definition, in North-West Russia all geographical regions are rural, although in the Leningrad oblast most of the inhabitants actually live in St Petersburg City and its suburban surroundings. Ukraine is more densely populated than North-West Russia, but only one region, Donetsk, is not rural according to the OECD standards. Belarus consists of 90% rural land by its own definition.

Natural ecosystems change, but perhaps not as drastically as human environments. However, nature in rural areas is not only affected by climate, geology and other site-specific properties, but is also much affected and sometimes more or less destroyed by human activities, especially wars, pollution, urban expansion, mining, energy installations, infrastructure, agricultural practices, etc.

Sustainable rural development does not imply that nature is left untouched. Unlike other mammals, humans have produced an extraordinary high number of individuals to provide for and have assumed the right to manage all resources on planet Earth to support their own expansion – but ecosystem balance is also needed for the future of mankind. If we want to survive as a species, natural resources such as biodiversity, minerals, agricultural and forestry land must be managed well and saved for future generations. Humans should find a way to balance their populations on a global scale in relation to the habitat needs of other species. Last but not least, in line with the UN Declaration on Human Rights, the standard of living, infrastructure, health services and education possibilities should be just and fairly distributed (between humans), so that they are enjoyed by rural people at the same level of quality as by urban dwellers.

A process aimed at local or regional definition of sustainable rural development should always involve local stakeholders. Thus, the freedom of local people to define their own needs and take part in decisions that affect their own lives is a cornerstone in defining how to achieve sustainable rural development.

Having said that, we can only give general comments on the key challenges for sustainable rural development:

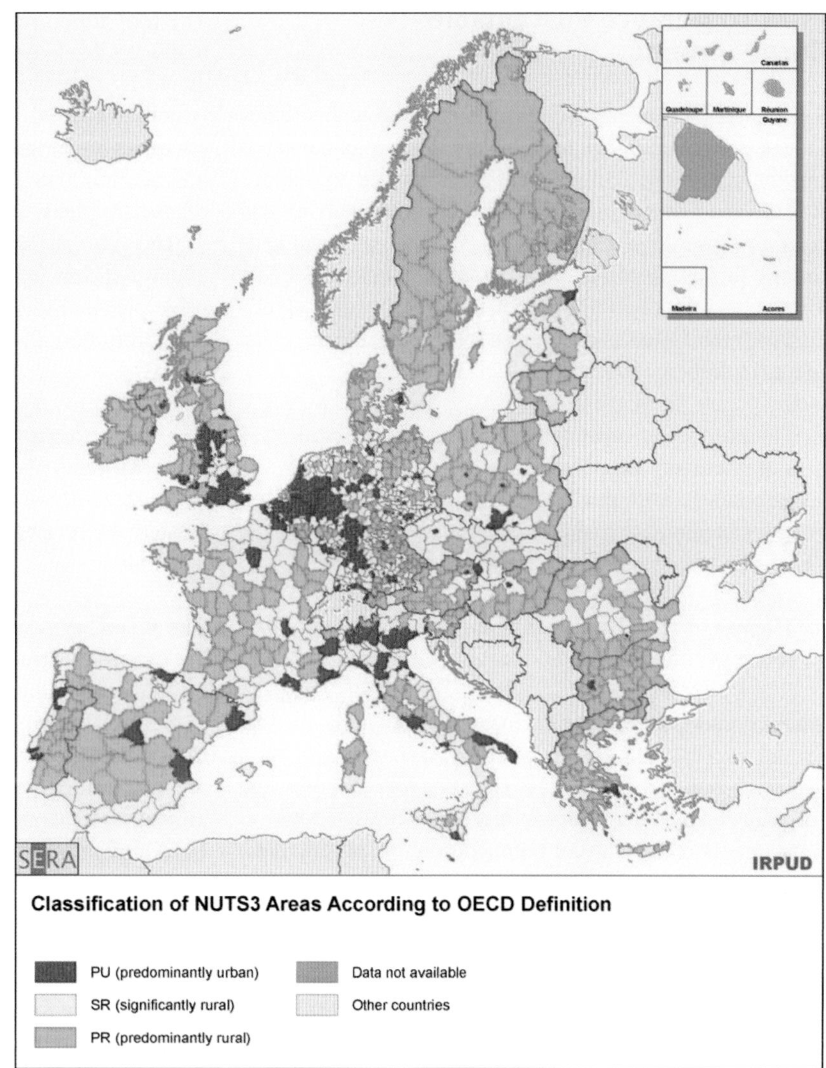

Figure 3. Classification of rural areas based on the OECD NUTS3 definition. NUTS= Nomenclature of territorial units for statistics. Source: Copus et. al., 2006.

- The organisation of human activities in the landscape to protect and manage global and long-term resources
- Keeping and maintaining ecosystems
- Supporting long-term biodiversity
- Establishing the necessary interactions between urban and rural areas
- Developing a sound economy, including job opportunities, etc.
- Developing good social conditions regarding inequities, gender issues, indigenous peoples, other minority groups, etc.

How to Achieve Sustainable Development

The general statements and norms connected with sustainable development do not help us very much in understanding the conditions and practical steps needed to achieve it. However, many researchers have contributed to this for more than 20 years. In his study on the physical conditions for sustainability, John Holmberg from Chalmers University of Technology in Gothenburg, Sweden, identified four fundamental conditions for sustainable development (Holmberg, 1992):

1. The productive capacity of the ecosphere must not systematically deteriorate.
2. Substances from the lithosphere must not systematically accumulate in the ecosphere.
3. Human-made substances must not systematically accumulate in the ecosphere.
4. The use of resources must be efficient and just, with respect for human needs.

These preconditions are easy to exemplify:

1. If non-renewable resources (e.g. phosphorus) are used up or renewable resources (e.g. fish) are used well above their capacity for regeneration, the productive capacity of the ecosphere will deteriorate.
2. When fossil carbon is combusted for energy purposes its end-product, carbon dioxide, systematically accumulates in the atmosphere, to the detriment of the climate in this case. In fact, it is a general rule that when this sustainability condition is violated the destructive influence of the end-product is noted long before the resource (e.g. heavy metals) is used up.
3. Human-made substances include e.g. non-biodegradable biocides but also other products detrimental to the ecosphere, such as PCBs toxic to reproduction capacity, and freons which slowly destroy the protective ozone layer. These two groups of substances are today illegal to produce in most countries.
4. The fourth principle is in fact not a physical one, but rather an ethical one. However it is now well understood to be necessary for social stability, which is needed for achieving sustainability.

The four conditions listed formed the starting point for a managerial scheme for working with sustainability introduced by the Natural Step Foundation. This foundation, which originated in Sweden but today is active in many countries including e.g. Canada, works mostly with industries but also with municipalities to help in the work of sustainable development.

The four physical principles focus on what to avoid when working with sustainability. There is also a set of principles that focus on the ecological conditions for sustainability based on Nebel and Wright (1996).

1. Ecosystems dispose of wastes and replenish nutrients by recycling all elements.
2. Ecosystems use sunlight as their source of energy.
3. The size of the consumer population is kept at a level so that overgrazing or over-use does not occur.
4. Biodiversity is maintained.

The practical use of these principles is easy to illustrate by examples from experience and they are discussed throughout the three books in this series.

Sustainable rural development described in this way can perhaps be accused of having a perspective that is too anthropocentric (giving mankind the right to govern over animals and plants). It can be challenged by those who believe humans should go back to their 'natural' place in the ecosystem (it is actually estimated that Earth in the long-term can support an optimum of 2 billion people, but we are approaching four times this figure already). It is important for all to study and discuss the issue of the place of humans in the food chain and in ecosystems. In this book we do so for our own corner of the planet, the Baltic Sea region. As often as possible, we compare this region with the Great Lakes district in the United States and Canada.

EU Policies on Rural Development

The overall aim of the European Union (EU) Sustainable Development Strategy is:

> *" to identify and develop actions to enable the EU to achieve continuous long-term improvement of quality of life through the creation of sustainable communities able to manage and use resources efficiently, tap the ecological and social innovation potential of the economy and ultimately ensure prosperity, environmental protection and social cohesion."*

The strategy sets overall objectives and concrete actions for seven key priority challenges, originally for the period up to 2010, many of which are predominantly environmental:

- Climate change and clean energy
- Sustainable transport
- Sustainable consumption and production
- Conservation and management of natural resources
- Public health
- Social inclusion, demography and migration
- Global poverty and sustainable development challenges

Strategies for rural development in Russia, Belarus and Ukraine are somewhat different than the EU approach. National strategies, laws and regulations exist, but monitoring and follow-up reporting are not in place to the same extent as in EU countries.

The concept of transition of the Russian Federation to sustainable development was approved in 1996. According to the Russian Survey on National Sustainable Development Strategies (2004), the strategy goal of state policy in the environmental sphere is '*...conservation of the natural systems, support of their integrity and life-feedback functions for sustainable development of society, the increasing of quality of life, improvement of health and demography situation, environmental safety of the country*'.

The Russian Action Plan on Ecological Doctrine Implementation (2003) includes a number of actions in the following areas:

- Pollution abatement and resources-saving
- Ensuring safety for highly dangerous types of activity and in emergency situations
- Development of the state system of environmental protection and natural resources use
- Development of appropriate legal base and enforcement
- Development of economic and financial mechanisms
- Ecological monitoring and information support
- Research and Development
- Ecological education
- Cooperation with civil society for state environmental protection policy implementation
- International cooperation.

Since 1995, government departments and agencies in Canada have been required by law to prepare sustainable development strategies, then update them and present these every three years to Parliament. In the USA, there is no government strategy for sustainable development, but recommendations have been issued, the most recent being the publication 'The New Sustainable Frontier – Principles of Sustainable Development (published by the US General Services Administration, Office of Governmentwide Policy).

Long-term Trends and Challenges

Which are the most urgent challenges in the coming years with the goal of achieving sustainable rural development? It already seems clear that rural citizens all over the world will be challenged by the need to provide enough food for a growing number of people. In the last few years the world market price of wheat has increased three-fold and it is predicted to continue to increase, especially as it competes with bioenergy production. Increased social standards will lead to higher demand for food. Important sustainability issues include type of food, whether it should be locally produced, and the amount of meat available.

Another area to be confronted by rural citizens is energy production. Many kinds of energy solutions, such as hydropower and wind power, have considerable impacts in the landscape. Are we going to sacrifice the rural landscape as the amount of fossil fuels declines? Devising alternatives is an important sustainability challenge.

Overall, the most difficult and important task for rural inhabitants will most likely be to protect, wisely manage and develop the ecosystem services provided by the landscape, which constitute the basis of our societies and our long-term survival as individuals. Developing and learning to manage ecosystem services is perhaps the most central task for the students of this series of books.

Part A

The Rural Landscape

Authors: Arvo Iital, Gregory McIsaac, Lars Rydén, Kalev Sepp and Valentin Yatsukhno

Coordinating Author: Arvo Iital

Landscape and Landscape History

1

Arvo Iital
Tallinn University of Technology, Tallinn, Estonia

The Origins of Landscape Science

Definition of Landscape

The definition of the term 'landscape' by e.g. geographers, ecologists and others can be quite variable. The original meaning was probably connected to a visual view of surroundings, as a picture or scenery, as has been widely adopted in art and literature. As a scientific term, landscape was introduced only in the early 19th century by Alexander von Humboldt, who defined it as 'the character of an Earth region' that is more than just the sum of its parts, as was indicated by a German bio-geographer Carl Troll (1939). According to the European Landscape Convention (2000), landscape means an area, as perceived by people, whose character is the result of the action and interaction of natural and/or human factors. Landscape can also be regarded as a provider of resources that includes land use, natural capital, etc., as a way of communicating through social order or customary law, or as a research object. This definition is close to the ideas developed by a Finnish geographer Johannes Gabriel Granö who combined natural and cultural themes including perception of landscapes through sight as well as other human senses (Granö, 1929). Thus, landscape includes two components tied to each other: one is objective, real and visible landscape (e.g. landform, vegetation pattern and texture, water bodies, buildings, human infrastructure) and the other is the subjective, virtual, non-visible landscape (Palang, 1994) including feelings generated by senses, a knowledge and past experience of the place, cultural associations, etc. Landscapes are heterogeneous in at least one factor of interest (Turner et al., 2001) and therefore landscape types and sub-types having similar features or attributes can be defined.

Elements and Components of the Landscape

The state of landscapes is mainly determined by the mixture of habitats or land cover types resulting from many causes, including variability in abiotic conditions (geology, relief, soils, climate, water), biotic interactions of fauna and flora that generate spatial patterns even under homogeneous environmental conditions, patterns of human settlement and land use and the dynamics of natural disturbance and succession (Turner et al., 2001). The socio-economic factors determining the state of landscapes include the economy, for example production and distribution of goods and services, political factors such as objectives and decisions, social factors determined by the population and tourism and cultural factors such as traditions and values (Messerli and Messerli, 1978). Socio-economic factors are driven by political means e.g. agricultural, forestry and energy policy, land use planning, environmental protection and promotion of the economy, and by the demand for natural resources, recreational areas and other ecosystem services.

The dominant vegetation type, i.e. forests, arable lands, wetlands, meadows, is usually recognised as the main factor characterising a specific landscape. The dominant vegetation establishes the resource base for the rest of the ecosystem (Turner et al., 2001). The natural vegetation structure is in turn determined by the soil types that are decisive for land use, e.g. forestry or agriculture. Some soils, for example loess, can be more suitable for today's agriculture. Therefore, the share of arable land in some regions of the Baltic Sea Region (BSR), e.g. in the south of Poland and in some areas in Germany, is very high. Other areas may need drainage or irrigation to be good for crop production. During the history of cropping, preferences with regard to soil quality have changed greatly depending mostly on the development of suitable agricultural technology, although the need for feeding people drove the modernisation of technology at the same time. For example, the earliest agricultural areas in thin calcareous soils in the north of Estonia lost most of their value for cultivation during recent millennia. In areas dominated by igneous rocks, as in most of Sweden and Finland and partly in north-west Russia, less fertile thin till soils prevail, so conditions for cultivation are poor and forest landscapes dominate. Similarly, sandy soils are generally of low fertility and too dry, and therefore rather unsuitable for agriculture. Interactions of climate, topography and soils have defined the vegetation zones in the Baltic Sea region, with boreal forests in the north and nemoral vegetation in Poland, Germany, Denmark, Belarus and partly Lithuania, and with a boreo-nemoral vegetation belt between these two zones (See Figure 1.3). Most wetlands in the Baltic Sea region are remnants of the post-glaciation period. Post-glacial land uplift and the eutrophication caused by nutrient enrichment have reduced many lakes to wetlands, while drainage programmes have reduced the area of marshland to a minimum, especially in Germany, Denmark and southern Sweden. Fortunately the area of wetlands in the north and east of Europe is still relatively high due to the lower population density and land use pressure.

Figure 1.1. Open wooded meadow in Matsalu National Park near Penijõe in western Estonia. The canopy contains much Ash (*Fraxinus excelsior*). Photo: Copyright Stuart Roberts.

Status of the Landscape

Depending on the degree of human interaction, landscape characteristics can be dominated by natural conditions or by human involvement. Thus a distinction can be made between natural landscapes and cultural landscapes and those that are somewhere between, i.e. semi-natural landscapes. We know that even habitats in remote areas (forests, mountains) have been somehow utilised or impacted and in Europe only a very few pristine 'natural landscapes' remain. In his classic definition, Carl Sauer (1925) describes the cultural landscapes as being fashioned from a natural landscape by a cultural group, i.e. the activities of man having imprints as rural, recreational and urban landscapes. Landscapes in the wilderness as well as landscape types that are far from natural conditions and that can be maintained only by permanent human involvement can be highly valued. This assessment can be based on ecosystem approach, on aesthetic, cultural, scientific or intrinsic landscape values, etc. Typical examples of landscapes that need permanent human involvement are alvar areas and wooded meadows that are nowadays in danger of being overgrown by bushes and trees, as well as the specific spruce fence landscapes in Sweden and Finland.

Traditional extensive farming practices are usually associated with the highest biodiversity, but higher concentrations of species of particular conservation interest can also occur in more intensively farmed areas. Areas where farming practices are associated with high biodiversity value are commonly referred to as High Nature Value (HNV) farming systems, where biodiversity conservation should be integrated into agri-environmental measures. The HNV concept, which first emerged in 1993, recognises the causality between certain types of farming activity and 'natural values' (Baldock et al., 1993). The HNV areas are typically low intensity, low input systems, frequently with high structural diversity. These landscape types can be highly valued even though they are far from natural conditions and can be maintained only by permanent human involvement, e.g. wooded meadows or other types of semi-natural vegetation that developed in conditions of low intensive agriculture or other types of semi-natural vegetation. The more recent concept of Traditional Agricultural Landscape (TAL) describes landscapes where intensive farming may have eliminated much of the natural value, while maintaining the most important traditional landscape features at the same time. In TAL the existence of high aesthetic and cultural values and ecological integrity are maintained using traditional management approaches.

Long-term History of Landscape and Land Use

Dynamics of Landscape Change

Landscapes are dynamic, both in time and in space. Today's landscape changes and processes that are either natural in origin or carried out by humans take place simultaneously and are associated with fragmentation of both natural and semi-natural habitats. These changes will lead to reformation of the habitat area and habitat quality.

It is very likely that before the development of the traditional agricultural landscapes, the natural landscapes formed a mosaic of different forest types and open patches. This means that otherwise homogeneous land cover types represented a variety of patches in different successional phases. The landscape mosaic that we can see nowadays describes the changes in natural conditions and human pressures over a long period when both expansion and contraction of cultivated area took place (Figure 1.2) accompanied by similar changes in the area and composition of natural landscapes. We can even conclude that new socio-economic formation tries to create its own landscape based on new ideologies and by changing the uses and values of previous landscapes (Cosgrove, 1998). In most part of the Baltic Sea region, the human impact has been the main driving force in shaping landscapes, especially during the past centuries. These landscapes are in one way or another man-made.

The Glaciation Formed the Landscape

The general shape of landscapes in northern Europe originates from the last Ice Age and the post-glacial history, reshaped by the human impact that is visible almost everywhere. Varying post-glacial climate conditions, geological properties and relief formed different soils and a variety of vegetation patterns. Heavy ice cover depressed the land and consequently vast areas were covered by fresh or sea water that went through several stages due to land uplift. In the centre of gravity of the continental ice cover in Scandinavia, the land has risen by more than 800 m since the last glaciation (Sporrong, 2003) and the mean annual rate of uplift has been nearly 10 cm. In large areas of the Baltic Sea region the land uplift continues even nowadays, being higher in the Bay of Bothnia, where it is about 8-9 mm/year, and decreasing to zero in southern Sweden and Latvia and even submerging south of that imaginary line. During and after the ice cover retreated, sediments transported from Scandinavian mountains

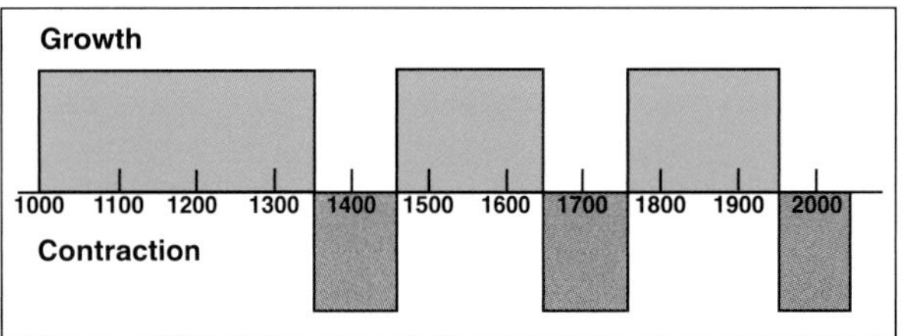

Figure 1.2. Expansion and contraction of cultivated area in Europe during the last millennium (Rabbinge & van Diepen, 2000).

Box 1.1. Landscape Types

Landscape boundaries, ecotones

In the Baltic Sea region there is a great variation in landscape types. These support human activities as well a rich biology through a large variety of habitats for plants and animals. The landscape varies with latitude (north to south), altitude (high or low), climate (especially wet or dry), and proximity to the sea (maritime or continental). They may be divided into vegetation zones, also called biomes (Figure 1.3).

Boundaries between different landscape types, the eocotones, often have special roles to play. For example ecotones around agricultural fields may absorb nutrients leaking from the field. Such ecotones constitute habitats for some birds and insects, and their removal in modern agriculture is negative for biodiversity. Forest edges, river shores and mountain sides are other examples of landscape type boundaries.

The science of landscape is basic for sustainable development since each type provides different ecosystems services and natural resources (chapter 2). Modern methods of landscape ecology rely on remote sensing, use of GIS, and characterise landscapes by e.g. the amount of carbon present in the soil, vegetation types, rainfall etc.

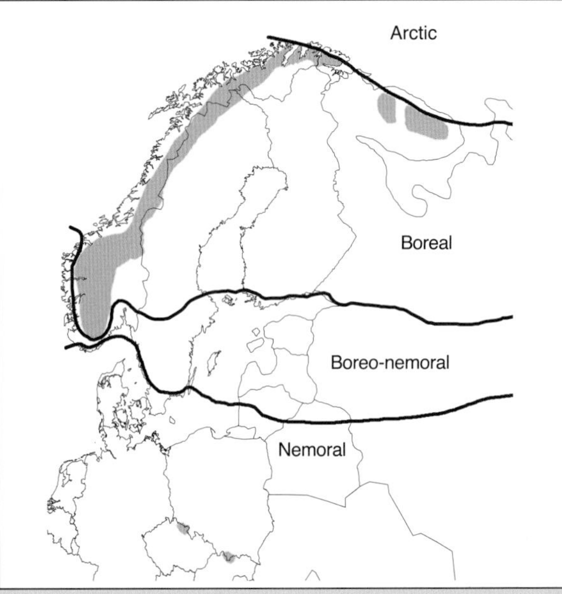

Figure 1.3. The vegetation zones in the Baltic region, with the four typical vegetation belts. Shaded areas are alpine zone, and subalpine and subarctic birch forest. (Adapted from Sjörs, in Rydin et al., 1999.)

Arctic-alpine areas

At high altitude, above the tree lines, the landscape is barren due to the climatic conditions. In the north the Scandinavian mountains are called fjell; in the south we have the Carpatian range. Plants and animals in the fjell belong largely to a group of arctic species found around the polar area.

In all the mountains, both low-productive dwarf-shrub heaths and higher productive grass/herb areas can be found. More to the north or at higher elevation, lichens play a very significant role. In the north the Saami traditional economy was based on reindeer herding. Today tourism may be even more important and hundreds of thousands of visitors spend summer months touring the mountains. Large parts of the mountains are protected as national parks. A big difference between the Scandinavian mountains and the Carpatian mountains is the much larger amount of wetlands and lakes in the northern region.

Coniferous forest, boreal forest – taiga

The forest landscape, with spruce and Scotch pine, dominates northern and central Sweden and Finland and the neighbouring parts of Russia. The pine is found in both dryer and very wet conditions, while the spruce does best in more fertile soils. Fires have always played a significant role in the dynamics of the coniferous forest, especially in drier climate. The number of higher plant species in such forests is low (but there is blueberry, lingonberry, crowberry and heather); the moss and lichen flora often dominate.

Few larger mammals are specialized to live in the boreal forest. Moose belong to the coniferous forests, while brown bear, wolf, and lynx, still typical, have often been pushed out of other areas by human activity. Birds in this landscape include Ural owl, Siberian tit, and Siberian jay. Even if the Northern coniferous forests are much influenced by forestry and other types of traditional human use, parts of them can be regarded as Europe's most natural landscapes.

Mixed coniferous – broad-leafed forests

The mixed coniferous-broad leafed forests covers large parts of south central Sweden, the southern part of Finland, the Baltic republics, and parts of neighbouring Poland, Russia and Belarus. This is a transitional zone where the coniferous trees are found on infertile soils and deciduous trees on better soil. Agriculture has during a long time changed large forest areas into open grazing areas or arable land. More recently forest has largely returned in less fertile arable land and grazing areas.

The mixed forest has in addition to the coniferous trees a number of deciduous tree species. Among them we have oak, important for biodiversity; especially old oaks which can be the home for a large diversity of insects, lichens, mosses and fungi, as well as birds and even bats. Other important deciduous trees are lime, ash, elm and maple. Mixed forests are often rich in bird species and mammals, including Roe deer, and in some areas, Red deer and Wild boar.

Broad-leaved nemoral forests

In the southern parts of BSR, broad-leafed forest is the original vegetation type, except in very wet areas, and it still constitutes an important landscape type. Among tree species are beech, hornbeam and maple. The economically valuable species beech and oak sometimes dominate.

Landscape Types

Figure 1.4. Karums Alvar is a small area of semi-natural grassland in the middle part of Öland, Sweden. Photo: Bengt Olsson.

Forests which have been used for grazing ,become more open, and may even form wooded meadows, although these disappear when not maintained. This landscape is often very beautiful and rich in flowers especially during spring, when Anemone and Corydalis species flower. During summer the forests are quite dark, with fewer plants, especially in the beech forests. Old forests may be very species rich and the habitat for a very large number of insects, birds, fungi and lichens.

Semi-natural grasslands

Semi-natural grasslands have successively developed during the last 6,000 years, mostly due to long periods of grazing. There are many types of semi-natural grasslands, some totally open without trees and shrubs, and others with trees and shrubs as a prominent part. Many grasslands are extremely rich in species, and very attractive for recreation.

Only a few percent of the semi-natural grasslands of the 1850:s northern Europe are left today. In Poland, the Baltic States, Norway and southern Sweden many areas survived into the 1960s, but since 1989, the regression has been tremendously fast. Recently, much work has been done to save and even restore semi-natural grasslands. The hilly landscape in south-eastern Sweden is probably the best stronghold for semi-natural grasslands in northern Europe today, and the Great Alvar on the island of Öland is Europe's largest continuous semi-natural grassland (Figure 1.4).

Arable land

The arable landscape has developed during thousands of years. Originally this landscape included many additional elements such as ponds, small fens, trees and stone fences. As agriculture was mechanized individual arable fields have grown in size considerably and a much more simplified arable landscape has been created, especially pronounced in for example Lithuania, Scania in southern Sweden and on the Danish islands.

Fauna and flora earlier typical for the arable landscapes are today threatened by forest takeover or large-scale agriculture that leaves little room for wild species. Plant species adapted to arable fields, e.g. *Centaurea cyanus*, are now becoming rare due to increasingly efficient methods of threshing. Birds living in the arable landscape are among the most threatened birds in Europe today.

Wetlands

Wetland is a broad term for landscape types with the water table close to the surface. They are called mires, shores and swamp forests. Drainage campaigns has reduced wetlands dramatically in the southern parts of the region, while in the North there are still large peat wetlands. Peat is often extracted and used as a fuel.

Many wetlands have earlier been open ponds or lakes, which successively were filled up with lake sediments and later with peat as wetland plants encroached. There are also wetlands dominated by trees and shrubs. *Alder* dominated swamp forests and *Salix* dominated wetlands along lake and river shores can for examples still be found in large regions of Eastern Poland and Belarus.

Wetlands can sometimes attract a large number of birds. Sandpipers and ducks are found in most types of wetland. The crane is a species typical for larger low-productive wetlands. The impressive black storch is found in swamp forests.

Rivers and lakes

The Baltic Sea region has an abundance of lakes, only in Sweden and Finland some 160,000. The majority of these lakes are small and have low nutrient levels. Usually mires, heath and coniferous forests dominate the catchment areas.

The nutrient poor lakes in the mountains, especially in the North, have been subjected to acidification with the consequence that all higher forms of life, including fish, have disappeared. This is in particular the case if the surrounding bedrock and soils have a low buffering capacity.

The number of oligotrophic nutrient poor lakes has declined during the last 50-100 years due to changes in land use. Draining to gain arable land in the late 19th and early 20th century led to lowering of the water table of many lakes.

The Baltic Sea coasts

The coastal areas around the Baltic Sea are different compared to other coastal areas. The brackish water of the Baltic Sea influences the shore meadow vegetation, since there are considerable water level fluctuations over the year.

Some coastal areas (in the Baltic States and Poland as well as in southern Sweden and parts of Germany and Denmark) have extensive shore meadows. These are important for a number of wetland birds, such as sandpipers, and several species of geese. The South-eastern Baltic coasts are famous for their sand dunes.

Lars Rydén

settled on the old relief, forming e.g. hilly moraine relief, end moraines, ice margin deposits and drumlins. Material transported by melt water formed large sandy plains, sandurs and eskers.

During different climatic conditions of the post-glacial period, the prevailing vegetation cover and thus the overall look of the landscape changed considerably. About 10,000 BC climate grew warmer for about 1,000 years, but only territories lying in present Germany, Poland and Denmark and in southern Sweden and some higher parts of the Baltic State region and the Russian catchment area were free of ice. The sea level before the ice shield was about 50 m lower than now, allowing direct connection between present Denmark and southern Sweden. Due to melting of the ice shield and lack of connection to the Atlantic Ocean, the water level rose step by step and finally reached up to 50 m higher than the present sea level. This stage is called the Baltic Ice Lake (Figure 1.5), when intensive sedimentation of fine particles in the fresh water body formed large varved clay plains that later became marshy. The percolation of water through the soil was restricted by permafrost, and evaporation was negligible due to the very short summer when the temperature rose above zero degrees. During this period birch migrated to the north, reaching Scandinavia. The prevailing tundra-like vegetation type near the melting ice cover provided grazing for wild animals.

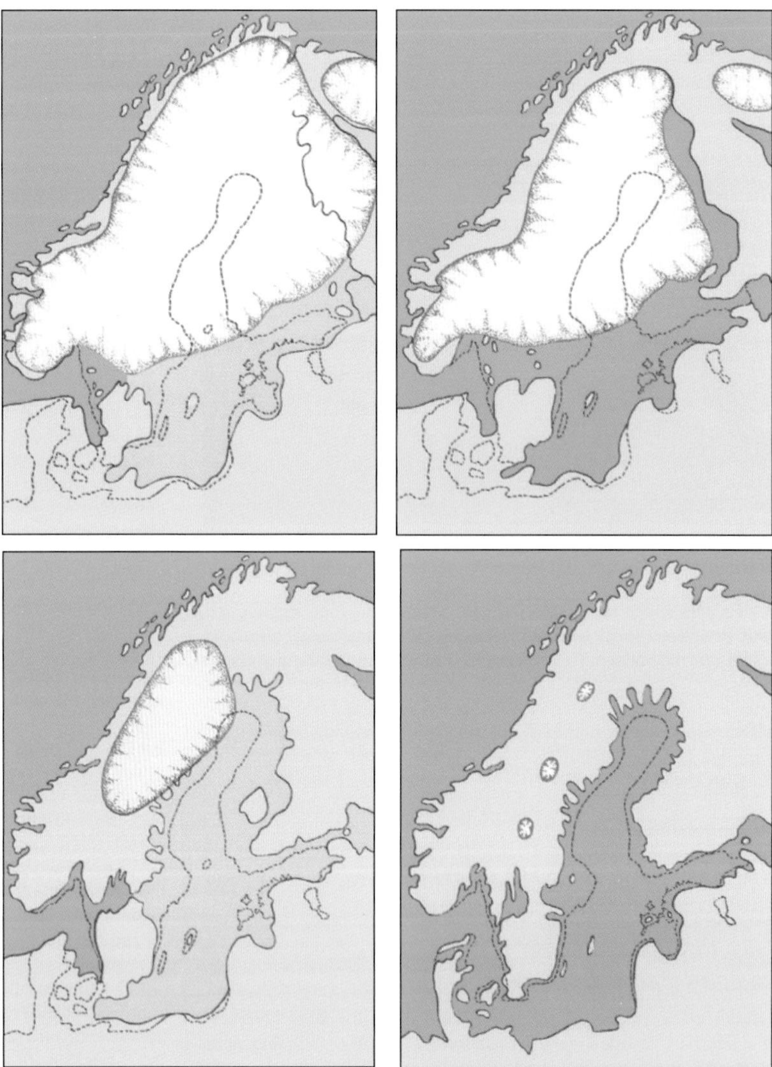

Figure 1.5. The main post-glacial stages of the Baltic Sea. From upper left to lower right: The Baltic Ice Lake up to 10,000 years BP.: The Yoldia Sea 10,000-9,400 years BP.: The Ancylus Lake 9,400-8,000 years BP.: The Littorina Sea from 8,000 years BP, which gradually changed into the Baltic Sea. Source: Isakar, 2003..

The First Humans

It is very likely that the first humans moved to the Baltic Sea region quite soon after the last Ice Age, following reindeer and elk. Step by step they settled near rivers, lakes and the sea. Later on, some headed further inland. The hunters, fishermen and gatherers of plants, fruit and roots of this time probably did not have any large impact on ecosystems, even though the area to support one person was relatively big (Palang et al., 2003). The population density was still very low. The main factor changing the shape of landscapes was probably fire, usually of nat-

Figure 1.6. Icetracks on coastal landscape. Photo: Ingrid Karlsson.

ural origin. Continuing melting of the ice cover and rising sea levels flooded large areas in present Estonia, Latvia, Lithuania, Russia and southern Sweden. The coastal line of the sea was very different to what we can see now and for example the large lakes in Sweden (Vänern, Vättern), Estonia (Peipsi) and Russia (Ladoga) formed a part of the former Baltic Ice Lake.

After the Baltic Ice Lake drained via the mountain plateau Billingen about 10,700 years ago and made a connection with the Atlantic Ocean, the water became slightly brackish (2-3‰). This period is called the Yoldia Sea (about 10,300-9,500 years ago). A further increase in the temperature during the Pre-Boreal period (about 11,500-9,300 years ago) raised the brackish water input and the sea level, accompanied by the land uplift after the ice shield melted. Finally the strait in central Sweden was closed. Birch and pine forests probably started to spread over what had once been tundra-like landscape. The transgression when water rose by nearly 10 m a century (Sporrong, 2003) gave an outlet into the Great Belt about 9200 years ago. Parts of former settlements on the coast of the sea were flooded during this period, called the Ancylus Lake (9,500-7,800 BP, before present). This was the case for example with Pulli on the bank of the River Pärnu, which is the oldest known settlement in Estonia. By at least that time humans reached southern Finland, since remnants of settlements in Lahti Ristola date back 9,250 years (Sporrong, 2003). Sand transported to the sea by rivers formed substantial dunes in many parts along the former coast. Due to the relatively warm and humid boreal climate, the overall vegetation picture was rather different compared with nowadays. Wetlands were common and the number of lakes much higher during this period. Open areas were found in the flood plains along the large rivers.

About 7,800-3,700 years ago, during the Litorina stage of the Baltic Sea, the connection to the ocean was better than ever before or since, and therefore the exchange of water between the sea and the ocean was intensive. The salinity of the Baltic Sea was fairly high, 15-18‰, providing much better conditions for many species. The sea level was only a couple of metres higher than now and thus the coast line looked rather similar to what we can see nowadays.

About 8,000-5,000 years ago, in the Atlantic Period, the climate became more humid and remained warm. The southern part of the BSR was covered by deciduous forests where the dominant tree species where oak, elm, ash and lime (Palang et al., 2003). Deciduous forests dominated even in southern Scandinavia and pine reached up to poor soils and high altitudes in Lapland. The remnants of this vegetation type can still be found, especially in the south of the region and in some sheltered areas, e.g. deep river valleys and coastal cliffs. It is likely that permanent habitation in this period reached to the islands of the Baltic Sea and developed for example on Saaremaa Island and on many Finnish islands during the Late Mesolithic Era (Kriiska, 2002). Around this time, the coastal settlements of Denmark and southern Sweden also expanded considerably (Andersen, 1993; Larsson, 1997).

Some 4,000 years ago, the temperature started to decrease, which led to immigration of spruce and pine forests to areas where oak elm and lime had previously dominated. In Western Russia spruce re-established already about 7,000 BP, and occupied vast areas in the former Baltic States and Finland during the period 7,000-5,000 BP (Björkman, 1996). From about 4,000 BP spruce forest expanded its distribution limits to the west. Spruce seedlings require sufficient insulating snow cover during the winter (Frey, 1983), which probably explains the expansion to the north in the period when the temperature started to decrease. At about 5,000-4,000 BP beech trees expanded into Poland, northern Germany and southern Scandinavia (Björkman, 1996). The invasion of this species has been explained by availability of habitats after the decrease of pre-existing dense woodlands due to human interference (Behre, 1988) and by a decreasing continentality in climate and milder winters. The forests became denser and darker.

During the next period, land uplift restricted the water input from the ocean and the Limnea sea level dropped to what we can see now. The water salinity decreased owing to freshwater input and continuing land uplift raised new islands from the water and reshaped the coastline.

The Man-made Landscape

The Neolithic Age

The first humans settled the Baltic Sea region very rapidly after the ice cover retreated, about 10,000 years ago. The hunters and fishermen who lived on coasts and nearby water bodies probably had quite a limited impact on the overall landscape pattern of this period (Lõugas, 1980). Humans who headed further inland burnt down forests to create more space and significantly influenced landscapes around their settlements, allowing invasion of new species such as beech. The landscape pattern was also changed by natural fires caused by lightning.

Figure 1.7. Stone wall in the province of Småland, Southern Sweden. All through the landscape farmers have removed stones from the fields to make way for arable land. Photo: Lars Rydén.

A gradual transition from hunter-gatherer to agricultural communities started in some areas in former Germany and Poland already about 7,000 years ago. It is very likely that human habitation multiplied during the long relatively warm era starting from the pre-Boreal Period. People settled near water courses and on the shores of lakes.

Towards the end of the warm period about 6,000 years ago, hunters and gatherers had invaded most of Scandinavia. The conditions for cultivation were more favourable in areas where the calcium-rich sedimentary bedrock allowed development of fertile soils, for instance in southern Sweden, former Denmark, Germany and Poland. These parts were the first to gradually change into cultural landscapes.

When climate turned cooler, opportunities to make a living with seasonal migration diminished. This created a need to intensify foraging, and it is likely that during the Late Mesolithic era, year-round villages began to arise in many places in the BSR (Kriiska, 2003). The practice of gathering firewood and timber probably generated an increase in sparse woodlands and open areas in the surroundings of year-round villages.

Loess and clayey till soils in particular are the earliest cultivated soils in this region. Step by step, a farming society based on cattle and goats and small cultivated fields started to dominate in the south of the area. A warmer period allowed cattle to be kept outside all year round and therefore additional grass production from meadows was not necessary. During the drier sub-Boreal Period starting about 5,000 years ago, when summers were warm but winters cold, cultivation was introduced in Scandinavia. Cultivation required more intensive cooperation and therefore the size of villages and population increased. Farming then continued to expand northwards, probably pushed by increasing population pressure in the south (Sporrong, 2003).

Findings of wheat, barley and oat pollen in layers of bog and lake sediments in Estonia dates back to the Middle Neolithic era, some 5,000 years ago. Evidence of farming during this period has also been found in Latvia and

Lithuania. However, farming probably remained a minor activity compared with hunting, fishing and foraging in the wild. Very little is known about cattle breeding during this period, but it probably spread during Late Bronze Age some 3,000-2,500 years ago. Extra fodder for winter time probably included twigs from aspen, birch, ash and other trees. Production and storage of hay probably started much later, when suitable cutting tools for this work were introduced in the Pre-Roman Iron Age approximately 2,500-2,000 years ago (Laul and Tõnisson, 1991).

Intensive farming allowed a much greater density of population than can be supported by hunting and gathering. This process speeded up burning of forests and the conversion of this land to agricultural land. The species composition of forests changed and the area of birch forests in the slash and burn areas increased, probably favoured by colder winters.

The Post-neolithic Period

The land reclamation activities of the post-Neolithic period involved clearing the fields of stones, which were stacked in the fields. Numerous stone heaps with a diameter of a few metres shaped the agricultural landscapes in many places in the BSR, for example in Kõmsi, Estonia (Lõugas, 1980). In older permanent fields the height of the stone heaps reached more than 1-2 m, but nevertheless it is still often difficult to see the heaps and burial mounds in the current landscape. Around 1000 AD, a landscape had developed with organised villages, which had fenced fields and grazing areas in the vicinity of buildings. By the early 11th century settlements extended to 63°N in Sweden and 62°N in Finland (Orrman, 2003). While in the south the farming of permanent fields was well established, most of the northern parts of the region were still dominated by hunter-gatherers and most of the landscape remained more or less natural. Around the Gulf of Bothnia, prehistoric agrarian settlement was limited to a narrow coastal zone and lower parts of the river valleys, with very few exceptions, due to clayey lime-rich soils and better climate, e.g. around Lake Storsjön in Sweden or large lakes of southern Häme in Finland and the shores of Lake Ladoga. The northern shores of the Gulf of Finland and the east coast of the Gulf of Bothnia were practically uninhabited and had no permanent settlement before the 11th century (Orrman, 2003). However, during the medieval period settlement in Finland spread from the coast to inland areas. A rapid expansion in settlement also took place around Lake Ladoga in Karelia. This expansion to marginally less fertile areas influenced farming technology. The use of iron shares for ards and ploughs spread in the region between 1000 and 1200 AD, making it easier to till heavy soils. In addition, slash-and-burn cultivation permitted the cultivation of rye even in heavy forest soils (Orrman, 2003). In the early medieval period, a shift to a crop rotation system took place in large areas in Germany and Poland and spread to Denmark and southern Sweden already in the twelfth and thirteenth centuries and to Finland before the mid 14th century (Orrman, 2003). This system required sufficient manure application and thus animal husbandry was a prerequisite for grain cultivation except in the slash-and-burn areas. In some areas in Denmark there was probably even some over-fertilisation and excess losses of nutrients. The crop rotation system, especially in the three-field system, included some land that was rested. Barley cultivation dominated, but later winter rye was introduced. Oats was also important but wheat was more or less a luxury product.

The Medieval Period

In areas where cattle farming was of greater importance than crop production, the proportion of meadows was high, exceeding the area of arable land in the southern Swedish highlands by about five-fold (Sporrong et al., 1995). The meadows with permanent grazing became plant species-rich, as we can see in today's wooded meadows. From the 11th to the first half of the 14th century the population growth continued and previously unoccupied less favourable areas were taken under cultivation. This process led to an increased number of rural holdings (Table 1.1). In early medieval times, settlement probably spread

Table 1.1. Late medieval rural settlement in Scandinavia and Estonia (Source: Orrman, 2003, modified)

Region	Number of rural holdings
Present Denmark	110,000
South Sweden	52,000
The Swedish provinces	75,000
Estonia	6,000
Finland	13,000

Figure 1.8. Farming in Sweden during the 18th century. Painting by Jan Eric Rehn, Petrus Strandberg, 1749. Source: Uppsala University Library.

to the remaining forest regions in Denmark. Population growth caused emigration from more densely populated areas in Denmark, southern Sweden and Germany to the more sparsely populated eastern parts of the BSR and the southern coast of the Baltic.

From 1600 to Today

The farming system in the Baltic Sea region changed rather slowly and forest fire, partly of natural origin, was still the main factor shaping the landscape. Repeated burning, a common cultivation procedure in different parts of the BSR until the 17th century, continued in some areas until the second half of the 19th century. In the 17-18th century, use of forests for manufacturing and production of heating wood increased considerably, rapidly enlarging the clearcut area. Around many big factories, mines and cities, the forests disappeared almost entirely, as happened for example around Tallinn in Estonia. The area of forests decreased by more than 50% in southern Estonia and northern Latvia and 30% in northern Estonia during the 18th century and formed only 19.8% and 24.4%, respectively, in these parts of the BSR by 1887 (Cvetkov, 1957). Increased wind erosion damaged agricultural land. Domestic animals needed additional feed during wintertime in the colder climate and collection of hay for fodder, brought from wetlands and meadows, became common practice. When the animals were kept inside for some part of the year, it was possible to collect manure for fertilisation and agriculture became more intensive. The land area under agriculture increased, but where manure was not available the soils became exhausted. Gradual specialisation and exchange of goods paved the way for a denser population outside the best agricultural regions.

The number of inhabitants was still rather low in Scandinavia until the 19th century, when the hunting-gathering lifestyle was replaced by farming almost everywhere.

From about the middle of the 18th century the area of fields increased quite rapidly. Population pressure was high. Meadows were turned into fields and much wetland was taken into use after drainage of the areas. A crop rotation system was widely implemented, made possible with the use of manure as a fertiliser. The size of farmsteads was probably restricted by labour costs for manure transportation. In the north of the region the climate restricted agriculture, so here hunting and fishing remained the most important way of living until the 20th century.

The Main Categories of Landscape Transformation

The main factors influencing the land use structure can be classified as natural, political and socio-economic (Sepp, Chapter 2, this publication). The impact of natural factors usually changes quite slowly.

The area under cultivation reached its peak at the beginning of the 20th century (Sporrong, 2003) due to population pressure and reached the limits for production without extra energy input (such as use of soil management machinery and chemical fertilisers). Consequently the area of forest was minimal at that time.

Today farmland can be found mainly in regions where the soils and climate conditions are more favourable, e.g. in Denmark, Germany, Poland, the Baltic States and in southern Sweden, the Central Swedish depression and along the shores of the Gulf of Finland and the Bothnian Sea (Figure 1.11). The forests have mainly retreated to the less fertile soils. The proportion of cultivated land varies greatly from few percent up to 70% in Denmark and in some areas of Germany and Poland.

Among the main factors determining the development of current land cover are land reforms, urbanisation and changes in social structure. Socio-economic factors include land amelioration (drainage, irrigation), forestry (deforestation) and concentration of agriculture.

Drainage

The increasing population required more and more land for food production in the BSR. Due to excess precipitation, drainage is needed in large areas of the Baltic Sea catchment and drainage of land was able to increase crop and forage production areas in landscapes with peat soils and wetlands. Thus drainage has been one of the main recent factors reshaping the landscape, e.g. in Denmark and in the province of Schleswig-Holstein in Germany most mires had disappeared by the 20th century due to drainage operations.

The first attempts to regulate water runoff with the aim of getting rid of excess water were made in the Baltic Sea region back in the Middle Ages. Water energy was first used for water mills. A river closed by a dam supplied water seasonally more evenly and helped to prevent floods.

In Denmark and Germany, intensive land reclamation campaigns started in the second half of the 19th century. Similarly in Sweden land reclamation through water drainage projects was most intensive during this period. Consequently, agricultural land area more than doubled in the 19th century and intensive drainage lasted until the middle of the 20th century, when about one-sixth of the total agricultural land had once been a lake or a wetland (Anderberg, 1991).

In Russia and the Baltic States, drainage was rather local until the 19th century (Karavayeva et al., 1991). Tile drainage started in the middle of the 19th century and during the first half of the century only some 7,400 ha were drained in the west of Russia (Karavayeva et al., 1991). In Estonia about 108,000 ha had been drained by 1917, mostly in forest areas, and the area increased to more than 350,000 ha by 1940 (Juske et al., 1991). Drainage reached its peak in 1960-1980, when, for example in Estonia, more than 56,000 ha were drained from 1966 to 1975 (Figure 1.10). Now about 727,000 ha, or more than half the agricultural area, are drained in Estonia, including 7,600 ha of polder systems. In addition, about 601,000 ha of forest land are drained and the total drained area forms about 30% of Estonian territory.

In Finland the systematic drainage of agricultural land started on bigger farms in the 1850s and land reclamation reached its peak during and after World War II, when more agricultural land was needed to feed the people and to settle Karelian refugees.

The history of drainage in Belarus dates back to the second half of the 18th century. At the end of the 19th century, extensive drainage works were carried out in the Polesie region. However, Belarus still had the largest marshlands in Europe before a large-scale land reclamation campaign started in the second half of the 20th century following the 'Land Drainage and Sovkhoz Building Act' of 1966. Now

Figure 1.9. Drained field. Photo: Ingrid Karlsson.

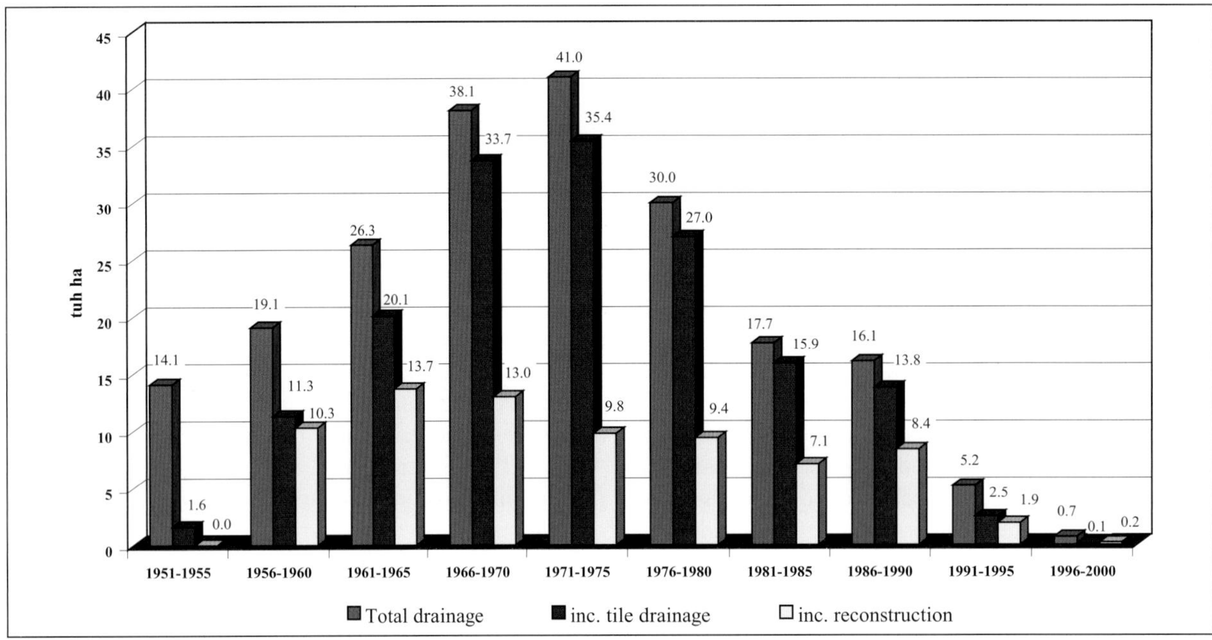

Figure 1.10. Mean annual area (thousand ha) of drained agricultural land in Estonia. Source: Estonian Ministry of Agriculture.

about 3 million ha of large former swamp areas have been drained and converted to agricultural land.

In Latvia quite extensive land drainage started in the 18th century in the east of the country. By 1995, almost 1.6 million ha had been drained. The first subsurface drainage systems in Lithuania were installed back in 1855, but large-scale drainage started in the second half of the 20th century and the total drained area is about 3 million ha. Nevertheless, the share of drained land in the Baltic States has remained relatively low compared with that in western European countries.

Drainage changed and removed habitats for many plant communities and thus shaped the pattern of landscape mosaic. The mires and large floodplains of unregulated rivers disappeared and were replaced by arable land and grassland. The dominant vegetation type of drained forests also changed, generating new spatial patterns.

Many drainage systems on the eastern coast of the Baltic Sea have not been maintained properly during the past 15 years. Many ditches and small streams are overgrown with bushes and other high vegetation, which is slowing down the water flow velocity, prolonging retention periods and thus enhancing the self-purification capacity of streams in agricultural areas.

Due to the climate, irrigation is only used for special crops such as strawberries, fruit trees, and other valuable crops in the Baltic Sea region. The area equipped for irrigation as a percentage of the total arable land area is relatively high only in Denmark and in some parts of Germany, Finland and Sweden.

Deforestation

Deforestation is the main factor contributing to landscape patterns. This process can be driven both by natural and human-induced processes. Natural causes of deforestation are fires caused by lightning, floods and storms. Natural fires leave mosaics of burned and un-burned vegetation, fairly common in many fire-sensitive areas in the Baltic Sea region. These disturbances are usually quite local and recovery through succession takes a maximum of one hundred years. Thus succession plays the most important role in creating a heterogeneous vegetation mosaic of forest.

Human activities contributing to deforestation are mainly forest harvesting, but partly also human-induced

Table 1.2. Changes in wooded area between 1960 and 1993 (km²). Source: BASICS, Baltic Sea region Statistical database on sustainable development, natural resources and environment.

Country	1960	1970	1980	1985	1990	1993
Belarus	-	75,030	-	71,920	73,834	73,720
Denmark	4,380	4,720	4,930	4,930	4,660	4,450
Estonia	14,616	17,220	19,019	-	18,692	20,220
Finland	217,610	223,710	233,210	232,220	233,730	231,860
Germany	102,100	102,150	102,750	103,380	103,930	107,000
Latvia	23,986	25,617	27,286	27,700	28,032	28,390
Lithuania	16,774	18,339	19,550	19,580	19,677	20,000
Poland	77,500	85,460	86,840	87,280	87,540	87,850
Russia	-.	-.	-	7,666,410	7,710,000	7,635,000
Sweden	276,500	278,000	279,200	280,050	280,150	280,000

forest fires. Burning of forests has been an attempt to produce more land suitable for cultivation. In some parts of Sweden it is mainly the use of fire together with natural fires that has contributed to shape landscapes of high ecological and cultural diversity, e.g. heathlands, open grasslands, meadows, and swidden (shifting) agriculture sites (Goldammer, 1998) and fire has significantly influenced the composition and structure of forest ecosystems.

Before the era of manure as a fertiliser, burning of forests was a means to get more fertile land (by adding phosphorus in particular but also micronutrients to the soil). The burning was repeated after about 15-30 years and a field produced by fire was usually in use for up to 8 years depending on the local conditions (Ratt, 1985). For example in eastern Finland the burning practice was used for more than 200 years (Pitkänen et al., 2003). This activity continued in some parts of the BSR (e.g. Poland) until the 1960s and it created a mosaic of open agricultural lands and forests of different ages and successional phases. At the same time the exploitation of forest through fire led to decreasing quality of soils and spread of erosion. In some cases, especially in Denmark and southern Sweden, burning turned large areas into heathlands or sand dunes.

The increased human population raised the demand for wood products, especially timber for construction purposes. In addition, in some areas of Sweden and Poland, iron production required charcoal and wood. Sweden had 30% of the world's iron production during the 1700s, but the share decreased rapidly in the 1800s. The Baltic Sea region was also the world's leading tar producer starting in medieval times, and this also decreased the area of forests. In the second half of the 1800s, large forests in Northern Sweden and Finland were taken into use. Annual wood production in Sweden doubled from about 20 million cubic metres in 1850 to 40 million cubic metres in 1900 (Palang et al., 2003). Again between 1950 and 1975, annual timber production increased by 70% to 65 million cubic metres before reaching a level of 78 million cubic metres in 2005 (State of Europe's Forests, 2007). The timber stand in Poland decreased from 36% at the end of 19th century to 20.8% in 1945 (Palang et al., 2003).

During the past 50 years the wooded area has increased in Poland, Lithuania, Latvia and Estonia but has remained almost unchanged in Sweden, Finland, Denmark, Germany and Belarus. The share of forest and other wooded land in land cover varies today from about 15% in Germany and Denmark to 70% in Sweden. More information on forestry is given in Part C of this book.

Expanding Agriculture

Over the past 2-3 thousand years, large parts of the Baltic Sea region once covered by forests have been transformed into agricultural land. Large areas (60-70%) of land in Denmark, Germany and Poland are in agricultural use nowadays, and agricultural use is also relatively high in Lithuania (Table 1.2). Poland farms 40% of the arable land in the BSR. The percentage of agricultural land in Estonia and Latvia is between 30-40%, but only about 6-12% in Sweden, Finland and the Russian part of the catchment (HELCOM, 2004) (Figure 1.11). Central and northern parts of Sweden and Finland are still typical lake and mire landscapes with very thin soils unsuitable for cultivation.

The area of agricultural land reached its maximum in the BSR by around 1900. By 1920 the total field area in Sweden had increased by more than six-fold compared with 1750, to occupy more than 9% of the total land area. By this time also about 65% of the Estonian territory was in agricultural use (Palang et al., 2003). After this maximum, the agricultural area decreased in both countries and has now nearly halved in Sweden and forms only about 18% of the land area in Estonia. In Denmark the area of forests has been reduced to 3% of the total land cover by about 1800 (Palang et al., 2003). Today the forest area in Denmark has increased to 16% of the total land area. In recent years, the number of agricultural holdings and number of active farmers have decreased in most of the countries around the Baltic Sea, while the average size of agricultural holdings has increased.

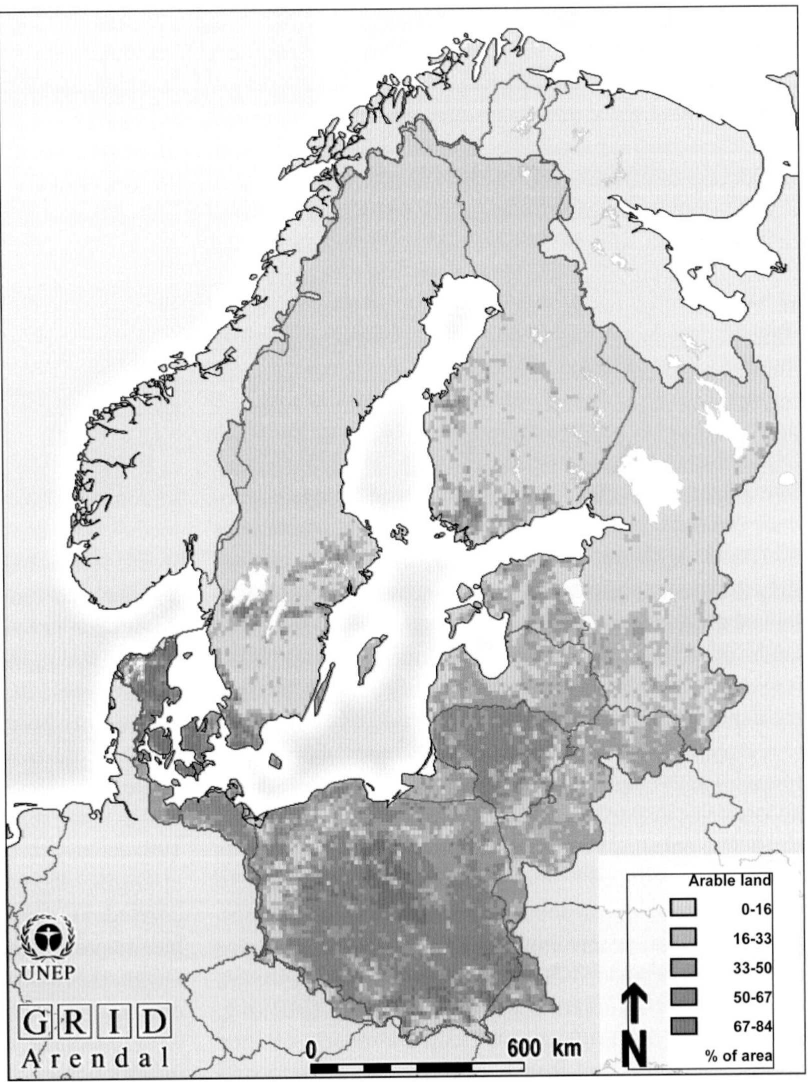

Figure 1.11. Arable land in the Baltic Sea region. Ratio of arable land out of total land use in the Baltic Sea drainage basin. The map displays the situation at approximately 1990. Hugo Ahlenius, UNEP/GRID-Arendal.

The impact of enlarging open agricultural land areas has been controversial. It has had negative consequences on the total area of wetlands and natural forests. Disruption of ecological processes, habitat loss and fragmentation are typical processes taking place in agricultural landscapes. Consequently, contiguous land cover (e.g. forest) can break down into isolated patches when the area cleared exceeds a critical level. At the same time fragmentation of landscapes decreases the inner area of patches and forms more borders in the landscape, increasing the overall ecotone area, the boundary or transitional zone between two ecological communities. This process has created more niches for the species of open habitats and light-rich forests. Agriculture also enhances the spread of weeds and other invasive species. Agriculture contributes to changes in soil nutrient content in different ways: soils can both become poorer due to agricultural crop uptake of nutrients or richer due to overfertilisation.

Today's Landscapes

Layers of Time

In most landscapes we can distinguish layers from different historical periods. Some very old landscape elements such as burial mounds, remnants of fortifications and stone walls around fields date back to the ancient prehistoric period, and are easily visible even today. Other human landscape influences are not that easy to detect. In many places in the BSR, buildings from medieval times can be found. The mosaic of estate landscapes with numerous parks and building complexes is dominant in many places in Germany, as well as in the Baltic States and in other areas. Windmills are specific visible landmarks still reminding us about earlier agricultural practices, especially in coastal areas. These traditional old landscapes still shine through even though they are largely changed by industrialisation, increase of field size due to intensive amelioration in more favourable agricultural areas, and the spread of urban areas (Figure 1.13). Thus, past functioning has produced today's landscape's structure, just like today's structure produces today's functioning and today's functioning will produce future structure (Forman and Godron,1986). We could actually call these types of landmarks the landscape memory.

Today, industrial landscapes dominate in some regions in all countries surrounding the Baltic Sea. New layers of elements add to the landscape 'cake' contributed by modern wind turbines, high grain storage silos, manure storage, waste water treatment facilities, etc. in the rural

Figure 1.12. Aerial patchwork landscape in Kåseberga, Southern Sweden. Photo: Christopher Line.

landscape. One of the more drastic examples of recent changes in land use in the BSR is the Chernobyl accident in the Soviet Union (Ukraine) in 1986. Since then, long-term radiation has affected e.g. 18% of the most productive farmland in Belarus and 20% of its forest area. This area is today forested but excluded from food or feed production and it has a very low human population.

Thus the landscape is a complex entity which operates over numerous temporal and spatial scales as described by Antrop (2000).

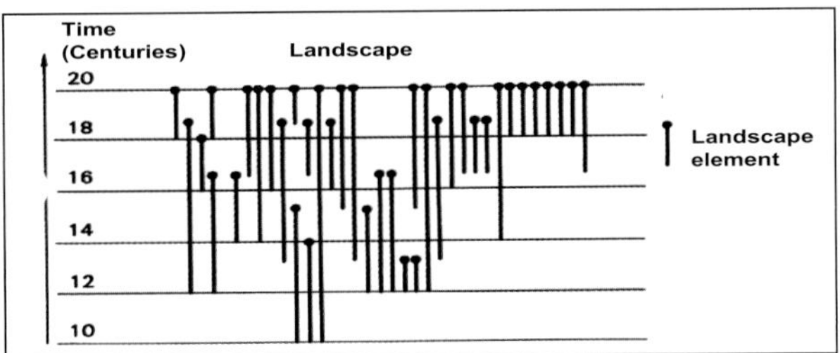

Figure 1.13. Different time layers shine through in the same spot. Source: after Vervloet, 1986.

The Sustainable Landscape – What is it?

The Baltic Sea drainage basin is roughly four times the surface area of the sea itself. About 48% of the region is now forested, with Sweden and Finland containing the majority of the forest, especially around the Gulfs of Bothnia and Finland. About 20% of the land is agricultural land, mainly in Poland and around the edge of the Baltic Proper, in Germany, Denmark and Sweden. Nearly 17% of the basin is unused open land, with another 8% of wetlands. Most of the latter are in the catchments of the Gulfs of Bothnia and Finland. The rest of the land is heavily populated.

We use landscapes for different purposes:

- To produce resources (e.g. forestry, agriculture, rearing animals, mining minerals)
- To give space for human infrastructure (buildings, transport, industry)
- For recreation
- For ecosystem services (i.e. flooding control, water supply)
- To support aesthetic, cultural and religious values
- To support components and structure of ecosystems

Very often these goals are in conflict with each other. Therefore optimisation of land use and a more sustainable approach with regard to landscapes are needed.

Characteristic features of sustainable landscapes are self-sufficiency and variety of ecosystems, high environmental quality and maintenance of natural resources. In urban and rural areas sustainable landscapes provide enhanced landscape beauty; less environmental degradation; more effective use of water, timber, fertilisers and other resources; more valuable wildlife habitat; and cost savings from reduced maintenance, labour and resource use.

The optimisation and management of landscapes should follow the basic principles of sustainable landscape maintenance. We should take into account that the impact of human activities in the landscapes can be visible after a time lag of several years. Fragmentation of landscape mosaic by human settlements and land use will not necessarily lead to a decrease in species diversity. In contrast, maintaining large monoculture agricultural fields can cause undesirable results. We should also remember that only those species that are suitable for specific climatic, hydrological, soil and geo-morphological conditions can be introduced. Otherwise, lots of resources would have to be spent to maintain communities by e.g. drainage, irrigation, fertilisation, chemical treatment. This is not in agreement with the principle of sustainable landscapes.

Sustainable landscapes will support abiotic landscape resources, e.g. local climate and water availability, as well as biotic resources such as biodiversity and ecological functioning. Sustainable land use also implies reduced inputs of resources and pollution, and maximised re-use of resources. Finally, sustainable landscapes look more attractive. Thus sustainable landscapes are valuable due to a number of criteria, including producing resources, providing a space for human infrastructure, recreation and ecosystem services, and supporting aesthetic, cultural and religious values as well as components and structures of ecosystems.

Landscape Functions and Ecosystem Services

2

Kalev Sepp
Estonian University of Life Sciences, Tartu, Estonia

Ecosystems Goods and Services

Definitions

In recent decades, the multiple benefits provided by ecosystems and landscapes have been described in a large number of studies, which provided the basis for a recent global assessment of ecosystem goods and services (de Groot, 1992; Costanza et al., 1997; Daily, 1997; de Groot et al., 2002; Millennium Ecosystem Assessment, 2005). In spite of the large body of literature on ecosystem (or landscape) functions, goods and services, there is still no clear consensus on final definition and typology and considering the complexity of man-environment interactions, there probably never will be (de Groot and Hein, 2007).

Many different types of environmental functions performed by natural, semi-natural and man-made ecosystems can be identified. Wande´n and Schaber (1998) identify functions which have information values (aesthetic, educational, scientific, orientation, signal), functions which have ethical values (e.g. right to existence for all living creatures), functions which have production values (e.g. production of food, fibre, fruits) and functions which have life support values (e.g. carbon fixation by green plants, protection of the soil against erosion, the maintenance of soil structure and fertility by a healthy soil flora and fauna, biological control of crops and fruits by insects). De Groot (1992), de Groot et al. (2002) and others (e.g. Millennium Ecosystem Assessment, 2005), provide slightly different lists of environmental functions.

According to Daily (1997), '*Ecosystem services* are the conditions and processes through which natural ecosystems, and the species which make them up, sustain and fulfil human life. They maintain biodiversity and the

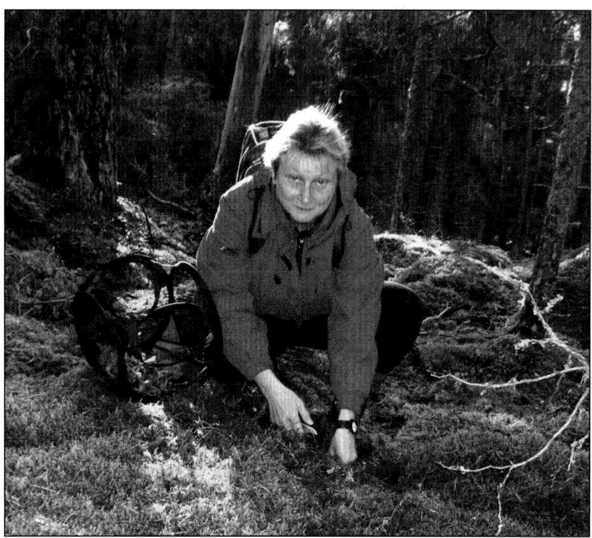

Figure 2.1. Possibility to pick mushroms and berries and enjoy wildlife and outdoor life are important ecosystem services provided by the forest. Photo: Ingrid Karlsson.

production of *ecosystem goods*, such as seafood, forage, timber, biomass fuels, natural fibres, and many pharmaceuticals, industrial products, and their precursors. In addition to the production of goods, ecosystem services are the actual life-support functions, such as cleansing, recycling, and renewal, and they confer many intangible aesthetic and cultural benefits as well.'

Daily's definition makes an important distinction between ecosystem services and ecosystem goods. Ecosystems goods are the generally tangible, material products that result from ecosystem processes, whereas ecosystem services are in most cases improvements in the condition or location of things of value. Daily explains that ecosystem services are generated by a 'complex of natural cycles', from large-scale biogeochemical cycles (such as the movement of carbon through the living and physical environment) to the very small-scale life cycles of micro-organisms. Daily's (1997) definition makes another key point about ecosystem services: they 'sustain and fulfil human life'. The emphasis here is squarely on human well-being, and thus in keeping with an economic perspective. Some might say that such an anthropocentric focus is too limiting – that it devalues the importance of ecosystem structure and processes to species other than humans, or that it runs the risk of ignoring ecosystem processes that contribute to human welfare but are not yet recognised as doing so.

Daily (1997) listed several ecosystem services, such as purification of water, mitigation of floods, and pollination of plants. As she mentions, these services 'are absolutely pervasive, but unnoticed by most human beings going about their daily lives'. Unlike these ecosystem services, most ecosystem goods do not go unnoticed, as they are the basic natural resources that we consume on a regular basis. Ecosystem goods have long been recognised as key elements of wealth; it is the grand contribution of the modern ecological and hydrological science to more fully recognise and appreciate the services that nature also provides (Brown et al., 2006).

The tidy distinction between ecosystem services and ecosystem goods was later obscured by Costanza et al. (1997), who, after noting the difference between goods and services, proceeded to lump them into the class of 'ecosystem services'. This lumping had the advantage of brevity, but tended to blur the distinction between the functional nature of ecosystem services and the concrete nature of ecosystem goods. This lumping was adopted by others, including de Groot et al. (2002) and the Millennium Ecosystem Assessment (Alcamo et al., 2003).

Figure 2.2. Provision of renewable energy from wind, water and sun are also ecosystem services. Photo: Lars Rydén.

The Millennium Ecosystem Assessment (MA, 2005) stated that ecological goods and services are the benefits people derive from the ecological functions of healthy ecosystems. Such benefits accrue to all living organisms, including animals and plants, rather than to humans alone. To avoid lengthy texts, MA (2005) also decided to use the term 'services' for goods and services, as well as the underlying functional processes and components of the ecosystems providing them. However, many authors see a principal difference between the use of the terms

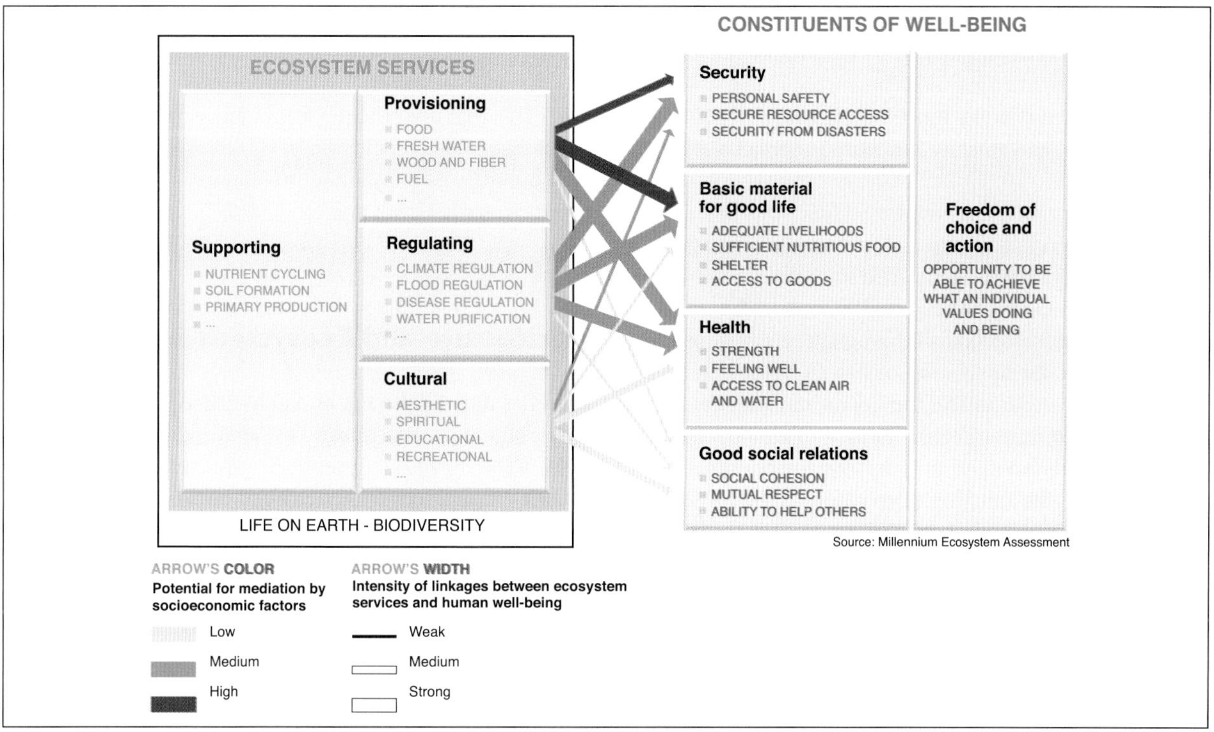

Figure 2.3. The support provided by ecosystems services to human well-being. Source: Millennium Ecosystem Assessment, 2005.

'functions' and 'service' as reflected in the definition by de Groot et al. (2002), which says that ecosystem (or landscape) functions are '… the capacity of ecosystems to provide goods and services that satisfy human needs, directly or indirectly.' Thus 'function' can be seen as the actual (functional) processes and components in ecosystems and landscapes that provide the goods and services that have, direct or indirect, benefit to human welfare (de Groot and Hein, 2007). There are situations where the distinction between function and services is difficult (regulation versus supporting services) and considering the complexity of ecological systems and their interactions with human society, a satisfying classification of functions, goods and services will probably never be found.

Although the difference between processes and services is more than semantic, it may not always seem so, especially when the terms used to summarise the processes are only slightly different from the terms used to characterise the service. For example, the function in which water infiltrates into watershed soils, is stored in those soils, and is later released downstream, has been called 'regulation of hydrological flows,' and produces the service called 'water regulation' (Costanza et al., 1997). The shorthand labels we attach to processes and services must not be allowed to blur the distinction between processes and the services they perform.

Figure 2.3 drawn from the Millennium Ecosystem Assessment (2005), illustrates how the biosphere supports the survival of society and the execution of economic activities, including agriculture, by pointing out that social and economic dimensions are dependent on the functioning of the ecological systems.

Four Kinds of Ecosystems Services

Four groups of functions (or services) are primarily distinguished by the Millennium Assessment: provisioning, regulating, cultural and supporting services, roughly corresponding to the production, regulation, information and habitat functions distinguished by de Groot et al. (2002).

The typology includes four categories: (1) provisioning functions; (2) regulation functions; (3) habitat functions; and (4) cultural and amenity functions (Groot et al., 2002).

1. *Provisioning functions* comprise functions that supply 'physical services' in terms of resources or space. This category has been divided into two classes: production and carrier functions. *Production functions* reflect resources produced by natural ecosystems, for example the harvesting of fish from the ocean. *Carrier functions* reflect the goods and services that are provided through human manipulation of the natural productivity (e.g. fish from aquaculture). In these cases, the function from nature is the provision of suitable substrate or space for human activities, including agriculture, mining, transportation, etc.

2. *Regulation functions* result from the capacity of ecosystems and landscapes to influence ('regulate') climate, hydrological and biochemical cycles, earth surface processes, and a variety of biological processes. These services often have an important spatial (connectivity) aspect; e.g. the flood control service of an upper watershed forest is only relevant in the flood zone downstream of the forest.

3. *Habitat functions* comprise the importance of ecosystems and landscapes to maintain natural processes and biodiversity, including the refuge and the nursery functions. The refuge function reflects the value that landscape units have to provide habitat to (threatened) fauna and flora, the nursery function indicates that some landscape units provide a particularly suitable location for reproduction and thereby have a regulating impact on the maintenance of populations elsewhere.

4. *Cultural and amenity functions* relate to the benefits people obtain from landscapes through recreation, cognitive development, relaxation and spiritual reflection. This may involve actual visits to the area, indirectly enjoying the area (e.g. through nature movies), or gaining satisfaction from the knowledge that a landscape contains important biodiversity or cultural monuments.

Contrary to Millennium Ecosystem Assessment (2005), the typology does not include the category 'supporting services/functions', which represents the ecological processes that underlie the functioning of ecosystems and landscapes. Their inclusion in valuation may lead to double counting, as their value is reflected in the other types of services (de Groot and Hein, 2007).

Agriculture and Ecosystem Services

Benefits and Problems of Agriculture

Covering over one-third of total global land area (FAOSTAT, 1999), agriculture represents humankind's largest engineered ecosystem. Among the Earth's major ecosystems, agriculture is that most directly managed by humans to meet human goals. As Tilman et al. (2002) state: 'Agriculturalists are the de facto managers of the most productive lands on Earth. Sustainable agriculture will require that society appropriately rewards ranchers, farmers and other agriculturalists for the production of both food and ecosystem services.' However, appropriately rewarding ranchers, farmers and other agriculturalists will require the ability to accurately measure ecosystem services in a verifiable quantitative manner.

Even though the problems agriculture has created for nature conservation are well-known, the acquisition of natural resources for immediate human needs neglecting the long-term view, development of urban areas, intensive use of agricultural lands, and population pressures continue to mount, more often than not at the expense of degrading environmental conditions.

The rural landscape has until recently been regarded simply as a positive externality of the productive activity, taken for granted and not further examined. Now, however, it is being realised that the agricultural landscape has also other functions – the environmental/ecological, the cultural/heritage and the amenity/scenic. Agricultural ecosystems both provide and rely upon important ecosystem services. Agriculture is in the midst of a change of conditions, which may cause it to change dramatically and in as yet unforeseen directions. So these other functions are coming under close scrutiny, such as producing separate public goods of increased value to society

Table 2.1. Examples of environmental functions, critical attributes and associated goods and services (Adapted from De Groot et al. 2002).

Examples of environmental functions	Critical attributes and characteristics (e.g. ecosystem processes and components	Examples of goods and services
1. Biodiversity-related functions (habitat functions: providing suitable living space for wild plants and animals, regulation functions: maintenance of essential ecological processes and life support systems)		
Refugium functions	Suitability to provide food, shelter and reproduction habitat	Maintenance of biological and genetic diversity. Nursery functions for wild species
Life support functions	Role of biota in movement of floral gametes.	Pollination of crops
	Population control through trophic-dynamic relations	Control of pests and diseases
		Reduction of herbivory (crop damage)
Genetic resources	Maintenance of wild relatives for plant species and animal breeds	Improvement and adaptation of cultivated plants and domestic animals
2. Landscape-related functions (information functions: providing opportunities for cognitive development)		
Aesthetic information	Attractive landscape features	Enjoyment of scenery (scenic roads, housing, etc.)
Recreation	Variety of landscapes with (potential) recreactional uses	Travel to natural ecosystems for ecotourism, outdoor sports, etc.
Cultural and artistic information	Variety of nature with cultural and artistic value	Use of nature as motive in books, film, painting, folklore, national symbols, architecture, advertising, etc.
Spiritual and historic information	Variety of nature with spiritual and historic value	Use of nature for religious or historic purposes (i.e. heritage value of natural ecosystems and features)
Science and education	Variety of nature with scientific and educational value	School excursions etc.
		Scientific field laboratories, etc.
3. Soil complex related functions (regulation functions: maintenance of essential ecological processes and life support systems)		
Soil erosion control	Role of vegetation root matrix and soil biota in soil retention	Maintenance of arable land
		Prevention of damage from erosion/siltation
4.Water complex related functions (regulation functions: maintenance of essential ecological processes and life support systems)		
Water supply	Filtering, retention and storage of fresh water (e.g. in aquifers)	Provision of water for consumtion (e.g. drinking, irrigation and industrial use)

as they become scarcer, and whose value should be made to play a role in the decision-making of the farmers. In environmental planning and decision-making, however, these benefits are often not fully taken into account and productive, multi-functional landscapes continue to be converted into more simple, often single-function land use types or turned into wastelands. Yet, increasingly studies are showing that the total value of multifunctional use of natural and semi-natural landscapes is often economically more beneficial than the value of the converted systems (Balmford et al., 2002). Food, fibre, and fuel production have been the overwhelmingly dominant goal of agriculture. Yet, as a managed ecosystem, agriculture plays unique roles in both supplying and demanding other ecosystem services (Swinton et al., 2007). Agriculture supplies all four major categories of ecosystem services – provisioning, regulating, habitat and cultural services – while it also demands supporting services that enable it to be productive.

In order to allow for the performance of environmental functions by (semi-) natural and agricultural ecosystems, certain ecological conditions have to be present. These ecological conditions are critical ecological processes, abiotic and biotic components of ecosystems and their inter-relationships. Identifying these critical ecological conditions by use of indicators is a possible way to systematically analyse which attributes and characteristics are necessary for the performance of environmental functions (i.e. provision of environmental goods and services) in a specific ecosystem (see Table 2.1).

Agriculture and ecosystem services are interrelated in at least three ways (Dale and Polasky, 2007):

(1) Agro-ecosystems generate beneficial ecosystem services such as soil retention, food production and aesthetics.
(2) Agro-ecosystems receive beneficial ecosystem services from other ecosystems such as pollination from non-agricultural ecosystems.
(3) Ecosystem services from non-agricultural systems may be affected by agricultural practices.

In some cases, tracing the interrelationships between agriculture and ecosystem services is fairly direct, as when pollinators increase agricultural crop yields or conservation easements on agricultural lands provide habitat for bird species enjoyed by birdwatchers. In other cases, the contribution may be more indirect or complex, for example when wetlands reduce the load of nitrogen in surface water originating from agricultural fields and destined for a coastal estuary where eutrophication causes hypoxic conditions and reduced fish productivity.

Agriculture's Ecosystem Disservices

Agriculture both provides and receives ecosystem services (ES) that extend well beyond the provision of food, fibre and fuel. In the process, it depends upon a wide variety of supporting and regulating services, such as soil fertility and pollination that determine the underlying biophysical capacity of agricultural ecosystems (MA, 2005). Agriculture also receives an array of ecosystem disservices (EDS) that reduce productivity or increase production costs (e.g. herbivores and competition for water). Some are planned, but most are indirect, unmanaged, underappreciated and unvalued – in effect, serendipitous (Swinton et al., 2007). A wide variety of ES and EDS confer benefits and costs, respectively, to agriculture. These are supplied by varied species, functional groups and guilds over a range of scales and influenced by human activities both intentionally and unintentionally.

These unwanted effects of agriculture – agriculture's ecosystem disservices – are not minor. Land use change associated with agricultural development results in habitat loss, cropland irrigation leads to the diversion of rivers and groundwater depletion, overgrazing results in rangeland erosion and can initiate desertification, invasive pests are introduced with the movement of agricultural commodities, accelerated nitrogen and phosphorus loading of surface waters results in aquatic and marine eutrophication – the list goes on and is well known (Swinton et al., 2007). However, ecosystems in agricultural landscapes can also ameliorate these problems, as can changes in agricultural management per se. Cropland can be managed to be more nutrient and water efficient, riparian zones can be managed to effectively remove nutrients and sediments before runoff reaches surface water bodies, and native communities and wetlands can be restored within a matrix of agricultural lands to provide habitats for beneficial insects and birds (Robertson et al., 2007).

Only in their absence do most become apparent. Pollination services, which have recently become threatened by honeybee colony collapse disorder, contribute to fruit, nut and vegetable production worth $75 billion in 2007 (USDA, 2007) – five times the cost of expected US farm subsidies. Wetlands and streams in agricultural watersheds can transform leached nitrate into a non-reactive form that keeps it from harming downstream ecosystems (Whitmire and Hamilton, 2005). These sorts of services (and disservices, in the case of effects that are deemed undesirable) place agriculture in a web of other services provided by ecosystems to society, a web formed by linkages within and inherent to the agricultural landscape (Figure 2.4).

We now recognise that agriculture is not so much a field-based enterprise as a landscape-based enterprise: Crops in individual fields are dependent on services provided by nearby ecosystems, whether native or managed, and nearby ecosystems are often influenced by their agricultural neighbours (Swinton et al., 2007). Neighbouring ecosystems provide food, refuge and reproductive habitat for pollinators and bio-control agents; they provide wildlife habitat; and they help to attenuate some of the unwelcome effects of agricultural production, including the escape of nitrogen, phosphorus and pesticides into non-agricultural ecosystems where they may produce undesirable impacts.

Ecosystem services (ES) and dis-services (EDS) to agriculture influence both where and how people choose to farm. For example, many major fruit-producing regions in temperate climate zones are located downwind of large bodies of water that help to regulate local atmospheric temperature changes (Ackerman and Knox, 2006) and reduce the probability of late frosts that might damage fruit blossoms. ES to agriculture affect not only the location and type of farming, but also the economic value of farmland. While determined in part by crop price, the value of agricultural land also depends on production costs linked to ES such as soil fertility and depth, suitable climate and freedom from heavy pest pressure (Roka and Palmquist, 1997).

The scales at which services are provided to agriculture are also critical to how management decisions are made. Many key organisms that provide services and dis-services to agriculture do not inhabit the agricultural fields themselves. Rather, they live in the surrounding landscape or they may move between natural habitats, hedgerows and fields. Table 2.2 summarises the major actors and scales of provision for the ES and EDS described.

The scales at which ES and EDS are rendered determine the relevant management units for influencing their flows to agriculture (Zhang et al., 2007). If they respond to factors on a small scale then it may be possible to manage them within a single farm. However, if they respond to factors on a larger scale, then the management actions of individual farmers must be coordinated with several different other decision-makers involved (Weibull et al., 2003). Table 2.2 reveals that scarcely any ES or EDS are provided only at the field level, so management will be more effective if performed at larger scales. The appropriate scale at which to manage will depend upon each specific provisioning ES and the supporting and regulating ES on which it relies. Table 2.2 also highlights the importance of a farm's landscape context in managing many of the supporting and regulating ES and EDS.

Services and Disservices Provided to and by Agriculture

Crops and Soil Fertility

The most important service provided by agriculture is its provision of food, fuel and fibre. Grain, livestock, fuel, forage and other products are used to meet subsistence or market needs, usually without regard to the provision of other services. Nevertheless, a number of other services are also provided.

The most important supporting service is the maintenance of soil fertility, which is fundamental to sustain agricultural productivity. Agronomic management that maintains or improves soil fertility, when employed in place of less sustainable practices, can be viewed as providing a mitigation service. A number of factors comprise soil fertility, and all of these are potentially influenced by agronomic practices. Micro-organisms (bacteria, fungi, actinomycetes) are critical mediators of this ecosystem service. For example, bacteria enhance nitrogen availabil-

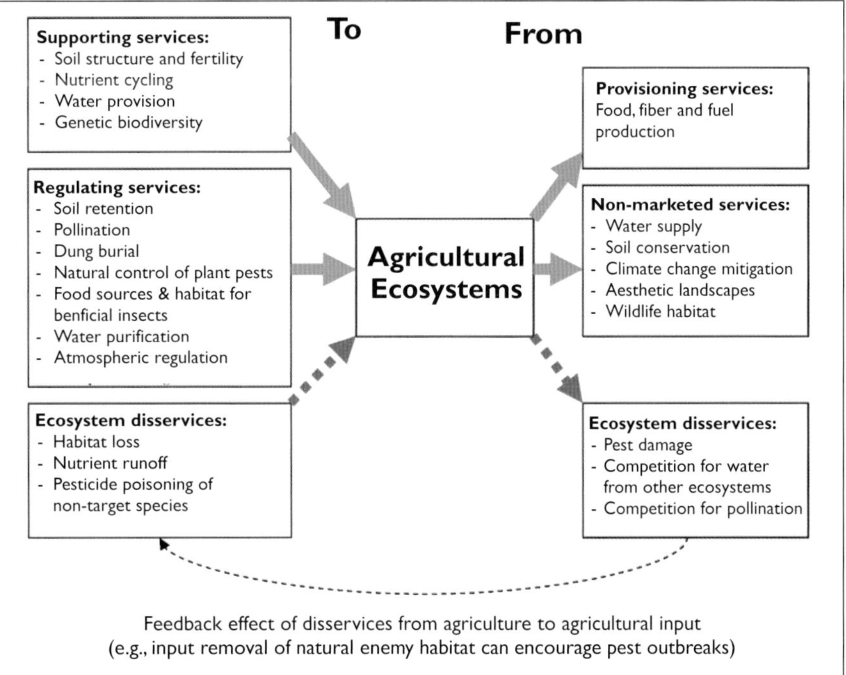

Figure 2.4. Ecosystem services and dis-services to and from agriculture. Solid arrows indicate services, whereas dashed arrows indicate dis-services. Source: Zhang et al., 2007.

Table 2.2. Major ecosystem services (ES) and dis-services (EDS) to agriculture, the scales over which they typically are provided, and main guilds or communities whose activities typically supply them (Zhang et al., 2007).

ES or EDS Services	From fields[a]	From farm[b]	From landscape[c]	From region/globe[d]
Soil fertility and formation, nutrient cycling		Vegetation cover		
Soil retention	Cover crops	Cover crops	Riparian vegetation; floodplain	Vegetation cover in watershed
Pollination	Ground-nesting bees	Bees; other pollinating animals	Insects; other pollinating animals	
Pest control	Predators and parasitoids (e.g., spiders, wasps)	Predators and parasitoids (e.g., spiders, wasps, birds, bats)		
Water provision and purification		Vegetation around drainages and ponds	Vegetation cover in watershed	Vegetation cover in watershed
Genetic diversity	Crop diversity for pest and disease resistance			Wild varieties
Climate regulation	Vegetation influencing microclimate (e.g. agro forestry)	Vegetation influencing microclimate	Vegetation influencing stability of local climate; amount of precipitation; temperature	Vegetation and soils for carbon sequestration and storage
Disservices	**From fields[a]**	**From farm[b]**	**From landscape[c]**	**From region/globe[d]**
Pest damage	Insects; snails; birds; mammals; fungi; bacteria, viruses; weeds	Insects; snails; birds; mammals; fungi; bacteria, viruses; weeds	Insects; snails; birds; mammals; range weeds	
Competition for water from other ecosystems	Weeds	Vegetation cover near drainage ditches	Vegetation cover in watershed	Vegetation cover in watershed
Competition for pollination services	Flowering weeds	Flowering weeds	Flowering plants in watershed	

a Services provided from within agricultural fields themselves.
b Services provided from farm property, but not necessarily in active fields themselves.
c Services provided from landscape surrounding typical farms, not from farmer's property.
d Services provided from broader region or globe.

ity through the fixation of nitrogen from the atmosphere. This occurs most often in plants that have symbiotic relationships with N-fixing bacteria, but free-living soil bacteria can fix nitrogen as well (Vitousek et al., 2002). Micro-organisms also enhance soil fertility by liberating nutrients from detrital organic matter (e.g. plant leaves) and retaining nutrients in their biomass that might otherwise be lost downstream (Paul and Clark, 1996).

ES and Insects – Crop Pollination and Pest Control

Regulating services are among the most diverse class of services provided by agriculture. Agricultural landscapes have the capacity to regulate the population dynamics of pollinators, pests, pathogens and wildlife, as well as fluctuations in levels of soil loss, water quality and supply, and greenhouse gas emissions and carbon sequestration (Swinton et al., 2007). Insects provide vital ES to agriculture including dung burial, pest control and pollination. Beetles in the family *Scarabaeidae* are especially efficient at providing dung burial services (Ratcliffe, 1970). They decompose wastes generated by large animals (a potential EDS from agriculture), thereby recycling nitrogen, enhancing forage palatability, and reducing pest habitat, resulting in significant economic value for the cattle industry (Losey and Vaughan, 2006).

Crop pollination is perhaps the best known ES performed by insects (Losey and Vaughan, 2006). The production of over 75% of the world's most important crops that feed humanity and 35% of the food produced is dependent upon animal pollination (Klein et al., 2007). There is increasing evidence that conserving wild pollinators in habitats adjacent to agriculture improves both the level and stability of pollination, leading to increased yields and income (Klein et al., 2003).

Natural control of plant pests is provided by generalist and specialist predators and parasitoids, including birds, spiders, ladybugs, mantis, flies and wasps, as well as entomopathogenic fungi (Naylor and Ehrlich, 1997). This ES in the short term suppresses pest damage and improves yield, while in the long-term it maintains an ecological equilibrium that prevents herbivore insects from reaching pest status. This important ES, however, is increasingly threatened by biodiversity loss (Wilby and Thomas, 2002) and modern agricultural practices (Naylor and Ehrlich, 1997).

For beneficial insects to provide the above direct ES to agriculture, a number of subsequent supporting and regulating services are required. For example, predators and parasitoids rely on a variety of plant resources such as nectar, pollen, sap or seeds (Wilkinson and Landis, 2005) as alternative food sources to fuel adult flight and reproduction. Non-crop areas can provide habitat where beneficial insects mate, reproduce and overwinter. Evidence shows that increased landscape complexity, which typically means increased availability of food sources and habitat for insects compared with mono-culture landscapes, is correlated with diversity and abundance of natural enemy populations (Thies and Tscharntke, 1999).

Water

Water provision and purification fulfil requirements for water of sufficient quantity, timing and purity for agricultural production. Vegetation cover in upstream watersheds can affect the amount, quality and stability of the water supply to agriculture (Zhang et al., 2007). Forests stabilise water flow to reduce differences in flow between wet and dry seasons (e.g. Yangtze basin; Guo et al., 2000). Forests can also stabilise soil to reduce sediment load in rivers. Wetlands and riparian vegetation can also improve water quality and attenuate floods (Houlahan and Findlay, 2004).

Genetic Diversity and Other Regulating Functions

Genetic diversity provides the raw material for natural selection to produce evolutionary adaptations. Similarly, breeders of crops and domestic animals utilise existing genetic variation to select artificially for desirable traits.

Figure 2.5. Pollination is one of the most threatened ecosystem services. Photo: Marcin Bajer.

Genetic diversity is important not only in avoiding catastrophic losses, but also in improving or maintaining agricultural productivity. Many important crops could not maintain commercial status without the regular genetic support of their wild relatives (de Groot et al., 2002). Genetic diversity at the species level can also enhance biomass output per unit of land through better utilisation of nutrients and reduced losses to pests and diseases.

Another (abiotic) form of ES to agriculture involves climate, including temperature and precipitation regimes but also the frequency and severity of extreme weather, droughts, floods, etc. Favourable climate confers a cost advantage to those who farm there. Suitable and stable climate relies on atmospheric regulation, which like many other ES is influenced by the functioning of multiple ecosystems.

Cultural Benefits of Agriculture

Additional services provided by agricultural landscapes include cultural benefits, the valuation of which can be especially difficult. These include open-space, rural viewscapes and the cultural heritage of rural lifestyles.

Crop pests, including herbivores, seed-eaters, and pathogens (specifically, fungal, bacterial and viral diseases) decrease productivity and in the worst case can result in complete crop loss. Revenue loss from insect pests and pathogens can be disproportionately high for crops for which the price depends heavily on quality, such as fresh produce (Babcock et al., 1992). Non-crop plants can re-

Box 2.1. Nature Protection

The Conservation Movement

As man enters and uses the landscape its original shape and functions are altered, sometimes with serious consequences for wildlife, environmental services and, not the least, culture and beauty. The conservation movement has been fighting this since a century or more, by promoting national parks and other protected areas. The first national park was established in United States in 1872; in Europe Sweden was first with a protected area in 1909 (in the archipelago) and a large national park in the mountains (fjell) in 1910.

As the disastrously rapid decline of diversity, loss of species and nature, were understood strong steps were made towards international criteria and standards for active nature conservation. The International Conservation Union, IUCN, was formed in 1948, best known for its red lists of threatened species. At the UN Rio Conference in 1992 the Convention on Biological Diversity, CBD, was signed by 192 nations. As its 10th Conference of the parties assembled in Nagoya, Japan, in 2010, biodiversity was still decreasing at an alarming speed, at least some 100 times the background value. The countries adopted a new ten-year strategic plan to protect biodiversity and committed themselves to protect 10% of the world's oceans and 17% of all land mass no later than 2020.

Protection and Conservation of Sites

The majority of legislative regulations for nature conservation in the European countries, including those in the Baltic Sea basin, support goals such as:

- maintenance of ecological processes and ecosystem stability,
- conservation of biodiversity,
- conservation of geological heritage,
- conservation and long term survival of species and ecosystems,
- creation of proper human attitudes towards nature, and
- rehabilitation of resources and areas of nature to the proper stage.

The IUCN (1993) defines a protected area as "land and/or sea especially dedicated to the protection of biological diversity, and of natural and associated cultural resources, and managed through legal or other effective means." Countries around the Baltic Sea understand this definition in different ways. In Europe, more than 40,000 sites are protected. Some of these are very small, known as nature reserves. A national park is defined as an area of at least 1,000 ha of specific and wilderness value with richness of diverse nature phenomena, nature monuments and beautiful, often primeval environment. Many protected areas are suffering from intensive agriculture, from air and water pollution, and a lack of sufficient sources for proper management, and also from intensive tourism.

Protected land covers 9.8% area of Denmark, but true national parks are lacking. In Finland, 30 national parks cover nearly 8,000 km^2. In Sweden, 23 national parks cover about 6,300 km^2.

Figure 2.6. Camping at Abisko, Sweden. Photo: Tomas Hellberg.

Some of them are unique, and the only "Arctic" national park within the European Union is found there. Nature reserves in Poland are divided into strictly protected and partially protected areas where certain kinds of human activity are allowed. The most spectacular and important National Park, the Bieloveza Forests, is divided about equally between Poland and Belarus. The only remaining traces of the European original deciduous forest are found here.

Conservation and Restoration of Wetlands, Meadows, Old Forests

The nature conservation value of wetlands got the highest recognition when the Convention of Wetlands of International Importance, especially as Habit for Water Fowl, also known as the Ramsar Convention, was signed in 1971 in the Iranian city of Ramsar. The signatories, the convention says, share a common belief in the value of wetlands as valuable and irreplaceable economic, cultural, scientific and recreational resources and commit themselves to proper management of wetlands for the present and future benefit of their people.

In addition to protection of wetlands, some countries have made great efforts to restore the once lost wetlands, where birds are quick to occupy the "new" territory. Artificial wetlands play an increasing role in wastewater management, as a cheaper alternative to clean water.

A traditional manure-driven agriculture with species rich natural hay-meadows and grazing areas dominated in the whole region into the early 19th century. Almost all these meadows, totally dependent upon mowing or grazing, have been lost in an even faster pace, especially if new forest is planted on it. However, there are also projects where the old meadows are conserved. The include restoration of the important bird area Matsalu bay in Estonia, Biebrza National Park in Poland.

Nature Protection

Figure 2.7.View of the lower basin of the Biebrza National Park, Poland. Photo: Frank Vassen.

Figure 2.8. Forest trail in Bialowieza National Park, Poland. Photo: Chad Chatterton.

European Union Biodiversity Policies

The European Union's 27 Member States includes a vast range of natural habitats and a great diversity of flora and fauna. Yet Europe is the most urbanised and, together with Asia, the most densely populated continent in the world. These factors have exacted a toll. EU's precious 'biodiversity' continues to be under serious threat, 42% of our native mammals 15% of birds, 45% of butterflies, 30% of amphibians, 45% of reptiles and 52% of freshwater fish are threatened. In Northern and Western Europe, some 60% of wetlands have been lost. Two-thirds of trees in the EU are under stress, while forest fires in the south continue to pose a problem.

The EU has been involved in efforts to protect the continent's natural heritage for the past 30 years. The Sixth Environmental Action Plan (EAP) 2002-12 highlights nature and biodiversity as a top priority. Under the EU Sustainable Development Strategy launched in Gothenburg in 2001, halting the loss of biodiversity in the EU by 2010 is a priority. As this ambition failed, as it did in the world as a whole, EU is now behind the new vision formulated at COP10 of the CBD in Nagoya.

European Union Directives and Conservation Policies

Two EU Directives deal with the conservation of European wildlife, focusing on the protection of sites as well as species. Council Directive 79/409/EEC on the conservation of wild birds, the Birds Directive, identified 193 endangered species and sub-species for which the Member States are required to designate Special Protection Areas (SPAs). As a result of this action, some severely threatened species are now beginning to recover. Council Directive 92/43/EEC on the conservation of natural habitats and of wild fauna and flora, the Habitats Directive, aims to protect other wildlife species and habitats. Each Member State is required to identify sites of European importance and to put in place a special management plan to protect them, combining long-term conservation with economic and social activities, as part of a sustainable development strategy.

The sites of the Habitats and Birds Directives make up the Natura 2000 network - the cornerstone of EU nature protection policy. The Natura 2000 network in 2010 included 22,529 sites, covering 719,015 km^2 or 13.7 % of EU27 terrestrial territory. It is co-financed through the Commission's LIFE programme and other Community finance instruments. The Natura 2000 Networking Programme will create a series of training events, themed workshops and practical tools to promote Natura 2000, good practice in site management and the benefits of networking, across Europe.

The European Landscape Convention is part of the Council of Europe's work on natural and cultural heritage, spatial planning, environment and local self-government. It sees the landscape as an essential consideration in striking a balance between preserving the natural and cultural heritage as a reflection of European identity and diversity, and using it as an economic resource. The convention was developed within the Conference of Regional and Local Authorities of Europe, CRLAE, and later adopted by the Council of Europe in 2000. The landscape is important as a component of the environment and of people's surroundings in both town and country, whether it is ordinary or outstanding landscape. The public is accordingly encouraged to take an active part in landscape management and planning, and to feel it has responsibility for what happens to the landscape.

Lars Rydén

duce agricultural productivity via competition for resources and allelopathy (Stoller et al., 1987). In fields, weed competition for sunlight, water and soil nutrients can reduce crop growth by limiting access to required resources (Welbank, 1963). Competition for ecological resources of value to agriculture also occurs at landscape scale. Water consumed by other plants can reduce water available to agricultural production. For example, trees can reduce the recharge of aquifers used for irrigation. Competition for pollination services from flowering weeds and non-crop plants can also reduce crop yields (Free, 1993).

The Monetary Value of Ecosystem Services
Being able to place values on ecosystem services is fundamental to designing policies to induce agricultural land managers to provide (or maintain) ES at levels that are desirable to society. Of course, food, fibre and fuel have markets that provide incentives to produce those ES, as well as measures of their value to society. However, many other ES lack markets. The value of those ES may differ between farmers and the consumers of the ES. Farmers (or producers in general) would often lose income by changing production practices to generate more ES.

Figure 2.9. Sheep managing the landscape. Photo: Ingrid Karlsson.

Policy and Management of Agricultural Landscapes

Not Only Providing Harvest
Nowhere is the need for the application of ecological principles more acute than in agriculture. Agriculture is the world's largest industry and has had an overwhelming effect on structuring the landscape. The Millennium Ecosystem Assessment (2005) found that several ecosystem services that relate to agriculture are in decline. Particularly noticeable are the worldwide declines in wild fish and fresh water. In many cases, declines in wild-fish stocks can be traced to over-harvesting (Jackson et al., 2001; Myers and Worm, 2003). Decreases in the supply and quality of fresh water in many parts of the world can be traced to increasingly intensive agriculture, both in terms of withdrawal of water from rivers for irrigation, and lower water quality from the flow of nutrients, sediments, and dissolved salts from agricultural lands. The global increase in crop production may also account for declines in air quality regulation, climate regulation, erosion regulation, pest regulation and pollination (MA, 2005). A major concern is that the increased agricultural production over the past 50 years has come at the cost of the ecological sustainability that will be necessary to maintain productivity in the future.

Current cropping systems focus on a single ecosystem service, the production of food, yet many other services (e.g. clean water and air, pollination, disease suppression, habitat for other organisms, carbon storage, maintenance of biogeochemical cycles, etc.) are possible and needed. Soil loss can also be regulated by agricultural management. Conservation tillage and the maintenance of plant cover year-round can reduce runoff and associated soil, nutrient and pesticide losses. The reduction of runoff also serves to increase infiltration, which increases the water available to plants and can improve groundwater recharge. At its heart, this is an ecological challenge: agronomic yield is in essence an ecological productivity, and the ways that organisms interact among themselves and with their abiotic environments determine the productive capacity of the agricultural ecosystem, the proportion of ecological productivity that can be harvested as plant or animal products, and the biological diversity and stability of agro-ecosystems. Thus, the good understanding of ecological principles among farmers and agriculture policy-makers is highly critical. The future adequacy and environmental impact of agriculture depends on how effectively we understand and manage the ecological, but also the social elements of agricultural ecosystems (Tilman et al., 2002).

Policy-makers have responded to the alarm launched by researchers with regard to the need for 'biodiversity conservation'. A reference to 'the conservation of biodiversity' is present in almost all conservation, land use management and environmental protection policies proposed at local, national and international scale. As can be seen from some reports and projects written at European Community (EC) level, policy-makers use biodiversity for various goals and objectives without much specification.

Farmers as Landscape Managers

A large number of countries have legislation that explicitly recognises the importance of the recreational, cultural, heritage, aesthetic and other amenity values embodied in agricultural and other landscapes. The European Union agro-environmental measures (EU Regulation 2078/92) include aid to farmers who adopt 'farming practices compatible with the requirements of protection of the environment and natural resources, as well as maintenance of the countryside and the landscape'. Within the EU, the national agricultural legislation of member states typically sets objectives for the protection and restoration of landscapes and also for providing public access to these landscapes.

Sustainable agriculture will require that society appropriately rewards ranchers, farmers and other agriculturalists for the production of both food and ecosystem services, but this will require the ability to accurately measure ecosystem services in a verifiable quantitative manner.

Measures adopted by OECD countries for agricultural landscape conservation and restoration can be categorised into three main types:

- *Economic incentives*, such as through area payments (e.g. Norwegian area and cultural landscape payments) and management agreements based on individual agreements between farmers and regional/national authorities, where payments are provided in compensation for restrictions on certain farming practices and maintenance of key landscape features (e.g. the EU Environmentally Sensitive Area Schemes).
- *Regulatory measures*, which may set certain minimum standards on the whole agricultural area and can designate certain areas of 'high' landscape value as national parks or reserves, and impose restrictions on certain management practices for farmers in these areas (e.g. the national park system created in France, see Bonnieux and Rainelli, 1996); or protect specific landscape features (e.g. the Hedgerow Regulations in the United Kingdom).
- *Community and voluntary based systems*, which set out to devolve the responsibility and management of natural resources, the environment and landscapes to farm families, rural communities and local governments.

Measuring the ***costs of landscape provision*** can help policy-makers determine the outlay by farmers in maintaining and/or restoring certain landscape elements. These costs may relate to cultural and heritage features, such as spending by farmers on the conservation of historic sites and/or buildings on farmland. However, expenditure could also involve costs incurred in hedge or stone wall maintenance that, while providing a positive externality in terms of the landscape, may also generate benefits for the farmer, for example, by providing a windshield for crops and livestock.

The difficulty for policy-makers is that there are few precise rules that indicate the 'correct' or optimal provision of landscape. Questions include how much is optimal, precisely which landscape features does society value, and to what extent do changes in policies and policy mixes affect landscape (Sinner, 1997). To help answer these questions, indicators of agricultural landscapes provide a tool to better inform future policy decisions by recording the stock of landscape features, determining how these features are changing over time, establishing what share of agricultural land is under public/private schemes for landscape conservation, and measuring/evaluating the 'cost' or effort of landscape provision by farmers and the value society attaches to agricultural landscapes.

Rural Development in the Belarusian Polesie Area

3

CASE STUDY Belarus

Valentin Yatsukhno
Belarusian State University, Minsk, Belarus

Ecosystems of the Belarusian Polesie

Geography

The Polesskaya lowland 'Polesie' is situated in Belarus, Ukraine and Poland and has a total area of 13.2 million ha. It is a unique natural region with very rich biological and landscape diversity. There are large forests and bogs preserved in their natural conditions, as well as vast floodplains which are unique in Europe. The rural landscapes of Polesie represent an outstanding combination of ecological, economic, historical and cultural values.

Belarusian Polesie is the largest region in Central and Eastern Europe where natural wetland ecosystems are concentrated, covering a total area of more than 680,000 ha. This is the northern part of the Polesie lowland and constitutes almost 32% of the territory of the Republic of Belarus (Figure 3.1). The core of the region is the Prypyat' river basin. Here 35 regional types of landscapes can be found and they all have various geological features, soil composition, climate and vegetation cover. Wetland ecosystems used to occupy more than 44% of the area. The floodplain in some of the upper parts is as wide as 20-25 km, while the central part and the river mouth is 3-8 km wide.

Figure 3.1. Polesie is the largest natural wetland ecosystem in Central and Eastern Europe covering parts of Northern Ukraine, Western Poland and a large part of Southern Belarus. Source: Author..

The Flora of Forests, Meadows and Mires

The flora of Belarusian Polesie includes a number of rare species. Over 1,400 species of higher vascular plants are found in the region, representing 96% of the whole flora assemblage of the country. More than 60 rare species are included in the Red Data Book of Belarus. The regional isolation of the Polesie flora and the presence of many natural boundaries created by geological water level differences of continuous or insular type are the main causes of the richness of specific regional and even zonal species. The boundaries of the floristic Polesie largely coincide with the borders of the hydrological Polesie. The present plant cover in the Belarusian Polesie consists mainly of forests (42.1%), meadows and mires (23.3%). Forest vegetation includes the following types: coniferous (61.1%), broad-leaved (7.9 %), small-leaved (12.4%) and native larch forests on bogs (18.6%). The most important tree species are: Pine (58.7%), birch (15.3%), black alder (13.5%), oak (7.2%), spruce (2.4%) and aspen (1.2%). Other broad-leaved trees (hornbeam, ash) and broad-leaved/coniferous (broad-leaved/pine, broad-leaved/spruce) species are also noticeable.

These forest types represent formations that have been typical in Western Europe but are rather unique nowadays. There are patches of forest types that are completely different from the Eastern European forests of south-taiga type both when it comes to tree species composition and the structure of the forest under-storey vegetation. The lower percentage of spruce forests and their ecosystem diversity in Polesie is also accompanied by mixtures of spruce with Western European-type species such as oak, alder and other broad-leaved species. Extensive areas are occupied by black alder forests typical of fen mires.

The Polesie area could be classified as steppe meadow. Its meadows are characterised by a great number of steppe grass species (*Agrostis vinealis, Festuca trachyphylla, Koeleria delavignei, Phleum phleoides*). Its special type of raised bogs is also attributed to a particular Polesie landscape type with a distinctive boggy vegetation complex.

The mires in Polesie also display a specific character. They occur over large areas and are occupied mainly by reed, large sedge, *Hypnum*-sedge and grass-sedge communities.

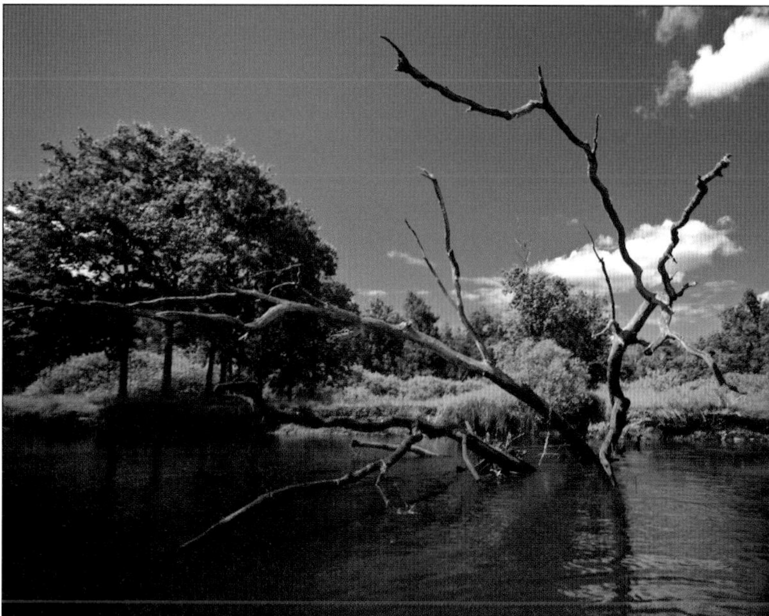

Figure 3.2. The river Ubort. Not far from Chernobyl. Gomel. Of Belarus. Pool Pripyat River. Belarusian Polesie. Photo: Oleg Gritskevich (Belarus).

The Fauna

The fauna is also characterised by a high diversity in these huge wetland areas. All Belarusian amphibians and reptiles, about 80% of all Belarusian birds, and 55% of its mammals are found on this territory. About 100 species of animals are included in the Red Data Book of Belarus.

Influence of Recent Human Activities

Hunting and Deforestation

Humans have only had an impact in the natural ecosystems of the Polesie area over the past 80-100 years. The early changes were mainly caused by timber felling and hunting. As a result, brown bear (*Ursus arctos*), beaver (*Castor fiber*) and lynx (*Lynx lynx*), as well as red deer (*Cervus elaphus*), moose (*Alces alces*) and wild boar (*Sus scrofa*) became almost extinct. However, beaver and ungulate species were successfully restored by the 1950-60s.

Drainage

During the second half of the 20th century, especially during 1966-90, more than 2.6 million ha of wetlands were drained in Belarusian Polesie. Later, reparation work on old drainage systems was carried out on more than 500,000 ha and 1.1 million ha were converted to agricultural use through these amelioration projects. Unfortunately, this led to an ecological catastrophe for plant and animal communities in this region. Fatal changes in different types of wetlands were observed in huge areas (Table 3.1). The whole Pripyat River catchment area was affected by the intensive drainage and land reclamation activities. Around 20% of its total area was drained and most of the small rivers were converted to channels. The dam constructions along the Pripyat River disturbed the natural development of floodplain ecosystems which depended on annual spring floods. In addition, water levels in the Pripyat river have increased. Thus many floodplain areas every year are over-inundated and wet. This causes degradation and destruction of the forest vegetation in some places.

Later there were also many examples of unsuccessful levelling of the bogs to turn them into rationally managed agricultural landscapes. This did not work, since oxidation of the organic matter proceeded very rapidly after lowering of the groundwater. As a result, biological diversity was severely damaged, while the agricultural value of the land diminished quickly.

The agricultural land created now consists of drained peat soils (about 700,000 ha). At first the collective farms set up here had some advantages, mainly because the organic matter of the soils contained more nutrients for crop uptake. However, within a short time it became evident that the drained and farmed peat soils were ecologically unstable. Now the state of the drained peat soils is causing concern because of decreased soil levels, problems with low pH, unavailability of micronutrients, etc. It is estimated that the total loss of organic matter in 1986-2000 was 43 million tonnes. A continuation of rational agriculture on these lands would require additional economic investments, training of farm workers, other agricultural machinery, other fertilisers and micronutrient applications and other measures.

One of the main reasons for the catastrophic impact of drainage in Belarus was the disregard for scientific arguments for conservation of undisturbed natural ecosystems with the purpose of maintaining biodiversity. In total, the agricultural land reclamation project caused a significant decrease in the number of different animal species, especially waterfowl.

Climate Change

Furthermore, the land degradation in Polesie has recently been exacerbated by negative climate changes, such as more frequent and prolonged droughts and other extreme natural phenomena (early frosts, disruption in the hydrological regimes, etc.). During the last 50-year period the number of droughts in the region increased 2.5-fold. The wetlands which were drained during 1960-1990 are most affected by these droughts.

The Chernobyl Radioactive Contamination

On top of this, the Ukrainian Chernobyl nuclear accident in 1986 influenced and is still strongly influencing the

Table 3.1. Changes in wetland area in Belarusian Polesie during 1959-2004. Source: Pikulik and Kozulin, 2000; Yatsukhno, 2006.

Habitat type	1959	2004	% change
Lakes			
Small forest lakes, km^2	23	23	0
Low productive lakes, km^2	1,117	1,117	0
High productive lakes, km^2	162	204	+21
Artificial water bodies			
Fish-farm ponds, km^2	24	192	+800
Water reservoirs, km^2	65	416	+640
Channels, km^2	5,000	32,157	+85
Rivers			
Highly waterlogged floodplains, km^2	3,700	688	-82
Moderately waterlogged floodplains, km^2	3,000	2,715	-10
Riverbeds, km^2	12,000	12,000	0
Small rivers, km^2	77,270	62,160	-20
Mires			
Open fen mires, km^2	10,765	3,800	-65
Wet mineral lands			
Wetlands with mineral soils	26,800	12,750	-52

Figure 3.3. Bug wetland in Pribuzhskoye-Polesie, Belarus which is a UNESCO biosphere reserve. Photo: Ivan Prakapiuk.

agriculture of Polesie. More than 1.8 million ha of agricultural land are polluted with Cs-137 at densities of over 1 Ci/km^2. As a consequence, 265,400 ha of fields were abandoned from agricultural use. The annual economic loss from agricultural production due to the Chernobyl accident is estimated at about US$ 70 million. The social and environmental costs are of course innumerable. About 70% of the overall radioactive contamination is in the Polesie region, and 88% of the population affected by the fall-out still resides here (1.4 million ha).

Reclamation, Use and Preservation of the Agricultural Landscapes

Implementation Policies

During the implementation of the 'Program on Dealing with the Consequences of the Chernobyl Nuclear Accident', the main attention focused on the radioactively contaminated areas with a dense human population. Agricultural activities were maintained on the 1.36 million ha contaminated by radioactive caesium and on the almost 0.5 million ha contaminated by Sr-90. The main aim of this programme is to produce foodstuffs suitable for human consumption. For this purpose, a special agricultural system has been introduced based on knowledge of radionuclide migration in soil and plants, as well as on how further migration through the food chain reaches humans. This system includes regulation of soil water regimes and use of appropriate crops, fertilisers and plant protection measures.

Principles of Reclamation

As a basis for agricultural production in the contaminated areas, the following principles of construction, formation and utilisation of reclaimed agricultural landscapes are used:

1. Maximal areal distribution of reclamation systems and agricultural land (arable and meadow lands, forest areas and forest belts, water basins, ponds, buffer, soil-saving and water-security zones) in accordance with the natural landscape types and reclamation systems (Yatsukhno, 1995). (Table 3.2) (Romanova and Yatsukhno, 2001). In such agricultural landscapes the proportion of land used for agricultural purposes is 0.7-0.8 70-80%.

2. Anthropogenic ingredients of landscapes (canals, reservoirs, fields, roads etc.) should be harmonised with natural habitats. This means that the landscape should keep its natural diversity factors such as water levels to enhance processes of self-purification and self-regeneration of natural habitats. To reach this goal, transition zones have to be created from agricultural areas to the various natural landscape types – forests, bushes, bogs, river valleys etc.

Table 3.2. Present and proposed optimal land use proportion of rural landscapes in Belarusian Polesie. (Romanova and Yatsukhno, 2001).

Land use	Present proportion, %	Optimal proportion, %	% change
Forests and shrubs	7	10	+3
Arable lands	48	31	-17
Meadows	37	45	+8
Mires	8	14	+6

3. Preventive measures need to be taken in the formation and utilisation of agricultural landscapes, for instance by preventing the lowering of the groundwater level in the adjacent terrains, diminishing contamination of waters through drainage systems, and preserving landscape diversity elements such as environmental niches, hibernation pits, rifts, etc.

4. The measures need to be integrated and compatible with agricultural production. Thus water levels, crop rotations, optimisation of the soil structure under crops, level of fertilisation etc. need to be incorporated into the maintenance of areas outside the actual agricultural areas.

Prospects for Future Sustainable Rural Development

Developing Agriculture

The rural inhabitants in this area have until recently lived in close connection to the natural environment. However, 'agricultural modernisation' has drastically affected the historically inherited values such as traditional ways of living and working, ethnic backgrounds, identity awareness, etc. In addition, it is high on the agenda for the development of Belarusian Polesie to restore the areas contaminated by radioactivity from the Chernobyl power plant catastrophe, both concerning its ecological and socio-economic values. In fact, the biological and landscape diversity in Polesie is a prerequisite for the preservation of its historical and cultural heritage, and for the sustainable development of the region as a whole.

Successful development of the region should be accompanied by reforms of agriculture, creation of a more diverse economy, and the breakup of the monopoly of large state agricultural enterprises. Alternative economic entities such as joint stock companies, cooperative farms, individual farms, share companies, associations, agro firms, holdings etc. should be developed. Crucial tasks in this transformation are land reform, the possibility to buy and sell land, land rental system reform, a reformed loan and credit system, etc. Approximately 30% of the agricultural land today can be expected to be put to uses

Table 3.3. Nature Protected Areas of Belarusian Polesie region, ha (Sheme...2007)

Natural protected area	Land area, ha
National Park	
Prypyatsky	82,254
Reservs	
Polessky radio-ecological	215,500
Zakazniks	
Landscape	
Mozyrskye Ovragi	1,141
Prostyr	3,440
Olmany mires	94,219
Strelsky	12,161
Mid-Pripyat	90,447
Vydritsa	17,560
Smychok	2,635
Biological	
Baranovichsky	29,019
Vetkovsky	5,900
Zhitkovichsky	15,000
Radostovsky	8,657
Shabrinsky	3,300
Babinets	850
Borsky	2,805
Buckchansky	4,915
Yelovsky	963
Falichsky Moh	1,700
Chirkovichsky	463
Buda-Koshelevsky	13,575
Selyava	260
Lukovo	1,523
Tyrvovichi	1,391
Zvanets	10,460
Luninsky	9,283
Buslovka	7,936
Sporovsky	19,384
Dnepro-Sozhsky	14,556
Hydrological	
Vygonoshchanskoye	43,000
Total area	712,497 or 11.7 % of Polesye region

other than agriculture because of its low agricultural productivity, and also because it is situated too far from large settlements (Yatsukhno et al., 1998).

In addition, better and more complex nature protection and management measures need to be introduced This includes restoration of the more traditional farming methods, used before collectivisation of the land and the large drainage schemes. Agricultural and ecological tourism, folk crafts, hunting, fishery, apiculture could be new ways of making a living in the area. However, this would require heavy investment.

Nature Protection

One promising strategy for future natural resource management is the establishment of nature protected areas. Today, the protected areas (zakazniks) of Belarussian Polesie cover 484,500 ha, which is over 11% of the region's area (Table 3.3). This area includes Prypyatski national park (82,200 ha), Polesski radiation-and-ecological reserve (215,500 ha) and 28 national reserves including 7 landscape, 1 hydrological and 20 biological reserves), Mid-Pripyat (90,400 ha), Olmany mires (94,200 ha), Zvanets (10,400 ha) and some smaller areas. However, Belarusian protected areas have to become a part of the European ecological network. The Polesie area would then be connected with its corresponding areas on the other side of the border (Poland, Ukraine, Russia). This would create a large and very valuable continuous area with similar ecologically and socially interesting features. This continuous and interconnected system should be seen as an inheritance given to future European generations.

The Baltic Waterscape
Lakes, Wetlands, Rivers and the Sea

4

Lars Rydén,
Uppsala University, Uppsala, Sweden

The Baltic Waterscape

The Waterscape Elements

The waterscape of the Baltic drainage basin is rich with its abundance of lakes, rivers, wetlands and the Baltic Sea itself and its coasts and archipelagos. In this chapter we will review this richness of surface water and try to understand its flows, how it depends on and influences the climate of the region, and how it is a resource for the rural landscape, its agriculture, fishery, forestry and beauty.

Considerable parts of the region are covered by water. The Baltic Sea accounts for 25% of the total drainage basin. A very long coastline touches nine of the countries in the region. The longest coastlines belong to Sweden and Finland.

There are more than 500,000 natural lakes larger than 0.01 km^2 (1 ha) in Europe; of these about 80 to 90% are small, with a surface area between 0.01 and 0.1 km^2. Three quarters of these lakes are located in Norway, Sweden, Finland and the Karelo-Kola area of the Russian Federation. The total volume of the lakes is 700 km^3. Generally, the Swedish and Finnish parts of the region are characterised by large numbers of lakes as compared to the southernmost parts. 9% of the area of these countries is covered by lakes.

Wetlands comprise close to 20% of the Baltic Sea catchment. This figure was much higher a century ago, as much of the wetlands have been drained. Thus more than half have been turned into agriculture, forestry and peat extraction. Still large natural wetlands remain, especially in the North. The decreased wetland areas have reduced the capacity of water to undergo self-cleaning on its way to the sea and is thus one factor contributing to the serious pollution situation of the Baltic Sea.

In large parts of the Baltic Sea region, especially so in the North, the rural landscape has a water surface within sight, a river or a lake. These have great importance for quality of life in the region. They give us pleasure; they contribute

This chapter is based on texts and information in the Baltic University course on Sustainable Water Management, Volume I *The Waterscape* with chapters *The Baltic Basin – rivers, lakes and climate* by Sten Bergström, Nicolai Filatov, Dimitrij Pozdnjakov, Artur Magnuszewski and Hans Bergström; *Wetlands in the Baltic Sea region* by Lars Lundin; *Lakes – origin, ontogeny and natural functions* by Peter Blomqvist and Anna-Kristina Brunberg; *Hydrology and water quality of European rivers* by Artur Magnuszewski, as well as Chapter 5 *The Baltic Sea* in the Baltic University book *Environmental Science*. The original chapters are fully referenced.

to a rich biological life; and always they were crucial for transport and communication. An important part of sustainable development is to take care of and cherish this waterscape for the pleasure and use by us and by coming generations.

River Basins or Catchments

The Baltic waterscape may be divided into catchments, also called river basins or drainage basins. A catchment consists of a river and all its contributories, including smaller streams, lakes and wetlands. A catchment in turn may be divided into smaller parts each consisting of a tributary stream to the larger river and its catchment, a process which may continue in several steps. The border of a catchment, called the water divide, can in many cases be recognised on the map as the highest point of a mountain range, but sometimes one need to track all the small streams to recognise where the water divide is located between two catchments.

Figure 4.1. National and international river basin districts. Modified from larger map. Source: European Commission, 2007.

The water input to the catchment depends on rainfall and such properties as topography, bedrock, and soil type. All water in a catchment is critically dependent on the activities in the catchment. This includes land use, for instance agriculture, which may contribute to eutrophication. Also potentially polluting activities, such as urban water effluents and effluents from industries, influence the water situation.

Catchments or river basins come in very different sizes and characters. Sweden's special position is noticeable. Sweden is a sparsely populated country, where heavy rainfall feeds the rivers. Catchments are limited in size, and many major towns are located along the coast. Other countries are drained by only a few river catchments; thus the Vistula and Odra rivers drain more than 95% of Poland. In small catchments the population tends to congregate in towns along the coastline and wastewater is discharged directly into coastal areas rather than into the river systems. Large catchments have a more uniform distribution of settlements, sometimes concentrated in the upstream area, for example the Vistula catchment and Silesia district in southern Poland.

The European Union Water Framework Directive, the first Framework Directive of the Union, requires that member states organise their water management according to river basins. Thus river basin authorities have been established in all 27 countries in the Union. The sizes of these vary greatly. Latvia has one single river basin authority – the only main river is Daugava – while Sweden has five such authorities. While a river basin authority typically is housed by a regional office, such as a county office, the work to manage the water in the basin typically is the responsibility of the local authority, the municipality.

The Flow of Water – From Mountains to the Sea

The flow of water in nature is described by the hydrological cycle. We see how precipitation in mountainous areas feeds small streams and brooks, which continue to lakes, wetlands and larger rivers. The rain that falls in the landscape penetrates the soil and adds to groundwater. Groundwater in turn flows into the rivers, which thus are receiving water all the way along their path from the sources to the river mouth where they end. When the water has entered the sea, in our case the Baltic Sea, it may again evaporate and add to atmospheric humidity and at some point be transported to higher areas where water condenses into droplets and forms rain, thus completing the hydrological cycle. Some water of course evaporates earlier from surface waters and thus makes a shorter hydrological cycle. In other cases it may collect in wetlands or lakes with a slow water circulation and then makes a longer cycle.

The energy for driving the hydrological cycle comes from the sun, which causes water to evaporate and also fuels the weather phenomena, which brings humid air to higher altitudes. The energy from hydroelectric power stations in some rivers thus ultimately comes from the sun.

When considering the flow of water the concepts of upstream and downstream are essential. Up-streamers typically have high quality water but are also in a position to pollute water. The down-streamers are thus at the mercy of the up-streamers to get enough water – these may not extract too much of what they receive – and high quality water. The down-streamers on the other hand most often have better conditions for agriculture and need to provide for the up-streamers.

Several of the large rivers in the world have during the last decades lost much of its water. The Colorado River in North America is not any longer the majestic sight it once was. Its water flow and thus depth have decreased by meters. In Asia the large rivers have decreased not only because of extraction of water in the cities they pass but also because of the receding glaciers – receding due to global warming - which since millennia are feeding them with melt water. We have so far not seen similar changes in the rivers of the Baltic Sea region.

Figure 4.2. River Dvina (in Latvia Daugava) near Polotsk, Belarus demonstrate a mature river landscape. Photo: Lars Rydén.

Climate and Water

The European Climate

Air-mass circulation determines Europe's climate. The relief of the continent makes it possible for air masses originating in the Atlantic Ocean to pass freely through the lowlands, except in the case of the mountains of Scandinavia. Polar air masses from areas close to Iceland and tropical air masses from the Azores can both reach the continent, bringing very different conditions of temperature and humidity.

Continental air masses from Eastern Europe have equally easy access westward. The almost continuous belt of high mountains separates southern Europe, and limits the interchange of tropical and polar air masses. Of the various climatic conditions, five air pressure belts can be distinguished. Driven by these pressure patterns, westerly winds prevail in northwest Europe. Winters get sharply colder eastward, while summer temperature increase southward. Northwest Europe, including Iceland, enjoys somewhat milder winters because of warm Gulf Stream waters.

Four regional European climatic types can be distinguished:

- Maritime climate (Svalbard, Iceland, the Faeroes, Great Britain and Ireland, Norway, southern Sweden, western France, the Low Countries, northern Germany, and north-western Spain);
- Central European (transitional) climate (central Sweden, southern Finland, the Oslo Basin of Norway, eastern France, south-western Germany, and much of central and south-eastern Europe);
- Continental climate (northern Ukraine, eastern Belarus, Russia, most of Finland, and northern Sweden);
- Mediterranean climate.

Table 4.1. The largest rivers in the Baltic drainage basin (Bergström & Carlsson, 1994).

River Mean annual flow for the period 1950-1990 (m^3/s)	
Neva	2,460
Vistula	1,065
Daugava	659
Neman	632
Odra	573
Kemijoki	562
Ångermanälven	489
Luleälven	486

Climate in the Baltic Sea Basin

The climate in the Baltic Sea region is that of the Atlantic-Arctic Temperate Zone and can be described as relatively mild. Winters are fairly mild in the south-western parts, getting colder towards the north and north-east, but, although long, they are not very severe, especially in Eastern Fennoscandia, where spring is late and summer is short. Frequent cold sessions during spring affect the climate in the whole region. Throughout the year the relative humidity levels are high and precipitation is abundant. These features are due to the geographical vicinity of the Baltic Sea, the Atlantic Ocean, the White and Barents Seas, as well as the dominance of intensive cyclonic activity during all four seasons.

Eastern Fennoscandia is notable for a peculiar climate resulting both from some specific features of the atmospheric processes in the Atlantic Ocean, Arctic Ocean and Siberia, as well as from the Great European Lakes' and White Sea effects on the drainage basins. The climate formation here is influenced by the high percentage of coverage of the territory by surface waters (lakes occupy 12% of the territory), forests and wetlands.

The duration and stability of the eastern circulation in this area is usually lower than that of the western circulation. It manifests itself mostly during the winter period through low air temperatures, a smaller number of cloudy days and lower precipitation. This type of circulation loses much of its vigour by April when the meridional type replaces it. By the beginning of the summer period, the western air transport takes a dominant role. The dominant form of atmospheric circulation over the territory throughout the year is the western transport (151 days), while the eastern circulation lasts less (94 days) and 120 days are governed by meridional circulation. For the western part of the region western and eastern transport is less (120 and 85 days, respectively) while meridional transport is more frequent (160 days).

Precipitation

In the northernmost parts of the basin more than half of the precipitation may be accumulated as snow and released during melt in spring, whereas the runoff has its peak during winter in the south. The mean annual volume of fresh water runoff from the land areas of the entire Baltic basin to the Baltic Sea amounts to approximately 450 km^3, Danish Sounds and Kattegat excluded. This corresponds to a flow of 14,150 m^3/s which means that the runoff from the land area of the Baltic Sea basin is only slightly less than that of the Mississippi River and greater than in any river in Europe. The average discharge of the biggest rivers in the drainage basin is presented in Table 4.1.

There is considerable inter-annual variability in the runoff to the Baltic Sea. The wet year of 1924 had a mean annual runoff of 19,500 m^3/s while the corresponding figure for the dry year of 1976 was as low as 11,100 m^3/s. The annual inflow of 450 km^3 is a tremendous volume of water, which, in theory, is available to the population in the basin. Evenly spread out over the surface of the Baltic Sea it corresponds to a depth of 1.2 m of water. Unfortunately the geographical distribution of this water is converse to the population density. Due to the high precipitation and

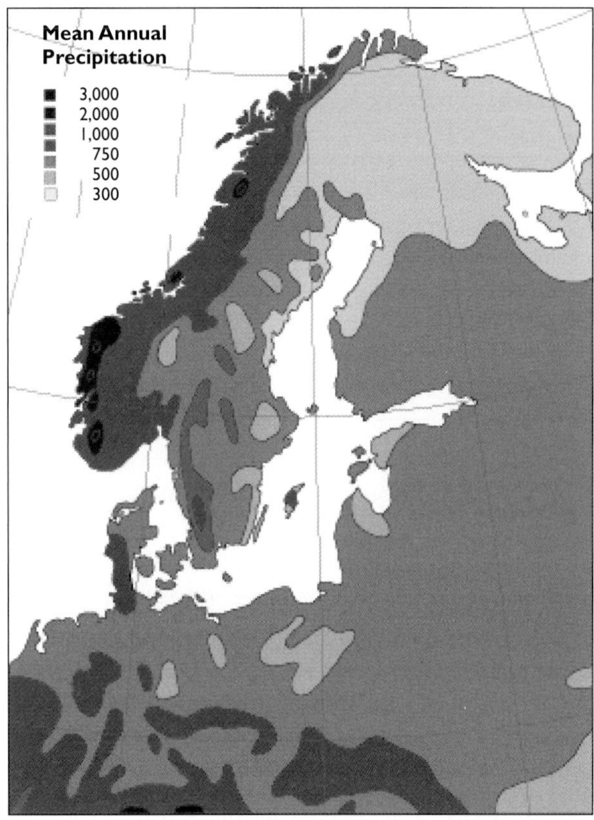

Figure 4.3. As a whole the Baltic Sea basin receives 450 km^3 precipitationper year. The amount of precipitation ranges from very wet areas in the Norwegian mountains with 3,000 mm annually, to drier areas on the north-eastern rim and southern agricultural regions with below 300 mm annually (data compiled by Lars Hedlund. Source: Rydén et al., 2003)

low evapo-transpiration of the north the available water resources are much greater there than in the south and particularly great in the northwest. This is in strong contrast to the population density, which is greatest in the south and very low in the northern parts of the area.

The Lakes

An Abundance of Lakes

Lakes are beautiful elements of the landscape appreciated for many different reasons: scenery, recreation, wildlife, fish production, swimming, skating, and boating. People simply love lakes. The lakes also have less well-known important functions as natural regulators of river flow and sediment and nutrient traps.

Table 4.2. The largest lakes in the Baltic drainage basin (data from MSSL-WCMC-UNEP, 1989; Raab & Vedin, 1995).

Lake	Area (km^2)
Ladoga, Russia	17,800
Onega, Russia	9,900
Vänern, Sweden	5,650
Peipsi, Estonia	3,100
Vättern, Sweden	1,900
Saimaa, Finland	1,500
Mälaren, Sweden	1,120
Päijänne, Finland	1,100
Oulojärvi, Finland	890
Pielisjärvi, Finland	870
Ilmen, Russia	550

Due to the recent glaciation, the northern part of the Baltic basin is very rich in lakes. Sweden has 96,000 lakes larger than 1 hectare and the corresponding figure for Finland is 65,000. Some of the lakes in the Baltic Sea region are the largest in Europe, such as Lakes Ladoga and Onega in North West Russia and Lake Vänern in Sweden. There are eight lakes which have an area of 1,000 km^2 or more (Table 4.2). Altogether lakes cover 9% of the land areas of Finland and Sweden. In the plains of the three Baltic States and Poland lakes are not as common.

The majority of the lakes occur in depressions in the land surface caused by the ice during glaciation or by glacial melt water from about the same time. When the stream water enters the lake, the velocity is greatly reduced and particles transported with the river from the catchment to a large degree settle in the lake. A more important sedimentation process in the lakes of the region is the settlement of dead biological material from lake water. The sedimentation causes the bottom to rise over time, giving changed pre-conditions for vegetation growth of many plants, and the lake may finally disappear, having been transformed to a peat land. Thus most lakes are short-lived in a geological perspective.

How Lakes Function

Lakes metabolize – produces and consume nutrients – in a pattern that decides its functions. The concentration of dissolved oxygen is here a crucial factor. Dissolved oxygen (DO) is essential to all aquatic organisms that breathe (including fish). There are three sources of DO in a lake ecosystem: Firstly atmospheric oxygen dissolves in the lake water at the surface and is transported downwards by wind-generated mixing, secondly photosynthesis by plants in the lake produces oxygen, and thirdly, there is a constant inflow of oxygen-rich water from the drainage area.

The main limiting factors for primary production in the lake ecosystem are phosphorous (P), nitrogen (N), and silica (Si). In addition to these elements, solar light is in many cases a factor that becomes limiting at depth or in a lake having a snow-covered ice. P and N reach the lake with inflowing water from the catchment, as wet deposition with rain and snowfall on the lake, and as dry deposition with particles from the atmosphere. P and N are recycled within the lakes, between living and dead biota. Lakes normally act as sinks for phosphorous, with a net deposition of P in the sediments. Part of the N reaching the lake is lost to the atmosphere by denitrification.

Nutrient-rich lakes, called *eutrophic*, are often recognized by their frequent algal blooms. Nutrients come with runoff from agricultural land, forestry land, impediments (indirectly from the air pollution) and from private sewers to these lakes. Nutrient-poor lakes, called *oligotrophic*, are often brownish due to humic substances and are more typical for forest areas and wetlands in less populated areas.

The biologic function of a lake is closely connected with its thermal regime. The temperature distribution determines the vertical stratification, which in turn determines the pre-conditions for vertical mixing. The lakes in the region typically have periods of summer and winter stratification separated by the autumn and spring circulation periods. The circulation periods distribute dissolved oxygen, taken up from the air, in the entire water body. The summer stratification is quite stable, with a strong temperature gradient and a corresponding strong density gradient. The density gradient efficiently reduces wind-induced vertical turbulent mixing and the supply of dissolved oxygen to the deeper layer during summer stratification, which may result in oxygen deficit in late summer.

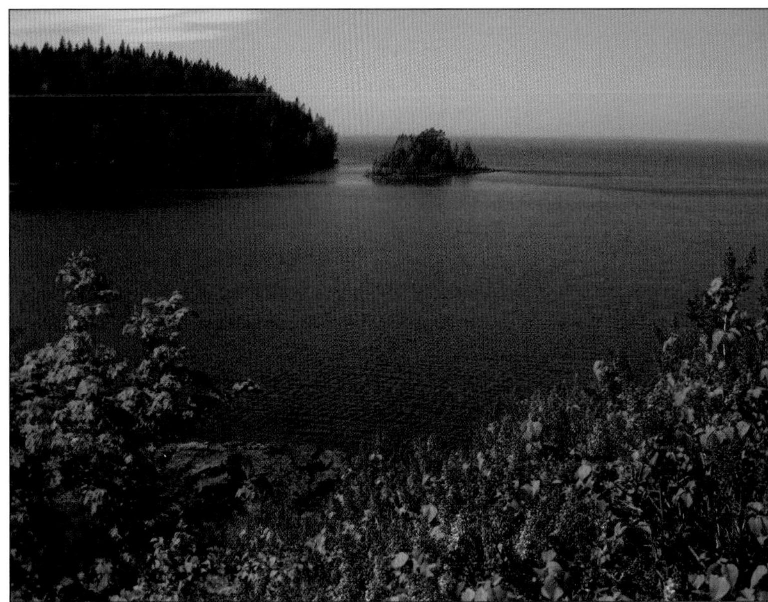

Figure 4.4. Lake Ladoga in Karelia, Russia is the largest lake in Europe. Draining into the Gulf of Finland through river Neva it provide freshwater for St Petersburg. Ladoga has also many environmental problems including eutrophication and pollution from industry. Photo: Jussi Huotari.

In a lake bottom the upper part, called the littoral zone, is illuminated and has green plants. The littoral zone therefore acts as a sieve for nutrients reaching the lake, and it provides larger animals, including fish, with an abundance of food from large plants to minute bacteria. This wide range of food items promotes a high diversity of larger animals in the biotope.

In the open water, the pelagic zone, we find the plankton – organisms which cannot swim. The phytoplankton is pigmented and can photosynthesise, but most often also "eat" organic carbon to supplement their growth. A most important group of phytoplankton in lakes are cyanobacteria (earlier named blue-green algea). Among the zooplankton we find e.g. *Daphnia* as one of the most common species. The basic production in the pelagic zone is carried out by plankton, eaten mostly by insect larvae and fish. Most fish species change their main diet as they grow. As fry, fish usually lives in the open water feeding on zooplankton, and then return to the littoral shore zone to feed on the organisms produced there when it is older.

Threats Against the Lakes – Eutrophication, Acidification and Chemical Pollution

Very many lakes in the agricultural landscape receive more nutrient loads than can be taken care of by natural cleaning processes and therefore become eutrophic. In the rural landscape eutrophication is reduced if there are buffer zones – stretches of land, which may absorb and use nutrients in the runoff from agricultural land – between the fields and the water. For lakes being recipients of outgoing water from a town or city, a well functioning wastewater treatment is equally very important. It is the phosphorus, which is most critical as it is often the limiting nutrient for biological growth. Nitrogen may also contribute to eutrophication, but lack of N is often compensated for by natural N fixation from bluegreen algae (bacteria). Thus N is less often limiting. If the P inflow is not too large the lake may self clean and excess P is then bound in the bottom sediments.

The excess nutrients may lead to growth of algae, sometimes to dead bottoms and deterioration of its biological and societal value. However lakes dominated by macrophytes, such as stoneworts (*Chara*), water lilies (*Nymphae*) and pondweeds (*Potamogoton* and others) are able to absorb comparatively large nutrients inflows to be used in its ecosystem. The macrophytes support rich communities of invertebrates, fish and birds. A second type of lake is dominated by phytoplankton and has less rich ecosystems. In these fish are often killed by lack of oxygen and instead we see algal blooms. If the macrophytes are removed – for example to make it easier to swim – one risk to transfer the lake to the less desirable kind of lake dominated by algal blooms.

Acid rain is another serious threat to lakes, especially in areas with low buffer capacity, which is the case in Norway, Sweden and partially Finland. During the 1960s, 70s and 80s acid rain caused by coal combustion in many large industries in most importantly England and continental Europe came with the prevailing western winds to the Nordic countries. As a consequence, many thousands of lakes and rivers became acidified. Many lakes, including a number of very good fishing lakes, especially in the north, had pH values below 5, even close to 4, were devoid of fish and for all normal purposes dead. In Norway similarly a number of rivers famous for salmon fishing were dead. It was not until the UNECE Convention on long range transboundary pollutants entered into force that the acid rain problem decreased. The Swedish Environmental Protection Agency had then, and continues to have, a project to lime these lakes to reduce acidification. The complete restoration of these lakes and rivers will still take long before it is completed.

In some cases lakes have been the receiver of chemical substances released from factories or, in a few cases, from landfills. If these lakes are upstream in a river basin the whole basin may be affected. A famous and well-researched case is Lake Järnsjön in southern Sweden, where a previous printing factory had released large amounts of PCBs (polychlorinated biphenyls). This substance, since the 1960s know as a serious environmental pollutant, had been bound to the bottom sediments of the lake outside the factory. It leaked to all water downstream along River Emån, and thus killed many species in the ecosystem, some of them rare and red-listed. In a major operation by the Swedish EPA to save the ecosystem of River Emån, the contaminated bottom sediments was removed and stored in a protected landfill.

Wetlands

Large Wetland Areas

In the Baltic Sea region, all countries originally enclosed large natural wetland areas. These wetlands developed during the Holocene period and have been considerably affected at later stages by human exploitation. The wetlands in the Baltic Sea catchment have attracted considerable interest as they occupy large areas, about 20% of the Baltic Sea basin, and have significant impact on surface water.

Today wetlands constitute only small areas in many countries. In Europe on the whole, 60% of the original 53 Mha (530,000 km^2; 1 Mha = 10,000 km^2), of mires have been turned to agriculture (50%), forestry (10%) and peat extraction for fuel and horticulture (10%). In Denmark and Germany, vast former wetland areas are now used for different purposes. In Finland, Estonia Latvia, Lithuania, and Poland, drainage has altered large wetland areas. In Sweden, exploitation varied greatly, with large differences in regional wetland utilisation. In the north, there has been a relatively small impact, while utilisation was much more comprehensive further south, especially in the present-day agricultural regions.

Finland, with its low coastal zones and extensive archipelago, has a large share of peatlands. Of the original almost 12 Mha, now remains ca 9 Mha. Of the drained area 0.6 Mha is used in forestry and about 1 Mha is used for agriculture, of which only 0.3-0.4 Mha is in use today. Peat winning is carried out, and the resulting peat accounts for 5% of Finland's energy demand. Peat is here considered a fossil fuel as it takes thousands of years to reform.

In the three Baltic States Estonia hosts large wetland areas and belongs to the most peat-land rich countries, with over 22% of the land area, one million ha covered by mires. Agriculture, forestry and peat winning make use of some the peatlands. In Latvia wetlands cover 39,000 km^2 or 10.4% of the land area. Large areas have been drained for agriculture, forestry and peat cutting, leaving about 70% unused. Lithuanian wetlands extend over 30,000 km^2. Drainage has been done mainly for agricultural purposes. Peat winning has decreased considerably since 1960, as it has encountered a strong opposition and preservation opinion.

Widespread wetland areas exist also in Poland, with 1.2 Mha of peatland, mostly fens. 86% has been drained and is now used as meadows and pastures. Large and important wetlands areas are the Biebrza and Note valleys in the northeast. Most of the un-drained area is found in these nature reserves, comprising a total of 1,500 km^2, or 14% of the peatland area.

Russia hosts the largest wetland areas, both in Northwestern Russia (1 Mha) and Kaliningrad. Of this territory, 80% is counted as an exploitable resource.

With the exception of Russia, Sweden is the country that encloses the largest peatland area in Europe, 10.4 Mha. In southern Sweden considerable use of wetlands for agriculture has taken place, a low estimate is that there is 0.6 Mha, of which an estimated 0.3 Mha might presently be in agricultural use. Forested peatlands cover 3.4 Mha and drainage has been carried out on almost 2 Mha. Peat winning today amounts to about 15,000 ha, Conservation involves first and foremost c. 4,000 km^2 mostly in northern Sweden and the high mountains. Another 0.4 Mha has been proposed to be protected based on the national wetland inventory.

Figure 4.5. The Djurholma bog in southwestern Sweden, which is 70 ha large, is a nature protected area. From the bird tower it is possible to sometimes see grouse playing. Much larger bogs of this kind is to be found in the northern parts of the Baltic Sea region. Photo: Guillaime Baviere.

Different Kinds of Wetlands

Wetlands are comprised of water-saturated bodies connected mainly to groundwater aquifers. They may have open water surfaces, shallow water with maximum depth of some meters. Most wetlands are found in landscape depressions or other relatively low lands. Often, soils underlying wetlands are almost impermeable. In systems with permeable soils, outflowing groundwater is able to maintain water saturation. At such locations wetland often turns into peatlands.

Peatlands are composed of low-conductivity organic material with high porosity, often > 90%. However, the low conductivity and the often flat extension mitigate large and fast water turnover. Thus peatlands are often flooded at high water input and gradually turn into shallow-water lakes. Eventually, after surface runoff, water levels in the peat are lowered to deeper horizons. Altogether, during high water access, peatlands are mainly transition zones containing water in already wet and high-discharge situations. Nonetheless, peatlands do not furnish additional water during drought. When there is need for water, peatlands keep it to themselves.

At suitable climatic conditions the peat-forming vegetation changes from vascular plants to Sphagnum mosses, and the peatland turns into a bog. At this phase, the peatland starts to raise, with the elevated surface becoming domed-shaped, the so-called raised bog. Later, after a considerable amount of time, pools begin to develop on the bog.

Bogs and fens are peatlands with a substantial layer of peat. When this layer is very thin, the wetland is called a mire, nonetheless still colonised by hydrophilic vegetation. The type of plants, and consequently the type of peat that is formed, is linked to the supplied water quality. Fens in mineral soils with a high nutrient content will be rich while those in poor environments, poor fens, are even poorer than bogs. Bogs are by hydrological definition furnished with precipitation water only, which is low in nutrients.

The Many Functions of Wetlands

Wetlands are not wastelands, even if this attitude has been and still is common. Wetlands have great value. In their natural states, wetlands – marshes, swamps, bogs and fens – constitute essential life-providing systems. They are recognised as coastal lands, lakes, ponds, rice fields and peatlands. Wetlands can be used in several different ways and are often of great interest. About two-thirds of the world's population depend on wetlands for their existence.

Wetlands constitute an ecotone – a border area - between terrestrial and aquatic environments. They have even been described as "the kidneys of the landscape" (Mitsch & Gosselink, 1993). As such, wetlands function for the immobilisation of contaminants, as nutrient sinks, sources of chemical substances and turnover of gases. Wetlands are crucial for the turnover of water and chemical elements such as metals. In this way they protect downstream water as they store nutrients and contribute to the self-cleaning of water. Phosphorus is stored in the sediments while considerable amounts of the nitrogen may be released to the air by denitrification.

Wetlands act as carbon sinks thus reducing climatic change. The energy input to the wetland comes mostly from sunlight as photosynthesis, even if some may be added with organic substances from surrounding. As wetlands in this way grow carbon is stored in the biomass. Globally 400-500 gigatonnes of carbon (Immirzi & Maltby, 1992) is stored in wetlands, roughly corresponding to the amount of carbon in the atmosphere. Compared to other soils, 20% of all stored carbon is found in peatlands. When a wetland is drained its organic material is decomposed by bacteria as oxygen from air enters, and then carbon dioxide is released to the atmosphere, adding to the greenhouse effect. On the other hand, in natural conditions, methane is released instead. Methane is 25 times stronger as a greenhouse gas. The release of methane is strongly mitigated by drainage. In addition, emissions of nitrous oxide (N_2O) are limited by drainage. N_2O has a greenhouse effect that is 250 times greater than that of CO_2.

Water to a wetland comes from precipitation, surface water inflow, groundwater discharge and inundation from rivers and the sea. In these ways wetlands store water and reduce the consequences of large rainfall and inundations. One of the reasons of serious consequences of recent floods in the Baltic Sea region, as well as in other parts of the world, is the transformation of wetland areas to other functions such as agriculture.

Wetlands are key biotopes for biodiversity protection. They form habitats for a large number of plants and soil-living fauna and as such often act as refuges for individuals and as pathways in spreading to other areas. In some cases, often involving bogs, certain specialised types find a niche where there is little competition. In other rich habitats, very demanding species manage to survive. Wetlands constitute a key biotope for many bird species. This was early recognised when one of the first global conventions for the protection of biodiversity, the Ramsar Convention, was signed already in 1973. Several protected wetlands are so called Ramsar sites. Also amphibians, another threatened animal group, find life space in wetlands. In case of forest fire, wetlands can also provide protection for many species.

Rivers and Streams

Rivers and River Basins

A river is a system comprised of the main river channel with all its tributaries and the area that the river system drains, called the catchment or the drainage basin. The climatic conditions influence the water input to the catchment, while characteristics such as topography, bedrock geology, soil type and land use determine the catchment response to rainfall.

Human activity affects river systems in numerous ways, for example, through urbanisation, agricultural development, land drainage, pollutant discharge and flow regulation (dams, canalisation, etc.). The lakes, reservoirs and wetlands in a river system act as storage elements, attenuate the natural fluctuation in discharge, and serve as settling tanks for material transported by the rivers.

The rivers of Scandinavia and the North European Plain have been shaped since the Pleistocene epoch. On the East European Plain, catchments are relatively large and rivers are long. In western, central and eastern Europe, rivers are largely 'mature,' i.e. their valleys are graded and their streams are navigable. Northern and southern Europe's rivers are still 'youthful,' with ill-graded profiles and are thus more useful for hydroelectricity than for waterways.

The main rivers to discharge into the Baltic Sea are the Neva, the Vistula, the Oder, the Daugava (Dvina in Belarus and Russia), the Neman, the Kemijoki and Luleälven Rivers. With minimum tidal influences, deltas (Neva River) and spits (Vistula River) have been created. Countries with long coastlines relative to their area, especially Sweden and Finland, are characterised by a large number of relatively small river catchments and short rivers in addition to some main and majestic water courses.

The river runoff volume and temporal discharge distribution from the rivers of the Baltic Sea region are governed by factors that include local conditions of rainfall, snowmelt and retention capacity. The river flow regimes of large catchments can be different from those of small catchments. Large rivers are much less variable because they integrate runoff over a large area, with different climate and physiographic conditions. The average annual runoff follows very closely the pattern of average annual rainfall and topography. Annual runoff is greater than 4,500 mm in western Norway decreasing to less than 250 mm in large regions of Ukraine and the southern part of the Russian Federation.

The rivers in the western area have higher discharges in the winter season and lower in the summer.

The rivers of mountainous and continental climates are fed by snowmelt, being highest in the spring and early summer.

Figure 4.6. Akkats Hydro power plant by Lule Älv river outside the small city Jokkmokk in Northern Sweden. The mural paitings entitled *Uvssat davás* in the Sami language (Doors to the West) are made by Bengt Lindström och Lars Pirak. Photo: Hans Blomberg/Vattenfall.

Changing and Controlling Rivers

Water is probably the most regulated natural resource in the world. The flow of most of the running water in our countries is regulated, especially in the large watercourses. And there are reasons for it: Unregulated watercourses have very irregular water flow. A natural river might even run dry during late summer and become flooded during spring when snow melts. In addition to this seasonal variation there is an inter-annual variation that might be considerable with large floods in wet years. In addition, water might be lacking where it is needed and too plentiful in other places. Thus the wish to control both the time and place of water supply is the background for the efforts to harness and domesticate this most basic of natural resources.

Rivers typically have many historical arrangements for regulation of its water levels. However, the large expansion of efforts to regulate water occurred during the 19th and early 20th centuries. Then, lakes were lowered all over the region, especially in Sweden, in order to create more agricultural land and many lakes were completely extinguished. Some 2,000 lakes drainage projects were carried out in Sweden up to about 1950. The agricultural area of the country increased by more than one million ha, but there were also serious environmental consequences of this. Wetland biotopes nearly disappeared, and biodiversity of course decreased. Draining of forests and swamps has caused much faster decomposition and outflow of nutrients and organic material. This may favour some species, but is a disadvantage to many more others.

Since the beginning of the 20th century many of the larger rivers in the northern Baltic Sea region, especially in Norway and Sweden but also Finland, have been extensively regulated mostly in connection with the construction of large hydroelectric power plants with dams and reservoirs. Reservoirs usually have a relatively short water residence time – sometimes just a few days – so they can be regarded as a hybrid between a river and a lake. Today only a few streams and rivers flow naturally with waterfall and falls. Therefore, it is of utmost importance to preserve what remains of these waters. Reservoir construction in Europe seems to be stagnant, mainly due to the lack of suitable sites and growing public opinion against the construction of dams and reservoirs.

Most lakes and streams are affected by regulations of some sort. Historically, waterpower was used to propel mills and saws and to refine iron. These early dams are now a part of our heritage, and have shaped the water landscape. A river basin often has hundreds of smaller dams or constructions to control water. Smaller dams, once built by individual farmers or other landowners, are often quite old and have not necessarily been legalized through a court process. There are often clear conflicts of interest in many water regulation projects, e.g. between industry (high water levels) and agriculture (low water levels).

Water regulation has an important impact on biology in or close to the water. When the annual rhythm of water flow changes, so does the condition for biological life. Calm-water species are different from those living in and by streaming water. Smaller or larger obstacles along the streams, such as mills and similar constructions, hinder salmon, trout and other fish that migrate, from continuing upstream. The most serious obstacles are the large hydropower dams. If the problems are too great an entire population or genetic variant of trout may disappear. On the other hand, ponds and reservoirs may become important water mirrors for ducks and other birds dependent on calm water.

In the agricultural landscape ditches, canals and pipelines are used to drain areas of water. Thus thousands of kilometres of drainage canals or ditches exist in the region, often being earlier streams and rivers now straightened and channelized. A major disadvantage with such drainage canals is that the water receives less efficient purification processes, such as denitrification. From water quality point of view it would be far better if the drainage canal ended in a natural creek, watercourse or wetland, rather than straight into the Baltic Sea. River regulation has been undertaken in many catchments of western and southern Europe. In e.g. Denmark, 85 to 98% of the total river network has been straightened. In contrast, in countries such as Poland, Estonia and Norway, many rivers still have 70 to 100% of their reaches in a natural state.

River Pollution and Restoration

The pollution of rivers is similar to the pollution of lakes, already described. Here only a few additional comments will be given.

The most important sources of river pollution are organic waste fed from domestic and industrial sewage. The decomposition and breakdown of organic matter is carried out by microorganisms and takes place mainly at the surface of the sediment and vegetation in smaller rivers and in the water column in larger rivers. Immediately downstream of a sewage effluent, organic matter decomposition reduces the oxygen content of the water and results in the release of ammonium. Further downstream, the concentration of organic matter decreases as a result of dilution and continuing decomposition. As the distance from the effluent increases, bacteria oxidise the ammonium to nitrate, and oxygen enters the water via the water surface, thereby increasing its oxygen content. Eventually the levels of organic matter, oxygen and ammonium reach those present immediately upstream of the sewage effluent. This process of recovery is called self-purification. Organic pollution is still a serious problem in many European rivers and will continue to be so for as long as large amounts of sewage water are discharged into the rivers without being treated.

Human settlement and associated clearance of forest, agricultural development and urbanisation greatly ac-

Figure 4.7. A sandy beach at Curzon Spit outside Kaliningrad. Photo: Lars Rydén.

celerate the runoff of materials and nutrients into rivers and lakes. This stimulates the growth of phytoplankton and other aquatic plants and in turn the growth of organisms higher up the aquatic food chain. The great variation found in extensively populated areas is attributable mainly to variation in the extent of wastewater treatment; well-functioning treatment plants can decompose up to 90% of the organic matter in the wastewater. In Norway, Sweden and Finland organic matter content is measured only as COD (COD=Chemical Oxygen Demand). In these countries discharge into rivers of organic waste derived from human activity is negligible and COD levels therefore are generally low.

The capacity of rivers to purify itself depends on the residence time of the water. This is greatly reduced by channelization, and thus the control and straightening of rivers and streams are linked to river pollution. Quite many projects to restore rivers to a more natural state are ongoing in the region, both to reduce eutrophication and improve fishing, as well as to improve the beauty and landscape values of the waterscape.

The Baltic Sea

The Sea

The Baltic Sea accounts for almost a quarter of the Baltic Sea basin, and is of decisive importance to all the countries along its coasts. It is special in many ways. The Baltic Sea is lying on a continent, and its average depth is only about 55 meters. It is more or less cut off from the oceans, and has only one narrow connection with the Atlantic through the Danish belts. As a result the Baltic Sea is a brackish water body, meaning that it is neither fresh water nor fully marine water, but with a salt concentration in between. In fact the Baltic Sea is one of the largest brackish water bodies in the world. Brackish waters are rather unusual on Earth, and few animals and plants are adapted to live in them. The Baltic Sea biodiversity is thus low.

The Baltic is also severely polluted by excess nutrients, it is nutrient-rich, eutrophic. As the drainage area is densely populated (85 million people) new nutrient is constantly added with runoff from agricultural land and effluents from cites and towns. This causes frequent large algal blooms and dead bottoms, as oxygen is consumed by the large amounts of sediment. The once very fish-rich Baltic Sea has today a shortage of fish both due to eutrophication and over fishing. The restricted water exchange with the Atlantic Ocean makes the pollutants stay long.

As a whole, the Baltic Sea basin receives 450 km^3 of rain and snow per year. This corresponds to 40 cm of water, if spread out evenly over the entire region, or 1.2 m on the Baltic Sea itself. Precipitation does not hit the region evenly. Average runoff, i.e. the difference between precipitation and evaporation, is much higher in the north than in the south. In the north, the precipitation is larger and the evaporation smaller, accounting for the differences. Most of the fresh water entering the Baltic Sea emanates from river input. From the amount of precipitation, one might get an intuitive idea about the half-life of water in the Baltic Sea, which is 25 years, corresponding to 30 m of water depth on the average. But this does not account for the whole story. Due to the salt water inflow the total exchange of water in the Baltic Sea is much larger than the net outflow. This is also valid for the exchange of water between the different basins in the Baltic Sea. However, the water exchange is fairly small which results in both the water staying brackish, and a slow dilution of pollutants.

The water cycle of the Baltic basin ends with an exchange of water with the seas that pass through the Danish Sounds. This is a critical factor for the concentration of oxygen and salinity and thus for the whole ecological system of the Baltic Sea. This exchange is a much more irregular process than inflow via rivers. The flow goes back and forth under the influence of climatological and oceanographic conditions. Typical flow rates may be in the order of ten times the average annual fresh-water inflow. Major inflows of highly saline water to the Baltic Sea have an episodic character. These events may occur about every ten years (Schinke & Matthäus, 1998) but are still of utmost importance for the salinity and oxygen conditions of the Baltic Sea. This is, however, normally only a temporary improvement due to the increased pollution load on the water body. The mean depths of the Danish Sound and the Belts are only 14.3 m, which is a most important obstacle for a free water exchange across the Danish straits.

Coasts and Islands

The Baltic Sea may be saluted for many positive aspects. Its short geological history of only a few thousand years after the last glaciation is the main reason why it has so many dramatic and beautiful types of scenery. This includes the largest archipelago in the world with more than 25,000 islands (some say 50,000 or more depending on how the concept "island" is defined) between Sweden and Finland, and many special coastal types.

Many people visit or live on and by the coast; the coast is an important cultural and natural resource. It is a resource for shipping, fishing, aquaculture, sailing, recreation, and industries using the coastal zone as a receiving system for emissions of various types of pollutants. The coastal zone is therefore a zone of interest for many parties, interests that often are in conflict with each other. For the Baltic Sea ecosystem, the coast is an area where several species reproduce. All estuaries and shallow, soft bottom bays in the Baltic Sea basically have very high bio-production.

There are great differences between the different coastal regions in the Baltic Sea. In the south, sandy coasts prevail, and in the north, rocky coasts. The archipelagos dominate the Swedish and the Finnish coastline, klint coasts are found in Estonia and on the west coast of Gotland, and lagoons in Gdansk Bay. Sweden has by far the longest Baltic Sea coast, about 35% of the entire coast.

There are seven large islands in the Baltic Sea and very many smaller ones. The Baltic islands, especially Gotland, Öland and Rügen, have turned into summer favourite landscapes for those who can afford. Tourist business is the main economic activity on these islands.

Threats Against the Baltic Sea

The Baltic Sea is the final recipient of pollutants from the entire basin and is of special concern in efforts to improve our environment. There are many reasons for being concerned. Due to its semi-enclosed character the Baltic Sea is very vulnerable to pollution. The water body is affected by contributions of fresh water and nutrients from rivers, pollution from industries, municipalities and shipping and by direct atmospheric deposition. The inflow of water with high salinity and oxygen concentrations via the Danish Sounds is another critical factor for the ecosystem of the Baltic Sea. The environmental problems of the Baltic drainage basin and the Baltic Sea are very complex. The Baltic Sea is sometimes described as one of the most polluted seas in the world. While eutrophication continues to be serious and worsening, the chemical pollutants, e.g. PCB, are decreasing since several years.

The Baltic Sea was the object of the first environmental convention agreed on in the Cold War period in 1974, and ratified in 1980. The most important result was the establishment of Helcom, the organisation, which coordinates activities and collects data on the Sea. The Convention on the Protection of the Baltic Sea was rewritten into a much stronger text in 1992. A number of rescue programs have been established to improve the situation of the Sea, but so far results have been meagre. Recently the Baltic Sea action programme, which now enters into force, severely limits the amounts of Nitrogen and Phosphorus which surrounding countries are allowed to let into the Baltic Sea. It remains to be seen if the coastal states are able to implement these requirements.

Mountains and Tundra
Landscapes of Beauty and Wilderness

5

Lars Rydén
Uppsala University, Uppsala, Sweden

The Two Large Mountain Systems of the Baltic Sea Region

Borders of the Baltic Basin

The Baltic Basin is limited in the north, south and west by large mountain chains and in the east by plains. The mountains – often forested and, especially in the north, wetland-rich parts of our region – account for an important part of the surface area and as well essential cultural economic and biological opportunities which need to be considered when discussing rural development.

In the northwest the Scandinavian Mountains at the border between Sweden and Norway form parts of the Baltic Sea region, with a very special nature, culture and economy. It is an important recreation area of Europe with many thousands of visitors every day.

At the very far north this formation continues east into mountain tundra, reaching 400-800 meters, called *tuturi* in Sami, into northern Finland and Russia. (The word *tundra* is related to tuturi.)

Also in the southern parts of the Baltic Sea region we find beautiful and dramatic mountain ranges. The Carpathians is a large mountain range extending all the way from Czech Republic, Slovakia and the Polish-Ukrainian border to Romania and Serbia. The Carpathians form the water divide between the Baltic Sea and the Black Sea. Again we see an extensive and beautiful mountainscape with its special biology, culture and economy. In contrast to the Scandinavian Mountains large parts of the Carpathians are well populated.

The Carpathians extends to the west and northwest into the so-called Sudeten Mountains which covers parts of Czech Republic (Bohemia and northern Moravia) bordering on Poland and further to the border to Germany. To the west of River Odra are the Silesian parts of these mountains with extensive mining industry also here with its special culture and economy.

Figure 5.1. Tatra mountain landscape in Southern Poland bordering the Slovak Republic. Photo: Lars Rydén.

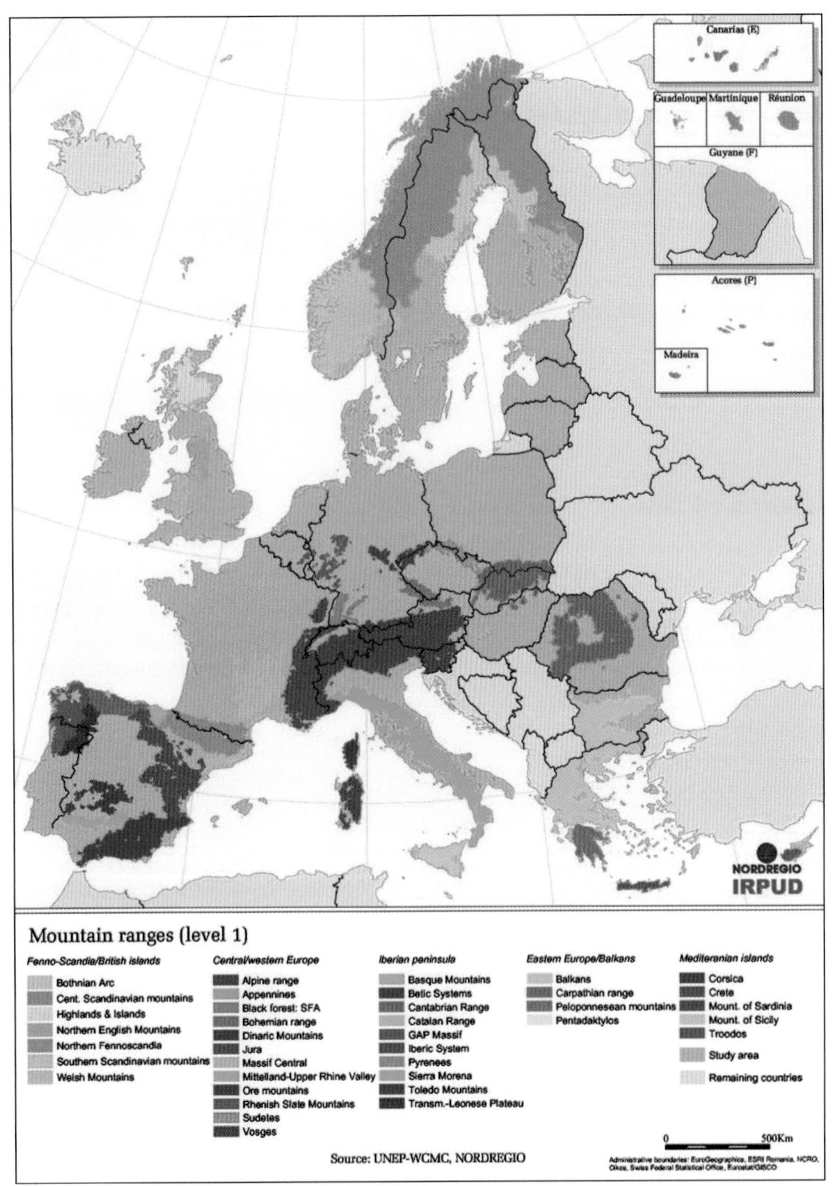

Figure 5.2. Mountain ranges in Europe. Source: UNEP-WCMC, Nordregio. Europen Commission, 2004.

The Scandinavian Mountains

The Scandinavian Mountains or the Scandes, also called *Fjells* (*Fjällen* in Swedish) is a mountain range that runs from the southern border between Norway and Sweden to the Arctic Sea along the Scandinavian Peninsula. The western sides of the mountains go all the way to the North Sea where they form the fjords on the Norwegian Atlantic coast; on the northeastern tip they reach up to northern-most Finland. The crest of the Scandinavian Mountains forms the western water divide of the Baltic Sea, and the border between Norway and Sweden. The entire length extends 1,700 km making then the longest mountain range in Europe. The widest part in mid Norway is about 370 km. They reach their highest points at about 2,000 m at the Arctic Circle. Galdhöpiggen, the highest peak in Norway, is 2,469 meter while Kenekaise, the highest peak on the Swedish side, is 2,104 meter. At their tip in northwestern Finland, called the North Cape, they are rather hills.

The mountains are thus not very high. This is the results of several hundred million years of erosion and weathering. Their estimated height when they were formed some 450 million years ago was about 5 times their present, that is close to 10,000 meters. The Scandinavian Mountains are one of the oldest mountains in the world. Some of the rocks are vestiges of the Karelid Mountains formed close to 2,000 million years.

In the north the mountains have many ice fields and glaciers, some quite dramatic in shape, making it possible to ski year around. But these are at present getting smaller every year – a development caused by global warming. Thus the heights given above are already several meters too large and authorities are today making new maps for the mountain climbers.

As in all mountains the Scandinavian Mountains have a very special ecosystem. The vegetation above the tree line is dominated by grassland with some dwarf birch (*Beltula nana*) and bushes (*Salix sp*). Below the tree line there is birch forest and further down mostly spruce. Here we also find much water in small and large lakes, rivers and creeks, and vast wetlands. The fauna and flora is special, in an ecosystem now threatened by increased temperatures. The characteristic reindeers barely exist as wild as they all belong to reindeer herding Sami families. Large areas have been protected as National parks. The two most well-known are Sarek National Park (with 8 peaks above 2,000 m), the second national park in Europe from 1909, and Stora Sjöfallet national park, both in Sweden.

The Carpathian Mountains

The Carpathians form a chain of mountains or mountain systems which stretch in an arc from the Czech Republic in the northwest to Romania in the south. The largest part is in the south, but extensive parts, the so-called Western and Central Carpathians (traditionally called the Beskids) are found in Czech Republic, Slovakia, Poland, Hungary and Ukraine. It is also here we find its highest section, called the Tatra Mountains, and the highest peak of 2,655 m the Gerlachovsky stit (peak) in Slovakia. The total length of the Carpathians is about 1,500 km; at its widest it is 500 km (in Romania), and the total area is estimated to 190,000 km^2.

The Carpathians is almost completely covered by forest – no part is above the tree line. There is no eternal snow, glaciers, dramatic waterfalls or large lakes. The very rich flora is similar to the one of the Alps and the fauna is interesting with important populations of e.g. brown bear. We also find extensive areas of virgin forests in this mountain system.

The mountains are fairly well populated and there are many important cities in or at the foothills of the not so high areas of the Carpathians. On the Slovak side there is Bratislava just south of the mountains, and Kosice, Banska Bystrica and Zilina in the hilly area. In Poland Krakow and smaller Przemysl on the Ukrainian border lies just north of the mountain, while the smaller cities of Nowy Sacz and Tarnow are in the mountains. In Ukraine Ivano-Frankivsk is in the mountains while the large city of Lviv is on its northern side.

The Silesian and Moravian Mountain Chains

In southwest Poland to the west of River Odra we find the Silesian parts of the Central European mountain system. These areas have considerable coal mining as well as mining for some metals such as zinc, copper and lead, and have developed a large heavy industry, coal mining, coke works, iron works, mostly using imported iron ore. Best known steel work may be Nowa Huta at Krakow, but other important centers are found in Katowice, Gliwice and Sosnowiec. The area is densely populated and almost forms a continuous urban district.

The Silesian area of Poland has an important German speaking minority and once had its own language. Further to the northwest the Sorbian (Slavic) minority represent another very special culture also connected to mining.

In the south and west of this area we find the Moravian Mountains on the Czech border, and the Sudeten Mountains on the German border, close to the most important city of Wroclaw (in German Bratislava) where the Odra River passes. These mountains are better known for their magnificent tourist sites rather than mining.

Life and Economic Activities in the Mountains

The Sami and Reindeer Herding

The Sami (Saami) is the indigenous population in the far north of Norway, Sweden, Finland and all the way to the Kola peninsula of Russia, an area called *Sapmi* in Sami languages. The original area of Sami people was considerably larger and extended further south, estimated to almost 400,000 km^2, but with time the Sami has been pushed north and become a minority in their own area, as the main (Germanic) population of the countries have moved north. Today there is a total of some 80,000 Sami still conserving their original livelihood in the four countries. Most of these live in Norway (about 50,000-60,000), while there is about 20,000 in Sweden. A very large part of the population with Sami roots has moved south and is found in the large cities, in particular Oslo and Stockholm or has been urbanized in the North.

The traditional economy of the Sami was the semi-nomadic reindeer herding. Today only a minor part, about 10%, of the Sami works with reindeers. Other important parts of the economy are fishing, hunting and handicrafts. More recently tourism has become an important source of income, as well as art and music. To an extent the Sami in the Nordic countries have been granted some legal rights to execute their traditional livelihood, while other rights, e.g. exclusive rights to fishing and hunting, have been lost. Legal processes for access to reindeer grazing and calving areas is still treated by the courts as conflicts with other land users is common and likely to increase due to the warming.

Since some time there is a Sami parliament in Sweden and radio broadcasts in the Finno-Ugric Sami languages. In the political struggle for their rights the Sami has protested against mining, against the Swedish government on a planned very large onshore wind farm, including 1,000 wind turbines to built in a reindeer winter grazing area, and against logging plans in Finland threatening the lichens, essential winter food for the reindeers. The Sami was badly hit by the Chernobyl disasters fallout as radioactive cesium was efficiently accumulated by the reindeers making the meat unfit for human consumption.

Figure 5.3. During the winter the reindeer gather at the farm and the reindeer herdsmen feed them on pellets and hay. Photo: Heather Sunderland (Rukakuusamu).

Mountain Tourism

Mountain tourism is an activity on the increase. In Sweden a 2002 study reports that 25% of the adult population (1,4 million persons) visits the mountains every year. Over a 5 year period almost half of the population has visited the mountains, 85% of them for leisure and during vacation time (Fredman, 2003). The larger parts of the visits occur in the winter period for skiing and scooter driving. During summer touring in the fjell (mountains) is dominating followed by fishing and canoeing. People spend time photographing, bird watching and in general enjoying outdoor life. 67% of the visitors use a commercial facility for living, and meals.

It is obvious that tourism constitutes a considerable part of the economy of these areas. Employment is created in restaurants, cafés, hotels and hostels. During winter it is slalom slopes and lifts, leasing of skis and other equipment, which creates economy; during summer it is fishing cards, canoes etc.

Southern Poland's mountains areas bordering Poland, Czech Republic, Slovakia and Ukraine similarly have an important tourism industry. The main centre for visit to

Polish Tatra Mountains, Zakopane, is visited by 250,000 tourists every year, for touring, skiing and other activities. The Bieszczady mountains to the west shared with Czech Republic is similarly very popular as is the Karkonosze Mountains with winter sports centres Karpacz and Szklarska Poreba, while the Carpathians in Ukraine has a growing number of visitors, not the least because of the cheap prices. More to the west and closer to the German border the Sudeten Mountains have a large number of very popular resorts for visitors.

Another form of visitors' economy mainly in the Carpathian and Sudeten mountains, are the spas. Spas have a very long tradition from Medieval times. People go to spas for health and social reasons. Popular spas include Krynica, Zegiestow and Piwniczna in Beskid Sadecki.

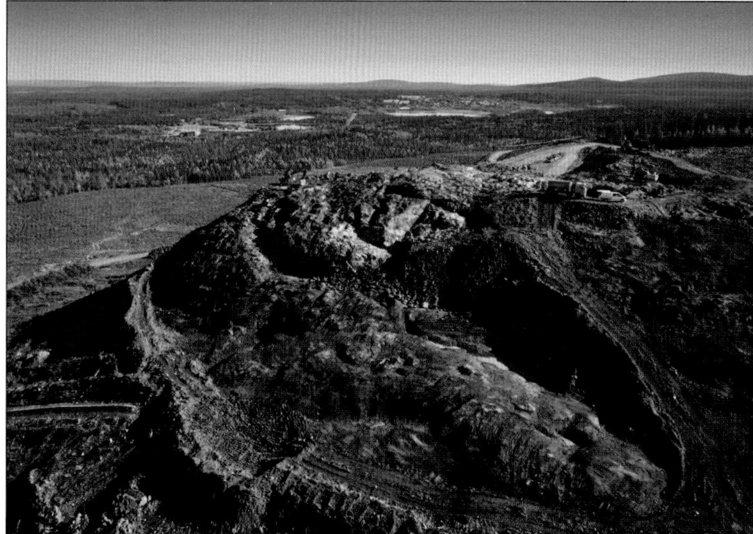

Figure 5.4. Gruvberget, close to Svappavaara, Sweden. Photo: Fredrik Alm. Source: LKAB.

Mining

Many mountains areas have considerable mineral deposits and developed mining industry. In North Sweden the Kiruna iron mine is the largest. Pit mining began at the site in 1898 and was followed by underground mining from 1960. Today it is the largest underground iron ore mine in the world. The state-owned mine is producing some 26 million tonnes of iron ore per year. Mining will continue for a considerable period as much is still left of the very large ore body of 4 kilometers length, 80-120 meters thickness and depth of up to 2 kilometers. The mining company LKAB is a main employer in the region. The Kiruna Iron mine is connected to the port of Narvik in Norway and Luleå in Sweden by railway, and to steel works further away.

The second largest mine in north Sweden in Boliden, closer to the Baltic Sea coast producing copper, zinc lead and most remarkable large amounts of gold, was closed in the 1960s. Further mines are found in the mountainous areas (Bergslagen) in mid Sweden. These mines were the most important in Europe for iron, copper and silver up to the 19th century. Some closed mines in these regions are presently reopened due to the increased world market prices of iron ore.

Slovakia had a very important mining industry in their part of the Carpathian Mountains. However in this case most mines are closed and historical. Classical and well known mining towns include Banská Bystrica once known for its abundant deposits of copper (and to a lesser extent of silver, gold, and iron) and Banská Štiavnica (today with a mining museum). During the communist period the Slovakian mining industry was still an important part of heavy industry and vital for the economy of the country. Today it is no longer competitive. The decline of the mining sector has significant social and economic implications. The three universities with mining specialties AGH (Academy of mining and metallurgy) in Krakow, Poland, the Technical University in Ostrava, Czech Republic and the Kosice Technical University, Slovakia, bear witness of the importance of the mining sector in the region.

The Mountains as Our Unique Nature Heritage

Mountain areas have ecosystems very different from the lower part of the landscape. The reasons are manifold, not the least strong winters with heavy snow cover, short summers with very intense light (in north of the region) and special nutrient conditions. Since the mountains were typically not heavily populated they were often left alone, were not significantly polluted, and rare species of the flora and fauna have survived. They often also constitute a refuge for large carnivores, such as wolves, bears, lynx, and wolverine, as well as many bird species, for example the large owls. They are also home to some unique animals such as the reindeer in the north and the Tatra chamois. In many cases the rivers, brooks and lakes are undestroyed and host several valuable fish species.

Since mountains were earlier considered of less economic interest it was easy to agree on protection status. The first national park was created in the Swedish fjell already in 1909. It has been followed by many protected areas in all of the countries in the Baltic Sea region. The mountains areas of the Baltic Sea region is thus biologically and environmentally of very high quality and by many considered a unique and common heritage to be protected and kept for us and future generations.

The number of people visiting the mountains for tracking, fishing, skiing, etc is today dramatically increasing every year. It is also clear that the visitors are increasingly coming from all of Europe and not only the closest countries. It seems that an important aspect of the development of the rural areas of our region is to protect and make our mountains available for us and coming generations.

History of Land Use in the Great Lakes Region

6

Gregory McIsaac
University of Illinois at Urbana-Champaign, USA

Ecosystems, biotic communities and social systems evolve and change in response to a variety of natural and anthropogenic pressures and constraints. This complicates the pursuits of sustainability, sustainable rural communities, species diversity and ecosystem processes. According to Ostrom (2009), understanding ecosystem dynamics and how a desired resource will respond to different management practices is an important component to establishing sustainable socio-economic systems. Sustainable management of common property natural resources tends to occur where the resource users are familiar with the resource, its dynamics and its limits; and where rules against overuse are clearly stated and enforced; and use is readily monitored. In the past these conditions have most frequently been achieved in managing resources at a relatively small scale. As remote sensing allows for large scale monitoring, sustainable landscape management can become more common. This chapter provides a brief overview of the long term co-evolution of the humans and the landscape in The Great Lakes region of the US. Much of what took place in the 19th and 20th centuries demonstrates unsustainable land use, which may serve as a cautionary tale, indicating mistakes that ought not be repeated. Various problems associated with unsustainable land use have been recognized and some corrective measures have been implemented. The longer term history may provide an understanding of the context within which local sustainable resource management efforts must operate to move the larger system closer to sustainability.

Great Lakes Region Prehistory

After the Recent Glaciation

The topography of the Great Lakes region was formed by repeated cycles of glacial advance and retreat over the last million years. The most recent glaciers reached its maximum extent about 20,000 years ago and extended south of the Basin. There is evidence of human activity in the region that is 13,000 years old (Walters and Stafford , 2007). At that time, glaciers and tundra covered the northern portions of the Great Lakes Basin. Between 10,000 and 12,000 years ago, 35 genera of large mammals went extinct in North America, including mastodons, mammoths and horses. The causes of this extinction event are uncertain, but may include climate change, extraterrestrial impact, and human hunting pressure (Faith and Surovell , 2009).

Figure 6.1. Native American Encampment on Lake Huron. Oil on canvas by Paul Kane, c. 1845.The Granger Collection, New York.

After the glaciers retreated, and the climate warmed, forests eventually dominated most of the landscape, with boreal forests in the north, deciduous hardwood forests in the south, and mixed conifer-deciduous forests in between. There were, however, significant climatic shifts over the last 10,000 years that caused shifts in the patterns of vegetation (Davis et al. 2000). Based on pollen evidence, precipitation generally increased during the last 8,000 years which has increased the proportion of mesic trees, such as sugar maple and beech. Increased precipitation probably also increased the areas of wet prairie, wetlands, numerous inland lakes that were found to be common in the Basin in the 19th century when systematic surveys were completed.

The First Settlers – Native Americans

Native Americans' use of fire also influenced aspects of the vegetation and wildlife in some areas, most notably to the south and west of the Basin, in Illinois, where frequent fires, some of which were likely of human origin, maintained prairie and savannah landscapes where rainfall was sufficient for hardwood forest. Native Americans probably had some influence on the composition and structure of the forest as well, through fire, selective tree removal, and gathering activities that enhanced seed dispersal, but the extent and significance of that influence is not well known (Williams, 2000).

Early Native Americans made use of the landscape through hunting, fishing and gathering plants for consumption and other uses. Wild rice (four species in the genus *Zizania*) was an important food source that was gathered in some regions of the basin. In the southern regions deer, bison, elk, turkeys were commonly hunted. In the north, moose, bear, caribou, geese and beaver, were more important game animals (Tanner et al., 1987). The lakes and its tributaries provided both avenues of transportation as well as an abundant source of fish (Bogue, 2000). Tools were made out of stone, bone and wood. Trees were harvested for fuel, shelter and other uses such as canoes building. The lifestyle appears to have been largely nomadic or semi-nomadic to take advantage of resources available in different locales during different seasons.

In the last 2,000 years cultivation of domesticated crops became an increasingly important aspect of Native American life in the southern portions of the Great Lakes Basin. Evidence for plant domestication in eastern North America, including the land that is now Illinois, is about 4,000 years old (Smith, 1989). In the Mississippi River Basin, 7,000 year old archeological evidence indicates that humans began to occupy river flood plains continuously during the summer months. This occupation caused disturbances to the flood plain environment that appear to have favored certain weedy invader plants, such as curcubita, goosefoot, sumpweed and sunflower, which have edible seeds. At some undetermined date, humans apparently began to intentionally cultivate these plants, and by about 3,000 years ago evidence of domesticated varieties is apparent from physiological differences between the cultivated varieties and their wild relatives.

Maize was probably introduced into North America from Central America about 1,700 years ago, but it remained a relatively minor crop until about 800 years ago when the common bean was also introduced. At that time, cultivation of maize-bean-squash complex became widespread in eastern North America, including the southern portion of the Great Lakes Basin. During the Medieval Warm Epoch (approximately 950 to 1250 AD) both wild and domesticated species could be found much further north than their present ranges.

With the expansion of maize and bean cultivation into North America, the cultivation of indigenously domesticated plants, such as goosefoot and sunflower, decreased. Nonetheless, there was still a great variety of domesticated crops grown in Native American fields, such as tobacco, peppers, cotton, amaranth, sunflower, and Jerusalem artichoke (Smith, 1992). Additionally, different varieties of maize with different cob shapes and sizes appeared in different regions. Early European explorers recorded the existence of short- and long-season maize varieties, indicating a sophisticated knowledge of crop breeding and husbandry (Tanner et al., 1987).

Native American population densities in the Great Lakes region seem to have been low and the human impact on the landscape, although uncertain, was also probably relatively small. One possible explanation for the low impact is the absence of large domesticated animals used as beasts of burden like horses or oxen in Europe. The primary source of power of Native Americans appears to have been human muscle and open fires. Additionally, the short growing season and the low productivity of the crop varieties probably limited human population density. In southeastern North America and Mexico, with longer growing seasons, higher population densities and permanent settlements were established, probably with greater environmental impact.

The European Colonization

The arrival of Europeans to the Americas and their release of domesticated pigs in the late 15th and early 16th Centuries introduced diseases that drastically reduced Native American populations throughout the Americas (Mann, 2005). In Hernando Desoto's 1539 brutal incursion across southeastern North America, he encountered "thickly settled with great towns" along the Mississippi River. One hundred and fifty years later, Renee-Robert Cavelier, Sieur de la Salle, found these areas largely abandoned (Mann, 2005).

Besides diseases to which the Americans had little or no immunological resistance, Europeans introduced horses and firearms (Holder, 1970), which many Native Americans adopted for hunting and war fighting, thereby changing the nature of their interactions with the environment and with other people. The initial European interest in the Great Lakes Region largely focused on the fur trade. Native Americans traded animal pelts in exchange for European products, such as firearms. In their enthusiasm for such products, the Iroquois people of the eastern Great Lakes region depleted the beaver population in their territory as early as 1641 (Tanner et al., 1987). Competition over beaver trapping and the fur trade contributed to a long period of hostilities between the Iroquois and the neighboring Huron people.

European Encroachment and Landscape Transformation

During the 1700s, much of central North America, including the Great Lakes, was officially designated as Native American territory, and many of the eastern Native Americans migrated into the Great Lakes region. This increased the population and competition and conflict over resources. There was also some westward migration of Europeans into Native American territory, most notably Finish forest dwellers, who had emigrated from forested areas of Finland, where hunting, trapping and gathering wild foods had been viable livelihoods (Warren, 1994). The British Isles and much of continental Europe had long been deforested and immigrants from those places were unfamiliar with hunting or clearing forest. In the westward expansion of European settlement in North America, Finnish immigrants often provided the first clearing. The Finnish frontier immigrants would build a simple living structure and clear a small patch of forest for growing crops, but would subsist to a large degree from hunting, gathering and trapping. As the neighboring population increased, hunting and gathering success would decline, prompting the frontier woodsmen to sell their land, move further westward, and repeat the cycle of setting up a homestead and pursuing their frontier lifestyle. Although the Finns came with skills and attitudes that were well suited to frontier living, they were unfamiliar with the American flora and fauna. In many areas, they learned about local plants and animals from Native

Americans with whom they enjoyed good relations and intermarried.

Before moving further west, the frontier woodsmen often sold their land to people who had less interest in and/or skills for living primarily by hunting and gathering. The buyers were more typically people who had traditional farming skills learned in the eastern states or in Europe, and they bought the land to pursue that livelihood. These farmers generally cleared larger areas for crops than the frontier woodsmen had, built more permanent structures, kept livestock and produced a little marketable surplus if there was access to a market (Cochrane, 1993).

Relationships between Native Americans and European-descended immigrants ranged from friendly to hostile. Some Native Americans readily adopted the practices of the European immigrants such as the use of log cabins, with glazed windows and fenced yards (Tanner et al., 1987). But as more Europeans encroached upon Indian lands in the early 1800s and cut down forests, the forest wildlife became more scarce and Native American hunting and gathering became increasingly difficult (Perlin, 2005). Through a series of treaties, forcible removal, and armed skirmishes, most of the Indian lands in the Great Lakes region were taken over by the US government in the 1800s, and then made available to European immigrants by various means: sale, auction or legislation (e.g., the Homestead Act of 1861).

In 1825 the Erie Canal was completed which provided a transportation link from the Great Lakes to the Hudson River and the Atlantic coast. This opened the Great Lakes region to more extensive immigration and commercial development, most notably in the abundant fish provided by the lakes (Bogue, 2000). Initially, settlement in the region occurred largely near the lakes and along the river corridors. After 1830, railroad networks were constructed and connected the interior landscape to urban markets, and consumed vast quantities of wood (Perlin, 2005). Between 1830 and 1900, several million immigrants arrived in the region and most of the land that was suitable for agriculture was converted from forest or prairie to cropland. As the southern forests disappeared, the northern forests were aggressively harvested for wood for the expanding population, railroads, steam ships, iron smelters and other commercial activities (Bogue, 2000; Cronon, 1991; Perlin, 2005). Large areas of old-grown coniferous forest were cut down and the tree trunks removed. The remaining slash was left behind, occasionally contributing to damaging wildfires.

Figure 6.2. View of Erie Canal by John William Hill, 1829.

The extensive logging and lumber milling practices had several negative impacts on the Great Lakes fishery. Tree removal led to greater erosion and sedimentation of streams and rivers which served as spawning beds for many fish species. Additionally, in some places logs were transported to saw mills by floating them down streams and rivers, which could also degrade habitat. Finally, sawing the logs into boards and useful wood products produced large quantities of saw dust and waste wood, which were often dumped into rivers or coastal waters of the Great Lakes further degrading the quality of the habitat for fish (Bogue, 2000).

Concern over destructive logging practices was expressed as early as 1867 in a document prepared for the Wisconsin legislature titled "Report on the Disastrous Effects of the Destruction of Forest Trees Now Going on so Rapidly in the State of Wisconsin." Similar deforestation occurred throughout the US and criticism of the practices became more vocal during the course of the 19th century. The American Association for the Advancement of Science recommended the creation of protected forest reserves on federal lands and in 1891 President Benjamin Harrison complied by stopping timber sales on federal lands (Perlin, 2005). This provided the basis of the National Forest System in the US. The US Forest Service

Figure 6.3. Clearing of land. Source: Perlin, 2005

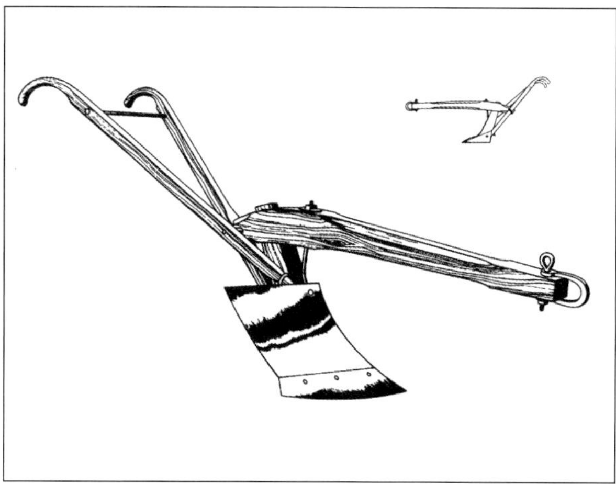

Figure 6.4. The John Deere steel plow from 1837 increased the amount of land a farmer could plow in a day because soil was less likely stick to its surfaces. Deere's cast-steel plow, which was pioneered in 1837. Prior to Deere's introduction of the steel plow, most farmers used iron or wooden plows which stuck to the rich Midwestern soil and had to be cleaned very frequently. The smooth sided steel plow solved this problem, and would greatly aid migration into the American Great Plains in the 19th and early 20th century. Source: Augustana College, Special Collection.

was created in 1905 to manage the forests for multiple uses, including production of wood as well as recreation and environmental conservation.

Pioneer Farming in the Great Lakes Region

Many of the early immigrant farmers to the Great Lakes region brought relatively simple tools that they had used in the East: wagon, plow, harrow, axe, rake, scythe, fork and shovel (Bogue, 1963). These early pioneers gravitated toward forested areas, which provided wood for housing, fencing and fuel, in part because they were familiar with clearing and farming woodlands. Although they may have had some experience with natural meadows, their wooden or iron faced plows were not suited to either cutting into the thick prairie sod or for working the fine textured soils.

In the 1820s and 30s farmers, blacksmiths and other innovators introduced various modifications to the plow that provided a sharper and stronger cutting edge (share) and smoother surfaces so that soil did not stick to either the plow share or the moldboard. John Deere's steel plows reportedly became a standard for excellence in the 1850's, but Deere was neither the inventor nor the only manufacturer of steel plows. Deere's primary contribution to the plow lie in manufacturing a large number of high quality plows at an affordable price (Bogue, 1963).

Even with improved plows, the initial breaking of the thick prairie sod required large teams of draft animals. After the prairie sod was first broken, the soil was surprisingly productive. Without applying fertilizer or manures, without even paying much attention to weeds, farmers would harvest yields that were equal to or greater than yields which east coast farmers had struggled for. The prairie soil and vegetation had accumulated plant nutrients and organic matter during the previous six to ten thousand years after the retreat of the glaciers. When the prairie sod was broken and the soil cultivated, these nutrients were released as the plant material and organic matter decomposed. In 1890, the Illinois Agricultural Experiment Station in Urbana reported only a minimal crop response to manures or commercial fertilizers applied to soils that had been used for continuous maize production for 15 years, and that this small response was not sufficient to justify the investment in fertilizer (Bogue, 1963). A smaller flush of nutrient availability occurred when woodland soils were brought under cultivation.

The settlers planted a mixture of crops and raised livestock both for home consumption and for the market. Crops included wheat, maize, oats barley, rye, flax, potatoes, vegetables and fruit (Bogue, 1963). Although pioneer farms were much more diversified than today's more specialized farms, maize was grown on a large portion of crop land acres because it gave high and reliable yields and the mature crop could stand in the field all winter without spoilage or much loss to wildlife. However, maize's low price per bushel did not justify transporting it very far and consequently much of it was fed livestock on or near the farm where it had been grown. Thus, by 1860, the Midwest (including the southern portions of the Great Lakes Basin) was becoming the nation's livestock and feed grain producer, complementing the agricultural and industrial specializations occurring in other US regions (Cochrane, 1993). A considerable quantity of wheat was grown because it brought a much higher price per bushel than maize. This rendered it a more attractive export crop, but yields were lower and much less certain than maize (Bogue, 1963).

Horses and mules were used for draft power, and a large portion of the oats that farmers grew was fed to their horses, with the remainder sold for human consumption. Land that was too wet to cultivate was initially used for livestock grazing. Through the 1870s, there was apparently a considerable quantity of communal grazing land as evidenced by occasional newspaper stories and editorials about settlers attempting to claim such land for private ownership (Bogue, 1963).

Many rural communities were settled by people of one particular ethnic or religious heritage. Amish families congregated together as their part of their religious practice emphasizing harmonious relationships with their fellow believers and avoiding dependency on nonbelievers. Some groups of families migrated from Germany as a group and established a new community in the US (Salamon, 1992). Others migrated individually and gravitated toward towns settled by people of similar ethnic heritage. To varying degrees, community relations and farming decisions reflected a continuation of some of the traditional attitudes and practices that had been common in Europe. Some of these traditions continued through much of the 20th century. After interviewing farm families in the 1980s, Salamon (1992) reported that many German descended farmers were oriented toward intergenerational continuation of the family farm and supporting their local community. These farmers tended to avoid taking on debt, and preferred to intensify their operations with livestock production. They also preferred to live close to town and were active in their church. At the appropriate time, the farm would be passed on to the next generation. In contrast, English-descended farmers approached farming as a business, and were more willing to take on debt in pursuit of higher economic return. Their farms were larger and less diversified. They were less likely to be active in community affairs or to want their children to take over the family farm or to enter farming as a livelihood.

Figure 6.5. Man and woman using a double-handled saw to clear trees from their land in Wisconsin 1905. Credit. Wisconsin Historical Society.

Wetland Drainage

In the 1800s, large areas of land in and near the Great Lakes Basin were wetlands. Both Native Americans and early European settlers tended to avoid these areas in part because of the difficulty they presented to travel as well as the presence of mosquitos and malaria. In 1850, the US government gave more than 26 million hectares of federally owned marsh and swampland to the states on the

Figure 6.6. Dredge boat. To dig dredge ditches to drain farm land for drainage district. A slip scraper was used to dig hole in middle of field till there was enough water to float this boat. It was prefabricated and had a steam shovel in front to dig it's way toward the river. Taken into the field by wagons and put together on site. Building on back is crew quarters. Photo from Moultrie county in Illinois around 1900. Source: Illinois Digital Archives, made available by the Arthur Public Library.

condition that money from the sale of the land to private individuals would be used to drain the land and render it more productive. Ohio, Michigan, Illinois received over 2 million hectares of this federal land. These states enacted laws to allow the formation of drainage districts that would organize multiple land owners in drainage projects (Bogue, 2000). In Illinois, much of the land was purchased by absentee owners, speculators and land barons, who in turn, leased the land to tenants, or sold it at a profit (Bogue, 1951). Large areas of wetlands were also being drained in Ontario.

There was experimentation with land drainage techniques between 1850 and 1880. Installation of clay pipes or "tiles" about one meter deep in the soil was a desired technique, but initially too expensive for all except a few of the wealthiest land owners. Open ditches were a common approach to drainage when the cost of tile drainage was too high. But the impediments to draining large tracts of land were as much social as they were economic or technical. The most efficient path for draining water from one farmer's land might cross the fields of neighboring farmers. Obtaining the necessary cooperation among landowners was the work of the drainage districts.

Wetland soils tend to have even greater accumulations of organic matter and stored nutrients than prairie soils. Once drained, these soils are highly productive cropland and thus there has long been a strong economic incentive for farmers to install drainage tiles. Additionally, drainage reduced mosquito habitat and the prevalence of malaria, while also reducing habitat for birds and amphibians. In the 19th and early 20th century many miles of clay tiles were installed using hand labor. By mid 20th century the process had been mechanized and plastic tubing has replaced clay tiles.

As the wet prairies were drained, and common grazing areas enclosed, livestock raisers found that the native grasses, such a big bluestem, did not survive or produce well under the drier conditions and more intensive grazing. They found imported bluegrass and timothy grass were more suitable than the native grasses for barnyards and forage (Bogue 1963). By 1900, cultivated crops and pastures of introduced forages replaced all but a few remnants of the native vegetation that once covered Illinois (Iverson, 1988) and other states in the Great Lakes region. Most of this transformation occurred in less than a century after the Native Americans had been forced west of the Mississippi River. In the process, many native species, such as bison, elk, wolf, and prairie chicken, either disappeared from the landscape or became very scarce.

From Farming to Manufacturing

At the same time that people were migrating into the Great Lakes region in the early 1800s, New Englanders were developing a distinctive system of manufacturing that emphasized mass production, low cost, and interchangeability of parts (Sawyer, 1954). This system took many years to develop and depended in part on the development of precision machine tools (Roe, 1916). It also involved significant investment of public and private funds. One of the key contributors to this development was Eli Whitney, who received many contracts from the US government to produce military hardware. While he was developing new machine tools to produce parts that would be sufficiently uniform to allow interchangeability, he did not always complete his contracts. In effect, these contracts were fore-runners of government research and development grants, although they were not intended as such.

Manufacturers in the US created many products, some of which were used on farms to increase labor productivity in harvesting, planting and cultivating fields. Advances in textile manufacturing equipment increased the demand for cotton. Manufacturing also created a demand for labor and an increasing percentage of the population would find employment in the manufacturing sector and decreasing percentage in agricultural production. In 1800, approximately 75% of the US population was directly engaged in agricultural production. In 1850, this had fallen to less than 60% and by 1900, less than 40% of the population was engaged in agricultural production (Rasmussen, 1960). As farms became increasingly mechanized, one family could farm more acres. Between 1900 and 1950, the average farm in Illinois increased from about 50 to 60 hectares ha in area. In 1990, it had jumped to 140 hectares and farms became more specialized in a smaller number of products such as corn and soybean. A similar trend toward larger farms occurred in other states but with somewhat different patterns of specialization. Wisconsin and Minnesota, for instance, have greater specialization in dairy production.

Increasing Influence of Science and Technology

By the 1890s, the native fertility of the cultivated soils was beginning to be exhausted. Some farmers began to notice declining crop yields that could be reversed by applications of manures, rock phosphate, lime, and rotations that included nitrogen fixing legumes. Around 1900, a rotation of maize-oats-clover became common in Illinois. The US Department of Agriculture, under the guidance of Secretary James Wilson between 1897 and 1912, increased its emphasis of scientific research in such areas as genetics, pathology, soils, chemistry and statistics. Wilson also influenced the Department's growing regulatory function with the passage of the Food and Drug Act of 1906.

In the 20th century, three major technological innovations further transformed agricultural land use in the Great Lakes Region: the use of the internal combustion engine to replace draft animals; the introduction of hybrid maize, and the use of industrially manufactured nitrogen fertilizers. Steam engines had replaced some animal power in the latter half of the 19th century, particularly for harvesting and threshing grain. However, the use of steam power never approached the use of animal power on farms in the US (Wik, 1953). Steam engines were extremely heavy, and required a great deal of fuel and water. Sparks from the engine exhaust could ignite a dry field waiting to be harvested. The weight of the engines is reported to have collapsed some bridges, and in some such incidents, the expensive engine was not recoverable. After 1910, internal combustion engines and liquid fuels became more readily available, and tractors began to displace the use of both steam power and draft animals. Draft animals, particularly horses, persisted on farms longer than steam engines and were still a common sight on Illinois farms in 1950. With the elimination of draft animals, however, land that had been used to grow their feed and forage was devoted to other purposes, such as the production of maize and soybean for hog, beef and dairy production. This led to farms becoming more dependent on a supply of fossil fuel rather than relying on internally produced feed and forage for draft power.

In the 1920s scientific research conducted by the US Department of Agriculture and the Land Grant Colleges began to produce practical results, particularly in the development of higher yielding varieties of hybrid maize. At first, farmers were either too poor and/or too skeptical to purchase and plant much of the new seed. But when economic conditions improved in the mid to late 1930s, nearly all maize grown in the region was hybrid varieties which provided higher yields per unit area and ushered in a new era of crop breeding.

The availability of inexpensive nitrogen fertilizers after about 1960 reduced the need for applying animal manures, or rotating grain crops with legumes to maintain soil fertility. Many farmers with the highly productive soils, particularly those in the "Corn Belt" south of the Great Lakes, found they could earn greater returns on investment by specializing in maize and soybean rather than with livestock. After 1960, much of the Corn Belt land that had been planted to hay for livestock forage was brought into a maize-soybean rotation. Much of this land is tile drained, and the combination of tile drainage, nitrogen fertilizer on maize and high soil organic matter soils contributed to high nitrate concentrations in drainage water, which is a drinking water hazard and a contributor to algae production in coastal marine waters.

Figure 6.7. Buried machinery in barn lot in Dallas, South Dakota, United States during the Dust Bowl, an agricultural, ecological, and economic disaster in the Great Plains region of North America in 1936. Source: United States Department of Agriculture.

The Great Depression, Dust Bowl and Expanded Government Programs

The combined crises of the Great Depression and the Dust Bowl of the early 1930s led to significant changes in government policies in conservation and economic assistance. The dust storms of the "dirty 30's" were the consequence of several factors. The years 1930-1934 were years of below average rainfall for much of the US, including portions of the Great Lakes region. The topsoil dried out and became susceptible to wind erosion where there was little or no vegetative cover, such as in cultivated fields. The worst wind erosion occurred on south western plains: Oklahoma, New Mexico, Texas, and Kansas, where above average rainfall in the 1920s had encouraged expansion of cultivation and wheat production (Worster, 1979). The wind-blown soil that appeared in Washington, DC and elsewhere during this period may have helped convince politicians to support the legislation that provided funds for technical and financial assistance for rural areas and farmers.

In addition to establishing soil conservation programs, described below, a variety of farm income stabilization programs were initiated by US Congress in the 1930s, some of which continue to the present day in modified form. These programs include crop insurance, price supports, loan programs and land set-aside programs. Although these programs benefit farmers in the short term, by providing subsidies that reduced the risks of economic losses from agricultural production, these programs helped attract financial investments in high tech agriculture (Strange, 1988). Over the decades, this contributed to production surpluses and regional specialization. Some critics have described this as a production treadmill with much of the net benefit being captured by land owners, equipment manufacturers, agrochemical suppliers, food processors and consumers rather than farmers who increasingly rent land from absentee owners. Since the 1930s, the numbers of farmers has declined dramatically.

A primary reason for low farm product prices was the excess supply in relation to the demand. This was partly a result of abundant land and improved production methods. To address the problem of excess production, the Cropland Adjustment Act of 1934 was the first of many subsequent land set-aside programs in which farmers removed portions of their land from production in return for either direct payments or for price guarantees. A farmer might be required to plant an annual crop, such as oats or barley, for soil conservation, but would not be permitted to sell any product from the land that was set aside from production. At times when the US Department of Agriculture officials anticipated periods of sustain surpluses and low commodity prices, set-aside programs were established for multiple years. For example, the Conservation Reserve programs of 1956-1969 provided funding to participating farmers to establish perennial vegetation for multiple years. These programs of long-term set aside were probably more beneficial to wildlife, such as pheasants, than annual set-aside programs (Edwards, 1994). However, when high commodity prices returned in the 1970s, the perennial vegetation was replaced with annual crops which reduced numbers of pheasants and rabbits.

The agricultural legislation of 1930s also created the Soil Conservation Service (SCS), which was renamed the Natural Resources Conservation Service (NRCS) in 1995. The SCS provided and the NRCS continues to provide technical assistance to farmers adopting soil and water conservation practices. In 1934, the SCS estimated that more than half of the nation's land was moderately or severely eroded (Schwab et al., 1993). More scientifically based soil erosion surveys have been conducted as part of the Natural Resource Inventory starting in 1977. In 1982, 25% of US cropland and nearly 40% of cropland in the Corn Belt was eroding at rates believed to be damaging to the long term productive capacity of the soils (National Research Council, 1986). In 1985 the Conservation Reserve Program (CRP) was initiated in which the US federal government paid an annual fee to land owners who took highly erodible land out of crop production. By 1992, erosion rates had declined considerably largely due to the CRP and the use of conservation tillage (Kellogg et al, 1994). In recent years erosion rates have continued to decline as conservation tillage and no-till have become more commonly practiced (US Dept. of Agriculture, 2009).

Despite reductions of soil erosion, the impacts of agricultural runoff on water quality continue to be a concern, due to sediment, nutrients and pesticides. A later version of CRP targeted cropland adjacent to streams for conversion to perennial vegetation in order to filter runoff and thereby buffer the receiving streams. The connection between reduced erosion from cropland and surface water quality is complicated, however. In some settings, a reduction in erosion from cropland has been linked with improved water quality. In other settings the improvement in water clarity has permitted the formation of algal blooms because of high concentrations of phosphorus in runoff. In yet other areas, there has been little or no discernible effect of soil conservation on water quality. Trimble and Lund (1982) examined the connection between soil conservation measures and sediment transport in the Coon Creek in southwestern Wisconsin, and reported that cropland erosion rates and sediment deposition rates in the stream valley declined dramatically after 1940 due to the implementation of soil conservation measures. However,

Figure 6.8. Maize being transferred from a combine to a truck for hauling during harvest near Champaign IL, circa 2008. Photo: T.P. Martins.

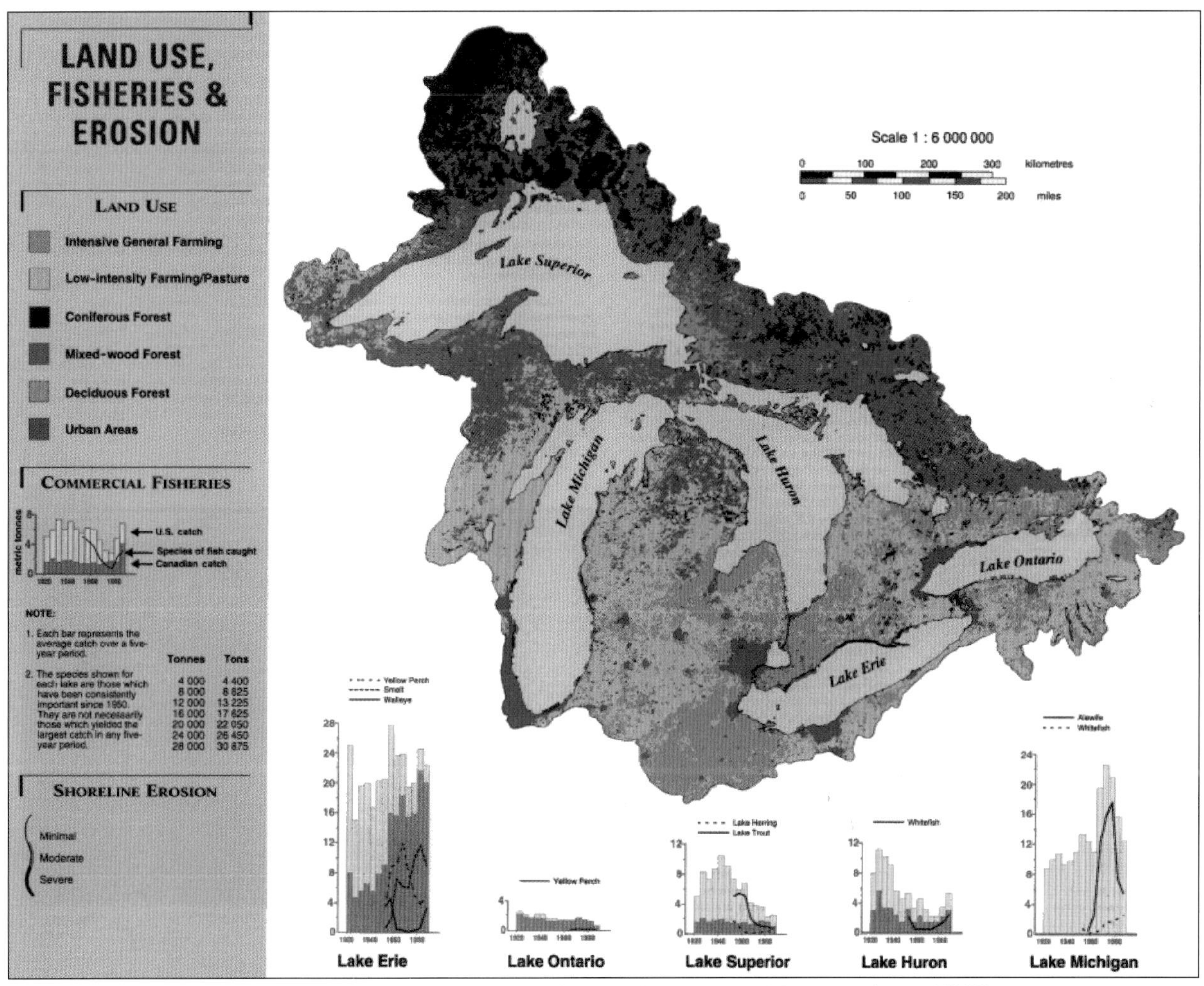

Figure 6.9. Land use, fisheries & erosion in the Great Lakes region. Source: US. Environmental Protection Agency, US EPA.

high rates of sediment deposition in the stream valley during the preceding seven decades left a legacy of sediment supply that will influence sediment transport in the stream for many decades into the future. We still have much to learn about the art of managing cropland in ways that protect or restore the aquatic ecosystems that receive agricultural runoff.

Population Rebound in Rural Areas

Depending on how "rural" is defined, between 18% and 36% of the population in the Great Lakes States could be classified as rural in 2000; and between 65% and 95% of the land area could be classified as rural (Cromartie and Bucholtz, 2007). For most of the 20th century, rural counties and communities have been losing population to urban and suburban areas. This has partly been a consequence of reduced demand for labor in farming, forestry and mining, and increased demand for labor in the manufacturing and service sectors. With many rural people migrating to urban areas for education and employment, a considerable number of rural schools and businesses have closed, thus forcing the remaining residents to commute longer distances for services, and to become less connected to their local community. It becomes difficult to attract educated professionals, such as doctors and dentists, to areas with declining populations and services. However, starting in the 1970s, there is evidence of a revival of many rural communities in the US and in the Great Lakes Region (Johnson, 1999). It appears to be driven by several factors such as urban residents seeking a rural quality of life that includes neighborliness and environmental amenities. These new rural residents include people raising young children, retirees and new immigrants to the US (Salamon, 2003). Several rural areas in the Great Lakes region offer environmental amenities as well as recreational opportunities and have been able to generate jobs and income from tourism (Johnson, 1999).

While the new rural residents are often initially welcomed by the long-time residents, there are also sometimes conflicts, particularly over environmental amenities. For example, the long-time residents tend to be accustomed to odors produced by local livestock facilities, while the new comers may find the odors offensive and seek to impose limits on the odor producing activities. Similar conflicts may also arise over forestry or mining activities that threaten recreation, wildlife or scenic views.

In recent decades an increasing number of conservation and ecological restoration activities have been initiated, partly driven by the information acquired from nearly a century of formal ecological science. Both private and federal agencies have engaged in a process to promote sustainable forestry practices. Remaining wetland areas have been given a modest degree of legal protection, and wetland and prairie restoration activities are enjoying an increasing amount of private, federal and state funding. Since 1972, the US and Canada have engaged in a process of ecological monitoring and restoration of the Great Lakes through the Great Lakes Water Quality Agreement. Although this Agreement focuses on the Lakes, the connection between land use and the lakes is recognized. Although it will likely take many decades to recover from the extensive changes that have occurred since 1800s, it is hoped that an adaptive process of discovery, education, and restoration will bring about positive changes for the people and landscape of the Great Lakes region.

Summary and Conclusions

The landscape of the Great Lakes region has been altered by natural factors and human activities. European settlement since 1800 has caused significant and rapid conversion of forest, prairie and wetland to agriculture. This process was initially driven by individuals seeking to provide for their families, but over time became a complex industrial, and governmental system. The environmental and social problems caused by these changes were recognized by a few during the 19th century, but there was insufficient capability to restrict destructive uses or plan more constructive land uses. Efforts to address the problems were often implemented only after the problem resulted in a crisis, such as large forest fires or the Dust Bowl. While some progress has been made in protecting forests and conserving soils, considerably more work can be done to improve the sustainability of rural communities and design landscapes that provide habitat for native species as well as healthy livelihoods for rural residents. Finer scale analysis than presented here is needed to guide local restoration and compatible rural development activities. At the scale of the Great Lakes Basin, state and national and institutions are needed to provide a framework for understanding the socio-ecological system, and developing policies and practices that enhance local sustainability and discourage unsustainable activities.

Part B

The Rural Society

Authors: Per G Berg, Elena Kropinova, Diana Mincyte, Lars Rydén and Marina Thorborg

Coordinating Author: Lars Rydén

From Traditional to Modern Rural Society

7

Diana Mincyte
New York University, New York, USA

Baltic Pre-history

The First Settlers

People have inhabited the Baltic Sea watershed area for almost 100,000 years, but it was only after the melting of the inland ice during the last glacial period (*ca* 70,000 BC to *ca* 12,000 BC) that agriculture was introduced and permanent settlements were built. Traces of the oldest permanent human habitation in the southern part of the region date back to around 12,000 BC, while the first agricultural settlers moved in and significant agricultural production emerged around 4,000-3,500 BC. Starting with this period, agriculture has played a central role in the social, political and economic life of the region with the notable exception of its most northerly regions, where indigenous populations continue a semi-nomadic lifestyle up to this day. There are four major stages in the development of rural societies in the Baltic basin: 1) Early history, 2) Feudalism and mediaeval state formation, 3) Industrialisation, and 4) Modern rural societies.

Neolithic Times to Bronze Age

During pre-historic times, the geography of the region looked very different, as most of the region was covered with ice and water and the Baltic Sea formed an enclosed freshwater lake. As the ice drew back, during the late Palaeolithic period, reindeer-hunting camps started to appear at the edge of the ice. There was a little forest with occasional arctic white birch and rowan patches, but as the climate became warmer the area became covered by taiga, attracting wildlife and people. Archaeological, linguistic and genetic evidence suggests that the peoples arrived first from the south-west and north-east. These peoples lived nomadic lives and depended on hunting, fishing and collecting roots, herbs, berries, seeds and mushrooms.

During the 6th millennium BC, the climate was warm enough to cover southern parts of the region, with forests of temperate broadleaved trees breeding deer and moose and providing a source of survival for the group of tribes belonging to the Kongemose culture living in the area. They continued to develop fishing and seal hunting techniques they inherited from their predecessors. Culturally and socially, these tribes lived the same lifestyle as others in northern areas of the globe, including Northern Eurasia and America. Archaeological data suggest that these societies were patriarchal, but not as strict and gender discriminatory as they became in settler groups. Numerous imported objects found in the graves testify to connections with the European mainland.

The first settlements emerged in areas constituting today's Denmark, Northern Germany, Poland and Southern Sweden. The process of settling first started with the establishment of fishing settlements near the water and then spread to include inland agricultural communities. These cultures included not only groups with advanced agricultural culture, but also those using primitive tools. Archeological sources show that they built fortified settlements and started making copper tools, jewelry, and arms. The processes of settling and the advancement of agricultural technologies in the Baltic region also led to

Figure 7.1. Iron age village at Lejre in Denmark with log canoes and a thatch roof building. This is one of several reconstructed villages to be found in the Baltic Sea region, such as Eketorp in Öland in southern Sweden and Hedeby in northern Germany. Photo: Kristian Mollenborg.

the development of politically much more centralised and hierarchical social systems in villages. With the surplus production of food that was enabled by farming and animal husbandry, during the 4th millennium BC local socio-economic systems were slowly transformed into broader trading economies, and labour was diversified. The sedentary lifestyle and food surpluses also led to an increase in population density and much later, in the first millennium AD, to the first major urban settlements in the region.

Life in the Neolithic and Bronze age villages meant being constantly preoccupied with food procurement. At that time food preservation techniques were limited and households, which included extended family members, subsisted on growing domesticated plants and animals and on the collection of wild plant foods and hunting. The groups living along the coastline and inland in today's Denmark learned to use domesticated dogs, goats, swine, and oxen. It is important to note that all the domesticated animals came from the Middle East and Asia with the exception of reindeer, which were domesticated by the Sami people. Animals lived in the same built structures as humans. During the Neolithic period people learned to milk goats and cows, and milk played an important part in rural economies. Milk was used as a protein source for drinking, but also as sour curd that resembled the present day cottage cheese. Since people did not keep hens, their diets did not include eggs. In addition to domesticated food sources, they also hunted deer, bison and wild boar. Cats were not domesticated, but mice and rats had not yet adapted themselves to live in human habitats.

The agricultural tools were wooden and weak, making it difficult to work the land. The early farmers practised slash-and-burn cultivation, which required them to move around often after the plots they had cultivated were exhausted of nutrients and allowed to be re-taken by brush. Using crude plows and stone sickles to cultivate grains, and with the development of milling techniques, their diets were enriched with wheat, barley, and millet. They stored their grain in pots and made it into heavy bread baked without yeast.

In these early times people dressed mostly in skins, but they also slowly acquired skills in handling textiles and started using woven fabrics made out of flax. Their fishing nets were also made of flax.

The Neolithic houses were very simple. Most of the dwellings at that time continued to be built using wood, bone, fur, leaves, grasses, and only later brick. Made of these materials, the huts had clay floors. There is no archaeological evidence of stools or tables or beds. In their households they used pots and woven baskets for keeping grains, dairy, and other foodstuff and often kept them hanging by the ropes from the ceiling. The children and young adults took the cows and goats out to graze, and brought them in at night.

The most common settlements in the region consisted of 20-30 relatively independent, self-sustaining households with approximately several hundred inhabitants. Collections of these settlements later led to the formation of more hierarchical social systems known as tribes. Villages, integrated units that were based on cultural bonds and economic interdependence, were not established until the Iron Age. The household was the centre of social organisation and agricultural production. Within the household, labour was distributed according to age and gender. It was arguably during this period that the division between the public and the private spheres was established, separating the feminine-domestic domain from the public life that involved males. However, Neolithic societies worshipped goddesses and were involved in cults celebrating female gods.

In these Neolithic societies there was little occupational specialisation, meaning that every household produced tools and procured food using their own resources and skills. Only later, with the improving technologies and increasing agricultural surplus, did specialisations such as pottery making or metalwork start to take shape. Simultaneously, complex systems of proprietorship and inheritance emerged, laying the foundations for more integrated systems of exchange and trading, as well as the emergence of slavery.

It should be noted that the so-called Neolithisation of the region was neither linear nor homogeneous. For instance, the people of contemporary Sweden's northern parts retained an essentially Mesolithic lifestyle into the 1st millennium BC.

Furthermore, due to major population migrations during the Neolithic period, groups of different ethnic and linguistic backgrounds and vastly different lifestyles lived next to each other. For example, the proto-Sami groups continued to lead a nomadic lifestyle, while the groups that were descendants of Indo-European migrants settled down and practised agriculture.

Iron Age

In the eastern and south-eastern parts of the Baltic watershed, the processes of settling occurred somewhat later. While the first traces of human activity in the territory of today's three Baltic States and Russia go back to around 10,000 BC, it was not until the 1st and 2nd Century AD that agriculture became the primary occupation and the key source of their food. At first, the land was cultivated collectively by clearing brush and forests. By the 5th Century, the Baltic, Slavic and Ugro-Finn tribes started using metal tools and draft animals, and the customs of inheritance were formed.

During the Iron Age, around 4th to the 1st Century BC, people in the south-western part of the region began extracting iron from the ore and peat-bogs. At that time the climate in the region became significantly cooler and wetter, limiting agriculture and leading to southward migrations and a significant decline in local cultures that lasted at least until 500 BC. Starting from the 2nd Century BC, the Roman Empire exerted its influence on local cultures and lifestyles, especially among the elite. While its borders encompassed only the most south-westerly parts of the Baltic basin, peoples living in this territory maintained active trade routes and relations with the Romans, as attested by finds of Roman coins and records showing that some of the Danish warrior aristocracy served in the Roman Army.

Through their interactions with the Roman Empire and in response to increasing competition for land and resources, the tribes living in the Baltic areas started forming more coherent and larger political entities that encompassed several tribes and that later emerged as mediaeval states.

Figure 7.2. Reenactment of iron age farmers tilling the land with a wooden ard (plow) in Lejre, Denmark. © Lejre experimental Centre.

Social Conditions During Early Middle Ages

The Vikings

Starting in the 5th Century and through 1050 AD, Norse cultures in the south-western regions of the Baltic watershed region lived through the Vendel and Viking periods that made them famous for long distance seafaring, trading, exploring, raiding and the colonisation of coastal areas of Europe, North Africa and even the Middle East and North America. These groups developed a complicated social structure including tribal, kinship and merit-based relations. While the majority of population in the Nordic region were involved in agriculture and local fishing, long-distance seafaring significantly affected the Baltic region and its societies through commercial and technological exchanges.

During the Vendel and Viking periods, rural settlements continued to grow in numbers and population density, with the wealth being increasingly concentrated in the hands of the most powerful families. These settlements also became integrated into large political unions that included vast territories. Instead of self-sufficient egalitarian households living as relatively independent units, the archaeological data reveal the emergence of hierarchical villages with magnificent buildings erected in the centre by the most prominent families and a number of huts built around the perimeter of the village and inhabited by poor farmers. During this period, the first military fortresses, court buildings and royal palaces were built by the noblemen.

In this period, four to five social classes could be identified in Baltic rural societies. The highest class consisted of the noblemen, who were born to the most prominent families such as ancestral kings and patriarchal chieftains. In the densely populated areas of the South and South-West Baltics, the tribal chief constituted an independent class from the kings, who were their superiors and to whom they paid their tribute. The royal-noblemen class was far removed from the rest of society and had a cross-regional culture of its own that it shared with West European aristocracies. The next class down consisted of powerful farmers or 'middle class', landowners who were preoccupied with building their wealth and political influence. The third class comprised former slaves and the poorest of the farmers who subsided on their small land plots and who were the primary source of hired labour in the village. At the bottom of the social structure were slaves, who performed the most difficult tasks and who built the wealth of the owner's family and the village. Most of the slaves were acquired as war prisoners or bought from other villages. Not surprisingly, many slaves were of different ethnic or cultural background. The descendants of slaves were also born into slavery and they could only be freed by their owners. In addition to the slaves who were acquired through warfare, free farmers too could fall in their social standing and be enslaved if they failed to repay their debt or as punishment for a crime.

Free Farmers

The households of free farmers remained relatively large, 20-30 individuals. While the data suggest that Baltic societies were organised around patriarchy, scholars argue that this was not as clearly pronounced in terms of economic exploitation, limited decision-making and exclusionary property laws as in the rest of Western Europe. Noble women were allowed to manage their property and make economic decisions. Unlike in Western Europe, noble women were buried in graves as rich and well decorated as those of their male counterparts.

The most powerful households in the village – such as free farmers (about 10-20% of rural population) and chieftains (about 2-5% of rural population) – owned up to 30 slaves and also hired help, but they were also part of the commons and shared pastures with the rest of the village community. Considering that the most valued property at the time was land, they possessed the best land and the most advanced tools to work it. They participated in the local and global markets that were enabled through Viking explorations, and they paid in silver and gold coins. Despite clear boundaries among social classes, upward mobility was possible and it was achieved through marriage. In some cases the position of the most prominent leader of the village was not inherited, and the chieftain had to prove himself in order to be elected and establish legitimacy among the village community. In the case of free farmers, land was owned by all the members of the family including sons and unmarried daughters. A dowry was given to daughters upon their marriage and most of it was paid in gold, not land.

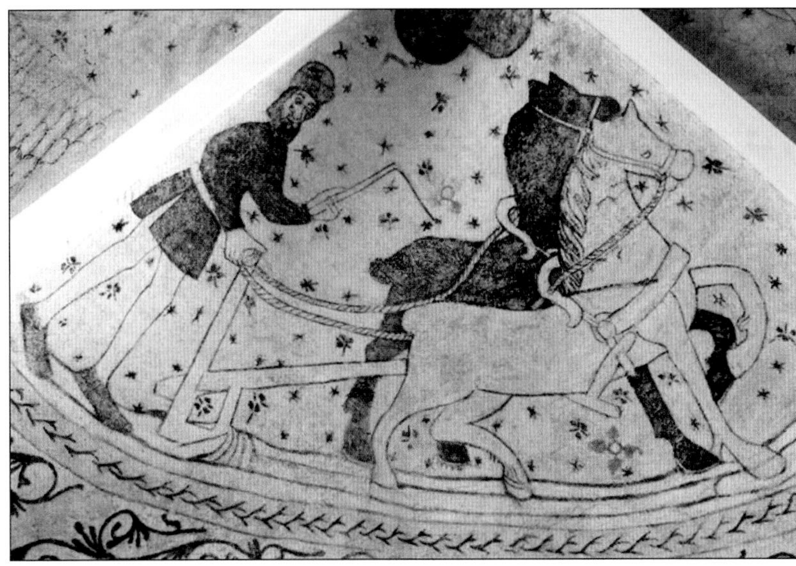

Figure 7.3. 15th century fresco from Rinkaby church by Albertus Pictor, Sweden portraing Adam (Old Testament, the Bible) plowing. Photo: Lennart Karlsson. National historical museum of Sweden in Stockholm.

During the Viking period, homes became larger and building techniques improved. Instead of clay and mortar, the homes of the free farmers were built using wood and bricks. In addition, the animals were moved away from human homes into sheds. Herds of livestock increased to 80-100 animals, especially in the territories of contemporary Denmark and Southern Sweden. The advancement of agricultural technology allowed farmers to switch from the Celtic land use system that was implemented in 200-300 AD to an infield-outfield system. Infields consisted of enclosed meadows and cultivated lands, while the outer parts of land, or outfields, were used as pastures. Stone walls separated the domains and allowed better control over livestock. The village during this period consisted of 5-7 settlements covering about 5 square kilometres.

The diet of the rural population also improved due to the advancement of food preservation techniques including drying, smoking, curing and fermenting, as well as freezing in the northernmost areas. Milk continued to be the most important component in the local diet, while cattle and pigs were the most important livestock. Most farms also had sheep which not only provided the households with milk, but also with wool used for clothing and even sails. With the development of trading routes, oxen became a valuable commodity in the south of contemporary Denmark. Similarly, groups living along the coast of contemporary Sweden sold herring, while the Baltic tribes traded amber, resin, wax, honey, furs and wood.

The Role of Women

By the end of the Iron Age, labour and life in the village were organised around gender relations. During the early Middle Ages, women were increasingly pushed into the domestic sphere and were often deprived of the right to own land or property. While the law statutes of the Duchy of Lithuania allowed elite women to inherit and manage property, women from lower social strata did not have any such rights. The average age of marriage for women in the 13th and 14th Century was 16 and they bore an average of 7-8 children. It was not uncommon for the children to be born out of wedlock before church marriage until well into the 17th Century and the only form of contraception used in villages was wet-nursing lasting up to 4-5 years. Starting the 15th Century, a major shift took place in Baltic families as the child-bearing age increased and the age difference between husband and wife started to decrease. By the 17th Century the average age at marriage for women in Denmark's rural areas reached 28 years and for men it was 31 years, while women had 4-5 children in their lives. This suggests that women in villages entered marriage as more mature individuals and as a result, they had more legitimacy and power in making strategic decisions compared with their predecessors in the Middle Ages.

Households of free farmers in the Middle Ages consisted of family members and slaves. As slaves were gradually replaced by hired servants and their numbers in the household decreased and the childbirth rate started to drop, the average rural household in western parts of the region consisted of only 6-8 persons. The size of household for the poor farmers and freed serfs was even smaller, about 4 people. This was because there were rarely any relatives or older generation living together with the family and young children were sent out to work on the estates.

Middle Ages

State Formation and Christianisation

It was during the early mediaeval period that the groups of tribes living in the Baltic Sea region formed the first unified states with established and coherent polities. While the boundaries of these early political units changed significantly in the course of the next millennium, the states in the region maintained their cultural and political identity throughout the Middle Ages and into the early Modern era. These political units approximately corresponded to the Modern countries of Sweden, Germany, Denmark, Poland, Prussia, Lithuania-Belarus, Russia and the Czech Republic. For the rural populations, the establishment of unified political units brought new systems of social and political control, as well as increased conflicts over the use of land and natural resources. With the development of the distinct political states, rural societies in the Baltic region continued to diversify and develop distinct cultural and social systems. The foundation of the hierarchical administrative systems in the early Middle Ages unmade the relatively homogeneous Iron Age cultures of Northern Europe and led to the emergence of strong place-based identities and idiosyncratic cultures.

In addition to the development of new political and administrative unions that connected villages into integrated administrative networks and spun the web of supervision and control over them, the Middle Ages also brought Christianity into the region, fundamentally transforming local belief systems, world views, rituals, lifestyles, diets and architecture. Christianisation started with the baptism of the Danish king Harold Bluetooth in the 960s and swept through the region, reaching the Grand Duchy of Lithuania first in 1250 and then in 1385 when the country was irreversibly Christianised. This new religion had many advantages for the kings, as it brought support from the Holy Roman Empire and political legitimacy in the eyes of other European powers. It also allowed the king to dismiss many of his opponents who adhered to the old mythology. The Church brought a stable administration that rulers could use to exercise some control over their subjects. Even though it took several generations to denounce pagan beliefs after royal families adopted Christianity, by the end of the 15th Century most of the region was fully Christianised.

During the Middle Ages, the Roman Catholic Church and local rulers became close allies. Thousands of church buildings sprang up and the economy flourished with the emergence of the Hanseatic League, an alliance of 70 trading ports that maintained a trade monopoly along the Baltic coast from the 13th to the 17th Century. Sea trading spread new agricultural technologies including metals from Germany and new agricultural techniques from Denmark. Even though many farmers resisted the introduction of metal tools due to their religious beliefs and saw them as violating pagan deities, agricultural technologies spread rapidly and enabled the cultivation of new lands, which was essential for sustaining the swelling population in the mediaeval Baltics.

A major interruption in this period of economic prosperity and growth was the Black Death, which reached the region in the 1350s, killing about one-third of the population and bringing famine and despair. During the years of Black Death the Church, the rulers and nobility reduced their taxation, enabling larger farms to better sustain themselves. Smaller and poorer farms that could hardly pay rents during the years of prosperity ended up losing everything. After slaughtering all the animals and letting their land fallow, these farms depended fully on the labour of weakened family members to subside. Not surprisingly, these small farms were unable to recover even after the plague passed. Due to the Black Death, the number of free, tax-paying farmers was significantly reduced and large areas of land were acquired by the ruling elites and the Church, along with families of destitute peasants. These processes led to a strengthening of the feudal system in the region.

Feudalism

Nevertheless, feudalism in the Baltic territories was different from in the rest of Europe. Unlike Western and Central Europe, where manorial estates were the most prevalent form of agricultural establishment and where peasants were considered the private property of the landlord, mediaeval rural societies in the Baltic region were dominated by medium and small-scale farmers who were also relatively free in terms of participating in economic activities outside of their lord's estate. In addition, peasants in most of the Baltic region were not subject to their landlord's jurisdictional power. In the case of medium-size alluvial farms, the farmers were not only legally free, but also owned their land and estates. Rather than paying a lord, these farmers were taxed by the Crown and required to furnish a knight and mounted horse in times of war.

Such 'soft' feudalism was mostly found in Denmark, Central Sweden, Lithuania and Poland, while more traditional feudalist societies with highly hierarchical and exploitative lord-vassal relations were prevalent in Russia, Prussia and the territories of contemporary Czech Republic. During the Renaissance and pre-Modern era, 16th to early 18th Century, regional differences were exacerbated due to the changing political landscape. The Polish-Lithuanian state was significantly weakened by internal quarrels and an unstable economy, and at the end of the 18th Century it was split among Russia, Prussia and the Austro-Hungarian Empire. The territories that were included into the Russian Empire experienced the loss of the mid-level alluvial farmers, who were turned into serfs. In Sweden, Denmark and Prussia, on the other hand, such mid-level free farmers flourished as they were the beneficiaries of the economic growth fuelled by the Hanseatic League. The spread of the Reformation as a counter movement to the Catholic Church removed the burden of taxation from peasant shoulders and also brought ideological justification for their independence. In Sweden, the 18th Century brought a transition from absolutism to a parliamentary form of government and rapid industrialisation. Farmers gained the right to purchase clear title to their lands and became relatively independent economic subjects in the globalising economy.

Russia followed an altogether different trajectory of rural development. The structure of Russian agriculture was founded on the peasant commune (*mir*), an institution dating back to Kievan Rus' in the 10th and 11th Century AD. A typical community consisted of peasants who pooled their labour and resources, but also practised a form of local self-government. They made decisions on land use, crop rotation and labour allocation and settled disputes in the village assembly, which was usually presided over by the village elder. In the 15th and 16th Century, such systems were increasingly transferred to the hands of lords appointed by Russian tsars and these communes were thereby turned into exploitative manorial estates and the peasants into the private property of the lords. This rural system in Russia survived until the 20th century.

18th to 20th Centuries

18th Century – Shifting Farms

The period from the mid-18th to the mid-19th Century saw the rapid modernisation of agriculture in the Western Baltics. At the beginning of this period houses and barns belonging to several families were still standing close together in a village and the cultivated area was split up into several small lots, the result of centuries of inheritance and marriages. By the mid-19th Century, however, farms were redeveloped and moved far apart, with each farm having a few large fields around it. The old village was split up and the farming land redistributed among the families. Introduced by the state authorities, these agrarian land reforms were enforced with military power. In addition, pasture that used to belong to the villagers collectively was divided into individual lots and cultivated.

Such a transformation was enabled by the introduction of new agricultural technologies as well as by the liberalisation of markets and the emergence of capitalist economies. After Jethro Tull developed seeding and weeding technologies at the turn of the 18th Century, his inventions spread throughout the region enabling larger fields to be worked with fewer hands. With the imple-

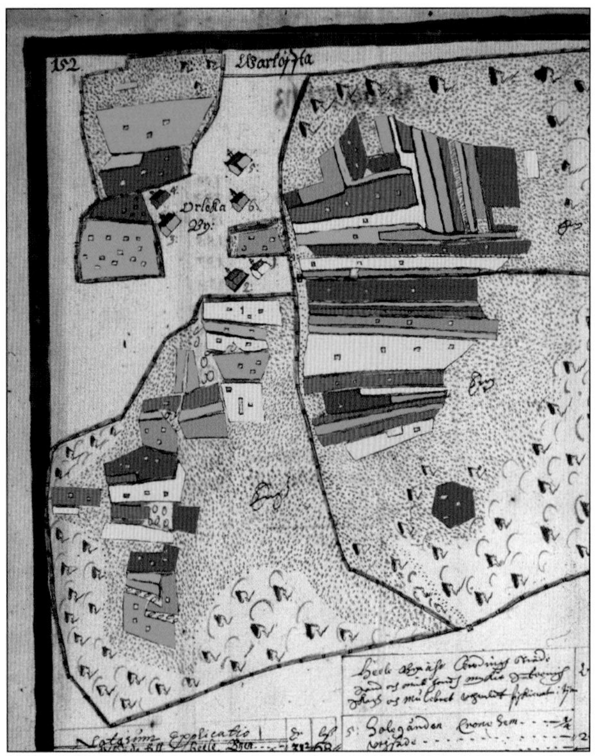

Figure 7.4. Before the 18th Century Sweden was a country of villages. Farmers lived close to each other in settlements, while their fields were inter-mixed as a way of compensating each other for the good and less productive portions of the land. Despite of its advantages, it was a less productive system than individual-based farms because tilling, sowing and harvesting required a lot of coordination on the part of the farmers and new technologies and techniques were difficult to implement. In the 18th Century authorities introduced a reform designed to improve agricultural productivity. The new law required that the number of fields in each farm was decreased and larger fields were formed. The above map represents farms in the Orleka village in west Sweden in 1645 before the reforms were implemented. Each of the six farms is marked with different colours, showing to the distribution of the land around the village. Note how small the patches of the land are, and how widely dispersed each farm is. Given the complexity of the rural landholding structure before the reform, it is not surprising that it often led to conflicts among farmers and affected rural communities, especially when individual farmers moved out from the village closer to their newly formed fields. But is should also be noted that the reform brought an extensive expansion of agricultural land and the incorporation of previously unused land. The reform was particularly successful in the fertile plains of southern Sweden, while in the regions where more diverse soil productivity patterns, as it was in the north, it stalled. Today's rural landscape in Sweden, with individual farms sited separately from the village in the landscape, is very much a consequence of the 18th Century land reforms. Source: Friden-Fröjered-Korsberga hembygdsförening.

mentation of selective breeding, the livestock reared on Swedish, Prussian and especially Danish farms was pure-bred and much more productive than just a century earlier. Furthermore, the use of root vegetables in fallow fields allowed the land to be used more efficiently and provided an important source of fodder to support more livestock throughout the year. As a result of these developments agricultural outputs grew, as did the wealth and influence of farm owners, who invested in buying land and building the first truly modern agricultural farms.

Despite the improvements in farming technologies, the life of smaller farmers remained monotonous and physically taxing. They continued to live on their farms growing their own food and selling their labour for money. For them, meat was a luxury they could only eat in late autumn, when they slaughtered their animals because they did not have enough fodder for the winter. They lived mainly on cereal-based porridge, potatoes, bread, butter and water.

Social Conditions and Class Structure

Life on the smallholder farms in the early Industrial era usually consisted of four stages: 1) childhood, 2) hired labour, 3) establishing a household/starting a family, and 4) living into the old age as part of the children's households. Most of the children stayed at home until Confirmation at about 14-16 years. By the mid-18th Century children received at least some formal elementary education, including lessons in reading and writing. Quite often their first teachers were their mothers, suggesting that literacy in rural populations in the Baltics was distributed evenly between the sexes. Unfortunately, the poorest of the farmers had to let their children start working at a much younger age, depriving them of their education. After spending 10 to 20 years working as hired help on larger estates, the young got married and established a new household on a piece of land that was partly or wholly inherited from their parents and relatives.

Figure 7.5. Harvest time 1909 near the Marinski Canal, close to Lake Onega, Russia. Photo: Sergei Prokudin-Gorsky. Source: Library of Congress.

Estate owners, on the other hand, were shielded from the economic and environmental pressures that shaped the lives of poorer farming populations. First, with better nutrition and hired help they were able to have more children whose mortality rates were considerably lower and most of whom grew into adulthood. Second, their children received a better education and were prepared for the jobs that the Industrial Revolution brought, such as the government and academic positions that were usually held by the nobles in earlier centuries. The aristocracy became less exclusive and social mobility increased, enabling the descendants of the rural elites to enter their ranks.

Overall, the concentration of farming land in the hands of the larger farmers and the increase in population in the region and Europe more generally meant that there were a lot of people who did not own any land at all. In addition to the poor farmers who were hardly able to hold onto their land, a class of rural proletariat without property started forming. A consequence of the modernisation of agriculture in the Western states of the Baltic region was that the numbers of the rural proletariat skyrocketed and wealth was increasingly concentrated in the hands of the wealthiest farmers, leading to the stratification of rural societies. Some of the landless succeed in finding jobs in the rapidly growing towns, where the developing industries needed more workers. However, many were forced to stay on the farms of their relatives as permanent labourers unable to form their own households.

A different set of challenges was faced by the peasants on the eastern coast of the Baltics, in the Russian Empire, who continued to live in serfdom. Despite rebellions and significant social unrest in the first half of the 1860s, they continued to endure exploitation, disparagement and physical abuse from their lords.

In the mid-19th Century, facing increasing pressures from abroad and criticism from the Russian intelligentsia, Tsar Alexander II abolished serfdom. Although officially emancipated from serfdom, the peasants' life changed very little. The overwhelming majority remained impoverished and continued to rent land and homes from their former landlords well into the 20th Century. The agricultural reforms including Stolypin's reform of 1906 that sought to develop a capitalist agricultural system 'from above' by banning collective land working systems, imposing private land ownership laws, and supporting the development of large-scale industrial farms. However this failed and most farms continued to function as manorial estates. Even though these reforms laid the groundwork for a market-based agricultural system for Russian peasants, they failed to be implemented on the wider scale, leaving most of Russia's peasants living in an essentially feudal society.

Figure 7.6. Fuel-powered agriculture represented by this Fordson tractor produced by Henry Ford between 1916-1928. The Fordson Model F was the first small, mass-produced and affordable tractor in the world. In Ford signed an export contract with the Soviet Union for which soon became the most important customer of the company. In 1924, the "Red Putilovite" factory in Leningrad started the production of Fordson-Putilovets tractors. These inexpensive and robust tractors became an important enticement for peasants towards collectivisation and were often to be seen on propaganda posters and paintings. Photo: Unknown. Probably 1930s in Hälsingland, Sweden. Source: Sockenbilder.

Modernisation of Rural Societies

In the 19th Century agriculture in the Western Baltic region flourished. New technologies such as drainage, fertilisers and steel plows significantly reshaped the landscape and rural lifestyles. Simultaneously, the development of steamships, the construction of railroad and road networks, the introduction of the electric telegraph and especially the liberalisation of the economy enabled the estates not only to sell their products in market towns, but also to enter the global marketplace. With these developments the predominantly agricultural economy shifted from village to private farm-based agriculture, as farms continued to consolidate and settlements became spread out even further than before. However, as in the previous century, these developments did not bring economic or social improvements for the growing rural proletariat. By the turn of the 20th Century, a mass exodus to the United States took place as Swedes, Poles, Lithuanians, Latvians, Estonians, Finns and Russians left their villages and became cheap labour for American factories, mines, farms and cities.

The 19th Century was also marked by the spread of nationalism, an idea that common language, history and culture constitute strong invisible bonds among groups who live in the same territory. In the Baltic region nationalism was built on rural nationalism, which regarded peasantry as the true steward of authentic national culture. In early forms of its inception Baltic nationalism was tied to liberation movements and called for constitutional reforms that would grant more rights to individuals as well as the liberation of nations occupied by Prussia and the Russian Empire, such as Poland, Finland, Estonia, Lithuania and Latvia. Despite the fact that national liberation movements relied on the ideals of agrarian nationalism, most of the members of these movements came from elite backgrounds and urban environments and had little to do with the daily lives and identities of rural inhabitants. In the context of national revival, rural societies continued to live as highly hierarchical systems organised around the ownership of land and resources, gender and age.

More broadly, the Industrial Revolution brought positive changes to the Western Baltic countries, significantly increasing their GDP and building wealth for their individual citizens. The introduction of taxation, voting reforms and the installation of national military service led to the establishment of Sweden, Denmark and Prussia as advanced nation states and avant-garde industrial economies in the world. In addition, with the 1917 Russian Revolution the Russian Empire crumbled, leading to the foundation of the independent nation states of Poland, Finland, Estonia, Latvia and Lithuania.

In these newly formed countries, extensive agricultural reforms were implemented that were designed to modernise and industrialise agriculture. In just two decades between 1917 and the beginning of World War II in 1939, these nations built agrarian economies by redistributing the land and giving it to the landless, supporting individual farmers financially and politically, and liberalising market economies. These reforms led to the further dissolution of the villages and the consolidation of individual farmers estates . Just as in the Western Baltics in the 19th Century, many of these estates did not succeed and mass migrations to cities and the US occurred. The largest and most advanced estates flourished throughout the 1920s and 1930s, while small and medium-sized farms started to get stronger only on the eve of the World War II.

The Russian Revolution – Collectivisation

For Russia, the Revolution brought a very different form of modern agriculture. Instead of individual farmers operating as relatively independent economic units, the new system was based on socialist ideals of collective ownership of land and resources. At first, the Bolsheviks viewed collectivisation as a natural process during which Russian peasants would pool their land and resources together to create large, efficient cooperatives. Due to persistent food shortages and misconceived ideas about peasants as enemies of the proletariat who were prone to retain their bourgeois inclinations, collectivisation was accompanied by public humiliation, violence, mass arrests and deportations. After having signed the agreement, the peasants were forced to hand over their land and livestock to the *kolkhoz* and work as agricultural labourers with little pay in kind. Those who refused to sign were taxed heavily and persecuted for evading the taxes. Even after joining collective farms, they were often considered enemies of the people or *kulaks*, who had to be liquidated as a class. Even though peasants resisted by destroying their own property and livestock, the government continued to take extreme measures to requisition grain from the peasants, sometimes even taking their seed grain.

The results of collectivisation were devastating. One estimate suggests that between the summer of 1929 and March 1930, the government confiscated land and property from some 7 million peasants and the number of *gulag* inmates increased from 28,000 to 2 million. Starting in 1932, a widespread famine swept through Russia and

Figure 7.7. Soviet propaganda poster by V.S. Korableva. "Come comrade and join our Kolkhoz!". Source: Sovietart.

Ukraine, killing 5-6 million people. Even during the years of famine, Stalin continued to export grain abroad and deliberately suppressed news of the famine to the outside world, thus preventing foreign aid from reaching the starving peasants. The modernisation of agriculture in the Soviet Union bore a high human cost.

Leaving Traditional Rural Society Behind

At the end of the 19th Century in the western Baltic region agriculture reached its peak. At least 85 % of the workforce was busy in the agricultural sector. Large state programs were initiated to stimulate the increase of farm-

Figure 7.8. Image of grain harvesting using combines. Photo: Ingrid Karlsson

land. In the east the peak was later but the same dynamics were present. Living standards in the countryside were still poor as compared to today's standards, particularly in Tsarist and socialist Russia, as it was for almost everyone at this time.

Since the turn of the 20th Century, the area of arable land in the Baltic watershed regions has been in decline, as less valuable land was reforested or set aside for pastures. With industrialisation, agricultural landscapes changed significantly through the increasing domination of monoculture production, consolidation of small-scale farms into larger units, and the growth of rural infrastructures such as roads, trains, and communication lines. Modern granaries, sugar mills, industrial livestock feedlots, meat processing facilities, and heavy machinery, replaced local barns and horse drawn plows and carriages. Rural livelihoods changed, too, as people became more mobile and, leaving farming behind, often found jobs and started commuting or relocating to urban centers.

In the backdrop of these major agrarian changes, it is easy for us to idealize and romanticize simple rural lifestyles, as they appear in the nostalgic images of the "traditional countryside." We should remember though that living in these "traditional" rural societies meant hardship, that relying on local cycles of nutrient turnover translated into shortage and even famine, that herding cows in the wooded meadows, driving horse-drawn carriages, or feeding pigs household leftovers required enormous amount of backbreaking labor, skill, knowledge, effort, and determination.

Given these issues, it is hopeful to see signs of new developments in Baltic rural societies that seek to balance the vision of traditional lifestyles with post-industrial realities, particularly in efforts to preserve local rural livelihoods, culinary and agricultural skills, and diverse rural landscapes. Various initiatives have been set up and funded by the European Union and the national governments across the region that include the maintenance of wooded meadows with their uniquely rich biodiversity, restoration of local breeds of domesticated animals such as cows, goats and even hens, and perhaps most importantly, the restoration of summer houses and dachas by the new inhabitants who are willing to come back to the countryside, even if for vacations

Demographic Development in the Baltic Sea Region

8

Marina Thorborg
Södertörn University, Huddinge, Sweden

Country Specific Demographic Development

Sweden

Sweden is the country with the longest running, most continuous population statistics in the world since the mid-18th Century. In 1570, Sweden had an estimated population of 450,000 people, while a century later it was 1.3 million. When annual population registration began, Sweden was home to 1.9 million inhabitants in 1755. Between the years of failed harvests in the 1860s and the negotiations about Norwegian independence from Sweden were peacefully concluded in Karlstad (1905), a quarter of the Swedish population of 4 million left, mainly for the Americas. Mass poverty was not the reason for leaving, as both income and employment were expanding in agriculture and even more so in industry during this period, but most left from areas with high tenancy rates and meagre soils. The demographic transition of Sweden from high birth and death rates to low rates was basically completed by the 1920s, with a birth rate of 17.6 and a death rate of 11.7 per 1,000 people per year in 1925.

Being untouched by World War I, Sweden enjoyed continuous population growth until the mid-1930s when the one-child family was slowly becoming the urban norm with a birth rate of only 13.8 per 1,000 against a death rate of 11.7 in 1935. In 1934 Alva and Gunnar Myrdal, both later ministers in the government, together wrote the warning book *Kris i befolkningsfrågan* (The Population Crisis), which contributed to a further enlargement of social welfare, particularly for working mothers in order to keep them in the labour market.

World War II, with Sweden being officially neutral, led to a population boom that receded only in the late 1950s. During the war almost 7,000 Danish Jews fled the Nazi occupation of Denmark, while Sweden temporarily accepted 70,000 children evacuated from the war in Finland and refugees fleeing both Nazi and Communist occupations of the Baltic states. Being a net immigration country from 1929 onwards – with work-related migrants from Southern Europe and refugees from the Soviet Bloc – Sweden enjoyed steady population growth until the mid-1970s. Simultaneously, rapid urbanisation with continued unbroken industrialisation since the 1870s led to a diminishing population growth rate, with most children being born in the least developed areas, i.e. the inland regions of Northern Sweden and to first generation immigrants.

From 1980, with birth and death rates slowly converging at 11.7 and 11.0 per 1,000 respectively, immigration was the main contributor to population growth. However, from 2007 the Swedish total fertility rate (the average number of children born to a woman over her lifetime) of 1.91 – among the highest in Europe – has approached the population reproduction level of 2.1. After World

War II, Sweden together with Japan and Holland could boast of having the longest life expectancy in the world, particularly for women, and the lowest infant mortality (Statistics Sweden, 2008; Magnusson, 1996, p. 308; Palm Andersson, 2001; Tables 1 and 6).

Finland

Finland was a part of Sweden from the 13th Century until 1809. From roughly doubling its population when statistics began in 1749 to 1809, it had 863,000 inhabitants after incorporation as a Grand Duchy into the Russian empire in 1809. After World War I, Finland with its 3 million inhabitants became independent and fought ferociously in World War II to keep its independence. However, because of a Friendship Treaty with the Soviet Union which Finland had to sign, it had to send back people fleeing the Soviet bloc, meaning refugees had to continue to Sweden. Today with around 5.3 million inhabitants and a slow population growth rate, Finland is still one of the most sparsely populated regions of Europe and an increasing part of its growth comes from immigration from eastern Europe after 1989. Except for a delay of half a generation because of wars and later industrialisation and urbanisation, Finnish basic demographic data are similar to those of Sweden (Statistics Finland, 2007; Table 1).

Denmark

Denmark with roughly 800,000 people in 1769 grew steadily until the early 1970s, when the population reached 5 million. From then on until the early 1990s it grew at a snail's pace, hitting the bottom in 1988-1989, a year in which it added only 524 people to its population. The rate picked up due to immigration, particularly from Poland and Lithuania. Being the former centre of a much larger country, the capital Copenhagen and its suburbs contain roughly half the population. In contrast to the rest of Scandinavia, Denmark has a vibrant agricultural sector and therefore its rural population has not been diminishing very fast. It is usually concluded in surveys that because of an unhealthier lifestyle, the Danes lag behind other Scandinavians in life expectancy and infant mortality (Statistics Denmark, 2008; Tables 1 and 7).

Germany

After World War II, when Germany was divided, West Germany had a population growth of almost 1% during 1950-1955, then slowly diminishing to 0.7 during 1965-70 and further to -0.1% in 1984-85. In addition to this, millions of Germans fled from Soviet-occupied East Germany. After Germany was reunited in 1990, its main population additions came from migrating Germans

Table 8.1. Total population in the Baltic Sea Region 1980-2010. http://esa.un.org/unpd/wpp/Excel-Data/population.htm

	1980	1985	1990	1995	2000	2005	2010
Belarus	9,658,500	9,998,503	10,259,700	10,274,231	10,057,810	9,825,102	9,595,421
Czech Republic	10,261,606	10,300,844	10,302,718	10,319,337	10,242,890	10,220,638	10,492,960
Denmark	5,123,026	5,113,701	5,141,034	5,233,364	5,339,501	5,419,444	5,550,142
Estonia	1,472,898	1,525,790	1,567,631	1,440,710	1,370,749	1,345,857	1,341,140
Finland	4,779,488	4,902,206	4,986,441	5,107,802	5,173,370	5,244,342	5,364,546
Germany	78,288,577	77,684,875	79,098,094	81,929,441	82,349,027	82,540,739	82,302,465
Latvia	2,513,349	2,582,011	2,663,905	2,492,095	2,384,972	2,305,528	2,252,060
Lithuania	3,430,089	3,561,668	3,695,890	3,629,104	3,500,028	3,415,748	3,323,611
Norway	4,085,621	4,152,560	4,241,485	4,359,096	4,490,859	4,623,298	4,883,111
Poland	35,577,214	37,201,804	38,056,174	38,391,778	38,302,444	38,165,040	38,276,660
Russia	138,655,363	143,642,108	148,243,501	148,698,582	146,757,517	143,843,159	142,958,164
Slovak Republic	4,961,607	5,141,880	5,270,072	5,368,894	5,404,845	5,415,496	5,462,119
Sweden	8,310,467	8,350,392	8,558,829	8,826,949	8,860,153	9,029,345	9,379,687
Ukraine	50,043,550	50,949,364	51,644,914	51,121,722	48,891,792	46,923,927	45,448,329

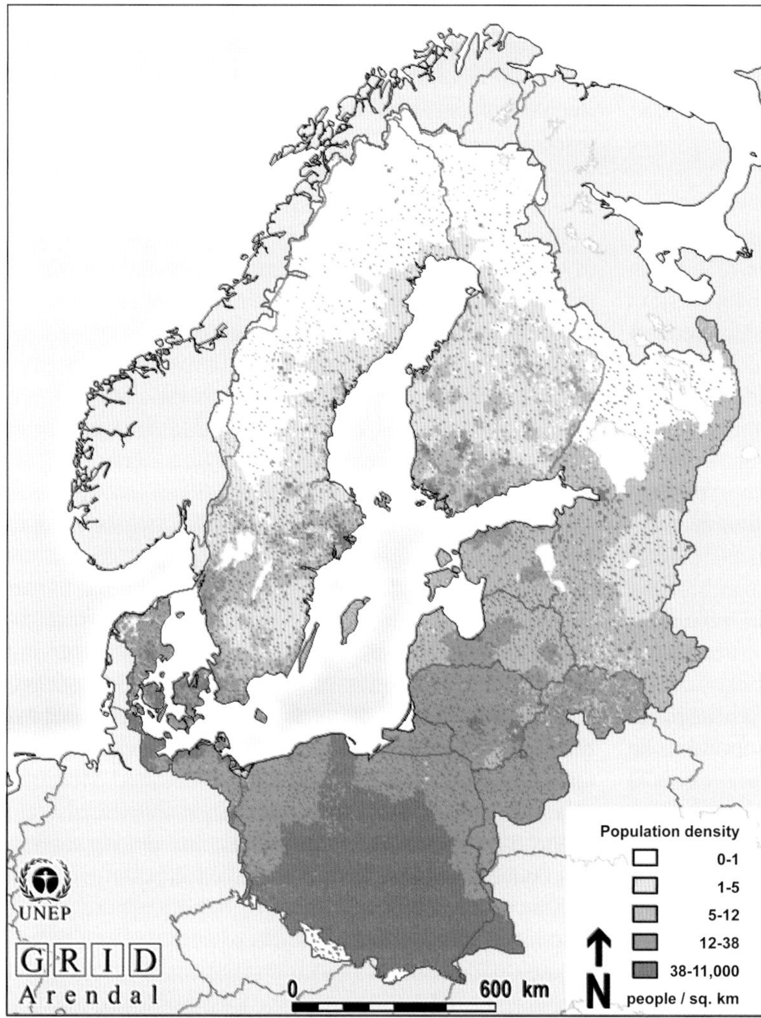

Figure 8.1. Population density in the Baltic Sea drainage basin at about 1990. Cartographer: Hugo Ahlenius. Source: UNEP;GRID Arendal.

from the former Soviet Bloc. In Germany the number of childless couples (28%) was higher than in other West European countries, contributing to the population decline. In the ensuing debate over this fact it was stressed that a society with a school, tax and pensions systems structured for only one provider per family (the man) meant that for a woman to become professional she had to forego child-bearing (See Vidal-Naquet and Bertin, 1991).

Poland

Poland was trice divided during the 18th Century – with the Polish language and the Catholic church as the main rallying points during the divisions – and after World War II the whole national boundary was moved west by 200 km, with its new western parts coming from the earlier German Reich and with 11 million Germans fleeing from the advancing Russian Red army in 1945 (Atlas till världshistorien, 1958).

From roughly 1 million inhabitants in the year 1,000, the population in Poland had doubled by the late 14th Century since it was less affected by the Black Death than Western Europe. When Poland entered a union with Lithuania in 1386 the total population was short of 8 million. By 1500 about 85% of all people lived in rural areas, a century later about 75% and this remained so until after World War II. According to the census in February 1946, two-thirds of the population were still rural inhabitants. Because of the Polish-Lithuanian Union, the three partitions of Poland in the 18th Century and frequent border changes, the population of Poland was long characterised by sizeable national minorities – roughly one-third of all – and had the largest Jewish community (3.3 million) in Europe before 1945. About 3 million Polish Jews were killed by the Nazis during World War II, either starving to death in enforced ghettos or killed in gas chambers in concentration camps. In the eastern areas taken by the Soviet Union from Poland during World War II, 40% of the population perished, while up to 250,000 more were deported to Siberia and arctic Russia.

The Jewish Minority

According to international and Polish researchers, almost 6 million Poles were killed during World War II, 5 million by the Nazis (3 million Jews and 1.9 million Poles) and about 1 million by the Soviets, though some scholars have been trying to revise the latter figure (Kuodote and Traceskis, 2005; Thorborg, 1997 & 2002b; Martinsson, 2008; Tao Yang, 2008; Bengtsson, 2007, p. 59 ff., p. 131 ff, p. 237 ff; Eurostat, 2009).

Post World War II Poland

After World War II, Poland became one of the most homogeneous countries in the world, with over 95% being Polish. Only in the new border areas did people from neighbouring countries live in any great numbers. A small exception was the Polish Tartars, paid soldiers in the late 1300s and numbering almost 100,000 in 1630, who having dwindled to less than 500 mainly settled in North-Eastern Poland. In the first post-war census in 1946, Poland had almost 24 million inhabitants, increasing to 25 million in 1950 and nearly 30 million in 1960. Poland showed a relatively rapid population increase in the post-war period well into the 1980s. The combination of Catholicism (usually a more pronatalist faith than different Protestant denominations) and *positive* population policies, i.e. social programmes and subsidies, contributed to this population growth. Later, through *negative* population policies such as restrictions on abortions in the 1990s and turbulence during the transition years, a somewhat slower growth rate ensued, with a peak of 38.3 million in 1996. In 2007, 40% of the population was still rural, the rural share having increased slowly since 2000 (European Commission, 2006; Eurostat, 2009; CSO, 2008, 2009; Table 1)

Russia and the Soviet Union

Two features distinguish Russia from the West. Firstly, throughout its history population data have often been used to serve ideological goals and have therefore either been kept secret, or not fully revealed. Secondly, compared with Western Europe Russia has been characterised by a significantly higher mortality rate with more deaths from infectious disease which has continued until this day. With the move to administrative modernisation, local self-government and the creation of *Zemstvos* in 1864, a wealth of scattered regional data on rural peasant households was obtained. The first all-encompassing census ever was taken in 1897 by something like 100,000 enumerators resulting in a total population, both permanent, (*postoyannoye)*, and present, (*nalichnoye*) of 127 million inhabitants. After the Bolshevik revolution in Russia in 1917, the ensuing civil war, food shortages, global influenza epidemic and mass migrations, a second census listed 147 million in 1926 in the entire Soviet Union, of which 93 million in the Russian Federation (Blum and Troitskaya, 1997; Kingkade, 1997).

From the end of the civil war in 1922 until the outbreak of World War II, according to most research on the issue one in 15 of the whole population in the Soviet Union disappeared and/or was killed in peacetime under the regime of the communist dictator Stalin. Millions were killed in the collectivisation of agriculture and the ensuing famine. Even during the famine years grain was exported, 5.83 million tonnes in 1930, 4.79 million tonnes in 1931, 1.61 million tonnes in 1932 and 2.32 million tonnes in 1933-34. When starvation had become widespread in 1932 and 1933 the Politburo, the leading organ of the Soviet Union, decided that no allocations of food, fodder or seed were to be made available for the rural areas but that grain collected by the state must go to the starving urban population. In the campaigns against the so-called *Kulaks* ('rich' peasants) in Ukraine at the beginning of the First Five-Year plan in 1928, according to new research, up to 4 million people were killed in peacetime. Mortality was high among the almost 15 million individuals sent to the *gulags*, prison labour camps, and among numerous ethnic groups subjected to forced deportations such as that of the Crimean Tartars to Siberia. These peacetime losses have been the subject of intensive and heated debates. This conflict is also apparent in the population statistics. In 1917, the year of the Russian Revolution, the population of Tsarist Russia was estimated at 185 million, while in 1931 the Soviet Union counted 161 million people. On the one hand there was a civil war until 1922, but on the other hand the average Russian woman was bearing 7.5 children in 1920 (Da Vanzo and Adamson, 1997; Applebaum, 2003; Wheatcroft, 2000; Courtois et al., 1999; Tao Yang, 2008).

Estonia, Latvia and Lithuania

The occupied states of Estonia, Latvia and Lithuania lost 14% of their population through mass killings and three waves of deportations to Siberia during the 1940s, in addition to those already killed during the German Nazi occupation. Most of the achievements of the Baltic states in significantly improving the standard of living during their independence between the World Wars was rapidly erased. World War II led to an estimated loss of about 20 million Russian men, with only Belarus losing more people during the war as a proportion of their population (Kuodote and Traceskis, 2005; Thorborg, 1997, 2000, 2002a; Martinsson, 2008; Tao Yang, 2008; Bengtsson, 2007, p. 59 ff., p. 131 ff, p. 237 ff).

The Soviet healthcare system received as much as 6% of Gross National Product in the 1960s, contributing to rapidly decreasing mortality and increasing longevity. However, after peaking in the 1960s it was prey to a so-called residual principle, meaning that after everything else was funded the health services got the leftovers, resulting in decreased spending per capita. In the mid-1990s health spending per capita was down to only 4% of what was spent on every American. About 10% of the Russian hospitals dated from before World War I and were not particularly updated, with 20% lacking running water (RAND, 2001).

A decreasing birth rate was something that all advanced industrial societies were exposed to when women in large numbers entered employment in the formal sector. However, for Russia the death rate increased significantly at the same time, which set it apart from the experience of modern, Western societies (Tikhomirov, 2000, chap. 4).

Russia was only slightly behind the West in life expectancy in 1965. Since 1965, life expectancy for men in the USA and Western Europe has been increasing by 0.2 years annually on average and in Japan even by 0.3 years, while in Russia it began decreasing by 0.1 year per year in 1965-1980, with even greater decreases in 1988-1994 and 1998-2000. Only during the anti-alcohol campaign under the Soviet leader Gorbachev in the mid-1980s did mortality rates stagnate, after which a concomitant sharp rise in male mortality, alcohol consumption and violence against women re-emerged (RAND, 2001; UNDP, HDR, 2002). Hence at the start of its dissolution in 1991, the Soviet Union was experiencing the continuation of a demographic crisis which had started back in the mid-1960s.

Life Expectancy and Gender Gap

Increasing Life Expectancy

In Scandinavia, Germany and Poland, life expectancy has shown a continuous increase over time. During the transition years in the 1990s in Poland, men and women added

Table 8.2. Life expectancy of men and women in selected countries of the Baltic region in 1900, 1950, 1990, 1995, and 2009.

Country	Life expectancy									
	Women					Men				
	1900	1950	1990	1995	2009	1900	1950	1990	1995	2009
Sweden	55	73	80	81	83	53	70	75	76	79
Finland	44	70	79	80	83	41	63	71	73	76
Denmark	55	72	78	79	81	52	69	72	73	76
Germany	47	69*	78*	80	82	44	65*	72*	74	76
Poland	42	63	75	77	80	41	57	66	69	72
Lithuania	42	67	76	75	80	41	60	66	63	70
Estonia	42	68	75	74	79	41	61	65	62	68
Latvia	42	69	74	73	77 e**	41	62	64	60	67 e**
Belarus	34	70	76	74	77	31	61	66	63	65
Russia	34	67	74	72	73	31	60	64	58	60
Ukraine	34	70	74	72	75	31	61	66	61	63

*=German Federal Republic, **=2008. Source: 1950 from Chawla et al. 2007. 1990 and 1995 from Kucera, 2007. 1900 from Dinkel, R. H. 1985. For Poland to Ukraine downwards in the table for both sexes. For Finland 1900 from US Bureau of the Census 2009, est. from CIA 2010. The rest from US Bureau of the Census, 2009.

about two years to their life expectancy, showing that their transition began earlier, was slower and proceeded more smoothly than in countries further east. In Poland life expectancy has shown a steady increase since 1950 without interruption. Although in the Baltic states life expectancy sank in the mid-1990, longevity in 2009 surpassed its earlier peak by at least three years (Table 8.2).

In contrast, the life expectancy of Russian men was higher in the Tzarist era 100 years ago than in the mid-1990s (Tikhomirov, 2000, chap. 4). Alcohol consumption is part of the explanation for the differences between the sexes in shortening life spans in some former Soviet Bloc countries. The largest fall in life expectancy during the 1990s was experienced by Russian men, who lost 6 years. Ukrainian men lost 5 years, Latvian men 4 and those in Belarus, Estonia, and Lithuania lost 3 years between 1990 and 1995 (Table 8.2).

At the beginning of the new millennium in Russia, life expectancy could differ by 18 years, with Russian men having the shortest life expectancy of all in the developed world (14 years less than the EU male average). This is particularly the case in rural areas, with a life expectancy of 51 in the regions of Pskov, Novgorod, and Karelia. This is a similar level to that in Germany and Scandinavia in the year 1900 (DaVanzo and Adamson, 1997; UNDP 2006/2007; RAND 2001; Table 1).

The good news, however, is that between 2005 and 2006, life expectancy for Russian men increased by an unprecedented 1.6 years, a 2.7% jump according to Russian statistics. Even if part of this is based on different methods of measurement or earlier under-evaluations, an increase of 1% is regarded as extremely high (USA Today, 2008).

Mortality

A continuously decreasing mortality rate has been the number one motor of population growth in the West. In Scandinavia, mortality has decreased steadily since World War II to be among the lowest in the world, with men aged 18-24 being the most accident-prone. While mortality rates for Poles decreased by more than 20% during the hardest transition years from 1990 to 2002, the mortality rate increased by about the same amount for people from the Baltic states. For Belarus and Ukraine it increased by 33% for women and 40% for men, while

Table 8.3. Mortality rates (per 100,000) for men and women in selected countries of the Baltic region in 1990 and 2002

	1990		2002	
	Women	Men	Women	Men
EMU*	68	145	(Add)	(Add)
Poland	102	264	82	204
Lithuania	92	246	103	303
Estonia	106	286	112	322
Latvia	108	295	118	327
Belarus	98	254	134	371
Russia	107	298	168	464
Ukraine	105	268	139	378

*= European Monetary Union. Source: USAID, 2007; Table 12

Table 8.4. Adult male death rate (per 100,000 males) from external causes in Russia and USA, 1999. Source: DaVanzo et al., 2003.

Cause of death	Russia	USA
Suicide	54	18
Homicide	31	21
Fall, fire, drowning	37	5
Motor vehicle accidents	23	6
Other external causes	52	6
Total	197	56

Russian women and men both suffered a 56% mortality increase (Table 8.3).

Russian men of working-age have a death rate due to external causes that is 4-8 times that of US men of the same age, and are five times more likely to end their days due to infectious and parasitic diseases (RAND, 2001; DaVanzo et al., 2003; Table 3). According to the World Health Report by the WHO, 50-66% of all cases of epilepsy, homicides, motor vehicle crashes, drowning, cirrhosis of the liver and oesophagus cancer were caused by alcohol in Russia in 2002 (USAID, 2007). To stop excess mortality – as was already accomplished with resounding success during Gorbachev's anti-alcohol campaign in the 1980s – a campaign to reduce alcohol consumption is currently being implemented with full force, with a 4% decrease in death rates between 2006 and 2007. While in 2006 there were 687,000 more deaths than births, this was reduced to 478,000 in 2007 and further to only 363,000 in 2008 (USA TODAY, 2008; Russian Federal, 2009).

Table 8.5. Sex ratio at 65+ and gender gap in longevity in selected countries of the Baltic region, 2009.

	Sex ratio at 65+	
	Males per 100 females (in %)	Women outliving men (number of years)
Sweden	80	5
Finland	69	7
Denmark	80	5
Germany	72	6
Poland	62	8
Lithuania	53	10
Estonia	49	11
Latvia	48	11
Belarus	47	12
Russia	44	14
Ukraine	49	12

e=estimate, *=2008, **=2009. Source: CIA 2010. Poland CSO. 2009. Column 2 from Table 1.

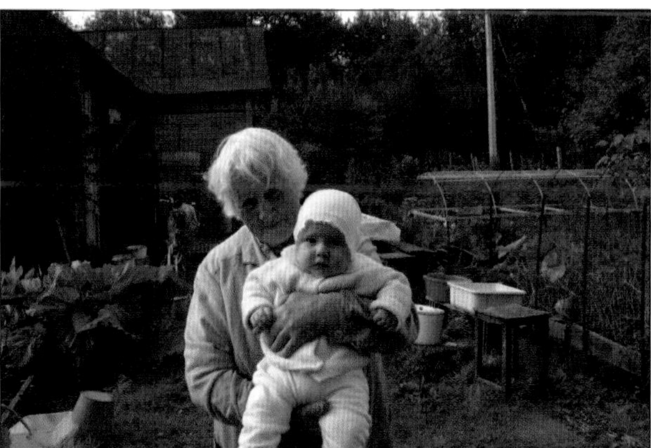

Figure 8.2. Babuschka with her granddaughter at the datcha. Photo by Igor Khomyakov.

Age Gender Gap

Given equal nutrition and medical care, women generally live 4-6 years longer in developed societies. In Poland and Finland (which has the highest consumption of strong liquor by men in Scandinavia), women outlive men by at most 7 years, also seen in the low male sex ratio at 65+, while in Lithuania women survive men by 8 years and Estonia and Latvia show a much higher difference of 10-11 years. The corresponding gap is on average 12 years in Ukraine, Belarus and Russia, reflecting the hardships

Table 8.6. Age structure of population (%) in selected countries of the Baltic region, 2009.

	Years		
	0-14	15-64	65+
Sweden	16	65	19
Finland	16	67	17
Denmark	18	66	17
Germany	14	66	20
Poland	15	72	14
Lithuania	14	70	16
Estonia	15	67	8
Latvia e*	13	70	17
Belarus e	14	72	14
Russia	15	72	13
Ukraine	14	71	16

e=estimate, *=2008. Source: CIA 2010. Poland. CSO. 2009

of the transition years added to and/or expressed in male drinking habits (USAID, 2007; Table 4).

The Russian situation is a combination of the skewed gender rate as a leftover from World War II, with 20 million men killed, and high male death rates, which peaked in the 1990s with a 14-year age gap (Thorborg, 1993, 2002a; USA TODAY, 2008; Table 4).

What further complicates the situation for the countries of the former Soviet Bloc is that although women live longer, their pension age begins five years earlier than men's. However, some countries have begun lengthening the working life in order to catch up with the European norm of 65 years for all, instead of 55 for women and 60 for men, which was the established Soviet norm (Thorborg, 1996a & 2002a).

The Ageing Society

Age Structure

The proportion of global population aged 65 + was 5% in 1950, 7% in 2000, and is projected to reach 16% in 2050. Transition to an ageing population was accomplished in Western Europe during more than a century, but is now predicted to occur within a generation in Eastern Europe,

Table 8.7. Population birth, death, infant mortality, net migration and growth rate in selected countries of the Baltic region, 2009

	Populationrate per 1,000 of birth, death, infant mortality, net migration and growth (in %)				
	Birth	Death	Infant mortality	Net migration	Growth
Sweden	10.7	10.2	2.7	1.7	0.16
Finland	10.4	10.2	3.5	0.6	0.08
Denmark	10.4	10.2	4.3	2.5	0.27
Germany	8.2	11.0	4.0	2.2	-0.06
Poland	10.0	10.1	8.7	-0.5	-0.05
Lithuania	9.2	11.3	6.4	-0.7	-0.11
Estonia	10.4	13.5	7.2	-3.3	-0.64
Latvia	9.9	13.6	8.6	-2.3	-0.60
Belarus	9.8	13.8	6.3	2.3 e	-0.37
Russia	11.1	16.0	10.3	0.28	-0.47
Ukraine.*	9.6	15.7	8.7	0.1	-0.62

e=estimate. * = 2008. Source: CIA. 2010. Sweden Statistics Sweden, 2009, Finland, Statistics Finland, 2009, Denmark Statistics Denmark, 2009, Poland. CSO (GUS). 2009. Ukraine. State Statistics Committee of Ukraine. 2008.

implying the most rapid ageing in the world. However, in the West the societies were already relatively well off before old age cohorts began swelling, meaning that pensions and healthcare systems were in place and functioning to a reasonable degree. In Eastern Europe, however, the rapid ageing of the population is taking place in still poor countries with inadequate welfare systems on the remnants of a former crude 'cradle to grave' social security system, with an even worse situation in the countryside for the old when the young and able have left (Chawla et al., 2007; Table 5).

According to estimates for North America, up to 70% of the total population is employed, in Western Europe up to 60%, while in Eastern Europe only about 50% because of the early pension age (Dempsey, 2007). With only half the population in the workforce, the pension base will be further eroded unless pension age and fertility rates can be rapidly increased.

Fertility

Sweden has recently experienced an upsurge in fertility approaching the replacement level, with a total fertility rate of 1.97 combined with the lowest infant mortality in the world, together with Japan and Norway. This is leading to positive population growth, which is also the case for the rest of Scandinavia. Germany is still struggling with a decreasing population since its society is not organised for full-time working mothers, with almost one-third of all opting to have no children (Statistics Sweden, 2009; Table 8).

The lowest recorded fertility rate in the world was in transition economies of Eastern and Central Europe in the mid-1990s (Table 8.7). Poland barely managed to grow well into this century by continuing to increase its birth rate, from 9.9 per 1,000 in 2000 to 10.0 in 2008, while simultaneously trying to halt its increasing infant mortality from 8.1 in 2000 to 8.7 in 2008, and its death rates from 9.6 per 1,000 in 2000 to 10.0 in 2008. Simultaneously, emigration from Poland fell from 19,700 in 2000 to 14,800 in 2008 (Poland CSO, 2009).

In 1981 the Soviet authorities adopted a comprehensive programme for maternity benefits resulting in continually increased fertility levels peaking in 1987, just when the anti-alcohol campaign was stopped, having passed the replacement level with a total fertility rate of 2.2. However, from 1987 to 1999 the birth rate shrank by 50% (Kingkade and Dunlop, 1999; USA TODAY, 2008).

Some argue that these pronatalist policies did not lead to a higher number of children but only shorter spacing between them and earlier births, as this quicker led to better housing and other benefits. Because the number of children that would otherwise have been born in the 1990s were already born in the 1980s, part of the decline in birth could be explained in this way (Thortonne and Philipov, 2007).

Figure 8.3. Photo: by Boris Tikhomirov.

However, in 2007 a law increased payments and maternity benefits in Russia, guaranteeing mothers education and other benefits worth 10,650 USD for bearing a second child and any thereafter, leading so far to the highest increase in births for 15 years, from 1.4 million in 2006 to 1.6 million in 2007. Therefore the Russian population decrease has slowed to almost zero, from 532,000 less people in 2006 to 212,000 less in 2007 and only 121,000 less in 2008 (USA TODAY, 2008).

At the beginning of the new millennium infant and maternal mortality rates could differ by a factor of 3, particularly between urban and rural areas, with the rural areas having the highest mortality. All indicators of maternal health worsened during the 1990s. There was a decline in the health of babies, pregnant women and those who had just given birth. However, during 2008-2009 Russia is planning to spend about 20 billion Roubles (about 1 billion USD) on new prenatal centres, according to the first vice-Prime Minister. Being harder hit by the population decrease than urban areas and housing a quarter of the population, the rural areas are to benefit from this investment (UNDP, 2006/2007; USA TODAY, 2008).

However, the reason for earlier births from the 1960s until the 1990s is specific to the former Soviet sphere, namely sterility in women arising from numerous abortions.

Abortions

In the West abortions were easier to obtain from the 1970s onwards, with each legal change being preceded by intensive debates on the grounds of ideology, religion and women's liberation. In contrast to popular notions, most of those undergoing abortions were married women in their late fertile age with already many children. As the first country in the world the Soviet Union legalised abortions in the mid-1920s, because of influences from strong, radical women – such as Inessa Armand and Alexandra Kollontai – who made up 33% of the early, leading Bolsjeviks. Abortions were severely restricted in the 1930s and temporarily forbidden in the 1940s, but allowed again from the early 1950s. (Thorborg, 2002c).

Because abortion had become the Soviet Union's number one method of birth control as safe contraceptives were not available, women often attempted to give birth to the number of children they wanted early in life and then rely on abortions to prevent further pregnancies. Unsafe abortions could be seen as one of the causes of maternal mortality, with 67 and 63 women dying in childbirth per 100,000 live births in Russia and Estonia, respectively, in 2000, compared with 20 for the advanced industrial countries. Hence to minimise the risks to their health and fertility, women began to choose earlier child births. In the post World War II period in many nations in Western Europe the age pattern of child-bearing changed, with the peak child-bearing age beginning to occur later in life, between ages 25-29. In contrast to this, the child-bearing peak age in the Soviet Union began to occur earlier, between the ages 20-24. Concomitant with these developments and in contrast to the West, Soviet women on average married at age 26.2 in 1965 but at age 22.0 in 1995 (UN/ECE, 2000; Thortonne and Philipov, 2007; Table 7).

In Eastern Europe abortion rates have been shrinking, particularly in Poland because of the re-emergence of the political power of the Catholic Church, leading to intensive debates and campaigns for very strict abortion laws. In addition, from the mid-1990s the average age at childbearing increased by 2 years to 25 in 2006 (Thortonne and Philipov, 2007; CSO, 2009; Table 7).

Hence, use of abortion as a birth control method during Soviet times led to both earlier childbirths and earlier marriage, in contrast to trends in Western Europe. A side-effect of this was increased sterility, thereby shrinking the

Table 8.8. Abortion rates in 1980, 1990 and 1999 per 1,000 women aged 15-44 and per 100 live births in 1995/1998, 2002 and 2008

	Per 1,000 women				Per 100 live births		
	1980	**1990**	**1999**	**2005**	**1995/1998**	**2002**	**2008**
Sweden	18	22	17	20	31	35	26
Finland	14	11	9	9	17	18	15
Denmark	21	18	15	15	25		19
Germany	14	20	17	18	40	35***	
Poland	17	7	1	0	1		0.1
Lithuania	59	62	23	14	55		21
Estonia	111	88	47	33	180	101	34
Latvia	108	87	35	27	110	73	30
Belarus	94	117	60	32	190	96	28
Russia	140	126	70*	54	200	139	45
Ukraine	107	97	62**	28	145	89	22

*=1998,**=1996, ***=1998 and per 100 live births 1995/1998. Source: UN/ECE, 2000; UNDY, 2005; UN Department of Economic and Social Affairs, 2007, Table 13; UNAIDS, 2008. For 1980, 1990, 1999: Thorton and Philipov, 2007. For Scandinavia and Germany OECD, 2007 and Federal Statistical Office, 2006. For 2002: USAID, 2007, citing UNICEF. For 2005 from Poland to Ukraine. UN. 2007. Statistics Division. Source:"Fellowship of the Minds" Abortion rates for 101 countries, by Dr. Edwin, blog at WorldPress.com 5/5-2012

Table 8.9. Family type and number of children in Russia, Sweden, Germany, USA and France, 2000

Percentage of mothers who have completed their families by number of children.						
No of Children	**Russia**	**Sweden**	**Germany**	**USA**	**France**	**Italy**
0	8	14	28	15	14	15
1	30	16	25	19	20	25
2	44	40	30	32	32	42
3+	18	30	19	34	34	18

Source: UN Population Division, 2006, in *The Economist*, 2007.06.16, p. 28

number of women able to have children. It is obvious that abortion is still used as the main birth control measure in Estonia, Latvia, Russia, Belarus and Ukraine and that even today, other contraceptives are not used to the same extent as in Scandinavia. For this reason it is interesting to compare family size in former Eastern Bloc countries with that in developed Western countries.

Family Size

Comparing family size in number of children by country demonstrates that Germany has the largest proportion of childless families (28%), while Russia has the smallest proportion (only 8%). Surveys in Eastern Europe and Russia indicate that if conditions were better, women would like to have more children. Most families have two children in the countries concerned. In Sweden, USA and France the population is still growing, with one-third of all families opting for a third child or more. Russia as well as Germany and Italy have shrinking populations, with three-child families making up less than one-fifth of all families (Table 8.9).

In addition to abortions, ensuing sterility and unsafe contraceptives that threatened women's health and child-bearing capacity, a new devastating scourge arrived on the scene in the 1970s, namely HIV/AIDS.

HIV/AIDS

Because of open interventions and information campaigns at a relatively early stage in the media and in schools, HIV/AIDS in Scandinavia never managed to reach epidemic proportions, considered to be 1% of the population. Although it was seen as threatening in the 1980s and 1990s, it has since been contained on a low level. In Eastern Europe and the Commonwealth of Independent

Table 8.10. HIV/AIDS adult prevalence rates, and people living with it and deaths from it, 2007.

	Adult prevalence rates	People living with it	Deaths
	in %	number	number
Sweden	0.1	6,200	less than 100
Finland	less than 0.1	2,400	less than 1
Denmark	0.2	4,800	less than 10
Germany	0.1	53,000	less than 500
Poland	0.1	20,000	less than 200
Lithuania	0.1	2,200	less than 200
Estonia	1.3	9,900	less than 500
Latvia	1.8	10,000	less than 500
Belarus	0.2	13,000 e	1,100 e
Russia	1.1	940,000	40,000
Ukraine	1.6	440,000 e	19,000

e=estimate. Source: CIA World factbook 2012 and from Burns, 2007.

States (CIS), HIV rates increased more rapidly than in any other region of the world from 1997-2007, growing from 630,000 cases in 2001 to 1.5 million in 2007, with 6-14,000 deaths due to AIDS in 2001 and 42-88,000 in 2007. In Estonia, Latvia, Russia and Ukraine a critical level has been reached, with over 1% of the adult population being infected (USAID, 2005, p. 7; UNDP, 2009; Table 9). As drug-related HIV has declined, sex-related HIV infections are increasingly affecting women (Burns, 2007).

Latvia and Ukraine have the highest HIV infection rates, followed by Estonia and Russia. These countries are border and transition countries in the process of opening up to the world, while a closed society such as Belarus has been less exposed. The central European countries of Poland and Lithuania, both Catholic and with more developed infrastructure to fight and contain HIV/AIDS, have managed to halt it before it reached the epidemic stage and are currently on a low Scandinavian level (UN, 2005; Table 9). Hence rapid HIV/AIDS proliferation appears to be contained in Scandinavia and Central Europe while still spreading in Latvia, Ukraine, Estonia and Russia, although some cities in Russia such as Moscow have managed to halt its further growth (Burns, 2007). Almost 60% of Russian children have various kinds of disorders because of alcoholism, venereal disease, drug addiction and the spread of HIV/AIDS (UNHDR, 2002). However, its accelerating proliferation is not only due to opening up of borders but also to a massive increase in migration since the dissolution of the Soviet Union, which is in contrast to earlier when movements of people were strictly controlled.

Migration

Being a net receiver of migrants since 1929, Sweden has a history of giving asylum to people fleeing persecution, and especially since World War II Sweden accepted refugees from the former Soviet Union and from East Germany and Poland. During this war a sizeable community from the Baltic states managed to flee from Nazi and subsequent Soviet occupations. Sweden also welcomed work-related migration from former Yugoslavia and Southern Europe and refugees from Hungary in 1956 and from former Czechoslovakia in 1968. In the latter two events people were fleeing the Soviet invasions of their countries. During the Vietnam war Sweden accepted some thousand of American men seeking to avoid the draft to active service. Later, many refugees from Latin America, Africa, the Balkans and Middle East have been given asylum. Because most migrants stayed in Sweden, becoming Swedish citizens, up to 18% of the Swedish population today is foreign born (Statistics Sweden, 2008; Magnusson, 1996; Table 10).

Finland and Denmark began receiving migrants from Eastern Europe in large numbers from 1989 onwards, with some earlier, seasonal population movements being re-established, such as Poles and Lithuanians going to Denmark. In the first phase of migration to Scandinavia many migrants and refugees ended up in either unskilled work in heavy industry or agriculture, thereby slowing the depopulation of the Swedish countryside. The whole Eastern European region is unique by simultaneously being a major receiver and sender of migrants. The dissolution of the Soviet Union in 1991 was initially followed by a heavy immigration wave to Russia. Between 1992 and 1998, up to 3.7 million Russians came to Russia from former Soviet republics. They contributed to repopulation of the countryside in European Russia. Hence even though the Russian population decreased by almost 8 million people, it had a migration balance and surplus of nearly 6 million people from 1990 to 2004, and in addition an estimated 10 million illegal immigrants from former Soviet states. Belarus was also helped in counter-

Table 8.11. Population in the Baltic region by country and main ethno/linguistic group in 1992, 2002, 2007, and other groups 2007

Country	Population (in millions)		Migration balance	Change in concentration of main ethno/linguistic group (in %)			Other groups (in %)
	1994	2010	1990-2004	1992	2002	2007	2007
Sweden	8.7	9.1				92	Sami and Finns
Finland	5.0	5.2				92	Swedes 6
Denmark	5.2	5.5				95+	Inuit
Germany		82.3				92	Turkish 2.4
Poland	38.6	38.5	-222,000	98	98	97	Germans 0.4
Lithuania	3.7	3.6	-246,000	80	83	83	Polish 7, Russians 6,
Estonia	1.5	1.2	-142,000	62	65	69	Russians 26, Ukrainians 2
Latvia	2.5	2.2 *	- 99,000	52	58	59*	Russians 28, Belo R. 4, Ukrainians 3
Belarus	10.3	9.6	+45,000	78	81	81	Russians 11, Polish 4, Ukrainians 2
Russia	148.4	139.4	+5,764,000	82	82	80	Tatar 4, Ukrainians 2,
Ukraine	51.7	45.4	-830,000	73	73	78	Russians 17

*=2008. Sources: CIA, 2010; Kucera, 2007. 1992 and 2002 from USAID, 2005, Table 34. For migration balance EBRD, 2002. Sweden 1994 and 2007: Statistics Sweden. 2008. Denmark 1994: Statistics Denmark, Table FT, Poland: CSO, 2009.

balancing its shrinking population by migration of many Belarusians from the former Soviet republics. Originally highly agrarian, with more than two-thirds of its population in rural areas until 1960, almost one-third still remains there (Kucera, 2007; Table 10).

The Baltic states of Estonia and Latvia today have a higher proportion of their own population than before 1989, since many Russians and Belarusians emigrated. Because the Russians in the population were urban, the degree of urbanisation in Estonia and Latvia gradually decreased during the 1990s (DaVanzo and Adamson, 1997; Chawla et al., 2007; Table 10).

Simultaneously ethnic Germans migrated from the former Soviet Bloc to Germany, which received over 4 million ethnic Germans, while Pontian Greeks went to Greece and Jews to Israel (UN, 2006).

Generally a westward movement can be detected, with Poles and people from the Baltic states moving to Western Europe and the Americas. In addition, both Lithuania and Poland have sizeable communities of migrants in the USA, some of them returning after 1989. Belarusians, Russians and Ukrainians also migrated by leaving first for Eastern Europe while their own countries were receiving immigrants from further east, many of them ending up in rural areas. While 69,000 Poles had left for OECD countries in 2000, only four years later as many as 169,000 from Poland, 68,000 from Ukraine and 65,000 from Russia were immigrants to OECD countries (UN, 2006).

Between 1991 and 2004, up to 2.5 million people emigrated from Ukraine. Of these, 1.9 million went to other post-Soviet states and 640,000 to the West. With the beginning of economic recession in 2008, some of this western-bound flow reversed, with up to 56,000 returning from the UK (the great majority being Poles) in the year from September 2007 (O'Grady, 2009).

Hence two flows of migrants can be distinguished: one to Western Europe from Central and Eastern Europe and one to richer countries of the former Soviet Union – such as Russia and Kazakhstan – from poorer ones such as those of Central Asia. Both push and pull factors are at work here. Young countries with growing populations are with some exceptions net senders of migrants, while old, more developed countries with stagnant or diminishing populations are usually net receivers. The problem here is for older, stagnant countries in Eastern Europe to adjust their institutional structures in such a way that they can receive more migrants to offset their declining populations and particularly their decreasing population in the countryside.

Demography and Rural Development

The Dramatic 20th Century

Through luck and skill Sweden kept out of two World Wars and in contrast to most other European countries it therefore enjoyed relatively smooth and slow demographic changes during the 20th century, with a decline in the birth rate (although this fluctuated 1960-2000), deaths rate, family size and rural population. Finland and Denmark, with a delay because of wars and occupations, displayed similar changes. Germany, through losing two world wars, and then being divided and later re-united, has experienced pronounced population changes at home and contributed to changes abroad.

Dramatic changes occurred in a number of demographic key variables in the transition countries of Eastern and Central Europe, especially in the 1990s. However, the transition upheavals did not cause these changes, but were merely reinforcing trends already well on their way during Soviet times. The 20th Century started with turbulence for Eastern Europe with war, revolution, civil war, terror and famine. The 20th Century ended almost as dramatically as it began with a break-up of the Soviet system and initially a deterioration of life for most people being visible in population data. However, in contrast to the beginning of that century, bloodshed was the exception and suppressed peoples regained freedom and independence. Hence the outlook for a higher quality of life was in sight.

Meanwhile, life expectancy declined rapidly in the 1990s, not yet having regained its former peak before 1991 for men in Ukraine, Belarus and Russia. Regional disparities in the life expectancy of Russian men widened, with the lowest level of 51 years on a par with that in Germany and Scandinavia in 1900. An already widening gender age gap was reinforced by this trend. However, of late a sharp turn-around has emerged and the very good news is that Russian men have made an unprecedented come-back in increasing life expectancy.

In Eastern Europe there was, and still is, a fear of a rapidly ageing population developing before the resources and institutions to deal with this are in place.

However, migration has counterbalanced some of these population losses. The whole East European region is unique by simultaneously being both a major receiver and sender of migrants. The new demographic situation of Eastern Europe is not fundamentally different from that of the most industrially advanced countries, with a change in family size, ageing and a decreasing population. So far, Russia and Kazakhstan have to some extent managed to counterbalance some of their population decline by immigration but resources for integrating these migrants have not yet been employed.

Improvements over time can be seen in better Human Development Index (HDI) ratings. However, this is mainly improving in some urban and rich areas, while in much of the countryside the situation is still deteriorating. Although rapid improvement can be seen in Poland and the Baltic states, there too the countryside is lagging behind in human development.

A number of different explanations have been forwarded trying to explain recent drastic demographic changes in Eastern Europe and the Baltic Region, such as the rapid erosion of many former pronatalist policies and subsidies. One theory is based on the phenomenon that during insecure periods people tend to delay getting married and having children, while another blames the sharp drop in standard of living in the early 1990s for a reluctance for young people to have families. Some other types of reasoning tend to emphasise the influence of Western values, stressing individual choice and increased opportunities for new behaviour, which in turn might have led to the postponement of major life decisions such as whether or when to have a family. Further along this line, some others focused on self-fulfilment and free choice resulting in more open norms such as more trial-and-error in finding a partner. Yet another explanation stressed Western influences and the realisation that more modern Western education was needed, so marriage had to be postponed.

A Widening Gap between Urban and Rural

All of Scandinavia has post-industrial societies with high rates of urbanisation and those active in agriculture make up less than 4% of the working population, while rural tourism is currently employing more people than agriculture. Because of well-developed infrastructure there has been migration out of urban areas to the countryside and increased commuting to urban work. Therefore sustainable agriculture, tourism and different green movements seem to be compatible.

As the demographic data show, most of the countries of Eastern and Central Europe are well on the way to a better life for the large urban segment of its population, while the countryside is lagging behind. In all transition countries the gap between urban and rural areas has been widening, reinforced by migration and a brain drain from rural areas of the young and educated. However, there is an increasing realisation at local, regional and international level that a large amount of resources needs to be directed to both social and physical infrastructure development in rural areas. The European Union, international organisations and NGOs are important in this context to further promote rural development.

It should be noted that sustainability of course requires that the population does not increase indefinitely. A necessary consequence of this is an ageing society. However, today in the aging societies in North Western Europe old people are both living longer and getting healthier. This means that medical expenses might increase less than the proportion of elderly. Hence a more healthy and sustainable society in the Eastern part of the Baltic Sea region might result if needed resources will be available. So far the largest deficits are found in the rural areas.

Economic Development and Work Opportunities in Rural BSR

9

Marina Thorborg
Södertörn University, Huddinge, Sweden

Post World War II Development

The European Union Context

Today working in agriculture is the primary means of surviving for fully 75% of the world's 1.4 billion poor living in rural areas (Collier, 2007). In the European Union of 2004 with only 15 countries, 4.1% of the workforce was employed in agriculture while in the 10 EU accession countries of 2004 up to 13.2% were. Through takeovers, entry of multinationals, and mergers, the agri-food sector had been radically transformed during the 1980s. At the turn of the millennium the agri-food sector contributed about 8% of industrial employment and 2% of total employment in the EU. In the subsequently enlarged EU, 90% of the area was rural, as was more than half its population. Until this enlargement, rural poverty was practically eliminated in the EU and Northern Europe. In 2007 (after Rumania and Bulgaria had also joined the EU), more than 93 million people or one in five Europeans lived under the poverty line, which is five times more people than in the early 1990s. Rural poverty in the EU is still double its earlier rate before 2004 and up to three times higher than in urban areas. For this reason, after 2006 in the EU Common Agricultural Policy (CAP), an extra infusion of just above 10 USD billion for rural development was earmarked for new EU members – among them Estonia, Latvia, Lithuania, Czech Republic and Poland – and the CAP budget was increased for a six-year period to almost 17 USD billion

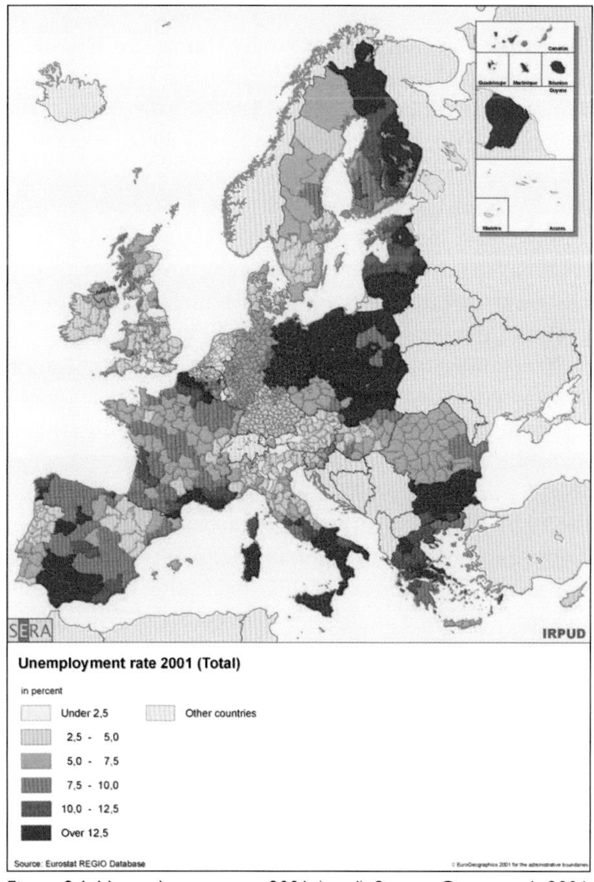

Figure 9.1. Unemployment rate 2001 (total). Source: Copus et al., 2006; Eurostat REGIO Database.

annually in contrast to the period 2000-2006, when funding for rural development was just below 10 USD billion per year. The basic CAP policy has been to support the price to farmers, while keeping market prices for their products low enough to avoid consumer protests through subsidy and export subsidy programmes. In return, farmers have to follow EU directives on quantity and quality of production (IFAD, 2007; Barthelemy, 2009). The EU Lisbon strategy of March 2000 was re-launched in 2006 to further stress the goal of making the EU 'capable of sustained economic growth with more and better jobs and greater social cohesion' (Wibberley, 2007).

This chapter deals with labour development, focusing whenever possible on rural areas and agricultural employment in Eastern and Northern Europe, where all countries are directly or indirectly affected by EU policies.

Box 9.1. Definitions

Labour utilisation generally refers to the number of people working as a proportion of the total number of people of working age, usually meaning from age 18 until official retirement age but in agriculture often from 15 years to retirement.

Distribution of income within a society can be described in different ways. Most often statistics give data for the richest 20% versus the poorest 20%. A more comprehensive measure was developed by the italian sociologist Corrado Gini. The *Gini coefficient* is a distribution measure from 0 to 1 where 0 represent a perfectly equal distribution and 1 total inequality where everything is owned by a single person.

Economic transition means liberalising economic activity, prices and market operations and reallocating resources to their most efficient use, developing market-orientated instruments for macroeconomic stabilisation, effective enterprise management, imposing hard budget constraints and establishing institutional and legal framework to secure property rights, rule of law and transparent market entry regulations (Kucera, 2007).

Soft budget constraints means the state is protecting the economic sector or parts of it by using a variety of mechanisms such as soft credit from state banks, monopoly protection, import restrictions, supply of heavily subsidised energy resources, tax privileges, non-tax settlement schemes, barter trade and cash subsidies from the budget.

Hard budget constraints means imposing strict financial discipline, the government ensuring uniform and even-handed enforcement of necessary regulations, promoting transparency, clarity and accountability of public activities and decisions and guaranteeing freedom of entry and exit of business activities.

Economic Development of Soviet Union and Russia

Through the Marshall Plan help from the USA, the war-damaged countries of Western Europe were quickly rebuilt after 1949, while Stalin, the Soviet dictator, acted in such a way that this help did not extend to Eastern Europe and the Soviet Union (McKay, 1996). Sweden, mostly through luck, managed to stay out of the war and with its undamaged infrastructure was able to enjoy a high growth rate from the late 1940s while becoming an immigration country (Magnusson, 1996; Porter, 1990).

In countries of the Soviet Bloc, rapid industrialisation and forced collectivisation of agriculture had absorbed the rural excess population as well as demobilised soldiers, the urban unemployed and unskilled labourers after World War II. During the 1950s and 1960s and well into the 1970s, these countries were reasonably successful in combating poverty and promoting equality through improvements in general education and health. Lifelong and full employment was guaranteed by the state. The built-in faults of this system were coming to the fore in the 1980s with low labour productivity in a system of 'soft budget constraints', meaning increasing demand for artificially low-priced goods, particularly housing and energy, leading to shortages in goods, accommodation and services. Some scholars refer to the best periods of Soviet rule as 'welfare colonialism'. However, in this stifling political system with curtailed freedoms, creativity and innovation were sorely lacking. With the dissolution of the Soviet Union in the early 1990s, an abrupt termination of state services and central planning followed (IFAD, 2007; Thorborg, 1993; Bengtsson, 2007; Table 1 and 2).

In the Soviet system people were not allowed to be idle, only resources were allowed to be idle and these learned reflexes continued into the transition era, contributing to a low unemployment level but with wages eroded by inflation and decreasing productivity. From 1990-1998 Russian GDP shrank by 46%, while hyperinflation raised consumer prices by 385%, leading to annual economic shocks. Although GDP growth resumed in Russia after the Rouble devaluation in August 1998, the GDP per capita in 2003 was lower than in 1973. However, with Russia emerging as a major oil exporter benefitting from booming oil prices, the 1990 level almost doubled by 2008 (Maddison, 2007; UN, 2005; Thorborg 2002a, b, c, 2003a; Tables 1 and 2).

Table 9.1. World GDP per capita (regional averages 1000-1998) in international dollars. Source: Maddison, 2001, Table B-21

	Year					
Region	**1000**	**1600**	**1870**	**1950**	**1973**	**1998**
Eastern Europe	400	516	871	2,120	4,985	5,461
Fmr Soviet Union	400	553	943	2,834	6,058	3,893
Western Europe	400	894	1,974	4,594	11,534	17,921
Western off-shoots	400	400	2,431	9,288	16,172	26,146

In countries formerly under illegal Soviet occupation, such as the Baltic States, political repression and memories of deportations to Siberia did not contribute to develop trust or enhance Russia's 'soft power', although an extensive industrialisation drive with massive Russian investment – followed by immigration – started from the 1960s onwards (Kuodote and Traceskis, 2005; Thorborg, 1997). When Soviet domination terminated, the states of Eastern Europe turned to the West as trust in the Soviet system and its attractiveness were totally eroded. A rapid decrease in standard of living ensued when social safety nets disappeared and subsidies were removed. However, Estonia and the Czech Republic recovered quicker than the rest of the transition countries (UN, 2005; Thorborg, 2003b; Table 2).

Agricultural Development in the Nordic Countries

Although Sweden went from being an agrarian country to an industrial one in the 1940s, productivity was higher in agriculture than in industry all through the 1970s and 1980s because employment in agriculture decreased by 75% from 1950 to 1980 and agriculture's share of GNP went down to 5% by 1980. Although family agriculture was still the model, basic mechanisation was completed by 1970 in combination with the disappearance of about 100,000 small-scale family farms, contributing to increased farm size and less demand for labour. In Northern Sweden small-scale agriculture was highly seasonal and almost always combined with forestry (as was the case in Finland), which was exposed to large-scale rationalisation in the late 1960s. The traditional form of mixed agriculture largely built upon the principles of self sufficiency was supplanted with specialisation either in grain or animal husbandry.

The other Nordic countries experienced similar developments but with a time-lag due to war and occupation. In Finland the family farm continued with its members contributing over 97% of the workforce at the turn of the millennium. The Finnish land reform in 1921 had resettled landless farm workers and tenants and after World War II another 40,000 families were resettled after being displaced from the areas occupied by the Soviet Union and therefore in contrast to most industrialised countries, the number of farms increased.

In 1950 Finland had 260,000 farms and the number was still around 200,000 by 1981. However full-time farmers earned only 70% of the average income of an industrial worker in 1984, so most farmers supplemented this with income from forestry. In the mid-1980s, 65% of farmers' income came from agriculture, 25% from wages and 10% from forestry. As in the other Scandinavian countries, the trend was towards specialisation. Denmark and the UK not only had the highest number of non-family farm workers in the EU, but Denmark also was the largest employer in the agri-food business, which accounted for 3% of all jobs, while in Sweden this was much lower than 2%. In Denmark, the most agricultural country in Scandinavia, the seasonal movement of agricultural workers from Poland stopped when the Iron Curtain blocked migration but was partly resumed after the break-up of the Soviet Bloc in the 1990s (Magnusson, 1996; Porter,

Box 9.2. A Short Note on Data

Information referring to the European national level is generally easier to find than information on rural-urban differences, while comparative national data on rural development are even harder to find. Estimates on the size of the informal sector vary widely and even more so for that sector in the countryside. Definitions of unemployment also diverge greatly, as do estimates of unemployment. According to the Centre for Rural Research at Exeter University working on EU data, 'Different statistical procedures and criteria mean that comparable data are not available systematically. EU and OECD definitions and thus data contrast markedly and there is considerable diversity between reporting countries despite efforts to standardise.' (Wibberley, 2007).

Table 9.2. GDP per capita performance and GDP growth rates in Eastern and Northern Europe, 1970-2010.

	GDP per capita in 1,000 USD #					Growth rate					
	1973	1990	2003	2008	2009	1973-90	1990-2003	2007	2008	2009	2010
Sweden	13.5	23.3	28.3	38.5	36.8	2.6*	1.4**	2.7	0.5	-4.4	1.2
Finland	10.8	20.1	24.5	37.7	34.9	3.7*	1.7**	4.4	1.2	-7.6	1.2
Denmark	13.4	24.1	30.3	37.8	36.0	2.0*	2.3**	1.7	-0.9	-4.3	1.2
Germany	13.2	19.4	23.2	34.8	34.1	2.5*	3.0**	2.5	1.3	-5.3	1.4
Czech Rep	7.4	8.9	9.8	26.1	25.1	0.83***	0.83	6.1	2.5	-4.1	1.7
Poland	5.3	5.1	7.7	17.3	17.9	-0.26	3.17	6.8	5.0	1.7	2.7
Lithuania	7.6	8.7	8.0	17.7	15.4	0.78	-0.62	9.8	2.8	-15	-1.6
Estonia	8.7	10.8	14.3	21.2	18.7	1.32	2.19	7.2	-3.6	-14.1	0.8
Latvia	7.8	9.9	9.7	17.7	14.5	1.39	-0.15	10.0	-4.8	-17.8	-4.0
Belarus	5.2	7.2	7.4	11.8	11.6	1.88	0.21	6.9	9.2	-0.2	2.4
Russia	6.7	7.8	6.3	15.0	15.1	0.99	-1.58	8.1	6.0	-7.9	4.3
Ukraine	4.9	6.0	3.5	6.9	6.4	1.20	-4.00	6.9	2.1	-14.1	3.7

In 1990 PPP (Purchasing Power Parity) in USD for 1990 and in for 2003 and 2008 in constant 2,000 USD.
* = 1970-90, ** = 1990-2000, *** = Czechoslovakia in 1973. Sources: The years 1973-2003; Maddison, 2007. For GDP per capita the year 2008 est. and for growth rate 2008 est.; CIA. 2009. Except for growth rates for Baltics the year 2008; Baltic Rim Economies, BRE 2009. The year 2009; Estimated growth; The Baltic states from Grundberg, S. 2009a. Sweden the 1st quarter of 2009 compared with the same quarter preceding year, from Grundberg, S 2009b. CIA 2010. Estimates. For 2010. WEO 2010. July. Estimates.

1990; Barthelemy, 2009). Sweden and with a certain time-lag Denmark and Finland experienced profound structural transformations of agriculture from the 1970s onwards, with sharply falling employment in agriculture (up to 90% during a brief period) and ensuing depopulation of the countryside. Similar developments occurred in Eastern Europe after the break-up of the Soviet Union.

A trend visible in Sweden and the other Scandinavian countries was towards higher part-time employment in agriculture, with up to 60% of the main income coming from other types of work (Official Statistics of Sweden, 2009). Labour market modernisation in the Soviet Bloc basically followed the Western pattern until the mid-1990s, with a time-lag of around one generation. This is clearly demonstrated by the fact that in Scandinavia, the relationship between the share of labour force in agriculture and its contribution to GDP was around 1:1, while in the Czech Republic and Latvia it was 1:2 and in Poland the relationship was 4:1. Denmark was the exception, with the contribution of agriculture to GDP being higher than its share of the agricultural labour force 1990-2001, showing its advanced degree of mechanisation and rationalisation (Prokopijevic, 2002; Barthelemy 2009; Tables 3 and 4).

Polish Agriculture

In Poland in 1921, less than 50% of farmers owned their own homesteads, a few rich landowners had large estates, while most cultivated small plots and more than 20% were landless. Because Poland was an important agricultural exporter, the world depression with decreasing demand hit Polish farmers particularly hard, resulting in a semi-starvation situation in the countryside for several millions of surplus farm workers who could not be absorbed by an industry expanding at a snail's pace.

After World War II, in 1945 almost two-thirds of the population in Poland were peasants. The death toll in the war hit harder in urban areas, although half a million farms were destroyed. With the social pre-war structure still roughly intact, the post-war communist state confiscated estates above 50 hectares and distributed this land to private farms. Simultaneously, in contrast to the pre-war situation, an expanding industry managed to absorb rural surplus labour or to supplement farmers' income. Until 1956, when collectivisation was attempted by the state, up to 1 million farmers left the land and production dropped sharply. Therefore in the late 1950s as a survival measure de-collectivisation ensued, with only 6%

of farms remaining collectivised. Because of this farmers remained suspicious of the state, even when essential infrastructure was developed. As the state favoured the few remaining collectives with modern equipment, credit and loans, many private small-scale farms continued to use horses for cultivation. The medium-sized farms (5-15 hectares) that initially dominated in the private sector after 1956 were divided so many times that by 1986 up to 60% of the farmsteads had less than 5 hectares to survive on.

When at that point the state for reasons of efficiency tried to re-concentrate land holdings, peasant resistance blocked this move. Then most peasants were not solely dependent on income from agriculture. Half the rural population commuted to urban jobs, while 15% had most of their income in the countryside from non-agricultural pursuits, another 15% had most of their earnings from agriculture and finally only 15% depended solely on the land for survival. Because private peasants had been marginalised in regard to physical and social infrastructure, the young and educated left the countryside. Only during the hard trough of the transformation years in the early 1990s did this trend reverse for a couple of years, when just as in the Baltic states people moved to the countryside for food security (SOEC, 2009).

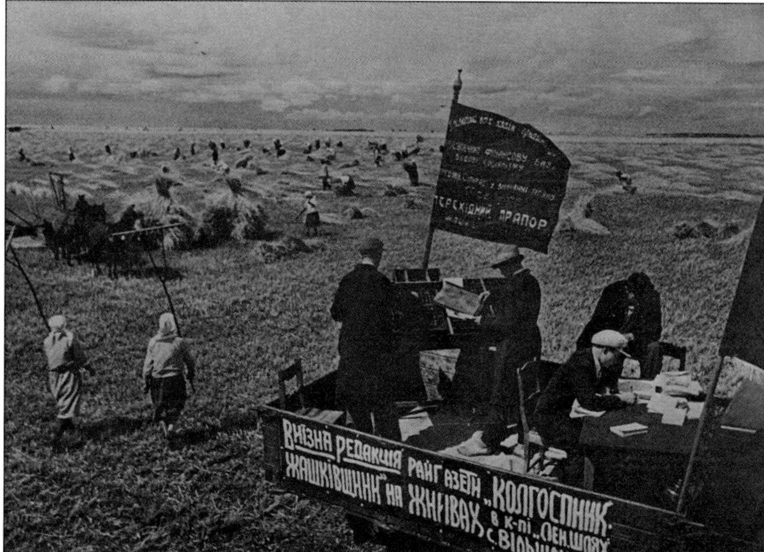

Figure 9.2. Journalist from up the newspaper, "Collective Farmer" at work in the fields of a cooperative farm outside Kiev, Ukraine. Source: Library of Congress.

Collectivisation and De-collectivisation of Farms

Soviet Agriculture

In contrast to this, the Soviet Union had already in 1928 at the start of their First Five-Year Plan chosen the Preobrazhensky model for development, built on massive resource extraction from agriculture geared towards a rapid build-up of heavy industry. By some accounts the collectivisation of Soviet agriculture lowered its production capacity by 25%, and cost the lives of 5-6 million people, where Ukraine alone (with the most fertile land) lost over 3 million people due to terror, anti-kulak campaigns and deportations to Siberia (Applebaum, 2003; Conquest, 1971 p. 39 ff; Courtois and Werth, 1997; Yang, 2008).

This mode of production came at a very high cost to the environment, with farming based on heavy mechanisation and intensive use of pesticides and chemical fertilisers. In this system the institution of the Sovkhozes (state farms) and the Kolkhozes (cooperative farms) was combined with a small plot for private production. These plots were typically about 1/3 of a hectare in size (Fainsod, Chap. 16; Thorborg, 1996a and b). The production from the private plots accounted for 25% of the total value of the agricultural output in the late 1980s, 33% in 1992, almost 50% in 1995, approaching 60% in 1998 and returning to 50% in 2004. According to Russian statistics, in the year 2000, for example, the value of the average return from 1 hectare of Russian agricultural land was 3.931 Roubles (131 USD) from former *Kolkhozes*, from large commercial enterprises it was 2,131 Roubles (71 USD), and from private households it was 37,719 Roubles (1,257 USD) (O´Brien et al., 2007).

Belarus

When states were reforming former state or collective land in the 1990s, three institutional problems had to be decided upon: how to transform rural wage workers, how to decide the size of farms and how to maintain productivity. These problems were solved differently over time in different countries. Initially in Russia and Belarus the state kept ownership of land, while as a rule in most other transition countries the aim of land reform was to create privately owned family farms. Although most of the land in Russia underwent some reorganisation, most opted for the safe shield of state subsidies rather than being dependent on the vagaries of the market. By the mid-1990s 280,000 private farms cultivated 5% of the arable land, while some had already returned to the old forms.

Although Belarus did not privatise land holdings, state farms and collectives decreased from cultivating 94% of all agricultural land to 83% in 2004. However, the share of agricultural output from family farms increased from under 25% of all output in 1990 to almost 50% after 2000, showing that 17% of all farmland produced almost 50% of all output. This is similar to the Russian situation. However, the agricultural labour force shrank from 1990 to 2007. Agriculture accounted for 20% of all employment in 1993, 14% in 2000 and 10% in 2007 (O'Brien, 2007).

Poland and the Baltic States

A major concern during this period was to hand back land to former owners and their heirs, some of them urban and many of them already at an advanced age. In Poland and Latvia de-collectivisation was complete. Therefore in Latvia agriculture and agricultural employment accounted for roughly 1:2 in 1990, almost 1:4 in 2001, and 1:3 in 2007-2009, showing increasing inefficiency. In Lithuania, Estonia and many Eastern European countries, actual land distribution occurred slowly at an uneven pace and rather unequally. Although Lithuanian farm workers were 50% more productive than their Soviet counterparts – partly because the communist leaders in Vilnius were allowed greater independence from Moscow in the late 1950s – they were not yet up to the level of Western farmers. With regained independence small-scale holdings multiplied and production and efficiency dropped, only basically being changed during the EU application period. In Ukraine, Lithuania and Belarus especially, the decline in real wages was around 60% between 1989 and 1998. In Ukraine a loss of output of about 60% was recorded by 1998, while during the same period employment only contracted by 12% (UN/ECE, 2000).

Privatising Russian Agriculture

In the first post-Soviet period the main institutional changes to develop private agriculture in Russia were the following:

1 December 1991: The right to leave the former state and collective farms and to receive land shares when leaving.
2 October 1993: Legalisation of private ownership of land and the right to sell and buy agricultural land.
3 July 2002: A law regulating procedures to be employed in rural land transactions.
4 2003. Separate laws for private farms and private plots (O´Brien, 2007).

One estimate reported in Russian agriculture 'a staggering unused potential, perhaps involving as much as 80% of arable land' (Leijonhielm, 2008). This can be explained by the fact that just as in Poland earlier under communist rule, small private and new farmers had great difficulty in getting sufficient credit for investment in fertilisers and mechanisation, because large farms continued to be favoured by the state in regard to credit, information, technology and extension services. (Griffin, 2002).

The area of Russian cultivated land almost halved from 1992 to 2006, which can be the explanation behind the increasing price of Russian food. Until the prices of most common foods were frozen in 2007, they had increased by 25-30%. After 12 years in the pulp business, it is not surprising that the new Russian president Medvedev also wanted to exploit the great untapped potential of Russian forests (Leijonhielm, 2008). Russia has a great potential for growth in its abundance of unused agricultural land and its mature forests.

However, a major problem is the depressed agricultural wages, with relatively very low remuneration for farm labour averaging 40% of the wages for the whole country. Because of low wages and pensions, more than a quarter of the income of the rural population is in kind, mainly produce from their own private plot. Poor families get almost two-thirds of their food in this way (UNDP, 2003). However, in Russia the more well-equipped and mechanised large-scale collective units continued into the new era. For this reason the discrepancy between labour input and productivity was smaller in agriculture. Overall, the

Table 9.3. Contribution of industry and agriculture to GDP (%) in countries of the Baltic Region in 1994, 2001 and 2007

	Share of GDP*							
	Industry				Agriculture			
	1994	2001	2007	2009	1991	2001	2007	2009
Sweden	32e	31e	29	27	5e	3e	1	2
Denmark	29e	28e	26	24	5e	4e	2	1
Finland	34e	33e	32	30	5e	3e	3	4
Germany	33e	32e	30	27	3e	2e	1	1
Czech rep	34	37	40	37	5	4	2	2
Poland	32	29	32	28	6	5	4	5
Lithuania	26	10	32	27	23	7*	5	4
Estonia	32	16	29	26	10	4	3	3
Latvia	23	17	21	22	8	4	4	4
Belarus	27	34	41	42	15	7	9	9
Russia	33	34	40	35	7	7/14	5/9.9	5
Ukraine	30	40	32	31	16	12	9	10

*= 2000. Source for the rest : EBRD. 2002. Except for the year 2007 from CIA, 2008, and 2009 from CIA, 2010. e= estimates.

Table 9.4. Employment in agriculture in countries of the Baltic Region as % of total employment, 1990-2007

	1990	2001	2003	2005	2007	2009
Sweden	3	2/3*	2	2	2	1
Finland	4	3*	3	4**	5***	5***
Denmark	4	3*	3	3	3	3
Germany	3	3	2	2	3	3
Czech Rep.	10	5	5	4	4	4
Poland	26	19	18	17		17e
Lithuania	19	16	16/18	14		14e
Estonia	12	7	6	5	5	3
Latvia	16	15	14	12/13	12	12e
Belarus	19	16	14	-	-	-
Russia	13	12/14	11	11	10/11	10e
Ukraine	20	22	19	19	16	16e

*= End of 1990s. e= estimates. Source : Barthelemy, 2009. **=2004 Source: USAID. 2007. Except for the years 2007 and 2004 Denmark, and 2003 for Latvia from CIA, 2008. *** 2008 for Finland agriculture and forestry from CIA, 2009. In digits 2001 for Russia, For 2009. CIA, 2010 except estimates.

difference between labour input in industry and industrial output was still greatest in Ukraine, followed by Russia, a legacy of the Preobrazhensky model (Casula, 2008; USAID, 2007). In recent years through a revival of agriculture Russia has changed into being a net exporter of grain from a net importer (CIA, 2010).

In Belarus state banks had to provide loans – basically without any chance of ever getting repaid – making up for example 25% of all loans, equivalent to 3% of GDP, in 2001. These subsidies from the government were not conditional on any reforms of an inefficient and overstaffed agricultural sector, which was performing badly and a drain on state coffers. Most of the farms were loss-making and not paying their energy bills (Smee, 2001). This was also visible in slower growth in per capita income and first in a quick shrinking of the agricultural sector – then even increasing between 2001 and 2007 – and in a slower decrease in agricultural employment (Tables 7.2, 7.3 and 7.4).

The Baltic States and Central Europe

In the Baltic States, Estonia in particular, a rapid decline has occurred in the number of people working in agriculture, almost reaching Western levels since 1991.

Table 9.5. Employment in agriculture in countries of the Baltic Region by sex in 2001 as % of total employment.

	Men	Women
Sweden	4	1
Denmark	5	2
Finland	8	4
Germany	3	2
Czech Rep.	6	4
Poland	19	19
Estonia	11	7
Lithuania	24	16
Latvia	17	14
Russia	15	8

Source: ILO 2002

Estonia had already carried out rapid and successful modernisation of its agriculture during its Independence in the 1920s and 1930s. In Poland, Lithuania and Latvia the proportion of agriculture in the economy has diminished to just above West European levels, while the workforce in agriculture has not shrunk accordingly, implying lower labour productivity, and also expressed as lower per capita income. However in Poland greater problems are that

Table 9.6. All-seasonal, part-time, seasonal and migrant workers in agriculture in selected countries in the Baltic region, latest data.

	Work type			Whereof migrants from:		% from
	All-seasonal	Part-time	Seasonal;	EU	Non-EU	sending countries
Sweden	24,000	19,000	8.000		3,000	
Finland	5,000	10,000	1,000		1,200	78 Russia, Baltics
Denmark	35,000		12,000	8,000+	2,000	90+ Poland, Ukraine
Germany	530,000	270,000	216,000 Poland			80 Poland
Czech Rep.	176,200	6,500				80 Ukraine, Belarus, Russia
Poland	153,200	20,000			16,000	75 Ukraine
Poland					4,000	25 other Eastern countries
Lithuania	3,000	16,000	3,000		small share	
Estonia	15,000	2,500				
Latvia	28,000	22,400	large grey sector			
Russia					1,500,000+	Ukraine

Source: EU countries: www.agri-in fo. 2009. Russia: Matthews, O. 2008.

almost a quarter of the 4 million working in agriculture are of pension age and that agricultural employment is very uneven between Polish regions, ranging from 9% in Silesia to 39.5% in Podlaskie, i.e. less developed agriculture in the East. The greying of the Polish agricultural workforce is also seen in the fact that the same number of women as men work the land – more than in any other country of the Baltic Sea region – and, as women survive men by 11 years, these women are widows (www.agri-info. 2009; Wibberley 2007). See also Chapter 8 in this book, Table 8.2 and 8.5.

In Estonia and Czech Republic, both the agricultural sector and its workforce shrank rapidly to Western levels – diminishing by 73% from 1989 to 2005 – which, combined with higher efficiency, contributed to a higher per capita income (Wibberley, 2007. Table 2, 3 and 4). Ukraine, Poland and Lithuania stand out as the most agricultural countries, but with the lowest agricultural productivity. Compared with the mid-1990s, in Estonia, Latvia and Poland industry and agriculture have either stagnated or decreased at the expense of services as a proportion of total GDP in conformity with general trends in the EU. This has not been the case in Czech Republic, Lithuania, Belarus and Russia, where industry was still on the increase until 2008.

However, in both Belarus and Ukraine, the agricultural share of GDP has almost halved. (Table 9.3 and 9.4). A new feature of the dissolution of the Soviet Union was the massive flow of migrating labour across Europe, usually from the East towards the more developed West with its higher wages (Table 9.6).

Unemployment, Poverty and Migration in Rural Areas

From Hopes of Westernization to Subsistence Farming
After 1945 and up to the mid-1970s, most planned economies of the Soviet Bloc were succeeding in improving general health and education, while simultaneously reducing income poverty through rapid industrialisation. In this process jobs were created not only for the urban unemployed and unskilled workers, but also for the rural poor. From 1950 until the mid-1970s, average life expectancy increased by up to 10 years, while infant mortality halved because of solid investment in social infrastructure and a broad distribution of benefits. The ideological framework was committed to an equal society, which included a system of entitlements for all such as guarantees of employment, social services and security.

Although the political system was not open, it provided the basic necessities of life. However, after the mid-1970s many of these positive developments stopped and even reversed. After the break-up of the Soviet system in 1991, high hopes for an easy and rapid transition to a functioning Western type of society soon evaporated when the economic system more or less collapsed. In much of the countryside former state and collective farms were dissolved and privatised, leaving part of the rural workforce without work and with few possibilities for alternative activities. In this situation with no alternatives, many jobless turned to subsistence or semi-subsistence agriculture or different types of self-employment on a small scale in order just to survive (UN, 2005).

Table 9.7. Income inequality in selected countries in the Baltic region 1989/91-2003/2004 and latest data, all in GINI-coefficients

	1989/91	1999/2000	2003/2004	2007
USA	0.40e	0.41	0.43e	0.45
Canada.	0.33e	0.33	0.32**	0.32e
Argentina	0.53e	0.53e	0.53	0.49
Sweden	0.25e	0.25	0.23	0.23e
Czech Rep.	0.19	0.23	0.24	0.27
Poland	0.27	0.34	0.26	0.31
Lithuania	0.26	0.35	0.31	0.39
Estonia	0.28	0.38	0.40	0.39
Latvia	0.26	0.33	0.39	0.33
Belarus	0.23	0.24	0.25	0.34
Russia	0.47*	0.43	0.42***	0.49
Ukraine	0.23	0.34	0.35***	0.41

*= 1995/96, and **= 2005 ***=2001/2002 Source: USAID, 2005, Table 17. NB The higher the number, the greater the inequality. CIA, 2010 for 2007. e=estimate.

Poverty

Since the collapse of the Soviet Union, poverty has increased rapidly in Eastern Europe at a pace almost unparalleled elsewhere and in some cases has contributed to increased ruralisation as urban dwellers have moved out of towns in order to have some food security. A particular feature of Estonia was the high level of subsistence economy for its urban inhabitants, with up to 75% of them getting their basic supplies of potatoes and cabbage for the winter straight from the countryside through family and connections. Latvia was the Baltic country with the most difficult transition both politically and economically. In the worst period, the third quarter of 1992, up to 80% of its population, could not afford a 'complete minimum food basket', while half the population had an income below the value of a 'crisis minimum food basket', on which people cannot live for long without permanent damage to their health. Similar hard times befell Lithuania, but it was helped by being the most agricultural and least developed of the Baltic states and therefore closest to a subsistence economy. The ironic twist is that this was hitting a country after 50 years with a planned economy and Communism, which earlier during Independence had a market economy and in the 1930s ranked third in the world in per capita meat consumption and second in the world in consumption of milk and dairy products! (Thorborg, 1993, 2000, 2002c, g).

For this reason, although agricultural production went down the agricultural labour force went up, with the number of people partly working in subsistence agriculture increasing, Ukraine being an example of this. This meant that agricultural productivity was falling, with more people engaged in agriculture and simultaneously less output, also leading to decreasing income from agricultural work. Here a kind of agricultural involution occurred – in the sense Geertz (1963) first described it in Java – with more people working part-time and informally producing less with more work-intensive methods. This occurred because some of the machinery owned by the state and collective agricultural sector was not used in new small-scale agriculture and, in addition, two-thirds of it was worn out (Wegren, 2007). Therefore agricultural income decreased and underemployment rose. According to some estimates the proportion of the population living in poverty increased fourfold due to rising income inequality combined with decreasing average incomes during the first half decade of transition (Table 9.7).

In the late 1980s, about 8% of the population in the transition countries of the former Soviet Union and Central and Eastern Europe were estimated to be living in poverty while during the trough in 1993-94, well over 30% of the population could be classified as poor. In Russia, for example, resurging economic growth reduced poverty from officially 42% in 1999 to just 20% in 2002 and 16% in 2007. Depending on different evaluation methods, poverty in Russia was 40% in 2000 according to household surveys, but 29% according to official data. In most years

Box 9.3. Work Opportunities in the Baltic Sea Region

Work and employment in the rural society is commonly divided into primary, secondary and tertiary sectors. The primary includes work in agriculture, forestry and fisheries as well as hunting; the secondary manufacturing sector includes industries, while the services sector is dominated by public jobs, such as schools and healthcare. The description below relies on an extensive study made for the European Commission and reported in 2007, Study on Employment in Rural Areas, SERA. Regrettably it does not cover Russia, Belarus and Ukraine, although some references to the situation in these countries are made.

Division between sectors

Jobs in the primary sector have declined dramatically since ever since some 100 years. In the west, where most agriculture today is industrialized, a few individuals may manage a farm of hundreds of acres or hundreds of animals relying on machinery. There are only 10 regions in the EU25 – one is eastern Poland – in which primary sector activities employ a majority of the workforce. Secondary and tertiary employment is overwhelmingly the most important sectors for employment. Even in the more peripheral rural regions the primary sector only reaches an average share of 19%, compared with 11% in the more accessible regions. Also in forestry job opportunities have been dramatically reduced with the introduction of new efficient machinery.

In 2001 the percentage employment in secondary sector industries in rural EU27 regions was at 28%, compared to the urban average of 25%. Tertiary employment rates across the EU27 in predominately rural areas were 57 %, (and much lower in the new member states in the east), compared to 74 % in urban regions. Tertiary sector growth has tended to be associated with metropolitan functions, in particular the growth of financial markets, knowledge-based industries, and public services such as education and healthcare. Generally speaking, the service sector employment is increasing, while that of manufacturing is stable or decreasing. Still changing policies and practices regarding public services including transport, telecommunications, housing, health and education, often impact particularly severely on rural areas and especially the less well off and less mobile people.

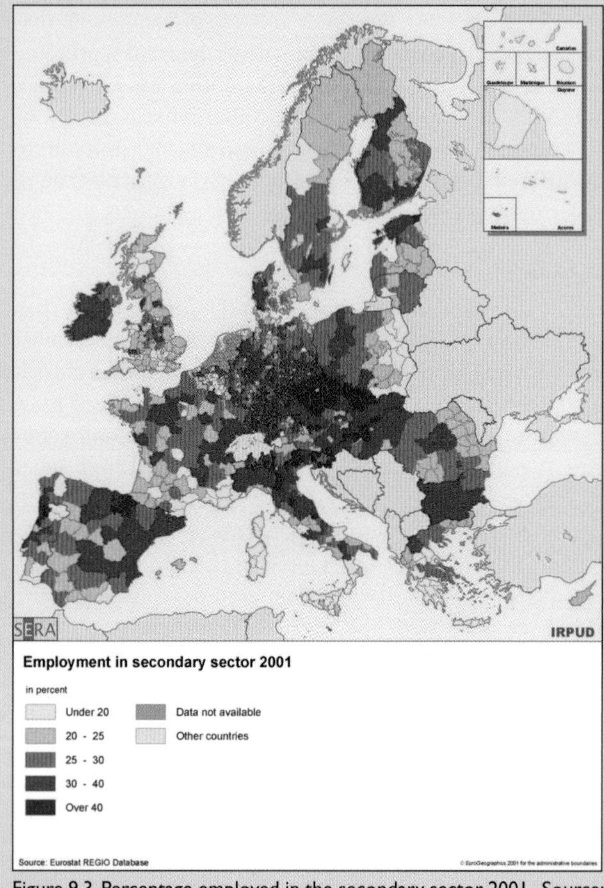

Figure 9.3. Percentage employed in the secondary sector 2001 . Source: Copus et al., 2006; Eurostat REGIO Database.

Rural labour market and the role of agriculture

Rural labour markets tend to be segmented along sectoral/occupational lines and typically operate within geographically extensive areas. However self-employment, or working for a locally based SME, are more compatible with farming than employment by a larger company. Those who are essentially "life-style" or "hobby farmers", together with non-farming members of farm households, probably have the option (skills and qualifications permitting) to look further afield, and across a broader range of occupations.

The range of enterprises within a rural economy exhibits a surprising amount of diversity and individuality, as shown in the general statistics. Many rural enterprises are location-specific, for example, the growth of certain crops depends on particular agro-climatic conditions. Location also drives the type of services that are on offer. For example, location by a major road or near to a thriving city will provide opportunities not open to more remote rural areas. Tourism depends on the proximity of the coast or a particular kind of landscape or climate.

Although agriculture is not directly involved in the employment growth it is indirectly linked to many secondary or tertiary jobs. This occurs in three principal ways: Firstly the "upstream" units supply the agricultural sector with inputs, such as seeds, fertilizers, machinery etc., while "downstream" is processing and marketing agricultural products. Secondly agriculture provides complementary jobs, as full-time working within agriculture is now relatively uncommon – many, if not most, farmers and farm households, are also active in secondary or tertiary labour markets. Finally through spin-offs, as the attractiveness of the

Work Opportunities in the Baltic Sea Region

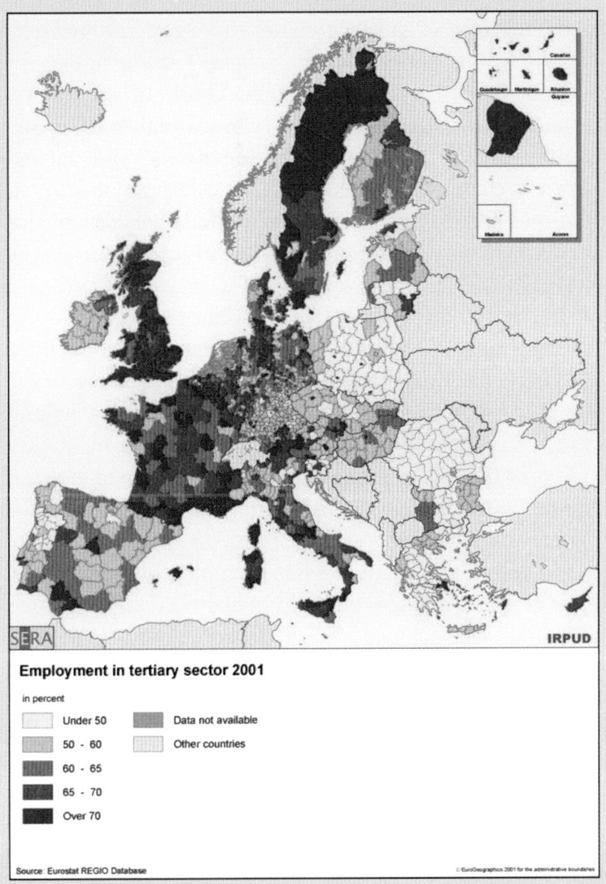

Figure 9.4. Percentage employed in the tertiary sector 2001. Source: Copus et al., 2006; Eurostat REGIO Database..

countryside depends on working farms, mills etc. which may increase tourism and make the area more attractive for the in-migration of people and businesses.

Agro-tourism

Agro-tourism is a common name for housing and feeding visitors on the countryside, mostly during summer and vacation periods. In addition to just offering a place to stay and eat, many also arrange activities such a canoeing, horseback riding, biking, and hiking especially in mountain areas. Also over day activities, such as cafés and kiosk services or selling homemade produce may be important in the season. The growth of spending on leisure and recreation activities has significantly boosted the size and importance of the rural tourist industry. Tourism directly employs over 9 million people across the European Union - 6% of total employment - and a much higher percentage in some regions. 13,000 farm units offering visitor facilities to tourists, providing an annual income of 850 million Euros. It also indirectly supports millions of jobs in connected services such as the hotels, restaurants and cafes, rising faster than any other sector during 2001-2003.

New and expanding areas - Nature conservation, Organic farming and Renewable Energy

Nature conservation supports employment and plays an important role in the development of rural economies. Within the European Union system farmers have new responsibilities for providing ecosystem services and goods, which is paid from the state budget in order to maintain a good environment and attractive landscape. This includes e.g. coastal management, grazing on meadows and management of wetlands. Many of the jobs associated with conservation-related activities are located in remote rural areas where there were few alternative employment opportunities. Tourism arising from conservation and land management activities often provided more employment opportunities than land management itself.

It has been claimed that organic farms employ between 10%-30% more people than non-organic farms, however few figures are available. The area under organic farming is increasing. In the EU-15 2002 covered 4.8 million ha or 3.7% of total farmland, an increase of 112% compared to 1998, an increase which has continued since.

The present EU and national policies for climate mitigation and introduction of renewable energies will be important for the rural labour market and a significant potential for employment growth. A doubling of renewable capacity in the EU by 2020 has been estimated to lead to approximately 30% of gross employment creation in the sector. In Poland the realisation of the renewable energy strategy objectives has been estimated to create 30,000-40,000 new jobs annually; in Denmark it has been projected to lead to the creation of 73,000 new jobs.

Other expanding sectors – Telework

While telework increases rural employment opportunities, it may also help employees improve the balance between work and home life, and offer new business opportunities. For ten EU countries studied the proportion of home-based respectively supplementary teleworkers was highest in Finland (10.8 and 6.0 per cent), while some large economies such as Germany and France were well below the average. In general telework is increasing. In the UK from 1997 to 2003 it doubled up to 7.5 % of the total workforce. It is not clear what proportion of teleworkers were rural-based.

Lars Rydén

the poverty rate of the rural population was 30-40% higher than that of their urban counterparts.

More women than men were poor, despite women having a higher educational level on average than men (Thorborg, 2002d). Women aged 31-54, meaning the age period when they have dependent children, were the poorest of all in the late 1990s, with a poverty rate 25% higher than that of men in the same age group. Up to 62-85% of families with many children and only one parent were considered to be in deep poverty in Russia (UNDP, 2003; Thorborg, 1999, 2002b; Burawoy, 1996).

Rural Unemployment

While in 2003 the poverty rate was estimated at 4-5% in Estonia and Lithuania, it was 17% in Poland and encompassed more than 27% of the population of Belarus. By some estimates 35% of the population was poor in Ukraine in 2009 (CIA, 2010). However, in most transition countries GDP declined more than agriculture and when economic growth restarted GDP rose more slowly than agricultural growth, meaning that agriculture softened the impact of transition (Griffin et al., 2002). For example, in Lithuania rural unemployment is 4-5 times higher than in the capital Vilnius, while on the national level unemployment only affects 3% of all. However, social inequality is increasing in some parts of the Lithuanian countryside, with agricultural productivity being stagnant or sliding backwards. In Lithuania every third person in the countryside is counted as poor.

In 2005 poverty was still increasing in Lithuania. Up to 100,000 people from the country have migrated to the rest of EU. Poorest is Eastern Latvia, with the highest unemployment in Latgale.

In 2006 Latvia was the poorest country in the EU, with only 46% of the EU average in per capita income. Even Estonia has experienced a widening gap between rich and poor, with the wealthiest 20% of the population accounting for 40% of GNP while one child in three still lives under the official minimum level of existence.

So far the recent economic recession has hit the Baltic countries hard (Svenska Dagbladet, 19/3, 25/3, 27/3 2009). In Poland a high level of unemployment peaked at 20% but fell back in 2007 helped by migration. The level of labour utilisation was the lowest of EU-15 and also lower than in neighbouring states. From the late 1990s labour utilisation decreased by 5%, going down to 54% during the past decade.

Withdrawal from the labour force usually began at age 40, particularly in the countryside, which is earlier than in the rest of EU, and accelerated after age 55, which during the Soviet period was the official retirement age for women (Allard and Annett, 2008; Thorborg, chapter on population in this book). As a rule, inequality increased rapidly during the early transition period and slowed down in the new millennium. Lack of employment possibilities and distance to markets in rural areas are considered key factors in explaining this rural-urban gap (IFAD, 2007. Table 7).

Internally, the wealth gap between rich and poor in all transition countries has been widening, going from a more equal Scandinavian level to a level closer to the Americas with both Russia and Ukraine, which among others have surpassed the USA and India in inequality (CIA, 2008; Table 7). The EU Agenda 2000 tried to break the link between leaving the countryside and leaving the country, with rules stressing enhanced national autonomy for 'diversification of activities in or close to agriculture' and for 'basic services required by the rural economy and rural population', focusing on job-creating areas such as green tourism, supply of community services, management of heritage resources and organic farming.

Experiences from Denmark show that organic farming leads to job creation but also increases labour costs significantly (by up to 38%), implying that this is only a solution for more resource-rich states (Barthelemy, 2009). For most transition states, having rural migrants in 'circular migration' to the West sending money home seems to be the temporary solution to problems of un- or underemployment in rural areas. Large numbers of migrants from non-EU countries – Belarus, Ukraine and Russia – work illegally in the EU and they are impossible to count, while migrants from EU transition countries often work in a 'grey' sector with employers not paying taxes or social benefits for them or sometimes just paying them in kind (www.agri-info 2009; Table 6).

Migration from Rural to Urban and Back

Agricultural employment has changed extensively during the post-war period, from often being the largest area of employment to almost the smallest one and with some countries losing up to 90% of their workers in less than a dozen years. During chaotic transformation years after the break-up of the Soviet Union, agricultural employment was able to act as a cushion. Sometimes a kind of agricultural involution occurred when more people produced less with less machinery but with food security as their main goal, also temporarily contributing to a reversed flow from urban to rural areas. In the increasingly affluent Scandinavian countries this return flow to rural areas began a generation earlier, when better infrastructure made it possible as a lifestyle choice while either still keeping urban full-time employment or beginning to work part-time in the countryside. Simultaneously, for tax reasons more and more people became part-time farmers. This of course revised the ageing and depopulation trends in rural areas, particularly those close to urban centres.

With the EU came more open borders, contributing to rural areas being used more extensively for recreation in other countries and thereby creating more seasonal employment in the countryside. Proximity to urban areas and developed infrastructure proved to be a crucial condition for continuous development of the countryside through attracting more people, slow outmigration and creating more rural non-agricultural employment, a sector still in its infancy compared with Southern Europe.

A great potential for employment in rural areas resides with tourism, which today is creating more employment than agriculture in the more developed countries of the Baltic region. It particularly contributes to part-time employment in rural regions where earnings from agriculture need to be supplemented. However, what is needed is often a more consistent policy, not only from local and national authorities but also from the EU so that small- and medium-scale undertakings and new activities such as tourism receive the attention they deserve. A large unused potential is waiting to be tapped. Promoting ecotourism could be a viable way towards both contributing to economic development by creating more employment in rural areas and simultaneously furthering sustainability in agriculture by being particularly suitable for family and small-scale agriculture."

Agro- and Rural Tourism in the Baltic Sea region

A Growing Sector

10

Elena Kropinova
Immanuel Kant Baltic Federal University, Kaliningrad, Russia

Different Kinds of Tourism in the Countryside

Growing Rural Tourism

Agrotourism is an alternative form of tourism and sustainable way of agriculture at the same time. It is rapidly developing in the Baltic Sea region. It focuses on the specifics of local agricultural, nature management, traditional rural way of life, and creating an economic background for development of nature-friendly methods of farming. Some countries, such as Germany, Denmark, Sweden and Finland are the pioneers in this sphere. The others- Poland, Lithuania, Estonia and Latvia- are actively adopting their experiences and trying to be integrated in this system, enter the existing organizations and create their own. Rural tourism development in Russia is currently in its initial stage. The most advanced areas in North-West Russia are the Leningrad and Kaliningrad regions.

Rural tourism has become quite popular in the Baltic Sea region over the past years. It is largely connected to a rather negative attitude to the farming practices that developed in the countries of Northern and Western Europe caused by excessive use of chemicals, disturbance of natural landscapes, and a sharp increase of ecosystem load. This, along with economic stagnation, led to unemployment, lowering of living standards and outflow of the population from rural areas. Developing the so-called farm tourism became one of the ways to revive rural settlements and maintain an adequate employment level. The European Charter for Rural Areas prepared by Council of Europe offers guidelines for rural tourism as a way of diversifying agricultural land use towards alternative forms, one of which being rural tourism. The document states (Council of Europe, 1996: 15-16).

> *1. Parties should take all necessary legal, fiscal and administrative measures to develop tourism in rural areas in general and agricultural tourism in particular, taking account of the carrying capacity of the areas concerned. In particular this can be done by encouraging the provision of rural hostels and by ensuring that farmers who offer tourist accommodation on their farm in addition to their agricultural activities are encouraged to do so.*
> *2. In implementing this policy, parties should aim for a balance between the indispensable development of tourism, the protection of nature and the potential offered by existing infrastructures and services by maintaining the quality of the landscape and the environment and preserving traditional architecture and materials."*

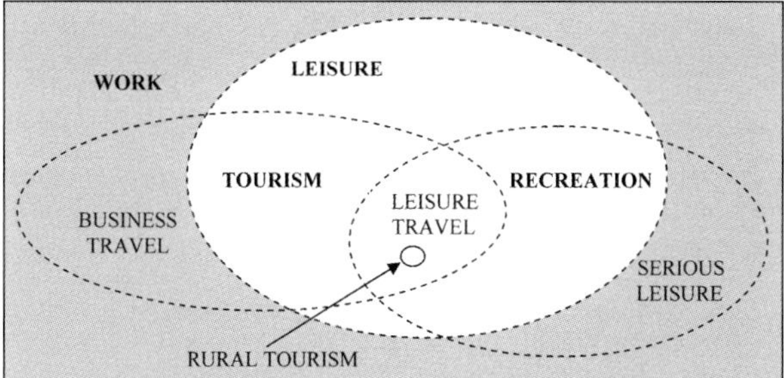

Figure 10.1. Relationship between leisure, recreation and tourism. Source: adopted from C. M. Hall and S. J. Page, 1999 (with authors modification),

According to UNEP, income from world rural tourism in 2006 amounted to over $150 billion, which is close to one-third of total tourism receipts (Makarenko, 2007). By estimation of the European Union Council of Tourism Development in Europe there are 200,000 farm and country tourism operators in Europe that offer over 2 million beds, give employment for 500,000 people and provide annual turnover of 26 billion euro (Makarenko, 2007) statistical survey shows that 35% of EU urban dwellers prefer to spend their holidays in rural areas. Their share is particularly high in the Netherlands – 49% (Biblioteka tourisma, 2010).

From Adventures to Ecotourism and Agriculture

Agrotourism is one of the sustainable forms of land use in rural areas . In the western part of the Baltic Sea region it is most commonly referred to as "agro-tourism" or "farm tourism", in the eastern part "village tourism" or "rural tourism". The place of rural tourism in the system of such definitions as leisure-tourism-recreation is somewhere inside the "leisure travel" zone, defined by C.M. Hall and S.J. Page (1999) (Figure 10.1) .

Rural tourism and agrotourism are almost synonyms. If by "rural tourism" we usually refer to tourism and recreation activities undertaken in rural areas and the arena for that is the whole countryside, for agrotourism the main component would be the agro-landscape. Jansen-Verbeke and Nijmegen (1990) used even more precise specification as "directly connected with the agrarian environment, agrarian products or agrarian stays".

Agrotourism is considered to be an alternative tourism due to its "individual oriented" approach and as an "alternative" ratio to the "mass tourism" which got a lot of

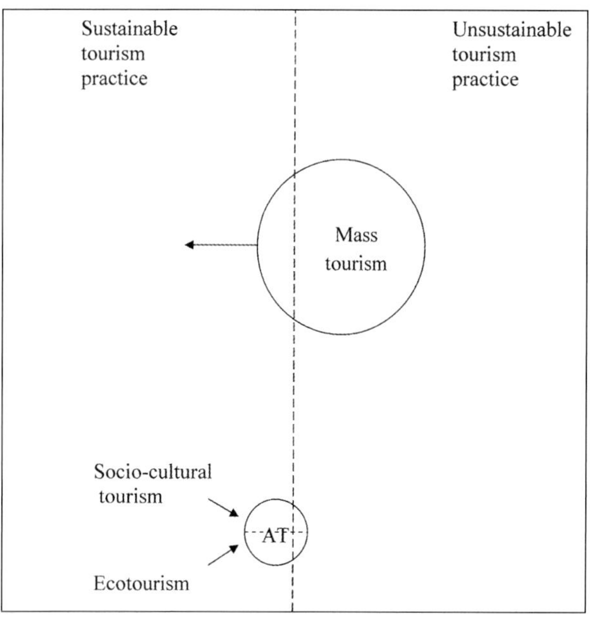

Figure 10.2. Tourism relationships. Source: Adopted from Butler 1996 in Weaver (ed. David A. Fennel (1999), p. 27).

criticism during the last decade. There could be both sustainable and unsustainable forms of agrotourism, though the sphere of our interest lies in the "sustainable zone" similar to the alternative tourism (AT) (Figure 10.2). We could not, however, completely agree with Butler's approach according to which ecotourism is placed between sustainable and unsustainable practices, since the main principle of ecotourism is sustainability.

Trying to find similarities between the different nature-oriented types of tourism David A.Fennel (2003) says that "Alternative Tourism includes, for example, rural or farm tourism, where a large portion of the touristic experience is founded upon the cultural milieu" of the farms. Ecotourism, on the other side, is more dependent upon nature and natural resources, which is the the main motivation for travelling. The description of Ecotourism by David A. Fennell and Ross K. Dowling (2003), who argues that it "is seen as ecologically and socially responsible, and as fostering environmental appreciation and awareness. It is based on the enjoyment of nature with minimal environmental impact", fits well into agrotourism too. But one could go further and affirm that if speaking about ecotourism we bear in mind nature, culture and education (and the importance of each of these three components is in the same order) - the socio-cultural influence is not of less importance then the nature and even sometimes plays the leading role as far as the "hosts"/owners of the farm are concerned.

Moreover, the interaction between tourists and nature mostly happens through these "hosts". In ecotourism the education is mostly directed towards information, whereas in agrotourism education is provided through active involvement of the guest/tourists into the day-to-day life of the inhabitants of the countryside, including participation in cultural and traditional village-events, obtaining crafts skills etc. "The educational elements of ecotourism , which enhances understanding of nature environments and ecological processes, distinguishes it from adventure travel and sightseeing…" (Fennell and Dowling, 2003). The same could be said about agrotourism. Rural tourism is more predictable and safe compared to adventure tourism.

So, even if rural tourism differs from ecotourism, socio-cultural tourism, adventure and events tourism it has some common features with them (Figure 10.3). It is a separate type of tourism but it includes some features and activities inherent to ecotourism, socio-cultural tourism and adventure tourism.

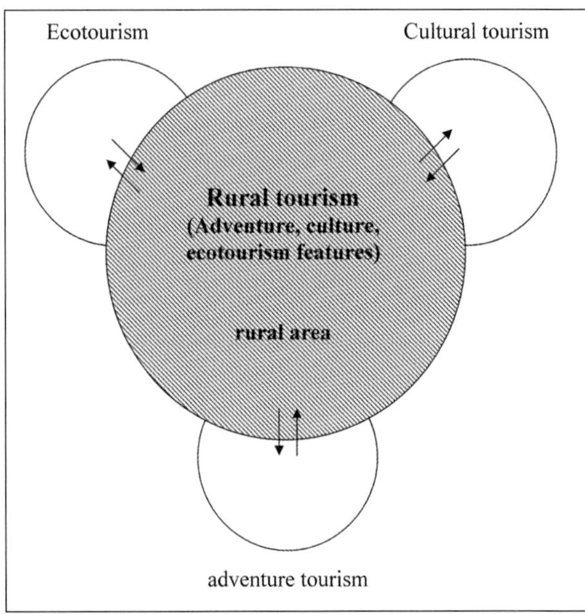

Figure 10.3. Rural tourism in the system of Alternative Tourism. Source: Adapted from David A. Fennell (2003), p. 32 (With authors modifications).

The Wide Content of Rural Tourism

Agrotourism consists of services provided by the farm: accommodation, meal, entertainments and other activities dependent on the possibilities of the farm and clients' demands. To provide that kind of services the following components are required:

- Attractive landscape,
- Farm/mansion house (as accommodation and activity facility),
- Farmland (plot of land attached to a house),
- Subsidiary plot,
- Landlord (farmer),
- Guests (agrotourists),
- Others (domestic animal buildings, garages, camping grounds, apiary, vegetable garden, agricultural fields, pastures, forestry areas etc.)

Moreover, agrotourism is not just accommodation of the tourists in the mansion house, but the functioning the whole set of functioning infrastructure such as proper transport communication between settlements, places for entertainment, natural or historical and cultural sights, information centers, restaurants, cafés, taverns, handicrafts workshops etc. Besides, the guest in the agrotourism is "guest" and he/she demands "home" ("family") comfort and personal attitude.

The agro-industrial complex and agrotourism activities are interconnected. Agrotourism activities depend on the peculiarities of the agro-sphere developed in the territory (Figure 10.4).

The rural area itself gives a wide range of opportunities for the interesting and active leisure, such as picnicking, herbs, berries and mushroom picking, hunting, cycling, , fishing, swimming, canoeing, campaigning, animal and bird watching, hiking, biking, nature studying, photography; By its term the farm as tourist accommodation facility opens the following options:

- gastronomic tourism;
- buying souvenirs;

- cooking;
- conservation (juice, jam etc.);
- spa treatments including sauna baths;
- participation in the rural life style etc.

Agrotourism May Contribute to Economic, Social and Environmental Development

The role of agrotourism for sustainable development of the Baltic Sea region could be viewed at three regional levels: economic, social and environmental.

Economically the image of the BSR rural area as nature-oriented with a wide range of activities (including accommodation) will increase the number of tourists in the region with the purpose of agrotourism , as will the number of days tourists stay (on average 3-5 days). This will improve the economy of the farmers and local communities in general with limited investments.

Constant improvement of service quality and the development of small and medium-size business through the introduction of environmental management will improve the quality of tourism. As the tourism industry has a multiplier effect in the economy, it will contribute to the development of other sectors of the economy in the region and promote a balanced development of the region in general. A new attitude towards agriculture has already developed and the process is going on.With increasing employment (first of all for women) in rural areas; the continuous migration from rural to urban areas could be halted; additionally, the visual environment of farms and villages will improve.

The quality of life is improved by the development of infrastructure and related industries, crucial for the local population. The infrastructure includes transportation, communications, domestic and social ("soft") infrastructure (health facilities, information centers, clubs, etc.) and is used to satisfy the needs of local population and the economy. A great number in the local population will be motivated to have better education through their involvement into the tourism activities. Private businesses will be started up.

Agrotourism development supports historical cultures and traditions in the region and the revitalization of the traditional handicrafts. By that it also serves the protection of the historical heritage of the region.

The development of agrotourism demands proper ecological conditions. The population where tourism activities are planned realize the necessity to protect nature and the landscape.

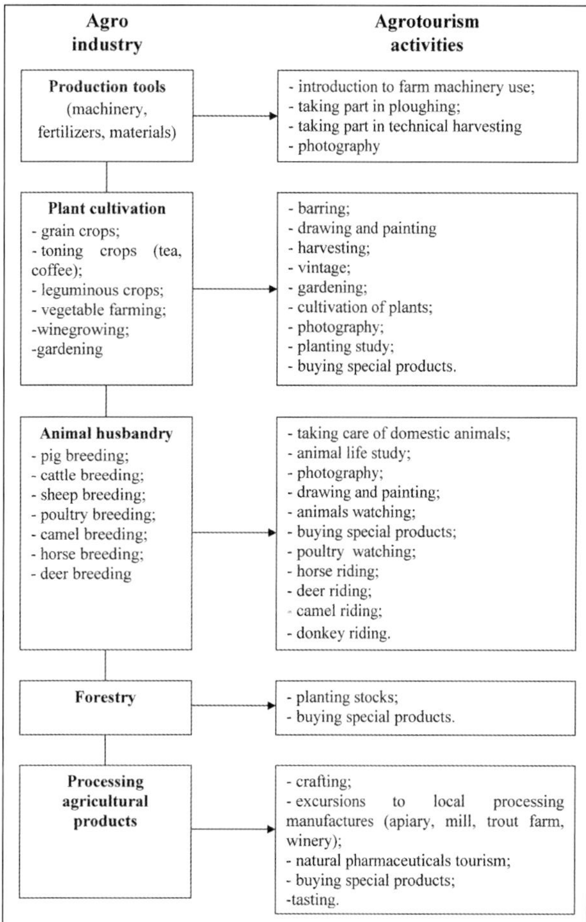

Figure 10.4. Interconnection between the agro-industrial complex and agrotourism activities.

Improving environmental conditions and promoting sustainable development is possible through monitoring, development of environmental management and ecotourism, development of ecological trails in sustainable environmental management, sharing of experiences and technologies through international projects, and the active participation of NGOs and universities and other institutions of environmental education.

Well managed agrotourism will require less material resources per unit of product value and will result in "softening" of the external impact on the environment

Environmental education takes place during excursions to nature and entertainment with close interaction with nature. Agrotourism could relieve overcrowded tourist destinations from overpopulation, when the distribution of tourists becomes more even in the area.

Rural Tourism in the Baltic Sea Region

Three Types of Countries

In the Baltic Sea region it is possible to distinguish three types of countries with different level of agrotourism development: Germany, Denmark, Sweden and Finland are the pioneers in this sphere. Secondly, Poland, Lithuania, Estonia and Latvia are actively adopting their experience and trying to be integrated in this system, enter the existing organizations and create their own ones. Thirdly, rural tourism development in Russia, Belarus and Ukraine is still in its initial stage of development with Kaliningrad and St Petersburg areas being the most developed so far.

Germany, Finland, Sweden and Denmark

The leader among the Baltic Sea countries in receiving tourists is Germany. There are about 20 000 farmsteads in the country and the German Agricultural Society (DLG) has been established. Around 1400 hosts in the entire country of Germany are awarded with the quality label of the DLG: "Urlaub auf dem Bauernhof" ("farm holiday"), "Urlaub auf dem Winzerhof" ("vineyard holiday") and "Landurlaub"("countryside holiday") (Bauernhof Urlaub Deutschland, 2010).

In Finland a holiday in small rural houses for 2 to 8 people is popular. The houses are equipped with everything necessary in relation to their size and desired living standard. This provides an opportunity for a comfortable holiday at a nice place close to, for instance, a pure lake having all kinds of amenities available (microwave, TV, etc.). This branch of tourism is a well-organized industry that offers services both to domestic and foreign tourists (Tourism Business No 6, 1998). Not only individual farm owners but also big players enter the service market. One of them is Lomarengas Ab Ltd, Finnish Country Holidays, which offers more than 4,000 classified holiday cottages with a minimum rent for one week (500-2000 euro) (Kommedschi. Otdich i Finlandij, 2010)

As an example it is possible to withdraw the "Green Triangle" - it is a tourist zone that unites 13 communes from Turku, along both sides of the historic road Härkäti, and to Häme. "Straw gallery", "Atelier of jewels and stones", and "Sculpture park" located here are evidence of sound cultural traditions and lively creativeness. "Black" sauna and golf courses, motor tracks and horse-riding "compete" here. Tourists can choose between accommodation standards from "a five-star farm" to a space outdoors under a shed" (Tourismitjeskij Katalog, 2001).

In Sweden rural tourism is also popular. There are about 500 farmsteads in Sweden (2002), which serve approximately 170,000 tourists annually. A holiday in Swedish rural areas is attractive among foreign tourists mostly to Danes, Norwegians and Germans. For example, in the catalogue of rural tourism in the Swedish south-eastern province of Blekinge there are 38 accommodation units, plenty of restaurants, museums and sights, small shops, service sector institutions, information and leisure centres. Some farms are also equipped to provide health resort treatments (Rural tourism Blekinge, 2000).

The catalogues of Danish tour operators has a rural tourism (agrotourism) section which provide holidays on Danish farms. A specialized agency is ready to find a suitable offer for a rural holiday (Birschakov, 1999).

Latvia, Poland and Lithuania

In early 1990s there were only 20 Latvian farmstead owners engaged in rural tourism. In 2002 there were over 180 of them. The most active entrepreneurs joined into the rural tourism association Lauku ceļotājs ("Rural tourist"). Information on rural tourism is available in catalogues and on the Internet. However, the list of activities is not very long. Some local governments support actively those entrepreneurs, who develop this sector. Tax policy is also liberal to them (Blumental, 2010).

According to the Ministry of agriculture there are 10,000 farms welcoming tourists in Poland and their occupancy rate reaches 80%. According to the data provided by the Polish Ministry of Agriculture and Food Economy, 80% of Polish farmlands is not polluted with harmful heavy metals (Oleszek et al 2010). This is a significant argument in favor of choosing a rural holiday.

Figure 10.5. Excursion on horseback in beautiful Latgale, Latvia. Source: www.adventureride.eu

Mazuria, a picturesque land of lakes and forests in Poland, offers over 55 beds on agrotourism farms. Guests can take part in field works along with host families, go fishing or hunting, ride a bicycle in the surroundings, and gather berries or mushrooms.

Poland is a member of the European Center for Ecological and Agricultural Tourism (ECEAT) which operates actively across the country. The organization's activities are aimed at supporting organic farming through ecotourism development. ECEAT-Poland offers various forms of accommodation on organic farms across the country. Furthermore, the organization represents the international foundation ECEAT, established in Amsterdam and cooperating with 23 ECEAT member countries (Lopata, 2010). This cooperation provides opportunities for Polish farmers to welcome foreign tourists, and for Polish tourists to have a holiday on a farm abroad. Some farmers managed to improve the economic outcomes of their activities considerably after having changed to ecologically clean (organic) farming. Tourists, who buy food from them during their holiday, often become regular customers.

It is important to distinguish between farms, where lands are cultivated with traditional methods, i.e. use of chemicals, and organic (ecologically clean) farms that meet ECEAT criteria. Organic farms apply ecological methods without any use of fertilizers or pesticides and 50% of food products offered to tourists are produced on the farm. Moreover, it is expected that these farms pay particular attention to the protection of the environment by saving water and energy, practices sorting of waste fractions and invest in the introduction of clean technologies. These farms usually also commit themselves to the use of natural local material, keep traditions, and invest in farm development. ECEAT provides training for those farmers who want to engage in organic farming. If a farm meets the standards of the Polish Association of Organic Farming (PTRE) or the Association of Ecological Food Producers (Ekoland) it can become a participant of the ECEAT-Poland ecotourism programme.

Abundance and diverse nature of some Lithuanian regions in addition to cultural heritage sites create favorable conditions for development of rural tourism in this country. These services become more and more popular among urban dwellers. Rural tourism develops into a satellite business for villages and gives opportunity to get 30-40% revenue. It is a significant field of tourism development in the region.

In Lithuania with the population of 3 million people about 680 farmsteads have been officially registered. About 30% of them are annually renovated. In 2006 there were 189,1 thousand agrotourists in Lithuania, which is 36,8% more than in 2005 (130 thousand people). It is notable that this kind of tourism is popular in autumn and winter as well. Thus, in December 2006 more than 16,000 guests spent their holidays in rural farmsteads, which is 34,2% more than the year before.

Many farms presented in catalogues offer their services in organizing conferences and seminars. However, lodging conditions in the places willing to offer these services are not adequate to the standards and investments are needed. Consumers of these services are holiday-makers from CIS countries. Rural residents are not ready to receive tourists because of lack of practice (language and communication barriers) and business skills (Augulavitje, 2000).

Researchers of Klaipeda University held a survey "Ecological farming and rural tourism as alternative activities for rural population in Western Lithuania". It showed that Klaipeda and Silute have the most favourable conditions for rural tourism (Eidukeviciene 2001).

The catalogue "Holiday in rural Lithuania 2001" contains 29 rural tourism establishments. 21 of them are in Klaipeda, 1 is in Kretinge and 7 are in Silute. In the catalogue the establishments are referred to the following types of rural tourism: 39% ethnographic, 15% modern with ethnographic elements, 23% modern, 23% other types.

Rural tourism development experiences of Sweden and Finland, having similar climate and nature, is particularly useful for the northern regions of Northwest Federal District of Russia (NWFD). For residents of the Kaliningrad region of NWFD, experiences of Germany and Poland and to some extent of Lithuania and Latvia are more relevant since Kaliningrad region shares its history as well as its natural and geographical characteristics with these more southern and coastal-near countries.

Developing Agrotourism in North-West Russia

North-West Russia

Rural tourism development in Russia is currently in its initial stage. That is why it is still not possible to find the organized statistic data for this type of tourism. Rural tourism can be referred more modestly to as "rural hospitality". It is, probably, even more correct from historic point of view, as Russian people always have been distinguished by their hospitality (Platnova, 2012).

North-West Federal District of Russia consists of 11 administrative units where the following tourism development zones are outlined.

- "The Heart of Russia": the Leningrad, Pskov, Novgorod regions,
- "The Russian North": the Arkhangelsk, Murmansk, Vologda regions, the Republic of Komi, the Republic of Karelia, the Nenets Autonomous District,
- "The Baltic coast": the Kaliningrad region,
- St.-Petersburg.

The overall area is of the North-West Federal District of Russia is 1,687,000 km2. The population is 14,600,000 (including St.-Petersburg - 4,700,000). According to the survey held within the framework of the project «North-West Russia: New Windows on Russia» the annual number of tourists visiting the region is 10-12 million. Rural tourism is one of the priorities for development of the region.

The main prerequisites of rural tourism development in this vast territory situated in various climate zones and with differing levels of urbanization are diverse unique landscapes that are not affected by urbanization, intensive agricultural production or other similar activities. At the same time there are limitations for tourism and agrotourism development such as the high sensitivity of many ecosystems in Russia to antropogenic influence, their fragility in districts attractive to tourists due to their "wild" nature or aboriginal household patterns.

Conditions for Tourism Development

Factors influencing agrotourism development can be divided into two groups: physical and geographic factors and social and economic factors. The list of resources offered by Cubb and Cubb (Cubb and Cubb, 1981) (Fennell and Dowling, 2003) for recreation in the nature can be extended, adapted and referred to as physical and geographic factors of rural tourism development in Northwest Russia (Table 10.1).

Social and Economic Factors

Another reason for the development of modern rural tourism is the agricultural crisis. Farming is replaced by agribusiness, and mechanization and modernizing change rural reality to a great extent. In many European rural regions agriculture actually stopped being the most important form of land use and activity of rural communities. (Vidy-turizma, 2010)

Therefore, even though physico-geographic characteristics are significant, rural tourism development is also directly dependent on social and economic conditions. Table 10.2 shows the examination of these factors in the Northwestern region of Russia.

Thus, we come to a conclusion that the highest level of rural tourism development has been reached in the Leningrad and Kaliningrad regions, and the Republic of Karelia. It became possible due to favourable physical and geographic as well as social and economic con-

Table 10.1. Physiographic factors influencing agrotourism development in North-West Russia

Social and economic factors of rural tourism development	Examination of North-West Russia
Small- and medium-scale farms capable of receiving tourists	At present every fourth resident of NWFD lives in rural area. Almost half of agricultural products is produced on farms and private auxiliary plots. About 300 rural households specialize in receiving tourists. In over 1000 settlements people are willing to start receiving tourists in their rural houses.
Development of traditional activities	Ethnic settlements (Russian, Pomorian, Karelian, Nenets, Lappish and Komi), northern folk crafts centres in Kargopol, Velikiy Ustuyg, Kholmogory, Kirishi, etc. People belonging to indigenous ethnic groups (Vepsians, Votes, Izhory, Ingrians) live in the territory and preserve traditional way of life and crafts. Main traditional folk crafts are weaving, embroidery, lace making, Velikoustyugskaya niello, carving and birch bark painting, bone carving, ornamental metal working.
Favourable institutional conditions for development of small and medium-sized business in rural areas	In the Federal special purpose programme "Social development until 2010" the objective of developing agrotourism is stated (section 3.6). "Establishing a territorial network of information and consulting centres, promoting agrotourism, and training for rural population on organizing non-agricultural activities for alternative employment in rural areas" are planned. A Law of the Kaliningrad region "On tourist activities in the Kaliningrad region" (regulation and promotion of rural and ecological tourism) is in place. NGOs have been established with the aim of rural tourism development (public association of farmstead owners has been established to coordinate development of rural tourism in the Republic of Karelia, "Rural tourism club" in the Leningrad region)
Cultural and entertainment events	There are tourist products "New Year on the Mill on the Chernaya river", "Christmas and in the green forest" (Luga district), "New Year with an ostrich" (Vyborg district), participation in Ivan Kupala Day celebrations (Feast of St. John the Baptist), development of tourist routes in historic villages, visiting wild geese staging area.
Trained human resource (household owners), having knowledge of basics of hospitality	In the Leningrad region the programme "School of rural tourism" has been established (work with rural population, information centres' staff, and officials involved in the agroindustrial sector, environmental protection and tourism). Regular seminars "Rural tourism development" are organized and involve visiting functioning guest houses, owners share their experiences, a number of Russian editions aimed at hospitality skills training were published. "Organization of rural tourism" published in 2003 in Kaliningrad is one of them. Study visits to Finland, Lithuania, Poland, Sweden and Irelands are organized to explore successful experiences of rural tourism development.
Development of additional kinds of tourism (sports, cultural and cognitive, adventure, and ecological tourism).	NW RUssia has a substantial potential for development of sightseeing and cognitive tourism, ethnic and event tourism. Cultural heritage is represented by archeological sites, ethnic settlements, ancient towns, craft villages, famous architectural ensembles, cult objects, old family estates. Abundant natural resources of the region provide the necessary prerequisites for development of water, sports, recreation tourism, adventure (hunting, fishing, rafting, boating, catamaranning, etc.) youth tourism, "weekend getaways", development of cruise routes and cycling routes.
Development of associated activities	Deer breeding, vegetable farming, flax growing, dairy cattle husbandry, pig breeding, poultry breeding, butter-making. Developing traditional activities is of particular significance.
Favourable social environment safe for tourists	Standard requirements to rural houses used for tourist accommodation and requirements to services rendered in this kind of accommodation establishments (the Leningrad region) have been developed; Principles and guidelines for rendering tourist services have been defined (the Kaliningrad and Leningrad regions, the Republic of Karelia); Recommendations for organizing rural tourism have been elaborated (the Kaliningrad and Leningrad regions, the Republic of Karelia); A catalogue of rural farms capable of receiving guests has been made (the Kaliningrad and Leningrad regions, the Republic of Karelia); Training manuals on rural tourism have been developed (the Kaliningrad and Leningrad regions, the Republic of Karelia); Tourist information centres have been established. The centres provide information about rural holiday options (the network of tourism information centres in the Leningrad region, Tourism information centre in the Kaliningrad region).

Table 10.2. Social and economic factors influencing agrotourism development in North-West Russia

Physical and geographic factors for the development of rural tourism	Conditions in North-West Russia
Geographic location	The area occupies northern and western territories of European Russia. The district has access to the Baltic and Barents seas, part of it is washed by the waters of the Arctic ocean. An ancient "Trade route from the Varagians to the Greeks", where Novgorodian Rus emerged, spread along the district's rivers and lakes. St. Petersburg is deemed to be the cultural capital of Russia. The district borders Finland, Norway, Poland, Lithuania, Estonia, and Latvia. The area has good transport connections: a well-developed net of railway and automobile roads, air connection, navigation, and ferries.
Climate and weather.	The climate is moderately continental, and on the coast it is marine. Bioclimatic conditions of the area are diverse. In the west they are comfortable (cold-temperate winters and warm summers), while in the north winters are severe and summers are temperately warm.
Topography and landforms.	Landscapes are quite diverse: from marine on the Baltic coast (in the Kaliningrad region) to mountain in Karelia and the Kola Peninsula. It provides conditions for development of various kinds of tourism: mountain tourism, rock climbing, rafting, hiking, equestrian tourism, recreational, ecological and rural tourism. Most of rural farms are situated on plains. The agriculture specializes in production of vegetables, potatoes, and flax, dairy cattle husbandry, pig, poultry and deer breeding. Butter production is well-developed.
Surface materials	Soil structures are diverse: from podzolic and peatbog in the north to soddy slightly-podzolic on noncalcerous moraine and brown forest soils in the west. The district is rich in minerals. Granite, marble, iron and colour ores, bauxite, wolfram, molybdenum and others are extracted. 90% of the world's amber are centred in the Kaliningrad region.
Water	North-West Russia differs from the rest of the territory in increased number of water bodies and has the highest number of lakes. Most lakes are situated in Karelia and the Russian Plain. There are over 7 thousand lakesThe extensive net of rivers (Neva, Svir, Pechora, Mezen, Onega, Northern Dvina) connected by navigation canals (Volgo-Baltijskij and Belomorsko-Baltijskij) provides conditions for development of water tourism and cruise tourism with possibilities to make stops in rural households. Special place of the Baltic Sea coast, the Curonian and Vistula lagoons allows to combine rural and recreational (health resort) tourism.
Vegetation	Large part of the area is covered with forests rich in berries (blueberries, raspberries, foxberries, bilberries, cranberries, blackberries) and mushrooms (yellow boletus, honey mushroom, cep, aspen mushroom, brown cap boletus). The following natural zones are represented: tundra, forest-tundra, taiga, mixed coniferous-broad-leaved forests. There are also small areas of broad-leaved forests in the Kaliningrad region which is the westernmost zone of Europe where they grow.
Fauna	There are plenty of sanctuaries and nature reserves in the district. There are 6 national parks. Forests are rich in fur animals, pine forest and wader birds. Hunting, fishing, and deer breeding are traditional activities of the local population.
Ecological conditions	Ecological condition of the environment is relatively steady. This is a favourable factor for rural and ecological tourism development. Exceptions are local polluted areas around large cities or industrial hubs.

ditions. Programmes for rural tourism in these regions have been developed, catalogues of rural estates are published (Figure 10.6), standards for receiving tourists and rendering services developed, associations of agrofarmers and rural tourism information centres established.

The level of rural tourism development in the Novgorod, Pskov, and Vologda regions may be defined as middle and lower middle. Weak integration processes, lack of a single regulating authority, fragmented character of the rendered services, and weak support by local authorities are the factors determining this state of rural tourism. The Arkhangelsk and Murmansk regions, the Republic of Komi and the Nenets Autonomous District have less favourable climatic conditions and are remote potential clients and, therefore, are regions with a low level of rural tourism development. Ecological and adventure tourism is more developed in these regions.

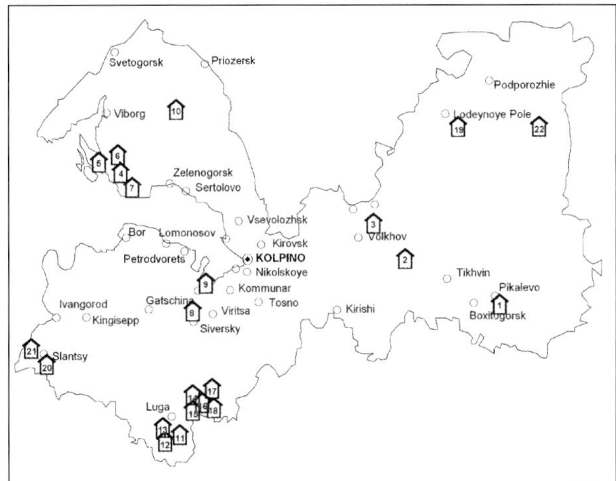

Figure 10.6. Distribution of the agrotourism farms in the Leningrad region. Source:Adapted from Catalogue of the countryside hostels, Project A way home – tourism in the countryside of Leningrad region, 2009

Recommendations for the Agrotourism Development in the North-West Russia

In the sphere of administration: to support the organizations dealing with agrotourism, including small private enterprises (guides, small guest-houses' owners etc.), NGOs etc., elaboration of programmes of agrotourism development and financial support from the government at all levels; formation of a data-base of agrotourism farms, lands and resources;

From the organizational point of view: to support construction/renovation and market entry for the new farmers converting their activities into agrotourism, to develop the concept on involvement of the new areas into the agrotourism activities by development of the infrastructure (for instance, on the development of the tourism potential of the Vistula spit); development of associations and chains of agorotourism enterprises.

In the sphere of education and research: to improve the regional system of education, retraining and life-long learning for the tourism industry (with special accent on ecological and sustainable tourism, especially in the rural areas and for the whole families; to provide research in the sphere of agrotourism, ecological and sustainable tourism; to organize international work-shops on exchange of experience in the sphere of agrotourism; to increase the ecological education of the local population; best-practice dissemination; explore and make an inventory of agrotourism resources (similar to other tourism resources);

In the sphere of marketing: to create the "nature-oriented" image of the North-West Russia in media; to open municipal agrotourism information centers; to support the creation of tour-operators "specialized" on agrotourism; to promote North-West Russia in the whole Baltic Sea region tourism market;

In the ecological sphere: to provide nature protection and nature preservation measures. Special attention should be paid to the unique natural objects.

It is important to pay special attention to "ecological tourism" infrastructure development. For example, when constructing bicycle roads' net some of the tourist routes should be more ecological (as ecological means of transportation will be used). Construction of wharfs at the Baltic Sea coasts at the Curonian and Vistula lagoons, and the Gulf of Finland will open nature objects not accessible by land for tourism.

In the sphere of finance, the financing of all these ideas should be supported from federal, regional and municipal sources as well as from sources of tourism companies interested in the development of the domestic and incoming tourism; the support of the agrotourism projects for instance through the Cross Border Cooperation Programme within European Neighbourhood and Partnership Instrument 2007-2013.

Therefore, for NW Russia the next step in the development of rural tourism and territories suitable for it is the elaboration of common standards, and an integrated set of catalogues, and the establishment of a common authority for rural tourism promotion in Northwest Russia aimed at creating a common information space in the Baltic Sea region.

Agrotourism in the Kaliningrad Region of Russian Federation.

The main accommodation facilities in agrotourism are country estates. Currently there are about 60 (400 beds) of those in the Kaliningrad region. They are distributed unevenly, mainly in coastal area, in Polessk and Nesterovsk districts (Vyshtenets lake) (Figure 10.7). They accommodate 1,500 holiday-makers annually (according to expert assessment the number is even around 4,500 tourists annually) (Otdel Turisma, 2010). Prevalent are internal

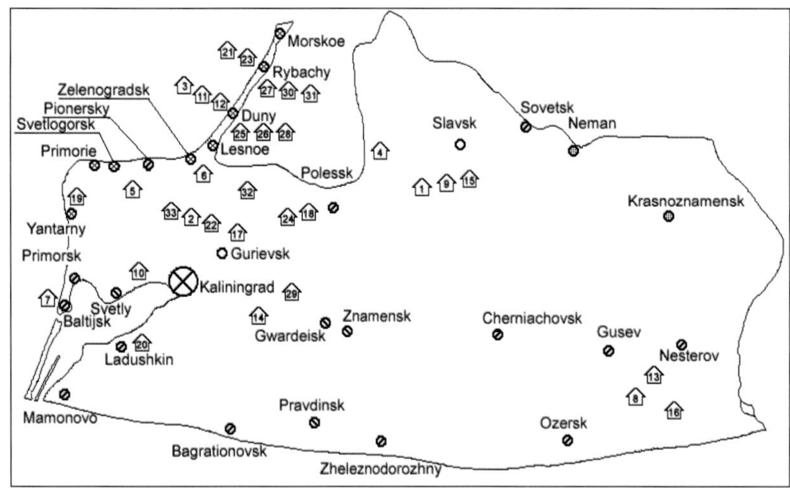

Figure 10.7. Distribution of the agrotourism farms in the Kaliningrad region. Source: Organization of agrotourism // Teachers guidebook. Kaliningrad: KGU, 2003. - 115 pgs., (co-authors N.Desiatova, V.Korneevetz)(in Russian)

tourists and visitors from other Russian regions (Moscow and the Moscow region, St.-Petersburg and the Leningrad region), as well as German residents.

In the summer of 2005 the Kaliningrad State University organized a poll to investigate the possibilities of agrotourism development in the area. In the diagram the answers on the question on the most preferred activities at the farm are presented (Figure 10.8). The analysis of the results indicates that women prefer the picking of the berries and mushrooms, and men – prefer above all fishing.

Here are the most interesting examples, of agrotourism in the Kaliningrad region.

Guests staying in "Zaeza" peasant farm (Nesterov district, village Ozerki) can take part in agricultural works, take care of animals, go mushrooming and berry picking, or enjoy homemade delicacies in addition to communicating with animals, getting to know how to use agricultural tools and machinery, or how to grow ecologically clean products.

"Flora world" estate museum (Gurjevsk dictrict, village Egorjevskoe) is unique in its home "botanic garden", where guests can look at an extensive collection of berry and ornamental crops, have advice on growing technologies or expansion of best berry varieties. The estate offers one-day tour, catering service included (buffet, barbecue) (Travel catalogue for tourism in Kaliningrad Region, 2009).

"Klyuken" country estate (Zelenogradsk district) is a child leisure centre. Children get unique opportunity of intense language training in addition to having outdoor rest and entertainment, and learn horse riding. Foreign native-speaking students are engaged in training. Catering is provided with ecologically clean products bought from the neighbouring farms. The hostess can share old Russian recipes for Russian stove.

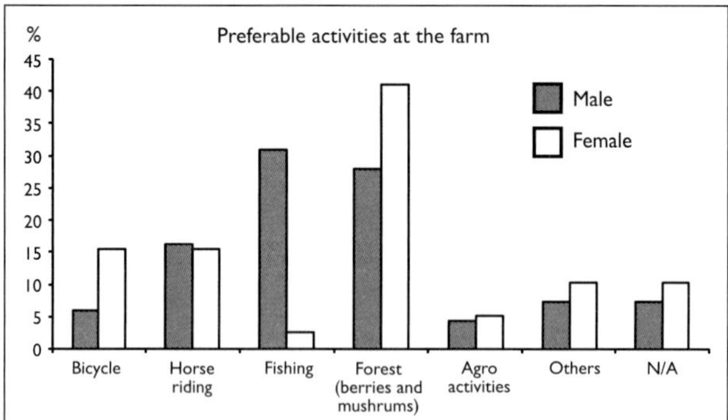

Figure 10.8. Preferable activities in the farm for male and female tourists (results of poll conducted in the Kaliningrad region, 2005)

The most sustainable form of agrotourism is the agropark. An agropark is a sustainable form of tourism in a rural area, comprising a territory with special mode of land use (with nature conservation functions prioritized). Several agrofarms have accommodation of rural recreants, and agrocentres with an extensive network of social sphere institutions and maintenance facilities.

Urbanisation and Urban-Rural Cooperation

11

Per G Berg
Swedish University of Agricultural Sciences, Uppsala, Sweden
Lars Rydén
Uppsala University, Uppsala, Sweden

An Urban-Rural Civilisation History

..."But in the agri-urban landscape of the pre-Hispanic Maya"....." food consumed in the city was also largely produced in the city. Since it minimizes transport energy costs, the agro-urban landscape is an efficient way of producing food"...
..."In fact, the data from the Maya lowlands indicate quite decisively that agricultural production is not the antithesis of urbanism, but to the contrary – and no less provocatively – an urban function."

[From the final report of the research project *The Urban Mind – Cultural and Environmental Dynamics* (Sinclair et al. eds.) investigating the pre-historic roots of the city – published by Uppsala University 2011]

The Roots of Urbanisation

Today it is clear that the fossil fuelled *urbanization* is one of the main drivers of global change (UNHabitat, 2007; IGBP, 2004; Aleklett, 2008). Also a massive depopulation and decomposition of *local rural functions* and *livelihoods* – and the effects of the modern industrialized agriculture – adds to severe planetary reverberations: more frequent droughts, floods, changes in atmospheric concentrations of gases and greater variations in temperature and moisture across the planet (IGBP, 2004). A common denominator for this development is an ongoing *separation of urban and rural* development. This separation is partly geographical and physical – as a quite recent breach in the place-bound co-evolution of urban and rural systems (Saifi & Drake, 2007). The separation is also partly functional and conceptual as our civilization has now lost its overview, control and understanding of resilient life support (food, fuel and fibre) and its relation to present human culture.

During practically all of its 7,000-years of history – since the foundation of Eridu, Ur and other early urban-like settlements around Euphrates and Tigris in present Iraq – the cities of the world were always closely intertwined with agricultural-, fisheries- and herding ecosystems. And through the millennia – old cities and conglomerates of Neolithic villages in pre-historic Americas, in ancient Turkey, along the Nile, by the Indus delta and in early Yangtze cultures – the urban and rural were perceptionally, geographically and functionally integrated – hence featuring the fundamental essence of a sustainable urban principle (Sinclair et al. 2011; Hyams, 1976). Even during modern time's industrialization, our current city cultures were in principle physically co-evolving with its life-support hinterlands and micro-regions (Saifi & Drake, 2007). The full separation of urban and rural has mainly been a post-modern invention of the last 60 years – through globalized markets for labour, food, fibres, fuel and minerals. And even more: this current time era with food specialization and extreme international trade now may have reached its peak. And the necessary *sustainability transition* in our current civilisation – fuelled by the climate-, environmental- and resource crises of the globe – today features a modern re-integration of urban and rural structures (Saifi & Drake, 2007; Gaffron et al. 2005; Itoh, 2003).

In an envisioned more robust future human culture, *the cities* will probably not be exclusively urban, but also encompass rural functions and a high consciousness about its life-support systems (Gaffron et al.,2008). For new rural human habitats – reformed for global survival – *the countryside* will most possibly link more efficiently to urban communication, urban transport systems and urban culture. Such partly new human habitats may be called *Resilient Citylands* (see below and Berg, 2010).

In this chapter we will discuss the process of urbanization as well as how cities and its surrounding rural landscape depend on each other and how their interaction is important - even crucial - for sustainable development.

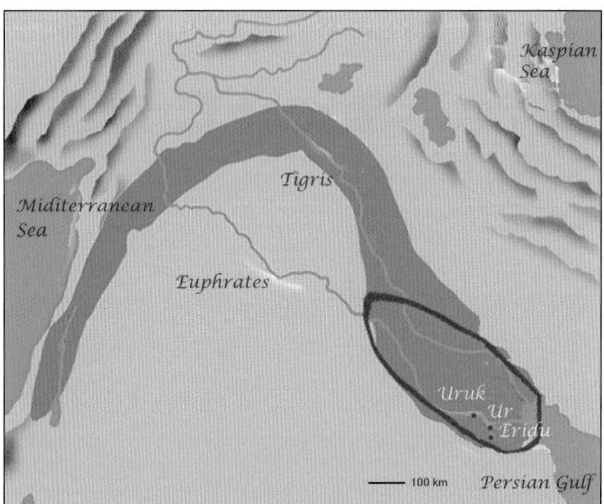

Figure 11.1. The Green Crescent in Mesopotamia by Euphrates and Tigris in Current Iraq. Three of the many cities in the ancient Sumerian state are considered by archeologists as some of the oldest urban formations in the world – Eridu is estimated to be 7,000 years old. Note that the cities were directly linked to the river and its fertile river delta landscapes. Map developed and edited by Per G Berg

Urban-rural Co-generation Until Second World War and After

During its 250-year history probably starting with Coalbrookdale in Western England – newly industrialized cities received its basic life support from its embedding productive fields, forests and waters. The industry cities grew initially along railway settlements as star rays into the surrounding landscape (Carstensen, 1992, Hall, 1988; Geddes, 1904). In the opposite direction, fibre- and energy yielding forest-, productive farmland- and fish-rich water landscapes reached inward towards the centre of cities in the form of green-blue wedges. The urban and rural interlocked structures were *co-evolving* all the way until the beginning of the 1930-ies in central Europe and until the 1950-ies in the Nordic countries (Berg, 2010; Saifi & Drake, 2007, Helmfrid, 1994; Carstensson, 1992). Already in the beginning of the 20-th century attempts were made in England to extract the magic, the labour markets and the cultural excellence out of the unhealthy, coal smoke-stricken cities and combine it with the healthy nature outside the city in Ebenezer Howard's *garden city movement* (Howard, 1902). Even in our own time, in the most radical examples of emancipation of nature from the urban fabric – the American sub-division – was paradoxically created as an effect of human private cravings for *both* the city *and* nature (Mumford, 1961). As the continuous villa-mats spread out throughout the private motorism-fuelled and land-consuming suburbs – eradicating any natural- or cultivated landscapes – wealthy citizens a few decades later desperately sought the new frontier and started to settle in *edge-cities*, in the new urban fringe between wilderness and urban structures (Garreau, 1985).

The practice of intertwining built and green/blue structures is now gradually degraded in Nordic cities but in our time this is instead developing in central European cities: Stockholm's *green wedges* (Florgård, 2004) and Copenhagen's *green finger plan* is now inspiring Paris, London, Berlin, Rome and Barcelona to find a new integration between urban and rural: For the *health* and *recreation* of its citizens; for improving the *ecosystems services* and even increasingly for slowly expanding the *primary production* in, near and over the free land areas surrounding the city (Bokalders & Block, 2010; Egnor, 2009; Gaffron 2005; 2008; Bolunda & Hunhammar, 1999).

Primary Drivers and Dark Clouds of Urbanisation

The first urban structures were built as market places for food and commodities, trade and labour, business, and communication. Functionally the first cities were *densely populated* settlements and legally they became organizational entities with exclusive *rights*. Socio-politically they got the preconditions for the establishment of a military-protected ruling class, living on the primary production *surplus*, created by the farmers outside and the craftsmen inside the fortified towns. The densely populated towns, eventually nurtured emergent cultural systems and art (Sinclair et al. 2011; Ahlberg, 2005). Even today people and business move to cities to find jobs, trading partners and housing. And both the traditional and the new sustainable city with its mixed-use, short-distance, walkable structures – could save time, money and resources for travel and transport, service and cultural experiences (Gehl, 2010; Gaffron, 2005). Living in cities also permitted individuals and families to take advantage of its human diversity, excellence in art, traditions, the magic of the city, sports and education and of specialized market commodities (Alexander, 1977; Jacobs, 1961).

Through an efficient, egalitarian and democratic governance, cities may also deliver broad education to all its inhabitants, an inclusive participation in the development of communities, a high quality health care and other public and commersial services for all citizens and a versatile transit system. Inside the cities, commodities, convenience and culture may be exchanged more efficiently than in sparsely populated areas simply because of scale and proximity (Gehl, 2010; Bokalders & Block, 2010; Gaffron et al. 2005; 2008).

If this is the positive vision of the city, the reality in the world cities is however a growing slum formation, social degradation, violence, drug abuse, poor and unhealthy housing, decreasing job opportunities, car-invaded streets or long-distance uncomfortable travel to work. In the Baltic Sea region such problems are less prominent but the *suburban* problems typically include segregation, high unemployment and social unrest. The intrinsic drawbacks in *all modern urban areas* are also always a relative deficit of nature, clean air, healthy environments, ecosystem services and basic life support with energy, water, food and matter (Berg 2010; Bokalders & Block, 2010).

Figure 11.2. Ironbridge. The village Coalbrookdale in Shropshire in Great Britain, with its world heritage bridge built 1776-1779, is today a symbol and considered the cradle of industrialization in England and in the world. The preconditions were ideal for this early development – with iron ore mining in the area, a new method to produce coke from coal, and the river Severn flowing into to Bristol Channel. The surrounding landscape is a rich agricultural landscape providing the life support of the emerging industry population. Photo: Klara Livsey Berg

Moving To the Cities – the Modern Urbanisation History

Up to the end of the 19th century most people in the world lived in the countryside. With few exceptions cities were small compared to today and in 1900, even in Europe, they housed less than 15% of the population.

A wave of urbanisation started when growing industries needed a larger and specialized workforce in the beginning and middle of the 19th century (Mumford, 1961). The fastest growing cities were found along rivers and by coasts where transport were easier. With the development of railroads, industrial cities were established also inland. During the decades after the 2nd World War, a new wave of labour induced urbanization occurred in new "*sleeping*" suburbs (Alexander, 1977; Schorske, 1963).

After the 2nd world war, agriculture were increasingly industrialized and mechanized and needed less labour. In many countries, the farm size gradually increased and smaller farms were abandoned. In the West this development started already after the 1950s while it occurred much later in Central and Eastern Europe. Still in the early 1990s there were more than a million small farms in Poland (Kronenberg & Bergier, 2010; Maciejewski, 2002; Rydén et al. 2003).

Another strong driver for urbanization in the Baltic Sea region (BSR) was population growth. During the 19th century and up to the first World War, a growing part of the population couldn't find life support and therefore emigrated to the Americas, e.g. to the United States. After that the Baltic Sea region population roughly doubled during the 20th century – this time swallowed by the growing cities. From the 1990s the urban share of the population in the West has typically reached 85% while in the East just above 70% (Rydén, 2003; Kronenberg & Bergier, 2010). For the world, currently the largest wave of urban growth in human history is taking place. Since 2008, more than half of the world's population – 3.5 billion people – live in towns and cities. By 2030 the projections are 5 billion people in cities, mostly in Africa and Asia (UNHabitat, 2007).

For the Baltic Sea region the population dynamics is more complex: Some central large cities, e.g. Stockholm, StPetersburg and Warszaw grow steadily, whereas remote smaller towns and communities are depopulated (Hanell & Tornberg, 2007). Some cities, e.g. Riga, decrease in size as many leave to find jobs elsewhere. Urbanisation in the BSR is however also expected to reach 85%. An opposite weaker sub-trend is *re-ruralisation* – when families move to the surrounding countryside to find primary production jobs and a new lifestyle.

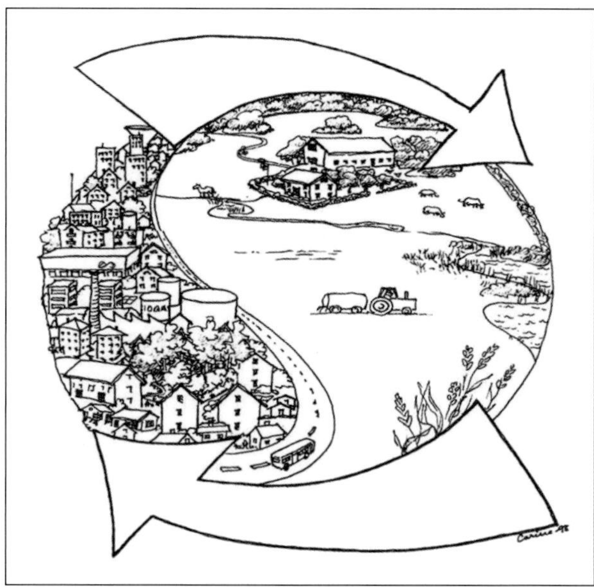

Figure 11.3. Urban-rural interdependency. Future sustainable cities will in a range of scales co-evolve with its local and regional hinterlands. Illustration: Carina Lindkvist.

The Vision of a Good City

Patterns of Urban Cultures

What is a good city? Cities were during most of its history environmental disasters, with air pollution, contaminated waters and epidemics. During industrialization, life expectancy in cities was much lower than in the countryside. The post-industrial era featured an improved sanitation, hygiene and housing standards but was instead followed by a new plague: excessive motorism again fouling the air, polluting the waters and contributing to accidents and an increased crime rate (Gehl, 2010; Hall, 1988; Alexander et al. 1977).

In city planning all through history – there has been a struggle for understanding and implementing a functional and attractive urban environment for its citizens creating wellbeing, security and support (Lynch, 1981). For its life-support, all dense human habitats must handle challenges of energy-, water- and food provision for its inhabitants as well as an efficient waste and waste-water management (Bokalders & Block, 2010). For any urban human habitat, also its wealth distribution, accessibility for citizens to public transport and other public and private services, culture, parks and waterfronts are important issues (Gehl, 2010; Alexander, 1977). The social aspects of a city are equally important, such as high quality relations between citizens, good education, strong local communities, a sense of security and what classic urbanist Jane Jacobs referred to as a "caring citizenship" (Jacobs, 1961). If the ambition is to include *all the citizens' needs and demands* – also mechanisms for public participation are crucial for creating the good city (Gaffron et al. 2005; Day, 2002; UNCHS, 1996).

Parallel with a new urban-rural integration as one basic principle for sustainable cities and rural areas, the understanding of the *flows and communications* within the urban

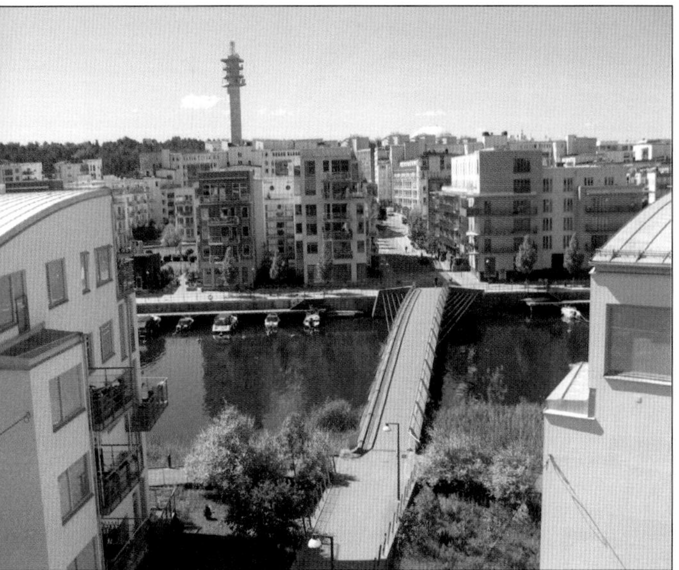

Figure 11.4. Hammarby sjöstad in Stockholm. Cities in the future can be expected to activate their 'inner town-country' boundaries (green spaces and networks) in all scales: for cultivation, water reuse, nutrient circulation, ecosystems services and for recreation. Photo: Saara Saukko.

environment has undergone a fast development. The walkable city with short-distances to all urban functions was the historic norm , whereas spread-out, zonated new world car-cities had up to now been the exceptions. It is only during the past 60 years that the cities have been increasingly invaded by private motorism – a plague currently spreading in all third world- and newly industrialised cities. At the same time many e.g. European cities now try to re-conquer the walkable city. Another influence during the past century still boosting the land-consuming, car-dependent city is the *modernistic project* including large-scale housing areas and sprawling villa areas, tied together with motorway arteries, junctions and an all over the cityscape covering iron-grid network of accessible streets. The *garden city* proponents: e.g. Ebenezer Howard (1902), Patrick Geddes (1904) and later Ian McHarg (1969) and Johan Rådberg (1982) argued in favour of more green-covered and healthy cities as a reaction to the coal-fired, disease-spreading hardscapes of the industrial towns.

The green healthy city ideals also included various aspects of *urban farming* (Wagner, 1921; Geddes, 1904). Another group of city planners, architects and debaters focused on the need to create *social*, *equitable* and *inclusive* cities: e.g. Lewis Mumford, (1961), Jane Jacobs (1961) and Christopher Alexander (1977). Only in the past few decades, attempts were made to *combine* urban green principles with the social and organizational function of urban areas in the emerging *Ecocities* plans and principles (Bokalders & Block, 2010; Gaffron et al. 2005).

From Declining Countrysides to Complete Communities

What are good rural towns and communities: As the countrysides' organization and livability are increasingly secondary to the needs in the urban areas – its citizens increasingly abandon its fields, forests and waters – as well as its small towns and spread-out communities, i.a. in the Baltic Sea Region (Hanell & Tornberg, 2007). And as the regions are drained of its brain- and practical experience powers in the countryside – also the urban environments get more impoverished (Alexander, 1977). The living community countryside with all its life support, ecosystems services and recreational capacities are gradually degraded due to its step-by-step loss of maintenance and caretaking.

This *rural flight* can only be countered through a development of the rural areas and towns *based on their own opportunities and requirements*. The necessary upgrading of the rural areas include tailor-made solutions for *combining services*, for a place and situation adapted *tax system*, for a higher *revenue from its natural resource capital* and for the local provision of food, waters, fibre, minerals and other natural resources (Kahiluoto, 2006; Svensson, 1993).

For reversing the rural flight trend also a development and maintenance of *complete rural communities* need to take place. Complete communities include all necessary ingredients for sustenance of the rural communities (Berg, 2010). And the definition of complete communities must be done from the *rural perspective*: what does the rural community need? What can they not survive without? Even a non-profitable shop or pre-school may need to remain since they are deeply connected to all other rural systems (SOU, 2005; Leader, 2000; Svensson, 1993). And one particularly important measure for reversing the rural flight is to *connect more closely the rural culture with the urban.*

Figure 11.5. Järna complete rural community. This small rural community with 6,000 inhabitants have over a period of 25 years developed a full production-consumption cycle – from the surrounding farms and greenhouses, to the Saltå kvarn and local wholesalers, to distribution to a range of farm shops and ordinary ICA and Coop shops in the local Järna town. The community also features bank, cultural houses, education and research. Photo montage: Per G Berg

Figure 11.6. Vauban eco-district in Freiburg. This well-known renewable energy neighbourhood have combined green areas in four scales with a tram-supported, bike-pedestrian mobility. Also the community culture is characterized by its mixed-use, socially diverse, and syn-aesthetical planning. Urban farming is implemented in e.g. kitchen gardens, garden plot areas and community fruit orchards. Photo: Varis Bokalders

The Emergence of Ecocities

Major approaches to achieve urban sustainability has for the past decade been to address its energy efficiency, the form of the city and the organization of its mobility. The simple hypothesis is that if the city is *densified* – there will theoretically be shorter distances between dwelling and various functions (Thwaites, 2007; Gaffron, 2005). Initially the critics identified the *modernistic project* as the main problem and the *compact city* as the main remedy for creating the sustainable city. This is – however – nuanced in more advanced ecocity architecture and planning where advantages and drawbacks of *both* models are discussed (Ibid). In times of fast expansion and growth of cities, waves of unreflected densification are typically the universal strategy to cope with a growing population, with a growing resource turnover and with the need for a higher capacity of the city machinery (Berg et al.2012, submitted; Rådberg, 1988).

A series of modernistic waves can be distinguished: e.g. within the first industrialization wave during the 19th century; at the expansion of suburbia and the car-society after 2nd World War – and today at the turn of the new millennium when *densification* is an economically motivated strategy for the transformation into resource efficient cities. *The Ecocityprojects* (2003-2008) in seven EU cities from Northern Tampere to Southern Barcelona have all emphasized that dense is better for the environment (Gaffron et al. 2005; 2008).

But the compact European city also exhibits "qualified density", a "balance of centralization and decentralization" and presupposes that apart from houses – also green areas, squares, commercial plazas and other public spaces are included in the densification strategy. Therefore, important part-goals for the formation of ecocities are also *short distances, mixed-use planning, integration of infrasystems* and a city for *all inhabitants* (Ibid). On the move in international ecocity planning is also the Gehl Architects call for *cities for people*, with human scale and human psychologically adapted streets and functions as key drivers for the new cities. And the potentially most radical transformation is from the *car-dependent hardscape city* to the *walkable green city*. This transformation is currently underway in a range of European cities: e.g. in southern Germany, in Holland and Denmark.

The New Urban Rural Co-operation

Cities' Eternal Dependency on Rural Production

Rural areas and nature's land and waters always and without exception provided and will provide the life support of the city with nutrients, energy, fibres, metals, other materials and clean water. The primary production inside the city was always limited, although city cultivation and the use and reuse of physical resources may occasionally have been quite efficient (Sinclair et al. 2011; Berg, 1993; Rådberg, 1992). However, today's relationship between town and country is invisibly global and is characterised by two major trends and their corresponding challenges.

First our way of organising and managing cities has led to a need for giant life support areas – including recycling areas – typically 1000 times larger than the corresponding surface unit of cities (Bokalders & Block, 2010; Berg, 2010; Folke et al. 1997). Secondly the *depopulation of rural areas and towns* has led to a new distribution between small settlements, medium-sized and large cities, with the latter becoming increasingly dominant (see Persson & Bro, 2002 and Alexander, 1977). The result has been higher energy consumption, increasingly resource-demanding food and materials production systems and a strong increase in long-distance travel and transportation of goods and commodities all over the globe (Bokalders & Block; Berg, 2010; IGBP, 2004).

New and simultaneously more sustainable town and country systems need to come geographically closer in the future in different scales and in a modern IT-based format. Today most foods, wood products, biofuels and biochemicals are produced for global markets. The world trade of food and other organic commodities has contributed to more people than ever in history having a sufficient standard of living – but also to more people than ever living in the utmost misery, poverty and without shelter (UNHabitat 2007). And – as many are aware of – we are living on borrowed time. The food is mainly produced with the aid of fossil oil and stored phosphates. The transport sector uses less than 5% renewable energy to move people, food, goods and raw materials over the surface of the earth. The food production systems of the world – from primary production in fields and animal stables to refined food in everyday kitchens and school restaurants – are facing a series of environmental/ethical problems and challenges. These include:

Figure 11.7. Resilient land use. Future primary production will probably use renewable energy, modern 'meadow-is-the-mother-of-arable land-cultivation' and produce most of the food, biochemicals, bioenergy and biopurification services needed by cities and communities within macro- and micro-regions. Photo: Per G Berg.

- how to manage scarce resources on a global scale and simultaneously produce food of a high quality, with acceptable environmental impact, for all people;
- how to transform food production from using stored to renewable physical resources;
- how to produce food with a minimum of environmentally hazardous chemicals;
- how to stimulate the choices of healthy food and sound eating habits;
- how to distribute healthy food according to equity principles;
- how to support reasonable working conditions, strengthening local communities in world rural areas and to prevent new waves of ruthless exploitation of land, forests, fields and waters;
- and how to find an efficient and ethically acceptable balance between biofuel and food production.

Some of the answers may emerge in how the future relationship between town and country is organised.

Box 11.1. How to Calculate the Footprint of a City

Rural Society

The ecological footprint (EFp) of a study population is the per capita footprint multiplied by population size (N): EFp= N(ef) We account for direct fossil energy consumption and the energy content of consumption items by estimating the area of carbon-sink forest that would be required to sequester the carbon dioxide emissions associated with burning fossil fuels ([carbonemissions/capital/[assimilation rate/hectare]), on the assumption that atmospheric stability is central to sustainability. (An alternative is to estimate the area of land required to produce the biomass energy equivalent [ethanol] of fossil energy consumption. This produces a larger energy footprint than the carbon assimilation method.)

Every effort is made to avoid double-counting in the case of multiple land uses and where there are data problems or significant uncertainty we err on the side of caution. Also, while we define the footprint comprehensively to include the land/water areas required for waste assimilation, our calculations to date do not account for waste emissions other than carbon dioxide. Accounting fully for this ecological function would add considerably to the ecosystem area appropriated by economic activity. Together these factors suggest that our ecological footprint calculations to date are more likely to be under-estimates than over-estimates.

Data from my home city, Vancouver, British Columbia, Canada, serve to illustrate application of the concept. Vancouver proper has a population (1991) of 472,000 and an area of 114 km^2 (11,400 hectares). However, the average Canadian requires over a hectare (ha) of crop and grazing land under current land management practices to produce his/her high meat protein diet and about .6 ha for wood and paper associated with various other consumption items. In addition, each "occupies" about .2 ha of ecologically degraded and built-over (e.g., urban) land. Canadians are also among the world's highest fossil energy consumers with an annual carbon emission rate of 4.2 tonnes carbon (15.4 tonnes CO_2) per capita (data corrected for carbon content of trade goods). Therefore, at a carbon sequestering rate of 1.8 tonnes/ha/yr an additional 2.3 ha of middle-aged North temperate forest would be required as a continuous carbon sink to assimilate the average Canadian's carbon emissions (assuming the need to stabilize atmospheric carbon dioxide levels).

Considering only these data, the terrestrial "personal planetoid" of a typical Vancouverite approaches 4.2 ha, or almost three times his/her "fair Earthshare." [An additional .74 ha of continental shelf "seascape" is appropriated to produce the average Canadian's annual consumption of 24kg of fish.] On this basis, the 472,000 people living in Vancouver require, conservatively, 2.0 million ha of land for their exclusive use to maintain their current consumption patterns (assuming such land is being managed sustainably). However, the area of the city is only about 11,400 ha. This means that the city population appropriates the productive output of a land area nearly 174 times larger than its political area to support its present consumer lifestyles. [The Vancouver Regional District (metropolitian area), with 1.6 million inhabitants and a land-base of 2930 km^2, has an ecological footprint of 6,720,000 ha, 23 times its geographic area.]

While this result might seem extraordinary, other researchers have obtained similar results. Folke et al. (1994) report that the aggregate consumption of wood, paper, fiber, and food (including seafood) by the inhabitants of 29 cities in the Baltic Sea drainage basin appropriates an ecosystem area 200 times larger that the area of the cities themselves. (The latter study does not include energy land.)

William E Rees

Source: Rees, 1996. (Rees together with Mathias Wackernagel has developed the concept of ecological footprint. See http://www.footprintnetwork.org.)

Uniting Two Perspectives on Town and Country

There are currently two dominant and distinct perspectives on the eternal relationship between town and country. One is the prevailing *urban* perspective, whereby planners, engineers and estate economics in the city regard rural non-dense areas mainly as a recipient for urban flows of waste, wastewater and foul air as well as suitable lands for industry localization (UNHabitat, 2007). Representatives of the urban perspective, however skilful they are in arranging settlement- and transport structures with a high capacity (Hall, 1988; Alexander et al. 1977), often underestimate the need for land surface, plant biomass, soil and water volumes in order to transform city waste streams in a sustainable way to harmless raw materials in natural and cultural landscapes, to neutralise the contaminants in wastewater and extract its nutrients – and to decompose the particles and volatile chemicals in the city air in soil microecosystems in order to produce clear, clean air again (Berg, 1990).

The urban perspective also typically lacks a nuanced insight about the different functions of city greenery: partly contributing to the *metabolism* of society using cascading or coupled urban biological processes, partly providing *ecosystem services* to the city, and partly for creating a *recreation* and *well-being* in the everyday life of city residents. The urban perspective, finally, even lacks an insight that rural communities need to be *complete* to survive and develop according to their own conditions (taxes, culture, profits from primary production). As a multiple reference to the urban town-country perspective, see comprehensive or master plans of i.a. Baltic Sea Region cities.

The second perspective on the town-country relationship, the *rural perspective*, is represented by the actors of rural areas – those who are committed to its *communities* including local primary production from its forests, fields and waters (Leader, 2000; SOU, 2005). The rural perspective is also carried by large land management enterprises and policy makers that are primarily interested in *production land* which is typically detached from its adjacent rural communities (Jordbruksdepartementet, 1989). These actors have – in different ways – advanced knowledge about land use and management, animal husbandry, production methods and agricultural policies. They also share a vast knowledge about agricultural, forest and water ecosystems. However, the rural experts and actors probably have more limited insights into how the city population demands food and other bio-products and how values about health and environment in the city are rapidly changing the conditions for the food production of tomorrow – for instance the growing interest for local production (Granvik, 2012).

In the rural perspective there is also seemingly a lack of active interest (or capacity?) in pushing for solutions of the organic waste disposal problem inherent in cities (Berg, 1993). There is also an apparent lack of interest to create small and large eco-cycles between town and country. Modern large-scale agriculture stake-holders also often lack the ability (or interest?) to utilise its own large nutrient flows from animal husbandry for linking it efficiently to primary production areas (Jordbruksdepartementet 1989).

Large and Small Rurban Circles and Cascades

Emerging attempts are now being made across Europe, within research as well as within planning to achieve a radically more sustainable urban development, among other measures to unite the two main urban-rural perspectives. An emerging 'common' perspective on the town-country relationship can also be expected to contain new insights that may provide strong leverage actions towards radically more sustainable cities and rural production systems in the future (see e.g. Bokalders & Block, 2010 and Gaffron et al. 2005 and 2008). Such a new common town-country perspective will be able to argue for *large-scale, efficient recycling between city centres and dense suburban areas* on the one hand and *large-scale primary production lands and waters*, characterised by resourcefulness, clean food chains and healthy food on the other (Ebbersten & Bodin 1997).

Figure 11.8. Culemborg cityland outside Utrecht. This Dutch best practice community has succeded in intertwining blue and green structures in different scales for primary production, ecosystem services and recreation. This community has also developed a high diversity of small enterprises in the area. Photo: Courtesy of Varis Bokalders.

In the short-term, such a new town-country perspective would also be able to argue for *medium-scale* and *small-scale* town-country systems that close the nutrient cycles around smaller cities and villages, near suburbs and in more genuine countryside town settings (Ibid; Berg 1993). For smaller communities, functional integration of social, organisational, economic and cultural resources within the landscapes in which they are embedded, constitutes a special survival factor, featuring *complete rural communities* (Granvik, 2012; SOU, 2005; Berg, 2010; 2007; 2006). In the future we can expect more resource efficient production-distribution systems on all scales. Those systems are expected to use renewable energy and a modern variant of the 'meadows-are-the-mother-of-agriculture', which has the ability to capture the valuable nutrients in cascades of primary production land, secondary land and efficient 'polishing ecosystems' (Ebbersten & Bodin, 1997).

The climate crisis makes it imperative to implement a renewable energy *transition* within the next 40 years, to reform *food production*, the *transport system* and to introduce new comfortable but radically more sustainable everyday habits within e.g. *habitation* (Bokalders & Block, 2010; Edman, 2005). A decrease in cheap oil supply may also trigger radical changes in the short-term perspective (within 10 years) in the co-evolution between town and country (Saifi & Drake, 2007). Visions about a radically reformed new town-country relationships need to be developed immediately, but can only realistically be implemented over a longer time period of several decades (Berg, 2010; IGBP, 2004; Odum, 1989).

The need to reduce the ecological footprint of the cities can result in a fast relative relocation of food production systems from global markets to macro-regional (e.g. the Baltic Sea- or Mediterranean Regions) or micro-regional (within for instance EU NUTS regions such as Mälardalen in Sweden) markets (Granvik, 2012; Granvik et al. 2012) .

Figure 11.9. Pfaffenhofen experimental area 45 km north of München is planned as an eco-settlement with sustainable residential areas, farms, recycling units and recreational areas. The plans are to be net producers of electricity and soil – produced from waste water sludge, compost waste and charcoal. Illustration: Rolf Messerschmidt at Eble Architects in Tübingen.

Resilient Citylands in the Future

Combining Urban and Rural

In the beginning of the last Century the biologist and city planner Patric Geddes (1904) described a sustainable city system with both urban and rural functions – a walkable city with gardens, parks and food production - but also with efficient public transit systems and a system of socially strong neighbourhoods. It was a city with rich spaces for entrepreneurs but also aware of its cultural assets. In Germany Martin Wagner (1923) defined a range of interlinked attractive green areas in different scales for the pleasure and utility of the citizens: small-scale intimate *entrance* green and *courtyard/garden* green; Intermediary *district green* to denote parks, small forests and fields and waters separating city neighbourhoods; and large-scale *wilderness green* with its forests, arable land, wetlands, river banks and waters. The functions of public green structure, were in turn elaborately described by landscape architect Ian Thompson in his book *Ecology, Community and Delight* (Thompson, 1999) implicating three fundamental landscape values: for life-supporting communities (urban agriculture), for regulating the climate (ecosystems services) and for providing pleasant garden- and park settings for the recreation and well-being of the citizens.

Urban and Rural Citylands

Such were the roots of what we could today describe as an extended and more comprehensive vision of a sustainable city – not mainly focusing on its physical (energy and matter) resources managed in a durable economic setting: But including all seven dimensions (physical, economic, biological, social, organizational, cultural and aesthetic) of sustainable human settlements – outlined in the foundation texts of the UN *Habitat agenda* (Berg, 2010; UNCHS, 1996). This *Cityland system* thus encompassed a new and modern relation between the city and its surrounding and interwoven countryside landscapes (Berg, 2010).

The urban cityland is not only urban but also contain rural properties; the *rural cityland* is not only countryside but also encompass a range of urban functions. *Resilient Citylands* is therefore a new version of urban-rural co-evolution with both its surrounding green areas and wedges and also with its *internal green infrastructures* – its systems of parks, greenways, alleys, street trees, verdure courtyards, gardens (Saifi & Drake, 2007; Florgård, 2004; Lundgren-Alm, 2001). *The Cityland* concept can guide us towards a deeper understanding of how biological and cultural systems can be united in different scales, with different values, with different purposes.

Figure 11.10. Houten bicycle town. This little suburb to Utrecht has been optimized for bicycles, which has lead to that 80% of all (person-kilometer) internal mobility is with bikes and the cars are lead around the community. A remarkable feature of the little town is its nuanced soundscape, few accidents and a high air quality. Photo: Varis Bokalders.

Functional Densification and Mobility in Urban Citylands

An urgent and current matter concerns how we can build or evolve current urban environments to become *green compact cities*. *Functional or qualified densification* signifies an urban development where townscapes can include all functions for a more efficient land use: houses, streets, pathways, squares, plazas, nodes, parks, gardens, schoolyards, pedestrian avenues, greenways and commercial and public service (Berg et al. 2012; Berg, 2010; Thwaites, 2007).

The new compact city has – accordning to Gehl Architects' characterization (Gehl, 2010) and Alexander et al. (1977) – transformed its former practical public spaces being transit zones between home and work to instead become the public living room for citizens' experience of the "magic of the city" (Ibid). The new compact green city also exhibit a *transport modal shift* – from dominating car-traffic, car-adapted spatial planning and adjustment of citylands to a *bike-pedestrian-public transit* dominated transport system (Bokalders & Block, 2010; Bach, 2002).

This new *or renewed* cityland transit network is created in close encounter or integrated with green links, along blue waterfronts, across parks, supported by new bike-pedestrian service nodes (with storage, renting, repair, rest, coffee-shops and utilities for the pedestrians and bicyclists (Bokalders & Block, 2010; Thompson, 1999).

The new bike-pedestrian-public transit networks and nodes are furthermore supported by intelligent transport systems (ITS) with information, guidance and tips in smartphone applications, on information boards at traffic nodes and distributed as small information screens throughout the urban landscapes of tomorrow (Gullberg et al. 2007; Bach, 2002).

Cityland Ecosystem Services

Green areas, water surfaces and flows in urban and rural communities are potentially important for the wellbeing of its inhabitants (Cooper-Marcus, 1997; Kaplan & Kaplan, 1989; Eriksson & Ingmar, 1989). These *ecosystems services* (Oberdorfer, 2007) can be measured e.g. by self assessment of citizens, using questionnaires but also more objectively in clinical studies where physiological effects in individuals can be estimated (Mitchell & Popham, 2008; Stigsdotter & Grahn, 2003).

An often used indicator for city development is that the inhabitants should live no more than 250-300 meters from a green area to actually go there (Lisberg-Jensen, 2008; Alexander, 1977). It is also established that apartments close to surface water or green areas are more expensive than those further away, reflecting the value of this asset in a city (Andersson, 1998).

Greenery in cities is not only important to humans. It contributes considerable to biodiversity. Thus birdwatch-

Figure 11.11. The seminar park in Uppsala. This park with its seminar buildings is the only remaining complete seminar environment in Sweden. It is a strategic and exclusive area for developing a district park from a mature park structure including pedagogic gardening, ecosystems services for north-West Uppsala and recreation for its inhabitants. Still the Conservative party and the Social democrats are determined to exploit the area for new apartment buildings. Illustration of a city park: Tim Andreaheim Landscape Architect student, 3rd year.

ers have reported that Berlin – that has a very high percentage of green areas – has the largest number of bird species in Germany (Oberdorfer, 2007). It is also notable that many species which were earlier only found in the countryside today is increasingly moving to the cities for finding food, which is less accessible in industrialised agriculture, that "too" efficiently takes care of the harvest (Ibid). For children and adolescents, the parks, green playgrounds and plazas in cities are more easily available than far away countryside. It is a highly valued resource for getting children acquainted with nature, for learning about nature protection and for play and moving the body (Uppsala kommun, 2002; UNICEF, 1989).

Greenery and water bodies also has an influence on the *microclimate* and *air quality* in a city (Ibid). A diverse green structure is important for breaking strong winds and for inviting in the sun in park glades, courtyards or other solar pockets. The urban temperature is reduced in parks, along green corridors or rivers, thus allowing ventilation of the city air. Green roofs have become more common also in large cities for their buffering of rain- or melting water flows but also for temperature regulation of buildings. Green elements also contribute strongly to the moisturizing of the city air – and the soil in green areas are instrumental for cleaning foul smells in the city air. Urban gardening and agriculture has a potential of reducing the ecological footprint of the cities. Houses may be designed so as to allow considerable areas for gardening in courtyards, along walls, on roof-tops or in greenhouses or balconies connected to the apartment buildings (Lundgren Alm, 2001; Thompson, 1999).

The monetary value of the ecosystems services of cities have been studied in several research projects and found to be considerable (Anderson, 2008; Lundgren Alm, 2001). To insert the rural in the urban is thus one way to decrease the ecological burden of cities.

Cities as Regional Cityland Centres

In comprehensive planning, there has been a shift from only planning for one (very urban part) of a city and within a comparatively short term future horizon (5-10 years). This was the situation in the early 1990-ies in Swedish planning (Nilsson, 2003). In newer comprehensive planning also other neighbouring cities are taken into account. Joint labour markets, common land, waters and other environmental resources enrich all participating cities. Intercity communication and transport can be improved and the futures horizons expand to 10, 20 and/or 40 years. And yet there has – up to now – been limited care in comprehensive planning for the region surround-

Figure 11.12. Farmers market in Katarina Bangata in Stockholm. Stockholm greater region farmers directly meet with the city consumers, representing a small-scale food market. Resilient cityland markets will also be medium-scale markets in the boundary zone between town and country and large-scale regional and global markets. From an illustration to a EU-financed SLU report (2006) about local food production by Hans Månsson, Bild & Mening

Figure 11.13. Cultivation in the new fringe zone. In many suburban areas in Baltic Sea region Cities there is a direct contact with forests, fields and water and yet there is very little attempts to make use of the production values and other values related to urban farming. In this example large green areas have been transformed into productive land.

ing the cities. City planning has still focused on urban infrasystems and settlement patterns and less interest has been devoted to the regional towns and smaller communities. Instead *county councils* (the government's local representatives) have targeted the landscape communities outside the cities (Gaffron et al. 2005; Helmfrid, 1993). A stronger commitment is needed, to see the values of surrounding towns and hamlets, to appreciate their often creative solutions for combining various countryside services, to acknowledge the need for tailor-made logistics and governance systems – e.g. rural laws and tax-systems (Svensson, 1993). A typical feature which need special solutions in the rural areas are informal economic methods.

The next logical step is, therefore, to include also issues about both the city and its surrounding communities in the comprehensive plans of tomorrow. Regional planning has started to take this course in several Swedish and Norwegian city-regions (see e.g. SLL, 2009) but also in several European Ecocity projects (Gaffron et al. 2005), as well as in Canada (Moffat, 2003) and New Zealand (Frame & Brown, 2009). For hundreds of years the functional regions were defined by their current transport means: they were not larger than it was possible to travel from one end to the other, often by foot or by horse and carriage, in one day (Carstensen, 1992). Today travel by car or public transport has expanded the regions now depending on efficient train- or bus traffic. With a full inclusion of all communities of different sizes – modern cities can again finally become real *regional centres of resilient citylands*, co-ordinating environmental resources, nature protection areas, transit systems, local economies, health care, public and commersial services and culture, for towns, small towns and hamlets in the countryside (Berg, 2010; Alexander et al. 1977).

The Strategic Boundary Zone between Town and Country

One of the new features of *resilient citylands* is the built/green-blue *interface zone* between more urban and more rural functions. Nordic cities had traditionally, and still have, a very long green/blue interface *line* between settlements and human cultures on the one hand and glades, meadows, forests, parks, arable fields, lakes, seas and rivers on the other (Berg, 2010). Throughout the history of civilization, edges between town and nature have proved to be the most preferred locations for habitation (Roseland, 2005; Berg, 1993; Odum, 1989). For *citylands* the edge *line* is expanded to a wider *zone*: in this zone will be the important *district* green areas for neighbourhood recreation (district parks, play grounds, sports grounds, orchards, stables for sheep, cows, horses and pigs); in this zone there could be room for urban agriculture with green houses and community gardens, where fruit and vegetables can be grown for urban and sub-urban dwellers; in this zone there is room for clean companies and clean micro-production; in this zone there is land for industrial combinates, refining the primary produce into food, fuel, fibre, boards and other building material; in this zone there is room for new recycling of waste industry; and in this zone there is room for the new generations or renewable energy (wind and wave power, Photovoltaics and solar heat collectors and bioenergy cultivations) and energy carriers (storage of bioenergy and electricity – see e.g. Bokalders & Block, 2010).

The future town-country relationship will therefore rely strongly on the organization and design of both *inner* boundary zones of the cities (settlements turning towards parks and community forests, fields and waters), but also between settlements and the *outer* nature, and between built areas and *outer* cultural landscapes. Preliminary theoretical research and map studies of the morphological dynamics of city growth indicate that a long and winding interface zone between urban and rural functions are strategic for creating resilient citylands accessible for many citizens to experience urban and rural recreation, urban and rural culture and urban and rural production (Berg, 2010).

Furthermore, supplementary small-scale, peri-urban production systems for food and bioenergy and urban agriculture may play a more important role than previously. It is reasonable to assume that world trade will continue to play a role in life support of world cities, but a relocation to relatively more local eco-cycles – where a larger proportion of basic bio-production and consumption may occur – seems to be a logical consequence of global change, the need for food security and local labour markets supplementing the global. An advancement of current knowledge about urban-rural: soil-plant *systems*; resilient crop production *systems*; forest *ecosystems*; microbial *systems*; ecotechnology *systems*; and resilient food *systems* (Berg, 1993; 1990) in different scales will play key roles in the long-term survival and development of the renewed cities, countrysides and citylands in the future.

Living in the Baltic Waterscape

12

Lars Rydén
Uppsala University, Uppsala, Sweden

Living by Water

Humans always settled close to water from the earliest times as evidenced by archaeological remains. It is natural. The coasts, lakes or rivers provided water, food, harbours and transport routes all essential for human society. Also today we see that not only cities have been built on coasts, river deltas, and along rivers or lakeshores, but the same is true for smaller towns and villages in the rural communities. It is clear that almost everyone appreciate the sight of a water surface or access to a shore. Properties on such sites have a higher financial value, both for year around farms or living houses, and for dachas and summerhouses. Compared to the south of Europe and to many other continents the Baltic Sea region is rich in waterfronts and many of us can enjoy life by water.

It needs to be kept in mind that there are some responsibilities connected to living by water. Wastewater should be treated before entering a recipient water body, a collective responsibility in a city or town. In individual farms or houses wastewater may be treated before entering a water outlet but alternatively, as is often done today, collected in a special tank and picked up and taken to a treatment plant. One also needs to be careful with all kinds of waste, including solid waste, as it is very destructive in a water body where it may spread over large areas. Construction of beaches, porches or larger arrangements such as marinas needs to include proper arrangements for waste management.

In some countries new buildings close to water shores are not allowed any longer, as the shore is considered an area, which should be accessible to everyone. There are also regulations, mainly in North Europe, stating that a person always has the right to walk along the shore of a lake, even passing a private property. Some local authorities have stopped constructions closer to the water line as an adaptation to climate change and predicted increase of surface levels and flood risks.

This chapter was based on texts and information in the Baltic University course on Sustainable Water Management, Volume I The Waterscape with chapters The Baltic Basin – rivers, lakes and climate by Sten Bergström, Nicolai Filatov, Dimitrij Pozdnjakov, Artur Magnuszewski and Hans Bergström; Wetlands in the Baltic Sea region by Lars Lundin; and Volume III River Basin Management with chapters Shipping - boats, harbours and people by Peter Norberg, Allan Nilsson, Pia Westfjord, Yngve Malmquist and Lars Rydén; Fishing and aquaculture; Tourism and recreation by Ebbe Adolfsson, Chatarina Holmberg and Beatriz Brena; Water regulation and water infrastructure by Lars Rydén, Inger Brinkman and Yngve Malmquist; as well as Chapter 5 The Baltic Sea in the Baltic University book Environmental Science. The original chapters are fully referenced.

Water Resources

Water is a most important resource for all humans. We need it for drinking, cooking, cleaning ourselves and for growing our crops. After the systems change in 1989-91 all former communist countries focused their environmental concern firstly on fresh water provision and wastewater treatment. Also in the poorest of municipalities this work was started.

Fortunately the Baltic Sea region is well provided with water. The annual average runoff for the Baltic Sea region as a whole is estimated at 5,000 m^3/per capita, per year (very close to European average). This is the water available for all purposes and needs. Most of it stays in the landscape, the so-called green water, and some is lost through evaporation, that is, is constantly transported into the atmosphere in the form of mist or vapour. The green water is necessary and most often sufficient for agriculture. The degree of irrigation in the Baltic Sea region is small compared to e.g. Southern Europe or the southern hemisphere.

The water extracted for society – industry, households and urban areas etc – is from the blue water running in lakes, rivers, canals, groundwater aquifers etc. In households it is typically 100-400 litres per day and capita or 40-150 m^3/per capita per year. It is clear that on the average society uses only a few percent of the water resources available. In general, 53% of the abstracted water (surface and groundwater) is used for industrial purposes, 26% is used in agriculture and only 19% is used for domestic purposes. Industrial water use is decreasing.

The water resources per capita show very large variations between different geographical regions. Low water availabilities are found in densely populated western countries with moderate precipitation (e.g. Germany and Denmark) and some eastern countries (Poland, Ukraine), mainly due to low precipitation. Water is plentiful in sparsely populated countries where precipitation is high, like the Nordic countries, and in countries with large trans-boundary rivers running through them. Latvia, Ukraine and the Czech Republic receive between 50 and 75% of their renewable water resources from abroad through such rivers.

Rivers and other surface bodies provide 70% of the water for all utilisation sectors, but groundwater is also an important fresh water source. In countries with extensive groundwater reservoirs, more than 75% is drawn from groundwater. Finland, with insufficient groundwater supplies, abstract more than 90% from surface water sources. For Europe as a whole, about 65% of the public supply is provided from groundwater which normally is of a better quality than surface water.

The degree of water use is critical. Thus while Sweden uses about 3% of its water resources, this figure is closer to 16% for Poland. At this degree of water use we start to see some recirculation of water in the society, that is, used water entering a river at some point is being recuperated at another point downstream. This reuse of water requires careful wastewater purification and management.

It is possible to indicate the amount of water needed for an item produced by its water footprint, meaning all water needed during the life cycle of the product. The water footprint for a kg of meat is typically 15 thousand litres, while it is ten times less for a kg of bread. Also industrial products have water footprints; high footprints occur for e.g. 1 kg cotton has a footprint of 10 thousand litres. In the Baltic Sea region water availability is, in a global comparison, large. We do not need to be too concerned about water footprints, while lack of fresh water resources is a growing problem in e.g. many Asian countries.

Shipping

The waters in the Baltic Sea region have been trafficked since the earliest of times. The Viking ships and Hanseatic cogs are part of our common history. But these were very few compared to our contemporary boat and ship traffic. Today both boating for pleasure with many tens of thousands of sailing and motorboats and trade with freight ships is enormously much bigger. The great majority of transport to, from and within countries occurs on ships. As an example in Sweden the share of freight on ship corresponds to 80% of all transport, a figure which increases even more if transport on trucks and trains which are carried by ferries is included. In addition there is considerable passenger traffic on ferries over the Baltic Sea, especially after the systems change in 1989-91.

Also on inland water ways there is an important traffic. The large rivers of Wisla, Odra, Neva, Daugava and Elbe are used by smaller ships and barges. The larger lakes, such as Vänern, Mälaren, Ladoga and Onega, have its transport including the adjoining waterways out to the larger seas. The fairly few large canals, e.g. Kiel Kanal in Germany and Göta Kanal in Sweden, also harbours boat traffic.

The intense boat traffic constitutes a real environmental danger. So far there has not been any main oil disaster in the Baltic Sea. However, the risk for such an event has increased significantly the last few years with the expansion of oil tanker traffic to and from Russian ports in the St Petersburg area. Recently the Baltic Sea was labelled a Particularly Sensitive Sea Area (PSSA) by the International Maritime Organisation (IMO), the UN body for Sea Security. This requires that oil tankers should be equipped with double hull. It remains to be seen if the Russian ships will adapt to this requirement.

Figure 12.1. Containership. Photo: Niklas Liljegren. Courtesy of Sjöfartsverket. http://www.sjofartsverket.se.

But already today pollution from ships is considerable. About 400 oil spills are registered each year in the Baltic Sea. Only few of these can be linked to a specific ship so that its captain could be taken to court. Many private boats are less careful with the management of toilet and household waste. The last few years cruiser with thousands of tourists are increasingly often visiting Baltic Sea ports, such as Visby, Stockholm, Helsinki, St Petersburg, Tallinn and Riga. Many of them empty toilet waste into the Baltic without acceptable treatment. Marinas are requested to have facilities for emptying toilet tanks on board small boats and a slow change is taking place.

With the use of modern information technologies sea traffic is better regulated. Main shipping routes are established in the Baltic Sea for larger ships. It is possible to have immediate information on all neighbouring ship traffic. These are part of several aids to avoid serious accidents.

Fishing

Fishing always was of great importance to the people living near the Baltic Sea. At one time it contributed a fair share to the protein intake. Today the large production of fish in the Baltic Sea itself is complemented with fish from aquaculture, especially in Norway, and inland fishing, not the least in the north. Both subsistence fishing and recreational fishing are performed in the Baltic Sea, along the whole Baltic Sea coastline, from the Bothnian Bay to the Atlantic environment in Kattegat and Skagerrak and in many different types of inland waters, lakes and rivers.

When compared to most other areas in Europe, the Baltic region provides very rich and variable possibilities for fishing. Commercial fishing is mainly performed in the open sea, with some taking place in the larger lakes, in mouths of rivers and along the coasts. The most important species for commercial fishing are cod, herring, and sprat. In the Baltic Sea these account for 90% of all catches. Other economically important species are salmon, sea trout, plaice and turbot. Coastal commercial fishing includes vendance and whitefish in the Bothnian Bay, perch, pike and pikeperch, along the entire Baltic Sea coast and flounder and eel along the southern coasts.

The fish stock varies considerably. During the peak period of 1973-1995 the average catch in the Baltic Sea was 760,000 tonnes with a maximum of 940,000 tonnes in the early 1980s. Today, however, the cod population is small. The decrease is due both to over-fishing and to low reproduction caused by oxygen deficiency and low salinity in the reproduction areas. Herring and sprat populations, conversely, have increased, helped by eutrophication. Environmental impacts have negatively influenced eel, flounder and salmon. Moreover the disease M74 casts a shadow over the future of the salmon in the Baltic.

In inland waters, commercial fishing is mainly focused on the large lakes, but also occurs in the mountain lakes of Lapland and in rivers in the southern Baltic regions. Important species include salmon, char, pikeperch, perch, pike, eel, vendance and whitefish. In Sweden alone the total commercial catch in inland waters amounts to approximately 2,000 tonnes annually.

Recreational fishing in inland waters aims at the same species as commercial fishing, although with a greater focus on perch and pike. Recreational fishing has grown strong over the last few years, and hundreds of thousands of fishing amateurs are found in every country. Anglers' associations are among the largest NGOs in our countries. Trolling for salmon and pike as well as more advanced angling for species of no commercial value are newly introduced fast-growing fishing methods. The annual catches within subsistence and sport fishing, dominated by perch and pike, are estimated at 40,000 tonnes in Sweden alone. The economic importance of recreational fishing cannot be calculated as precisely as the yield of commercial fishing. The recreational value itself, however, justifies a high price per kilo, especially when more desirable species like trout, char, salmon and pike are considered.

The bottleneck for many fish stocks is the availability of suitable spawning areas. This is especially valid for salmon, trout, grayling and whitefish spawning in running waters but also for many marine species that utilise shallow water areas. Shallow and protected areas with stable temperature and nutrient conditions form the most important environments, i.e. shallow bays in the sea and in inland waters. Small running-waters are often very important, especially for salmonids, and in exposed coastal areas they constitute the dominating production areas for fish fry. Care should be taken to protect spawning and growth areas since they are already so affected that the production of species of importance to fishing is limited. Many times streams and rivers have been restored by anglers associations to ensure the right conditions for fish reproduction.

Table 12.1. The Baltic fish catch (tonnes) by every country and main species in 2006 (source: ICES and Finnish Game and Fisheries Research Institute). From http://www.helcom.fi/environment2/biodiv/fish/en_GB/commercial_fisheries/.

	Sprat	Herring	Cod	Flounder	Other	ICES 22-28 Southern Baltic	ICES 29-32 Northern Baltic	Total
Sweden	97,584	53,166	12,252	169	2,767	144,415	21,523	165,938
Finland	19,020	79,955	673	99	10,036	8,474	101,306	109,783
Poland	55,890	20,544	15,080	9,428	3,686	104,628	0	104,628
Latvia	54,638	21,762	4,567	1,163	631	82,465	296	82,761
Denmark	42,323	6,989	21,425	2,839	4,573	76,530	1,619	78,149
Estonia	46,689	23,192	703	352	2,104	21,778	51,262	73,040
Germany	30,779	26,206	9,558	1,017	4,400	68,258	3,707	71,960
Russia	28,324	9,780	3,747	1,237	4,271	43,702	3,657	47,359
Lithuania	10,814	1,172	3,301	376	158	-	15,821	15,821
Total	386,061	242,766	71,306	16,680	32,626	550,250	199,191	749,439

Tourism and Recreation Services

The great importance to us of water is demonstrated more clearly than ever in our free time. During vacations and in general during leisure time, boats, beaches and baths are more popular than ever. On sunny summer days the coasts of the Baltic Sea and many of the lakes in its basin are lined with millions of happy people enjoying water or being close to water.

Today, tourism and recreation form a dominating part of the service sector, worth billions of Euros annually in the Swedish economy alone. The use of water by tourism and recreation is fully comparable to other uses of water, such as fishing, shipping, etc., in pure economic terms. The tourism and recreation sector clearly contributes to the well being of people and as such deserves as much care as the other sectors when planning for the best management of water and river basins.

Tourism, recreation and outdoor activities may also have more or less serious impacts on the living environment. Walking along the shoreline, swimming in the sea and skating on the lake in the winter normally have no negative effects on the environment. Facilities used in connection with these activities, such as roads, parking lots and overnight cabins, might, however, disturb nature and cause damage. These facilities, especially if inadequately designed or misplaced, most often have considerably more environmental impact than the simple activity itself. This may include severe impacts on water resources.

Public beaches must meet certain criteria of water quality so as not to risk the health of the visitors, in particular children. Such beaches should not be situated close to sewage effluents and the risk of contamination of the water from restaurants, cafes and toilets should be taken into consideration. Microbiological tests should be carried out regularly as required by EU directives. The eutrophication of the Baltic Sea and its shallow bays is a special problem, as algal blooms typically appear during the warmer periods in the summer. Some of the algae, such as cyanobacteria, are slightly toxic. If these algae appear in large quantities, the beach has to close. Public beaches give rise to disturbances of plant and animal life and should not be located too close to sensitive shallow waters. Conflicts between visitors, local residents and plant and animal life are commonplace, especially concerning loud music, boating, water-skiing, etc.

Figure 12.2. Discovering the waterscape by paddling a canoe along the small Ljustorp river in northern Sweden. Photo: Leonard Broman.

Visiting nature protection areas, nature reserves or national parks when so allowed is a special kind of tourism dependent on the beauty and protection of the landscape and its waters and wildlife. Both in the protected and the everyday landscape, including the waters, environmental care and good natural resource management should be applied in all activities, such as forestry and agriculture. Environmentally attuned working methods and natural consideration should achieve this. Especially in the north a strong nature interest makes this an important concern for nature lovers and bird watchers, and in general what is today called eco-tourism.

Use and Restoration of Wetlands

Several hundred years ago, the first thought to enter the mind of a settler or farmer when he saw a suitable wetland was, 'How should this be drained?' This was very natural considering the more or less constant shortage of food and shortage of acreage for farming in times when harvest per ha was very low and artificial fertilizers were not yet invented. Thus, the single option for increasing food production was to increase the farmed land area. Especially in the southern Baltic Sea states and surrounding areas, at least as far up as Estonia and south Finland, agriculture has taken over large wetland areas. Many wetlands were found especially suitable to farming, including cattle grazing and cultivation of grain. Later, in the late 1800s, forestry on wetlands, mainly peatlands, attracted increasing interest. In Finland, Estonia and Sweden, forested peatlands are very productive and cover major areas. In this way the wetlands have been utilized for human activities, mostly agriculture, forestry and peat extraction in almost all the countries in the region. Peat has proved to be outstanding as a growing substrate and provides important material in horticulture.

More recently the natural values of wetlands have gained an upper hand and the focus has changed towards conservation and preservation. Natural wetlands have large biological and water storage values, which are now more appreciated, and food can anyway be imported from elsewhere. Naturally, wetlands with open water are of considerable importance to fishery in both inland and coastal waters. Wetlands are of considerable value for wildlife and game, recreation, berry picking, mushrooms and special vegetation. In modern agriculture with considerable leaching of nutrients, and a current desire to put a limit to it, wetlands are being recreated to act as retention areas, especially for nitrogen and phosphorus. Large drained and channelled areas have in this way been restored to a more diversified landscape with meandering watercourses and a frequency of wetland ponds. This natural cleaning of man-made nutrient runoff is gaining increasing interest.

Hydro, Wind and Wave Power

The rural landscape is an important provider of renewable energy and the waterscape is not an exception. On the contrary hydropower is the most important source of renewable electricity in the region.

The best sites for hydropower in the Baltic Sea region are found in the mountainous northern areas. The first hydroelectric power stations in the region were built on the rivers in northern Sweden and Norway at the end of the 19th century, when the technology for the transfer of electricity over large distances developed. The development of large-scale hydropower stations continued in these areas up to the 1980s. In comparison, the landscape in the south, where large geologically "older" rivers are found, is very flat. The Wisla River in Poland has thus

Figure 12.3. Since the beginning of the 19th century about 3 million hectares of wetland has disappeared in the Baltic Sea region mainly because of drainage to create farmland. In recent years however some wetlands have been recreated such as this one in Dalarna, Southern Sweden. The photos show Ansta before (left) and after restauration (right). Photo: Peter Sennblad(left) and Kajsa Andersson (right). Courtesy of Länsstyrelsen in Dalarna.

only one large power station at Plotsk, while the Daugava River has two power stations, one in Salaspils, Latvia, and a small one in Belarus. As the result of a century of exploitation of large rivers, Norway has the world's largest production of hydropower electricity per capita. In Sweden, 50% of all electricity comes from hydropower plants. Also in Finland hydropower is an important energy provider.

Wind power has increased dramatically over the last decades. Maps of average wind speed demonstrate clearly that normally the best places for wind power are found outside the coasts. Especially northern Germany and Denmark has been pioneering this technology and today more than 25% of Denmark's energy needs are covered by wind power electricity. Large wind power fields with hundreds of units are found in the Baltic Sea south of Öland, south of Gotland and east of Uppland between Sweden and Åland. Wind power is in a phase of expansion to meet the increased demands for renewable electricity.

Wave power is a more recent addition to the technologies of producing renewable electricity. Here a float on the surface of the sea is connected to a generator on the bottom by a cable. As the waves moves the float up and down electricity is generated. The technology is under development and presently for the first time a several hundred-unit wave power field is built on the Swedish west coast.

There are also small-scale technologies adapted to smaller streams. Small-scale hydropower may be installed in rivers e.g. at traditional dams and streams used earlier for mills. A small hydropower installation is only serving a few households or a small industry but is still valuable. A technology under development intends to use the energy in streaming water by a rotating device on the bottom; also this is a small-scale device.

Equally solar power is installed in the region at a rapidly increasing rate.

While solar, wind and wave power are intermittent sources of energy, hydropower is not. In fact the large dams and reservoirs of the large hydropower stations have an enormous value as "batteries" of the national energy system and may compensate for moments when the wind is not blowing and waves are small.

Especially wind and hydropower intervene in the landscape in a way that not always is accepted by the local population. In these cases a compromise has to be made to balance the requests of renewable energy and preserved natural environment.

Part C

Forests and Energy

Authors: Per Angelstam, Marine Elbakidze, Agnieszka Karczmarczyk, Ingrid Karlsson, Józef Mosiej, Aleh Rodzkin, Lars Rydén, Valery Tikhomirov and Katarzyna Wyporska

Coordinating Author: Kalev Sepp

Sustainable Forestry

13

Ingrid Karlsson
Uppsala University, Uppsala, Sweden

Sustainable Forest Management in a European Perspective

The Large Value of Forests

Forestry and forest-based activities are important parts of rural income-generating activities but are also extremely important for many different types of ecosystem services. Examples of goods and services provided by forests are: Raw materials for timber, pulp and other fibre-based products, fuel wood, berries, mushrooms, herbs, recreation, tourism and ecological values such as biodiversity of plants and animals, filtering air pollution, cleaning water, protect against soil erosion, moderate drought and other natural hazards.

The long-term horizons in forestry, with rotation periods of up to 150 years and more in the cooler climates, require special attention to be given to planting methods, forest management and careful selection of tree species for various habitats.

European Forests

In all Europe, 44% of the land area (about 1 billion ha) is covered by forests. This is about 25% of all forests of the world. More than 80% of Europe's forests are found in European Russia. In 2006, about 3.8 million people worked in the European forest sector (including forest industries). Employment is slowly declining, the decline being mostly in the pulp and paper sector (FAO, 2009).

Many of Europe's forests are planted, but this started in many cases a hundred years ago or more. In the north the species composition is rather limited due to the cool climate and mainly native species (boreal forests) are planted.

The major threats to forest resources are environmental (fires, pests, storms). The area of forests has increased by almost 13 million ha in the past 15 years. The area of protected forests has also expanded by about 2 million ha and now comprises 5% of Europe's forests. Furthermore, wood volumes and forest biomass carbon reserves are also increasing (UNECE and FAO, 2007). All this is good news and indeed partly due to the intensified European cooperation in this area.

Criteria for Sustainable Forestry

On a European level, a set of pan-European Criteria and Indicators for Sustainable Forest Management were established by the Ministerial Conference on the Protection of Forests in Europe (MCPFE) in the early 1990s. MCPFE has 46 member states including all states in the Baltic Sea Region. Within the borders of these member states are located 98% of the forests on the European continent.

MCPFE has agreed on the following definition of sustainable forestry (UNECE and FAO, 2007):

> *Sustainable forestry is the stewardship and use of forests and forest lands in a way, and at a rate, that maintains their biodiversity, productivity, regeneration capacity, vitality and their potential to fulfil, now and in the future, relevant ecological, economic and social functions, at local, national and global levels, and that does not cause damage to other ecosystems.*

Furthermore, MCPFE has developed six criteria for sustainable forest management to safeguard the ecological,

Box 13.1. Forests and Sustainable Development

Forests have a key role in sustainable development. The most telling example may be Easter Island in the middle of the Pacific Ocean, where a once vivid society after destruction of the forests only could house a small and desperate population in a barren landscape. The story has been told repeatedly, but a most convincing version is in the book *Collapse* by Jarred Diamond. In his book Diamond analyses a dozen societies which collapsed, all of them characterised by the loss of forest resources. Most of these examples refer to the history but some are contemporary, e.g. the development in present day Montana, USA, is on a track reminding of the ancient collapses.

Forests in Europe today are increasing; the forested area reached a minimum around the beginning of the 20th century, when agriculture expanded to use also less profitable, previously forested land; much of this has later been reforested. There was, however, a previous deforestation crisis in Europe, which occurred in the beginning and mid of the 1700s. Large area of forests was then almost clear-cut, due to the large demand for timber, mostly in the mining industry. In Saxony (today a state, bundesland, in Germany, then a kingdom) timber was used in the silver mines for building shafts and heating the ore. Carl von Carlowitz, head of the 'Oberbergamt' (Royal mining office) in the Erzgebirge district of the Kingdom of Saxony, was given the job of solving the problem. Carlowitz made a number of proposals for resolving the resource-crisis:

• Practising "Holtzsparkünste" (the art of saving timber) by applying energy-saving stoves in housing and metallurgy and by improving heat-insulation of buildings.
• Searching for 'Surrogata' (substitutes) for timber, such as peat.
• Cultivating new forests by "sowing and planting of wild trees".

In 1713 von Carlowitz published the book *Sylvicultura oeconomica*, the first comprehensive handbook of forestry. The 400 page book deals with the question, how to achieve 'Conservation and cultivation of timber, a continuous, steady and sustained use'. The concept of *Sustainability* (Nackhaltigkeit) appears for the first time in his book on forestry.

Also in mid Sweden forest was a critical resource. Wood was burned to heat the rock and crack the mountain to mine the iron ore; it was used to reduce iron from its oxides, and to melt it in the blacksmiths' ovens. Sweden was then the largest iron exporter in the world, feeding the wars in Europe. Here Count Carl Johan Cronstedt of the newly (1739) formed Swedish Academy of Sciences, was asked to tackle the problem. Cronstedt was architect and highly active in mining affairs. After experimentation Cronstedt together with General Fabian Wrede introduced in 1767 the 'kakelugn' a channelized stove, which very efficiently took up and stored the heat. It made Swedish energy technology the best in Europe, and meant much to reduce wood use for heating. Swedish homes got a reputation for being warm and nice.

It is interesting to see that the ways to deal with the resource crisis were then the same as today. Management skills - as in the handbook on forestry - and technological solutions - such as the channelized stove and insulation of buildings - and substitution for example by the use of peat are all on today's agenda.

Figure 13.1. A planted forest in mid-Poland. plantation of forest monoculture have been a state priority since the 18th century. Today for example only 10% of forests in Sweden are so-called natural. Photo: Krzysztof Ciesielski.

Today again forests are in focus in the sustainbilty discussion. Half of the original forests of our planet are gone. In the climate negotiations deforestation in the world have been recognised as a main source of emissions, accounting for up to 25 % of global greenhouse gases, and in the discussion on a global treatment the out-phasing of the fossils fuels are accompanied by the so-called RED, REDD and REDD+ Programmes which address "reduced deforestation and forest degradation" in developing countries. Almost the entire deforestation dilemma refers to tropical forests on the southern hemisphere. The boreal forests in northern hemisphere, including northern Europe, may however significantly contribute to reducing the emission by serving as a sink of atmospheric carbon dioxide, and they are included in the REDD negotiations.

Lars Rydén

Box 13.2. Carbon Nutrient Circle

A growing tree uses its above-ground parts (mainly leaves and needles) to capture CO_2 from the air. Each tree over its lifetime can capture about 1 ton of CO_2 in North European climate. However, in colder climates forests grow slower and are less effective in taking up CO_2. Photosynthesis converts solar energy, CO_2 and water into carbohydrates which remain in roots, stem and branches throughout the lifetime of the tree. The CO_2 remains captured if the stem and/or branches are converted to products such as timber, paperboard, paper and other fibre products and can be stored for several hundred years.

Furthermore, a large proportion of the forest industry's products are recycled and/or reused, which also prolongs storage. If the tree dies and is left to break down naturally, it releases its carbon, which is oxidised into CO_2 again. This happens rather slowly. A faster conversion to CO_2 occurs if the forest burns down or if the tree is purposely cut down and used as fuel wood. An equivalent amount of CO_2 is taken up by growing trees. The cycle is thus almost closed if the cut areas are quickly reforested (nutrients and some CO_2 are released into water and air for about 5-6 years after cutting, but good forest management strives to minimise these leakages). CO_2 accumulation is maximised by maintaining longer forest rotations (Paul et al., 2002).

Thus, using renewable forest products instead of non-renewable oil, gas or mineral resources as raw material helps to counteract the greenhouse effect which warms up our planet. Europe's forests will be increasingly valued as a carbon sink in the light of the climate change threat.

Ingrid Karlsson

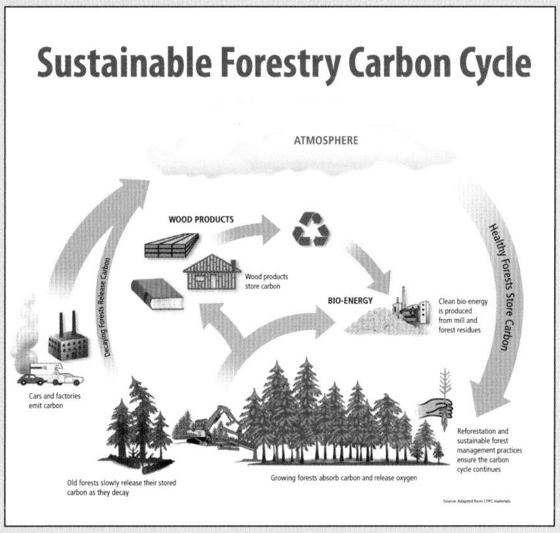

Figure 13.2. The forestry carbon cycle. Source: http://www.bcclimatechange.ca/media/documents/Sustainable-Forestry-Carbon-Cycle.pdf

economic and socio-cultural functions of forest (EFI, 2009):

1. *Maintenance and appropriate enhancement of forest resources and their contribution to global carbon cycles.*
2. *Maintenance of forest ecosystem health and vitality.*
3. *Maintenance and encouragement of productive functions of forests (wood and non wood).*
4. *Maintenance, conservation and appropriate enhancement of biological diversity in forest ecosystems.*
5. *Maintenance, conservation and appropriate enhancement of protective functions in forest management (notably soil and water).*
6. *Maintenance of other socio-economic functions and conditions.*

The Use of Forests

There is an increased demand for wood fuel in Europe. Since the mid-1990s, the EU and its Member States have introduced policies to increase the share of renewable energy in total energy consumption to combat climate change, meet Kyoto Protocol targets and address concerns about rising fuel prices. Energy security has also become an important issue on the political agenda (FAO, 2009). Chapter YY (p. xx) provides more information on different forms of bioenergy.

Socio-economic functions are of special concern for rural employment in logging and timber industries in the countryside, but also in relation to the production, processing and trading of non-wood forest products (NWFP; for instance Christmas trees, berries, mushrooms, tourism and hunting). Ten percent of European forests are managed primarily for the protection of soil and water.

Multiple functions of forest are dependent upon people's traditions, values and knowledge about the forests and on how to find their way in the forest. More attention should be given to increasing biodiversity and to keeping the different types of natural ecosystems for economic reasons, since NWFP is increasing in economic importance. This in turn needs society's support in the form of information, education, legislation, economic incentives, infrastructure investments, etc. This of course needs policies with strong cross-sector coordination.

Certain aspects need to be given more attention, such as gender issues and indigenous people's rights to their traditional forest use. The power relations when using the different natural resources in the forest have very often been to the disadvantage of women and minority groups. In some cases recent National and European initiatives have been taken to counteract these disadvantages, for instance in securing the Scandinavian Sami people's rights to land for reindeer grazing. These issues are sometimes controversial and public debate is intense at times.

Free access rights for the public to forest land is either common practice or protected by law with some exceptions in North Europe. More than 90% of the forests in Europe are open to public access (FAO, 2009). This is described below in more detail for each country in the Baltic Sea region.

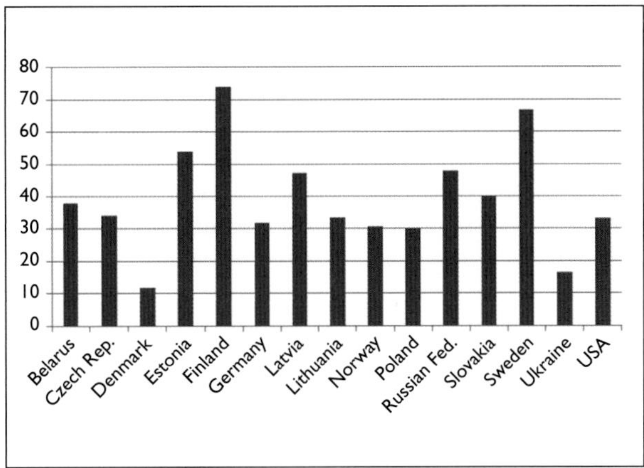

Figure 13.3. Forest area as % of total land area. Source: FAO, 2005; Appendix 3, Table 3.

Table 13.1. Ownership of forest land in 2000. Source: FAO, 2005 Appendix 3, Table 5.

Country	Public	Private	Other	Total forest area (1,000 ha)
Belarus	100	0	0	7,894
Czech Rep.	76.7	23.3	0	2,648
Denmark	28.4	71.6	0	500
Estonia	37.5	22.4	40	2,284
Finland	32.1	67.8	0.1	22,500
Germany	52.8	47.2	0	11,076
Latvia	54	45.1	0.9	2,941
Lithuania	77.3	22.7	0	2,099
Norway	14	86	0	9,387
Poland	83.2	16.8	0	9,192
Russian Fed. (European part)	100	0	0	808,790
Slovakia	52.4	43.2	4.4	1,929
Sweden	19.7	80.3	0	27,528
Ukraine	100	0	0	9,575
USA	42.4	57.6	0	303,089

Sustainable Forestry in the Baltic Sea Region

The Baltic 21 Forestry Sector

As can be seen from Figure 13.3, the rural areas around the Baltic Sea are to a large extent forested. Only Denmark and Ukraine have less than 30% of their total land area covered by forests. The Baltic Sea region is one of the most forested and least populated corners of Europe. In the chapter on land use history (p. xx), maps show the gradual decrease in forests in Europe during the last centuries.

On the Baltic Sea Regional level, a Forest Sector was established within the Baltic 21 framework in the year 2000. A Baltic 21 Forest Action Plan 2005-2008 was decided in 2005 (Baltic 21, 2005). The four most important

Table 13.2. Percentage of total forest used for different functions (Source: Olmos et al., 1999; FAO, 2005; Appendix 3, Table 6)

Country	Production	Protection	Conservation	Social Services	Multiple purpose and others
Belarus	51	28	6	15	0
Czech Rep.	75	6	7	12	0
Denmark	39	7	16	0	39
Estonia	72	2	6	0	0
Finland	91	0	7	0	2
Germany	0	22	19	42	17
Latvia	0	6	14	2	79
Lithuania	70	10	9	3	8
Norway	63	28	2	0	8
Poland	64	21	5	11	0
Russian Fed.. (European part)	77	9	2	2	11
Slovakia	10	18	5	13	55
Sweden	73	0	12	0	15
Ukraine	48	30	3	19	0
USA	12	0	20	0	68

themes for the Baltic 21 Forest Sector's work according to this plan are:

- *Sustainable management of private forests*
- *Multiple use of forests*
- *Transparent timber flows in the Baltic 21 region*
- *Increased use of wood as a renewable and environmentally friendly resource*

Ownership of Forests

When analysing the impact of forestry on rural development, it is important to consider ownership of forest land. Differences within the Baltic Sea Region have very little to do with climatic or other 'natural' properties of the forest. The ownership, e.g. the power over how to use forest land and its natural resources, has been decided for political and economic reasons. According to some researchers, state forestry lacks incentives for economically efficient timber harvesting and forest management in general (Lazdinis et al., 2009).

Historically, forests were considered public areas. With an increasing need for arable land and increasing possibilities to make money from forest products, privatisation of forests has taken place. Some interesting comparisons can be made from studying Table 13.1. For instance, in Norway and Sweden more than 80% of forest land is in private hands, while the US has close to 60% and Germany has about 50% of private forest land. In Russia, forest resources have remained publicly owned to 100% even since 1990, when the Soviet Union was dissolved. Russia has huge resources of arable land and forest land – on a global scale, Russia has 25% of all forest land in the world (including both its European and Asian parts).

Ownership differences are highly important when discussing rural development and people's possibility to earn their living in the countryside. Practical livelihood decisions are very much dependent on how to interpret international human right laws, private ownership, and the principle of state sovereignty over natural resources (see Table 13.1 and Table 13.2).

Forestry in the European Union Part of the Baltic Sea Region

14

Ingrid Karlsson
Uppsala University, Uppsala, Sweden

Sweden, Norway, Finland and Denmark

A History of Forestry

Soils in Sweden, Norway and Finland were shaped by the glaciers that receded only 10,000 years ago. This short geological history and the fact that the countries are located so far north in Europe are the reasons why land, which is not agricultural land, has a low productive capacity, with a predominance of coniferous forest and relatively slow vegetation growth. However, there is a considerable variation in climate due to the large north-south extent of the countries (from 55°N to 69°N). Forest land in Sweden and Finland in particular is characterised by a high abundance of lakes and wetland areas.

Sweden has about 22 million ha of forest land and Finland about 20 million ha. Denmark is small in comparison, with only 0.5 million ha forestry land. The trend for the standing volume of forest cubic metres is positive: in Sweden alone, the increment is close to 120 million forest cubic metres each year.

All Fenno-Scandinavian countries have a strong history of privately owned forest land. This started back in the 19th century, when industrialisation in England generated a demand for timber imports. Timber enterprises in England, France, the Netherlands, Norway and later also firms established in Sweden and Finland could buy the right to cut old timber wood (often 200-400 years old and very high quality for construction purposes) for low prices from private farmers who saw very little value in their forests.

By the beginning of 1900, most parts of southern and central Sweden were deforested and large parts of northern Sweden as well. Laws were then enforced to stop the buying of land and cutting without replanting. This led to the aggressive lumber companies moving east and south, to Finland, Russia and the Baltic states, where his-

Figure 14.1. Spruce forest. Photo: M. Gerentz. Source: SLU

tory partly repeated itself. In Russia, the cutting was not as successful as in Scandinavia and in the Baltic States. The transportation of timber to the coast was much more problematic in Russia, since many rivers had their outlets to the north, where harbours were clogged by ice for large parts of the year (Perlinge, 1992). Since that time, in Sweden and Finland, forests have been highly valued natural resource assets.

Access Rights

In Norway access rights are different depending on how far away the land is situated from the farmhouse. At a distance from the farmhouse there are no limitations on access, but public access is only permitted close to houses during times when the soil is frozen or has a snow cover. All mushrooms and berries except for the cloudberry (which is considered to have a very high economic value) are allowed to be picked by the public.

Sweden and Finland have more production forest than any other country in the Baltic Sea Region, but they also have a long tradition of general access to all forestry land. Thus, even if Table 13.2 in Chapter 13 does not reflect this fact, all forests are in reality multipurpose forests, since all people have the right to pick e.g. mushrooms, berries and flowers in forested areas. For this reason protected forests are not specified. Private owners cannot prevent the general public trespassing on their property and everyone also has the right to camp for one night on private property (outside the house areas). However, the public are not allowed to walk in growing crops and can be fined for littering. In Sweden the most recent Forestry Act was passed in 1994. It contains several multipurpose considerations and states that environmental values have the same status as meeting production goals.

The laws in Denmark are somewhat different. In Denmark there is free access to public forests (36% of all forests) and only limited access to private forests. Forest properties smaller than 5 ha are allowed to be closed entirely and the larger ones can only be accessed via roads and paths and only during daytime (Saastamoinen, 1999).

Production Forests

Sweden and Finland are today (2007) the most active countries in Europe in producing and trading forest products in Europe (Swedish Forest Industries, 2008). In a global perspective, Sweden and Finland are also the second and third largest overall exporters of paper, pulp and sawn timber (next to Canada). New developments are mainly found in fuelwood production, mainly in the manufacturing of wood pellets. Sweden is the world leader in wood pellet production and also in consumption. In 2005, Sweden used more than 1.6 million metric tons of wood pellets for heating and for the production of electricity. On the global scale too, there is a fast growing market demand for wood pellets (FAO, 2009).

Large companies own about 25% of forest land in Sweden (Swedish Forest Agency, 2009) and about 9% of forest land in Finland. In both Sweden and Finland

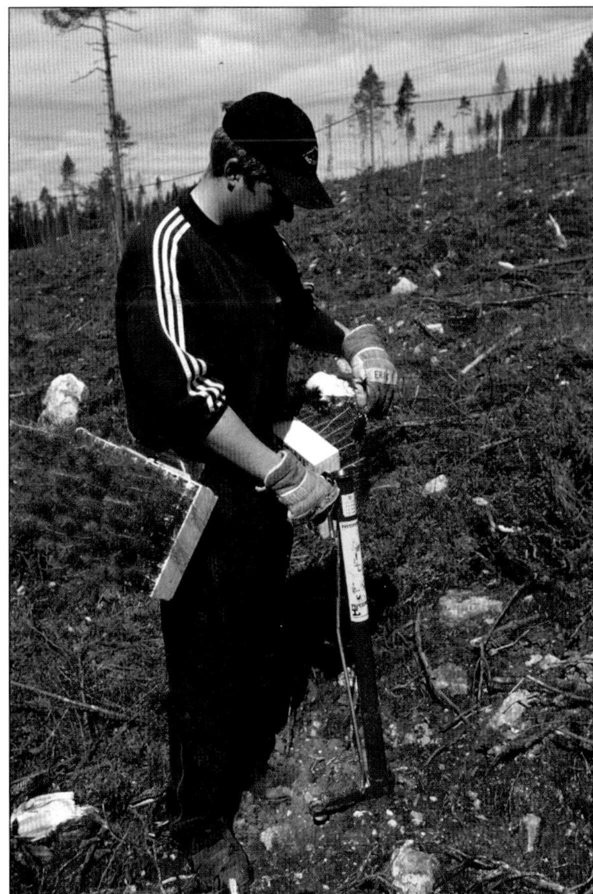

Figure 14.2. Planting of tree seedlings on clear-felled area. Photo: M. Gerentz. Source: SLU.

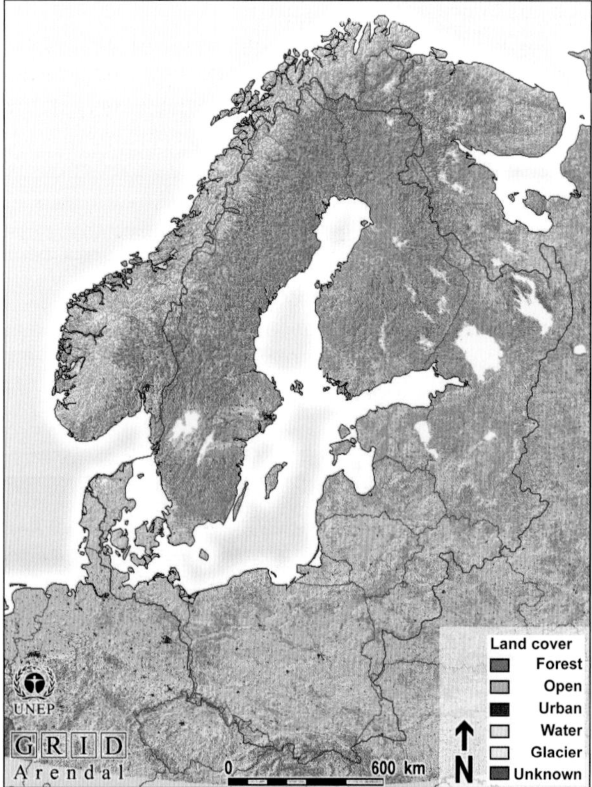

Figure 14.3. Land cover in the Baltic Sea region. Source: GRID/Arendal.

private owners are mainly farmers or small family enterprises. This means forestry is very important for rural employment and also for the rural identity. Most farms combine agricultural and forestry production. In Finland, the background to the high percentage of small forestry-dominated farms is very special. Many of the combined agriculture/forestry farms were created after 1945, when about 400,000 Finnish refugees came from Karelia after the war against the Soviet Union. The refugees were mainly small-scale farmers and were given land by the government in a forced land reform, as a way to solve the acute food shortage problem.

For both Sweden and Finland, a production goal ensures that the majority of forest land is used cost-effectively and with responsibility for efficient regeneration and productivity. However, equal weight is being given to ecological considerations. Safeguarding of biodiversity is for instance the responsibility of all landowners and is also protected through different special regulations and through creation of national reserves (Royal Swedish Academy of Agriculture and Forestry (KSLA), 2009).

In order to keep up with the recent developments concerning production and ecological considerations, education, training and information are needed. Many such programmes are carried out in Scandinavia. In recent years, more than 100,000 woodlot owners and other foresters have been reached by these programmes (Borealforest, 2009).

Sweden and Finland have signed and ratified about 25 different international conventions having impacts on forests and forestry, and they are also very often in the lead in terms of processes, especially concerning biodiversity and climate issues with implication for forestry.

The main stipulations of the current Swedish Forestry Act, in many ways similar to the Finnish, are:

- Mandatory reforestation after final felling (within three years in Sweden, within two to seven years, depending on regeneration methods and other relevant circumstances in Finland)
- A ban on the felling of young stands
- An obligation on forest owners to carry out preventive control of insect pests
- Special management regimes for valuable hardwood forests and upland forests
- A general duty of care for objects or sites of natural, historical or heritage value in the forests.

Regulations are controlled by the National Forest Authority through regular satellite imagery and fines can be levied on those not complying with the rules, which have legal status.

In Scandinavia, representatives from forestry, authorities, environmental and employees' organisations are also involved in the creation of forest certification systems on the same lines as the principles laid down by the Forest Stewardship Council (FSC). Sweden was the first country to work out a national standard approved by the FSC (Borealforest, 2009).

Estonia, Latvia and Lithuania

Forestry Cover After Soviet Occupation

All three of the Baltic states have a forest cover similar to that of the Scandinavian countries with a species composition mainly consisting of Scots pine, Norway spruce and birch, and comprising between 30-50% of land area (Estonia being the most forested, see Figure 13.3).

After World War II, all the Baltic states eventually became part of the Soviet Union, having been occupied first by Soviet Union, then by Germany, then by the Soviet Union again. Rural areas and their inhabitants were severely damaged by the war and by the occupation. More or less all educated people and people in leading positions, including the Jewish minority (during the German occupation), were reported to have been killed or deported for different reasons.

Of course these experiences resulted in forests and forest management that were completely different after World War II than before. Large areas of forests were damaged by warfare. People with knowledge about management of forests were no longer in place. In many cases Russian-speaking people, including those in the military forces, replaced the people who had been displaced or killed and all agricultural and forest land was nationalised. A period of planned economy with centralised decision-making started, with guidelines being set by the state. According to Lazdinis et al. (2009), the Soviet forestry of Lithuania was characterised by lack of economic incentives, entrepreneurship and managerial skills and top-down decision making.

Since 1990, all three Baltic countries have had a period of restitution of private forest land to its former owners, a privatisation process that is not yet finished. The average private forest holdings are quite small, in Lithuania somewhat less than 5 ha, and in comparison with those in the Scandinavian neighbouring countries are sub-optimal and difficult to manage, since essential forest operations are fragmentised.

In Estonia and Lithuania the Ministry of Environment is responsible for forestry affairs, while in Latvia the responsibility lies with the Ministry of Agriculture and Forestry.

Access Rights

The Baltic states have similar traditions to the Scandi navian countries concerning access rights to forests. Local people as well as tourists have free access to Baltic forests, including the right to pick berries, mushrooms and medicinal plants.

According to the Estonian Forest Act, camping in the forest as well as picking berries, mushrooms and other non-wood products in state, municipal and private forests without bound or mark is the right of every citizen.

Production Forests

State forest enterprises have been restructured and the number of staff has been sharply reduced. New knowledge and skills are needed in both private and state businesses. The ways in which forest resources are governed have been significantly modified – for instance, accountability in state forestry has become an important issue. This means for instance that annual reporting and auditing of accounts have become the norm. Illegal logging, which was quite a widespread practice in the beginning of the 1990s, has drastically declined. New state forest laws and forestry strategies are in place.

All three Baltic States joined the European Union in 2004, and this led to regulations on European and international levels concerning forestry having to be complied with in their national legislation. Export values of wood products, paper, furniture and assembled wooden constructions are on the increase, along with increasing imports of roundwood and sawn wood for further processing. The Baltic States can compete with Sweden and Finland in these industries, since wages are still much lower. Of the three Baltic countries, Latvia has most export income and is also the country in which the forest sector has the greatest importance, comprising 10-14% of GDP. Growing stock and protected areas have also increased in the past 10 years (1997-2007; Lazdinis et al., 2009).

Almost 4 million hectares of FSC-certified forest can be found in the Baltic Sates (UPM Forest AS, 2006)

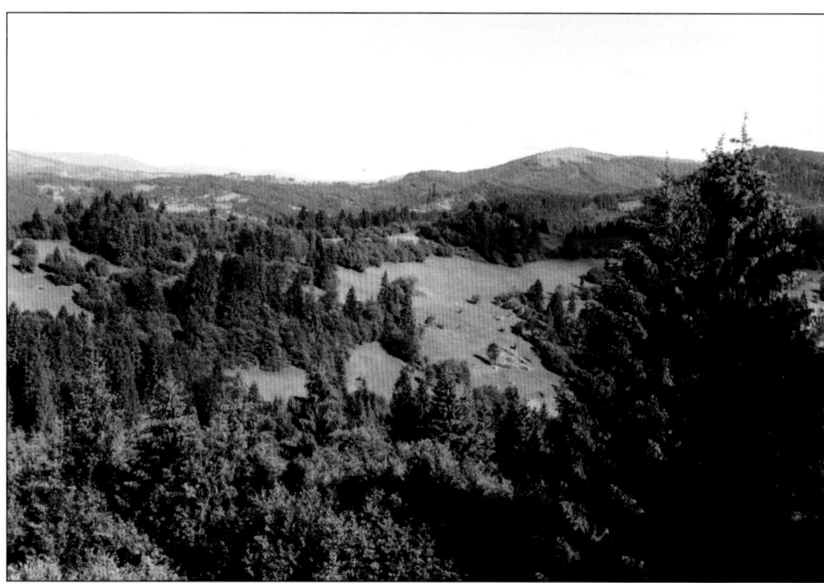

Figure 14.4. Forest in Poland. Photo: Lars Rydén.

Southern Baltic Sea region

Germany

The total forested area in Germany was about 11 million ha in 2000 (see Table 13.1), about 31% of the total land area. Forests were of course destroyed and damaged during World War II and reforestation took place. Since then, forest area has increased by around 6%. Consumption of wood by the wood working industry exceeds the fellings inside Germany. Germany is also the fifth largest exporter of pulp, paper and sawn timber (after Canada, Sweden, Finland and Russia), which means that this country processes more wood than it produces within its borders. Thus, Germany imports large quantities of wood, both as raw materials for its industries and as processed wood products.

Large parts of German forest land are protected. Public access to the forests is restricted, but access through roads and paths is guaranteed by law and regulations.

Poland

Forests cover close to 30% of Poland's land area (see Figure 13.3) and coniferous forests, mainly Scots pine, dominate. Forest production does not contribute to export income to a great extent and although there is a slow trend towards increasing privately owned forest areas, the employment provided by the forest sector is shrinking. Protected forests constitute a large proportion of the state forest area, about 21% of the total forested area (Table 13.2).

Wood resources in Poland have been growing for the past 20 years, for instance in 2006 the harvested volume made up 56% of the growth (MoE Poland, 2009).

In comparison to the post-Soviet countries, changes in forest ownership were not as drastic in Poland. The large and medium-sized private forest estates were nationalised after World War II but small forest plots remained private. Those private plots were mainly located in the south. Private forest land currently constitutes about 17% of the total forest land and generally has lower quality than the state-owned forest. The total number of private forest holdings (owned by individuals) is 900,000 and the average size of these private forest plots is only 1.43 ha (MoE Poland, 2009). However, this is due in part to Polish tax policies: forest land has lower tax than agricultural land, so some agricultural land is allowed to naturally regenerate into forests, a rather slow process. Private owners did not have the right to manage their own forest land during the communist times and only recently received this right.

One other reason for the poor condition of the private forests may be that there has been very little or no possibilities for education and training of private forest owners. In contrast, the state forest sector has been reasonably well-managed by professionals with high standards.

The state plans to increase private forest land areas from today's 17% to 23% by 2015. Some agricultural co-operatives, which have not been cultivated for years, are also expected to be converted to forests through natural succession. These lands may be privatised, too.

In south-west Poland, the health of the forests is rather poor due to industrial and other pollution, while in north-east Poland the forests are in better health. Nitrogen deposition is generally higher in central Europe than in the north. Sulphur deposition is still too high, so soils have become more acidic in Central Europe. Pollutant deposition has dropped, but crown condition surveys indicate vulnerability (UNECE and FAO, 2007). The deterioration of tree health is more often seen in spruce trees. When there are high N levels in soil and water, trees may become more susceptible to pathogenic fungi, insects, frost and collapse under wind or snow (MoE Poland, 2009).

Since 2004, 80% government subsidies with support from the European Union are available for farmland afforestation. These subsidies not only apply for replanting but also for tree maintenance for the first five years, along with an afforestation premium to compensate for the loss of income from farming (MoE Poland, 2009).

Czech and Slovak Republics

A third of the land area of the Czech Republic is covered by semi-natural and production forests (Figure 13.3). Most of this, about 60%, is managed by the state and the remainder belongs to municipalities and regions (15%), forest co-operatives (1%), and private owners (23%). Protected areas have expanded to a great degree recently.

Article 19 of the Forest Act of 1995 states that individuals are entitled to enter forests at their own risk to collect any forest berries and dry waste wood for their own needs, but they may not damage the forest or interfere with the forest environment. Instructions of the owner or tenant and the staff of the forest must be followed. The regulation is interpreted as being valid for picking mushrooms too.

Forests and Forestry in three Eastern European Countries

15

Per Angelstam and Marine Elbakidze
Swedish University of Agricultural Sciences, Skinnskatteberg, Sweden
Valery Tikhomirov
Belarusian State University, Minsk, Belarus

Russian Federation

Basic Information about the Forests

Globally, the Russian Federation has the richest forest resources in the world. Russia's forest cover ranks number one, with around 886.5 million hectares (or 23% of the global forest area) (Hansen et al., 2010). It is in second place in terms of growing wood stock, with a total of 80.7 billion m^3, which amounts to 55% of the world's growing stock of coniferous species. In terms of total carbon stock in forests (185.9 billion tonnes), Russian ranks number one. The forest landscapes in Russia play a major role for the conservation of unique biodiversity and in stabilising the global climate through carbon sequestration (World Bank, 2004). Much of the forest is located in remote areas with slow biological growth and fragile environments, especially in the north and far east.

There are different forest zones in the Russian Federation, from forest tundra and boreal to forest steppe. The main forest tree species are larch (*Larix* spp.) pine (*Pinus* spp.), spruce (*Picea* spp., *Abies* spp.) birch (*Betula* spp.) and aspen (*Populus tremula*) in the north and in the mountains, and oak (*Quercus* spp.) and beech (*Fagus* spp.) in the south. The coniferous forest species cover more than 80% of forested area and more than half of the forested areas are situated in regions with permafrost.

The forest cover has been decreasing continually during the last 500 years, with the most drastic changes happening during the 20th century. However, at the end of the 20th century (1983-2006) the forest cover increased by 6 million hectares (http://rainforests.mongabay.com/deforestation/2000/Russian_Federation.htm).

Brief History of Forest Use

Until the 12th century the use of the forests and forest lands in contemporary Russia was not regulated and forest wood resources were abundant. The development of forests as property with different ownerships began in the form of certain restrictions on forest uses, such as to support bee-keeping and hunting. The right to put boundary-marks on rocks, trees and trunks to delimit different forest holdings appeared for the first time in the 11th century (Hensiruk, 1964 ; Hensiruk et al., 1968). In many regions of Russia the forests were cleared for agriculture development. The people held the land in common, and those who did not belong to the village society did not receive a share of the land. Products from the forests were only used for self-subsistence and people did not pay taxes for this use. Hence, the forests were not considered important property (Teplyakov et al., 1998).

From the 13th to the late 16th century, forest property rights were given to patrimonial estates in some regions in Russia. One of the reasons was that wood became a subject of trade between different regions due to the development of the sawmill industry and charcoal production. This created an opportunity to transfer forest land as an inheritance or to other persons, as formulated through appropriate legal acts (service, protective, negotiated, inherited and others) (Teplyakov et al., 1998).

The first Russian Forest Code was adopted in 1649. The Code gave final judicial clarification concerning forest ownership with the following property divisions: landlord forests, royal family forests, state forests, state servants' forests, preserved forests, and border forests (Teplyakov et al., 1998).

One of the first laws on forest protection was issued in the 17th century. According to this law, it was prohibited to carry out logging and hunting along the big rivers and along the country's borders. Use of all forest land should be according to the needs and interests of the state. The main requirements were that (1) the logging of timber for ship-building was strictly prohibited, (2) all important trees, e.g. oak, had special signs, and local priests in the churches had to explain the restrictions on using such trees to the local people, (3) it was prohibited to use trees suitable for the building of churches or palaces as firewood, (4) the use of a saw instead of an axe for logging was prohibited; (5) making potash from the felling debris was prohibited; (6) harvesting peat for heating was prohibited (Hensiruk, 1964, 1992).

From the 18th century only state forests were regulated, and the private owners were allowed to use their forest property according to their own will. Rights to use forest products and charges for the use of wood from the state forests were introduced. Forestry thus developed into a separate societal sector with strict rules concerning the use of forest resources. Norms for logging, forest regeneration and forest plantation were defined, and forest administrations were established. Most of the forests belonged to the state (Hensiruk, 1964, 1992; Hrushevsky, 1995). The first record about sustained yield forestry was noted in a law from 18th century, adopted under Catherine II. It stated that: 'commercial and state interests demand that the future abundance of the forests be insured by a precise relationship between harvesting and reforestation' (Teplyakov et al., 1998). The first legislative acts concerning forest protection with the aim of controlling logging were introduced in 1888. These two laws aimed at establishing control over forest use on both state and private land.

During the Soviet era, all forests and forestry activities belonged to the state. The role of forestry was to support industry by supplying cheap raw material. Very limited silvicultural and ecological considerations were taken (e.g. Elbakidze et al., 2007). This exploitative approach led to large areas of clear-cut and young forests dominated by deciduous trees. Originally the forest administration was represented by the state forest management units (*leskhoz*), which were responsible for forest management, protection and conservation. In the 1970s integrated management units (*lespromkhoz*) were established to combine forestry and industry functions. In general, due to limited regulation and control, forest wood resources deteriorated further (Pipponen, 1999).

At the same time, the Soviet system for biodiversity conservation was in many ways successful. The system of strictly protected areas (*zapovedniks*) was developed from the 1930s (Boreyko, 1995; Weiner, 1999). Zoning of forest landscapes to satisfy protective, nature conservation and social functions was developed already in the 19th century. In April 1943 forests were divided into three groups where 'forests with protective and social functions' belonged to the first group. The second group included forests with ecological functions and certain limitations for exploitation, and forests available for exploitation belonged to the third group (Teplyakov et al., 1998). The areas set aside were substantial. For example in the Troitsko-Pechorsk region (4,100 km^2) in SE Komi Republic, a total of 40% was set aside for nature conservation and social functions (Angelstam et al., 1997, 2004).

Forestry at Present

Since 1991, after the disintegration of the Soviet Union, the development of the forest sector in the Russian Federation as an independent state has been in a state of flux and turmoil. The transition period from a socialistic planned economy to a market economy has been accompanied by economic and political crises. New Russian forest legislation has been discussed in terms of how to: (1) create and adopt market relations in the forest sector; (2) divide rights and responsibilities between federal and regional authorities; (3) divide tasks between public forest management and private forest industry; and (4) determine forest ownership.

During recent decades, revised Forest Codes have been adopted four times – in 1993, 1997, 2001 and 2007. The first Forest Code (1993) was inherited from the Soviet time, and was not appropriate for the transition towards a market economy. The main arguments for reforming the forest sector in Russia stated at political level were: (a) only 20% of forest wood resources were used by the commercial forestry sector; (b) as an owner of forests in Russia the state was ineffective under market conditions; and (c) improving the forestry sector would be possible only through radical transformation of the system of governance.

Following the Forest Code of 1997, forest management was divided between the federal and regional levels. The regional level decided on the level of revenues from forest use, and the federal level by and large accounted for the costs. On average the costs for management, protection and conservation were twice those of the revenues from forest use. As a result, state forest management units were forced to carry out commercial intermediate cuttings to cover the costs. The Forest Code of 2001 had the main goal of radically improving the economic situation in the forest sector to gain more economic benefits from Russia's natural resources.

The present Forest Code (2007) has a number of key strategic goals: to establish a new balance of power between Federation, Subjects of Federation and Private Business; to separate forest management and forest administration; and to establish a competitive and market-orientated environment in the forestry sector, including forest management.

At present the centralised system of governance in the forest sector has been replaced by a de-centralised system (e.g., Nilsson and Shvidenko 1998, Carlsson et al. 2001, Krott et al. 2000; Levintanous 1992; Solberg and Rykowski 2000). The most fundamental changes in the forestry sector since 2007 are:

1 The responsibility (power) over forests has been moved from the Federal level to the Subjects of the Federation (e.g., Republic, oblast etc.).
2 New institutions have been established for forest administration on the federal and regional levels. The Ministry of Agriculture is responsible for the forest policy and law making functions. The Federal Forestry Agency delegates decision making functions to the regions and is responsible only for forest policy implementation. At the local level, there has been a radical reform of forest management. The local state forest management units supervise how forests are used and are free from any commercial activity. New state forest enterprises have been established for commercial activities.
3 A new relationship between the state and private business has developed. Private business is responsible for the forest industries, silvicultural activities and forest protection.
4 Abolition of the system with three groups representing protective functions (group 1), multiple use (group 2) and industrial use (group 3).

The condition of forests and the potential for development of the forest industry are very diverse in Russia due to the large differences among regions in their natural biophysical conditions and history of forest use. The European part of the different forest zones is being gradually transformed by its economic utilisation (Angelstam and Törnblom, 2004; Angelstam and Kuuluvainen, 2004; Angelstam et. 2005; Shorohova and Tetioukhin, 2004; Volkov and Gromtsev, 2004). The official harvest statistics describing the historical development of wood harvest in the Russian Federation's Komi Republic is illustrative (Figure 15.1). The history of local forest use in Komi is

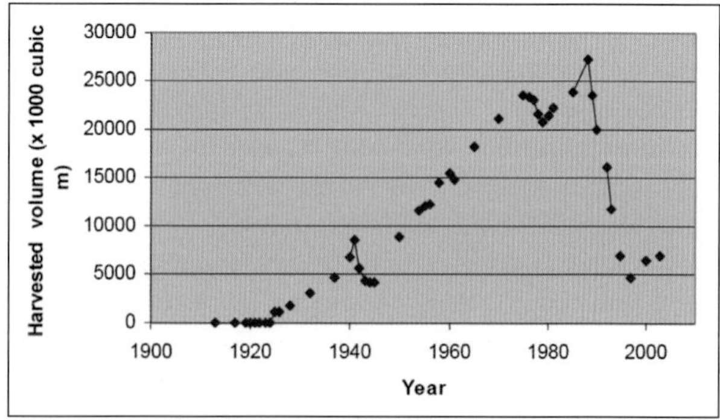

Figure 15.1. Graph showing the annual harvest of wood in the Komi Republic in the Russian Federation during the past 100 years. Source: Compilation of official forest statistics in the Komi Republic.

ancient. Logging for export of wood was long confined to high grading close to rivers of large valuable trees used for ship-building. While local forest industries supporting mining and salt boiling occurred early on, industrial forestry commenced only after WW2. Logged volumes increased from 5 million m^3 annually before WW2 to more than 25 million m^3 in 1990. This was again followed by a reduction to 6 million m^3 annually, a 75% decline (Figure 15.1).

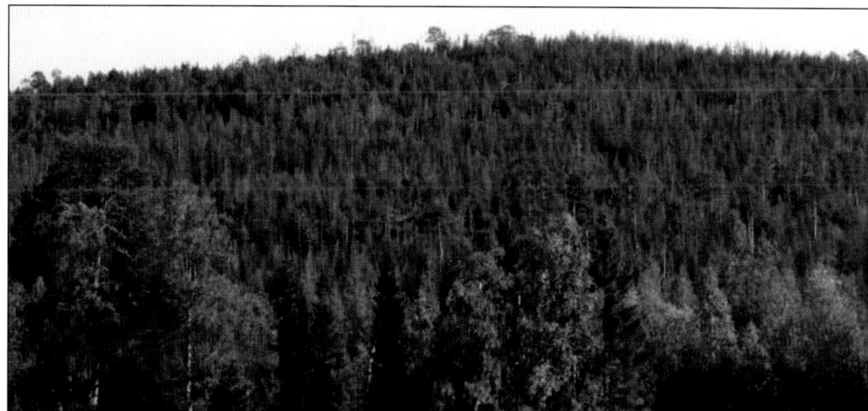

Figure 15.2. Naturally dynamic pine forest in a remote area of the Murmansk Region in north-west Russia (2007). Photo: Marine Elbakidze.

The former system of forest groups, with group 1 forests satisfying different protective functions such as buffer zones along streams, roads and villages, resulted in an active zoning of landscapes into different functions. Therefore, at the local level, forest landscapes in north-west Russia have abundant forest resources, either because the some older forests have not yet been harvested, for example in remote parts of the Komi Republic, Arkhangelsk or Murmansk regions, or because the forest has recovered by natural succession after intensive logging in the early twentieth century (Figure 15.2). However, at other places they have probably been subjected to more recent unsustainable exploitation, also known as wood mining or cut and run practices, with very limited wood resources left, and the logging camps and villages deserted, or with very limited potential for the near future (e.g. Knize and Romanuk, 2005). In the light of these changes, as noted by Lehtinen (2004): 'the forest actors of the European North need to carefully examine the new signals in forest trade, emerging from green developmentalism and new tourism entrepreneurship'.

The Kovdozersky state forest management unit (400,000 ha) in the southern Murmansk region provides a good illustration of the economic and socio-cultural challenges (Elbakidze et al., 2007). During the Soviet period forestry was the main industry in the area. The harvesting activity was very intensive during this period, and annual allowable cuts were often exceeded. The amount of forest harvested peaked at 596,600 m^3 in 1955. Since 1991 the harvest has not exceeded 10,000 m^3. As a consequence of previous forest exploitation (often referred to as 'forest mining'), young and middle-aged forests dominate in the area (Figure 15.3). It is important to note that in this region, and in general in NW Russia, only stands older than about 120 years are harvested. At present, the local and regional forest industry has virtually disappeared. The annual allowable cut is 55,400 m^3, and only 10% of this was harvested in 2004 and 2005 (Elbakidze et al., 2007).

During the past decade state investment in the forest management has been very low, which was the main rea-

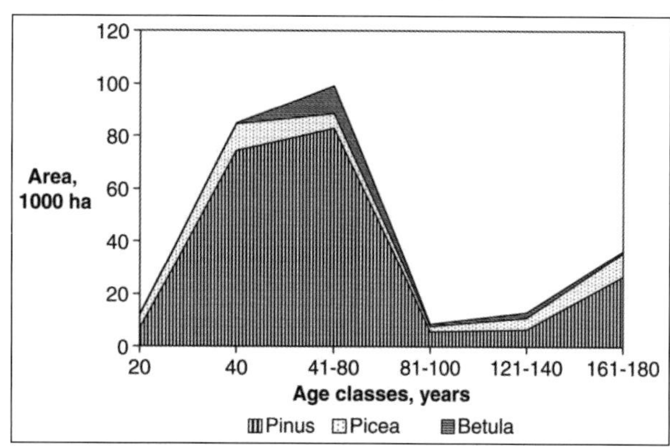

Figure 15.3. The area of main tree species in the Kovdozersky state forest management unit in the Murmansk region of north-west Russia Source: Archives of the Kovdozersky leshoz. Zelenoborskyy, Murmansk oblast.

Table 15.1. Summary of silvicultural system development in the Kovdozersky state forest enterprise (leskhoz) (Murmansk region, Russian Federation) (Elbakidze et al., 2007).

Kovdozerskiy leskhoz (total area is around 500,000 hectares) (Murmansk region, the Russian Federation)	
Final harvest:	
• log	Mainly by assortments and seldom by tree-length logs
• pulpwood	30% of pulpwood after final felling
• branches	Left in the forest after final felling
• stumps	Left in the clear cuts after final felling
Intermediate harvest	
• Sanitary cuttings	The total area of sanitary cuts is up to 0.01% of total leskhoz's area per year. At present sanitary cuttings are made mainly after windfall
• Commercial thinning	The first time is in the young forests (aged up to 40 years). Only 5% of the area which should be done is actually treated. The second time at a stand age of 40-60 years. This is done in only 1% of the area where it should be done. After the second commercial thinning there is 30% saw-wood and 70% pulpwood
Regeneration	
• Seed trees/scarify	The last time this was done was in 1998 on big clear cuts (more than 200 ha)
• Plantation	Forest plantation was carried out on an area of 0.01% of total leskhoz's area in 2005
• Leave undergrowth	Undergrowth is left after final felling if the size of clear cuts is more than 100 ha
Means of intensification	
• Draining	No
• Nitrogen fertilisation	Not at present. It was stopped 15 years ago
• Other fertilisation	No
• Genetic/selection	Selection work to improve the quality of tree species
• Exotic species	Cembra pine and Larix were introduced

son for the poor forest management in many local state forest enterprises. Many of them had to reduce or stop some silvicultural activities due to lack of finance. The Kovdozersky local state forest enterprise is an example (Table 15.1). Unlike previously, according to the Forest Code (2007), forest leasers are responsible for forest management.

In general, the Russian forest sector is now at a stage of integration into international markets. In 2002, timber harvest was about 180 million m^3 and the export value was about $4.5 billion. Increased commercial value and volumes logged can be expected, based on continued increases in domestic and international demand for forest products. Domestic forest product consumption is estimated to grow from 80 million m^3 of roundwood equivalent in 1994 to about 125-165 million m^3 by 2010 (World Bank, 2004). Overall market prospects are positive. The main aim now is to shift production from exporting raw wood and basic commodities to higher value-added products. However, improved forest road systems and other transport infrastructure, training, favourable legal and policy framework and overall improvement of the business climate are needed, which requires considerable new investments in sector modernisation (World Bank, 2004).

Ukraine

Basic Information About the Forests

Ukraine was part of the Soviet Union until its independence in 1991. Next to Russia, Ukraine is the largest

European country, covering 603,548 km^2. The forested area in Ukraine is 9.4 million ha, or 15.6% of the total land area.

Forests range from mixed hemiboreal and broadleaf forests in the north to steppe-forest woodland in the south. The forests in the Carpathian Mountains range from temperate to mixed forests with a boreal character close to the tree line (Figure 15.4). Forests in the Crimean mountains range from Mediterranean shrub to broad-leaved and coniferous forests (Hensiruk, 1992).

Figure 15.4. The Carpathian Mountains in the Western Ukraine are one of the most forested regions. Photo: Marine Elbakidze.

As a result of climatic conditions and anthropogenic influence during historic time, forests are very unevenly distributed in Ukraine (Buksha, 2004). The forest cover in different regions varies from 3.8% in the steppe zone to 70% in the Carpathian Mountains. The majority of forests are concentrated in the northern and the western parts of Ukraine. The largest forest cover is found in the Carpathian Mountains (40%), Polissya (29%) and Crimea (26%). By contrast, the forest cover is lower, and includes forest plantations, in the forest-steppe (8%) and steppe (3%) zones. Conifers occupy 42.6% of the forested area, with pine trees accounting for 36% of this figure. Deciduous forests cover 57.4% of the total area, with beech (*Fagus sylvatica*) and oak (*Quercus robur*) comprising 33% of this figure (Nilsson and Shvidenko, 1999).

More than half of Ukraine's forests (55.8%) are classified as protective and protected forests. Thus, forest management is restricted, for certain categories of forests final fellings are not allowed or rotation ages are much longer than in commercial forests. Other forests, mainly used for wood production, are classified as commercial forests (Forest Code of Ukraine, 2006). The area of the protective and protected forests has been increasing since 1991 due to the creation of new protected areas.

Massive forest fellings took place during World War II, and subsequent intensive forest planting occurred. Today, commercial forests aged up to 20 years comprise 31% of the total forest area, from 20-40 years ~45%, from 40-60 years ~13% and older than 60 years ~11% (Shvidenko and Andrusishin, 1998; Hensiruk et al., 1995). Currently, about 15 million m^3 of timber is harvested in Ukraine per year. Each year, enterprises of the State Forestry Committee of Ukraine cut and sell more than 7.6 million m^3 of wood, of which 5 million m^3 is industrial wood.

The Ukrainian forests are characterised by high productivity (Figure 15.5). The annual total average increment is 4.0 m^3/ha. The annual total increment varies from 5.0 m^3/ha in the Carpathian Mountains to 2.5 m^3/ha in the steppe zone. The total growing stock on forested areas is 1.74 billion m^3 (Nilsson and Shvidenko, 1999). The average wood stock is 185 m^3/ha.

Brief History of Forest Use

The forest landscapes in Ukraine remained more or less natural in terms of tree species composition until the 15th century. The forest was used by local people for hunting, bee-keeping, collecting non-wood products and was cut down only for agricultural purposes. From the 16th century forest usage became economically profitable. The forest areas began to decrease due to anthropogenic activity and their species composition and qualitative structure was altered (Hensiruk, 1992; Kubiyovych, 1938).

Figure 15.5. Productive beech forests (Fagus silvatica) remain in the Ukrainian Carpathians.The height of these beech trees is more than 45 metres. Photo by Marine Elbakidze.

Figure 15.6. Bark-beetles (Ips spp.) are one of the main 'destroyers' of introduced Norway spruce forests in the Ukrainian Carpathians.Tracks of bark-beetle larvae in the bark of Norway spruce. Photo by Marine Elbakidze.

In Ukraine commercial forest exploitation began in the 18th century, and along with railway building the forest industry started to alter forest landscapes completely. The wood was exported to Germany, France, England and Poland. Focusing on sustained yield production of wood, monocultures of Norway spruce (*Picea abies*) were created in the Carpathians and Scots pine (*Pinus silvestris*) in Polissya. In addition, wood was intensively used for potash production and as a source of energy for iron and glass manufacturing and sugarbeet processing. Forest cutting led to reduction in the proportion and area of beech and mixed spruce-beech-fir forest areas in the Carpathian Mountains, and a strong decline and regional disappearance of beech and oak (*Quercus* spp.) forests in central and north-western parts of Ukraine (Hensiruk, 1992; Hensiruk et al., 1995 ; Holubetst and Odynak, 1983; Holubetst et al., 1988; Kalynovych and Sytnyk 2003; Krynytskyj and Tretiak 2003).

In eastern Ukraine, agriculture's role became more significant due to the increased demand for bread in western European countries in the 18-19th centuries. In fact, until 1914 Ukraine was the European continent's leading exporter of grain (Davies, 1996). The need for new agricultural land caused a disastrous reduction in forest areas in the forest-steppe region. The area of forests in this zone was diminished to a fourth (Hensiruk et al., 1995). Some forest restoration started in the middle of the 19th century on small areas in steppe and forest-steppe zones of Ukraine, as well as in the Carpathian Mountains (Vakaluk, 1971).

The first legislative acts concerning forest protection with the aim of controlling logging were compiled only in the second part of the 19th century. In western Ukraine, a forest protection law was passed in 1852 and in the Russian-governed part of Ukraine in 1888. These were the first large-scale attempts at forest restoration in the Carpathian Mountains and at creating forest protection strips in steppe regions to mitigate wind erosion.

Data about the condition of forests in Ukraine during the Soviet period are contradictory. According to official information, forest area increased gradually. For instance, from 1961 to 1988 the forest area in Ukraine increased by 20.9% (Hensiruk et al., 1995) and from 1988 to 1996 by 1.2% (Forestry in Ukraine: the Strategy of Development, 2003). At the same time, in the Carpathian region of Ukraine monocultures of coniferous even-aged stands were created, which are characterised by low ecological stability (Hensiruk et al., 1995). As a consequence, the area of forests damaged by insects, fires and windfalls has increased during recent years (Hensiruk, 1992) (Figure 11.6). Due to the

Figure 15.7. Logging operations on steep slopes without any ecological considerations are still being conducted in the Ukrainian Carpathians. Photo: Marine Elbakidze.

Chernobyl accident in 1986, a large part of Polissya's forests in northern Ukraine became contaminated with radioactivity. Around 3.5 million ha (37%) of forest area were affected, of which 157,000 ha (1.6%) now have no potential for use due to radioactive contamination (Buksha, 2004; Nilsson and Shvidenko, 1999). The large-scale drainage of Polissya's wetlands in northern Ukraine decreased groundwater levels and caused forest drying.

Forestry at Present

Forests in Ukraine are state property. However, according to the new Forest Code (2006) communities and private people are able to own forests with some limitations. The forest lands are under the management of different state organisations including the state forestry committee (66%), and the ministries of agriculture (26.4%), defence (2.2%), emergency (1.6%), transport (1%), ecology and natural resources (0.8%) (Forestry in Ukraine: the Strategy of Development, 2003).

The forest industry is still a minor economic sector amounting to 0.2-0.4% of GDP. In budgetary terms, forestry expenses are twice the revenues from forest resources use (Forestry in Ukraine: the Strategy of Development, 2003; Synyakevych and Soloviy 2002). Payment for forest resources exploitation remains very low. The state as an owner of forest resources earns on average 3.9 hrn (€0.6) per cubic metre of logged merchantable timber. This is significantly less than in other countries (Forestry in Ukraine: the Strategy of Development, 2003).

As a country in transition it is very important to evaluate the heritage in forestry from the previous political systems for understanding what should be changed or remain under the new political and economic conditions. The debate concerning the 'socialist heritage' in Ukrainian forest management shows that it should be critically analysed for the future development of forestry. There are opinions that the Ukrainian forestry during the Soviet time (especially in the second half of the 20th century) 'could be judged as sustainable' (Polyakov and Sydor, 2006). The main proponents of such opinions argue that the Ukrainian forest management under a socialist centrally planned economy did a good job in providing environmental benefits from the forests to the citizens, as well as in preserving and multiplying forest resources (Polyakov and Sydor, 2006). Their opponents presented an opposite view (Nijnik and Van Kooten, 2006). They argued that under the command-control economy, the forest resources were excessively exploited and that inadequate attention was paid to silvicultural investments, despite official rhetoric to the contrary.

Today the principles of Sustainable Forest Management (SFM) have been adopted into the national legislation and forest programmes. The main trend of the official forest policy is thus to provide a balance between the conservation of forest ecosystems and the continuous, multi-purpose use of forests. In Ukraine, legislative frameworks of forests and forest resource management are formulated in the Forest Code of Ukraine (2006), the Law on the Environmental Protection of Ukraine (1991), and other legislative documents and governmental regulations that play a fundamental role in developing environmentally sound forest operations.

The Ukrainian Forest Code stipulates that forests have primarily soil protective, water-conservation, air-cleaning and health-giving functions, while their economic use is considered as having limited importance (Forest Code of Ukraine, 2006). According to the political and legislative documents the main goals of forestry in Ukraine are to: (1) conserve biological diversity in forests; (2) extend forest-covered territory to an optimal level in all natural zones; (3) protect forest function and

Figure 15.8. The traditional village system found in Europe's forest and woodland landscapes is characterised by a centre-periphery zoning from houses, gardens, fields, mowed and grazed grasslands to forests (i.e. the ancient system with domus, hortus, ager, saltus and silva). This view of the village Volosyanka in the Skole district of Ukraine's west Carpathian Mountains illustrates this. Beginning in the left part of the picture, the church in the very village centre is surrounded by houses that are located in the bottom of the shallow valley. The private gardens have many fruit trees and shrubs. Further to the right there is a fine-grained mixture of grasslands, some individual fields of which has been mowed and have hay-stacks and some not yet, and fields, like the potato field in the foreground. To the right there is forest, which is grazed by cattle moving in and out along specially designed fenced trails from the farm houses in the valley bottom. In addition, above the tree line on the top of the mountains, there are open grazed pasture commons. Photo: Per Angelstam.

limit forest exploitation; (4) improve social protection of forestry workers; (5) increase the resistance of forest ecosystems to negative environmental conditions; (6) improve forest management legislation according to international principles of SFM; and (7) encourage the development of forest research and education (Forest Code of Ukraine, 2006; Zibtsev et al., 2004; Buksha, 2004; Hensiruk, 1992 ; Essmann and Pettenella, 2001; Polyakova et al., 2001).

During recent decades the forest landscapes have been under severe threat from unsustainable logging methods, past replacement of natural tree species with introduced Norway spruce, habitat loss and fragmentation due to intensified forestry and infrastructure development (Hensiruk, 1964; Trokhimchuk, 1968 ; Holubetst and Odynak, 1983) (Figure 15.7). On the other hand, due to economic reasons and the need to develop local livelihoods, local people have had to come back to their traditional land use practices of the village system (Elbakidze and Angelstam, 2007 ; Bihun 2005). These were commonly practised for centuries, before the socialist period, and played an important role for maintenance of biodiversity and cultural heritage, and thus for rural development in Ukraine and Europe (e.g. Mellor and Smith, 1979). The recent privatisation of land has led to a revival in the social and cultural value of forests in Ukraine, which were often an unbroken part of families' cultural and natural heritage for generations (Elbakidze and Angelstam, 2007) (Figure 15.8).

There are, however, several opinions about the role of Ukrainian forests today and in the future. The first is ecologically orientated, and declares that the forest sector in Ukraine does not have economic importance. Instead forests play a profound ecological function, and should therefore be appropriately protected and harvesting practices should be reduced (Listopad, 2000). The second is economically orientated. The main thesis here is that exploitation and forest management and harvesting intensity in Ukraine are lower than in most European countries. Thus, forest sector utilisation has to increase substantially to fulfil economic needs at national, regional and local level (Bobko, 2003). Finally, a third view is that forests have ecological as well as economic and social functions (Polyakova et al., 2001; Synyakevych, 2004, 2005). Implementation of SFM according to the international discourse will help to combine these dimensions in the forested landscape (Essmann and Pettenella 2001; Krott et al. 2000).

Belarus

Basic Information About the Forests

Belarus is located in the transition between the southernmost boreal forest and the temperate forest zone and is thus dominated by mixed deciduous and coniferous. The main tree species are Scots pine, Norway spruce and birches. At present 30% of the total area is forested. Young forests constitute 36.6%, middle age 14.2%, and mature and "over mature" 4.8%. The forested area occupies about 8.3 million ha. The total stock of timber is 1.3 billion m^3 (Anon, 2010).

The forests are state owned and a large proportion are managed by the Committee of Forestry (about 7 million ha or 76.1% of the total forested area). The remaining forested land is under the management of the Committee of Defence, collective farms and associations, research institutes and local administrations (Anon, 2010). Depending on their commercial value and their location, the forests are divided into two groups. The first group of forests having water protection, sanitary and other protective functions make up 44%, while the second one, which is of commercial value, constitutes 56% of forests (Anon, 2010). Around 14-15 million m^3 of timber are harvested annually in Belarus, allowing the demand in the domestic market to be fully met, and nearly 2 million m^3 of industrial wood to be exported.

Forest-based Industries

The Republic of Belarus has a developed timber, woodworking and pulp and paper industry, which increased its production 2.8-fold over the period 1991-2005. The timber industry of Belarus has been subject to intensive privatisation: businesses with private and foreign categories of ownership produce over 70 and 6.4% of the total products, respectively, and employ 75 and 5.8% of the total sector's industrial and production potential.

The Belarusian forest industry is export-orientated in terms of numerous types of goods: fibreboard, furniture and plywood, sawn timber, wallpaper, matches, etc. In 1996-2005, the export potential of the forestry increased 4-fold.

Use of Forested Land

In 1955, Belarus had 23% forest land, now it has ~40%. From 1965 to 2000, the annual forest land increase was about 33,800 hectares. In 2001-2006 it increased to 51,900 ha. Nowadays the area forest land is equal to the agricultural area, which is ecologically beneficial for Belarus and all the region.

Table 15.2. Land use changes in Belarus, 2001-2005

Type of lands	2005		+/- compared to 2001	
	$x10^3$ ha	%	$x10^3$ ha	%
Farms and other agricultural land	8920.1	43	+9.3	+0.1
State forest land	8299.5	40	+209.0	+2.6
Land for nature protection and recreation	879.2	4.2	+46.5	+5.6
Industrial, transport, and military areas	690.1	3.3	-1211.7	-15.0
Private land	1284.1	6.2	-147.5	-10.3

The increase in forested land in Belarus in the past decade is a result of degraded and low productive agricultural land being converted to forest according to a decision by the Belarusian government. A large amount of land polluted with radionuclides was reforested after 1986. The role of forestry is thus not only production of natural resources, but also rehabilitation of destroyed land. Reforestation in Belarus is also occurring on obsolete military and industrial lands, while unused private land is transferred to other farmers or to forest lands (Table 15.2).

Forest historically has a multifunctional role in the life of Belarusian inhabitants. It is a source of wood for building and energy, herbs for medical purposes and food for domestic animals. There was never starvation in Belarus because when the harvest was bad in farmers' fields, the forest fed people with mushrooms, nuts, berries and the meat of wild animals. Nowadays skill in gathering mushrooms and berries is part of the culture of Belarusian people.

The forest in Belarus has a very important recreation function. Every weekend a lot of people go to the forest to walk, picnic or gather mushrooms and berries, or to hunt in the season.

Energy Production in the Rural Landscape

16

Lars Rydén
Uppsala University, Uppsala, Sweden

Energy in the Rural Landscape

Rural Society and Renewable Energy

One of the largest difficulties for sustainable development is the overwhelming dependency of most societies on non-renewable fossil energy supplies. The consequences of the large use of fossil carbon are twofold – first that supplies will come to an end; secondly that the end product – carbon dioxide – builds up and cause environmental damage. As for all non-renewable the effects of end products is felt typically before the source is emptied; here it is foremost carbon dioxide causing climate change although there are also a number of other serious pollution problems caused by combustion of fossil fuels long before global peak oil has been reached.

Non-renewable fossil fuels are concentrated sources of energy, stored by Nature after processes which took many millions of years. Renewable energy, continuously produced in nature, is on the contrary on the contrary spread evenly over a surface area, just as sunlight, and has to be harvested. The rural society therefore has an increasingly important role in supplying the society with energy. This is already seen by the increasingly larger role played by bio-energy, small-scale hydropower, wind power and more recently solar energy.

Energy production opens up new opportunities for the rural society, and is a main strategy for policies for rural development. We see new goals for rural development, new employment and a new economy in many countries. Moreover, planning for energy production could benefit the local society since it makes it possible to have locally owned production which in turn could mean better opportunities for starting local agricultural production, industries and services As an example the value of Finnish bio-energy production and processing in 2008 was 950 million Euro and provided 3,613 employment opportunities many of them at farms as a secondary activity. In Germany likewise a large number of new job opportunities from bio-energy production are reported.

The increasing role of renewable energy may be part of a transition to a sustainable society. It requires, however, that proper concern for other components in the sustainability agenda, such as biodiversity protection, is included.

Local Energy Production

Renewable energy is by nature most often local. But is it possible to provide all energy required from local sources – to build energy autonomy? This would be an important option and perhaps survival strategy for many rural societies. Obviously the possibilities for a municipality to provide all energy needed for itself varies dramatically with the circumstances. For the Nordic countries energy autonomy is probably a comparatively realistic option due to the reasonable small population and larger land area, and a geography e.g. allowing for large-scale hydropower plants as compared to the more densely populated continental Europe. Still there are a number of such projects in e.g. Germany, Austria, and the Netherlands.

Energy autonomy projects are so far most common for small communities, that is, towns in a rural setting (see box). In larger cities energy self-sufficiency projects are typically created in neighbourhoods often relying on more or less advanced technologies, such as passive

Box 16.1. Cases of Local Energy Resilience

The small town of Güssing, close to Graz in Austria, is an extraordinary case. From 1992 within eleven years, Güssing became self-sufficient with regards to electricity, heating, and transportation. Today more than 60 new companies and over 1,500 new "green Jobs" have been created and the share of commuters to other regions have decreased to 40%. Since Güssing generates more "green" energy than the regions needs, the value added to the region is over $28 million per year. Finally, green-house gas emissions were reduced by over 80%. The steps to energy autonomy include: 1992: New mayor elected; 1994: Public energy use cut 50%; 1996: 3 MW biomass CHP power plant, 1998: CHP power plant expanded to 8 MW; 2004: Installation of an advanced biomass gasifier. http://blogs.worldwatch.org/the-model-region-of-gussing-%E2%80%93-an-example-of-the-austrian-grassroots-strategy-for-energy-independence/

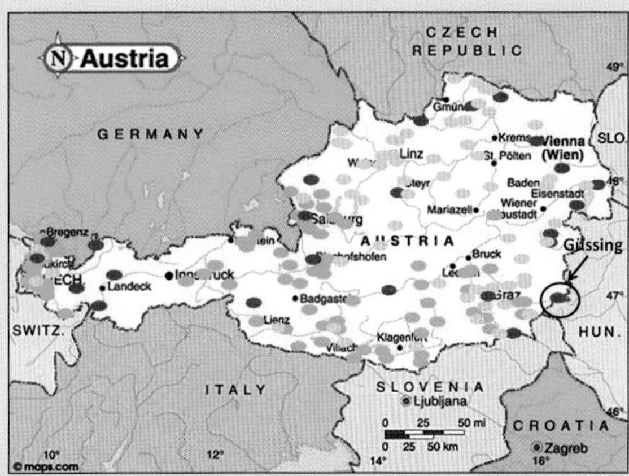

Figure 16.1. Energy independence growing on a regional level in Austria. The map depict regions indepenent of electricity, heat and/or transportation (red), regions with growing energy independence (yellow) and regions with high energy efficiency standards (green). Source: WorldWatch Blogs, 2011.

Växjö decided in 1996 to become "fossil fuel free". Växjö has since built two biomass plants and requested for the municipality green electricity. In 2000 the municipality developed the "local initiatives award" and in 2007 was awarded of "Sustainable Energy Europe Award". It is clear that Växjö there is political consensus of the fossil fuel free policy and several times the members in the city council take part in energy projects run by the municipality.

In Samsø in Denmark with 114 km² the 4,000 inhabitants changed their daily lives for greater energy efficiency. 21 wind turbines generating 28,000 megawatts annually have been built to meet the community's electricity demands and public transportation system; the surplus to sell is 10%. Farmers have adapted their tractors and other vehicles to consume ethanol or other fuels distilled from locally grown plants, like canola. The community experiments with electric cars as distances are very short, less than 50 kilometers. http://www.ipsnews.net/news.asp?idnews=49273

energy houses and smart grids. Much of the energy autonomy is also established on the household level, that is, houses are equipped with PV solar cells on the roofs for electricity production and/or with solar heat panels. Such solutions are available for any building, including those in towns or individual houses on the countryside.

Energy efficiency measures are an important part of making local energy supply sufficient. Especially in the heating sector the needed energy may be reduced substantially by energy efficiency projects. District heating is one of the most efficient. In Sweden close to 90% of houses are today connected to district heating using bio fuels. In the heating sector thus the vision of local energy supply are already close to a reality. The actions of households are important, as they may choose to improve insulation, change heating system or actually provide their own heating through e.g. heat pumps or panels for solar heating.

Local electricity production is still in its infancy, much due to the circumstance that national supplies are mostly safe and sufficient. However discontents with the changes in prices have made a number of both individuals and local municipalities develop their own local generation of electricity. Most important is probably electricity from power stations using bio-fuels, but wind power and hydropower for local needs increase rapidly. For the local communities which today are energy independent on electricity wind energy seems to be by far the most important source.

Probably the most difficult issue for local energy is fuel for transport. Imported fossil fuel by far dominates the market. Other options develop, however, such as buses using locally produced biogas, buses using locally produced biodiesel, cars on bio-ethanol and a few electric cars.

Estimations of the extent of locally produced energy today are close to guesswork. It is however obvious that it is not unimportant. Heating in the housing sector accounts for some 40% of the energy need and is mostly provided for by local sources, and that the other two energy sectors – electricity and fuel for transport – is marginally taken care of locally. If these are estimated to 5% each we will still arrive at a total of 50% local energy supply at least in the Nordic countries.

Policy/strategy Options and the Food-energy Dilemma

A country, region or municipality which decides to become fossil fuel free is confronted with a number of policy options. One of them is how to manage the resources they have in terms of available land. Should it be used for growing energy crops or food crops? In developing countries this choice may be critical, as bio-energy developments can pose a threat to food security because it may compete with the same natural resources. In the Baltic Sea region it is not critical unless we import food or energy, e.g. bio-ethanol; then we are part of the game. In our local markets it is more than anything a question of price.

Bio-energy development may also provide opportunities for increasing welfare. It can generate employment and raise incomes in farming communities and provide a sustainable source of energy that is an affordable substitute for imported fossil fuels. Investments in bio-energy may increase harvests for both food and fuel crops.

The most common strategy for improving sustainability in municipalities is rescaling. Both up-scaling (e.g. from individual heating of houses to district heating) and down-scaling (e.g. from district heating to heat pumps) are common. Striving for energy autonomy is typically downscaling from dependency on global or national sources of energy.

Local energy policies have repeatedly been shown to be beneficial for the local business life. It is obvious that producing energy locally offers work opportunities, and money used for buying fossil energy is then instead used for local business. An extreme example is Güssing in Austria (see box) where a completely new commercial sector developed based on local energy production and the competence developed in connection with this project.

Support of local energy production at least in the beginning requires some policy tools, especially economic ones. A most efficient one is the feed-in tariffs used in Germany, which guarantees that (extra) electricity produced locally will be bought by the national grid for a set (good) price. The economy of an investment is thus secured and has therefore made Germany number one in local electricity, especially from PV (photovoltaic cells) on roofs. Positive incentives include governmental subsidies for changing heating system from fossil dependent to e.g. pellet boiler. This incentive has been used in Sweden. Negative incentives include carbon dioxide taxation. In Sweden this is 1 SEK (about 10 Eurocents) per kg, enough to make use for fossil fuels for heating less attractive, while it is typically much less in other countries.

Heating Houses

Heating has since centuries in most countries in the Baltic Sea region been provided for by wood. In a well forested region this should be no problem. However resource constraints have during periods been a reality also for wood. In the 18th century the forest crisis made wood a limited resource. One result of this was the development of the tiled stove, which improved the energy efficiency of wood combustion several-fold (see p. 165). Today we are in a similar situation. We have to stop using coal –traditionally used for heating e.g. in Poland – or oil, earlier the standard in Sweden – or natural gas, the normal source in Latvia e.g. for heating houses. Reducing the need for heating, improving resource efficiency, and exchanging the resource used are all strategies required, and quite easily applied in a rural setting.

In the heating sector the needed energy may be reduced substantially by energy efficiency projects. In Sweden IVL (Swedish Environmental Institute) estimates that 20% of the energy demand in the housing sector (150

TWh) can be reduced by efficiency measures. New buildings are increasingly low-energy houses.

District heating, even in smaller towns or villages, is important since the use of fuel improves dramatically by having a more advanced boiler possible in a district heating network. In individual houses efficient pellet burners, or modern stoves using bio-fuels, are far better than the old time classical stoves.

There are several other technical options. Solar heating is one. Solar panels may be mounted on the roof of one house or expanded to many houses or even to the municipal scale. Thus in Kungsbacka in Sweden 48 one-family-houses cover 70% of its annual consumption of hot water from a 900 m^2 solar panel field, one of the largest in the world. The solar panel field in Aeroe in Denmark is another system heating the whole town. These very advanced solar panels may provide hot water and heating between March and November.

Another option is a heat pump. Many households – in 2010 estimated to 800,000 in Sweden – use heat pumps. These rely on electricity but are up to five times more efficient than direct electricity for heating.

Mapping Local Energy Resources

A rural local authority, which adopts a policy of energy production or energy autonomy, may start by mapping their energy resources. Energy appears in many different forms and one should be able to list at least 20 or so sources. In a second phase each of these resources need to be looked at in more detail. How much, which investments are needed, which is the payback time for investments are obvious questions. Finally one needs to assess which mix of resources will provide the best price and the best energy security.

The mapping of *local energy resources* should be divided in three categories: electricity, heat and fuels. An example of the resources to be included is listed in Table 16.1.

Data on wind speed or waves may be obtained from the meteorological institutes. Size of wetlands is found on a ordinary land use map. Forest production and agricultural production is the subject of local farmers and forest companies etc. A local energy company is a very good partner in a project of this kind, while the large international companies often are not interested.

Table 16.1. Mapping of local energy resources divided into the three categories electricity, heat and fuels.

I. Electricity	
Solar	Solar cells (direct sunlight to electricity)
	CSP (Concentrated Solar Power
	Combination panels for electricity and hot water
Water	Hydropower (Small scale from water flows from reservoirs and lakes
	Streaming water (developing technology)
Wind	Map average wind speed
Wave	Map average wave at the coast
II. Heat	
Solar	Solar panels for hot water
	CSP (Concentrated Solar Power)
	Combination panels for electricity and hot water
Geothermal	Heat pumps relying on renewable electricity
Biomass	Wood chips
	Wood pellets
	Other (straw etc)
III. Fuels	
Solid Biomass	Wood or wood waste from forestry
	Energy forests
	Peat
	Household waste
Ethanol	Crops harvest to ethanol
Bio-diesel	Oil crops (rape seed) to biodiesel
	Cellulose wood or straw (second generation bio-ethanol)
Biogas	Slaughterhouse and fishery waste to biogas
	Reed and other biomass from wetland
	Agricultural waste from farms
	Manure
	Sludge from wastewater treatment

Table 16.2. Production of hydropower in the nordic countries and the European Union. El (GWh) samt procent av den totala elproduktionen år 2008. Source: Wikipedia, 2012.

Land	2003	2004	2005	2006	2007	2008	%
Norway	106,216	109,373	136,441	119,726	134,736	140,522	98
Sweden	53,598	60,178	72,874	61,859	66,262	69,211	46
Finland	9,591	15,070	13,784	11,494	14,177	17,112	22
Iceland	7,088	7,134	7,019	7,293	-	-	-
Denmark	21	26	22	23	28	26	<1
EU 27	338,307	357,147	341,744	344,348	344,236	359,185	11

Renewable Electricity Production

The Dilemma of Intermittent Sources

Hundred years ago electricity for a town was produced locally in an electricity works. Later, when the technology of long distance transfer of electricity developed, larger national facilities, hydropower stations of power stations using fossil fuels, became the norm and electric current became something coming out from two holes in the wall.

Today locally supplied electricity is again an interesting option after having taken the decision to reduce the dependency of fossil fuels and thus reduce CO_2 emissions. The renewable resources include wind, water and sun. But these are different from power stations as they are only working when the wind, water or sun is available. We may save water in a reservoir, but sun and wind cannot be stored. These sources are intermittent. This may the biggest dilemma with locally produced electricity. Only for very limited use may an ordinary battery be sufficient, e.g. in remote places where electric lights in the evening come from a solar cell on the roof using daylight sun.

New and better batteries will hopefully one day be aviable but today it is far from sufficient for storing electricity on a regional scale. In a modern European country the most realistic option is to sell excess electricity to the national grid and get it back when the intermittent sources are silent. In Sweden this is working well since the large hydropower plants provide the storing capacity needed. In other countries where this opportunity does not exist, storing capacity in practice relies on power plants most often using fossil fuels. However power plants, especially smaller power plants, may be run using bio-fuels. In this case a system – consisting of intermittent sources and the power plant – completely or almost completely sustainable can be built. An example is Enköping in Sweden where the power plant is using forest wood waste and wood chips from an energy forest. It is a CHP, combined heat and power plant, in which the hot water is used for district heating and electricity is used for the town. There are also more advanced technical solutions such as pumped-storage hydroelectricity, or moving the problem by importing or exporting electricity to neighbouring countries or reducing demand when intermittent sources are low.

In practice countries such as Denmark, which has much wind power, install excess production capacity using fossil fuels to be used when the wind is low. In other countries nuclear power has a similar role. Nuclear power has the advantage of not emitting carbon dioxide when running, but still it is not a renewable resource. Another important aspect is to learn to reduce peak demand, by using electricity more evenly during the day and night.

Hydropower

Hydropower is by far the most import renewable energy source. In the Baltic Sea region Norway has the largest hydropower sector followed by Sweden and Finland, but it is also important in Latvia and Poland. In Sweden there are about 1,900 hydropower stations, and 85% of the rivers are exploited. Hydropower many be regulated and for this reason has an important role in the energy mix of a country. Hydropower today accounts in Norway for 140 TWh (98%), in Sweden for 69 TWh (46%), and in Finland for 17 TWh (22%) of the electricity use in the countries.

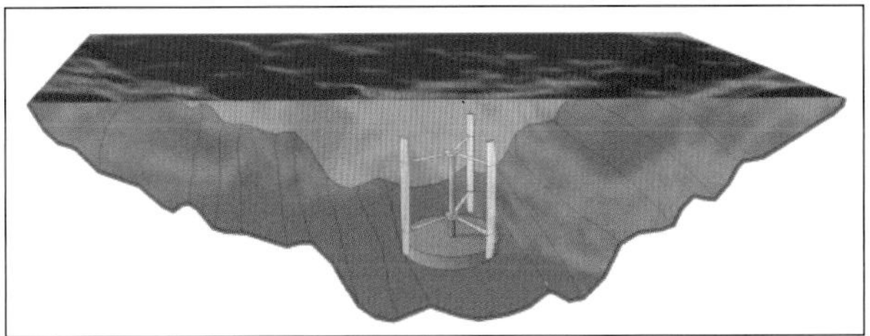

Figure 16.2 *Streaming water electricity.* Electric energy may be extracted from the rural landscape in many ways. To the established hydropower, wind power, and solar electricity we may add this new method of generating electricity from streaming water. The technology is similar to the one used in wind power. A main difference is that water has a density 800 times larger than that of air. The energy density of a water stream of 1 m/sec thus corresponds to the energy density in air at 9 m/sec. Streaming water electricity is predicted to be mostly useable for ocean currents at coasts, but it can also be used in rivers. An advantage is that it does not require any large constructions, such as water reservoirs, and it is not visible from the outside making it much less provoking in the landscape. Streaming water electricity is studied at Uppsala University to develop new ways of renewable energy production. Illustration by Karin Thomas.

Hydropower has been used for hundreds of years. However the big development took place in the end of the 19th century. The turbine then replaced the water wheel and thus made it possible to install a generator to produce electricity. At the same time the technology for long distance transfer of electric power developed and made it possible to use electricity from the far north of the Nordic countries for the urban centers further south.

The large hydropower stations influence large land areas for its upstream reservoir or dam. Land used for valuable nature and human settlements may have to be abandoned. The stations also influence the seasonal migration of fish and may kill substantial amounts of fish in the turbines. Some stations compensate for this by building stairs for fish upstream migration and cultivating fish fry for implantation. Still the environmental costs are substantial.

One way to get around the problem is to use smaller mini- or micro-hydropower. These are stations often built where a dam has existed for centuries for a small industry or mill. In the mid 1950s Sweden had about 4,000 small hydropower stations with a capacity under 1.5 MW. In 2008 only 1,500 of these were still running producing a total of 1.5 TWh (more than wind power!). It is estimated that another 2.5 TWh would be possible by renovation and starting old and abandoned mini stations. Micro-hydro stations have an important role to play in the economic development of remote rural areas, especially in the mountains.

The technology for small-scale hydropower is in a phase of rapid development. One system uses a combined turbine and generator in mobile machine housing. It can be installed under water in existing dams with only minor changes. It is thus invisible from the surface and also well adapted to the water fauna and flora. A German station with a capacity of 500 kW is expected to generate approximately 2.75 million kWh of electricity a year according to the company. This corresponds to the power consumption of more than 600 four-person households. Another construction uses a water wheel at the bottom of a stream, thus no dam is needed. This streaming water electricity is presently under testing.

Wind Energy

Wind power is the conversion of the energy in wind – moving air – to mechanical energy and most often to electricity in a rotating wind turbine. Wind power in the shape of windmills and wind pumps has a long history (and even longer if we add sailing!). The use of generators to convert the power of the rotating wings into electricity was made only shortly after the generator was introduced in the end of the 19th century. The modern wind turbine was introduced much later by Danish inventors. The first turbines had capacities of 20-30 kW; today the largest turbines may deliver up to 7 MW capacity. Wind energy in 2010 provided 2.5% of global electricity supply and is increasing rapidly with 28% yearly (2010 figures).

Wind turbines may be installed as a single, often not so large, unit to provide a farm or smaller group of households with electricity. More often however they are built as a group of turbines, forming a wind farm. Very many of the wind farms are built off shore. In Sweden the largest planned wind farms are in the Scandinavian mountains and others in the Baltic Sea off shore. The most successful wind energy countries in the Baltic Sea region are Denmark and Germany. The largest off shore wind farm in Denmark is *Horns Rev* on the Jutland west coast with a capacity of 209 MW. For the year 2010 7,8 TWh (21%) of Danish, 35,5 TWh (9%) of German and 3,4 TWh (2%) of Swedish electricity was provided by wind energy. The

Figure 16.3. Solar plant farm in Sala Heby, Southern Sweden. Photo: Heby Municipality. Sala Heby Energy AB, SHE.

installed capacity was 3,734 MW in Demark, 27,215 MW in Germany and 2,046 MW in Sweden. Most of these belong to the big power companies. However increasingly we see small companies as well as individuals or groups of individuals planning, financing and installing smaller wind turbines as part of local energy supply. It remains to be seen how large this trend will become. .

A wind turbine uses comparatively little land and the (formal) ecological footprint of wind power is small. It is however comparable to hydropower in the sense that landscape intrusion is large. A wind turbine can be seen and heard over large distances; this is not always so popular. The Swedish Energy Authority in 2008 indicated 423 areas with a total area of 9,673 km² of national interest for wind power in the country. Of this 5,817 km² are on land; if fully utilized these would be able to produce about 20 TWh.

Technical development of wind power continues. Of special interest is so called vertical wind power, which may be both more efficient and needs to be less tall, and in addition is almost silent. Only pilot scale vertical wind power exists presently

Solar Electricity

The conversion of sun light into electricity may either rely on photovoltaic (PV) cells or so-called concentrated solar power (CSP). In PV sun light is directly converted into an electric current. In CSP the sun rays are focused by mirrors into a small area to heat a liquid to high temperature which is pumped into a turbine to produce electricity. Research on how light can be transferred into an electric current exists since 100 years and commercial PV cells since the 1980s. From a slow beginning the development of commercial solar electricity has since the mid 1990s increased rapidly in response to higher oil prices and concern over climate change. The global increase is estimated to about 40% per year since about 2000. At the end of 2010 installed capacity was 40 GW. Germany, with an installed capacity of 17.4 GW, (together with Japan and China) is world leader in the field. The German solar PV industry installed 7,400 MW in nearly one-quarter million individual systems in 2010. Globally solar PV provided 12 TWh of electricity in 2010, about 2% of total electricity.

Solar electricity, more than any of the other renewable electricity sources, illustrates that renewable electricity depends on surface. It is thus an interesting opportunity for rural landscapes. Surprisingly to many the solar irradiation is enough – also in mid Sweden – to make a fairly small surface (25 by 25 km) enough for supplying all electricity needed in Sweden. In practice it is not so easy, but it illustrates that the sun is sufficient in large parts of the Baltic Sea region, although obviously not during winter far north. Since 2011 the largest photovoltaic plant is Finsterwalde Solar Park in Germany, with 80.7 MW capacity and Ohotnikovo Solar Park in Ukraine with 80 MW capacity. There are also some PV parks in Czech Republic (about 1,700 MW) but very little in the rest of the Baltic Sea region. The environmental impact of these is minimal as is the ecological footprint (not regarding the LCA of the cells which may be more problematic).

Presently the world market price for solar electricity is estimated to 1.1 Euro/W by the end of 2011 (Bloomberg New Energy Finance) and the price is falling rapidly. The payback time for PV systems are thus estimated to be about 8-12 years. Since they are expected to last 25-40 years PV electricity is since some years profitable. Solar electricity is, as is wind power, an intermittent energy source and thus requires some kind of back up. This is presently the largest problem with the technology.

Wave Electricity

Wave power produced along the coasts is in its infancy, but a promising technology. At present a first wave power farm consisting of several hundred units is installed on the Swedish west coast. It will be less intrusive as the only thing one can see are the floating devices on the surface. The generators on bottom seems to be very compatible with marine life and is colonized by sea stars and other animals and plants.

Bio-energy Production

Solid Biomass

Solid biomass was always simply firewood to be burned in a stove to give heat, or used in the kitchen to cook. Today biomass is still mostly wood or wood products such as wood waste from forestry (roots and branches), or sawdust made into pellets for easy management, or wood chips. To this should be added grass and trimmings from agriculture or horticulture, and various domestic refuse mostly household wastes. Classical crops may also be used for energy purposes, such as barley or oat. In practice this is a question of price, markets and practical circumstances.

Wood biomass is produced either from forestry or special energy forests mostly from Salix cultivation (See chapter 16). For forestry products such as wood waste or pellets there is no competition with food production. Energy forests may compete with food production as the land could be used differently.

Solid biomass in all its forms may be used in power plants to produce heat and electricity. In individual households pellets is more convenient to use for heating since they may be handled a little like a liquid, such as oil, to avoid the necessity of everyday's management of the boiler. Still many people like to use wood for a tiled stove or a modern stove. The drawback with this is that

Figure 16.4. Biogas-production on the farm. This pig farm in mid Sweden, with an average occupancy of 3,000 pigs, use all manure for biogas production. The gas is used in a combined heat and power equipment, which provides all electricity and heat needed for the farm and a surplus sold to the electricity grid. To the right the anaerobic digester, also called fermentation tank. Photo: Lars Rydén.

flue gases contain much smoke, particles, aromatic substances and dioxins. Efficient cleaning of flue gases is in practice only done at larger facilities such as municipal power plants.

Wood is considered a renewable source of energy. However this should be said with the reservation that the time it takes to replace a tree is long, many decades even 100 years. With the concern that GHG emission should be reversed within only few years the climate mitigation contribution from wood biomass is limited.

The use of biomass is increasingly important in the countries of the Baltic Sea region. In Sweden biomass accounted for 139 TWh in 2010, an increase of 9% from the year before. More than 32% of all energy use in the country is bio-energy. About 90% are forest products and an additional important part is byproducts from the industry (e.g. black liquor from pulp production). In Germany bio-energy accounts for 4,9% of overall primary energy, or 7.3% of total fuels and 6.3% of total heat (2007 data).

Biogas

Biogas is produced when all kinds of organic matter is fermented (biologically broken down) in the absence of oxygen or air. Biogas consists of methane, also the main component in natural gas, as well as water and carbon dioxide, which has to be removed before it can be used as a fuel. Biogas is formed in many different situations, most notably in landfills as much organic material, e.g. food waste, is stored, and when ruminants, most importantly cows, digest grass. Biogas can just as natural gas be used in all kinds of combustion processes. It is thus useful for heating, for producing electricity in a power plant, and for motor vehicles. The residuals from the fermentation can be used as fertilizer as all phosphorus and most nitrogen is retained. An important concern is to carefully stop all leakage from the process since methane is a strong greenhouse gas.

Biogas is produced in a fermentation tank using the substrate - the food waste or other organic material - and a proper brew of microorganism. It is not often as simple as it may sound. The process is very different for different substrates, it may be very long, several weeks or even months, and the process of producing a good bio-methane from the biogas is added. The economic reasons for interest in biogas are both a question of taking care of organic waste as it is the production of a renewable fuel. However the technology is developing and biogas production increases.

Germany is Europe's and thus the Baltic Sea region's biggest biogas producer. In 2010 there were 5,905 biogas plants in the country mostly used for electricity production in CHPs with a net production during the year of 12.8 TWh which is 12.6 per cent of the total generated renewable electricity in the country. Denmark has also a relative large biogas production. In 2009 Danish authorities reported 60 biogas stations at sewage treatment plants using wastewater sludge as substrates, 20 municipal plants to treat manure, food industry waste etc and another 60 on-farm facilities, in addition to facilities connected to landfills and some industries. Figures from 2006 report a total energy production of 1.1 TWh. In Sweden a handful of cities have fermentation plants to produce biogas for city buses and there are a few facilities on farms. The production of biogas increases dramatically in the country.

Biogas production offers a means to take care of manure at farms, straw and other agricultural waste as well as wetland bio-production, food waste and waste from slaughter houses, fishing industries etc. But it is also a way to process biomass. Biogas in Germany relies primarily on co-fermentation of energy crops; in 2011 ca 800,000 ha was used to grow energy crops for biogas. This is the outcome of governmental subsidies and has resulted in a new development in rural districts especially in southern Germany.

In Sweden biogas is mostly used for motor vehicles. The authorities estimated in 2011 that projected Swedish biogas production should be able to meet the demand for all buses in the country. Biogases buses give rise to very little air pollution and much less noise than ordinary diesel buses and are thus more convenient in city streets with much people.

Bio-fuels – Bio-ethanol and Biodiesel

Liquid bio-fuel is mainly bio-ethanol and biodiesel. Bioethanol is produced by fermentation of sugar, a process just the same as used for wine or beer making. Sugar is received from starch crops such as corn or sugarcane or sugar beets but it may also be other crops. New technologies allow ethanol production from cellulose that is wood, trees and grass. This so-called second generation

Figure 16.5. Rapeseed field near Eslöv in Southern Sweden. The fatty acids from the oil in rapeseeds can be used for bio-diesel after methylation. Photo: Håkan Dahlström.

Figure 16.6. Bio-dieselbus in Cambridge, UK. Photo: Hamster. Source: http://www.flickr.com.

bio-fuels require that the cellulose is hydrolyzed in a special step. It is an area in rapid development.

Bio-ethanol is used as fuel for motor vehicles substituting fossil oil products. Motors for ordinary petrol can also use ethanol with very little adjustments. Today in the European Union by law petrol includes 5% ethanol. This could be increased to 10% without any technical problems. Ethanol cars use a mix of 85% ethanol and 15% petrol (E85) as fuel. Ethanol increases the octane number of the fuel, allows higher compression, and reduces exhausts.

Biodiesel is produced from oil, mostly rapeseed oil, by transesterification with methanol to get fatty acid methyl esters. This is a fairly uncomplicated process and can be done on the farm where the vegetable oil is produced in an oil press. Biodiesel may replace ordinary (mineral) diesel fuel in a standard diesel motor, although one often uses a mix of mineral and biodiesel. In Europe much diesel is mixed with 5% bio-diesel.

Europe produced 53% of world bio-fuels in 2010; Spain, Germany and Italy were important production countries. In total 2010 worldwide bio-fuel (ethanol and biodiesel) production reached 86 billion liters of ethanol and 19 billion liters of biodiesel, an increase of 17% from 2009.

Sweden had the largest number of bio-ethanol vehicles – 200,000 cars use E85, 600 ethanol buses use ED95 (2010 data) – very much the results of considerable governmental subsidies. Still using bio-ethanol as a renewable fuel for cars is often referred to as "transition stage" on the way to electric cars. An important reason is that a combustion motor is only 25% as efficient as an electric motor. Another reason is that ethanol often is grown and harvested with conventional machinery on farms which use fossil fuels. Thus emission reductions of cars using bio-fuels are far from the potential it would have if the production of the fuel would be more sustainable. Hybrid cars offer today an intermediate solution. While bio-ethanol cars may approach a decline, biogas vehicles seems to increase.

Biomass Production in Energy Forests
Short Rotation Plantations

17

Józef Mosiej, Agnieszka Karczmarczyk and Katarzyna Wyporska
Warsaw University of Life Sciences – SGGW, Warsaw, Poland
Aleh Rodzkin
International Sakharov Environmental University, Minsk, Belarus

Energy Forest – Short Rotation Plantations

Energy forest is a forest grown and used for biomass production, that is, for energy purposes. Energy forest, properly called short rotation plantation (SRP), is fairly new, developed since the 1970s (Venturi et al., 1999). It includes the production of rapidly growing species of trees; the most popular are willow *Salix* and poplar *Populus*. Short rotation plantation can grow in a wide variety of climate and soil conditions. While poplars are commonly cultivated in drier areas, willows have been found to be the most suitable crop for regions characterized by a short period of vegetative growth and a higher level of precipitation. To obtain a good result the soil has to be of good quality and prepared carefully, weeds have to be removed and the plantation fertilized as with other crops.

SRPs usually have a rotation cycle ranging from 3 to 6 years, in some cases even 1-2 years. They involve fast growing tree species planted at very high density with up to 10,000 trees per hectare (Calfapietra et al., 2010). The annual yield of biomass produced could then be as high as 20 tonnes (Mg) of dry matter per ha per year, if the soil and moisture conditions are optimal, and appropriate fertilisers are used. In average it is possible to harvest from 15 Mg dry matter (d.m.) per year of the rotation cycle to 20 Mg d.m. of biomass from a 3 years plantation of willow.

The harvest of the plantation is done during winter when the ground is hard enough to allow the very heavy harvesting machines. The fields are then clear-cut. The harvesting machines cut the wood into wood chips directly. The chips are then dried before being used as a fuel.

Energetic value of dried biomass can be as high as 274 GJ per ha for one year plantation to 1,262 GJ per ha for a 3 years rotation cycle. It gives an energetic efficiency (measured as relation of energy value of biomass and energy input to plantation) from 22,5 to 42,0 for one and three years plantations respectively. To compare, energetic efficiency of rape amounts only 3,53 (Czart, 2005). The 5-7 cm stubs shoot new plants and after another 3-5 years it is possible to harvest again. After 20-30 years the field needs re-plantation.

Industrial and Economic Aspects

With a good organization, SRPs are economically a good choice. The concentration of willow plantations to a relatively small area will scale up the operations enough to allow the farmers to establish an industrial infrastructure for processing willow biomass and distribute the produced wood chips in the most cost-effective way.

Energy forests give a renewable solid fuel. They contribute to local independence from external fossil fuels,

Figure 17.1. Willow plant plantation near the combined heating power station in Enköping, Sweden. The plantation is fertilized with affluents from the nearby waste water treatment plant and produces 10% of the input of biomass to the power station. Photo: Lars Rydén.

and reduce emissions of green house gases and climate change. They also reduce air pollution from burning of coal, oil and gas. Around 1-2 ha of SRP can cover energetic needs of a single household, but to be profitable at least 50 ha of SRP is needed. A very important factor for a cost effective business is to assure that there is a local biomass market.

Reliance on locally produced biomass is an advantageous economic solution for energy supply. Compared to being dependent on imported fossil fuels, it increases energy safety, and in most cases also reduce costs, however, depending on the prices which fluctuate with markets. Local production obviously also provides local work opportunities. If wastewater is used for fertilisation (see below) it also provides a low cost method to take care of nutrients in the wastewater before it is released to the water recipient.

Energy forest production should be seen in the perspective of the increasing need for producing renewable energy, to reach the 20% goal of total production to 2020 according to the European Union Agreement. The present level of renewables is for the 27 EU member states 18,3% (2012) although this figures varies considerably in the different member states.

Use of Energy Forest Biomass

Biomass cultivated in order to generate energy can be used in a wide variety conversion products and processes. These fall into three major categories:

- direct combustion,
- gasification,
- hydrolysis and fermentation.

These produce electricity, heat, combined heat and power (CHP), and ethanol, respectively. As an example we may take Enköping municipality in Sweden (Börjesson and Berndes, 2006) where the power plant use a mixture of wood chips from energy forest and wood waste from the forest industry in a combined heat and power generation. The plant provides close to 50% of all electricity consumed in the town (about 40,000 inhabitants) and all heating needed through district heating.

The production of bioethanol from woodchips requires hydrolysis (so called second generation bio fuels) which consumes quite much of the energy and thus has a smaller yield. Bio ethanol may be used as a car fuel, but it is more often produced from other crops.

Metal Adsorption and Soil Decontamination

Before certifying an area for energy plantation and sludge fertilization, it is necessary to determine the condition of the soil. Areas where the limits of the concentration of hazardous metals in the soil are exceeded could be used for energy plantations, but without sludge fertilization. In such cases nutrients should be provided by irrigation only.

Salix has an excellent capacity to take up metals from the soil. This may be used for environmental protection.

Salix equally offers a good possibility to absorb cadmium from contaminated arable land and caesium from the soil. Since caesium (Cs-137) is the main radioactive element after a nuclear fallout or contamination, including the Chernobyl fall out, energy forest has a role in the decontamination of such soils. Caesium and potassium competes in the metabolism of the plant and thus if uptake of caesium is intended one needs to reduce potassium fertilization. Strontium (Sr-90) is also one of the elements in the radioactive fallout, although after some time it is present in much smaller amounts; it is absorbed by Salix in the same way as caesium. These operations are less efficient than with cadmium since Cs accumulates preferably in the roots and Sr in the leaves.

Energy Forest in the European Union

Energy forest is not a main alternative for biomass production in EU. Only few countries have a sizeable stand of SRPs. In some European countries the areas of SRP range between some thousands and tens of thousands of hectares. Swedish plantations seem to be the largest, although it only amounts to about 14,000 ha which translates to about 0.5% of the total arable land in the country and currently contributes about 1% of Sweden's wood fuel requirements (Gonzáles-García et al., 2012).

In Poland in 2005, the area of willow plantations for energy totalled 6 000 ha (Stolarski et al., 2008) and in 2009 it was 8 700 ha. The interest was preliminary highest for willow, which is a natural component of Polish vegetation, but also non-tree species *Virginia mallow* and *Miscanthus* has been used.

The potential for energy forests is however much larger. As an example Poland, with a vegetation period from 210 days (Gdańsk) to 215 days (Kraków) and annual precipitation of 500-700 mm, has favourable conditions for producing willow biomass. From 1.5 to 2.1 million ha of agricultural land in Poland could be used for SRP. Likewise the potential for energy forest plantations in the Baltic countries, is large. The land suitability for willow, poplar and *Miscanthus* cultivation has been estimated to be 353,000 ha in Estonia, 481,000 in Latvia and 1,332,000 ha in Lithuania, or 19%, 7.5% and 20.6% of the available agricultural land, respectively (Fischer et al. 2005). So far there are only small scale plantations in most EU countries (eg. Vande Walle et al., 2007).

Wastewater and SRPs

Wastewater for Irrigation and Fertilisation of SRPs

Effluents from wastewater treatment plants (WWTPs) can be effectively used for irrigation of energy forest plantations. By avoiding a direct discharge of the wastewater to the recipient and rather channel it to an energy forest plantation an additional treatment step in which nutrients are removed is achieved. Sludge, as a residue from wastewater treatment, could also be used to fertilize SRPs. In areas with limited access to modern treatment facilities, such as sparesly populated rural regions, SRPs may be a low-cost alternative to the construction of cost-intensive, high standard treatment of wastewater.

Figure 17.2. Poplar (*Populus*) plantation irrigated with wastewater within WACOSYS 6 FP UE project. Photo from the first year of experiment. On the left site – reference part irrigated only with water. Photo: www.wacosys.info

The use of SRP to take care of wastes, such us wastewater or sewage sludge, from the society has been identified as one of the most attractive methods for achieving environmental and energy goals, while simultaneously increasing farmers' income (Dimitriou and Rosenqvist, 2011). It has been estimated that from 7 to 20 Euro could be save per kilo of nitrogen by using natural instead of mineral fertilizers (Rosenqvist et al., 1997).

To get 20 Mg of dry willow biomass per hectare, about 150 kg of nitrogen, 18 kg of phosphates and 60 kg of potassium are needed (Pertu, 1993). Therefore, the content of available nutrients in the soil, sludge and irrigation water should be determined.

Currently, willows in particular seem to meet the requirements for efficient treatment / utilization of wastewater by irrigation because of their fast growth, level of water and nutrient uptake rates and coppicing ability. On the assumption that 15 m^2 of SRP are required for wastewater treatment from 1 person with a daily discharge of 100 liters, 10 ha of SRPs would suffice to treat wastewater from 6,500 people during the vegetation period.

The Role of SRPs in Development of Wastewater Treatment in the EU

The application of wastewater on SRPs has enormous potential in regions where treatment is currently ineffective or unavailable, as in sparsely populated rural areas. From 49 to 93% of the population in the Baltic states is connected to advanced wastewater treatment systems (tertiary treatment). For those which are not decentralized wastewater treatment systems are important. SRPs could then be an alternative to other biofilters (e.g. constructed wetlands), because they combine treatment and production.

Based on a Northern Ireland case study Rosenqvist and Dawson (2005) concluded that the most important economic factor, when considering wastewater irrigation of SRP, is the possibility of reducing cost of conventional wastewater treatment (£5,83-£14,8 per kg N compared to reduced cost for the farmer which was only £0,66 per kg N). Thus wastewater treatment can be the main driving force for introducing SRP in a region.

The amount of sludge produced in wastewater treatment plants is continually increasing as the number of people connected to wastewater treatment plants increases. Sewage sludge from urban wastewater treatment plants generated in the Baltic Sea region countries in 2009 exceeded 3,000 thousand tonnes. From the beginning of 2005, sewage sludge disposal in landfill sites has been banned in the EU. One potential solution for the growing volume of sludge produced could be the use of sludge for increasing wood biomass to generate energy.

SRPs thus offer double advantages. Firstly SRPs represent an economic solution enabling highly efficient biomass production and low-cost wastewater and sludge treatment. Secondly they could contribute to local independence from external fossil fuels and fluctuations in their prices, to reduced environmental pollution and increasing local employment. The main advantages of wastewater/sludge use on SRPs are:

- effective wastewater treatment (high nutrient uptake and high transpiration rate),
- increase in the rate of biomass production without the use of mineral fertilizers,
- reuse of nutrients by introducing 'waste' into the biological cycle,
- decrease in the volume of waste,
- protection of surface waters.

Figure 17.3. Treatment of municipal wastewater treatment plant effluent in soil-willow system experiment. Results show high removal of phosphorus an medium removal of nitrogen from wastewater (see above). Photo: Agnieszka Karczmarczyk

All in all, the potential of SRPs arises from biomass production and wastewater/sludge treatment. This makes the approach a very interesting opportunity for farmers and will further contribute to sustainable rural development.

Environmental Functions of SRPs

The role of closing the nutrient cycle in the environment as a way of making the environment sustainable is being described in the literature more and more often (Boyden and Rababah, 1995; Karczmarczyk and Mosiej, 2007). Many scientists point out the advantages of using wastewaters rich in nutrients for irrigation (Mant et al., 2003; Labrecque and Teodorescu, 2001). A possible risk is that the wastewater may contain other pollutants (e.g. heavy metals), which then may accumulate in the environment. Thus it is recommended to use nutrient rich effluents from wastewater treatment plants for irrigation (Mosiej and Karczmarczyk 2006).

In years 2004-2006 at Warsaw University of Life Sciences SGGW (within the SPB program connected with WACOSYS 6FP project) have run an experiment with irrigation of willow with wastewater treatment plant effluent. The WWTP was overloaded that time, and average total phosphorus and total nitrogen concentrations were 9,66 mg/l and 41,5 mg/l respectively. Pots with willow were irrigated with the different loads of wastewater 1; 3

and 5 mm per day. As the result of irrigation, decreasing of nutrients concentration in wastewater were observed (total phosphorus concentration varied from 0,7 mg/l to 2,2 mg/l; total nitrogen from 16,8 mg/l to 28,1 mg/l). In general reduction of total phosphorus was high (84%) and reduction for total nitrogen medium (47%). The highest removal of nutrients were obtained using low irrigation rate (1mm). The results showed that using wastewater for irrigation of SRP's can be a promising way for the protection of wastewater recipients.

The willow (*Salix viminalis*) is one of several plants used for energy plantations and wastewater treatment. It has several advantages. The plant's demand for water is high, so it could be cultivated on irrigated fields (Pulfold and Watson, 2003). It grows well, even if soil is polluted with heavy metals. As a non-food crop, it could also be fertilized with sludge. It can improve surface water quality by treating WWTP effluents. It is also identified as the most energy efficient carbon conversion technology to reduce greenhouse emissions (Styles and Jones, 2007). Fast growing tree species irrigated with wastewater contributes to meeting EU targets for increasing amount of renewable energy and improving surface water quality.

Fast-growing Willow in Belarus

The Potential for SRPs in Belarus

The Republic of Belarus does not have an adequate potential for domestic fossil fuel. Presently about 5% of Belarus' demand for energy is met by local renewable resources. A National State Program was approved to increase this input to 25% by 2012. The largest resources of renewable energy in Belarus are biomass, wind- and hydropower. Belarus has about 9.5 million hectares of forests, 5.7 million hectares of arable land, and 3 million hectares of pastures. Part of these areas may be used for biomass production by cultivation of fast-growing crops such as willow. The yield of willow biomass crops can reach 10-15 tonnes of dried wood or 5-6 toe (tonnes of oil equivalents) per hectare. The potential area for willow biomass production in Belarus is estimated at 0.5 millions hectare, which means that the annual energy potential of willow biomass systems in Belarus is 2.5-3 millions toe.

Willow biomass cropping systems simultaneously produce not only energy and economic value, but also environmental and social benefits. These include reduced SO_x and NO_x emissions, no emissions of additional CO_2 to the atmosphere, reduced soil erosion and pollution from non-point source of agricultural lands, and enhanced agricultural landscape diversity. Willow plants may be successfully grown on different types of lands and also have potential in reclamation of degraded and polluted soils.

Nowadays we see several experimental plots of willow plantation in different regions of Belarus. The adaptive technology of willow production have been developed and approved by Belarusian producers. There is no big industrial plantation of SRPs yet, even if there is some progress in this direction.

A special paragraph concerning SRPs production was included in the Belarusian national Programme for developing local and renewable energy sources during 2011-2015. In accordance with this Programme a harvester for SRPs has been transferred to the country. From 2012 we plan to test clones of willow and poplar and include them into the National State List of Belarus if the result are good.

Willow Plantations on Peatland

Another environmental benefit of willow plants is reclamation of cut-over peat. The area of such lands in Belarus is 20-30 thousand hectares. The problem is the absence of adequate technology for willow production on cut-over peat, which is very heterogeneous, poorly drained, low density and nutrient-poor.

A field study conducted at Lida region, in western Belarus, willow clones (Salix viminalis) was planted on peaty soils in a cut-over peat landscape. The soils in experimental plots were characterised as heterogeneous and available water capacity was moderate to high. The aim of the experiment was to study the scope for willow in unfavourable soil conditions.

Degraded peat soil conditions are not favourable for successful plant cultivation. As a result, once peat harvesting has ceased it is impossible to grow any cultural plants for some years, with the most critical period being the time after planting. We expected the same problems to be typical for willow and therefore examined willow survival and rates of willow growth during the first couple of months post-planting. Weed control is crucial in

Figure 17.4. Willow plants on site (2), with a low degree of peat decomposition and peat depth > 50 cm. Four month after willow plantation". August 2010

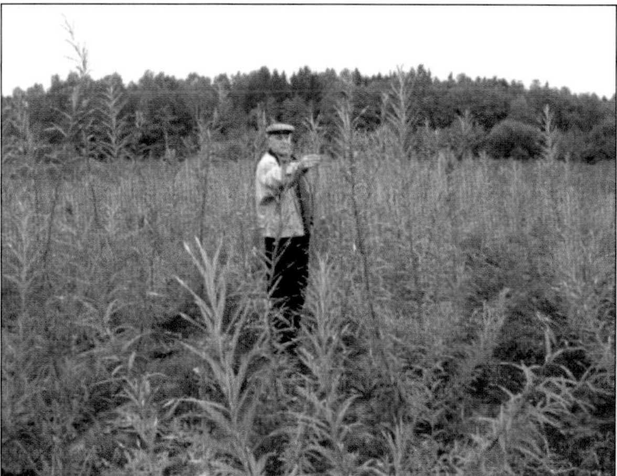

Figure 17.5. Willow plants on site (1), with a high degree of peat decomposition and peat depth > 50 cm. Four month after willow plantation". August 2010

this period because of competition between weeds and young willow plants.

Adequate rates of survival and growth of willow require fertiliser treatment, as cut-over peat soils have a low content of N, K, P and microelements. Our studies showed that fertilisation increased willow plant height by 20-50% depending on cultivar. The most positive effect was observed on the peat soil with the highest content of nutrients.

Cut-over peat soils are very heterogeneous, with widely varying nutrient content and different degrees of peat decomposition, so the cultural practices most suitable for a particular type of peat soil must be specified. To establish the best conditions we investigated the scope for willow cultivation on soils distinguished by different depth of peat layer and degree of peat decomposition.

The field experiment included 4 different soils: Peat layer depth larger than 50 cm and (1) high degree and (2) low degree of peat decomposition; (3) Peat layer depth larger than 30 cm and high degree of peat decomposition; (4) Sandy-peaty soil with peat layer depth larger than 30 cm and with sandy insertion. The crucial factor for willow plant development proved to be not only the nutrient content of the soil, but the level of peat composition. The contents of P and K were higher in soils with low peat decomposition, but the plant was growing better in soils with higher degree of peat decomposition.

Willow Plantation on Radioactively Polluted Areas

One of the key environmental problems in Belarus is the effective use of agricultural lands contaminated by radio nuclides, mainly Cs137, from the Chernobyl disaster and by heavy metals from traffic and industrial activities. After the Chernobyl disaster the area of radioactively contaminated agricultural soils in Belarus is about 1.3 million ha, including 0.8 million ha of arable lands. The optimal system of cultivation of this type of soils is a serious problem, since traditional crops such as grass and cereals accumulates radionuclides.

An alternative to traditional agricultural crops is fast growing willow. which can be used for renewable energy. In a series of field studies during 2007-2011 we studied the environmental aspects of willow production in polluted areas. The field experiments were conducted at Krichev district in Mogilev region in eastern Belarus, close to the Russian border. This region has a high level of Cs-137 contamination as well as much pollution of heavy metals (Rodzkin et al. 2010).

The concentration of cesium-137 in different parts of willow biomass was measured and transfer factors calculated for leaves, roots and wood. The results varied dependent on the levels of nitrogen, phosphorus and potassium fertilization. Potassium levels turned out to be a key factor for Cs-137 accumulation, which is expected since cesium is known to compete with potassium in the metabolism. The optimal dose of potassium was found to be 90 kg/ha.

We calculated that the concentration of cesium-137 in the wood after a 21 year period, normal time for re-plantation, will not be higher than permitted levels even with cesium 137 levels in the soil of 1480 kBq/m^2 (maximum 140 kBq/m^2 ; allowed levels for firewood is 740 Bq/kg). The concentration of cesium-137 in the roots increased gradually to 3,000 kBq/m^2 after 21 years.

A future problem may be the utilization of more polluted roots. There are two alternatives. The first is to recultivate the plantation already after 12-15 year, not after 21. Then parts of roots can be used as firewood. An alternative is to leave the roots in the soil, then plough the plot and plant new trees.

The yield of willow wood on the experimental plots was about 11-12 tonnes of dry biomass per hectare annually. We concluded that about 0.8 million hectares of radioactively polluted arable land in Belarus, today partly excluded from agriculture could be used for willow biomass production (Rodzkin et al. 2010).

Part D

Planning, Management and Assessment

Authors: Alexander Feher, Jonas Jasaitis, Agnieszka Karczmarczyk, Ingrid Karlsson, Józef Mosiej, Kristina L Nilsson, Lars Rydén, Michelle Wander and Katarzyna Wyporska

Coordinating Author: Alexander Feher

Spatial Planning and Management

18

Kristina L Nilsson
Swedish University of Agricultural Sciences, Uppsala, and Luleå University of Technology, Luleå, Sweden
Lars Rydén
Uppsala University, Uppsala, Sweden

The Aim of Spatial Planning

The Origins of Spatial Planning

Spatial planning refers in short to "the methods used by the public sector to influence the distribution of resources and activities in spaces of various types and scales". Spatial planning includes all levels of land use planning, that is urban and rural planning, regional planning, environmental planning, national spatial plans, and planning on international levels.

There are numerous definitions of spatial planning. One of the earliest comes from the *European Regional/Spatial Planning Charter* (often called the 'Torremolinos Charter'), adopted in 1983 by the European Conference of Ministers responsible for Regional Planning (CEMAT). It reads

> *Regional/spatial planning gives geographical expression to the economic, social, cultural and ecological policies of society. It is at the same time a scientific discipline, an administrative technique and a policy developed as an interdisciplinary and comprehensive approach directed towards a balanced regional development and the physical organisation of space according to an overall strategy.*

This definition sets spatial planning in a broad and interdisciplinary context. Spatial planning challenges in this way the understanding of planning focusing merely on land-use planning and on blueprints. Indeed, spatial planning includes strategy building and is closely intertwined with regional and environmental policies. Even the term European spatial planning is ambiguous and probably best understood as territorial policy-making on European level.

Developing Methods and Tools of Spatial Planning in Europe

Numerous planning systems exist around the world. Especially in North-western Europe spatial planning has evolved greatly since the time after the Second World War. In 1999, the European Spatial Development Perspective (ESDP) was signed by the ministers responsible for regional planning in the EU member states at a meeting in Potsdam, Germany. Although the ESDP has no binding status, as the European Union has no formal authority for spatial planning, the ESDP has influenced spatial planning policy in European regions and member states, and placed the coordination of EU sectoral policies on the political agenda, as ESDP provides the possibility of widening the horizon beyond solely sectoral policy measures.

The ESDP provides the first European strategy for the development of the territories of Member States. The aim is to translate the policy aims for European spatial development into examples of good practice at transnational and European level as well as at national, regional and local level. In doing so, the objective is to demonstrate concrete and visible ways of applying and supporting the policy orientations laid down for the European territory.

There are several financial instruments on an EU level to support this. A ministerial meeting in Tampere in 1999 underlined the importance of utilising EU Structural Funds according to the guidelines set out in the ESDP. The ESDP Action Programme support practical policies through actions jointly approved by the Commission and Member States. The Action Programme includes the idea of "ESDP Demonstration Projects". Finally the Interreg program, financing regional development projects, is another vitally important instrument for the application of the ESDP for cross-border and transnational co-operation on spatial development and planning.

On the European level a number of steps have been taken to support planning in member countries. In 1997 the EU Commission Services published a compendium on European spatial planning systems providing an overview on the various approaches to spatial planning within the EU. It was followed by the Study Programme on European Spatial Planning (SPESP), and a research network to support European territorial policies. In 2002, following on the SPESP experience, the European Spatial Planning Observation Network (ESPON) was established to provide territorial evidence for European policy-making covering 29 countries, and after 2007 even 31 countries, that is the 27 EU member states, the three EEA states Norway, Iceland and Liechtenstein, and finally Switzerland.

The European Spatial Development Perspective is certainly the document which kick-started much of the spatial planning thinking at the European level. But the ESDP is merely the first, and so far, main point of reference. The story continued via the elaboration of an evidence document, the Territorial State and Perspectives of the EU, mainly based on ESPON findings. The evidence document resulted in a policy document known as the Territorial Agenda of the EU. This Agenda still has to prove itself, but its mere existence suggests that the momentum of European spatial planning has been sustained from the start of the ESDP. In policy terms these years meant steps in the creation of an intergovernmental spatial policy agenda offering itself as a frame of reference for other policies, including existing EU policies and planning for sector development in Europe.

Spatial Planning and Sustainable Development

Planning and management is one important instrument for implementing sustainable development. There are high demands and expectations on spatial planning to support the society with physical structures to make it possible for people to act and live in a more sustainable way.

During the last decades there has been a growing awareness and international agreements at both UN and EU level for the protection of the environment. In addition the predictions of climate change requires activities to decrease environmental burden and at the same time adapt the physical environment to the effects of climate change. The environmental and climate issues were first in the 1970-1980's defended mainly by environmental NGOs. Today these issues have entered into the official agendas, regulations and rules. The concept of sustainable development is often included in all official planning documents and it is uncomplicated to find cohesion at the general visionary level. On the detailed planning level, when the visions are to be concretised, it is more challenging to achieve consensus between actors with a manifold of sector interests and values.

The Brundtland concept of sustainability is often divided in ecological, social and economic dimensions to make it more manageable and understandable. This means that all these dimensions are to be considered in planning situations. A more detailed description on how to implement this in practical planning and management work is given in below.

Legal Frameworks and Authorities for Spatial Planning

European Level

Generally, the actors at European level are weak when it comes to means and instruments to exercise territorial policies. The competence and means for real action

Figure 18.1. In Latgale, the most eastern part of Latvia, several local authorities have formed Latgale Planning region as an established legal entity for cooperation in spatial planning. Latgale Planning Region is a derived legal entity established in accordance with the Regional Development Law on June 2006 under the supervision of the Ministry of Regional Development and Local Governments. Its activity has been financed from the state principal budget. (http://www.latgale.lv/en/padome). Latgale is not so modernised as the western part of Latvia and has a beautiful landscape and rich wildlife. Photo: Päwels Cacivkins

lie with the Member States regions and local actors. Therefore, most "European actors" can only influence via non-binding guidelines, convincing arguments and discourses. The European Commission has furthermore the possibility to influence via funding schemes, such as the Structural Funds and the Interreg programs, or via regulations. However, there is no regulatory power in the field of spatial planning or territorial policies at European level. Thus the regulatory influence comes via other policy sectors which may influence territorial development and spatial planning.

The EU commission works with funding, based on rules to be followed to be able to reach the funding. In this way the commission forces the regional and local authorities to follow the intentions of the EU policies. We may see the funding programs as "carrots" and non-funding as "sticks".

In the European Union the two main actors are the European Commission, mostly represented by the Directorate General for Regional Policies (DG Regio), and the intergovernmental co-operation where the Member States come together to shape policies. Both actors have been active in territorial policy-making at European level for a long time.

Whereas the intergovernmental setting appears natural in a field where the European Community does not have an explicit mandate, the contribution of the European Commission is more subtle and mostly act via various sector policies. The EU Regional Policy has also taken some deliberate steps to influence spatial planning. Spatial issues and territorial cohesion are increasingly acknowledged in the three-annual Cohesion Reports. But most importantly the European Structural Funds, i.e. the main instrument of European regional policy, are partly used to promote territorial thinking in Europe and thus indirectly also spatial planning.

The Renewed EU Sustainable Development Strategy was adopted by the European Council in June 2006. It is an overarching strategy which deals in an integrated way with economic, environmental and social issues and lists the following seven key challenges:

- Climate change and clean energy
- Sustainable transport
- Sustainable consumption and production
- Conservation and management of natural resources
- Public health
- Social inclusion, demography and migration
- Global poverty

Tackling climate change is one of the biggest challenges. The EU integrated energy and climate change policy from December 2008 intends to direct Europe towards a low-carbon, energy-efficient economy. The quantitative targets for 2020 is to cut greenhouse gases by 20% (30% if international agreement is reached), to reduce energy consumption by 20% through increased energy efficiency; and increase energy from renewable sources to 20%.

National and Regional Planning Level

Generally, the powerful instruments for spatial planning and territorial policies lie, differing for each country, with the state, regional or local authorities. The responsibilities for the national planning are lying on various ministries. In Table 18.1 the national responsible ministry, planning instruments and legislation is summarised for Baltic Sea region states.

The influence of the regional authorities varies between the European countries. In many countries, such as is the case with Germany, the regional authority works out spatial

Table 18.1. Competent Authority legal responsibilities for planning and management From COMMIN (see further http://commin.org/en/planning-systems/national-planning-systems/nations.html)

Country	National level	Regional planning	Most important legislation
Belarus	Ministry of Architecture and Construction	Comprehensive planning specialized (sectoral) planning and Regional planning	Planning and Building Law
Denmark	Ministry Environment	Regional spatial development planning.	Planning Act
Estonia	Ministry of Internal Affairs	Spatial planning and development planning.	Planning Act
Finland	Ministry of the Environment	Regional development and regional land use planning	Nature Conservation Act, Building Protection Act, Antiquities Act, Environmental Protection Act, Water Act, Land Extraction Act, Highway Act
Germany	Several ministries and states (Länder)	Spatial planning, state development planning	Federal Spatial Planning Act, Federal Building Code, Federal Nature Conservation Act
Latvia	Ministry of Local Municipalities and Regional Development	Inter-municipal planning, Regional land use planning and regional development	Planning Law
Lithuania	several ministries	1. Regional strategic planning, 2. Regional development planning, 3. Regional territorial planning	Law on Territorial Planning
Norway	Ministry of Environment and the Ministry of local government and regional development	County planning and Inter-municipal planning	Planning and Building Act
Poland		Spatial Planning	Spatial Planning and Management Act
Russia	Several ministries	Planning scheme	Urban Development Code
Sweden	Mostly the ministry for Environment	Regional development programming, regional planning	Planning and Building Act

plans for the regional territory. The regional plans serve as guidance for decisions on comprehensive plans, detailed development plans and area regulations. The planning instruments are connected to formal planning legislation for regional plans for the entire nation/region or sectors in the nation/region. The plans may, if they are of importance for the region, indicate fundamental features of the use of land and water areas and recommend principles for the location of buildings and constructions.

In other countries, as for example in Sweden, the regional authorities, with exception of the Stockholm region, do not conduct any spatial plans. The regional bodies carry out regional development plans focusing on economical development. Instead the local authorities are the main and independent bodies for development of physical planning issues.

Planning on Municipal and Local Level

The local level is most often the key level for planning of physical structures. The planning area can be comprehensive for the entire local authority territory, as for example is obligatory in Sweden. It can also cover the entire urban territory for a city, a part of a city, a housing area or just a block. It is a local authority task to plan for the use of land and water. It can be made by a *comprehensive plan,* a general document for a larger territory. It relies on, and sometimes is requested by, the legislation of the country. A comprehensive plan is a plan for the entire area for which the local authority (most often the local authority, but in some countries regional authorities or even regional offices of state authorities) is responsible. It should identify future land use regarding e.g. building sites, transport infrastructure, agriculture, and forestry. The comprehensive plan should have a long term perspective. In most countries the comprehensive plan, in contrast to the detailed plan, is not considered law and thus is rather a policy document.

A detailed plan is binding document for detail land use. The detailed plan identifies the suitability of a site for development and give the exact location and character

Table 18.2. Comparison of planning systems at municipal and local level. From COMMIN (see further http://commin.org/en/planning-systems/national-planning-systems/nations.html)

Issues	Notes on the situation in the Baltic Sea region countries
1. Territorial organization	Several forms of local authorities exist. In some countries the local planning authority is also handling building permits.
2 Local planning authority bodies	Local committees or local supreme authorities have responsibility for initialization and adoption/ endorsement of plans. In some countries legally notified instruments exist to cooperate between municipalities.
3 Forms of planning	There are different land use and spatial planning instruments at local levels.
4 Regulation instruments of local plans	In some countries land use zoning categories are required in local plans including future directions.
5 Overall local plan	In most countries the overall local plan is legally binding. Then statutory zoning and land use categories are shown on the plan map. The time horizon of the overall plan is normally limited.
6 Detailed plans	In many countries the municipality has a free right to initiate a detailed development plan. This is valid for a specified time limits set for the public handling of detailed development plans and is the time horizon/ validity of these plan(s) positively limited?
7 Development control	The plans normally includes land use zoning categories, and categories of building permits. However these require building applications.
8 Implementation	Public acquisition of land is regulated by the local plan. Countries have particular instruments for covering of urban development costs.
9 Reactions against planning decisions	Conflicts in planning and building matters are mostly led before court and often special or administrative courts. In some countries affected groups may appeal against planning and building decisions.
10 The public costs of handling detailed development plans and building matter	The initiators may have to pay for public handling of development plans and building matters.

and design of buildings, infrastructure etc. The detail plan gives the formal rights and responsibilities for authorities and developers of a smaller territory. This may concern continuous development or a new single individual building. The detailed plan is accompanied by permits for the entrepreneurs to start building. The detailed plan is considered to be national and local regulation.

An overview how planning on municipal and local level is conducted in various ways in the countries of Baltic Sea region (Table 18.2) is found in the COMMIN, The Baltic Spatial Conceptshare, documents. Here we find for each country which municipal authorities are responsible for the planning, and which legislation and instruments that are available in each country.

Detailed plans and projects are worked out only when there are public or private actors interested to make future changes in urban or rural areas. There must be enough public or private interests and funding as a driving force for the planning. That is to say that everything that happens in the future can not be foreseen and planned in advance. The role of legislation and protection planning is one way to defend public values and common interests when private and individual interests plan for new developments.

Spatial Planning and EU Policies

Rural Development Policies

In the rural context the landscape with all its assets, including natural resources, is the key resource to take care of in planning and to manage properly. Without a well-managed and productive landscape the rural society will be bereaved of its key resource and indeed its condition for long-term survival.

The rural landscape and development is in most European countries not under spatial planning rules and regulation. That is to say, there are no formally adapted plans for development of rural areas. But rural development is still a main concern in European policy. Most rural development is encouraged by EU funding. Valuable natural resources and landscapes are, however, protected by legislation when projects or investments are planned.

Some 90% of the territory of the EU is "rural", and this area is home to more than 56% of the EU's population. In the Baltic Sea region urbanisation is high, in highly populated areas some 75%. The urbanisation increases even at an accelerated pace. At the same time many families move outside the city borders searching for cheaper ground (relevant also for enterprises) and a life closer to the nature. This can cause urban sprawl without clear difference between urban and rural areas. The pattern of typical urban sprawl, can be found e.g. around Berlin and Hamburg and in large Polish cities such as Łódź and Warsaw and to some extent in Riga.

The development of many kinds of rural trade and business is stimulated by the EU rural development policies. In particular farming and foresting are influencing the rural landscape. Many types of farming and harvests are today mostly steered by EU funds. The EU rural policy aims to improve the living conditions for the rural population, which often is not as good as for those living in towns and cities, to improve the rural economy, and to protect the landscape. The values of the rural landscape, should be properly addressed by spatial planning. These values include beauty and recreation, the production of food and raw materials, and nature protection and mitigating climate change. Rural life is attractive also today if access to adequate services and infrastructure is available.

The present EU rural development policy is valid for the period 2007-2013.

Financial Instruments for Rural Development

As described earlier there is no spatial planning legislation on the European Union level. Instead the Union uses other means of influencing rural development. The most decisive are the economic incentives.

There are a number of EU financed programmes addressing rural areas. Most relevant and forceful are those financed by the EU structural funds. Leader+ is one of four initiatives designed to help rural actors to consider the long-term potential of their local region. It aims to encourage the implementation of integrated, high-quality and original strategies for sustainable development, and has a strong focus on partnership and networks of exchange of experience. A total of EUR 5 billion was spent for the period 2000-2006. Action 1 of the program asks for the establishment of Local Action Groups, LAGs. Action 2 asks for cooperation between rural territories, while Action 3 focus on networking to collect and disseminate information at the national level on good practice, the exchange of experience and know-how. It supports technical assistance for cooperation in best use of natural and cultural resources; improving the quality of life in rural areas; adding value to local products, the use of new know-how and new technologies to make products and services in rural areas more competitive.

An important and influential part of the EU policy is the Common Agricultural Policy (CAP). CAP is implemented through economic instruments using a large part of the EU budget. The territorial impacts of the CAP are largely unsupportive of territorial cohesion in Europe, although there is scope in the given instruments to do more in that direction. Furthermore, one has to consider that the analysis of the instruments and expenditures of the CAP excludes the largest component of the support received by EU farmers in the form of the higher prices paid by consumers within the EU.

Equally the Structural Funds have been of decisive influence. Their main objectives are to reduce disparities in GDP and unemployment between regions. In doing so, they have contributed to territorial cohesion by stimulating regional and local innovation and development. However, they have done so less consistently than might have been anticipated. The assessments have revealed a complex picture; this shows that while money went to

Box 18.1. The European Union Rural Development policies

"With over 56% of the population in the 27 Member States of the European Union living in rural areas, which cover 91% of the territory, rural development is a vitally important policy area. Farming and forestry remain crucial for land use and the management of natural resources in the EU's rural areas, and as a platform for economic diversification in rural communities. The strengthening of EU rural development policy is, therefore, an overall EU priority." http://ec.europa.eu/agriculture/rurdev/index_en.htm

less-favoured parts of the EU, the differences between regions within a country have been left largely untouched or even accentuated. The funds have, however, boosted competitiveness through leverage effects on national policies: local and regional levels of governance have been empowered, resulting in innovations, strategic planning, and new partnerships.

Urban Policies

According to UN statistics the level of urbanization in Europe is currently 74.6 per cent with an expected annual growth of 0.3 per cent per year between 2000 and 2015 (UNCHS 2001a). Urban policies are certainly relevant for all regions, since even dominantly rural areas have some towns and villages, even if not large cities. There are also several important documents regarding local and urban development within the Union. These are also relevant for the very important rural-urban partnership.

The EU *Leipzig Charter on Sustainable European Cities* is a document of the Member States adopted in 2000. In the charter is argued that integrated urban planning approach is a prerequisite for sustainable development of European cities. Its key themes concern strategies for upgrading the urban fabric and for enhancing local economies and labour markets, clean urban transport and the integration of migrants.

On the international level The Sustainable Cities Programme (SCP) is a joint UN-HABITAT/UNEP facility established in the early 1990s to build capacities in urban environmental planning and management. The programme targets urban local authorities and their partners. It is founded on broad-based stakeholder participatory approaches. This programme focuses a facility to package urban Environmental Planning and Management (EPM) approaches, technologies and know-how.

Urban development and rural-urban partnership are topics addressed by many Interreg projects. Almost all ESPON studies and Interreg projects under all three strands address the issue of rural-urban partnership and polycentric urban development, some of these more explicitly than others. Taken together they cover a wide range of activities, from studies, via the development of strategies or strategic partnerships to infrastructure investments. The perception and understanding of polycentric urban development and rural-urban partnership varies accordingly.

Transport Policies

Transport infrastructure is fundamental for the mobility of persons and goods and for the territorial cohesion of the European Union. The growth in traffic between Member States is expected to double by 2020. The investment required to complete and modernize a true trans-European network in the enlarged EU amounts to some € 500 billion from 2007 to 2020.

Most transport infrastructures have been developed under national policy premises. The European governments agreed to establish a Trans-European transport network (TEN-T), allowing goods and people to circulate quickly and easily between Member States. It aims towards a single, multimodal network integrating land, sea and air transport networks. The European Community is supporting the TEN-T implementation by several Community financial instruments and by loans from the European Investment Bank. Grants are allocated both for project preparation and implementation phases. They are also aimed to feasibility and comprehensive technical or environmental studies and costly geological explorations. This is to help to overcome early stage project difficulties, and to the works phase.

The European transport investments have contributed to cohesion in relative terms, although they may actually widen the absolute economic gap between regions. The TEN transport infrastructure projects planned for the period up to 2020 have a decentralising effect, and is thus favouring peripheral regions. Infrastructure policies have larger effects than pricing policies, and the magnitude of the effect is related to the number and size of projects. However, even large increases in regional accessibility produce only small benefits in terms of regional economic activity. Generally, the overall effects of transport infrastructure investments and other transport policies are small as compared to those of socio-economic and technical macro trends.

Cultural Heritage Policies

Cultural heritage refers to material as well as non-material expressions. This includes the traditions, ideas and values that we consciously or unconsciously acquire from previous generations. The view of what constitutes a cultural heritage in all its diversity changes with time. It is however most often a historic environment and can include everything from individual objects and buildings to larger parts of the landscape. The Baltic Sea region has a very rich cultural heritage and many castles, churches, parks etc have protection status. Cultural heritage and historic environment work refers to activities that promote cultural heritage and historic environment conservation, e.g. by protecting, caring for, researching, disseminating knowledge about, and developing these aspects.

The historical perspective and long tradition are important strengths. In recent decades, the emphasis of public cultural heritage work has changed from the physical conservation of ancient monuments and the maintenance aspects of social planning evident during the 1970s. Via the everyday environmental and ecological issues of the 1980s, it turned towards a more holistic view in the 1990s, in which cultural heritage was regarded as a resource, where both its material and non-material aspects were integrated. The emphasis has thus shifted from "monuments" to "environment" to "heritage". In the revival work of the 21st century, history, dialogue and diversity have come into focus, as has a wider cooperation both with and beyond the traditional heritage sector.

The European Landscape Convention (ELC) promotes the protection, management and planning of European landscapes and organizes European co-operation on landscape issues. It also promotes the public involvement in matters concerning the landscape. It is the first international treaty to be exclusively concerned with all dimensions of European landscapes. The Convention underlines the fact that the landscape is a common good as well as a common responsibility. The landscape comprises a variety of values - cultural, ecological, aesthetic, social and economic. The use of natural resources and development of landscapes is often a matter of negotiation. A close co-operation between national and local authorities, private organizations and the public is necessary to achieve a sustainable development of the landscape. The ECL, an initiative of the Congress of Regional and Local Authorities of the Council of Europe, basically to protect the landscape, was adopted by the Council's Committee of Ministers in July 2002, and went into force in 2004, as the necessary ten states had ratified it.

The EU Framework Directives and Thematic Strategies

The EU environmental legislation includes well over 200 legal acts. Most are directed towards a special medium or sector, such as water, air, nature, waste, or chemicals. Others deal with cross-cutting issues, e.g. access to environmental information, and public participation in environmental decision-making. The acts of legislation are grouped into 17 policy areas. Those most relevant for planning work refer to Air, Civil Protection and Environmental Accidents, Climate Change, Industry and Technology, Land Use, Nature and Biodiversity, Noise, Soil, Sustainable Development, Waste and Water.

The most important legal instrument in this sector is the Environmental Impact Assessment, EIA. More recently the Strategic Environmental Assessment, SEA, has been introduced to broaden the number of projects which will be assessed and also broaden the aspects considered, especially to social and economic aspects. EIA and SEA are further presented at page 218.

The 1992 Rio UN Conventions promotes the principle of sustainable development. The Convention on Biological Diversity, signed during the Rio Conference, intends to stop the frighteningly rapid loss of biodiversity on earth. There are important efforts within the European Union to protect biodiversity. Based on the Birds Directive from 1979 and the Habitats Directive from 1991 the Union formed the Natura 2000 network. This includes many thousands of sites in member states, in which wildlife riches are better conserved, managed and protected by being included in this network, significantly enriching the Community's biodiversity.

The proposal for a framework Directive (COM (2006) 232) on soils sets out common principles for protecting soils across the EU. Within this common framework, the EU Member States will be in a position to decide how best to protect soil and how use it in a sustainable way on its own territory. Today there is a thematic strategy on soils.

Cleaner rivers and lakes, groundwater and coastal beaches are of high priority in European Environmental policy. A fundamental rethink of Community water policy, asking for a more integrated approach to water policy, culminated in mid-1995. A new European water policy and framework legislation to reach "good status" of surface waters and groundwater developed on a river basins approach. A Directive to introduce *integrated river basin management* for Europe, Directive 2000/60/EC, the EU Water Framework Directive (WFD) was finally adopted in 2000.

EU Supported Planning Cooperation in the Baltic Sea Region

The Swedish initiative Visions and Strategies around the Baltic Sea, VASAB, immediately after the systems change in 1991, became a first trans-national – regional – planning cooperation in Europe. It inspired the creation of the EU for regional cooperation and strategies, the Interreg, already introduced above. There are seven Interreg programmes in Europe, including one for the Baltic Sea region and one for the North Sea region. The first programmes lasted three years (I-III) while the present Interreg IV is a seven year programme (2007-2013). With the establishment of Interreg IIC trans-national co-operation and spatial planning issues got a formal platform and instrument in the EU. This was later continued as Interreg IIIB (2000-2006). The territorial co-operation has been integrated into the mainstream Structural Funds system under Interreg objective 3 "Territorial Co-operation".

Among the cooperative schemes in the Baltic Sea region also COMMIN, the Baltic Spatial Conceptsphere, is important. It is a partnership of 28 partners in 11 countries in the Baltic Sea region. It is an example of the impact of spatial planning and development policy in the region, but also illustrates the considerable heterogeneity among the Member States.

Enlarging the geographical scope, CEMAT, the European Conference of Ministers responsible for Regional Planning, is an obvious actor at the pan-European level. As the CEMAT is part of the Council of Europe framework, it covers not only the 27 EU Member States but in total 47 countries. The CEMAT can also be considered as a form of intergovernmental co-operation.

Today all of these actor groups plus various other actors are in one way or the other active in shaping territorial policies for the region and Europe. Each of them has a different understanding on what territorial policies or spatial planning at European level is. Furthermore, each of them has different intentions and means.

In 2009 The European Commission adopted a Communication on the EU Strategy for the Baltic Sea Region. This is the first time that a comprehensive strategy, covering several Community policies, is targeted on a 'macro-region'. The macro-region around the Baltic Sea includes the eight member states bordering the Baltic Sea, but close cooperation between the EU and Russia is also necessary in order to tackle jointly many of the regional challenges. The same need for constructive co-operation applies also to Norway and Belarus.

The Strategy aims at coordinating actions by Member States, regions, the EU, pan-Baltic organizations, financing institutions and non-governmental bodies to promote a more balanced development of the Region. Four cornerstones of the Strategy have been singled out as crucial:

1. Environmental sustainability (e.g. reducing pollution in the sea);
2. Prosperity (e.g. promoting innovation in small and medium enterprises);
3. Accessibility and attractiveness (e.g. better transport links);
4. Security (e.g. improving accident response).

The most important result of the regional strategy so far is the adoption of an action plan for the Baltic Sea, in which the states, among other obligations, have accepted very far reaching reductions of the nitrogen and phosphorus loading, which will decisively influence the way agriculture is conducted in the region.

Planning Processes

Processes of Planning Practice

Planning practice deals traditionally with how to distribute the use or protection of land and water areas. A main part of planning concerns localisation and shape of new or regenerated built up areas or infrastructure. Planning also deals with protection of valuable areas or resources as example heritage and natural environments. In later decades to these physical issues are in many cases added economical and social issues. Plans are based on, and adopted by, political bodies and worked out by professional planners. Knowledge and interests from other actors, as stakeholders and citizens, are involved in democratic planning processes.

Basic data for the planning processes includes a prognosis on existing conditions and development of areas regarding e.g. the physical situation, buildings, vegetation, infrastructure, demography, mobility, and economic activities together with estimations of the future development.

A rational planning process starts with collecting basic planning data, conducting a planning programme with a vision, and formulating the planning goals. Next step is to find alternative proposals of the future development of the planning goals based on the background and interests of the actors and stakeholders. The planning process is a way to clear out different interests and values between the actors and give stakeholders and interest groups opportunities to influence, criticize or at least receive information on the future plans.

The drivers for planning are firstly public actors. These have the task to distribute land for suitable purposes, establish comprehensive built up and infrastructures, such as communications networks, green structures, schools, children and elderly care, wastewater treatment plants, or to establish protected territories. Other drivers are often public or private actors concerned and interested in various development aspects or projects. These may be buildings, housing areas, commercial centres, energy projects, etc.

The planner needs to identify problems, and establish a platform to address conflicts of interests between actors and stakeholders, and at best allow for exchange of ideas how to address such conflicts.

Pro-active Planning

In the planning process, planners are able to determine a wide range of interconnecting issues that affect an area. Each step of the process can be seen as interdependent, and may be reiterated as needed. The steps are executed in order or in parallel as best fit the purpose. While spatial planning is complex, in practice it never follows a technical rational procedure from goals to results. The planning practice processes can then be described as a spiral where each round takes in new basic data and knowledge to reach a higher level of the planning outcome.

The final plan consists of a written document with objectives, visions and description of the plan together with attached maps and other illustrations as needed. Maps are normally available in computer format, a so-called Geographical Information System, GIS, (or on urban level, Local Information System, LIS, with very high resolution) or AutoCad. A GIS map consists of several, even a large number, of layers, each with a special kind of information, such as roads, buildings, water networks etc. Statistics of different properties of the area, which have been collected in preparatory steps, may be added to the GIS.

The planning team must first address the issues and context at stake. (For a comprehensive plan, as mentioned, this is a political issue.) These may be requests for new habitation, industrial production, areas asked to be set aside for nature protection, energy production, etc. If habitation is expanded, social services need to be included, such as schools, health services, areas for commercial services etc, and access to the area through roads. Requests for developments from private and public interests are often part and drivers the process.

The local authority may have policy goals, scenarios or "visions" for the long-term development. The visioning process of a community will be discussed further below. Data for the area to be planned typically describe environment (e.g. air pollution), traffic development, demographic trends, economic developments, social conditions, etc, but of course data should be collected regarding any relevant topic in the planning process. These data may be used as indicators as is described below.

The information gathered and the stated goals are used to identify trends and make forecasts and write a first planning proposal. A typical comprehensive plan begins by giving a brief background of the current and future conditions. Following the background information are the community goals and the way in which these goals may be implemented into the community. Comprehensive plans may also contain separate sections for important issues such as transportation, housing, culture heritage, outdoor recreation etc.

Next step is to propose actions to implement the plan, projects or an entire program for each of a number of selected issues. In some areas alternative plans may be drafted, especially with regard to budget options. The programs and plans should during the entire process be communicated with other actors, stakeholders and interest groups. This may be done through exhibitions, published reports, hearings etc. The plan may as well be distributed to the most relevant stakeholders to give them opportunity to comment on the proposed plan.

Figure 18.2. Gaming as way to do planning. In 2009 a group of farmers and other stakeholders in western Poland took part in a game organised by teachers and students of AGH University in Krakow as an innovative way to evaluate different way to develop the watershed. Photo: Piotr Magnuszewski.

The proposals should be evaluated. Some such evaluations are legally required, e.g. environmental impact assessment, EIA, (see below). The zero option, that is to leave an area as it is, should be one alternative included in the EIA. In general the evaluation may concern all kinds of negative and positive effects of a program or plan.

After proper preparations the local government finally adopts parts of or the whole plan. This general decision is most seen as a policy decision. In order to implement and carry out the plan decision are needed on each of a number of projects, each with its own budget, time line, and other details. In connection with such decisions a detailed plan is prepared and accepted. Collected data may be defining the goals to be reached – e.g. a certain level of air pollution, or traffic flow – and as such reported to the political level.

Urban and Rural Planning

Planning work typically always addresses economic development and demographic trends, although these two aspects of development may be the least easy to actually plan. Aspects which may be planned in detail includes nature protection, infrastructure and buildings. In between these extremes there is e.g. school development, which is also very much "planneable", as schools have to be made available for new groups of children. In the rural context agriculture, forestry and nature protection are among the most important to address in planning work. Still agriculture is much dependent on policy decisions. The CAP, common agricultural policy of the EU, is crucial for what farmers in the EU are able to do on a commercial basis.

The urban areas are growing all over the globe hosting approximately 50% of the population. Urban areas are complex systems of buildings integrated with infrastructure. That is the main reason why most planning activities are made within the urban areas. Urban - that is city and town - planning is an integration of the disciplines of land use planning and transport planning, to explore a very wide range of aspects of the built and social environments of urbanizations. Urban planning is a synergy of the disciplines of urban planning, architecture and landscape architecture. Another key role of urban planning is urban renewal, and re-generation of inner cities with changing use of buildings and areas, as for example new development of brown fields.

The quality of public spaces, urban man-made landscapes and architecture and urban development plays an important role in the living conditions of the urban populations. These so-called soft locational factors are important for attracting knowledge industry, businesses, a qualified and creative workforce, and for tourism. Therefore, the interaction of architecture, infrastructure planning and urban planning must be increased in order to create attractive, user-oriented public spaces and achieve a high standard in terms of the living environment. Urban development is the sum of all the cultural, economic, technological, social and ecological aspects influencing the quality and process of planning and construction. Urban development and regeneration include preservation of architectural heritage. Historical buildings, public spaces, green structure and their urban and architectural value are of great importance.

The urban green structure includes parks, gardens, avenue trees, wild green nature, and cemeteries. Nature and other green areas in a town or village are important for its social well-being, for its ecology, air and water, as well as for making a city attractive. Green areas in cities and towns are connected to each other and generate entireness – a green structure – independent of ownership or maintenance. They are also important parts of a city's building history, identity and character. A green structure function as lungs and kidneys for the urban areas while it contributes to urban biodiversity, preserves a good local climate, good air environment and provide space for ecological ways to clean storm water. Green areas also give possibilities for leisure and various out-door activities, as it provide informal meeting places, arenas for concerts, theatre, exhibitions, manifestations etc.

Water Planning

Planning adresses both land and water, and water needs a special notion. Water protection, regulations and management will be part of any comprehensive plan and many of the detailed plans. Water is since ancient times by far the most regulated natural resource, and even small streams may have hundreds of dams and other regulations to allow for drainage, defined water levels, abduction of water, hydropower, etc.

Water management is regulated in the EU Water Framework Directive. According to this directive all surface water in the Union should by 2014 (in most areas postponed) be in a "natural state". What this exactly means may partly be decided on at national level but, regardless, for a main part of European rivers, lakes and coasts it amounts to considerable environmental improvements. Water is to be administered by River Basin Authorities. These regional authorities are today assigned in all EU15 states, and soon in all EU29. Water need to be continuously monitored, a considerable task, mostly to be made by local authorities. This can be complicated while the water does not follow the administrative borders of local, regional and national territories.

Restoration of surface water are today more important than ever. Restoration organisations are established in many countries on the national (EPA) and regional level (county administration). In part of the Baltic Sea region (especially Norway, Sweden and Finland) restoration of acidified water by liming is a large task on-going since many years already. In more southern areas, and very much so in the Baltic Sea itself, eutrophication is the main problem. In 2008, as mentioned, a Baltic Sea Action plan was agreed on among the coastal states of the Baltic Sea.

The number of water restoration projects in the region increases. These include building wetlands to manage nutrient loads, to restore streams to natural conditions by removing dams and channelization to promote fish life, and removing old industrial sites to allow for waterfront habitation.

A main concern in water management will be diverse interests of stakeholders such as farmers, urban areas, industries and nature protection interests. These conflicts of interests need to be taken care of and balanced mostly by local and regional authorities on all levels.

Environmental Impact Assessment, EIA and SEA

If the planned development is foreseen to cause a significant impact on the surroundings this is normally examined as part of approval of a building permit. Each larger plan, program and development project needs an EIA, Environmental Impact Assessment. The EU EIA Directive is one of the oldest EU environmental directives, and it was in addition preceded in many countries by national regulation. Later on a Strategic Environmental Assessment, SEA, Directive has been adopted and is now

Figure 18.3. The small town Reszel in north-eastern Poland illustrate how urban and rural space is integrated and contribute to each other for the benefit of both. Photo: Johan Anglemark.

mandatory. The idea of an SEA comes from the regional development /land use planning and should ensure that plans and programmes take into consideration the environmental effects they cause and how to strategically avoid negative affects.

Today most often the Strategic Impact Assessments is made before the EIA; the results generated in the SEA are later used for the EIA. The structure of SEA (under the Directive) includes

- "Screening", investigation of whether the plan or programme falls under the SEA legislation,
- "Scoping", defining the boundaries of investigation, assessment and assumptions required,
- "Documentation of the state of the environment", effectively a *baseline* on which to base judgments,
- "Determination of the likely (non-marginal) environmental impacts", usually in terms of Direction of Change rather than firm figures,
- Informing and consulting the public,
- Influencing "Decision taking" based on the assessment and,
- Monitoring of the effects of plans and programmes after their implementation.

The EU directive also includes other impacts besides the environmental, such as material assets and archaeological sites. In most states this has been broadened further to include economic and social aspects of sustainability.

The EIA will ask for an estimation of the effects of the project for pollution, emissions, but as well intrusion into the landscape etc. A main concern is if the proposed plan is compatible with existing legislation, that is, in compliance. Important legislations concern existing Environmental Quality Standards, EQS (limits), the directives on biodiversity (birds, wetlands), protection of the landscape, and protection of natural resources. Another concern is if those influenced are prepared to accept a foreseen impact on the environment.

The EIA often leads to considerable disagreements and protests. Thus the building of a railroad in northern Sweden (close to the city of Umeå) was contested on the basis of its intrusion into an area important for bird re-

Box 18.2. Via Baltica Expressway

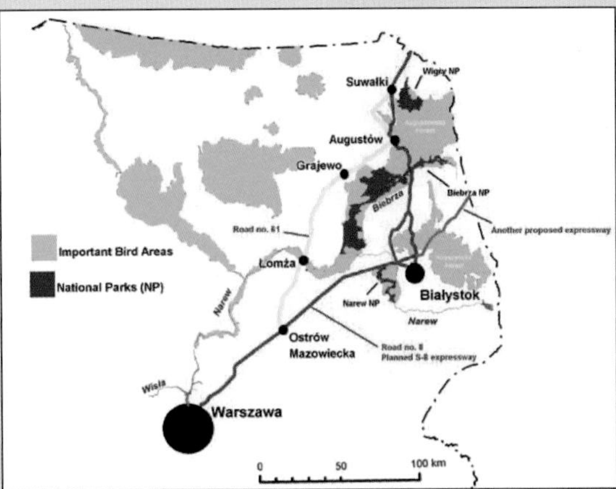

Figure 18.4. Planned route (red) of Via Baltica with alternative and later realised route (grey) through Rospuda valley.

Figure 18.5. View of Rospuda river valley. Photo: Mariusz Chilmon.

Controversial planning of the Via Baltica Expressway in Poland judged unlawful. Via Baltica, the expressway from Helsinki-Tallinn to Warszawa-Prague, was originally proposed to run straight through the Augustow and Knyszyn primeval forests in north-east Poland. Both sites are listed as Special Protection Areas under the Birds Directive and are proposed Sites of Community Importance under the Habitats Directive – Europe's major laws for the protection of natural environment, and are as well Natura 2000 sites. The plan was fiercely opposed by Polish and European environmental NGOs, who addressed the case to the European Commission. It decided in March 2007 to refer Poland to the European Court of Justice (ECJ) for breaching EU environmental law by planning construction of the Via Baltica through the protected Rospuda Valley. In September 2008 the Highest Administrative Court (NSA) in Poland ruled the section of Via Baltica expressway planned to cut pristine wetlands in Rospuda river Valley within a protected Natura 2000 site to be illegal. Polish Prime Minister Donald Tusk in March 2009 announced that Poland will choose an alternative route for the expressway that will relieve the town of Augustow of heavy transit traffic without harming Rospuda. The new bypass will now be constructed close to the nearby village of Raczki. (http://www.viabalticainfo.org/The-solutions-strategic-analysis). Landscape in Rospuda wetland. There are several alternative routes for transit traffic travelling from Warsaw to the Polish-Lithuanian border. In one alternative backed by Polish environmental NGOs, the route can cross the city of Lomza, which would not only be a shorter route but would also bypass the designated Natura 2000 sites. This existing road (no. 61) is also being modernised under the EU funds but with lower technical parameters than are required for the international standard Via Baltica. It has been closed to heavy lorry transit for a few years, and all transit traffic is currently directed via road no. 8, threatening the most valuable nature areas in the region. (see http://www.viabalticainfo.org/Map-of-possible-alternative; http://bankwatch.org/documents/Rospuda_valley_road_alternatives.jpg)

production. The building of the main road "Via Baltica" through and area in north-eastern Poland, nick-named the Green lungs of Poland, gave rise to large protests and was even taken to the European court (Box 18.2 above). The presently proposed expansion of the road network around Stockholm (Förbifart Stockholm) has been contested since it has been projected to lead to increased private car traffic and reduced municipal transport, and thereby a considerable increase in emissions of carbon dioxide, much in conflict with present efforts to reduce emissions of greenhouse gases.

In many countries cases like these are judged in special environmental courts. These are ordinary civil courts but specialising on environmental issues. In other countries an environmental conflict is taken to the county office, or the regional office of the state authority. There is in many cases the possibility to appeal to higher court, and especially to the European Court in The Hague, if the EU regulations are believed to be violated.

Also during operation the environmental impact of an activity is regulated. When a building permit has been granted, the activity itself, e.g. an industrial production, needs to be licensed. This is today regulated in several EU Directives. Especially significant is the IPPC directive, Integrated Production and Pollution Control. As required in this directive an activity of a certain character requires an integrated permit in which all disturbances on the surroundings are considered together. Activities which require an integrated permit includes land fills, industrial production, power plants etc. The permit prescribes maximum levels of the impact, such as amount of emissions, amount of waste, noise, etc.

Planning for Protection

Re-active planning or planning for protection of land or water is a way to defend certain values as natural resources, natural and cultural values. It can be about valuable nature objects and areas, landscapes, cultural heritage of buildings and entire built up areas. Such sites may be protected by reserves or in adopted plans. Larger areas are the national parks and thus under national administration, while smaller areas, which may be a lake, a meadow or a wetland, are under county or municipal administration. Up to some 10 percent of the territory of a country are protected. Protection exists on several levels, from no-entry (e.g. the archipelago under bird breeding periods) to areas which still includes farming and forestry, although under defined conditions. The conservation level needs to be detailed in the comprehensive plan.

Modern nature conservation concerns both people and nature on land and in water. It requires skills in dialogue and local participation and management. In most European countries, any plant or animal that is in danger of extinction or plundering may be given protected status. This means that it is forbidden to pick, catch, gather, kill or in any other way injure the species in question. Valuable nature areas as open landscapes, forests and wetlands are protected by various nature legislation and is often not planned by spatial plans. On the European level the Natura 2000 network consists of all sites registered by EU member states as protected under either the Habitats directive or the Birds directive. The member states are obliged to keep these sites in "a good conservation status". There are many thousands of such sites, only in Sweden close to 4,000.

Both nature and cultural conservation sites promote tourism. Tourism may be the fastest growing economic sector in the region today, and thus this is a strong argument in favour of increased conservation. Quite many cultural heritage sites, such as castles, mansions etc are used for conferences, concerts, exhibits etc and allow tourists to visit. A comprehensive plan should at best indicate the conditions under which a site may be visited and used for the different purposes and activities.

Planning for protection may also be understood as proper management of natural resources in an area. This may include regulation of hunting and fishing, which historically was very important in planning. It may also refer to how much of a resource, such as water, to use, or much timber can be taken from a forest, although these aspects are more often included in the license, or permit, for the area.

Implementation – Planning on Project Level

Planning on a project level is the implementation or part of the planning, when something is to be realised. A project can be a building or a construction that is projected and presented so it can be understood of those influenced by the project.

Detailed plans and projects are conducted when there are public or private actors interested to make future changes in urban or rural areas. There must be enough public or private interests and fundings as a driving force for the planning. That is to say that everything that happens in the future can not be foreseen and planned in advance. The role of legislation and protection planning is one way to defend public values and common interests when private and individual interests plan for new developments.

Sustainable Development in Planning and Management

Planning for Sustainability

As follows from above, to plan for more sustainability is a complex issue. The processes can either be seen as a systematic process based on environmental scientific knowledge or, as discussed below, a communicative process between actors and stakeholders involved in the planning. Here it will be treated as a systems approach to manage sustainability dimensions in planning processes or as a way to assess plans.

Only few planning projects have been carried out systematically with regard to sustainable development. Among the national level projects the Japan for Sustainability (JFS) project, published in 2007, is particularly relevant. It was carried out over a two year period by a group consisting of university researchers, interest organisations (NGO) and some companies. No authority, neither on state nor on local level, was part of the group. The report is interesting since all the typical stages are included and a result calculated. Sustainable development processes for municipalities, companies or other organisations have also been reported but most often with a less complete or systematic approach.

Even if there is no scientifically established method of how to conduct a complete planning process using sustainability principles, there is enough experience, that one may safely say that a best practice has been established. Alan Atkisson's ISIS system may be the best tried out in several cities, companies and other organisations. ISIS stands for

Indicators	Measurement and Assessment of Sustainability & Related Performance
Systems	Understanding Linkages, Dynamics, and Leverage Points
Innovation	Creating and Diffusing Change: Using a Cultural Systems Approach
Strategy	Commitment to Integrated Implementation and Follow-Through

It is possible to describe most systems using a 6 (or 9 in some versions) step procedure, consisting of the following.

1. Agree on what is sustainable development (*the concept*) among those concerned. This phase should at best also include awareness of the importance of systems thinking and the awareness of limits, since these are fundamental for understanding sustainability.
2. Agree on a *framework* to be used to describe and work with the "system" (the area or society to be planned). There are several such frameworks; the classical – ecological, economic, and social – is seldom sufficient for a planning project.
3. Agree on a *vision* for the area in a future time, such as 20-50 years ahead.
4. Decide on a number of parameters to be followed, *indicators*, to measure and monitor sustainability.
5. Decide on which parts of the society or system to address, and in a process of innovation, find ways to improve these and design a number of projects.
6. Run projects often over a period of some 2-3 years. The whole process is then reiterated for continuous improvement.

The six steps may be carried out in a different order (e.g. some starts with the indicators). Additional steps not listed above include agreements, especially on the political level, but also with citizens. After the six steps the process and the results are evaluated. Most often this leads to a reconsideration of each step in the process including the definition of sustainability, the vision, the indicators and finally what to address to improve sustainability, that is, what projects to run in a following round.

Definitions of Sustainability

To work in practice with sustainable development it is basic (see e.g. Atkisson, 2008) to

1. Understand systems in general
2. Understand sustainability in general
3. Distinguish between "development" and "growth" in goal-setting, that is, understand the physical limits of the system.

It is easy to find several hundred definitions of sustainability in the literature, all of which are somehow related to the situation in which they were developed. However a group which intends to work in a multi-year planning activity needs to develop their own understanding.

As an example we may cite the JFS (JFS = Japan for Sustainability) project, in which the group agreed on the following, so called judgment criteria:

1. "Capacity and Resources"
2. "Fairness across Time"
3. "Fairness across Space"
4. "Diversity"
5. "Human Will and Networking" which they considered important from the viewpoint of global citizenship.

It is easy to recognise the Brundtland Commission concern for next generation (intra-generational equity) in number 2, and the inter-general equity (e.g promoted at the Rio Conference) in no 3, while the others are less established.

It is also possible to have simpler versions, such as "Create welfare within existing resources", but they tend to be less useful in practical work.

Visions, Scenarios and Goals in Planning Processes

To increase sustainability of a region or an area one needs to know towards what goals one is heading. *Goals* are possible and estimated to be achieved during the planning period. The goals are discussed and set up mostly in the planning programme. *Prognosis* are quantitative predictions of probable future development. *Scenarios* are based on values and interpretations of a future development and a way to outline a future filled with a mani-fold of uncertainties.

Scenario technique is a way to create images of the future. A scenario is a systematic prescription of a future situation and of a possible development from the situation today forwards to the prescribed situation. Scenarios are often giving a simplified image of the whole and of the connections between different sectors in the society, with contribution from many knowledge fields. To present various possibilities of development often alternative scenarios are worked out. Scenario technique is a method of forecasting.

Visioning is an important part of sustainability management. The plan or the vision may be exhibited to the public and discussed broadly; the vision, just as a plan, does not have legal status but rather is a policy document. A vision is evaluated using a number of sustainability goals.

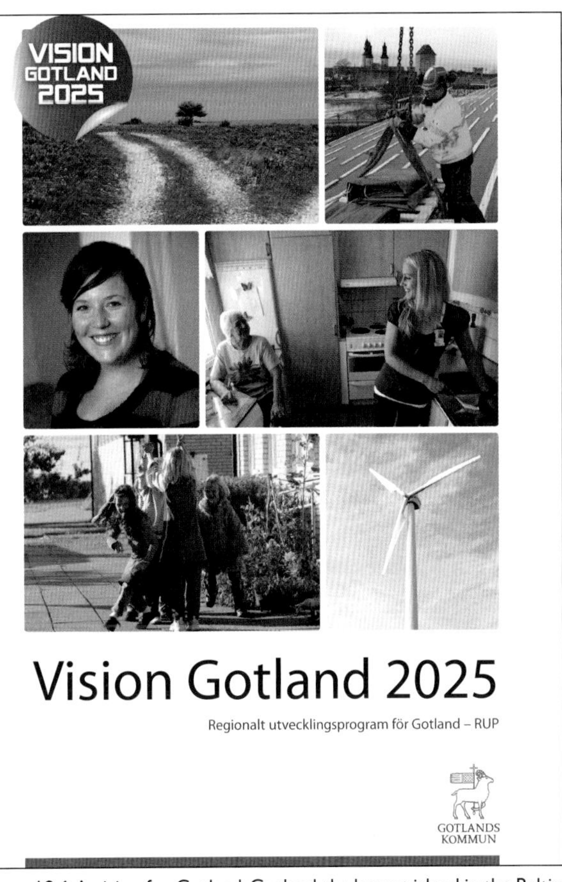

Figure 18.6. A vision for Gotland. Gotland, the largest island in the Baltic Sea, published its vision for a sustainable society for 2025. The Vision covers a number of areas as illustrated on the cover of the 28 pages document (http://www.gotland.se/imcms/38064).

Visions normally are restricted to a few areas of special interest for sustainability. A case may be the Swedish Göteborg 2050 (Göteborg is the second largest city in Sweden). The visioning was carried out in five main areas

1. Sun city (energy)
2. Urban structure (includes green areas)
3. Transport (traffic infrastructure, public transport)
4. Food (e.g. includes health and wellbeing)
5. Recycling (includes waste management)

The Global Community Initiative, GCI, have a long experience from visioning procedures. They always include the community as broadly as possible in the process, e.g.

by creating different citizen groups, and by making results available as the process continues, through exhibitions, in campaigns, or in festivities. Especially in an US context, where the local authorities are less strong than in Europe, it is important to have support from many stakeholders, including the private sector. The experience is that people often get enthusiastic about discussions on the long term future of their community, and that differences in opinions become less strong when it deals with a very long term perspective.

The Framework (Description) of the System

To work with sustainability management is to work with a system (the society and its land). For this purpose a good and useful systems description is needed. The classical system description – ecological, social and economic aspects or dimensions – is not so good for practical work, although it has been adopted by the business world as " the triple bottom line". Sustainability reporting has established the parts corresponding to these three dimensions, and it has been adopted by the GRI (Global Reporting Initiative) both for business and authorities.

More developed framework for sustainability includes Atkisson's compass with

N (North) Nature (the ecological or environmental aspects)
S (South) Society (the society part of the rather diffuse "social" aspect)
E (East) Economy (the economic aspects)
W (West) Wellbeing (the human part of the social aspect)

The Compass is rather well motivated in theory, as have been described by Atkisson (2009). It makes the rather unclear "social" dimension a little less unclear.

Other frames include the Global Community Initiative's 5 requirements, and an interpretation of the UN Habitat's as 7 resources. A more detailed frame was developed in the Baltic University Urban Forum project. In the project it was concluded that for local authorities sustainability is best made operational as resource management, and five resources were defined

1. Material resources – all material flows in the municipality, water, energy and waste
2. Urban space resources – all area to be planned in the municipality
3. Human resources – all inhabitants in the municipality
4. Societal resources – the city administration and all its services, institutions
5. Economic resources – companies and all other economic units

It is noted that these resources are not exchangeable and they are all limited. *Sustainable development is here understood as proper management of limited resources!* Each of them is discussed in larger detail in the project reports.

Regardless of the frame used at some level each aspect of the system has to be allocated to one of the parts, partly in an arbitrary way. The resource system or frame allows this to be done in a slightly more systematic and inclusive way.

Sustainability Indicators

It is essential to have adequate information on current developments and trends for the system in question. This information is given by so-called indicators. Choice of indicators is a serious question, as much effort is invested in following the indicators. They thus need to be important and meaningful, and relate to the vision.

There is no end to the number of indicators one may find. It is instructive to look at the economic pages in a daily newspaper; it is filled with hundreds of figures, all of which may be called economic indicators. Similarly one may compare to a medical diagnosis, which again may have many different figures, depending on the medical problem. Some are general, like body temperature, while others are special. In the same way a sustainability planning team needs to ask what indicators they need. Typically a set of environmental, economic, and welfare measures are used. Experience from the Urban Forum project showed that already today a typical municipality has some 60 indicators in common use.

The indicators are related to the framework chosen. Thus, if the three dimensional (environmental, economic and social) system is chosen, one needs indicators for each of these, as proposed in the GRI system. If the Compass is used, there will be four classes of indicators, and if the Urban Forum resource management system is used there will be five sets of indicators. Proposal for indicators are

Figure 18.7. Alan AtKisson discussing sustainability indicators at a workshop on management of sustainable development using the pyramid model. Photo: Krysztof Cielinski.

found in the basic reports of each of the projects. The Japan for Sustainability project, which used the Compass, reported 5 basic indicators for each of the four directions of the Compass. Each of these had 10 datasets to be calculated. That is the whole project used 20 indicators and 200 datasets.

Indices are composed of several component indicators. Some indices are well established. Ecological footprints (consisting of six indicators) are monitored according to an established method, and there is an understanding what the sustainability value is (1.8 ha/cap). For social aspect of SD the human development index (three indicators are combined) is used; an acceptable level of that is, according to the United Nations, 0.8.

It is important that the indicators are measured over a time period. Then a trend is given and one sees how it is changing. Some indicators which rely on standard measures, such as many environmental and economic data, are often available over a long time. Others need to be either constructed from historical data or monitored in a new project.

It is essential that the "sustainability values" of the indicators are available. This is the value that the indicator would have in a sustainable society, that is, in the vision. Sometimes it is easy to define the sustainability value. For example the use of non-renewable resources, such as oil, should be zero. In other cases it is less easy. What the unemployment rate is in a sustainable society is not easy to say. Some theory argues it should be 2-3%. This uncertainty is typical for many of the social indicators. Still one should assign a value to each of the chosen indicators. The discussions needed to do this are typically very useful to deepen the understanding of what sustainability is and what one needs to do to achieve it. Of course, it should be added, that the values given are provisional. They will be reconsidered at least each management cycle.

The sustainability values of the indicators are used to calculate the sustainability of the society (system). If the sustainability value is 100 and the present value for an indicator is 60 then for this indicator the sustainability of the system is 60%. The total value for the system is most often calculated as a non-weighted average of all used indicators.

Management and Project Work

The final goal is to implement the sustainability plan. This corresponds to the implementation of a spatial plan and one need to follow the legal process required. Never-the-less there is some specific characteristics typical for the sustainability process.

Indicators are often used in so-called "back casting". Here the values for the present and the future vision are plotted and the track "from future to present" is indicated by a line. This process allows us to establish intermediary goals for a specific year in the future, typically three years ahead, e.g. in energy use, traffic change etc. Back casting has been used in air pollution work and reaching the Kyoto protocol for reducing emissions of greenhouse gases.

A creative way to address what to do is to ask for the best "levers" in the system. What needs to be changed to get many more beneficial changes as a consequence? This is where system thinking is needed. For example improving public transport will also reduce air pollution if private car use decreases. In the more advanced versions of systems analysis computer models are used, but one gets very far by just drawing the systems and all interdependences on a piece of paper. This forms the basis of a strategy for changing the system and to spur innovations, that is, creative solutions for what to do.

In practice in turns out that very few communities use such a systemic approach. Most common is to focus on technology, e.g. how to work with heating, or waste management. A lack of systems view may in the worst case lead to no result if several processes counteract each other. Best is to look at both technology, the social changes needed to support it and design a "portfolio" of projects which support each other.

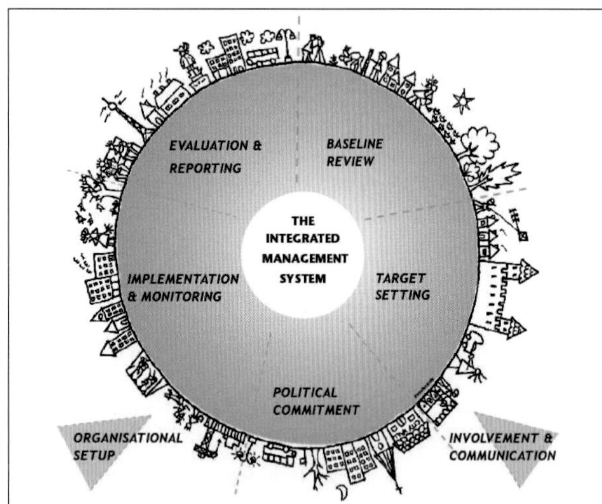

Figure 18.8. The MUE25 cycle is a variant of the classical Deming cycle (Plan-Do-Check-Act) It was used in the Managing Urban Europe project (MUE25) for Sustainable Urban Development. The model is equally useful for managing sustainble rural development.

There are many interesting ways to make the planning work interesting and more inclusive. One is to play games on a system which is designed according to the area to be planned. This method was used for planning of a river basin in Poland. In this case, the stakeholders formed teams, which played against each other. Students helped the farmers to handle the computers and the university teachers facilitated the process. As a result the consequences of different planning proposals became very concrete and clear. A more theoretical method is to model the system in question and calculate different scenarios. Modelling science today allows considerable detailed studies with environmental, economic and social parameters to be followed into long term future.

Management Cycles

In order to successfully implement the projects one needs to have support from all the concerned levels in the society. Some projects, e.g. the Managing Urban Europe 25 (MUE25), focused on this aspect. They defined a management cycle consisting of five steps

1. Baseline review (present value of indicators)
2. Target setting (the visioning process)
3. Political commitment
4. Implementation and monitoring (project work, and following the indicators)
5. Evaluation and reporting

The MUE25 cycle is a variant of the classical Deming cycle (Plan-Do-Check-Act), but includes specifically political commitment. The ISIS method asks for "Agreements and Actions"; this is more general since the ISIS method is much used in companies. It should also be added that the way to work is very similar to the environmental management systems, EMS, already adopted by hundreds of thousands of companies and quite many authorities.

The projects are implemented typically over a 3 year period. Then a new turn starts with review of vision, indicators, targets etc. Continuous monitoring and adaptation is needed and in particular the indicators need to be monitored.

Planning and Democracy

Three Planning Perspectives

Important changes today are challenging the way we organise and carry out local or municipal planning in the European countries. The underlying paradigm has moved from hierarchical regulation and control to network democracy, partnerships, new public management and governance. As a result, major restructurings of the institutions and legal frameworks for local planning and development are being implemented in several countries. Demands for efficiency have also resulted in new policy regimes and new roles for both professionals and politicians.

Planning was after WWII very much seen as a technical issue. The task of the planners was to use an effective, rationalistic method to achieve the best way to satisfy a list of requirements and reach the defined goal. This way to deal with planning was part of a larger view of development of society at large, as objective, rational and dependent on the application of proper instruments: The planner defines the goal, weighs the alternatives carefully and selects the best according to defined criteria. This, so-called *rationalistic planning,* is the result of economic, scientific and technical knowledge applied in a step-by-step linear process. Often the quantitative measured issues of the plan get priority over the qualitative/soft values.

The rationalistic comprehensive planning tradition has been hardly criticised for not being in accordance to planning practice. A more project-oriented planning, with many actors and stakeholders involved, has been more common during the last decades. Especially at the local level more cooperation in and between projects was achieved through a negotiation process between the actors. This is commonly called *negotiative planning*, meaning that several actors, most typically private actors such as business and building companies, but sometimes also groups of citizens, negotiate with the authorities about the plan. A dialogue is created between interested inhabitants, companies and public authorities to raise the understanding between each others' interests and arguments.

With increasing complexity qualitative uncertainties and plurality of values in the planning process also have increased. Planners meet these uncertainties with increased flexibility to include new circumstances and/or new information as they arise. Instead of a linear order, as in rational planning, one may introduce a cyclic order with several moments. This is called *strategic planning*. The planning agenda then includes alternatives to reduce complexity, and remove uncertainties as the process continues. The process is aimed to find strategies to manage a vision from idea to a concrete goal. The dilemmas, occurring in practical planning processes, must lead to active choices in relation to politics. A strategic planning process can be used for different purposes. It may be used either to set a democratic planning process into practical operation using strategies to handle a high number of stakeholders and actors. Or it can be used by powerful actors to achieve goals in their own interests, using strategies to avoid undesired hindrances.

Partnerships and Governance

In recent years we have seen an increasing a mutual understanding that the state or local agencies in most European countries have no longer the sole sovereign political and financial power for planning and implementing plans. Then to plan for future changes and be able to implement the plans, actors and stakeholders enter into different types of coalitions, so-called *partnerships*. These include a mix of public and private actors, each capable of bargaining on their own behalf. Partners are expected to bring something to the partnership, and share responsibility for the outcomes of their activities. Disadvantages include an unclear relation of responsibility between the population and their political representatives. Partnerships may also develop towards closed institutions, where the dominating stakeholders cooperate to the benefit of their own interests.

Another societal change during the last decades has been an increasing variation of politics, values, ethics, ethnicity etc. In parallel the inhabitants have become more involved and critical to the centralised rational spatial planning ideology. The traditional representative democracy, limited to voting, has not been able to respond to the criticism. It lacked elements of participation and discussion of proposals. There was too little of listening, mutual understanding and changing others views. Increased participation in the political process is called *participatory* or, more often, *deliberative* democracy.

Increased distribution of the responsibilities of realisation, economy and maintenance make for a higher degree

Table 18.3. Participation. Requirements for information on planning. http://commin.org/upload/Comparison_of_Planning_Systems/COMMIN_Planning_Systems_5_Participation.pdf

Issue	Part of the issue
1 Which are the duties to inform during planning work	Duties at the initiation of planning, for the proposed plan before adoption, and after adoption
2 Who has right to get access to information	Right to access to information for the public, owners of real property, and neighbours
3 Which information methods may be used	Role of hearings, meetings, etc. and how they are used
4 Which are the public opportunities to challenge, and appeal the plan	The legal basis for an appeal after adoption and the consequences for the further handling of the plan
5 Legal status of the public information process	May the public involvement in the planning process be limited; May a new planning procedure be made if these rules are violated

of *governance* in societal issues. The concept of governance has been much used in contemporary debate on public administration. The criticism against how traditional authority works, the bureaucracy, includes not only how decisions are reached but also how services are delivered. To see the difference one may compare policy decisions-making to "steering" and service delivery to "rowing" the boat of society. The argument is thus that bureaucracy is a bankrupt tool for rowing. In its place one proposes a kind of entrepreneurial government, which stresses competition, markets, customers and measuring outcomes. This transformation of the public sector may be summarised as less government but more governance. It is sometimes called a new public management.

Communicative Planning

The new institutions and regimes are influencing the organisation of spatial planning, which will require another type of planning profession than the traditional rational and strategic planning processes. This leads to so-called *communicative planning* processes. It is characterised by an ideal dialogue between actors and stakeholders. Individuals are supposed to be influenced only by good arguments and differences in power, status or prestige should have little effect on decisions. In a communicative process all stakeholders or representatives of stakeholder groups participates to exchange ideas, sort out what shall be judged and see what is important and assess proposals for changes. All parties are expected to be aware of, and accept, contradictory standpoints in a learning process. The stakeholders are assumed to be involved from the start of the planning process and be active during the whole process. Possible conflicts between parties are identified and solutions are expected to be reached in consensus through forms of deliberative dialogues. Understanding, integrity and truth between the parties give legitimacy to the decision-making.

The participation of all interested in the development of the plan is partly regulated by law, but as example differently in different Baltic Sea countries. Lists of the issues which may differ between countries are given in Table 18.3.

Managing Conflicts

As described above any spatial planning process is certain to be confronted with conflicts arising from many actors and stakeholders having different demands and interests on the same area. These are often so many that methods for handling such conflicts are useful. A *conflict map* is a map in which each smaller territory (sub-area) is marked and the conflicts of interest noted. Thus for each mark (number or letter) on the map a conflict is listed. To take a river basin as an example conflicting interests may be fishing vs. hydropower, nature conservation vs. road or railroad, shipping vs. recreation, water extraction vs. outflow from industry or agriculture further upstream.

It is also possible to construct a *conflict matrix*, that is, a table. In this each sub-area has a column and the separate interests/activities a row. Some 10-15 rows in such a matrix are common. In the box where a sub-area and an interest meet, the degree of the interest is indicated by a figure or a filled, half-filled or empty symbol. For example all boxes where forestry is going on or planned get a mark. If many different interests are marked in the column for one sub-area there are conflicts and coordination needs.

Planners are recommended to deal with these coordination needs or conflicts as early on as possible in the process. Possibilities for multiple use or cooperation should be looked at. If this is not possible one needs to find solutions. E.g. effluents from an industry may be diverted to a special treatment plant, and not allowed to be discharged to the river. A swimming place may be slightly moved to

Box 18.3. Conflict Resolution

Cornell University after much experience, especially in the Catskill upstream New York City, made a list of eight principles of how to deal with conflicts in planning processes.

1. *Conflicts are normal* – do not avoid them, outcome does not need to be negative. Ask: who benefits, who pays, who feels threatened and why; are there different values, do we have proper data?
2. *Seek a constructive outcome* – find a non-confrontual arena for dialogue, focus on process not positions, seek consensus that something has to be done.
3. *Power, perceptions and values* – find out how power, both legal and extralegal means, is used by the partners, find out how decisions are made.
4. *Conflict context* – follow the process of conflict resolution: make a report, identify concerns (listen), generate options, study feasibility of alternatives, write agreement.
5. *Can the conflict be saved* – cooperation is needed, not possible to win a conflict, avoid blaming others, benefiters should pay, agree on prevention rather than remediation.
6. *Conflict management strategies* – break down the conflict to component parts, translate to simple language, scientific facts are not perceived as neutral, a variety of perspectives, avoid "martyrs" who refuse to change, promote a negotiated agreement.
7. *Shape alliances* – recognition that cooperation is required to reach the goals, common outside threat promotes building of alliances, find a by all recognised coordinator.
8. *Public issues education* – facilitates and assists conflict resolution, broadens range of viewpoints, public experience are given credence, all views are given serious attention.

allow for a marina, if there are equipments to collect boat wastewater. Difficult conflicts arise when large interests come into the picture, such as large hydropower plants, which change an entire landscape, or main infrastructure, such as main roads, which also may require bridges.

Conflict solutions include the assessment of the importance of each separate activity for the local or regional authority or country. Such assessments are difficult to make and balance against each other. The broadest view possible should be used not to exclude important aspects. Environmental (or ecosystems) services are too often forgotten in such assessments, even if they are essential, as economic interest tend to dominate. Methods and arenas to estimate the monetary value of ecosystems services are available.

Challenges in Planning for Sustainable Development

The concept of sustainable development is a pluralistic concept filled with values. Hence it gives opportunities for different interpretations. Planning is not so much a mechanism for implementing sustainable development as an important forum in which different interpretations and methods of sustainable development are introduced, contested and accepted. There is no prior *conception* of sustainability (as opposed to the broader, consensual concept) independent of this process.

The different definitions have in common, however, that they stand for a better society in the future in which society and the natural environment exist in harmony, an objective which most of us are willing to support. When it comes to the actual content of the various expressions and the realisation of the aims included in the concepts, different groups and individuals have different interpretations. This reflects a diversity of values and relations to the environment and ecology, as seen in the discourses on sustainable development. Based on these values different strategies for achieving sustainability may be adopted.

The techno-central, or instrumental, approach relies on technology for solving the environmental problem. The concept of ecological modernization relates to environmental re-adaptation of economic growth and industrial development. On the basis of enlightened self-interest, economy and ecology is believed to be possible to combine to achieve sufficient resource productivity. Others maintain that life style changes are needed to approach sustainability, that is, it is not enough with efficiency, we also need sufficiency, to reduce significantly resources flow in our societies.

All the diverse perspectives and definitions of sustainable development challenge the planning practice. A social sustainable way to manage these challenges is to discuss and search for consensus of what can be sustainable for each planning conditions. It would be an important part of the planning programme.

A Rural Country in Transition
Alternatives for Lithuania

19

CASE STUDY
Lithuania

Jonas Jasaitis
Siauliai University, Siauliai, Lithuania
Ingrid Karlsson
Uppsala University, Uppsala, Sweden

20th Century Rural History

Developing Rural Society in the Early 1900s

In the beginning of the 20th century 'rural areas' in Lithuania were perceived as isolated and stagnant areas, only used for primitive agriculture. Lack of infrastructure and means of communication and transportation confirmed this opinion, in spite of the fact that most of the population lived and worked in the rural areas. Later, in the Independent Lithuania (1918-1940), the rural economy became more appreciated as being of significant value for the existence of the whole state. The better-off farmers became the backbone of the emerging middle class, and education was improved in rural areas. Woodworkers, carvers, stonemasons, stove-makers, metal-beaters, potters, rope-makers, etc. were also part of the rural village society. In the villages there were also weavers, knitters, tailors and shoemakers, and their products could often be very interesting and valuable folk art. In 1940, 75% of the people in Lithuania still lived in the rural areas, most of them being farmers and farm workers (Aleksa, 1999).

In the beginning of the Second World War, Lithuania was occupied first by the Soviet Union, then by Germans. Lithuanian soldiers took part in the war on the German side. The German influence and occupation led to great human losses to Lithuanian society, not least the extinction of the more than 300,000 Lithuanian Jews who were killed or sent to a certain death in concentration camps.

The Soviet Union again occupied Lithuania from 1944 onwards and more people were resettled, killed or sent to work camps in the Soviet Union (gulags). The numbers actually imprisoned in the gulags are still debated by historians from different countries. However, they were many. During and after the war, there were also many Lithuanians who went into exile in countries in the West.

The Soviet Period

The outcome of the war was that independent Lithuania was made part of the Soviet Union. The impact on rural areas of these traumatic events was that a great number, especially men in their most active age, were not present. This affected rural activities such as farming, handicraft and small businesses, but people with intellectual skills such as teachers were also lacking. The enforced collectivisation of agricultural land destroyed farmers as a social class, and the civil activity of rural inhabitants was devaluated. Rural people's impact on state development diminished. Old farmsteads were abandoned and a new society in the rural areas, consisting of blockhouse villages to house farm workers on the big state farms and

Figure 19.1. The Plokštine missile base is located near lake Plateliai, in Žemaitija National Park. It was built in 1962 and armed with R-12U intermediate range ballistic missiles with nuclear warheads. After the collapse of the USSR the base was turned over to the national park administration who have turned it itno an 'Exposition of Militarism' and with guided tours. Photo: Andrius Vangas.

collective farms, was formed. Most private businesses, professions and craftsmen were replaced by industry. In addition, farming experts, military personnel, engineers and other experts settled in Lithuania from other parts of the Soviet Union, as a part of the common strategy of the Soviet Union leadership to unify the different parts of the federation.

Lithuania's urbanisation was very intensive after the war, agricultural production was intensified and industrialisation was rapid. The number of people directly involved in primary agricultural activity decreased very rapidly, as the mechanisation of agriculture released labour to jobs in new industries in urban areas. This in turn made a great impact on education, professional structure, residence and even on everyday life. Lithuanian farm workers were 50% more productive than the Soviet average and 50% of the country's farm products were exported to other Soviet states. A positive development for rural areas during Soviet times was that quite large parts of valuable natural landscapes were saved as protected areas.

Post-Soviet Rural Lithuania

After the breakdown of the Soviet Union in 1989-1991, factories, rural schools and even collective farms closed down. Many reforms were made and quick decisions were taken which were positive for some but negative for most common people. During only a few years most of the agricultural land was privatised, but at the same time (1989-1994) agricultural production decreased by 50% (Iwaskiw, 1995). It was a turbulent time. Unemployment increased rapidly, and health care and other social welfare structures were neglected (since these were usually connected with state industrial companies, or state or collective farm organisations). This of course caused great disappointment and difficulties, especially for common rural people.

After the first difficult years of negative trends, living standards rose rapidly during the first decade of 2000. In 2001-2008 (until the financial crisis hit the world in 2008), Lithuania had one of the fastest growing economies in Europe.

The globalisation trends have had more impact on the rural economy and rural inhabitants since EU membership. During 2002-2007, scientific studies showed that the professional structure of the rural population again changed dramatically. Rural residents in the non-agricultural sector increased from 35 to 45% and rural business people increased from 2 to 4%. Retired and disabled people made up about 30% and unemployed people on welfare schemes about 10%. Many people also emigrated from rural Lithuania to other countries during these years (Jasaitis, 2005; Jasaitis, 2006a; Jasaitis, 2006b; Jasaitis, 2006c; Jasaitis & Surkuvienė, 2006).

Rural Lithuania in the European Union

Joining EU

When Lithuania joined the EU in 2004, agricultural workers constituted 13% of the total employable population (Statistikos...., 2007). Now even greater changes were introduced for the rural population. The agricultural sector was affected by EU policies and subsidies and an increasing number of rural citizens could have training for jobs outside the agricultural sector.

In 2008-2009 Lithuania was struck particularly hard by the financial crisis. In 2009, real GDP decreased by 18.5%. This caused high unemployment, cuts in public spending, great difficulties for private businesses, etc (Grant, 1997).

Negative Impacts on Rural Society

In spite of modernisation the rural part of the country still has a negative image among urban people, and this prevails even among decision-makers. The popular belief is that the main task of rural areas is the agricultural sector. Decisions affecting rural citizens are made without their participation, and this divides the country. The prolonged, but unfinished, land reform and many other policies discourage people from living in rural areas.

The landscape is sometimes destroyed by vandals and the activities of businesses seeking a fast profit. For instance, deforestation is a common problem, causing loss of biodiversity and increased erosion. Rural local roads are damaged by heavy vehicles and heavy agricultural machinery but the roads are left without maintenance. Agricultural land is left untilled, and ruins of useless Soviet-era buildings and wrecks of damaged machinery make the landscape ugly. Outskirts of local forests have become a dump, with no one responsible for cleaning this up. Not even the municipal police seem to care.

Urban Life

On the other hand, life is not satisfactory for common people in urban areas either: for instance very little attention has been given to enhancing the environment. Air, water and soil pollution is increasing, waste handling is poor, the traffic situation is very problematic, drinking water supply is of low quality, etc. Fuel and electricity prices are increasing. There is no space for children's games, sports activities or neighbourhood collaboration. There are no flowers around residential blocks and their interior is deteriorating. Added to this is the recent rise in unemployment.

Fortunately some new positive trends can also be noted. New forms of traditional and non-traditional farming are being developed, new commercial products and other activities are being created in the countryside, and new concepts of residence in suburban or rural areas are being realised.

Aspirations of Rural People in Lithuania

Attitudes of Countryside Populations

Social science research has recently been carried out to investigate people's ideas on future sustainable development in rural Lithuania. Questions were asked on what kind of society they would like to create, what social stratification they would welcome and what they think about respecting private property (of the employer, the neighbour or the state). This research revealed that people with the most experience of 'collective property' had trouble understanding how to value the concept of private property. They also had trouble perceiving their own responsibility for the state and society, and e.g. for taking part in self-governing. For those convinced that the state has to care for everybody, it is hard to image a vision of personal prosperity which each individual is expected to create their own long-term strategy of personal activity.

The results show that people actually cannot articulate their wishes because they do not know the meaning of the concepts used by the researchers. The respondents were clearly not able to identify objects in nature and describe their availability. They were unable to recognise many of the objects of wildlife (plants, trees, birds, etc.) in a natu-

Figure 19.2. View of the small village Medingenai, in western Lithuania in 2005. Photo: Patrick Wilken.

ral environment or to understand the interactions between ecosystems (Jasaitis, 2006c). They did not understand the importance of agriculture and ecology. Most of them were unable to understand why it is important not to dump litter and did not know how to behave in the forest, in the meadow, by the lake or at the river. Their knowledge of nature was not based on personal experience.

Seeking New Ways

An analysis of migration processes also showed changes in the structure of rural and urban population: 1) People looking for jobs are moving to cities; 2) more prosperous social groups are trying to obtain private households in suburban areas.

These tendencies are strongly related to changes in business development: more and more jobs can be created by small flexible business firms in residential houses, and modern industrial factories can be established in suburban areas, where good infrastructure (highways) and fast internet networks have been installed.

Another area investigated through interview surveys was people's ideas about spiritual communication and communication between generations. Possibilities for meeting places or household communities where people with similar professional or business interests could meet were also perceived as activities suitable for rural areas.

In conclusion, alternatives for sustainable rural development were the following, according to the respondents' views: 1) well planned housing areas (including infrastructure and public services); 2) multi-structural diversified economics; 3) functions for recreation, rehabilitation and tourism; 4) educational and experience-enhancing activities; 5) preservation of ethnic and cultural heritage; 6) preservation and management of natural landscape.

The local rural communities have the best possibility to determine the kind of services needed. Research information from settlements and townships can become the basis for planning training and adult education for people looking for new careers. Training in business management, small business methodology and the basics of cooperation is also needed. Legislation, economic incentives, better planning and increased cooperation between different political levels in society are other suggestions. However, the main question is who should pay for all the necessary changes and which areas should be prioritised.

Development Opportunities

Alternatives for Future Rural Development

A radical rethink is needed of concepts such as *villagers, rural economics* and *rural functions*. The main task for policymakers now should be to balance traditional and modern functions of rural areas to the benefit of the citizens and the society as a whole. The question here is how to include long-term, careful treatment of natural resources in the definition of sustainable development, and whether alternative sources of energy can be developed for rural use and a healthy rural life style promoted (Treinys, 2005;Treinys, 2006). Several projects have been proposed for an alternative rural development (Lietuvos..., 1997; A Typology of..., 1999).

There is an increasing interest in the former life style and old buildings in the countryside. Many buildings and facilities have been restored as weekend cottages or long-term holiday homes in the Lithuanian villages. The activity of organisations such as 'Tribe houses' *('Giminės namai')*, which promote a healthy lifestyle, organic food, creation of family leisure time areas and everyday communication with nature, is becoming increasingly popular.

Rural areas may also develop as suburban fringes to large cities. New suburban areas are planned, which have appropriate planning of infrastructure, and fit the surrounding environment, have parks, recreational areas, shopping malls, schools, and cultural centres.

Land Reform and Restructuring of Agriculture and Forestry

A very bureaucratic and legislative procedure of privatisation of rural land has been carried out recently. When Lithuania became an independent state, small parcels (down to 2 ha) were given to rural people who had no land. The problem was that the vast majority of these owners did not have any suitable farm buildings or agricultural machinery (Jasaitis, 2005). In addition, the new land owners were not familiar with the economic complexity of small-scale farming. Only in very rare cases were these owners able to develop a business activity such as growing herbs, seedlings and saplings, agricultural tourism, out-of-school teaching of children, etc. The majority of the owners of these small farms today are retired people, working their land with very old-fashioned methods. For them this land reform was positive, since they can generate some income as a supplement to their pension. The younger private land owners more often use the land for building large, well-equipped houses.

The question is what should be done for the future with these land reform plots and what should be done with remaining large state farms and collective farms.

Large- and Small-scale Tourism

The main tourist attraction in Lithuania is the beaches, but they are often overcrowded and alternatives are needed for rural tourism (Rural development, 2005). In nearby EU states, rural areas have a diversity of tourism alternatives, such as: private health services, sport centres, recreation areas, rehabilitation centres for disabled people, amusement parks, adventure parks, outdoor museums, restaurants, pubs, coffee places, youth camps, museums at historical or religious heritage buildings, shops for traditional handcrafts, etc. These alternatives do not always need large investments – some of them could be set up on a very limited scale. However, apart from better infrastructure and public services, in relation to tourism there is also need for improving legislation and marketing of such activities. Payment of fees for different activities also needs to be discussed.

Restore Identity and National Pride

National heritage need to be maintained and issues such as identity, local history, language and ethics need to be taken up to ensure that people are proud of the region where they were born (Wheelen & Hunger, 2008). Possible options in achieving this are school textbooks, museums, research policies and research funding.

There are several important issues for the creation of a common identity. Collection of narrative folklore, folk songs, adages and other samples of national verbal creativity; development of regional studies and using such material in the context of formal and non-formal education; practical training in ethnic crafts and traditional rural folk creativity; creation of special tourist routes, devoted to ethnographic or historical studies; analysis of national ethic heritage in different regions (lifestyle, means of communication, folk traditions, etc.) in collaboration with cultural centres, sport or religious organisations, youth clubs and so on.

A good example of the activities suggested is The Local Action Group (LAG) of Siauliai district, which took part in the EU LEADER+ programme. They appealed to the local rural communities and asked for help in recording and evaluating the resources of local heritage objects. The results of this campaign exceeded all expectations. Hundreds of historical, architectural, literary and nature objects were documented: imposing buildings (churches, manors), old cemeteries, monuments, memorial homesteads, memorial barrows, etc.; but also landscape objects: mineral springs, lakes, rivers, multi-bole trees, hills, valleys, etc. (www.zum.lt/min/failail/partnerystes_organizavimas.pdf)

The Aesthetic Dimension – Cleaning up

It is necessary to revive the work of the Society for Beautifying Lithuania, which was created by writer Juozas Tumas-Vaizgantas, Prof. Povilas Matulionis and others. This needs to be made part of people's attitude again, so that e.g. they avoid littering the landscape. There is therefore a need to inform and educate, perhaps have practical campaigns with schools, or fund this function using tax revenue.

Landscape and Maintenance of Water Resources

20

Józef Mosiej, Agnieszka Karczmarczyk and Katarzyna Wyporska
Warsaw University of Life Sciences – SGGW, Warsaw, Poland

Managing Water in Rural Areas

Sustainability and Management of the Rural Landscape

In European countries with a high level of agriculture, modern rural development includes projects with the aim of shaping, improving and sustainably developing the rural landscape. Such projects formulate and fulfil agricultural, economic and infrastructural aims together with the aims of nature protection, water resource conservation and landscape management.

The impact of agriculture on the environment can be mitigated by using environmentally friendly methods of agricultural production and multifunctional use of rural space that improves the rural landscape by maintaining diverse ecosystems. Sustainable development of the rural space must consider both the rural landscape with its patchwork of habitations and nature resource, and the traditional way of management with extensive enclaves of arable land, wetlands and natural land with a high diversity of flora and fauna.

Supporting national functions such as 'feeding', 'resources' or 'living', rural areas should have a landscape function as well as recreational and ecological functions. The environmental and recreational potential of a given landscape is characteristic of the area and contains cultural values which are sparse or simply do not exist in urban and industrial areas (Pijanowski, 2006).

Rural development projects should at best allow general issues to be resolved, while balancing interest and conflicts between the different functions mentioned above. They need to specify guidelines for spatial planning, which should include the protection of water and soils, which are the basic resources in agricultural production (Rajda, 2005).

This chapter will mostly refer to the conditions in Poland. Poland has a large agricultural sector, much of which is traditional and still with a large proportion of small family farms. At the same time the knowledge and understanding for actions to protect the environment is limited in a rural population, which since 2004 is pushed by new European Union legislation to improve its environmental standards. Conditions in Poland are partly similar to those in the other Baltic Sea region countries which joined the EU by 2004. A big difference exist, however, between the former Soviet Union countries and the rest of Central and Eastern Europe since the farming was collectivised in the Soviet system which created big units. Many of these are still are running but under a different ownership and management.

The Role of Water in the Landscape

In this concept of rural management, the water factor is perhaps the most important one. Water has different areas of use such as *productive* in agriculture and forestry, *social* e.g. tourism and recreation and *ecological*, nota-

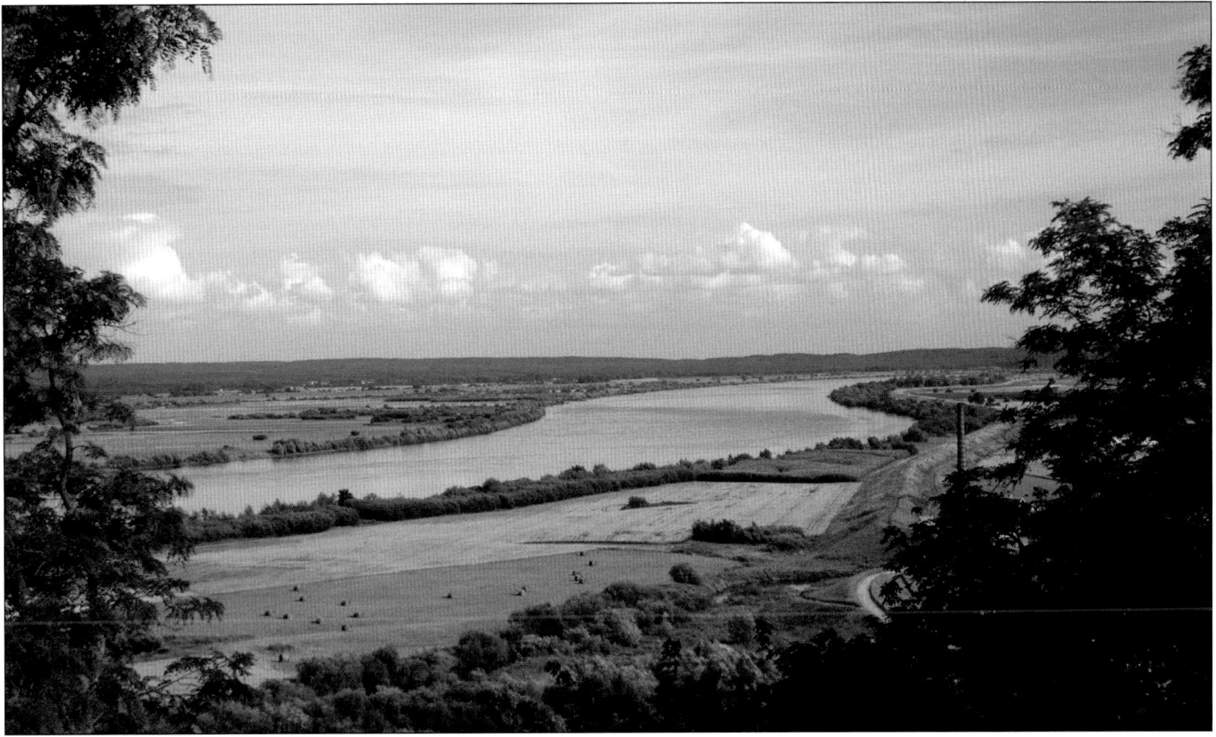

Figure 20.1. Vistula river in Poland, north of Warsaw illustrating the tight contact between the rural landscape and water. Photo: Sebastian Kruk.

bly habitat protection. Limited access to water can cause friction in the agricultural landscape and a shortage or surplus of water can affect biodiversity, especially in water-reliant ecosystems.

In addition to its productive (production of biomass) functions, water in the agricultural landscape plays different roles such as:

- Management of habitat conditions (soils, microclimate)
- Transport of chemical substances (solvent and substances carrier) and energy (changes in states of aggregation of water connected with heat absorption or emission)
- Aesthetic values of landscape management
- Management of conditions for biodiversity protection (small reservoirs, ponds, wetlands, marshes and extensively used, reclaimed grasslands in watersheds)
- Absorption, reception and reduction of anthropogenic threats caused by agriculture and habitation.

As regards the economic and ecological function of water in a given area, the decisive factor is not its absolute amount but the time during which this water is taking part in different processes, in other words, the time that water spends in the landscape. This time is dependent on the degree of surface cover by flora and fauna, and on the time it takes for rainfall water to reach rivers (Kędziora et al., 2005).

The role of water in spatial management cannot be viewed separately from economic, social and ecological functions of rural areas or without the context of the agricultural policy of state and regional authorities. It is also important to consider the conditions caused by existing ventures from the field of drainage and water engineering, supporting the economic needs of agriculture; and spatial management plans for habitats in rural areas (Rajda, 2005).

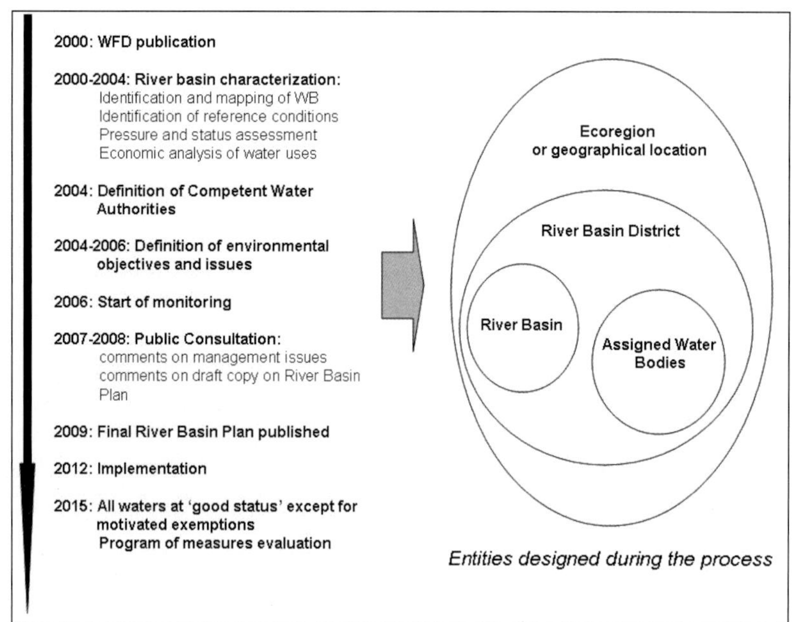
2000: WFD publication
2000-2004: River basin characterization:
Identification and mapping of WB
Identification of reference conditions
Pressure and status assessment
Economic analysis of water uses
2004: Definition of Competent Water Authorities
2004-2006: Definition of environmental objectives and issues
2006: Start of monitoring
2007-2008: Public Consultation:
comments on management issues
comments on draft copy on River Basin Plan
2009: Final River Basin Plan published
2012: Implementation
2015: All waters at 'good status' except for motivated exemptions
Program of measures evaluation
Ecoregion or geographical location
River Basin District
River Basin
Assigned Water Bodies
Entities designed during the process

Figure 20.2. The main steps and deadlines of the Water Framework Directive (WFD) implementation. Source: Steyaert and Ollivier, 2007.

The Water Framework Directive (WFD)

During the last few years there has been a marked change in the approach to management of water resources. Water is regarded as a 'restricted and sensitive resource, essential for sustaining of life, development and environment'. A new European water policy was introduced in the mid 1990s. It was based on the essential role of water in all ecosystems: 'water is not a product as any other but is a hereditary good that has to be protected and treated as such'. In year 2000 the Directive 2000/60/EC, the EU Water Framework Directive (WFD) was finally adopted and has now been implemented in all member states.

Some priorities of water management, such as techniques for water resources management, have become subordinate to sustainable development rules. Instead of focusing on the usage and supply of water to satisfy different parts of the economy, the aim is sustainable usage and protection not only of water itself, but also of water ecosystems and water-reliant ecosystems. Integrated water resources management takes in the natural, social and economic properties of water resources and connects them to the environment (WWF Polska, 2005).

According to the sustainable development approach management of rural areas, including water resources, should be considered in spatial planning and not violate the environmental protection requirements. Development plans should consider agricultural production space, residential areas with their technical infrastructure, degraded areas and protected areas including water biotopes. The present socio-economic conditions in the Baltic Sea region require a new view on the water factor in rural management.

The EU Water Framework Directive asks for integrated river basin management for Europe. It uses a river basins approach and has requested that all member states establish River Basin Authorities to implement the Directive. The base of the legislative text is that all surface waters and groundwater should reach "good status". Cleaner rivers and lakes, groundwater and coastal beaches are of high priority in European environmental policy.

Protecting Water

Agriculture and Environmental Protection

The impact of agriculture on the environment is significant because, unlike other economic activities, farming forms part of an ecosystem rather than being external to it. Agriculture manipulates the natural environment to produce food through a range of different practices, such as land drainage, tilling of soil, diverting natural water sources, irrigation and applying nutrients and pesticides. These practices affect the soil, air, water, biodiversity and landscape.

Rural areas are thus dealing with problems of environment pollution, which leads to disturbance of equilibrium and degradation of ecosystems. Even if this may be serious farmers are in reality foremost confronted with everyday financial problems. The majority of farmers, especially those with small farms, farm in the traditional way, that is, the products of the farm are only for family use. Animal density on this kind of farm is rising, but it is still low and environmentally friendly (Manteuffel et al., 2003). Choices made by farmers in terms of specialisation of agricultural activities lead to more efficient production, but may also result in negative environmental effects. The main forces behind this choice are economic efficiency and changes in market conditions. What may follow in terms of agriculture intensification, an increase in the use of mineral fertilisers, and a decrease in buffer strip areas both contributing to environmental pollution.

Legal Base for Protection

Pollution of water means that surface water and groundwater resources in Europe do not meet the requirements of the EU Water Framework Directive. According to this Directive, there is a broad range of tools that can help minimise the impact of agriculture on the environment. It is usual to choose a number of instruments that work on the appropriate scale, from the catchment and river basin to the actions taken at farm scale. All of these instruments need to have an appropriate legal basis. In parallel, the instruments have to be supported by a system of data collection and analysis to assess the effectiveness of actions from the point of view of the environment, society and the economy. Monitoring is very important in assessing the effectiveness of any actions taken (Kowalik, 2003).

But not only legal measures are used in the efforts to safeguard water resources. Farmers have to be willing and able to implement environmental protection measures. The most important condition for success is therefore the relationship of the farmers to the environment. The impact of agriculture on the environment depends on long-term and short-term decisions by farmers, mainly concerning manure management. The correct decisions can result in integration of economic aims with good agricultural practices, available technologies and the way of usage in the context of possibilities and limitations of political and economic situations. Most importantly actions to develop farming and farm infrastructure have to be accompanied by educational programmes to inform the rural society about the importance of environmental protection and sustainable development of rural areas, as well as the development of the competence needed for modern farming and specifically water and environmental management.

Water Protection Action

Actions taken for the protection and the use of water resources in rural areas need precise assessment of how agriculture influences, both positively and negatively, the environment (Pierzgalski, 2002). It is important to identify the kind of infrastructure that rural areas should be equipped with to ensure a balance between social and economic growth, while at the same time not degrading the resources of the environment. Development of infrastructure in rural areas is supported by regional policy and by structural funds of the European Union.

There are several kinds of projects which farmers may do to improve the environment and protect water quality.

- The construction of buffer strips between the fields and surface water contribute to the absorption of nutrients in run-off water and reduce the eutrophication of water.
- Making water courses retain water longer, e.g. by building wetlands such as small ponds and increase meandering, also contributes to reduced environmental impacts as nitrogen undergoes de-nitrification and phosphorus is bound to sediments.

- Using winter crops reduced run-off during winter months as the nutrients then are taken up by the crop.
- Limitation of number of animals per farming area is important to reduce manure production to a level which is in balance with the fields available.

The first two actions improve the environment as it is restored to more natural conditions, and contribute to a richer water and fish life. The two last actions are legally required by some countries in regions where nutrient run-off is especially serious.

Actions should at best also improve the quality of life by creating new work places that respect the social and economic aspects and the multifunctional development of rural areas.

The problem of developing infrastructure for manure management, wastewater collection, and drinking water supply for the citizens has to be considered in the following categories (Wierzbicki and Krajewski, 2003):

- Economic to create suitable conditions for technical and technological development in rural areas, to meet competition from of the old EU countries and to obtain capital funding.
- Economic to choose suitable solutions and technical and technological equipment, following the specifications required by EU, and also the conditions of investment processes to make the most of funding and competitiveness in the EU.
- Political, to make the integration of Poland into the EU efficient.

Eutrophication – the Main Problem

Manure as Natural Fertiliser

The main impact of agriculture on water is eutrophication, that is, excess growth of algae caused by excess plant nutrients, nitrogen and phosphorus, released into the water. The origin of nutrients is almost entirely excess fertilisers from fertilisation of the crop by either mineral or natural fertilisers i.e. manure either in solid or liquid form. Slurry, liquid and solid manure are natural fertilisers rich in nutrients and therefore when used reasonably, in accordance with local climate, soil and water conditions, they contribute to increases in crop yields and lower the costs of production. It is also in accordance with the general view of sustainable development as it recycles a key resource, the nutrients. When used in agriculture it is important not to overdose and to properly take the climatic conditions into account.

Figure 20.3. Fertilising fields with manure very often leads to excesss nutrients reaching surface water and groundwater with run-off from fields causing eutrophication, the most serious environmental problem in the whole Baltic Sea region. Photo: Karolina Kabat.

Extensive and uncontrolled use of slurry and manure for fertilising leads to extensive water pollution. Collecting and storing manure in leaking or overflowing containers results in point pollution of surface waters and groundwater. Agricultural effluents have a high biological oxygen demand (BOD). For liquid manure it is 50 times higher than for raw municipal sewage. When effluents with high BOD reach rivers, the level of dissolved oxygen decreases immediately; it may even result in the death of fish and invertebrates.

From an aesthetic point of view, it is important to maintain natural landscape values and limit the influence on local societies. Odour is a side-effect of animal production. It comes from farm buildings and from manure storage tanks and pads, as well as from manure/slurry spreading. It may be avoided by proper manure handling.

The Nitrogen Balance

The potential agricultural pressure on water quality is indicated by the 'gross nitrogen balance', which relates to the potential surplus of nitrogen on agricultural land. This is estimated by calculating the balance between nitrogen added to an agricultural system and nitrogen removed from the system per hectare of agricultural land. The gross nitrogen balance indicator accounts for all inputs and outputs from the farm, and includes all residual emissions of nitrogen from agriculture into soil, water and air.

At EU-15 level, the gross nitrogen balance in 2000 was calculated to be 55 kg/ha, which is 16% lower than the 1990 estimate of 66 kg/ha. In 2000, the gross nitrogen balance ranged from 37 kg/ha (Italy) to 226 kg/ha (the Netherlands) (EEA 2006). For Poland the gross nitrogen balance for the period 2002-2004 was calculated to be 45 kg/ha, ranging from 16.1 kg/ha in *dolnośląskie* voivodship to 75.2 kg/ha in *kujawsko-pomorskie* voivodship (Kopiński et al., 2006).

The availability of regional gross nitrogen balances could provide a much better insight into the actual likelyhood of nutrient losses to water bodies, when combined with data on farm management practices and climatic and soil conditions (EEA, 2006). The data given witness that eutrophication of European waters is a main and serious problem.

Protecting Groundwater from Nutrient Leakage from Agriculture

Experiences gained from the treatment of groundwater show that water resources, once polluted, are lost for 100-200 years. Contaminated groundwater is very difficult and expensive to clean. Therefore the protection of resources and appropriate handling, if the resources are intended to serve future generations, are crucial (Sadurski, 2001).

Appropriate manure management diminishes the danger of pollution. The environmental effects are not visible immediately after building the infrastructure for safe storage of animal manure, as better quality of surface waters and shallow groundwater, less acid rain, smaller global warming will only be noticeable after a period of years (Dobkowski and Skopiec, 2003). Good manure management is extremely important especially when livestock production is carried out near areas with sandy soils, sensitive to water pollution.

Proper action for reducing nutrient leakage may give dramatic improvements. Implementation of a programme to limit the water pollution by nitrates in Denmark in 1987 resulted in a 28% reduction in nitrate losses from agriculture and retention of 50% of nitrates on the farm. Within agricultural river basins, a 20% reduction in pollution in inflowing waters was recorded and the eutrophication process was also reduced.

In Sweden, a programme to limit nitrate emissions to the aquatic environment using a number of policy instruments achieved a 50% reduction in emissions from agriculture (Table 20.1). Research has shown that the most effective way of reducing nitrate emissions, apart from extensive farming, is appropriate manure management.

Activities that lead to improvement of the quality of shallow groundwater can be divided into three groups:

1) Building tanks for slurry and using environmental friendly techniques for spreading slurry on green areas and arable land. This would require farm infrastructure for environmental protection development and active protection of water resources, *in situ* pollution limitations, etc.
2) Building deep wells and appropriate location of shallow wells, activities which can make clean, unpolluted water accessible for people living in areas where water is already degraded.
3) Purification of water rich in biogens flowing from the catchment area before they reach larger water basins.

Experiences from Practical Projects

Table 20.2 summarises data on the motives of farmers in Poland which joined a so-called Rural Environment Protection Project, which subsidised the building of better manure storage facilities. The data show that reasons of taking part in the project were mainly economic (all the farmers), ecological (in the areas valued by tourists), quality of the production improvement (on the areas where similar projects were conducted in the past) and aesthetic. Farmers also indicated other motives, such as 'the wish to impress the neighbours' or the possibility to implement new technologies.

Farmers who have decided to build containers for manure storage can see no importance in this activity. At the beginning the most important thing is to build the container at the lowest possible cost, but after a year of use of the container the only return on their investment is the environmental protection benefit.

It is clear that the interest of clean surface or groundwater is not a priority for farmers and cannot be achieved

Table 20.1. Effectiveness of activities for reducing nitrate emissions from the agricultural sector in Sweden effectiveness (Mosiej & Wyporska, 2004)

No.	Activity	Nitrogen runoff reduction [t/year]	Reduction in comparison to starting year (1993)
1	Reduction in intensity of crop production by lowering prices and having a fertiliser tax	5,000	10.2%
2	Reduction in animal production	2,300	4.7%
3	Liquid manure storage and limitations on agricultural usage	5,400	11.1%
4	Academic research and licences for agricultural equipment	2,400	4.9%
5	Leaving stubble over the winter period	3,300	6.8%
6	Reduction in area of cereal production	4,000	8.2%
7	New protein feedstuffs	1,000	2%
8	Animal health improvement	1,000	2%
Total		29,400	49.9%

Table 20.2. Farmers' motives for accession to the Rural Environment Protection Project (Swatoń et al., 2002).

Percentage of interviewees questioned in the local implementation team	Torun	Elblag	Ostrołeka	Total
Problem - motive	%	%	%	%
a) Possibility of realising the investment with financial support	77.20	100.0	56.70	72.70
b) Contribution to lower environment pollution	42.50	55.20	48.50	45.70
c) Aim to improve the aesthetics of surroundings and get rid of odours	56.90	48.30	38.10	49.80
d) Recommendations by advisors from CAC and LIT	23.40	27.60	9.30	19.10
e) Possibility to implement new techniques and methods of farming	18.60	27.60	39.20	26.30
f) Future requirements of international conventions	37.70	44.80	36.10	37.90
g) Aim to increase production quality	15.00	13.80	21.60	17.10
h) Aim to improve the effectiveness of production	13.20	24.10	22.70	17.40
i) Aim to improve the conditions and hygiene of working	24.60	34.50	33.00	28.30
j) Possibility to decrease the labour requirement	11.40	6.90	19.60	13.70
k) Wish to impress the neighbours	1.80	0.00	4.10	2.40

only because they are encouraged to do so. There is a need for other policies. These include regulation, economic action, and information campaigns.

Countries are authorised to use legal means based on the water framework directive. Another important piece of legislation is the Nitrate Directive, which limits the use of nitrate for fertilization and requires that member states identify nitrate vulnerable zones on the basis of monitoring the sensitivity of groundwater and surface waters to nitrate pollution.

Also economic instruments may be efficient. Thus a tax on mineral fertilisers was used in Sweden for a period, which importantly reduced nutrients run off from agricultural soil.

Finally information may have an important place in the policy tool repertoire. Creating investment subsidies without thorough preparations and proper ecological education is not sufficient to guarantee good manure management and rural environmental protection. Advisory services and local seminars are important means to reach those aims.

Managing Water, Matter and Energy flows

Changing the Landscape Water Cycle

Adjusting water circulation is an act of interference with climate, environment and soil of an ecosystem. The ability to modify the distribution of solar energy used for water evaporation when air or soil is heated is of great importance for water circulation and habitat conditions.

Natural ecosystems are in the state of relative balance /homeostasis/. This means that the energy supplied to the ecosystem is equal to the amount of outgoing energy. If additional energy is added in the form of human labour, mechanic energy or chemical energy, an artificial ecosystem (e.g. agroecosystem) is created. If drainage causes a change of natural water conditions the flow of energy and matter will change. The deposition of organic matter in the soil is qualitatively and quantitatively dependent on the hydrothermal conditions. Changing the natural water conditions of soil by drainage or irrigation on the one hand increases the biological activity of soils, on the other hand affects the hydrochemical regime of the system soil - minerals – plants, and leads to increased outflow; it promotes the leaching out the nutrients and leads to migration of enormous amounts of minerals.

Managing Local Climate Through Heat Balance Adjustments

The amount of solar energy used for evaporation depends on biotic factors, such as vegetation type, percent of vegetation cover and its condition, and the humidity of the habitat. A more developed vegetation cover increases evaporation. As plants grow higher the wind speed increases in the leaf area, and when the roots are deeper the plants have better access to water. This means that in the same microclimatic conditions, more water evaporates from forest than from grassland and more from meadows than from farmland. Evaporation from areas without vegetation cover cannot be larger than the water transport from deeper layers of the soil to the surface. Evaporation occurs only at the few millimetres of topsoil. Plant productivity of the area depends on the balance between solar energy used for evaporation and for heating the air.

That distribution may be influenced by appropriate technical and agricultural operations. Increased drainage leads to decreased evaporation, and an increased share of solar irradiation is used to warm the environment. Conversely, by retention of water in the basin leads to increased evaporation; a smaller share of the solar heat is used for warming the environment. Coordinating water balance with balance of radiation may be used to create permanent changes in the internal circulation of water in e.g. agro-forestry. At the current level of agricultural production and water management in Poland 60-70% of the energy is used for evapotranspiration and the rest to heat the habitat. An optimal radiation for agriculture should aim to 80% evapotranspiration.

Table 20.3. Radiation balance for different vegetation types. (Ryszkowski, and Kędziora, 2008)

Land cover type	Share of radiation used for evapotranspiration/evaporation	Share of radiation used to heat the habitat
Fallow	0.55	0.40
Forest	0.88	0.07
Field Crops	0.75 - 0.80	0.20 - 0.25
Shallow water reservoir	0.86	0.14
Steppe without plant cover	0.14	0.86

The water retention in the landscape, extent of forest cover, soil moisture in agricultural lands, in addition influences precipitation.

Table 20.3 summarizes the radiation balance of evaporation and heating for a variety of vegetation types. Forest evaporates almost twice as much as fallow. On areas not covered with vegetation, dry steppe, only 14% of the energy is used for evapotranspiration. As most solar energy heats the air, an updraft of hot air is created drying not only the steppe but also adjacent areas. On the contrary in a highly moistured area, most energy (86%) is used for evaporation. The amount of energy required to evaporate 1 mm of water is enough to heat 10 cm of water by 6 °C (Kędziora, 2005).

The Role of Matter/Mineral Transport

One purpose of rural landscape engineering is to control and reduce the transport of matter in water streams to combat erosion, lifting silt, reduce loss of nutrients and reduce eutrophication of the recipient. The intensity of the matter turnover depends very much on management of the catchment area. Important factors include intensity of farming, distribution and type of vegetation cover, topography (slopes, valleys), and drainage. Rapid leaching of nutrients from the upper layers of the soil increases both by irrigation and drainage. With increased agricultural production the retention of matter in local circulation decreases, water and wind erosion increases, as does humus mineralization and leaching of the released minerals, mostly nitrogen and phosphorus. These are all important causes of eutrophication (Somorowski, 1996; Ryszkowski and Kędziora, ?).

The amount of substances dissolved and carried by the rivers to the sea is a measure of the intensity of land use. Vistula River in Poland transports on average 47 tons matter per km^2 per year from its basin, some from precipitation, but most from leakage from agricultural land. The background (natural) level has been estimated to 24 t/km^2 year. At the dawn of history the rate was much lower as the water table was lower and the amount captured by peat deposits was higher. It has been estimated that around year 1000 transported matter was about 12 t/km^2. The flow of matter from land was, however, higher, as part was captured by wetlands. The natural losses of chemical components important for agricultural production a thousand years ago has been estimated to be about 30% lower than today (15-18 t/km^2) (Maruszczak, 1988).

Landscape Management Preserves Scarce Water Resources

Land management practices that regulate water condition in a field (runoff, evaporation, retention), may significantly change the thermal conditions of the soil. So for example, draining excess water from arable land in springtime causes faster warming of the soil, spring irrigation of the valley meadows contributes to faster thawing of the soil and earlier beginning of vegetation; summer irrigations cause increase of the soil moisture and at the same time lower its temperature. Changes in the catchment, such as afforestation or building artificial water reservoirs, increases the water storage capacity of the area and thus reduce surface runoff, which in turn influences the local climate.

To secure optimal use of scarce water resources one should avoid fast draining of excess water from the catchments during winter and spring, as this reduce water supplies for the summer and more energy goes into heating of soil and air. Proper management in the agricultural landscape must be consistent with the two cardinal rules:

- to maintain as long as possible and as much as possible water in the landscape (with its reasonable redistribution), which minimizes the unproductive drainage of water out of a water basin and increases the retention of a surface and groundwater in the catchment,
- to get a maximum amount of water passes from the soil into atmosphere through the plants, and as little as possible by direct evaporation from the soil.

These effects may be obtained by proper management of the landscape. Introduction of plants into the landscape will increase evaporation from the surface of the whole area, but will reduce evaporation from fields lying between the riparian zones. Trees reduce wind speed, increase temperature and reduce evaporation from fields between riparian zones. The tall trees with deep root system in riparian zones evaporate more than crops. The effect is greater the drier the climate.

Assessment of Sustainable Land Use

21

Alexander Fehér
Slovak University of Agriculture, Nitra, Slovakia
Michelle Wander
University of Illinois, USA

Indicators of Sustainability

Monitoring Sustainable Development Requires Indicators

The Brundtland definition of sustainable development articulated by the World Commission on Environment and Development (1987) was among the first of many efforts to formalise policies and practices that will protect agricultural capacity. Definitions of agricultural sustainability typically require that practices produce healthy food and fibre for current and future generations in an equitable manner without degrading natural resources. It is widely held that sustainable agriculture is based only on a functional and productive system with high biodiversity and system self-regulation (cf. Bell and Morse, 2000). Proponents of sustainable agriculture frequently advocate systems modelled on nature that maintain production without loss or degradation of soil or other natural resources, and suggest that key elements of optimised systems include nutrient recycling where nutrients are supplied in proportion to the system within which they reside (Wander, 2009). Plant-soil interactions and organic matter reserves develop as characteristics of agricultural systems, and this feedback determines the degree to which sustained production can be maintained. The development of indicators that reflect progress toward sustainability has become a high priority for academics, policymakers and planners. Assigning appropriate indicators can be difficult and must consider the scale of application and objectives (Bossel, 2001).

What is an Indicator?

An *indicator* is a datum (value, level, etc.) that reflects (shows) the presence or amount of a factor under measurement. Indicators or sets of indicators are typically developed within the context of frameworks for application. An indicator is a parameter or value derived from several parameters which provide information about a certain observed phenomenon (or resource) from the point of view of its quantitative and/or qualitative properties affecting, in a given time and space, the environment as a whole and/or its individual components. These components are analysed according to how they affect the health condition of a population, the ecosystem structure and the productivity of a given space. Managers must identify the measurable phenomena thought to support sustainability. Different suites of indicators are often suggested for application at local, regional or national and international scales. The information and indication levels (scaling from a farm level to a world-wide assessment) can be presented as an information iceberg including a hierarchy from raw data to highly aggregated indices (Figure 21.1).

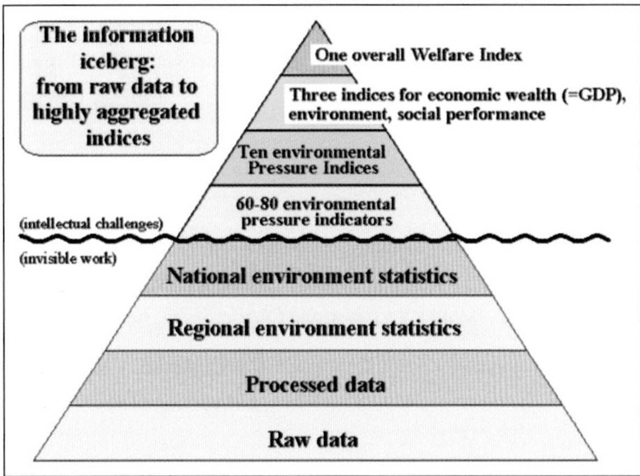

Figure 21.1. Example of an information iceberg: hierarchy of information and indication levels (according to Jesinghaus, 1999)

Summarising different sources, a good ecological indicator can be said to have the following properties:

1. Measurable (possible quantification) and statistically valid.
2. Relevant/representative, responsive (changes in a reasonable time frame so that response to action can be evaluated), sensitive to small variations in environmental stress.
3. Ease of handling and technically feasible.
4. Cost-effective.
5. Applicable in different areas
6. Can be updated.

The indicators usually include parameters on different assessment levels (from on-farm level to global level), holistic indicators are rare. The indication methods called the Direct Measurement Method (DMM) and Ecological Model Method (EMM) have been replaced by the Ecosystem Health Index Method (EHIM) to assess very complex and dynamic systems by ecologists. EHIM is a good example of the kinds of multi-criteria indicators that are a sum of other metrics. It includes selection of basic and additional indicators, calculation of sub-EHIs, determination weighting factors, calculation of a synthetic EHI from sub-EHIs and ecosystem health assessment (EHI 0 means the worst state, EHI 100 indicates the best healthy state). The EHI is calculated according to the equation:

$$EHI = \sum^{n} \omega_i x \text{ subEHI}_i$$

where EHI is the weighted sum that represents a synthetic ecosystem health index, subEHI_i the *i*th sub-ecosystem health index for the *i*th indicator, n above Σ the number of considered indicators and ω_i the weighting factor for the *i*th indicator.

The agri-environmental indicators, in comparison with other ecological or environmental indicators have special demands that must be considered (Table 21.1). Many indicators proposed in the literature are impractical, e.g. a farmer will probably never calculate an exergy and emergy ratio, even though it provides a solid theoretical basis for understanding agri-ecosystem integrity. It is expected that the on-farm indicators will give farmers information about changes at an early stage of land use decision making. Many indicators do not give any basis for practical purposes, and therefore ‘easy to understand’ indicators are recommended on local (farm) level.

Indication Frameworks

The Pressure-State-Response (PSR) Model

Indication frameworks are based on targeted phenomena (outcomes) that are sometimes evaluated at different assessment scales. The Pressure-State-Response (PSR) model outlines the way that indicators are commonly applied within such system-based frameworks. System-based frameworks evaluate sustainability based on attributes of the system. This example (PSR) has been developed and adopted by the OECD (for agriculture economic and social assessments). This model includes three main levels, reflecting the three components of sustainability (Figure 21.2):

- Pressure: Human activities affecting the environment.
- State: Changes in the environment.
- Response: Response of society.

Table 21.1. Attributes of agri-environmental indicators (Piorr, 2003).

Scope of indicators
Inform about status and development of complex systems
Provide sufficient information about sustainability of land use systems
Be responsive to changes related to human activities to rapidly indicate success and failure of activities
Able to show trends over time
Work as umbrella indicators summarising different processes and/or environmental aspects
Policy relevance
Provide a representative picture of environmental, agricultural and rural conditions, pressures or society's responses
Be simple and easy to interpret for different users
Provide a basis for regional, national and international comparisons
Be either national in scope or applicable to regional issues of national significance
Assist individual decision-makers in the private sector as well as trade and industry
Analytically sound
Be theoretically well founded in technical and scientific terms
Be based on international standards and international consensus about its validity
Lend itself to being linked to economic models, forecasting and information systems
Measurability and data required
Have to be controllable
Readily available or made available at a reasonable cost/benefit ratio
Adequately documented and of known quality
Updated at regular intervals in accordance with reliable procedures
Have a threshold of reference value against which to compare it, so that users are able to assess the significance of the values associated with it

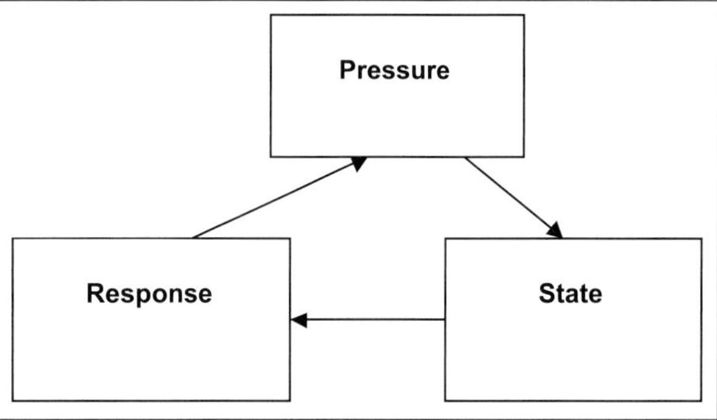

Figure 21.2. Basic framework scheme of the PSR indication model.

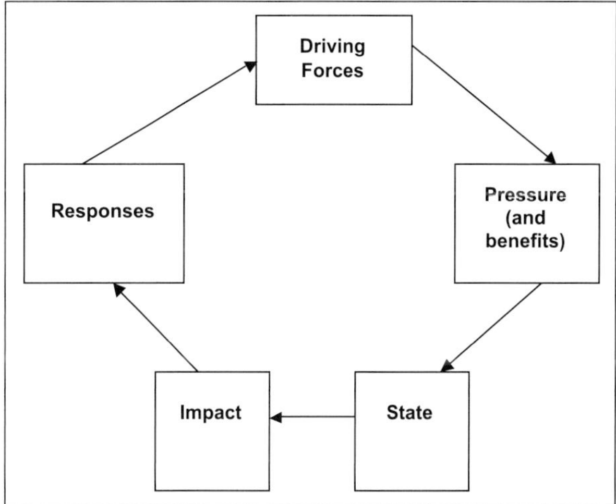

Figure 21.3. Basic framework scheme of the DPSIR indication model.

These three levels create a circle where the Response is followed by a new Pressure on the environment. The main indicators can be classified in one of these indicator groups (P, S or R). Several organisations (e.g. UNCSD, also OECD) use a model called DSR. In DSR models Pressure is substituted by Driving Force, which includes non-environmental variables (but sometimes Pressure and Driving Force are used as synonyms). Driving force indicators are targeted at the causes of change in environmental conditions in agriculture (farm management practices, etc.), state indicators characterise the effect of agriculture on the environment (e.g. impacts on biodiversity) and response indicators include actions taken to respond to the changes.

The DPSIR Framework

The most advanced model used by OECD is called DPSIR and is characterised by 5 stages (Figure 21.3):

- Driving force: Basic sectoral trend.
- Pressure: Human activities affecting the environment.
- State: Changes in the environment.
- Impact: Effects of the changed environment.
- Response: Response of society.

There are various combinations of these indication elements, e.g. DPR, PSR. These indicator frameworks consist of systems indicators (ecological, economic, social), and include process indicators (resources and outcome indicators) and structure indicators (contextual and sector indicators).

A number of groups have launched efforts over the past decade to develop indicators of environmental outcome. The National Research Council's 'Ecological Indicators for the Nation (NRC, 2000) and The Heinz Center's The State of the Nation's Ecosystems (Heinz Center, 2002 and 2008) are two prominent examples in the US. While these and other groups have gone to great lengths to identify indicators, determine their appropriateness as indicators of environmental outcome, and establish data availability, they have made no attempts to develop interpretations of indicator status or change. The lack of interpretations or thresholds for outcome stems at least partly from the complexity of the task at hand.

Soil and Conservation Related Frameworks

In the US, the frameworks that have historically influenced agriculture are those administered by the United States Department of Agriculture (USDA) and the Natural Resources Conservation Service (NRCS). These have focused on soil and conservation related indicators developed for determination and application at the farm scale. There is active interest in indicator and framework development with the growing recognition that historically important soil conservation tools – the Soil Loss Tolerance Standard (T) and the Revised Universal Soil Loss Equation 2 (RUSLE2) – fall short of what is needed to fully sustain soil and water resource quality (Cox, 2008; Tugel et al., 2005; Ritcher, 2007). There is interest in developing dynamic soil properties as indicators for use as:

- soil tests, where critical values are understood to warrant particular responses,
- monitoring aids used to evaluate trends and verify the benefits or harm caused by adoption of practices such as crop diversification and/or residue removal and
- as benchmarking tools to determine programme eligibility or rank parcels in terms of their risk or suitability for selected land uses. NRCS and USDA have identified a list of dynamic soil properties for potential inclusion in the Soil Survey that could form the basis of such a system.

Sustainability Frameworks

Sustainability frameworks under consideration rely on a Principles, Criteria and Indicator (PC&I) approach to sustainability assessment that relies on a thematically structured list of principles, criteria and associated indicators (Baelermanes 1988). Such frameworks incorporate indicators and combine them into a process for interpretation against a suite of goals or standards. These kinds of 'sustainability' frameworks contend with problems of indicator selection, scale of implementation and strategies for performance evaluation (Van Cauwenbergh et al., 2007). A systematic approach is emerging for content-based disciplinary frameworks that develop indicators to characterise specific functions or processes of concern (Lopez-Riduara, 2005).

Assessment Tools in Agriculture

General Requirements on Indicators in Agriculture

Two kinds of indicators can be developed: *physical indicators* based on 'endogenous' variables (proposed by ecologists for 'strong' sustainability) and *economic indicators* based on 'exogenous' variables (proposed by economists for weak sustainability). In the economic approach monetary values characterise the natural capital (resources).

Polyfunctional land use requires a multi-criteria analysis and it is necessary to define possible alternatives clearly – suitability indicators confronting various prospects and non-reductive models enabling better understanding of various types of causal relationships (multi-objective integrated representation; cf. Shaxson, 1998).

Many territorial indicators up until this point have been static without considering changes or trends. These kinds of indicators fail to evaluate ecosystems as complex adaptive systems and do not take into account non-linear trends, discontinuities, and multifaceted stability. They also do not include system resilience, ability to recover from stress, or resistance or capacity to absorb or sustain disturbances without degraded function. For instance the ecological footprint is only suitable to determine man's dependence on a particular area and an emergy analysis only examines an energy budget. The indicators have to integrate ecosystem structure and function and indicate changes (response) to environmental stress. In addition, they have to be quantifiable and easy to interpret (Meyer, 1992 etc.).

Indicators should be applicable to all levels of agricultural activity from the small family farm to agri-business on a national scale. For smaller units the indicators should be detailed. Even valuable data are useless if they do not support decision making. It is not advisable to overwhelm the data (coefficients etc.) with statistical calculations because the user can lose confidence and might not understand the scope of the value (Benites and Tschirley, 1997).

Methods and Systems for Analysis

A series of methods and systems are used to evaluate the performance of agricultural systems. These rely on a number of approaches based on physical, biological, or economic parameters Different methods have different degrees of importance (Table 21.2) and assess different aspects of agri-ecosystems (cf. Doherty & Rydberg, 2002).

Life cycle assessment (LCA) evaluates the impacts of a product (material or services) on the environment throughout its life. It focuses on material and energy flows and is used mainly in industry (applicable in agriculture but it can be difficult to find reliable data). Its results can be easily understood.

Cost-benefit analysis (CBA) is an economic analysis method and it is orientated towards cash flows. Its main weakness is that many environmental objects do not have a monetary value or it is very difficult to identify such a value, but the results are very clear and interpretable.

The *ecological footprint (EF)* is about carrying capacity. It is generally used in environmental sciences and in sustainable development. The results used to be shown for a land area affected by man but this method is not very precise and does not include all the influences and functional relations. However, it produces results that are clear to the public.

Emergy analysis (EMA/EA) measures values of resources, services and commodities in a quantitative way on the basis of the solar energy ('the system necessary for a product or service'). It is holistic but the results are not easily interpretable.

The *index of biotic integrity (IBI)* focuses on ecosystem health evaluation. It is about the ability of an ecosystem to maintain a community of organisms. It can be presented by an Amoeba chart that includes different species (see below).

Positional analysis (PA) is a planning tool that analyses the effects of decision actions on systems and possible action conflicts. It can directly support decision-making and can be used in local context with holistic results.

Human appropriation of net primary production (HANPP) compares potential primary production of biomass in a region with actual and exploited biomass of plants. In comparison with EF, it is more convenient for a limited area (with clear boundaries).

The use of modern technology, e.g. geographical information systems (GIS) and internet-based surveys for documentation of facts and phenomena dispersion, is recommended. Data gathering can be very expensive and therefore many subjects look for indicators based on currently available data.

Table 21.2. Selected assessment tools and frameworks.

Pressure State Response (PSR) and Driving Forces-Pressures-State-Impacts-Responses (DPSIR)	Assessment tool	OECD	
Environmental impact assessment (EIA)	Assessment tool	Enterprise or production system;	Regional or national
Principles, Criteria and Indicators (PC & I)	Assessment tool	Enterprise	Regional or national
Life Cycle Analysis (LCA)		Enterprise	Multi scale
Cost-Benefit Analysis (CBA)		Enterprise	Regional or national
Ecological footprint (EF)			Farm scale
Ecopoints (EP)			Farm scale
Environmental Management for Agriculture (EMA)			Farm scale
SOLAGRO			Farm scale
ECOFARM			Farm scale

Main Ecosystem Health Indicators

Landscape and Land Cover Indicators

Agricultural landscapes have three important features: structure, functions and values (cultural, maintenance costs, etc). All these landscape items can be assessed. OECD uses these main landscape indicators:

- Physical appearance and structure of landscape (components of landscape structure)
- Landscape management (management schemes to maintain and restore the landscape)
- Landscape costs and benefits (the value society places on landscapes and the costs of maintaining and enhancing these).

Landscape structure is the basic landscape indicator. It is based on landscape typologies with a region-focused approach. Landscape structure is evaluated from two points of view:

a) Environmental features and land use patterns (habitats, changes in land use etc.)
b) Man-made objects (cultural features on agricultural land).

Landscape management includes the share of agricultural land under public and private schemes for landscape maintenance and enhancement. Landscape value is analysed from two perspectives:

a) The costs of maintaining (or enhancing) landscape provision by agriculture
b) The public valuation of agricultural landscapes.

Landscape monetary values can be indicated by Contingent Value Methods (CVM). However, landscape value indicators are scarce and need international harmonisation (Table 21.3). They are state (S) or response (R) type, e.g. number and distribution of identified heritage objects, number of trained heritage professionals, etc.

Soil, Water and Nutrient Indicators

The soil is a specific part of the ecosystem that needs special indicators because it is a complex organic and inorganic system. According to the USDA Natural Resources Conservation Service (1996), soil quality indicators can be categorised into four groups:

- Visual indicators (obtained from observation or photographic interpretation), e.g. exposure of subsoil, changes in soil colour, runoff, windblown soil
- Physical indicators (arrangement of solid particles and pores), e.g. topsoil depth, bulk density, porosity, texture, compaction
- Chemical indicators (chemical properties), e.g. measurements of pH, salinity, organic matter, nutrient cycling, contaminants
- Biological indicators (micro- and macroorganisms, and their activities or byproducts), e.g. earthworms, nematodes, respiration rate (to detect microbial activity), ergosterol (fungal byproduct), decomposition rate.

Research explicitly addressing the soil quality concept began in earnest in the early 1990s as investigators sought to validate holistic approaches to soil assessment and test the efficacy of minimum data sets that could be developed for use by frameworks evaluating agricultural sustainability. Approaches to measurement and scale of application ranged from farmer-orientated, applied projects to research-orientated efforts evaluating indicators and their relationship to outcomes of interest and policy-scale efforts seeking to link practice with programmes or economic inducements and/or quantify programme success. Many efforts to develop soil quality indicators have sought farmer participation with the assumption that their local knowledge of context is an important orientating factor for point-scale evaluation of soil quality (Wander et al., 2002; Liebig et al., 1996; Schjonning et al., 2004).

Soil organisms are indicators of soil quality but direct soil biodiversity measurement is expensive and therefore its substitution is desirable (Büchs, 2003). The faunal indicators for soil quality must form a dominant group and occur in all soil types, have a high abundance and high biodiversity and play an important role in many soil processes. One of the animal groups that fulfils these conditions is the nematodes. Natural conditions are often independent of management intensity, so it can help farmers to improve their management practices only partly. Soil microorganisms are attracting interest because they react

Table 21.3. Possible classification of landscape indicators (Eiden, 2001).

Landscape dimension	Thematic indicator group	Indicator item
Landscape features	Landscape composition (e.g. landscape/land-use components comprising the landscape, contextual information)	Stock and change in broad land cover categories Stock and low land coverland use matrices
	Landscape configuration (e.g. structural arrangement of landscape elements)	Fragmentation Diversity Edges Shape
	Natural landscape features (state and change)	Stock and change of biotopes and habitats Hemerobie (naturalness) Habitat/Biotope fragmentation Habitat/Biotope diversity Habitat/Biotope quality
	Historical-cultural landscape features (state and change)	Point features Linear features Area features
	Present-cultural landscape features (state and change)	Point features Linear features Area features
Human perception	Visual and aesthetic value	-
Landscape management, conservation and protection schemes	Cultural landscape protection/conservation	-
	Nature conservation/protection	-

rapidly to stress by altering community structure (species richness and composition), activity rates (e.g. metabolism) and biomass production. Important processes such as nitrogen turnover are controlled by microbiological processes (Dilly and Blume 1998; Stenberg, 1999). In Germany a soil quality index has been developed to describe environmental conditions that influence invertebrates, (e.g. spiders, beetles) or plant species in the Czech Republic. *Collembola*, *Oribatida* and *Nematoda* are proposed for soil monitoring. There is active work on nematodes in the Netherlands and the US.

Biota are advocated as soil quality indicators because they play a key role in the transformation and circulation of organic matter and nutrients that respond to changes in the environment and micro-climate promptly. Despite this fact, measures of biomass or respiration continue to be explored but have not been included in interpretive frameworks. Modelling frameworks may be needed to help us use indicators such as soil bacterial activity, which reflects the set of factors that regulate the nutrient cycle, from management decisions or outcome assessment.

Weeds can also be used for indication of soil conditions (see next section). The soil nutrient balance can be assessed by nitrogen and phosphorus balance and organic carbon content in soil, the physical properties by soil erosion and compaction, chemical pollution by contaminants content, acidification or salination. The main soil processes and their state can also be evaluated on the basis of thermodynamic criteria (entropy). A complex system of soil dynamic properties assessment has been developed by USDA/NRSC.

Frameworks for Soil Indicators

Interpretive frameworks for soil indicators vary from the farmer to regulatory scale. The following example was developed for farmers participating in a study of tillage effects on soil quality (Wander et al., 2002). Data were summarised for individual farms and land uses (Figure 21.4).

Visual summaries have a utility that quantitative estimates lack, but the use of indicators in scoring functions helps producers consider trade-offs in soil function. For example, data from the same study showed contrasts in outcomes for the nutrient and water quality functions for the conventionally tilled (CT), no-till (NT) and non-disturbed (ND) scenarios (Table 21.4).

Water in the agricultural landscape should be of good quantity and quality. From the point of view of produc-

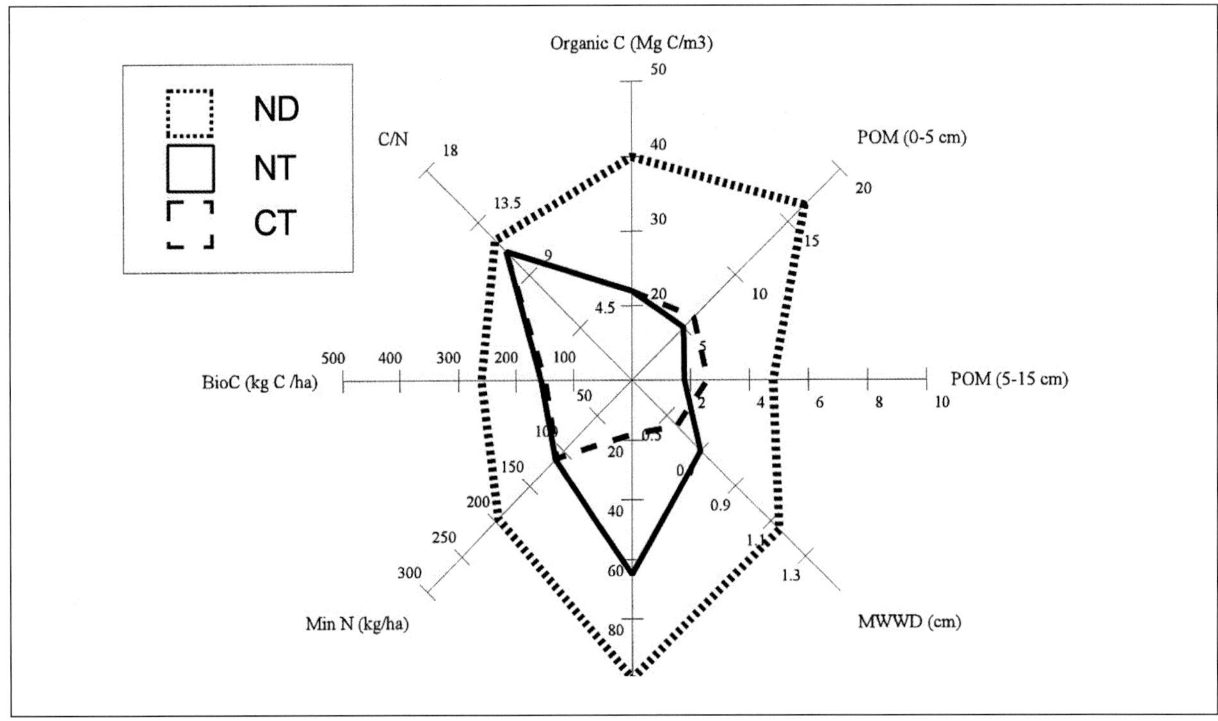

Figure 21.4. Soil organic matter quality (a radar diagram). Conventional tillage for maize-soybean systems = solid line; no-till for maize-soybean = hatched; undisturbed or minimally disturbed grass-covered areas = light dashed area that is the benchmark for local region.

tion, two of the most important indicators are the water use intensity and the water contamination. The EU Common Agricultural Policy (CAP) supports improving the state of irrigation infrastructure and irrigation techniques and protecting water quality in respect of pesticides and nitrates. Water and nutrients are dynamic natural elements in change, and therefore the balance (water and nutrient inputs, flow and outputs) is considered the object of assessment (e.g. soil surface nitrogen balance). Soil, water and also air are polluted by agricultural activities that are assessed by indicators included in many schemes (e.g. pesticide soil contamination, water contamination, methane emissions to air).

Biodiversity Indicators

The quantitative links between landscape patterns (matrix) and biodiversity have been also studied but it is difficult to find appropriate indicators of overall species richness of the landscape. *Mosaic indicators* are in the process of development, using e.g. amoeba charts presenting selected indicator species or habitat conditions. This type of diagram is excellent for a rough comparison of different states (different methods of landwork induce different changes in the landscape).

Table 21.4. Scoring functions computed for the Illinois Soil Quality Initiative computed using Karlen and Stott's (1994) approach.

Soil function indicators	Calculated values
Soil water relations = f(residue cover, porosity, aggregate stability, C content, macropores)	CT 2.45 NT 3.10 ND 4.60
Nutrient supply = f(available N, P, K, C content, pH)	CT 4.25 NT 4.00 ND 4.00
Rooting environment t= f(POM5-15 cm, bulk density, penetration resistance, C content, pH)	CT 4.35 NT 2.95 ND 4.10

The Biodiversity Action Plan for Agriculture issued by the EU Commission proposes a set of indicators for evaluation of biodiversity focusing on reduction of agricultural inputs, crop patterns benefiting flora and fauna, species in need of protection, high nature-value habitats, ecological infrastructure (e.g. field boundaries, non-cultivated patches), valuable habitats and endangered species.

Biota are singled out as promising indicators because they are sensitive to the changing agricultural landscape. Historically, biodiversity was characterised based on species richness and abundance or dominance of species. Today diversity is no longer used as a measure of system health and we know that higher biodiversity does not mean higher ecozoological stability. Species richness is considered along with genetic variability, including diversity sub-species (species genetical plasticity) and life habit. The challenge is to understand the functional role organisms play as they interact with changing environmental conditions. Managers increasingly argue for systems that achieve an acceptable level of resistance and resilience. There can be no single biodiversity indicator but the indicator depends on the biodiversity entity to be evaluated and is influenced by professional motivations. In determining ecosystem sustainability indicators, the following species properties are decisive: available quantitative data on species abundance, the species must be sensitive to interference by man, accessible and accurately measurable and with an indicative value for the ecosystem conditions.

Research on indicators is actively evaluating plant and animal species; the greater motility of animals allows them to respond to management faster than plant species and so more work has been done on animal indicators. Organisms such as spiders and beetles, which react in very short time periods and can be tied to particular trophic levels, are among the more popular indicators. This explains why faunal indicators are more commonly used in frameworks than plant species. Prominent examples are water quality indicators. Soil nematodes provide a good example of this as community composition and life cycle characteristics reveal much about the disturbance frequency, habitat quality and nutrient enrichment level of a soil.

In order for bioindicators to be useful, it must be possible to relate them to ecosystem function and, ideally, some course of management that could enhance indicator performance. Each organism and its community reflects a complex of mutually responding factors in the environment. Each organism responds to the presence of new or changing factors in a different way and these responses and changes indicate it. Degree of plant community degradation can also indicate changes in the environment (quantitative and qualitative changes in the species composition of biocenoses). Some bioindicators are selected because they represent harmful agents (disease-causing species) or degradation of communities (invasive species). The indicative channel between the habitat and invasive species is bi-directional (habitat ⇔ species). While the habitat conditions define the group of species preferring the given habitat type, the occurrence of a certain species also indicates the environment's character (Figure 21.5). A plant or animal community category can predict a more frequent occurrence of some species. For example, the relative abundance of native species and biomass reduction indicates landscape degradation (with possible exceptions).

Weeds can be used for rapid and visual indication of soil conditions, e.g. for soil structure, nutrient content, moisture, cultivation, etc. In addition, weed species may

Box 21.1. Ecosystem Health Indicators in the North American Great Lakes Basin

Indicators for ecosystem health have been proposed after a detailly analysis. The Great Lakes indicators can be regrouped according to environmental compartment (e.g., air, water, land, sediment, biota, humans) by Great Lakes issues (e.g., contaminants and pathogens, nutrients, non-native species, habitat, climate change). The main indicators evaluated in the Great Lake Basin are the following ones:

- Toxic contaminants.
- Land use: localization of large urban areas, recreational and industrial activities, occurrence of rare species etc.). Current land use decisions throughout the basin are affecting the chemical, physical and biological aspects of the ecosystem.
- Invasive species: occurrence of invasive non-native species and its impact on Great Lakes ecology and economy.
- Habitat status: localization and stadium of habitats (diversity, degradation), e.g. watershed, tall-grass prairie, island. Many factors, including the spread of non-native species degrade plant and animal communities.

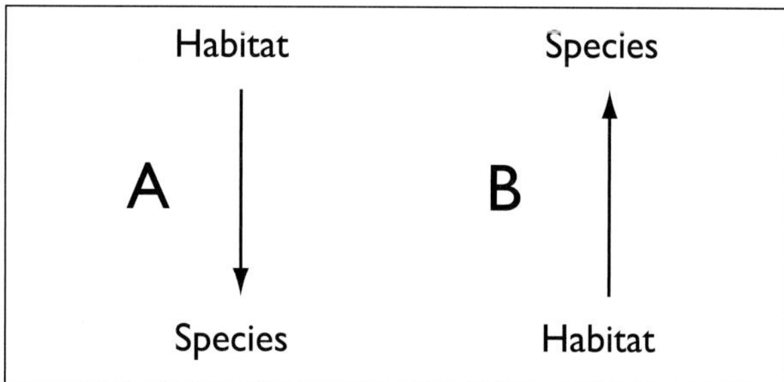

Figure 21.5. Two pathways of biodiversity indication. A. Habitat conditions indicate which species can occur there. B. Occurrence of a certain species in a habitat indicates the character or soil-climate conditions and intensity or frequency of the environment degradation (e.g. unwanted neophytes indicate potential environmental and/or economic losses in the system) (Fehér and Končeková, 2005).

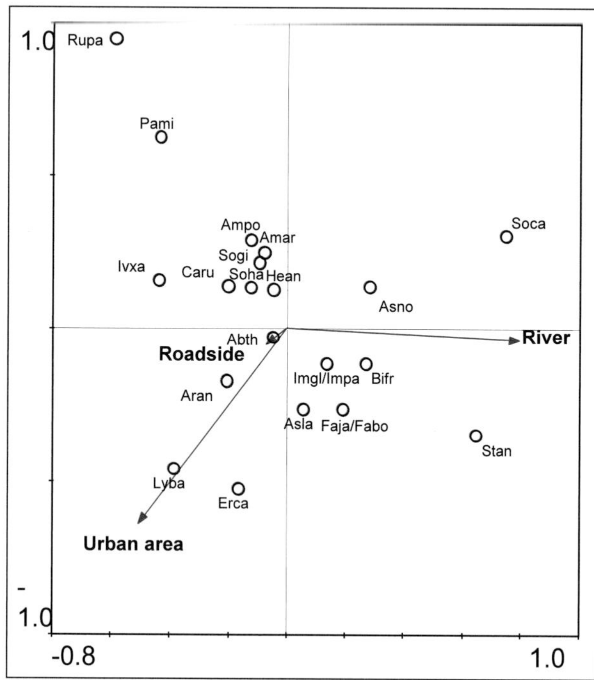

Figure 21.6. Statistical restriction of expansive weeds in the Žitný Ostrov Region, Slovakia (canonical correspondence analysis according to the bond with a certain type of preferred habitat, Fehér and Končeková, 2005). Abbreviation of species: *Abth – Abutilon theophrasti, Amar – Ambrosia artemisiifolia, Ampo – Amaranthus powelli, Aran – Artemisia annua, Asla – Aster lanceolatus, Asno – Aster novi-belgii, Bifr – Bidens frondosa, Caru – Cannabis ruderalis, Erca – Conyza canadensis, Faja/Fabo – Fallopia japonica* and *F. x bohemica* (evaluated together), *Hean – Helianthus annus, Imgl/Impa – Impatiens glandulifera* and *I. parviflora* (same position), *Ivxa – Iva xanthiifolia, Lyba – Lycium barbarum, Pami – Panicum miliaceum* and other invasive *Panicum* species, *Rupa – Rumex patientia, Soca – Solidago canadensis, Sogi – S. gigantea, Soha – Sorghum halepense, Stan – Stenactis annua.*

have different ecotypes growing in different habitats and growth characteristics of weeds also may indicate soil conditions (Hill and Ramsay, 1997). Figure 21.6 provides an example of a visual framework that allows the user to quantify the expansive weeds in an amoeba-type indicator (amoeba-chart, ray diagram, cyclogram, radar-diagram). Changes in the irregular, amoeba-shaped line indicate changes in agro-ecosystem biodiversity. An indicator expressed like this does not fully replace other indicators. It helps to evaluate ecological conditions of the environment (ecological gradient) and the effect of man on the agricultural landscape.

For ecozoological biodiversity evaluation with invasive species, it is advisable to use indicators of the amoeba chart that also include rare, protected and endangered species of synanthropic plants. The most common agri-biodiversity indicators are based on evaluation of rare species (McRae et al., 2000). In addition, the proportion of invasive and expansive species to ecozoologically valuable species should be considered. The indicator takes the abundance of individual species into account only semi-quantitatively (in cases where the number of sites is shown, information about the size of a population may be lacking). A species may also be quantified by the rate of infection in the given area. The amoeba chart is used also in evaluating the ecological integrity. This diagram is easy to use, which is its strength. It allows for quick and direct evaluation of the 'health' of an ecosystem and is very cheap. The weak side of the amoeba chart is the fact that it does not replace other methods, and it is difficult to define whether a certain phenomenon has appeared as a consequence of man's activity or is of natural origin. Finally, it evaluates symptoms, not causes. In the case of expanding weed populations, it fails to update the species scope of the indicator at various space and time horizons.

Economic and Social Evaluation of Rural Development

Economic Indicators

Economic indicators of sustainable agriculture typically focus on efficient resource use, the competitiveness and viability of agriculture and rural development (e.g. diversification of income sources). The social indicators often relate to labour opportunities and access to resources and services. The European Commission promotes the socio-economic function of multifunctional agriculture in maintaining the viability of rural areas and balanced regional development by generating employment in primary production and the supply and processing/distribution chains.

The economic and social indicators relate not only to agriculture but also rural development. The Rural Development Regulations of the EU state that rural development plans must include provisions to ensure the effective and correct implementation of the plans, including monitoring and evaluation. The economic and social indicators analyse:

- Stocks (state and flow indicators on stocks)
- Efficiency
  - in the economic dimension: output indicators (quality and quantity)
  - in the social dimension: indicators of employment and institutional efficiency
- Equity
  - in the economic dimension: indicators of the viability of rural communities and the maintenance of a balanced pattern of development
  - in the social dimension (territorial, sectoral, social and ethical indicators): indicators of access to resources/services and opportunities, equal opportunities, labour conditions and animal welfare.

In economic evaluation, a distinction is made between market and non-market outputs. Efficiency indicators link both types of outputs and can be proposed to combine them with competitiveness and viability indicators. During the process of indicator development, non-market environmental and cultural amenity values have been created. Economic indicator sets are based on the valuation of marketed goods (on the basis of individual preferences). There are two kinds of preferences: the revealed preferences (observed, actual preferences) and stated preferences (expressed preferences). They consider use values (e.g. for recreational activities) and non-use values (based on willingness-to-pay e.g. for aesthetic beauty of the landscape).

Economic assessment uses a set of methods based on different direct and indirect approaches, e.g. hedonic price analysis (estimation of implicit prices for individual attributes of a market commodity), market prices, contingent valuation (scenario construction), multi-criteria analysis (identifying decision criteria), etc. From a practical point of view, there are some economic techniques that are in use with efficiency, e.g. cost-benefit analysis (CBA) of investments, natural resource damage assessment (NRDA, payments for natural resources injuries) or environmental costing (ECo, e.g. for health damage).

Socioeconomic Indicators

Examples of economic and social indicator fields and/or indicators for sustainable agriculture and rural development include:

Stocks: Number of people employed in agriculture, age structure of agricultural labour force, agricultural education and training, fixed assets and stocks in agriculture, investment aids.

Efficiency: Quantity (in energy terms), organic agriculture, capital productivity, labour productivity, land productivity, energy efficiency.

Equity: Migratory balance, age structure, poverty rate, jobless households, early school-leavers.

Economic productivity, social responsibility and environmental protection together make up an inseparable whole. Agricultural production needs to be directed more towards sustainable land use (cf. Agenda 21, Chapter 14). Any planning of sustainable land use includes means and instruments for land use strategy. This strategy implementation should be in a suitable location for various land users and aim for the improvement of space and physical conditions of agricultural landscape in long-term use. It should include the protection/conservation of natural resources in balance with people's needs. In order to achieve productive and sustainable agriculture, it is necessary to determine a reliable and exact evalua-

Stock of natural resources affected by agriculture	Environmental emissions from agriculture	Farm management practices and resource use efficiency
Land use • land use changes *Soil resources* • soil erosion • soil organic carbon • soil biodiversity *Water resources* • total agricultural water use • groundwater use and recharge *Biodiversity* • genetic level • species level • ecosystem level	1. Water emissions *Nutrient balances* • nitrogen balance • phosphorus balance *Pesticide use and risks* • aquatic • territorial • human health risks *Water quality* • risk indicators • state indicators 2. Air emissions *Ammonia emissions* 3. Atmospheric emissions – Climate change *Agricultural energy balance and greenhouse gas emissions*	*Resource use efficiency* *Farm management* • nutrient • pest • soil • water • biodiversity • whole farm

Table 21.3. Agri-environmental indicators proposed by OECD (2001).

tion of ecological conditions and relationships. Policy-makers need indicators interpretable for them (e.g. Reid et al., 1993). Many indicators for sustainable development have been accepted on an international level (e.g. annex of Agenda 21; for European agri-environmental indicators see Washer, 2000). At present there are several lists of indicators for sustainable agriculture, e.g. the OECD, EEA, UNEP, USDA etc. (OECD, 2001; EEA, 2004; Parris, 2002). For the time being, a universal (holistic) indicator for evaluation of changes in agri-ecosystems has not been created, but minimum composite indicators are expected to combine a set of assessment criteria. The OECD uses its own agricultural indicators classified into four groups (Table 21.3). The OECD has its own database. The indicators rely on existing figures or new uncollected data. EUROSTAT provides statistical information required by the EU Commission (it includes also the Farm Structure Survey, livestock and crop production data and the Economic Accounts for Agriculture) and also the Farm Accountancy Data Network (FADN). The priorities of the European Environmental Agency (EEA) include agri-environmental issues such as soils, land cover, etc.

European Union Assessment of Agriculture

There are many useful sources for assessment in the EU, e.g. the Farm Structure Survey. The LUCAS project (Land Use/Cover Area Frame Statistical Survey) provides geo-referenced information. There are many activities in research and development of assessment and indicators of agriculture. The Joint Research Centre has developed European geo-environmental databases on soil, land cover, river basins and climate, the European Environment Agency collects information on air emissions, land cover, water quality and nature or biodiversity. To develop EU agri-environment indicators, a project has been started called IRENA (Indicator Reporting on the Integration of Environmental Concerns into Agricultural Policy). Within this project, indicator fact sheets and some reports have also been produced (based on DPSIR framework). There are many other projects, e.g. AIR, FAIR and ELISA (the Environmental Indicators for Sustainable Agriculture) in the EU, which has identified 22 state indicators related to soil, water, air, biodiversity and landscape. According to the EU Commission the indicators for the integration of environmental concerns into the CAP are important in transparency, accountability and ensuring the success of monitoring, control and evaluation (European Commission, 2001; Commission of the European Communities, 2000, 2001). These indicators promote the effectiveness of policy implementation and may support the Global Assessment process. The indicators for assessing the integration of environmental concerns into CAP need to:

- Identify the key agri-environmental issues that are of concern in Europe today
- Understand, monitor and evaluate the relationship between agricultural practices and their beneficial and harmful environmental effects
- Assess the extent to which agricultural policies respond to the need to promote environmentally friendly agriculture and communicate this to policy-makers and the wider public
- Monitor and evaluate the site-specific environmental contribution of Community programmes to sustainable agriculture
- Map the diversity of agri-ecosystems in the European Union and candidate countries (this has particular relevance in expanding to the EU's trading partners the specificity of the farmed environment in Europe).

Indicators to Survey and Analyse Rural Development
A possible set of headline indicators focused on key issues without complexity has been proposed (nitrogen balance for harmful and beneficial processes, bird species in agricultural land for site-specific state, landscape diversity for global environmental impact, and others).

There are not only international but also national indicators developed for the specific conditions of a country. These indicators can be adopted from international indicator sets. For example, in Finland four landscape indicators have been evaluated and proposed for national use: edge density of field margins (structure), change in openness of agricultural landscape (function), utilisation rate of rural tourism accommodation (value) and building permits for houses and farming purposes in rural areas compared with cities and densely built-up areas (value) (Hietala-Koivu, 2002). After the Millennium Ecosystems Assessment 2005 (MA) it is clear that no single indicator can represent the totality of the various drivers of changes in biodiversity or in ecosystems. Some direct drivers of change have relatively straightforward indicators, such as fertilizer usage, water consumption etc. Indicators for other drivers, including biological invasions, climate change etc. are not as well developed, and data to measure them are not as readily available. Changes in biodiversity and in ecosystems are usually caused by different interacting drivers. Case studies of deforestation and desertification reveal that the most common type of interaction is synergetic. Based on the findings of the sub-global assessments of the MA and recent literature only few examples of causal linkages for ecosystem change can be given. Indicators thus are of limited value for analysing the causes of ecosystem change.

Box 21.2. Indicators for the integration of environmental concerns into the Common Agricultural Policy (CAP) of EU

1. Area under agri-environment support
2. Regional levels of good farming practice
3. Regional levels for environmental targets
4. Area under nature protection
5. Market signals: organic producer price premiums
6. Technology and skills: holder`s training level
7. Area under organic farming
8. Quantities of nitrogen (N) and phosphate (P) fertilisers used
9. Consumption of pesticides
10. Water use intensity
11. Energy use
12. Land use: topological change
13. Land use: cropping/livestock patterns
14. Management
15. Trends: intensification/extensification, specialization
16. Trends: specialisation/diversification
17. Trends: marginalisation
18. Soil surface nutrient balance
19. Methane (CH_4) emissions
20. Pesticide soil contamination
21. Water contamination
22. Groundwater abstraction
23. Soil erosion
24. Resource depletion: land cover change
25. Genetic diversity of species
26. Area of high nature value, grasslands, etc.
27. Production of renewable energy resources
28. Species richness
29. Soil quality
30. Nitrates/pesticides in water
31. Groundwater levels
32. Landscape state
33. Impact on habitats and biodiversity
34. Share of agriculture in emissions, nitrate contamination, water use
35. Impact on landscape diversity

Source: European Commission, 2001

Part E

Policy Instruments and Governance

Authors: Hans Aage, Motaher Hossain, Ingrid Karlsson, Eugene Krasnov, Marja Molchanova, Józef Mosiej, Karin Hilmer Pedersen, Lars Rydén and Isa Zeinalov

Coordinating Author: Lars Rydén

Policy and Policy Instruments

22

Karin Hilmer Pedersen
Aahus University, Aarhus, Denmark
Lars Rydén
Uppsala University, Uppsala, Sweden

Rural Development and Environmental Policies – Old and New

Increasing Role of Rural Development

Rural development plays an increasingly important though complex role in meeting the economic, social and environmental challenges of the 21st century. While farming and forestry remain crucial for the economy in rural communities, increasing attention is paid to sustainable use of natural resources and to alternative sources of income for example tourism. This chapter looks at problems, incentives and institutions affecting policy decisions and choice of policy instruments in relation to rural development and sustainable agriculture and forestry. For illustrative purposes the empirical focus is the Baltic Sea Region occasionally including the USA. The message, however, concerning the development and implementation of sustainable rural development goes beyond the region.

From 19th Century Focus on Production

In the industrial society dominating the last century rural areas were thought of in terms of its economic contribution made by forestry and agricultural production. In Europe and elsewhere the focus was on productivity and efficiency, but throughout modern history the means to achieve these goals were different. On one side of the Baltic Sea countries associated with The European Union (EU) and its Common Agricultural Policy (CAP) increased productivity through direct and production-linked income subsidies to farmers. The consequence was over-production illustrated with 'wine-lakes' and 'butter-mountains'. On the other side countries which belonged to the now cracked Soviet communist system sought productivity through centrally developed and decided production plans. In these cases, however, agriculture did not generate substantial surpluses contributing to general affluence but rather endemic shortages and deficits. Despite these differences the focus on production cherished by both systems had hazardous consequences to the environment causing water pollution, soil degradation, and decreased biodiversity. Adding to theses challenges, the focus on production efficiency made the agricultural sector a main contributor to Climate Changes through emissions of carbon dioxide (CO_2), methane (CH_4) and nitrous oxide (N_2O). Looking only on carbon dioxide emissions, for example, the agricultural sector contributes with 9.2 per cent of CO_2-emissions in the European Union (EEA, 2010).

To 21st Century Focus on Multifunctionality

In the beginning of the 21st century rural areas are conceptualized in quite a different manner. Concerns about agricultural production as such have lost their hegemonic position and a socio-economic dimension was since the 1990s added to EU agricultural policies and the CAP system. This meant that production related subsidies shifted towards other issue areas such as food safety and quality, animal welfare, countryside access, culture and heritage. Multifunctionality also meant that earlier domination of centralized and state-led decision making changed towards bottom-up and local self-governance in a public-private relation (Derkzen and Bock, 2007). However, new ways of thinking agricultural production, rural development and environment in terms of multifunctionality are not un-challenged. These challenges constitute the framework for this chapter on how policy is made, which policy instruments are chosen and how efficient they may be. The description of David Easton's model of the political life (Figure 22.1)will serve to structure the rest of this chapter.

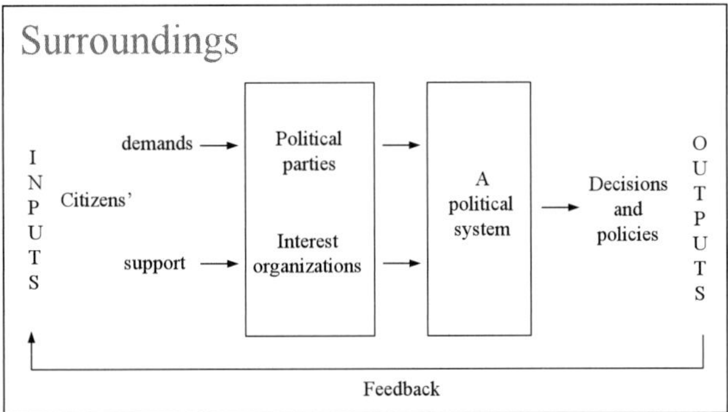

Figure 22.1. A model for studying political life (Easton, 1967).

The Political Life – A Frame for Political Decision Making

The Conditions of Policy-making

Policy is about *making authoritative decisions* on the distribution of wealth and values which are generally valid in society. To paraphrase Abraham Lincoln's famous saying in a democracy this requires government *by* the people (political participation), *of* the people (citizen representation) and *for* the people (governing effectiveness). Following suit David Easton (1967) modelled the political life as an input-output structure in which the political system on the one hand is dependent on input and on the other hand constitutes the locus of decision making forming the systems output. The model then captures the feedback mechanism in which output consequences turns into new input demands and support by citizens meaning that if citizens do not approve of governing effectiveness this will inevitably impact on their demands to and judgements of the political system (Figure 22.1).

As illustrated by the model political decisions and the political life are not performed in a vacuum, but is influenced by *surrounding circumstances and conditions*. Surroundings include for example the global and international context, discourse related to the topic, the general economic situation in a country, physical availability of resources, and technological innovations. These surroundings do not determine the outcome of the policy process, but they constitute the setting in which interests and values are formed and communicated into the political system.

The *input to the political decision system* comes from the citizens. Citizen's demands as well as support go through either political parties or interest organization. In the process media plays an important role in formulating and communicating inputs to the political system. The political system addresses the institutions - constitutions, governments, parliaments and the judiciary - active in deciding about rural policies. The output of political decisions takes the form of policy instruments and their implementation through state and local administration of which advantages and cut-backs will be discussed. The final section of the chapter is dedicated to reflections about how decisions today may feed back to new inputs for the future.

Tragedy of the Commons

G. Hardin characterized the human behaviour with respect to natural resources as the *tragedy of the commons* (Box 22.1). The core of the concept is a collective action problem caused by 'open access for individuals to exploit common resources in their own interests, while bearing but a fraction of the costs of doing so' (Hardin, 1968). 'The tragedy' occurs because individual rationality contradicts securing the collective good. The traditional

BOX 22.1
The Tragedy of the Commons:

The Herder's Game
Imagine a common pasture used by two herders (common land). The maximum capacity of the pasture is 10 cattle. The optimal 'cooperation' strategy would be for each herder to graze five cattle on the pasture, which would give each herder five well-fed cattle at the end of the season, and each would get 10 units of profit. However, one herder may choose a 'defect' strategy and graze more than five cattle on the pasture. This is a rational solution for him, as the additional animal will bring in extra income, while the function of overgrazing the pasture created by the extra animal will be shared with the other herder. Thus, the defection will result in a net gain of + 11, while the other herder may end up with less than before. However, if in the absence of mutual contact both herders choose to defect they may both – in the extreme case – end up with zero outcome as overgrazing will destroy the pasture.

		Herder 1	
		Cooperation	Defection
Herder 2	Cooperation	+ 10/+ 10	6/ + 11
	Defection	+ 11 / 6	0/0

political responses to problems of 'the commons' have turned in different directions arguing for 'more state', 'more privatisation' or 'more deliberation', i.e. intensive inclusion of all stakeholders in the actual distribution of rights, coupled with comprehensive efforts of moral persuasion. We will turn to these differences in the section on policy instruments.

Introducing Sustainable Development in Policy-making

The self-interest dominating ideas behind individual rationality and the *tragedy of the commons* focus on the environment as a resource for economic utilization and thus an input to economic development and growth. This perception of the natural environment changed tremendously since the concept of *sustainable development* was launched by the United Nations *Brundtland Report* in 1987. Before publication of the Brundtland Report, the environmentally negative consequences (externalities) of economic production were either not given any consideration or were believed to be absorbed by nature through diffusion. However, awareness of the environmental hazardousness behind blind focus on production increased due to severely polluted lakes and rivers and hot spots of heavily polluted areas. The concept of *sustainable development* tried to solve the inherent problem between production interests and resource preservation by conceptualising development through three fundamental components: environmental protection, economic growth and social equity. In doing so a key message of the report was to support integration of environmental consideration into any policy decision (World Commission on Environment and Development, 1987: 313):

> *"The ability to choose policy paths that are sustainable requires that the ecological dimensions of policy be considered at the same time as the economic, trade, energy, agricultural, industrial, and other dimensions on the same agendas and in the same national and international institutions."*

While integrating considerations on environmental protection into other policy decisions sought to create a win-win situation solving the conflict between environment and production rationale, the Brundtland Report also pointed out the moral aspect of environmental protection in terms of protecting resources for future generations. Thus, according to the report sustainable development means: *"development which meets the needs of the present without compromising the ability of future generations to meet their own needs"*. Thus sustainable development tries to solve two dilemmas: the one between production and nature and the other between the material well-being of present and future generations.

Judging between the two dilemmas is not easy. Future generations do not by themselves have a voice and countries and regions face different socio-economic realities. Affluent societies where people generally are materially well-off tend according to Ronald Inglehart (1990) to take more value in environmental issues in contrast to less well-off societies where people are more concerned about their subsistence. These differences not only distin-

Table 22.1. Agricultural statistic 2010. Source: World Development Indicators 2012.

	Rural population (% of total population)	Employment in agriculture (% of total workforce)	Agricultural production value added (% of GDP)
The Russian Federation	27	10	4
Estonia	31	4	nn
Latvia	32	9	4
Lithuania	33	9	4
Poland	39	13	4
Germany	26	2	1
Denmark	13	3	1
Sweden	15	2	2
Finland	36	5	3
USA	18	2	1

guish between countries but also between social groups within countries. Table 22.1 reveals the differences in the general well-being as measured by country BNP for the Baltic Sea region and USA as well as economic differences in agricultural workers income. It is seen that the former Soviet-dominated countries are much less off than the Nordic countries and USA while at the same time productivity in the agricultural sector is much lower. That the change in real farmers' income is considerably higher in theses countries reflect their lower starting point.

Environmental Policy is Transboundary

The socio-economic data from the countries bordering the Baltic Sea illustrates different interests when it comes to deciding between a clean environment versus immediate production. Despite differences the countries share an interest in a healthy Baltic Sea, which serves as a resource for fishing and a zone for recreational use. The coastal states are, however, not the only responsible for the Sea's environmental problems. Production further upstream in the Baltic Sea catchment area also contributes to the Baltic Sea environmental situation. But these countries - in the so-called 'hinterland' - may have little direct interest in protecting the Sea. This illustrates the transboundary character of pollution, which makes environmental policy essentially global and demand international cooperation to reach effective solutions. International agreements, however, requires consensus and a compromise between different interests in which the above-mentioned dilemma play a decisive role.

Ecosystem-based Management

The dilemma between production and environment assumes *a priori* a trade-off in which a healthy environment always comes as a cost of production and economic development. This 'truth' has been challenged by among others advocates for an ecosystem-based management approach (Box 22.2). Integrating whole ecosystems, different sectors, human beings and a long-term perspective in the formulation and implementation of environmental policy is an essentially new way of looking at the environment. In contrast to earlier species and sector-oriented policies this development in managerial science may help to overcome the dilemma between production and environmental concerns and pave the way for an environmentally sound economic development. Technological innovation can also contribute to less polluting production methods, as does increased recycling and use of renewable energy resources, both contributing to weaken the trade-off. Thus, science and technology as part of the surroundings in which policy decisions are taken contribute with new knowledge which aims at turning environmental protection into a win-win situation. The surroundings, however, do not determine the outcome of political decisions, but merely serve as preconditions, which may or may not be decisive when weighing between concrete interests.

BOX 22.2
The Ecosystem-based Management Approach

From	To
Individual species	Ecosystems
Small spatial scale	Multiple and integrated scale
Short-term perspective	Long-term perspective
Humans independent of ecosystems	Humans as an integral part of ecosystems
Management isolated from research	Management adapted to research
Sector-orientated management	Integrated sector approach

Source: Olsen et al., 2006.

The Policy-Makers

Citizen's Demand and Support

In democratic societies political decisions reflect the interests of the majority of the citizens through general elections. Consequently the size of the rural population matters. Relatively few people live in the rural areas. This means that as voters this group of people does not count much. On the other hand the agricultural sector does employ a reasonable number of the countries labour force. Event though agricultural production does not count much as percentage on Gross Domestic Product it does count enough to be a considerable economic factor in most countries (see Table 22.1).

Knowledge about prevalent values in society is traced through public opinion surveys. The European Commission has since 1973 commissioned a Europe-wide public opinion poll taking the temperature of European citizens' attitudes. In addition to the regular Eurobarometer which is conducted for a similar sample of question for economy and political institutions every six month, special surveys are made with focus on concrete issues. According to a special survey in 2007 concern for the environment comes next to economy, unemployment, growth and inflation (Eurobarometer 67, 2007). In contrast to the environment in general, global warming is an issue with cause increasing concern among citizens. On average, about 60% of EU citizens regard global warming as a matter to be dealt with at the earliest opportunity and believe that policies aimed at reducing GHG emissions by at least 20% by 2020 should urgently be put in place (Eurobarometer 67, 2007). Interestingly with respect to global warming citizens not only acknowledge its urgency, but also the necessity for international cooperation and especially the need to act at EU level. Citizen's view on environmental issues and global warming are not static, but change over time. In a follow up survey in 2009, 23% hold the view that the risk connected to global warming has been greatly over stated (Eurobarometer 300, 2009).

While the surveys show a general concern about the environment, variation between EU member states should be highlighted. First, in general attitudes differ between the more affluent old EU-15 member states and the less prosperous new EU-12. While only 3% of the population in the new member states hold environment as one of two most important issues, 8% do so in the older member states (Eurobarometer 67, 2007). This does not mean that citizens are not concerned about the environment only that the economy comes first. Second, when it comes to global warming the strongest support for the question of whether the EU should urgently deal with global warming is found in Greece, Cyprus and Sweden, and the lowest in Estonia, Latvia, Lithuania and Poland. While these differences may also reflect economic variations, the Swedish position suggests that they may just as well indicate a reluctance in member states across new and old members to hand over too many decisions to the EU in casus climate policy. Given that economic concerns are more salient among citizens in the new EU member states, they may be more inclined to keep decisions on environment at the domestic level, where they have more control.

Citizens' demands to the political system go through two intermediary factors: political parties that compete directly over their decision-making abilities, and interest organisations that indirectly pursue the interests of their constituents. Note here that political parties and interest organisations (or NGOs) are active on state, regional and local level – as well on supranational level in the case of the European Union.

Table 22.2. Rural population and land use in countries of the Baltic Sea region.

	Rural population			Rural population density	Land area	Land use					
	% of total				1000 sq. km	Arable land		Permanent cropland		Other land	
	1980	2002	1980-2002	2001	2001	1980	2001	1980	2001	1980	2001
Russia	30	27	-0.3	32	16.889		7.3		0.1		92.6
Estonia	30	31	-0.3	62	42		16.0		0.4		83.5
Latvia	32	40	0.6	51	62		29.7		0.5		69.9
Lithuania	39	31	-0.9	37	65		45.2		0.9		53.9
Poland	42	37	-0.2	104	304	48.0	45.9	1.1	1.1	50.9	53.0
Germany	17	12	-1.4	86	349	34.5	33.9	1.4	0.6	64.1	65.6
Denmark	16	15	-0.2	35	42	62.3	54.0	0.3	0.2	37.4	45.8
Sweden	17	17	0.3	55	421	7.2	6.5	0.0	0.0	92.8	93.4
Finland	40	41	.05	97	305	7.8	7.2	0.0	0.0	92.2	92.8

The Political Parties

Concern for a clean environment is not a traditional issue in political parties' profiles. Rather studies place environmental concern as a new post-material policy dimension, which co-exists with the traditional economic based left-right dimension (Inglehart, 1990). These changes in citizen's attitudes influence the constellation between political parties. In the beginning of last century and the early days of party formation, farmers representing rural interests organized political parties dedicated to pursue their interests. However, as demographic changes depicted in Table 22.2 shows the number of farmers as percentage of the population decreases the traditional farmer's parties have to attract other views which paved the way for a focus on environmental and animal welfare issues.

In the early 1980s new protest parties with the focus on environmental issues were formed in fourteen European countries including Finland, Germany and Sweden (Müller-Rommel 2002). The Danish political path was different, which did not mean that the environmental issue was not strong, but rather that the existing parties succeeded to absorb and integrate environmental concerns into their party programmes. While 'green' parties in the beginning played a marginal role in government, they have become increasingly important. Increasing electoral success, as well as specific parliamentary situations where additional mandates were needed to form a majority, has paved the way for Green parties to join coalition governments. The first 'green' party to join a government was the German federal green party *Die Grünen* in 1998 which went in coalition with the Social Democrats (SPD). In contrast, despite the fact that the Swedish *Miljöpartiet de Gröna* was part of the election coalition in 1998, it never entered into government.

In the Baltic States and Central and East European countries today's party formation is of recent history due to 50 years of Soviet-communist rule. In general, political parties were formed in the turbulent period of regime transformation in the early 1990s, but in some cases political parties could re-build on the pre-soviet party organization. The Polish situation is an illustrative case. Although the Soviet rule was defined as a one-Party rule, Polish farmers organized in a pseudo-independent political party. After the regime change the moderate interwar Polish Peasant Party (PSL) was 'reborn'. Adding the suffix 'Renewal' marked its distinction from the Soviet area Party organization, which did not cease to exist. In the process of party organization after 1990, the environment did not play any role, despite the fact the protests against the communist rule originated in environmental concerns (Nørgaard and Pedersen, 1994). This development emphasises that during authoritarian rule expression of environmental concerns could be allowed as long as it did not directly confront the ruling system, while on the other hand expressing environmental concerns served as a channel for more far-reaching critique of the system.

Table 22.3. The importance of group size; a numerical illustration. Source: Source: Pedersen and Svendsen (work in process).

	Citizens (large group)	Producers (small group)
Main policy goal	Environmental protection	Production and market protection
Number	500 millions	100 millions
Individual benefit (Vi)	€ 1	€ 5 millions
Total benefit in clean environment	€ 500 millions	€ 500 millions
Total cost (C)	€ 1 million	€ 1 million
Individual net benefit (Ai = Vi - C)	€ 1 – € 1 million = –€ 999.999	€ 5 millions – € 1 millions= € 4 millions

The architecture of EU has added a second layer to citizens' influence on policy making. At European level environmental interests are organized in the *European Federation of Green Parties*. The influence of this organization is, however, limited as again environmental policies are decided within the context of other policy issues.

The Interest Organisations

Coordinating and articulating demands through non-governmental interest organisations (NGO) serves the aim at influencing the political decision making process policy decisions in different ways. The classical model of interest group politics in democratic political systems is based on the idea of open access to the political system. This open ac-cess enables a plurality of interest groups to pursue their specific interests and thus constitute a system of interest representation based on checks and balances in which no single interest will be able to monopolise the political process (Truman, 1951; Lipset, 1959). However, citizens do not have equal incentives to direct their demands and support for the political system through interest organisations.

The question is why some interests are better or more influential than others. The 'logic of collective action' argues that small and privileged groups are better at organising and acting in support of their private interests, which is not the case with large groups. According to Olsen (1965), this 'logic of collective action' comes about because there are high incentives to join a group that seeks benefits only for the members of the group (private and concentrated interests), while there are low incentives to join a group that seeks benefits for all in a society (public and diversified interests). When public interests are at stake it is individually rational to 'free ride' because all will reap the benefit of public policy without sharing the burden of interest representation. This 'logic' is illustrated in table 22.3. If the total benefit for a clean environment equalized € 500 millions and the total costs equals € 1 million, the individual benefit for small group producers is so much higher than the individual benefit for large group citizens. Thus, following an individual rational calculation it pays off for small group producers to engage in lobbying activities supporting their interests, while this is not the case for the individual citizen. Consequently, environmental groups do not easily attract large numbers of members and their economic capacity to influence the policy process is accordingly comparatively weaker. The result of this unbalanced influence is that the interests of small and privileged groups will often triumph over the common interest, despite the latter having numerical superiority (Olson, 1965, pp. 127-128).

Although participation in environmental interest groups from a rational point of view is 'irrational', environmental groups have played, and continue to play, an important role as channel for environmental activists and a source of information for political decision-makers and administrators. Sometimes they serve as partners in public reconstruction and development programmes which on occasions may change them from being genuinely participatory and having a grassroot's character to being quasi-public institutions.

The actual political power of environmental groups is difficult to measure because of the grassroot's character, voluntary commitments and often with no membership records. Moreover, environmental groups have a tendency to pop up like mushrooms when media accentuates an environmental problem only to disappear when the news effect fades out. With new views on environment, for example within the mentioned eco-management approach, environmental groups are encouraged to increase cooperation across boarders. The Baltic Sea NGO Forum and the Baltic Sea Foundation for Environmental and Regional Development are cases in point coordinating activities and exchanging experiences. Launched in 2005 the Baltic Sea Foundation for Environmental and Regional Development takes a holistic view of the environment, civil society and development and invites environmental groups from all countries in the Baltic Sea Region to join in activities for the benefit of the whole region (Baltic Sea Foundation, 2012).

While interest representation is a legitimate element in a democratic political system, there is a distinction between legitimate lobbying, which strives to pursue the specific interests of the organisation's members, and illegitimate attempts to influence public decisions and practices through corruption. Corruption circumvents democratic decisions towards private interest and at the expense of the public interest. According to the non-governmental watch dog, Transparency International (TI) the commonality of corruption differs between countries. On a scale from 1 to 10 where 10 is 'corruption free' the countries around the Baltic Sea score between 9.4 (Finland, Denmark) and 2.4 (Russian Federation) (see Table 22.4). The Transparency International index relies on different surveys capturing how people perceive corruption to be common. Perception-data does not necessarily give a picture of the actual level of corruption. Due to media stories about corruption scandals perception-data tends to overestimate its' commonality. At the same time no country is 100 percent corruption free and when it comes to environmental policies vested private interests in either effecting future policy decisions or circumventing existing policies may tempt otherwise un-corrupt people into illegitimate deals.

Table 22.4. Perceived corruption in countries of the Baltic Sea Region, 10 indicates no corruption and 1 a high level of corruption. (Source: http://cpi.transparency.org/cpi2011/results/).

	Transparency International Corruption Perception Index, 2011
Belarus	2.4
Czech Republic	4.4
Denmark	9.4
Estonia	6.4
Finland	9.4
Germany	8.0
Latvia	4.2
Lithuania	4.8
Poland	5.5
Russian Federation	2.4
Slovak Republic	4.0
Sweden	9.3
Ukraine	2.3
EU average	6.0
USA	7.1

Science and Media

Science has a key role in the political process. Especially from the 1960s the number of scientific discoveries on how activities in the society impact on the environment and ecosystems has formed a strong base for political decisions. A number of individual chemical substances have been outlawed. The pivotal role of science in policy is well illustrated by the climate change debate where policies entirely rely on results from the research community.

Of course not all research results are welcome by those who become affected, and conflicts between business interests and research have become common. Lately several instances have gone so far that business has accused science to have a self interests in the results of the research. In the United States the so-called 'climate deniers' have a big role in policy making, especially in the congress. This anti-science lobby builds on a tradition from the time when the adverse effects of tobacco smoking were denied by tobacco companies. We did so far see only limited such trends in Europe and the EU climate policy remains one of the strongest in the world.

Likewise media has a pivotal role in the political process in most societies. The media have even been called the "fourth power of the state," then meaning that the first power is the government, the second the legislature and the third the judiciary. No politicians can afford to neglect the media in an elective democracy since he or she depends on it to be re-elected. Good journalists are able to highlight environmental issues very efficiently. In particular this has been efficient in cases when individuals or even entire cities have been badly damaged by bad environmental performance, such as emissions from factories or poisoning of water. Many similar stories can be told about poisoned fish, destroyed forests, threatened nature reserves, where media both informed and influenced the citizens, politicians as well as authorities to act.

In the best case media works as a continuing education forum where each and everyone may learn about environmental changes and is able to react accordingly. This key role of newspapers, radio and TV has become less critical in these days as Internet allows very many more actors to be heard and address the general society. At the same time cheap, open access and general availability of the Internet empowers the citizens' group vis-à-vis the small producer groups.

The Political System

Constitutions

The constitution defines the character of a political system at the most general level. The constitution states the formative institutional rules that regulate power and expertise, determining for example who is eligible to make decisions, what actions are allowed or constrained, what procedures must be followed, the kind of information that must or must not be provided (Ostrom, 1990: 51). Defining the fundamental structure of the society and thereby setting limits for political decision-making, constitutions can only be changed through specific procedures for example by demanding an oversized majority, and/or that a new elections must be held between two separate voting for constitutional amendments. This requirement on the one hand demands a prolonged process, and on the other hand that amendments are approved by two separately elected parliamentary secessions.

Countries around the Baltic Sea today all have democratic constitutions describing the division of power between the legislature, the political executive (governments) and the judiciary. Within the formal institutions actors are relatively free to make decisions about what is valued and how resources are distributed between citizens and citizen groups. This also includes decisions about which environmental policies a country will follow. However, some constitutions include a clean environment as a 'right' for their citizens. Making the environment a constitutional right sets restriction on which decisions is constitutionally legitimate, and in cases where legitimacy of a legal act is doubtful citizens may ask the High Court or the Constitutional Court to censure it. For example the Polish Constitution from 1997 enhances environmental protection in two ways. First, the Constitution makes the protection of the natural environment a legitimate cause to limit individual freedoms and rights (article 31) and second, it obliges public authorities to protect the environment (article 74) (see Table 22.5). Including environmental protec-

Table 22.5. A healthy environment as a Constitutional guaranty. (Authors' emphasis. The Polish Constitution, 2nd of April 1997. At. http://www.sejm.gov.pl/prawo/konst/angielski/kon1.htm accessed 14th August 2012).

Article 31	
1.	Freedom of the person shall receive legal protection.
2.	…
3.	Any limitation upon the exercise of constitutional freedoms and rights may be imposed only by statute, and only when necessary in a democratic state for the protection of its security or public order, or to protect the natural environment, health or public morals, or the freedoms and rights of other persons. Such limitations shall not violate the essence of freedoms and rights.
Article 74	
1.	Public authorities shall pursue policies ensuring the ecological security of current and future generations.
2.	Protection of the environment shall be the duty of public authorities.
3.	Everyone shall have the right to be informed of the quality of the environment and its protection.
4.	Public authorities shall support the activities of citizens to protect and improve the quality of the environment.

tion into constitutional rights is a recent phenomenon. In the Polish case constitutional amendments after the regime shift made the inclusion relatively easy because constitutional amendments were in any case to be made.

Rule of Law

To have a ood government work i practice requires that rule-of -law is respected in the country. This exists when a proper power distribution exists, and a law which guarantees the basic rights and institutions to be respected. Presently the three Baltic States have advanced extremely well to establish states based on rule-of-law. In the recently publish Word Justice Project Estonia and Poland are the best among their group of Central and Eastern European States (World Justice Project Index 2011). In particular Estonia has successfully reduced corruption to a low level, which is much less so for example for Latvia.

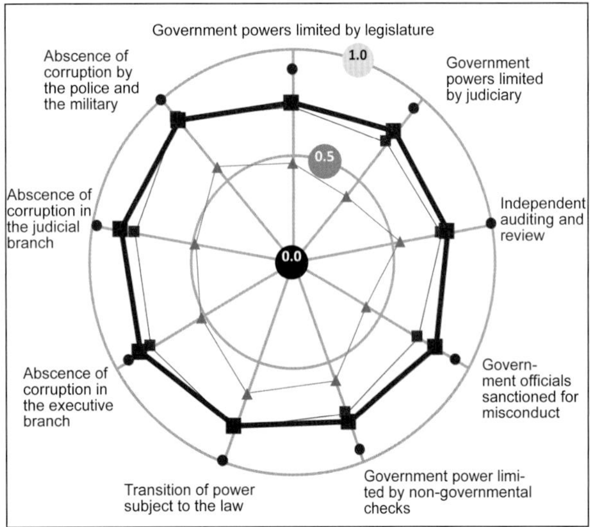

Figure 22.2. The World Justice Project (WJP) 2011 Index reports from 66 countries in the world, including several in the BSR, using nine dimensions of the Rule of Law, monitored by more than 50 different parameters. Here 9 parameters used to measure *Accountable Government* in Estonia are shown as an example. 1.0 means fully implemented and 0 absence. The thick blue line connects vaues for Estoina, the thin green line average values for 12 CEE and CA states, and the thin red line values for countries in the same income group. Estonia's values are 0.73 to 0.84, makes it the best country in its group of 12 in CEE and Central Asia. The corruption value is 0.86 making Estonia the most successful of the former Soviet Republics to reduce corruption. Source: http://worldjusticeproject.org/sites/default/files/WJP_Rule_of_Law_Index_2011_Report.pdf

Table 22.6. Government international commitments – two key global conventions as international indicators.

Ratification year/ country	Biological Diversity	The Kyoto Protocol
The Russian Federation	1995	2004
Estonia	1994	2002
Latvia	1996	2002
Lithuania	1996	2003
Poland	1996	2002
Germany	1994	2002
Denmark	1994	2002
Sweden	1994	2002
Finland	1994	2002
USA	...	...

The Convention on Biological Diversity (signed at the Earth Summit in Rio de Janeiro, 1992) promotes conservation of biodiversity among nations through scientific and technological cooperation, access to financial and genetic resources, and transfer of ecologically sound technologies.

The Kyoto Protocol (adopted at the third conference of the parties to the United Nations Framework Convention on Climate Change, Kyoto, Japan, 1997)

BOX 22.3
International Principles Guiding Environmental Policies

The *polluter-pays-principle* is designed to pass on the costs of environmental protection measures to the 'producers' of products. In practice, the principle is often formulated as a requirement that the polluter achieve a certain target level of emissions.

The *precautionary principle* is based on the notion 'if in doubt, don't do it'. This means that preventive measures must be taken if there is reason to assume that an action may create hazards to human health or harm living resources and ecosystems even though there may be no conclusive evidence of a causal relationship between the activity and its alleged effects.

The principles of *Best Environmental Practice* and *Best Available Technology* encourage diffusion of knowledge about how human activities and production can be maintained simultaneously with preventing and eliminating pollution effects.

The *proportionality principle* can be seen as a safeguard, especially of economic interests, as it indicates that the costs and efforts engendered by environmental protection measures should be proportional to the gains.

In the other end of the scale we find the Russian Federation and Ukraine where corruption is among the worst in the world, not to mention Belarus where democracy from the transition years have been completely eradicated by the present regime (See also Table 22.4). These three countries are among the most important agricultural states in Europe.

International Obligations

When the national constitutions are silent about rights to a healthy natural environment, participating in international organizations and through international agreements, countries may be just as obliged politically to make environmentally sound policies. Global environmental obligations are placed within the framework of the United Nations. Counted from the 1960s about 200 global conventions towards a clean environment have been issued. With respect to rural policies most relevant are the three Rio conventions, developed at the UNCED conference in Rio de Janeiro in 1992 – The Climate Convention, the Convention to protect Biological Diversity and the Convention to Combat Desertification and Land Degradation. All countries in the Baltic Sea region have signed these conventions (Table 22.6). The legal obligations of international conventions are relatively weak. The moral and political commitments from individual states are therefore imperative for environmental protection. At a general level, however, the four principles described in Box 22.3 constitute a shared baseline which guides national policy decisions.

In contrast to international conventions, supranational governments as the European Union and the United States federal government impose much stronger obligations on state or national government. Although the European Union was formed as trade cooperation, the integration process has encapsulated almost every aspect of political decisions. While the history of EU agricultural policies goes back to the 1960s, environmental protection came on the European Union agenda in the early 1980s and has expanded in terms of areas regulated ever since.

The value of EU policies depends on efficient implementation by every member state. In practice, however, harmonization is not always the outcome. EU legal framework comes as *regulations*, having direct legal force upon member states, or *directives*, which need to be transformed into national law. Directives may therefore in principle be implemented differently by member states, but the EU Commission censures both the timeliness of transformation and the content of national rules. In both cases insufficient or lenient transformation can be sanctioned by the European Court of Justice. Despite this process harmonization of EU regulations is questioned by political scientists (for example Faulkner et. al. 2004; Dimitrova 2010).

Policy Output

Restoring or Securing

Environmental policies fall between policies aimed at restoring harmed natural environment and policies aimed at securing the environment from future degradation. While most debate focuses on the latter, especially when it comes to choices between different policy instruments which essentially aim at managing individual behaviour in a proactive way, it suffices to dwell a moment at reactive policies. It makes a huge difference whether the policy is *re-active*, aimed at cleaning up after former generations, or whether it is *pro-active*, trying to regulate human activities in order to prevent future pollution.

Reactive policies address both restoration and remediation. While restoration not always comes as an indisputable good (see Box 22.4), remediation does. Remediation faces a technical problem, *how* to clean up contaminated areas without causing additional harm to the environment, and who should pay the bill. Remediation has been especially important in former communist countries. Although the communist system did have strict environmental legislation, deviation from rule was the norm rather than the exception. Cleaning up after polluting military installations left by the Red Army in the early 1990s in the Baltic States and Eastern Europe is a case in point. Remediation policies raise the question of *who* is going to pay. In many cases it is not possible to find a person, company or organisation to hold responsible, or those responsible may either not be willing or able to cover the expenses. Consequently, cleaning up policies is most often paid for by the state and thus, the taxpayers.

Proactive policies are what most peopled associate when referring to environmental policy. Proactive poli-

Box 22.4
Restoration policies – the Case of Lake Tang, Denmark

In 1921 a hydroelectric plant was constructed at Tange, a small village in the middle of Denmark next to the Gudenaa River. For the hydroelectric plant to work a barrier was build across the river, separating it into an upper and lower part and establishing the Tange water reservoir. Besides serving as a water reservoir for the plant, a quite beautiful nature resort was formed with a big lake, leisure activities, bird's habitats etc. However, at the same time natural flora and fauna were prevented from moving along the river and especially the Gudenaa salmon were threatened. Even though a fish ladder was constructed the Gudenaa salmon disappeared 1930 and other species have been drastically reduced.

During 2000-2002 a new, small population of salmon was discovered. This happened almost simultaneously as the Tange hydroelectric plant's licence to utilise the water from the Gudenaa River expired. This created the momentum for a *nature restoration policy* debate arguing that the original river flow should be re-established, thus optimising the path of salmon to the upper reaches of the river. This would imply dismantling of the plant and the disappearance of the Lake. Immediately a counter organization to the preservation of Lake Tange was formed.

There is not optimal solution to the dilemma between restoring and conserving. In the Case of Lake Tange the solution has so far been to install new and improved alternative water courses for the salmon to bypass the hydroelectric power plant which, however, is a fairly costly solution.

cies are aimed at protecting the environment from possible damage caused by human production and/or exploitation of natural resources. Thus, at the core of proactive policies lays the question *how* to manipulate individual behaviour so it does not harm the environment. In this sense, policy instruments are tools used by the policymakers to alter society. This can be done by influencing the individual incentives personal obligations, willingness or commitment (see Box 22.5). Thus, the choice of policy instrument is not apolitical but raises almost as many, or perhaps even more, conflicting interests than the political decision itself.

Policy instruments

Three Kinds of Instruments to Conduct Policies

In technical terms, policy instruments are a set of techniques used by the executive power of a country to implement its policies (the following is mostly based on Andersson et. al., 2000). Public policy instruments are generally divided into three classes:

- regulations,
- economic means, and
- information/moral suasion.

Regulations

Regulation (also called command-and-control instruments) comprises a range of means such as standards, bans, permits, zoning use restrictions, etc. Direct regulations are institutional measures aimed at directly influencing the environmental performance of polluters by regulating processes or products used, by abandoning or limiting the discharge of certain pollutants, and/or by restricting activities to certain times, areas, etc. Within countries belonging to the OECD, regulation has traditionally been the most commonly used policy instrument in environmental protection.

Choosing the legislative approach raises the problem of control. It is one thing to formulate a legal text telling people how they should behave. It is a different thing to make sure that people are actually doing so. This is especially a problem in the agricultural and forestry sector because farmers normally have more knowledge about their behaviour that the controllers ever can obtain. The increasing number of people working in smaller production units intensifies the problem of control. The problem is even more severe in Russia, the Baltic States and Poland, which struggle with a substantial informal economy that by nature is hard to control.

Economic Means

Changing the economic situation and thus making environmental behaviour rational has a positive and a negative outcome. It can be achieved either through economic support or by taxation. New measures such as environmental accounting add natural resources and pollutants to the assets and liabilities traditionally measured in standard accounts at national or local level or at the level of

> **BOX 22.5**
> **Policy Instruments:**
> ***Public Regulation Based on Should, Would and Could***
>
> *'Should'* reflects a traditional 'hard law' legislative approach in which environmentally sound behaviour is mandatory and backed up by control and even punishment in the case of non-compliance.
>
> *'Would'* reflects an economic approach. Regulations are designed to make environmentally sound behaviour economically rational, thus making the individual 'want' to act in accordance with environmental concerns.
>
> *'Could'* reflects a 'soft law' self-governing approach in which moral arguments and knowledge are used to persuade individuals to change their behaviour.

individual firms or development projects. The economic instruments include:

- charges and taxes (effluent charges, product charges, tax differentiation),
- subsidies,
- deposit-refund systems,
- market creation (emissions trading, liability), and
- financial enforcement incentives (non-compliance fines, performance bonds).

Economic policy instruments involve either the handing out or the taking away of material resources. In other words, economic instruments make it cheaper or more expensive to pursue certain actions. Charges and taxations have a long history to regulate agricultural production especially related to the use of nutrients. Acknowledging the theoretical strength of emission trading schemes to decrease CO_2 emission, ideas to include agriculture into emission trading scheme may constitute a new way simultaneously to minimise the impact of agriculture on climate change and serve as an independent income for rural areas (Pedersen and Svendsen, 2011).

Information and Moral Suasion

The third approach, information and moral suasion, attempts to change an agent's behaviour on a voluntary basis. This could be accomplished via education, transfer of knowledge, training, persuasion, recommendation, and negotiation. One important instrument in this category is voluntary agreements between governmental agencies and private enterprises. A shift towards prevention and sustainability in environmental policies may require governments to use instruments such as negotiation with stakeholders and joint agreement and action plans between sector ministries (OECD 1994). Voluntary agreements are therefore likely to gain importance in the future. The efficiency of voluntary agreements depends on private parties' capacity to self-regulate and their moral commitment. However, the fact the private parties may face a less favourable regulation if they do not change behaviour works as a constraining element.

Evaluation of Policy Instruments

Policy Instruments are evaluated in terms of effectiveness, efficiency, cost-effectiveness, and equity. Effectiveness concerns the extent to which a measure, such as an investment, succeeds in reducing environmental impacts in relation to the set policy targets. Efficiency has to do with the extent to which the costs of a policy are justified in terms of its effects and if it maximizes the effects minus the costs (Semeniene and Zylicz, 1997). A cost-effective policy seeks the least costly method of attaining a specific environmental quality goal. Equity relates to the balance between costs and benefits across the parties concerned. Hence, it has to do with burden-sharing and fairness.

It is difficult (but not impossible) to design policies that combine the notions of effectiveness, efficiency, and equity. As Weale (1992) aptly observes, "no country ... has discovered how to combine technical effectiveness with political responsiveness and economic efficiency. The solution to that problem still awaits discovery." Despite the judgement between different policy instruments is indefinite, a choice has to be made and each type of policy instrument has its strengths and weaknesses.

A major advantage of regulations is that they are most suited to effectively prevent hazards and irreversible effects. Furthermore, regulations frequently provide polluters with incentives to develop technology. Provided that there is effective enforcement, these instruments are able to achieve the desired environmental goals. The point is that enforcement is often problematic, because of the great number of controls, administrative requirements, staff, legal procedures in case of non-compliance, and so on. A second drawback is that command-and-control instruments tend to become weakened by bargaining and negotiation between representatives of the polluters and the environmental authorities. Thirdly, regulations are expensive for society in that they are often not efficient in economic terms.

Economic instruments, such as environmental taxes and charges, minimize total abatement costs in that they constitute a permanent incentive to reduce pollution. Furthermore, they provide a source of revenue. However, a number of problems and uncertainties arise in connection with the use of these instruments. First of all, the rate of charges and taxes are not always set at a level that assures effectiveness in environmental terms. Secondly, charges and taxes may be inappropriate for controlling toxic and hazardous substances if the time lag is too long before use of the substances is curtailed. The best way to control these substances is by means of direct regulations and bans. Thirdly, there are distributive implications, which must be taken into consideration when economic instruments are used. For instance, energy taxes may have negative effects on poorer households.

Voluntary agreements also have their pros and cons. On the one hand they offer flexibility and transparency. On the other hand, control by environmental authorities over actual implementation is minimal.

Policy Instruments Come in Packages

It should be noted that in real life policy instruments tend to come in packages. For example, regulations are almost always followed by some kind of information. Moreover, the application of policy instruments tends to require some kind of organisational arrangements, such as authorities, legal bodies, etc. The existing organisation partly determines what is possible to do.

The choice of policy instruments is also connected to an "administrative culture" that is quite different if the command and control or information and suasion dominate. What we see is that the shift towards prevention approaches and sustainability requires that governments use instruments such as negotiation with stakeholders and joint agreements and action plans to a much larger extent than traditionally, both within the governmental offices, that is, between sector ministries, and between authorities and other stakeholders in society. This is even more apparent on the local level, where often the municipalities are not economically strong enough to implement a policy and thus need to agree with other actors, especially the business sector, to achieve practical results.

Implementing Policies

Choice of Implementing Agencies

European and region rural development programmes are committed to subsidiarity and the partnership model is a key aspect of area-based development. Subsidiarity refers to the starting point for development projects resting with the people concerned at the local level, with shared decision making and responsibility. Even though the responsibility and participation are placed at the level of ordinary people, rural development programmes are mostly externally designed. Thus projects based on the partnership model do not, as one could expect from the name, emerge from the grassroots. Rather they usually include a mixture of elected representatives, the private sector and NGOs. In this way the partnership model facilitates inclusion of different local stakeholders.

Management of natural resources has traditionally been organised by economic sectors such as fisheries, mineral exploitation or agriculture. This approach has resulted in extensive conflicts among users and it is becoming increasingly evident that the approach is inadequate in meeting the need for sustaining the goods and services that flow from healthy ecosystems.

The Ministerial Level

The task to execute and implement the policies decided by the parliament is given to the responsible minister and his or her ministry. At first environmental matters were distributed to ministries of agriculture, industry, etc., and it was not until the 1980s that the environment was given its own portfolio, a special minister.

Each ministry has a number of agencies or institutions to carry out the policies agreed on. Agencies of agriculture, forestry and fishery are often very old, sometimes hundreds of years. However environmental protection agencies, the EPA, were mostly formed in the aftermath of the UN Stockholm Environmental Conference in 1972.

In Germany, the Federal Ministry for the Environment, Nature Conservation and Nuclear Safety was set up in 1986. It has the general responsibility for the elaboration and coordination for environmental policy. The Ministry is supported by its agencies the Federal Environmental Agency, the Federal Research Centre for Nature Protection and the Federal Office for Radiological Protection. In Poland, the Ministry of Territorial Management and Environmental Protection was established as early as 1972. This ministry was reorganized several times in the 1970s and 1980s and in 1989 it became the Ministry for Environmental Protection, Natural Resources and Forestry. Presently it is called the Ministry of Environment.

The importance of EPAs has increased quickly the last years, and they have often got a wider agenda including protection of natural resources. The need to balance a production policy against a protection policy is thus present in the very core of the implementation of policy. The EPAs often have national responsibility for monitoring and follow-up activities regarding the environment in the county, and has its own research budget, and the EPA is often responsible for large restoration projects, for example in Sweden the liming of surface waters.

Regional and Local Level

The conditions and the prerequisites for local and regional authorities to formulate and implement policy vary greatly between the countries in the Baltic Sea region.

The Nordic countries have a long tradition of local self-government. Municipalities and counties are financially strong and they are responsible for environmental infrastructure, such as sewage treatment plants, district heating and waste management. Municipalities in the Nordic countries are responsible for environmental issues on local level, while counties are solely responsible for regional environmental issues.

In Germany the principle of local self- government for towns and villages is written into the constitution, but the system differs from the Nordic countries in that Germany is a federal country with strong States or Länder. The Central and Eastern European states around the Baltic Sea more recently started to implement local and regional self-government. In most of these countries the municipal entities are too small to generate sufficient revenue to perform all tasks and to keep a broad base of competence. However in the whole region local and regional authorities are typically undergoing administrative reforms to become larger and stronger and having more responsibilities.

In all countries local authorities have a planning monopoly which obviously is crucial for development policies. Another factor is that the local level works close to citizens and close to the problems and needs within their territory. However rural municipalities in most countries are smaller and weaker than cities; this makes local rural development policies less forceful.

The local level is typically responsible for the monitoring and control of environmental policies. In the Nordic countries this is made by municipally run inspectorates and thus by the municipality. In the East the typical agent is a local/regional office of a national inspectorate, and then the local level is not involved. It is perhaps good for safeguarding national equity but not for fostering local responsibly. Critical issues include national parks and protected areas, biological diversity, chemical pollution, waste management and water safety.

Feedback - From Policy Outcome to New Demands

Nature protection and environmental policy have significantly reoriented during the last century. New environmental problems especially the risk of climate change and the following need to adapt to extreme weather situations have dramatically changed our understanding of nature and of human impact on natural processes. However, the road from production concerns to care for clean and healthy environment has not been straightforward nor have the inherent dilemmas between interests disappeared. In this context rural development takes it own place split between need for an economic sustainable future and healthy environment. These concerns may not contradict each other. Both should be taken into consideration. The request for democracy to rule not only by and of the people but also for the people is imperative for good governance today as is has been before. In this process increased inclusion and citizen participation with a view to environment will be the way to go.

Policy of Rural Development in Poland

23

CASE STUDY
Poland

Józef Mosiej
Warsaw University of Life Sciences – SSGW, Warsaw, Poland

The Policy Conditions

Development of Rural Areas in Poland

Of the total area of Poland (312,685 km^2) 168,000 km^2 (54%) are used for agriculture and a further 89,000 km^2 (28.5%) are covered with forest. The total population is 38.15 million inhabitants, of which the working population represents 13.5 million persons, 16.9% of whom are employed in the agriculture, hunting and forestry sectors. The rural population represents 38.2% of the total (Poland Central Statistical Office, 2007). With regard to these data, it is clear why rural development is an important aspect of the development of the country.

Major problems regarding rural development include

- excessive employment in agriculture,
- fragmented farm structure,
- poor education,
- poor access to finance services,
- insufficiently competitive processing sector and
- underdeveloped rural infrastructure.

Since 1989, that is after the shift in political system, Polish rural policy and thus rural development has overcome many challenges, and made several main changes. These include price liberalisation, opening up the national economy, removal of state subsidies for agricultural food products, establishments of major institutions responsible for government agricultural policy and, finally, the adjustments of policy needed to join the EU in 2004.

Economic Development of Polish Agriculture

Agriculture in Poland is one of the most important sectors from an economic perspective and its importance is greater in Poland than in other countries in the EU. It has an influence not only on the social and economic situation of the rural population, but also on the natural environment, structure of landscape and biodiversity. However, the overall effect of agriculture on macroeconomic indicators is relatively small. In 2004 the share of agriculture in GDP was around 4.5% (Ministry of Agriculture and Rural Development, 2006b), while the total GDP per capita in the country was PLZ 24,153 (about 5,000 Euro).

The productivity in agriculture is thus low, and is only 14 % of EU-25 average (Eurostat, 2007). This low productivity is the result of

- fragmentation of farms,
- unfavourable agricultural systems,
- low economic capacity of agricultural holdings,
- excess labour in agriculture and
- insufficient equipment on agricultural holdings, e.g. modern machines and facilities.

Figure 23.1. Old combine harvester on the Lubartow Plateau, to the north of Lublin in Poland. Photo: Trevor Butcher.

At present, with the financial support of the EU, the transformation of rural areas is underway. The EU is co-funding investments in agriculture and the environment and the implementation of comprehensive agri-environmental programmes, including subsidies for farmers who implement environmentally-friendly methods of production. The aim of these instruments is to stimulate multifunctional development of rural areas and modernise agriculture. However, the efficiency of implementation and consequently the capability to absorb the transfer of huge EU funding heavily depends on effective functioning of Polish institutions and administrations and the formulation of wise and deliberate policies. These policies should be supported with scientific evidence and knowledge (Motyka, 2007).

Economic Policy Tools, Subsidies and Taxes

In general, development of agriculture and rural areas in Poland is currently working in three directions:

1. Price support and marked stabilisation.
2. Subsidies for agricultural production and interest on intervention credits.
3. Structural policy for rural areas and agriculture.

Subsidies have been designated for soil protection, plant protection, biological improvement, and organic farming. Subsidised credit is available for purchase of agricultural land, management of agricultural holdings by young farmers, services to agriculture, fisheries, the agri-food sector and processing industry, restoration of holdings affected by natural disasters, investments in agriculture, food processing and creation of new jobs outside agriculture.

Structural changes in agriculture and rural development are specified by macroeconomic policies aimed at economic growth, rising employment rates, education, reduction of poverty and maintenance of production potential and production volumes. These policies are based on equal development opportunities for all regions, as well as a multifunctional rural development. A crucial issue has been to keep up policies, which support natural resource utilisation and environmental protection.

Results of Agricultural Polices

Protection of the Waterscape

There are two competing aspects of agricultural influence on the natural environment. The positive aspect is that long-lasting agriculture shapes the mosaic and diverse landscape, as well as guaranteeing good conditions for a diversity of plants and animals. The negative aspect is that agriculture degrades the environment to some extent through excessive and irrational fertilisation, non-adjusted agricultural techniques and non-compliance with good agricultural practices.

The use of nitrogen (N) in Poland remains at around 30 kg/ha, which according to the Code of Good Agricultural Practice is satisfactory in comparison with the average N usage in Western European countries, which is 55 kg/ha. This low level of N application in Poland is caused by low usage of mineral fertilisers. However, natural fertilisers (manure) can pose a danger to water quality and must be carefully stored and applied in such a way that water resources are protected from contamination.

Effects on Biodiversity

The rural landscape in Poland is fascinating with its biodiversity. It is believed that this landscape is the best preserved in the EU on account of favourable natural conditions and unique anthropogenic influences such as uneven industrialisation and urbanisation, traditional ex-

Figure 23.2. Countryside fields near the village of Barniewice in northern Poland. Photo: Andrzej Otrebski.

tensive farming still being maintained in large areas and the existence of large old woods. The Polish landscape is characterised by a diversity of habitats with mosaic biological structure. There are about 365 different types of plant assemblages and about 45 types of plant habitats used as meadows and pastures are situated on agricultural land. Some agricultural land neighbouring Nature 2000 programmes needs particular care.

Traditional production methods and spatial development patterns maintained to the present, create an original cultural landscape with peculiar rural architecture – complexes of traditional wooden houses, churches, chapels and communities, water-mills and barns. Preservation of these buildings will contribute to the image of past and present Polish agriculture at local and regional level.

Effects on the Environment

There are some unfavourable circumstances that can endanger a good rural environment. Some of them have their origins in the past, for example cultivation of poor soils and soils susceptible to erosion, inappropriate water management in agricultural catchments, lack of education with regard to agricultural practices, lack of adequate agricultural equipment and point-source heavy metal pollution of the soil.

In recent decades there has been a marked decrease in populations of birds in farmland areas. It seems that the biggest threats are abandoning habitats that are of marginal importance for agriculture, simplification of landscape structure and excessive intensification of agricultural production. New threats have been recognised recently that are related to the failure of Good Agricultural Practice that farmers need to follow in order to fulfil agri-environmental requirements (Ministry of Agriculture and Rural Development, 2005).

These dangers relate to (Ministry of Agriculture and Rural Development, 2006a):

- changes in the traditional system of plant cultivation and animal breeding, resulting in intensified agricultural production.
- failure to cultivate grasslands, leading to the degradation and overgrowth of land, which in turn causes the disappearance of rare birds and plants.
- delay in the utilisation of environmentally friendly agricultural production technology.

Russian Land Use
Environmental Legislation

24

CASE STUDY
Russia

Eugene Krasnov, Marja Molchanova
and Isa Zeinalov
Immanuel Kant Baltic Federal University, Kaliningrad, Russia

The Land Code of the Russian Federation

Principles for the Use of Land

The basic principles of rational land use in the Russian Federation are stated in the Land Code and other legal acts of the Federation (see Table 24.1). These principles provide for the following:

- Prioritisation of land protection as the most important component of environmental and production facilities in agriculture and forestry before the land is used as immovable estate.
- Prioritisation of human life and health protection.
- Prioritisation of preserving the most valuable lands and lands of specially protected territories.
- Land mapping into categories in accordance with its target purpose.
- Fee-paying basis for land use.
- Identification of the future use of land parcels and objects connected with them.

Agricultural Land

According to article 77 of the Land Code agricultural lands are lands outside the limits of settlements providing for the various needs of agriculture.

Arable lands include tilled land, hayfields, pastures, land under orchards, vineyards and other perennial plantations. Arable land makes up the most valuable part of agricultural land, and has a high level of protection as expressed in article 79 of the Land Code.

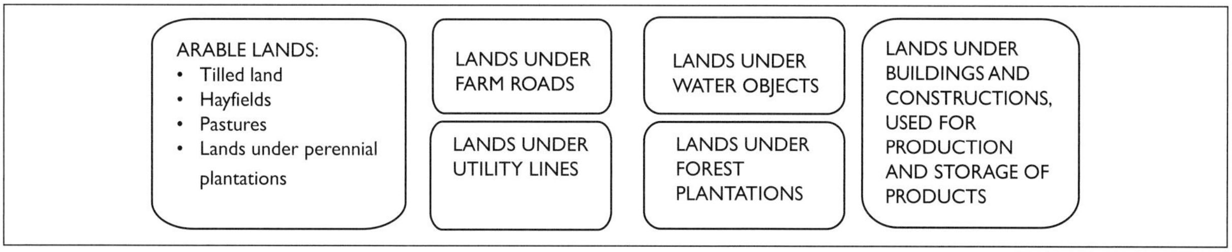

Figure 24.1. Composition of agricultural lands.

Table 24.1. Laws regulating land use in Russia.

Nº	Legal document	Year of enactment	Purposes
1	Law of the Russian Federation on Land Charge	1991	Establishes the methods of payment for land and the order of payments for different categories of land users, based on the target purpose of the land.
2	Law of the Russian Federation on Land Reclamation	1996	Land improvement.
3	Law of the Russian Federation on Government Regulation of Agricultural Land Fertility.	1998	Legal aspect of ensuring the fertility of agricultural lands.
4	Law of the Russian Federation on the State Land Cadastre	2000	Regulates relations arising in the course of activities in maintaining the state land cadastre. Establishes obligatory cadastral land inventory and open access to data contained in the land cadastre. Determines the order of making entries in the land cadastre and composition of the documents.
5	Land Code of the Russian Federation	2001	Basic principles, regulating relations in Russia.
6	Law of the Russian Federation on Land Planning	2001	Establishes legal foundation of land planning with the purpose of rational use of lands and their protection, creation of enabling environment and natural landscape improvement.
7	Law of the Russian Federation on Environment Protection	2002	Legal foundation of environment protection.
8	Law of the Russian Federation on Transfer of Agricultural Lands	2002	Regulation of transactions with land (sale and purchase).
9	Law of the Russian Federation on Peasant (Farm) Holding	2003	System of standards, connected with use and protection of lands in peasant (farm) management.

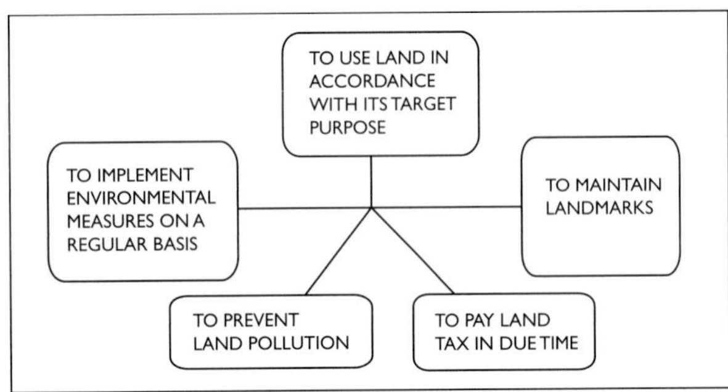

Figure 24.2. Basic duties of land users.

Agricultural land is used for the production of agricultural products, for planting shelter forests, for research, learning and other purposes connected with agriculture (article 77 of the Land Code).

Duty to Preserve Soil

Land users are obliged to implement a number of measures to preserve the soil (Figure 24.2), These include the protection of land from water and wind erosion, flooding, swamp formation, salinisation, drying and other negative factors. Land users are also obliged to prevent weed invasion, to maintain the achieved reclamation level, to restore disturbed lands and use the soil for agriculture in due time to maintain soil fertility.

Failure to fulfil these conditions is counted as 'soil damage' and implies administrative action.

Land Planning

Legal Regulation of Land Planning

Land planning in compliance with the Law on Land Planning is the foundation for land use. It includes mapping of land status, planning and organisation of the harmonious exploitation of land and the protection and maintenance of soil fertility (Figure 24.3).

According to articles 9 and 42 of the Constitution of the Russian Federation, 'every person has the right to an enabling environment'. The land is considered to be the foundation for life and the activities of the people of the country.

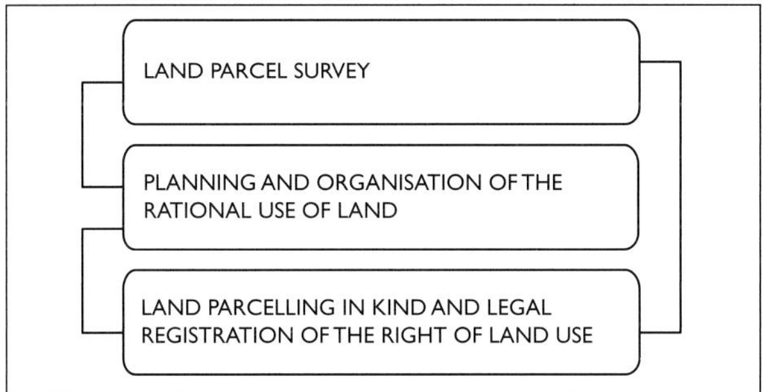

Figure 24.3. Land planning.

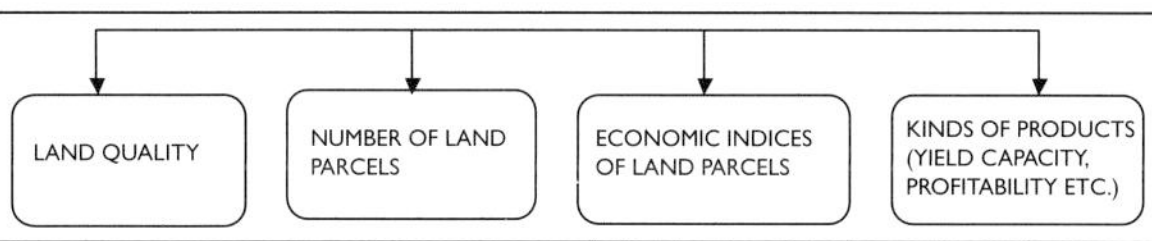

Figure 24.4. Basic provisions of the State Land Cadastre.

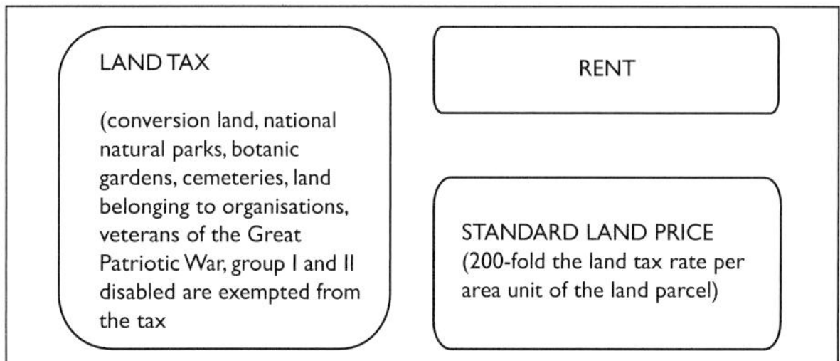

Figure 24.5. Methods of paying for land.

Threats to Land and Soil

In spite of these stated objectives, there is a real threat of soil exhaustion and deterioration of the ecological situation in general. This situation depends on the poor economic development of rural society and the lack of readiness of the community to understand the significance of these problems. In Russia this threat is especially serious as many agricultural properties are not economically competitive. Thus, for business reasons, Russian farmers preferably produce oilseed rape, soybean and forage crops. This deteriorates the soil status and damage ecosystems, in particular those dependent on pollination by bees and thus bee-keeping.

Unfortunately the situation reflects the low ecological culture of rural communities. It remains uncorrected as the systems for monitoring and calling to account those responsible for environmental offences remain undeveloped.

Land Monitoring

According to article 67 of the Land Code of the Russian Federation, a system must be established for observation, assessment and monitoring of the condition of lands in the territory of Russia. The basic objectives of monitoring include:

- Timely identification of changes in the soil status, assessment of such changes, forecasts and recommendations concerning prevention and elimination of the results of negative processes.
- Provision of information concerning maintenance of the State Land Cadastre, official supervision of land use and protection, other functions of governmental and municipal management of land resources, and land planning.
- Providing citizens with information about the condition of land.

State Land Cadastre

The State Land Cadastre is a systematic summary of documentary data, obtained as a result of registration of land parcels, their location, target destination and legal status (Figure 24.4).

The Land Cadastre is maintained for the purpose of information support concerning:

- Public and municipal management of land resources.
- Public control of land use and protection.
- Activities directed at soil preservation and enrichment.
- Land planning.
- State registration of the rights to immovable estate and associated transactions.
- Economic appraisal of lands and consideration of their cost.
- Fixing of a reasonable land fee (Figure 24.5);
- Other activities connected with the possession, use and disposal of land parcels.

Persons found to be in violation of the land laws are called to account for disciplinary, financial, administrative, criminal and civil responsibility.

Economic Instruments *Three Interlinkages Between Ecology and Economics*

25

Hans Aage
Roskilde University, Denmark

The Basic Interlinkage – Lessons of History

A Conflict Betwen Economics and Environment

Throughout human history environmental problems have always been with us; they have caused us to inhabit strange places of the globe, to eat cereals, to kill each other. Our history is rife with environmental disasters (although of a relatively local nature so far) in which cultures perished after depleting their own resource basis, e.g. the catastrophes of Easter Island in the 16th century and of Lake Aral in the 20th century, which was transformed into a salty desert after the water level had fallen by 13 metres and the water content had been reduced by two-thirds since 1960 as the result of large-scale cotton cultivation and irrigation (Rydén et al., 2003:27,197,541.).

The basic interlinkage between ecology and economics is that economic activity depends upon, and damages, the environment. Economic activity is the origin of environmental problems. It is not the cure, although this used to be a popular belief, especially among economists: 'Over time, the environment and economic prosperity are not opposing concepts, but rather complementary entities' (Lomborg, 2001:32,210). Now, environmental issues are being taken increasingly seriously by influential economists (Arrow et al., 1995,2004; Stern, 2007), but unfounded optimism concerning future economic growth is still widespread.

The Naive Belief in Economic Growth

Thus the 2006 Stern Review assumes 1.3% annual GDP growth as the baseline for the next century (Stern et al., 2007:161.). Likewise, the Danish report on future social welfare assumes 2.0% annual productivity growth and furthermore claims that this is 'well substantiated'.[1]It is nothing of the sort; it is an unfounded extrapolation of recent, exceptional historical experience, namely average growth rates of GDP per capita in the 20th century. Global GDP per capita changed little until 1000 A.D. During the following 800 years it grew by 0.05% per annum on average and in the 19th century by about 1%. Since 1900, global GDP per capita has increased by a factor of 5 (1.6% p.a.), total GDP by a factor of 17 (about 3% p.a.), energy consumption by a factor of 12 (half the original oil resource is used up), water consumption by a factor of 9 (one-third of total resources is being used), and global population by a factor of 4, from 1.6 to 6.1 billion people (Maddison, 2003; McNeill, 2001; Aage, 2002).

A repetition of the 20th century is physically impossible. Little *is* known about future GDP growth. Yet, something is known for sure about exponential growth: that it eventually grows very fast and that it eventually draws to a close, the only questions remaining being when and how.[2]

The true lesson of our environmental history is quite different. We have displayed a stunning improvidence and lack of long-term foresight or, positively phrased, we have an inborn, impressive ability to repress perplexing problems, which were always abundant, and concentrate on doing something more or less sensible. The fundamental problem with which mankind has wrestled – with varying success – throughout history is to achieve a balance between:

- Our desire to live comfortably and increase the supply of commodities, first and foremost to withdraw from the starvation limit by increasing food production.
- Our desire to proliferate.
- The capacity of our natural base to sustain production (Ponting, 1991:17)

The core problem is the old but increasingly painful awareness that economic activity today may endanger the life and welfare of our descendants hundreds of years from now, and that we do not know how to prevent it. It forces us to weigh our own survival against that of other human beings, to look across the globe and across centuries and to live under uncertainty, including a positive but unknown probability of future, man-made cataclysms. This awareness transgresses the habitual limits of our rationality and morality.

A Mistaken Interlinkage – Economy and Sustainability

Resource Availability is Not Fixed by the Market

Concerning the supply and optimal use of resources and environment, three different classes of issues can be delineated and considered separately, related to science, politics and economics, respectively. Compared with the first and second groups of issues, the third group, related to economics, is a very minor one.

The first class of problems concerns sustainability, the environmental effects of economic activity, the magnitude and nature of resources and the available and prospective technical options, including possible substitutions in consumption and production. These are science problems, and naturally they must be investigated using methods of the natural sciences.

Economists, however, have long cherished strong opinions on these topics. Now, this is finally changing for the better, but in the 20th century the shining growth optimism of Marx and Engels prevailed among economists, and mainstream economists figured prominently in the formation of environmental awareness in the last third of the 20th century as a blimpish rearguard party (Aage, 1984, 2008). Resources and the environment more or less disappeared from general economics textbooks, which often include chapters on economic growth containing highly relevant empirical evidence without at all mentioning ecological problems or nature as a basis for, and limitation to, economic activity. Words such as ecology, environment, pollution, green taxes and resources simply do not figure in the index.[3]

The core economic argument has two parts: firstly, that there are plenty of resources and plenty of carrying capacity and resilience of the environment; and secondly, that if there were any problems they would quickly and automatically be resolved by market mechanisms.

The first part of the argument against the doom-sayers amounts to neglect or outright denial of the finality of nature. Sometimes it is based upon extrapolation of historical trends, assumptions about substitutability and automatic technological progress or presumptions that economic growth improves the environment. Sometimes it is just postulated that Planet Earth 'is so incredibly much larger than all our needs' (Lomborg, 1998), that 'we have more and more oil left, not less and less', and that our oil reserves can be compared with a 'refrigerator' which, when near-empty, can simply be replenished 'in the supermarket', because 'new oil fields will be continuously added as demand rises' (Lomborg, 2001:125; cf. also the article entitled Plenty of Gloom in The Economist, 20 December 1997, pp 21-23). This might be true given a sufficiently short, very short, time horizon. Yet, the very basis of contemporary environmental awareness is that Planet Earth is limited in relation to human capabilities and global economic activities. What we do know for certain is that the number of unknown reserves will go down at precisely the same rate as the sum of used and known reserves goes up.

The suppression of resources and the environment in economics is partly justified by the fact that according to comparative analyses of growth rates in various countries in the 20th century, resource endowments had very limited explanatory power (Maddison, 1991:56-60). The confidence in continued growth relies upon 'successful adaptation to resource scarcity' (Maddison, 1991:58), but in order for this kind of analysis to make sense it must be assumed that certain possibilities for substitution exist. It must always be possible to substitute non-renewable resources with greater inputs of labour, man-made capital and renewable resources. According to Solow (1992:9), 'Without this minimal degree of optimism ...there is no point of talking about sustainability'. This assumption is the backbone of the particular brand of economic eco-optimism. If possibilities for substitution are very large (the elasticity of substitution between exhaustible resources and other inputs is bigger than unity, and the productivity of reproducible capital is sufficiently large), the effect is that according to Solow (1974:11), 'the world can, in effect, get along without natural resources'. Note however that whether this assumption is valid is not at all an economic problem; it belongs to the realm of science.

The second part of the economic argument is that market prices will reflect scarcity, and until now 'market prices give no reason to believe that natural resources are a limit to economic growth' (Mankiw, 1997:244 - the only reference to natural resources and the environment in this macroeconomics textbook). Furthermore, because of the market mechanism, scarcity of a resource causes an increase in its price, thereby creating incentives for exploration, substitution and innovation, which will eventually eliminate the scarcity:

> *'In fact, prospectors usually discover new natural resources when prices rise, and technological progress has been rather successful in finding substitutes' (Maddison, 1991:58)*

This argument is based on the economic theory of the market price of a raw material with known deposits (including a typical hint at a historical argument); it will equal extraction costs plus an increment for scarcity that increases over time by an annual percentage, equalling the rate of interest (Pearce and Turner, 1990:271-276, cf. section Long-term Exhaustible Resources below.).

However, the market is a peculiar place to search for information on the magnitude of resources and likely technical advances in the future. The sensible thing to do would be to directly address geologists and engineers.

In addition, the problem with the effect of those market-generated incentives is that the causation chain has two links that are both weak. Firstly, price rises have to happen early and strongly enough for measures towards substitution and technical development to be taken in due time. However, since the scarcity increment may only make itself felt right before depletion, prices will only rise if geological conditions cause sufficiently rapid increases in the extraction costs. This first link of the causative chain can be corrected politically by means of administrative regulation, taxation and subsidies, and also by tradable permits (Cf. Arrow et al., 1995).

Secondly, those endeavours have to succeed. The magnitude of resources and the possibilities for technological advances are scientific problems of an entirely different nature than economic effects reflected as rising prices. If the laws of supply and demand do not provide sufficient incentives, they can be corrected by government policy. As for the laws of nature, they do not lend themselves to amendment by decree. Using economic methods in the sphere of sustainability is mistaken and ideological.

Politics and Ethics: Cost-benefit Analysis

The second class of problems are the painful political and moral problems of how we want to allow for the welfare of future generations and to distribute the rights of exploiting resources and environment between rich and poor people. The contribution of economics in this sphere is equally mistaken and ideological. The method is to short-circuit all these political and moral problems by computing monetary values for everything, everywhere, everybody, at every time and comparing them in order to achieve seeming consistency and rationality. This is the principle of social cost-benefit analysis, which defines the social good as monetary values of human lives, global warming, diseases, children, the spotted owl, time saved by fast traffic, unspoiled wilderness, etc., etc.

Cost-benefit analysis is widely used for environmental assessments, including long-term effects of global warming. Thus the DICE model (Dynamic Integrated model of Climate and the Economy) (Nordhaus, 1994, 2007:697-701), a stylised model of various economic aspects and possible scenarios of global warming for the next century, is constructed upon a host of heroic assumptions, including growth rates of total factor productivity (1.5%, and then decreasing) and social discount rates (5%). Cost-benefit analysis is appropriate for comparing projects which are small, short-term and well defined. If used for long-term, extensive problems the results become very sensitive to the choice of assumptions, many of which are completely arbitrary, and results are invalidated by fundamental theoretical weaknesses, which include interpersonal comparisons of utility, the rate of discount, assumptions of substitutability, monetary values of human life and uncertainty.

Interpersonal comparisons of utility is the very idea of cost-benefit analysis. Individual utilities are measured as monetary values, and they are added in order to obtain total, utilitarian social welfare. However, an extra dollar of consumption is likely to be worth more to a poor person than a rich person. Thus, the Stern Review assumes a value of $\eta=1$ (unit elasticity of the marginal utility of consumption) (Stern, 2007:46,161-163). This arbitrary value means that utility grows with the logarithm of consumption and that an extra dollar is worth ten times less if the original level of income is ten times higher.

The rate of discount: For short-term private decisions, present values of future amounts of money are computed by discounting, reflecting the private choice of either consuming income now or depositing it in a bank account at some rate of interest for future consumption. However, attempts at social cost-benefit assessment over long time spans are ruined by the discount rate problem. A discount rate of 6% implies that 30 years from now, $100 will only count as $17 today, while 100 years from now it will be reduced to 29 cents. And 6% is 'what most economists might think are decent parameter values' (Weitzman, 2007:707). This means that if the rate of discount is positive, future generations will have no weight; if it is zero, present generations will have no weight. There are several suggestions on how to formulate the optimisation problem over time with a reasonable allocation between generations, e.g. by including the condition that welfare must not decrease over time, or by applying a discount rate approaching zero over time (Pearce and Turner, 1990:211-238). But this is all arbitrary, and the whole exercise rests on shaky theoretical grounds and belongs more to ideology than to science. Most long-term cost-benefit analyses use discount rates of 3-5%, but the Stern Review does not discount the utility of future generations at all; it uses a low value of the pure time discount rate at $\delta=0.1\%$ for one reason only, namely the probability that the earth could perish, so that prospective generations will not exist (Stern, 2007:45-47,161-163). Together with $\eta=1$ and an assumed growth rate of 1.3%, this implies a discount rate for income of $r = \delta + 1.3\eta = 1.4\%$ (the Frank Ramsey equation). This is far below the conventional 5-6% and fundamentally changes the calculation of costs and benefits of climate change and CO_2 reductions.

Assumptions of substitutability: When adding the monetary value of various goods the possibility of substitution is a basic assumption. Therefore price calculations are well suited for marginal decisions that allow substitution, e.g. whether to have gherkins or beetroot with roast pork. Substitution is also presupposed when attempting to calculate so-called true savings, i.e. savings adjusted for natural resources spent and environmental deterioration, namely possibilities of substitution between human capital, man-made physical capital and natural capital. Most economic calculations show that true savings are positive and hence fulfil a weak sustainability criterion, but this depends upon the assumption of substitutability, e.g. that less North Sea oil can be compensated for by more lessons in the French language.[4]

Monetary values of human life are arbitrary and differ widely. Thus the standard is about 3 million USD in the USA, 1 million USD in Denmark, and 150,000 USD in the Netherlands (Danish Ministry of Finance: Manual for cost-benefit analysis, Finansministeriet, 1999:63). Just imagine that physical constants, like gravitation or the velocity of light, differed by a factor of 20 from one country to another.

How to Manage Uncertainty

Of course, the best forecast for our future would hardly be the best decision basis. The task is not to find the best forecast for the future and then act as though that forecast were certain. If there is some probability of less positive scenarios with serious consequences, it can be rational to try warding them off, thus taking precautionary action upon a less probable forecast. After all, few people would consider their fire insurance premium to be wasted just because their houses did not burn down during the insurance period. The risk of fire can be described in terms of probabilities that can be subject to actuarial computations, but a more fundamental uncertainty is a distinguishing feature of environmental problems because of the risk of discontinuous, irreversible and cumulative changes, which renders marginal cost-benefit optimisation absurd (Arrow et al., 1995; Weitzman, 2007). No company sells insurance against the effects of climate change. The characteristic of serious environmental problems is their incalculability. Human activity has often proven to have ever more extensive impacts that we had never suspected and many environmental effects have come as total surprises: the impacts of DDT in the 1960s, eutrophication in the 1970s, the gap in the ozone layer and the greenhouse effect in the 1980s, and mad cow disease in the 1990s.

We do not know how to handle these ethical problems. We are no wiser from choosing some arbitrary numbers, like the η and δ of the Stern Review, as we cannot attribute any genuine meaning to them, either as moral standards or as objective knowledge. The debate on the proper magnitude of η and δ is as futile as alchemy (Cf. comments upon the Stern Report by William Nordhaus and Partha Dasgupta, The Economist, 16 December 2006, p 8; Nordhaus, 2007; Weitzman, 2007.). It is probably not so that 'the approach has the virtue of clarity and simplicity', but rather the virtue of exposing our fundamental ignorance and bewilderment. Indeed, 'such excises should be viewed with some circumspection' (Stern, 2007:30,31).

Everything boils down to the δ and η of the Stern Review (2006), namely the many attempts to solve the problem of the rate of discount and the distribution between rich and poor in a simple and consistent way. The approach is simple and dangerously so, as the inherent contradictions are only suppressed, not solved, simply because the real world including man is contradictory.

When comparing welfare across generations, across the globe, under uncertainty, the quest for consistency and rationality is mistaken and leads to precisely the opposite: a distorted and irrational perception of reality. Growth rates and discount rates, on which computations rely, are largely guess-work. Cost-benefit analyses covering long time spans invariably end up in paradoxes. Even for modern physics, time remains a mystery.

The main justification of the quest for rationality is the assertion that priorities are made, at least by implication, and therefore they had better be explicit and rational. The motto is a substitution of simple principle for complicated reality: we must choose, ergo we can choose. Sometimes it might be wiser to realise our ignorance and the impossibility of consistent choice, witness Aischylos, Shakespeare, Racine, Corneille and Schiller. For example, would it not have been better if the wealthy princes of the Italian Rinascimento had spent resources on feeding and educating the poor rather than erecting the duomo in Florence and financing art treasures? It is impossible not to say yes to this question, but to say yes is equally impossible; the poor are always with us, and an affirmative answer would imply rejection of philosophy, literature, music, architecture, science, religion and all other expressions of culture and civilisation.

The Operational Interlinkage – the Use of Economic Instruments

A Role for Economics

Now for the third class of problems. What are the contributions of economics? Squeezed between the first two classes of problems – relates to science and politics – there is little room left for economic analysis, the contribution of which is to examine the effects of economic incentives under various institutional arrangements, once the answers to the first two classes of problems are known. Adequacy of supplies and optimal use of resources are technical, scientific and political issues, not primarily economic.

However economics can contribute substantially, although marginally, to environmental policy. First of all, there is a need for book-keeping, for tracing the short-term macro-economic effects of environmental changes and policies. Secondly, economics gives useful insights into resource price developments if left to a competitive market. Thirdly, economic analysis is useful concerning institutions, incentives and effects of various policy instruments, e.g. analysis of pollution taxes vs. tradable permits (Cekanavicius et al., 2003).

The Imperative of Political Regulation

A basic insight from economics is that problems of resources and environment cannot be left to the invisible hand of market forces. The fundamental theorems of microeconomic welfare theory prove that market allocations fulfil a minimum efficiency requirement called Pareto efficiency, which means that resources, labour and capital are not wasted but will provide utility at least for someone. Contrary to cost-benefit analysis, Pareto's minimum efficiency concept does not imply comparisons of utility of different persons, and therefore it says nothing about distribution problems. There are further snags to it, because several preconditions must be fulfilled; if not, the market mechanism will not allocate efficiently, because of market failures, namely (Stiglitz, 2000:76-88):

1. Imperfect competition.
2. Externalities, i.e. economic effects upon other market agents that are not reflected in prices and account books. An important example is air pollution.
3. Public goods, i.e. goods that are not private. A private good can be used by one person only, and payment can be collected. There are several types of public goods, for example a lighthouse. An important example is fish stocks in the sea and other types of commons, i.e. goods with common ownership.
4. Incomplete markets. An important example is the insufficiency of markets for long-term decisions. Markets are essentially myopic.
5. Information failures.
6. Macroeconomic disturbances such as unemployment and inflation.

Thus, allocation problems in relation to resources and the environment are beset by market failures: all resource and environment problems involve long-term decisions (cf. section 3.2); pollution problems are normally externalities (cf. section 3.3); and many resources are not private goods, but rather like common land (cf. section 3.4). Therefore, political regulation is imperative. Whether government allocation will actually work, when the market does not, is no evident question, as market failures are not the only failures – there are also plenty of policy failures.

Long-term Exhaustible Resources

Long-term decision problems are handled by the market by means of a rate of interest. This also applies to utilisation of an exhaustible resource. The owner has a choice between two options: either he can extract it now, sell it and deposit the profit in a bank account and draw the profit plus interest one year from now; or he can leave the resource in the ground for one year and then extract it and sell it. A market equilibrium requires that prices, extraction costs and the interest rate make the owner indifferent between these two options. Therefore, the profit (the resource rent), i.e. the price less extraction costs, must increase by the rate of interest during the year, and the resource price at time t must satisfy:

$$P_t = M_t + R_0(1+r)^t = M_t + R_0e^{\rho t}$$

where P_t is the price of the resource at time t, M_t is extraction costs at time t, R_0 is resource rent at time 0, r is the rate of interest and ρ is rate of interest if computed continuously.

The resource rent thus increases by the rate of interest over the years. Whether this price and the corresponding rate of extraction are optimum for society is another problem. If the discounting principle of cost-benefit analysis is accepted, it is not impossible, but this is highly problematic, as discussed above.

It is also problematic whether resource prices will reflect future resource scarcity. The market price will depend on market agents' preferences for present relative to future consumption, which does not necessarily reflect market agents' assessment of future raw materials supply: A low price could just as well owe to the fact that the market is myopic, so that the scarcity price increment would be minute until a few decades before depletion. The movements of the market price for oil since 1973 do not follow an exponential growth path.[5]

We cannot trust the market mechanism to allow for generations yet unborn, even though a profiteering owner of an oil well will let the oil remain in the ground if prospective future price rises are sufficiently high. It is true that in theoretical terms market equilibria over long spans of time are possible, and that in theory there is no difference between those living a hundred years from now and, say, those living in Denmark today. Yet, in practical terms

Box 25.1. Taxation or Tradeable Pollution Permits

Assume that there are two polluting enterprises and that total emissions are 225 units, 75 from enterprise A and 150 from enterprise B. The political target is 75 units of emissions, so that emissions reduction in the two enterprises, R_A and R_B, should amount to:

$R_A + R_B = 150$

Total costs of reduction (TCR) and marginal costs of reduction (MCR) for the two enterprises are different, but both functions reflect that the cost of one further unit of reduction (MCR) increases with the amount of reduction already carried into effect:

$TCR_A = 0.10R_A^2 + 10R_A,$
$MCR_A = dTCR_A/dR_A = 0.20R_A + 10,$
$0 \le R_A \le 75$, cf. Figure 25.1.
$TCR_B = 0.04R_B^2 + 5R_B,$
$MCR_B = dTCR_B/dR_B = 0.08R_B + 5,$
$0 \le R_B \le 150$, cf. Figure 25.1.

The minimum cost solution for R_A and R_B, given that $R_A + R_B = 150$, is obtained by substitution and differentiation:

$TCR = TCR_A + TCR_B$
$= 0.10R_A^2 + 10R_A + 0.04(150 - R_A)^2 + 5(150 - R_A)$
$dTCR/dR_A = 0.20R_A + 10 + 0.08R_B(-1) + 5(-1) = 0$
$0.20R_A + 10 = 0.08R_B + 5$ or $MCR_A = MCR_B$,
cf. Figure 25.1.

The minimum TCR solution becomes:

$R_A = 25, R_B = 125$ and TCR = 1,562.5,

as illustrated in Figure 25.1, where TCR is the sum of the two hatched areas below the MCR curves.

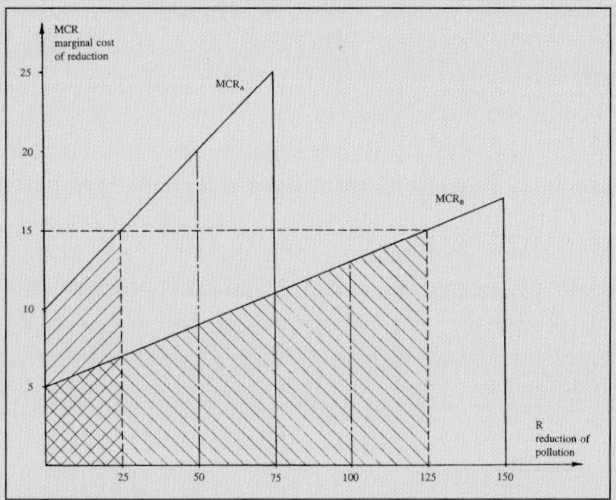

Figure 25.1. Distribution of pollution reduction costs between two enterprises by means of taxation and tradeable pollution permits.

This solution can be obtained by means of various policy instruments. One possibility is specific government decrees for emissions for each of the enterprises, but normally the government does not possess specific information on the cost functions of the enterprises. If the government roughly decrees that both enterprises should reduce their emissions by two-thirds, total costs of reduction will become TCR = 1650, exceeding the minimum of TCR = 1562.5, cf. the two vertical dot-and-dash lines in Figure 25.1.

Instead, the government can charge the enterprises a price of 15 per unit of emission. Then, as illustrated in Figure 25.1, enterprise A will reduce emissions by exactly 25 units, because up

markets only function in the short run, and there is another, rather more fundamental problem. There is always a large number of possible market equilibria. They produce widely different distributions of the final consumption among market agents, which is precisely the issue here. Which distribution is realised depends on how resource control is distributed at the opening of the market, that is today, when the present generation owns all natural resources. The problem confronting future generations is that they do not own anything. It is equally decisive for those living in Denmark how many resources they control, in the short term especially labour and capital.

If future generations are left at the mercy of the market and an interest rate of say 5%, it will require considerable price rises before the market will save anything for posterity. It is possible that the utility value to us of a barrel of oil is 132 times greater now than in a hundred years and 17,000 times greater than its utility value in 200 years, which would correspond to a 5% discount rate. Still our great-grandchildren are likely to view things differently. Whether a hundred years is a long time obviously depends upon the point of view, i.e. from which of the two extreme points of the time span it is observed.

Taxation or Tradeable Pollution Permits

to 25 units the reduction cost per unit is less than 15. Further reductions will cost more than 15 per unit, and the enterprise will prefer to pay the pollution charge. Correspondingly, enterprise B will reduce emissions by exactly 125 units.

It makes no difference whether the pollution charge for the enterprises takes the form of a tax on emissions or a cost of tradable pollution permits in a cap-and-trade scheme that requires enterprises to buy tradable permits for every unit of pollution.

Furthermore, if government supplies 75 units of tradable permits, the market equilibrium price will become exactly 15 per permit. At a price of, say, 10 per permit, enterprise A will demand 75 permits, and enterprise B 87.5 permits; the total demand will be 162.5 units and the price will increase, as it exceeds the supply of 75. At a price of 20, enterprise A will demand 25 units and enterprise B 0 units, that is a total of 25, and the price will decrease.

It makes no difference for the amounts of pollution, the price of permits or the incentive to reduce pollution whether tradable permits are sold at auction or given away for free or to whom they are given, as long as they are given as a fixed amount that does not vary from year to year according to actual amounts of emissions; in the latter case there will be no effect upon emissions. If 75 permits are given for free every year, e.g. 50 to enterprise A and 25 to enterprise B, an extra permit will still be worth 15 for both enterprises. As long as the number of free permits does not depend on actual annual emissions, a unit of pollution still costs the enterprises a price of 15, and 'grandfathering' will not imperil incentives to reduce pollution. Thus, the minimum TCR solution can be obtained by all of the four instruments:

1. Specific government decrees to each firm, if government has full information.
2. A pollution tax of 15 per unit.
3. 75 tradable pollution permits sold by auction.
4. 75 tradable permits distributed by grandfathering.

Taxes and tradable permits have essentially identical effects. There are, however, some differences between them:

Firstly, pollution is regulated by price (the tax) of pollution fixed by government in case 2 and by quantity (through the cap) in cases 1, 3 and 4. If government wants a specific quantity, it might be unable to find the proper tax rate in the first place, and it might be necessary to adjust the tax rate in the following years. If it is important to obtain a specific quantity effect at the outset (e.g. for a shoal fish like herring, which can be completely fished up in a short time), quantity regulation will be the solution. For more long-term problems (e.g. CO_2 emissions), a tax that is adjusted during a span of years might be sufficient.

Secondly, fiscal effects are different. In cases 2 and 3 the polluter will pay, and government receives a revenue, while in cases 1 and 4 there is no government revenue. The possibility of grandfathering is probably the main reason for the popularity of tradable permits as opposed to taxes. If permits are given away, not once and for all, but annually depending upon actual amounts of pollution of individual enterprises, there will of course be no effect upon pollution at all.

Thirdly, with a tax the price of pollution will be stable, whereas the price of tradable permits can be highly volatile, causing problems for investment planning for pollution reduction. The cap-and-trade schemes for carbon permits in the EU and, since the mid-1990s, for sulphur dioxide permits in the USA, have shown volatile prices, in the USA by more than 40% a year (The Economist, 16 June 2007, p 78).

On top of the costs of reduction come the costs of measuring and monitoring emissions, which may be considerable or even prohibitive, especially when pollution comes from many, diffuse sources. These costs are the same for the four policy instruments above.

It is possible to take the welfare of future generations into account without relying on price effects of interest rates. Thus, in Norway, but not in Denmark, part of the resource rent income from North Sea oil extraction is deposited in a government Oil Fund, which is not consumed but invested for the benefit of prospective generations. This policy also mitigates the so-called Dutch disease problem (from the discovery of natural gas in the Netherlands in the late 1950s), namely that large resource rent incomes tend to create a balance of payments surplus and thereby increase the value of the local currency and reduce the competitiveness of other sectors of the economy.

There is one further argument for strong government interference with natural resources, namely that governments need money. The pure resource rent does not originate in any productive activity, but simply from ownership of the resource, and taxation of the resource rent is a rare example of an efficient tax in the sense that it will not distort economic decisions; another example is a head tax and other types of lump-sum taxes. Most other taxes, like an income tax or an alcohol tax, inflict distortions upon economic activity, in these particular cases a distortion of the supply of labour and a (beneficial) distortion of alcohol consumption. In addition, it is compatible with widespread notions of justice that the user right of natural resources should belong to the people and not to any particular individual. It appears that there are heavy arguments for heavy taxation of resource rents.

This is especially evident in a country like Russia because of its heavy dependency upon oil, gas and raw materials, which constitute about three-quarters of exports. Competition is not essential from the Russian point of view, and it makes little sense to give away resource monopolies to private capitalists. Taxation of the resource rent is an alternative to public ownership, but the difference between them is negligible. It is not at all obvious concerning property rights of natural resources that 'private and privatized enterprises outperformed public enterprises all over the world' (Åslund, 2002:260).

Environmental Policy Instruments

No market and hence no market price exist for many ecological resources. Urgent problems are linked with emissions to the environment caused by resource consumption, and even if certain types of pollution, notably the most concentrated ones, have been successfully eliminated, other and more elusive pollution problems have increased. However, there is no such thing as a market for air with a low CO_2 content, or for seawater not contaminated with nutrients. Governments must take charge.

If a government decides to reduce a certain type of pollution by e.g. two-thirds, and there are several polluters with different costs of emission reduction, how can this political target be obtained at minimum cost to society? This is illustrated in detail in a numerical example (Box 25.1), which compares four different ways for governments to reach the target:

1. Specific government decrees to each firm, if government has full information.
2. A pollution tax of 15 per unit.
3. 75 tradable pollution permits sold by auction.
4. 75 tradable permits distributed by grandfathering.

All these policy instruments are incentives for centrally and politically fixed allocations, i.e. what is normally termed a planned economy. Moreover, the differences between the instruments are easily overrated. Tradable permits are used as an instrument mostly in relation to pollution, notably CO_2 emissions. Curiously, they are more popular than taxes despite the fact that their effects are largely identical, probably because they are erroneously considered more consistent with predominant market fetischism ideology[6] – but most likely because tradable permits are usually handed out for free in the first place, whereas taxes must be paid from the outset, and also because cap-and-trade schemes allow rich countries to pay poor countries to cut their emissions without involving government money. Even administrative regulation can become a purely economic incentive in the form of fines, if the public ignores the stigma incurred by the criminal offence of infringing laws and regulations (Aage, 2002:648-650).

No doubt, there are good reasons for using economic and other incentives in environmental policies. Yet they should not be mistaken for a market economy, which is something entirely different, namely that the market is allowed to determine spontaneously and decentrally how resources are to be allocated. On the contrary, environmental policy and regulation means central planning: that the allocation (amount of pollution, rate of extraction) is fixed politically in advance, before incentives and markets come into play.

Common Resources Management

Fish stocks and common pasture are a sort of public good, as it is normally difficult to prevent anybody from using them or to collect payment for them. However, they are not pure public goods such as a lighthouse, which can be used by additional ships without harming other users. This does not apply to fish stocks and common pasture, and because of these characteristics there is a tendency for overfishing and overgrazing, 'the tragedy of the commons', if utilisation is left to individual decisions in the market and not regulated by the government.

The reason is a discrepancy between social and individual marginal returns and marginal costs. A numerical example which shows sustainable fishing yield as a function of fishing activity (number of fishing-boats) can illustrate the problem (See Box 25.2).

In principle the problem is easily solved. The fishermen could cooperate, but as the number of fishermen increases, cooperation becomes more difficult, and they could well end up at point C in Figure 25.2. The prob-

Box 25.2. Fishing with Sustainable Yield

The curve in Figure 25.2 shows sustainable fishing yield as a function of fishing activity (number of fishing-boats, B), i.e. the yield after some years with a constant number of boats, so that fish stocks and the annual catch have stabilised. A given annual yield (for example 12) can be obtained with a small and a large number of boats (2 and 6); in the first case the stable stock is large and fishing therefore relatively easy; in the second case the stock is smaller, but the same annual yield can be obtained if more boats are operated. Fish prices are assumed to remain constant.

$STY = -B^2 + 8B$	social total yield
$SAY = STY/B = -B + 8$	social average yield
$SMY = dSTY/dB = -2B + 8$	social marginal yield
$STC = 2B$	social total costs
$SAC = STC/B = 2$	social average costs
$SMC = dSTC/dB = 2$	social marginal costs

SAC and SMC are identical and are shown as the horizontal dot-and-dash line in Figure 25.2, SAY and SMY are the two other dot-and-dash lines.

If government decides the fishing activity, it will increase the number of fishing-boats until the net addition to total yield from the last boat (SMY) is equal to the costs of the last boat (SAC = SMC, as all boats have identical costs). This maximises total social return (the resource rent):

$STR = STY - STC$ social total return (resource rent)
$dSTR/dB = -2B + 8 - 2 = 0$, or
$SMY = SMC$, which is obtained for
$B = 3$, $STY = 15$ and $STR = 9$, point A in Figure 25.2.

Then resource rent is at its maximum of STR = 9, i.e. the distance AB in Figure 25.2. It is not the maximum sustainable yield (MSY), which is 16 and would be reached with 4 boats. As the resource rent is positive with 3 boats, social average costs are less than social average yield (SAC < SAY), and SMY = SMC = SAC; hence:

$SAC < SAY$
$SMY < SAY$

This implies that if new boats are added to the fleet of 3 boats already fishing, the additional catch (SMY) will be less than the average (SAY), and the new boats will thus reduce the average. If left to individual decision this situation, point A, will not be stable. An additional potential fisherman compares his costs and his returns. His individual costs are equal to social marginal and average costs (all boats have identical costs). But his individual yield exceeds social marginal yield, and therefore he will start fishing. He only considers his individual returns which equal the social average, as all boats get the same amount of fish. He disregards the fact that his fishing will depress the average yield of the boats already fishing (social average returns are declining).

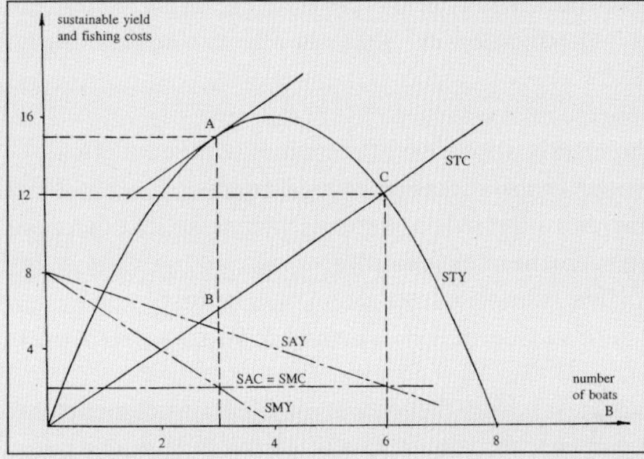

Figure 25.2. Fishing activity and sustainable yield with and without government regulation.

$IMY = SAY > SMY$	individual marginal yield,
$IMC = SMC = SAC$	individual marginal costs.

This will go on as long as
$IMY > IMC$, and the end result will be:

$B = 6$, $STY = 12$ and $STR = 0$, point C in Figure 25.2.

Total fishing costs will increase, the catch will decline, and the resource rent will be eliminated because of over-fishing.

lem could still be solved, namely by substituting one single owner for common ownership, and the single owner could be government or any individual. This also applies to the externality problem of pollution, which is closely related to the common ownership problem:

If costless negotiation is possible, rights are well-specified and redistribution does not affect marginal values, then:

- the market allocation of resources will be identical, whatever the allocation of legal rights,
- the allocation will be Pareto efficient, so that there is no problem of externalities,
- if a tax is imposed, efficiency will be lost.
  Coase's theorem, 1960 (Layard & Walters, 1978:192).

However, it is very difficult to establish ownership rights to e.g. clean air, and there will certainly be huge transaction costs in such a market. Furthermore, government regulation of fisheries has proved extremely difficult, and most of the world's fish resources are extremely overexploited because of the other part of the problem, namely the distribution of the profits, the resource rent (Hanley, Shogren and White, 2001:22-24,152-159).

All of the policy instruments (decrees, taxes and tradable fishing quotas) could be used for this problem, as well as for pollution and externalities. Taxation of catches is highly unpopular. Tradable quotas are used in some countries, e.g. New Zealand, Australia and Iceland. In Greenland quotas for shrimp are given away for free for an indefinite span of years; they are tradable, but few are traded, and prices are not public. In Iceland there is a tax on yield value less costs and wages of 6%, increasing to about 10%.

When ownership has been established, the owner faces the same problem as the owner of an exhaustible resource, namely to maximise resource rent over time, only more complicated because fish is a renewable resource. Reproduction of the fish is taken into account here as well as price changes, but many other possible model complications are left out, e.g. discontinuities, rigidity of capacity adjustment, uncertainty and interaction between several fish stocks.

If extraction costs and fishing costs are ignored, the price rule for the exhaustible resource can be formulated as:

$$\Delta P/P = r$$

where P is the resource price, ΔP is the price change during the year and r is the rate of interest.

When considering additional fishing the owner of the fish stocks must take into account not only price changes and the rate of interest, but also that his decision will influence the increase in the fish stocks, so the rule becomes:

$$F'(X) + \Delta P/P = r$$

where X is the fish stock and F(X) is the annual increase in the fish stock, and F'(X) is the annual percent change in the stock.

When fishing costs depend upon the size of the stock, the rule becomes more complicated. Generally, the optimal fish stock is lower the higher the unit price, the lower the fishing costs per unit and the higher the interest rate. If the price is constant and the interest rate required by the owner is higher than the marginal growth rate of the stock, F'(X), the consequence will be that the renewable resource becomes extinct (Pearce and Turner, 1990:241-261).

Case Study: Agricultural Pollution Policy in Denmark

The Problem: Eutrophication of the Baltic Sea

In the second half of the 20th century the environmental problems in inner Danish waters became increasingly severe. Recurrent episodes of oxygen deficit harmed – and continue to harm – the fish stocks, including the 1997 catastrophe of the Mariager Fjord, with massive fish deaths and extinction of significant parts of marine life. On its way to the ocean all water from the Baltic Sea and its feeder rivers, including polluting substances, pass through the shallow Danish waters. However, the water from the Baltic Sea entering Danish waters is presumably less polluted than the water it replaces, partly due to hydrographical conditions, namely that polluted water can be retained in the profound areas of the Baltic Sea. According to data from the late 1980s, Poland contributed 33% of the total nitrogen pollution in the Baltic Sea, the Soviet Union 25%, and Denmark, Sweden and Finland together 39% (Aage, 1998:215; Hansen, 1998; Aage, 2002).

The main culprit is intensive Danish agriculture, and the main problem is nitrogen leaching to the sea, about 311,000 tonnes in 1985. Since 1987, three government Action Plans for the Aquatic Environment have aimed at reducing eutrophication from the pollution of coastal waters with nutrients.

The First Plan – Reduction of Nitrogen Leaching

Plan I (1987-1993) aimed at reducing nitrogen leaching to the sea by 49%. For agriculture the target was a reduction of 127,000 tonnes i.e. 20%, but only 51,500 were achieved. The policy instruments were mainly administrative. Besides, there were some expectations concerning voluntary agreements, which did not materialise. For municipal wastewater the planned reduction was 15,000 tonnes by means of construction of new municipal wastewater cleaning plants, and this plan was overfulfilled with a realised reduction of 22,371 tonnes, but at a heavy investment cost. It is estimated that the costs of municipal wastewater cleaning were 70 DKK per kg reduction in annual nitrogen leaching. The corresponding costs of agricultural nitrogen leaching reduction were 6 DKK per kg (Economic Council, 2004:224-227; Jacobsen, 2004; Hansen, 1998). These costs are total social costs, i.e. total costs for society of resources spent, irrespective of who bears the burden of the costs, whether it is government, municipal tax-payers, farmers or other parties.

The Second Plan – Sustainable Agriculture

Because of this disappointing outcome, Plan I was amended by a Plan for Sustainable Agriculture in 1991 with obligations for farmers concerning accounts for the use of mineral fertiliser and concerning education in technology for spraying fields with chemicals. In 1998 total nitrogen losses were reduced to 207,000 tonnes annually, down from 311,000 in 1985, a reduction of 33% but still far from the original target of 49% for 1993.

Plan II (1998-2003) finally reached the original 1993 target, namely annual nitrogen leaching of at most 162,000 tonnes in 2003 or a reduction of 48% compared with the level of 1985. The instruments were again requirements for accounts of fertiliser usage and stricter norms for fertiliser usage. For every farm, an economic optimum use of nitrogen in mineral fertiliser was estimated, corrected for the nitrogen content of manure for farms with livestock, and the maximum permitted nitrogen utilisation was set as 90% of the economic optimum. Furthermore, the intensity of agriculture was reduced by increasing the area used as fallow, wetland and woodland and by introducing subsidies for organic farming. In 2002, nitrogen contracts were introduced in order to reduce nitrogen where costs were lowest. Farmers were asked to offer a certain reduction in their nitrogen quota in return for compensation. However, all bids were accepted and the costs became very high. The scheme was discontinued in 2004 (Jacobsen, 2004:103).

The average costs in Plan II were 15 DKK per kg reduction in annual nitrogen leaching. The costs of the 90% norm for nitrogen used were 13 DKK. The most cost-effective options were better utilisation of animal manure at 5 DKK and creation of wetlands at 7 DKK, and the most expensive was subsidies for organic farming at 80 DKK per kg nitrogen reduction (Jacobsen, 2004:95).

The Third Plan - Management of Nitrogen

Plan III (2004-2015) aims at a reduction in nitrogen discharges to 141,000 tonnes or less, i.e. a 13% reduction compared with the level of 2003. The instruments include stricter regulations on growing late crops that accumulate nitrogen, better utilisation of the nitrogen in livestock manure, establishment of new areas of wetlands and woodlands, establishment of crop-free buffer zones along streams and lakes and general set-side of agricultural land, partly by means of voluntary agreements.

Estimated reduction costs are on average 25 DKK per kg nitrogen leaching reduction and vary from 10 DKK per kg nitrogen reduction by using late crops to 90 DKK per kg by establishing new forests and about 300 DKK per kg by establishing biogas plants. Cost estimates differ according to the absolute size of intended effects and the valuation of beneficial side-effects (Jacobsen et al., 2004:97,128; Economic Council, 2004:226; Jacobsen, 2004:95; Hansen et al., 2003:20,27).

Comparing the Three Plans

The widely differing cost-effectiveness of various instruments in all three plans is partly explained by the fact that the plans had several other purposes than reducing nitrogen discharges. Other types of pollution also had to be reduced, especially phosphorus and pesticide pollution in the sea and in surface water and groundwater resources. Other purposes included general nature conservation, protection of biodiversity, and provision of recreational services for the population.

However, it is widely considered that there is room for improving the cost-effectiveness of policy instruments, especially by introducing economic incentives. So far instruments have been mainly administrative, with an element of voluntary agreements. The use of pollution taxes – or tradable pollution permits – is complicated by heavy monitoring costs, because of the diffuse character of pollution sources. One possibility is to tax mineral fertilisers as a proxy for pollution, and a tax on phosphorus input to agriculture is in fact included in Plan III.

A more cost-efficient instrument would be a tax where the tax base for individual farms is nitrogen input in fertiliser and feed less the nitrogen content in farm output. This comes close to a tax on nitrogen losses from farms to the environment, except that nitrogen accumulation in late crops would not be taken into account. The tax would provide proper incentives for farms to allocate nitrogen reductions efficiently inside individual farms and between farms, as illustrated in Box 25.1. Monitoring costs would probably also be lower than for the administrative instruments currently used. The order of magnitude of efficiency gains from using a tax compared with administrative instruments is estimated at 3 DKK per kg nitrogen loss reduction, or about 20% for plan II (Hansen & Hasler, 2007:55-59; Jacobsen et al., 2004).

A tax (or tradable permits) would not eliminate the need for supplementary administrative regulation, because the level of nitrogen pollution permitted is lower than average for some particularly sensitive areas, so that it is not only global nitrogen leaching that matters, but also its local distribution.

Long-term Democratic Decisions: Environment Boards

Besides the operational contributions to ecological science concerning book-keeping, developments of resource market prices, and the analysis of institutions and policy instrument incentives, there is an important general lesson for environmental policy and democracy to be learned from economics.

At the core of environmental policy problems is the inborn myopia of human nature and the inability to compare future hardships against present gains. Long-term foresight is not the forte of the free market, or of politicians. Thus the need for long-term decisions presents a problem for the two principal mechanisms of democracy: the market and the political system. However, examples exist of successfully coping with the time problem. Thus in monetary policy the problem is the balancing of present gains (printing money instead of collecting taxes) against future hardships (destruction of the monetary system). A workable, democratic solution has in some cases been successfully achieved, namely that democratically elected politicians devolve monetary authority to an independent central bank, which enjoys confidence and is circumscribed by strict laws. A more extreme form of independent monetary authority is the system of 'currency boards', as known in several former British colonies and recently in the Baltic States and Argentina. Correspondingly, one could imagine an institution of 'environmental boards'. In Sweden the Vattendomstolen (Water Court) is an administrative body with some independent, discretionary powers to make decisions concerning construction plans, which may affect the environment, especially construction of hydroelectric power plants.

Environmental issues are taken increasingly seriously by influential economists as witnessed by the manifesto of Arrow et al. (1995, 2004) and by the impressive Stern Review (2006) and Weitzman (2007). Hopefully, the changing attitudes among prominent economists herald a new, constructive role for economics in environmental policy. It is badly needed, as moral reorientation is required if we want to move ahead in less blind darkness than we used to do in the past (this is the true lesson of history) and if we want to approach the global environment and the global distribution – the major challenges of our time – in a civilised manner without resorting to the familiar regulatory mechanisms, namely wars, famines, migrations and pandemics.

Endnotes:

1. Andersen & Pedersen, 2005:191,200; the confidence in future growth rates of about 2% is widespread among economists for obscure reasons, cf. Weitzman, 2007:707,720.
2. Suppose that Judas kept his 30 pieces of silver and deposited them at a moderate 3% rate of interest. If they weighed 249.6 g in the year 30 A.D., the amount to day, 1977 years later, would be 5.976*1024 kg, which equals the total mass of Planet Earth. A fairly good approximation is that a capital on interest at r per cent per annum doubles every 70/r years.
3. This applies to the excellent and widely used textbooks by N.G. Mankiw (2000) and M. Burda & C. Wyplosz (1993).
4. Interestingly, the fronts regarding green amendments to national accounts have been reversed: Environmentalists used to criticise economists for not including environmental effects; now, when attempts are made to do so and true savings appear to be positive, economists are still being criticised, though the criticism has switched sign. Previously, economists used to say, How can I put a price on the lark's song? Now the environmental organisations are saying with contempt, Two pounds of larks, or two French lessons? .
5. Moreover, for oil, an appreciation based on calorific value only would seem short-sighted, since oil is a combination of chemical compounds with many other and more sophisticated applications than combustion.
6. World Bank, 2003:32; The Economist, 23 April 2005, pp 11,78-80. However this market fetishism ideology might now be on the retreat, cf. The Economist, 9 September 2006, p 9 and 16 June 2007, p 78; Aage, 2008.

Voluntary Instruments and Sustainable Consumption

26

Ingrid Karlsson
Uppsala University, Uppsala, Sweden
Motaher Hossain
University of Helsinki, Finland
Jahangirnagar University, Dhaka, Bangladesh

Economic Level and Environmental Impact

Consumer Behaviour

The core concept in sustainable development is to ensure the conditions for the present *and future* generations to obtain a good living. However, in attempting to find a balance between human welfare, economics and the environment, it soon becomes apparent that there are different views on what a 'good living' comprises and how it can be secured for this and future generations.

Individuals, households and groups acting independently have a great impact on the environment. For example, it is estimated that consumer behaviour on household level accounts for slightly less than half the carbon emissions in the US (Cutter et al., 2002). Individual choices also have a significant direct impact in the areas of transportation, housing, energy-using appliances, solid waste, water and food (National Research Council, 2005). Recent results from Denmark show that Danish households contribute to air pollution mainly through consumption of fuel in private vehicles, consumption of electricity, consumption of different alternatives for heating, consumption of food and consumption of different recreation and entertainment activities (Wier et al., 2003).

Environmental quality is also indirectly influenced by individuals and more or less independent groups in their roles as voters and citizens, households, investors, leaders, small business entrepreneurs, experts, researchers and members of non-profit organisations.

It is obvious that farmers have a great impact in rural areas. In areas where farming is a family business, which is the case in most Scandinavian, Polish, German and three Baltic states, the decisions made by individual farm households are very much connected to the private finances of the farming family. The decisions made by family farms are comparable with household individual/ voluntary decisions.

Lifestyle and Environmental Impact

The impact on the environment of individual households mainly depends on their standard of living, but is also greatly influenced by values and personal lifestyle. The study from Denmark referred to above showed that type of housing and consumer age have the greatest impact (Wier et al, 2003). Young people living in flats within urban areas have the least impact on environmental air pollution, mainly because of their low consumption of cars for transport and household energy for heating in the winter time.

Thus, a person who voluntarily wants to contribute to low environmental impact will choose to have no car and only travel by bicycle, on foot or by public transport and will live on a low technological and energy-consuming level, with holidays only spent in the local area. On the other hand, many strive for a lifestyle that is very bad for the shared environment, e.g. using the most comfortable transport, living in large detached houses outside the city and spending all their holidays in exotic and expensive resorts.

Most of us would claim to have chosen a lifestyle somewhere in between, for reasons that are obvious and important to us. What could make us change our behaviour? What voluntary activities are most effective as drivers of change?

As an example relevant to rural areas, we can study the recent increase in the number of private cars in the Baltic Sea region (see Figure 26.1). Owning a car is a lifestyle component considered absolutely essential by many consumers. The private car is often needed for individuals and families to be able to live a reasonably good life in sparsely populated areas.

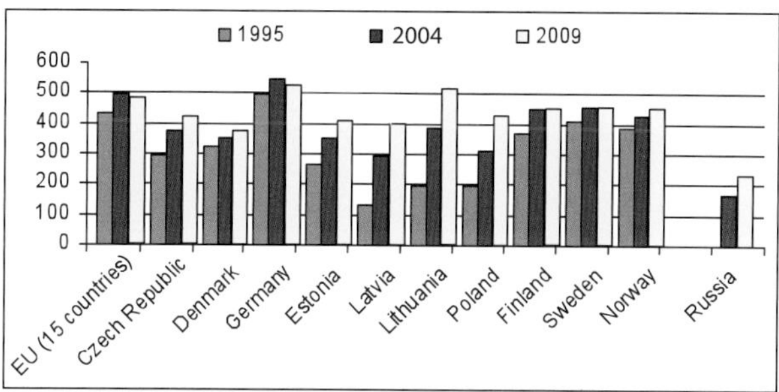

Figure 26.1. Motorisation rate (private car ownership per 1,000 inhabitants) (data for 1995, 2004 and 2009). Source: Eurostat.

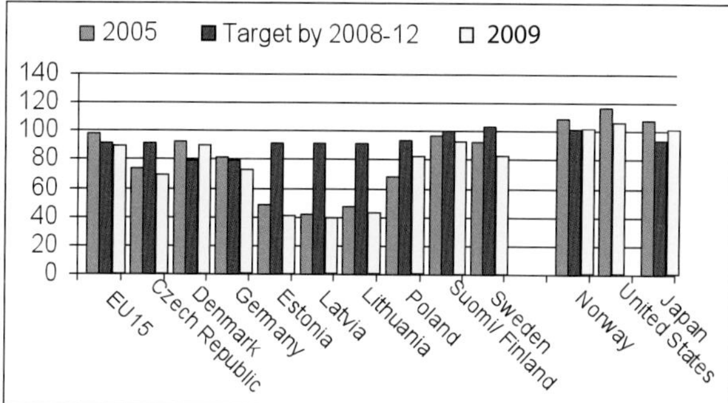

Figure 26.2. Greenhouse gas emissions and targets set by the Kyoto protocol. For US and Japan 2009-figures are from 2008. Source: Eurostat.

Car Ownership and CO_2 Emissions

Of course, well-planned infrastructure would include good public transport in all parts of the country. However, this is not the case except in the vicinity of the largest cities in the most developed areas. Even if consumption behaviour in different countries of the Baltic Sea region is uneven today when it comes to motorisation, most people in all these countries would regard having one car per family as the minimum for living a good life. Is this ideal possible? Elsewhere we have shown that passenger cars emit carbon dioxide, and their manufacture requires metals such as aluminium and platinum, which are limited resources and demand large amounts of energy to be produced. The European level of CO_2 emissions in 1990 must comply with the Kyoto Protocol. However as Figure 26.1 shows, all the countries in the Baltic Sea region have increasing numbers of cars, despite recent increases in fuel prices and taxes. In 2012, the price of car fuel in Sweden was around 1.6 Euro per litre.

In 2009 Russia had 225 private cars per 1,000 inhabitants. However, the steady increase in economic growth in Russia indicates that this number will increase rapidly. During the past 10 years, there has been 50-100% increase in the number of private cars in the three Baltic countries and Poland (Figure 26.1). In Scandinavia, the numbers of cars is approaching the level of 1 car for every other citizen, which is a level already passed 10 years ago in Germany.

Since the Kyoto Protocol Agreement was signed by most countries in Europe and other countries with high consumption, there has been a slow but steady downward trend in CO_2 emissions. The need for a reduction in greenhouse gases is agreed among climate experts, but the questions are how this can be implemented, and by whom. All or no-one is responsible, but obviously Denmark, Germany, Norway and Japan will have to work hard to reach their targets, while Estonia still is far below its target. The US did not even sign the Kyoto Protocol, despite having a greater impact on global greenhouse gas emissions than most other countries.

Greenhouse gas emissions from countries in economic transition around the Baltic Sea rapidly increased during

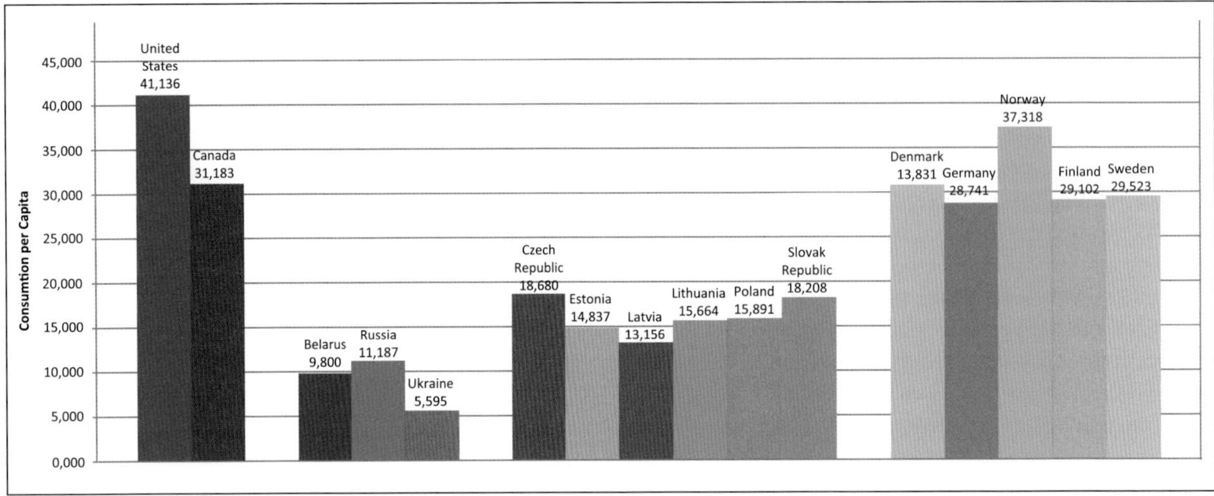

Figure 26.3. Final consumption per capita in USD adjusted by purchasing power parities*, year 2010. Data from UNECE, 2012.

* Purchasing Power Parity (PPP), NCU per US$:In broad terms, PPP is the relative cost of the same representative basket of goods when valued at the domestic prices of two different countries. In other words, PPPs are the rates of currency conversion that equalise the purchasing power of different currencies. A PPP is similar to a consumer price index in that it compares an overall price level of two different economies. It is different, however, in that the two economies compared are separated in space rather than in time. PPPs are, therefore, currency converters in addition to being spatial price comparisons. When countries share a common currency, such as the twelve countries of the euro area, and there is no need to convert to a common currency, PPPs are simply spatial price relatives.PPPs, and not exchange rates, should be used in international comparisons of real income.

the 1990s and early 2000s, especially in Estonia, Latvia, Lithuania and Poland. The debate on lifestyles and the need to voluntarily restrict the use of cars has apparently has yet become an issue in these countries. In fact it is unlikely to become an issue until the number of cars is equal to that in neighbouring countries.

Within the Baltic Sea region, there is a division between more and less wealthy countries. In the former Soviet Bloc countries, both those within the EU and those outside it, economic development and consumption are increasing rapidly but there is a fairly wide gap between rich and poor, so that the poorest people have not really had much opportunity to consume more than they used to in the past. Figure 26.3 shows the three different groups of economic performance within the Baltic Sea region, and compares these with the levels in the US and Canada. Obviously, a private car is one of the first items bought when people have more money in their pocket.

What is Voluntary?

Individual Choice and Responsibility

For an individual to make sensible voluntary choices, such as choosing to have the first, second or third car for the household, information and awareness are needed so that such choices are made consciously and deliberately. However, unconscious behaviour can also have a strong impact on choices and keeps individuals tied to habits that may sometimes be good but more often are bad (an example of the latter being gambling, which can destroy individual health, family finances and personal relationships.

Thus, the first step for a person who wants to make better voluntary choices is to develop critical thinking. The disadvantage of this is that the person must feel responsible for their conscious choices. Energy is required to observe, think, enquire and plan, prior to investing money or effort in buying new things or changing consumption pattern.

The moment of choice is always NOW. If individuals do not make their own choices, there will inevitably be someone else who will do this for them, or they will fall into the trap of doing what they have always done (unconscious behaviour/habit).

A voluntary choice is something done because the individual WANTS it (i.e. has values and goals that match this choice). Other people may provide advice, but individuals can never blame others for their choices if they have made these consciously. This means having to distinguish between opinions and facts and understanding the limits for the choices made (e.g. laws, physical ability, long-term economic regulations, etc.). It also means being very aware of the source of the facts influencing choices. Such facts should be reliable and understandable.

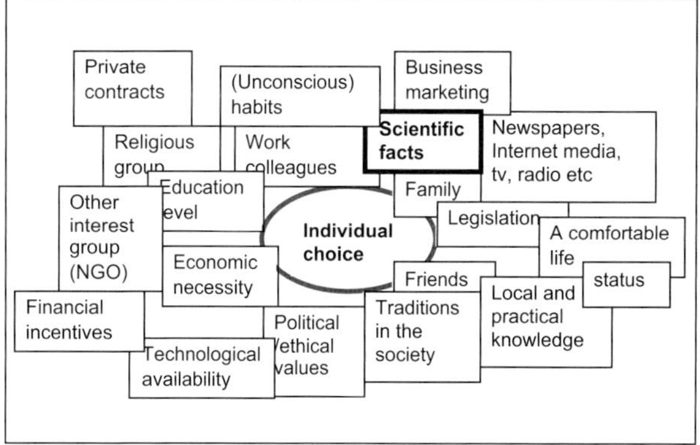

Figure 26.4. Factors affecting individual choice.

The Reasons for Choices?

An individual voluntary choice could be good for the individual, but at the same time have a negative impact for many others. Thus personal choice is seldom based entirely on the individual's own desires and dreams, but must take into account how it will affect family, neighbours, friends and society as a whole. Very often individual choice becomes a group choice, and when group dynamics are involved, different specific psychological processes within the group will influence the choice.

Voluntary driving forces for changing behaviour are described by Stern (2002). Some additions to his suggestions are provided below (see also Figure 26.4). Examples are given for each suggested driver of behaviour:

1. *Personal capabilities and constraints:* Literacy, social status and professional skills affect judgement capacity; personality, and habits determine unconscious behaviour.
2. *Value (ethical/political) arguments*: e.g. a vegan does not eat meat or even buy leather shoes
3. *Lifestyle (identity) arguments*: A high-ranking business person most often drive a high status car.
4. *Group dynamics arguments*: Individuals with higher status in the group have a stronger voice than those with lower status, and sometimes the norms of the group are more important than individual opinions.
5. *Convenience arguments*: When it is too much effort to learn which food is most environmental friendly I buy what is more tasty.
6. *Technological feasibility arguments*: Electric cars are much more environmentally friendly but the batteries must be charged more often.
7. *Private economic arguments:* If going by train costs four times as much as driving, even the environmentalist will choose the car.
8. *Private contract arguments:* A private agreement such as cooperation on the management of a shared water source with a neighbour.
9. *Forcing arguments (institutional and legal)*: Legal constrains may result in more sustainable behaviour.

Voluntary Measures will Succeed when They Show Social and Economic Benefits

The Role of Non-Governmental Organisations

There are benefits for society as a whole when individuals in that society use voluntary measures for change. Individual voluntary research or critical reports, newspaper articles, letters to the editor, etc. by individuals often reveal problems that need to be tackled by society even before politicians or the media are aware of these problems. Thus, individuals or Non-Governmental Organisations (NGOs) often act as whistle-blowers. If environmental activists organise in large groups, they can have a large impact in opinion-forming and they often play a lobbying and ultimately a political role. Voluntary measures such as waste sorting and household recycling were first started by individuals and are now a major task for city councils. The recycling and reuse of resources is of high economic importance since it reduces the costs of

Box 26.1. Sustainable Consumption

In the last fifty years the world has experienced an exceptional increase of consumption. In addition the population of the world is increasing. All of this consumes resources which are limited and scarce.

Consumption may represent different kinds of activities to different people and different places in the world. The social dimension of consumption is important. Consumption may be seen as 'not just a matter of satisfying material greed, or filling your stomach. It is a question of manipulating symbols for all sorts of purposes' (Bauman, 1992: 223).

It is a commonly accepted fact that current consumption and production systems are not compatible with a sustainable society and has considerable negative environmental consequences, including emissions of greenhouse gases, pollution, reduction of water supplies, and reduction of biodiversity. (Michaelis and Lorek, 2004). Thus, we now need to promote sustainable consumption.

Definitions of Sustainable Consumption

It is difficult to usefully define sustainable consumption. Here we will see sustainable consumption as "the use of goods and services that respond to basic needs and bring a better quality of life, while minimizing the use of natural resources, toxic materials and emissions of waste and pollutants over the life cycle, so as not to jeopardize the needs of future generations". This definition was established at the groundbreaking Symposium on Sustainable Consumption in Oslo, Norway in 1994). The definition was subsequently adopted by the UN Commission on Sustainable Development in 1995.

Sustainable consumption is thus an umbrella term which brings together many issues. We could discuss it in terms of social and environmental impact of consumption practices, consumer rights and responsibilities, sustainable consumption behavior, sustainable lifestyles and households, sustainable consumption challenges in agriculture, consumption reduction, sustainable products/service substitutions, and consumers as recyclers.

Rights and Responsibilities of Consumers

To achieve sustainable development through sustainable consumption we should be aware of our rights and responsibilities as a coumers. According to Consumer International (CI, 2007), formerly International Organization of Consumers' Union (IOCU 1987), the basic consumer rights and responsibilities include (shortened descriptions):

- The right to satisfaction of basic needs.
- The right to safety - to be protected against products hazardous to health or life.
- The right to be informed - to be given facts needed to make an informed choice,.
- The right to choose - to be able to select from a range of products and services.
- The right to be heard - to have consumer interests represented.
- The right to redress - to receive a fair settlement of just claims.
- The right to consumer education .
- The right to a healthy environment

Consumer responsibilities include:

- Solidarity: The responsibility to organize and protect our interests.
- Critical Awareness: The responsibility question price and quality of products.
- Action: The responsibility to assert and act to get a fair deal.
- Social Concern: The responsibility to be aware of impact of consumption on other citizens,.
- Environmental Awareness: The responsibility to understand the environmental consequences of our consumption.

How to Promote Sustainable Consumption

We, as consumers, have to behave in a way that will promote sustainable consumption. One has to be 'a responsible consumer, a socially aware consumer, a consumer who thinks ahead and tempers his or her desires by social awareness, a consumer whose actions must be morally defensible and who must occasionally be prepared to sacrifice personal pleasure to communal well-being' (Gabriel and Lang, 1995: 175-176). We can reduce the impact of our food consumption by: eating more vegetables, fruits, and grains and less meat; eating meat that is produced in the least harmful way—grass fed, organic, antibiotic- and hormone-free; giving preference to organic foods; buying in bulk to reduce packaging; avoiding disposable paper and plastic products; using reusable appliances; and buying from small, local sources whenever we can (Sierra Club).

Sustainable consumption of energy demands us to be more efficient in producing and consuming energy. We have to find out and develop alternative and renewable sources of energy. Care should be taken to reduce the use of fossil fuels.

A lifestyle of environmentally friendly consumption may also include taking care of environmental effects of consumption. With this in mind one could for instance use environmentally friendly products, manage waste by separating and recycling, reduce one´s impulse buying, etc. However, there is no single formula for sustainable lifestyles (Autio and Heinonen, 2004).

Governments and different non-government international bodies also have responsibilities to behave as promoters of sustainable consumption and to formulate policies and regulations supporting sustainable development through sustainable production and consumption.

Trade-off Between Consumption and Environmental impact

The main challenge of sustainable development may be to find consumption behaviors that minimizes environmental impact. Thus we should try to find a trade-off between consumption and its impacts on environment. This is not an easy task. Experts have identified that there is a lack of political will and lack of information about sustainable consumption and production patterns. Furthermore, prices do not reflect environmental and social costs and often governmental subsidies are given to unsustainable activities. There are important barriers such as lack of technology transfer and of capacity building (UNEP and CI, 2002).
However, there are also some positive examples. In Scandinavia, deposit schemes for glass, plastic and packages and many other fractions exists since many years in many municipalities also including rural areas. This type of local service is spreading to many other countries. Thus, recycling of waste could be one of many practical ways to reduce the resource consumption.

Md. Motaher Hossain
University of Helsinki, and Jahangirnagar University, Dhaka, Bangladesh

waste collection and management of landfills. Some of the reused material is economically valuable for private firms, one example being the reuse of newspaper in paper mills.

NGOs can be very different from each other. They can be based on religious, political, ethical, neighbourhood or other common values. Within the Baltic Sea Region there are for instance clear religious divides between Protestant/Catholic and Russian Orthodox Christians, giving rise to group pressure, traditions and habits that affect consumer attitudes and choices very strongly and very differently in various local contexts.

However, tradition/history is perhaps the most important factor for both individual and group choices. The most obvious voluntary choice made by individuals in the former Soviet states since the Soviet Union separated into independent states in 1990 is the large number of people moving from rural to urban areas, especially in Russia. This reaction to the living conditions in rural areas started very soon after 1990 (Libert, 1995, p. 163) and has continued up until now, in many cases leaving totally empty villages and uncultivated farm land, but the signals to governments from this 'voluntary behaviour' should be very strong: Something is fundamentally wrong in the rural development policies of these countries.

Voluntary Measures Must be Based on Good Quality Information

Information is needed in order for individuals to make better choices, and the role of society is to make this information as effective as possible.

Individual decisions should ideally be based on economic considerations, availability, attitudes and trustworthy information. Thus society needs to secure funding for independent research. Important characteristics of essential information that must be supported by governmental agencies are (Wilbanks and Stern, 2002):

- Information quality and reliability should be ensured
- Broader citizen involvement should be encouraged
- Voluntary action should be catalysed and supported (to ensure an inflow of corrections and new ideas to politicians and scientists)
- The capacity to act effectively should be improved
- Voluntary partnerships should be promoted (e.g. Finnish National Commission on Sustainable Development (FNCSD, 2007).

Consumer Action

Consumer action is a more active form of voluntary action than just choice of consumption, acting as a driver for change to more environmentally sound behaviour of individuals and households. One example of this is the action introduced by e.g. Greenpeace to refuse to buy cod from the Baltic Sea due to overfishing (Greenpeace, 2006). Another example is the action by animal rights groups against animal fur producers.

Funding of Voluntary Organisations

Individual actions, NGOs, independent studies, etc. are often the result of individual initiative. For example, NGOs are generally funded by membership fees and voluntary financial donations.

An example of an economically very important individual initiative is the creation of the Soros foundation, the Open Society Institute, in the 1980s. The Soros foundation in turn has funded many NGO-type voluntary initiatives and also independent studies in central and eastern Europe.

Voluntary Measures in the Rural Sector

Corporate Social Responsibility (CSR)

Business principles and codes of conduct can make a difference in the business sector, but only if this is demanded by consumers. Thus, business may introduce some voluntary market-specific measures for marketing and business reasons, but never to the extent that economic margins are substantially reduced.

Corporate social responsibility (CSR) can be defined as voluntary action by businesses over and above compliance with minimum legal requirements, in order to address their own competitive interests and the interests of the wider society.

Eco-labelling of Agricultural and Other Rural Products

Some 15-20 years ago, a debate began in Scandinavia on the pollution of lakes, rivers and the sea by paper mills.

At that time, most of the paper produced was bleached using chlorine, which was very detrimental to water ecosystems. Prompted by this debate in the media and action by environmental organisations, the industry very quickly developed alternative methods for bleaching and today chlorine-bleached paper has disappeared from the market.

Recently, many private enterprises in Scandinavia, Germany and North America have started to label their products to meet the expectations of the environmentally-conscious minority of consumers. For instance, in Sweden 8% of agricultural land is used for organic farming and the demand for some organic products the demand cannot be met. Eco-labelling systems have been developed, mainly for forestry, organic agriculture, mining, fishing, timber, paper mills and textile fibres.

Many of the major supermarkets in Scandinavia, e.g. COOP, ICA, Willy's etc., aim to meet consumer demand for products produced in organic farming systems and/or with a label showing that the product is produced under socially fair circumstances. This labelling is voluntary and is provided sometimes within the supermarket's own trademark system, sometimes in cooperation with other actors. Lobbying organisations have started their own labelling philosophy and are working to make it more widely known and accepted by different food trade actors. One example is the fair-trade label, where the premium on the product indicates that the workers involved in agricultural production, processing, storage, transport and packaging have decent working conditions and wages.

Agricultural products with such voluntary labelling that have significant market share include dairy products, meat, eggs, fruit, vegetables, bread, flour, jam, canned vegetables, tea, etc. However, there is higher demand for organic products than for fair-trade products. The highest percentage of voluntary labelling exists for dairy products; e.g. in 2007 organic farmers produced about 6% of Swedish milk (Swedish Dairy Association, 2007). Today other products are under debate. For example, products with large amounts of 'built-in' energy (beef, bottled water) are heavily criticised by environmental organisations.

This pattern of conscious consumer demand can generally be seen in Western Europe and North America, i.e. in countries with a high standard of living. Similar trends have only been seen in the largest cities of Poland, the Baltic States and Russia, while in Belarus and Ukraine they do not yet exist. Voluntary labelling has increased in the EU-25 area, from 11 systems in 1997 to 478 in 2007, most of these issued in Italy, France and Germany (Eurostat, 2007c). A more comprehensive way to ensure sustainable development with respect to all different aspects of economic, social and ecological sustainability is for an organisation or private firm to voluntarily join an environmental management and/or environmental certification system.

Voluntary, Economic and Policy Issues Need to Go Hand in Hand

Information, communication and dissemination of legislation, political measures and economic incentives are needed for the individual or group to make an informed choice. Thus, voluntary measures largely depend on what is decided in the surrounding society locally, regionally, nationally and internationally. The need for information and communication between different levels calls for increased networking and continuous updating of information. There must also be legislation in place to ensure communication of independent information, stop criminal acts and stop the most aggressive types of marketing of products that clearly undermine health or the environment.

References

Introduction

CIA Factbook. https://www.cia.gov/library/publications/the-world-factbook/

Ecological Footprint Atlas, 2010. http://www.footprintnetwork.org/en/index.php/GFN/page/ecological_footprint_atlas_2010. (retrieved 20120903).

European Commission, EC, 2006. *Study on Employment in Rural Areas*. http://ec.europa.eu/agriculture/publi/reports/ruralemployment/sera_report.pdf (retrieved 20120903).

European Union EU, 2009. *Sustainable Development Strategy*. http://eur-lex.europa.eu/LexUriServ/LexUriServ.do?uri=COM:2009:0400:FIN:EN:PDF (retrieved 20120903).

Holmberg, J., 1992. *Resources-theoretical principles for a sustainable developmen*t. Licentiate thesis, Institute of Physical resource Theory, Chalmers University of Technology and University of Göteborg. (In Swedish).

Homberg, J., Robèrt, K-H. and Eriksson, K-E. 1994, Socio-Ecological Principles For A Sustainable Society Scientific background and Swedish experience Paper presented at the *International Symposium "Down to Earth: Practical Application of ecological Economics"* October 24-28, 1994 in Heredia, Costa Rica.

ICLEI, International Council for Local Environmental Initiatives. 1994. *Local Agenda 21 Participants Handbook — Local Agenda 21 Model Communities Programme. Local Environmental Initiatives*, ICLEI, Toronto. http://web.idrc.ca/openebooks/448-2/ (retrieved 20120903).

IUCN, UNEP, WWF. 1991 *Caring for the Earth: A Strategy for Sustainable Living*. http://data.iucn.org/dbtw-wpd/edocs/CFE-003.pdf (retrieved 20120903).

IUCN and WWFN, 1992 *Caring for the Earth: summary of a world strategy for sustainable living Health Promot*. Int. (1992) 7 (2): 135-145. See http://heapro.oxfordjournals.org/content/7/2/135.extract (retrieved 20120903).

McNeill, J.R. 2000. *Something new under the sun: an environmental history of the twentieth-century world*. New York: W.W. Norton & Company, 421 p.

Nebel, B.J. and R.T. Wright,1996. *Environmental Science*. 5th edition. Prentice Hall.

Russian Survey on National Sustainable Development Strategies. 2004.

Russian Action Plan on Ecological Doctrine Implementation. 2003.

The New Sustainable Frontier – Principles of Sustainable Development (published by the US General Services Administration, Office of Governmentwide Policy)

UNEP, Grid Arendal. http://maps.grida.no/baltic/ (retrieved 20120903).

World Commission on Environment and Development (WCED), 1987. *Our Common Future*. New York: Oxford University Press.

Chapter 1

Anderberg, S. 1991. Historical land use changes: Sweden. In: Brouwer, F. M., Thomas, A. J. and Chadwick, M. J. (eds.) *Land use changes in Europe: Processes of change, environmental transformations and future patterns*, The GeoJournal Library, Dordrecht: Kluwer Academic Publishers, pp 403-426.

Andersen, S.Th. 1993. Early agriculture. In: Hvass, S. and Storgaard , B. (eds.) *Digging into the past. 25. Years of archaeology in Denmark*. Copenhagen: Aarhus Universitetsforlag, pp 88–91.

Antrop, M. 2000. Background concepts for integrated landscape analysis. In: *Agriculture Ecosystems & Environment*. 77, pp 17-28.

Baldock, D., Beaufoy, G., Benne, G. and Clark, J. 1993. *Nature conservation and new directions in the common agricultural policy*. London: IEEP.

BASICS, Baltic Sea region Statistical database on sustainable development, natural resources and environment. http://www.grida.no/prog/norbal/basics/index.htm (retrieved 20120903).

Behre, K.-E. 1988. The role of man in European vegetation history. In: Huntley, B. and Webb III, T. (eds): *Vegetation history*. Dordrecht: Kluwer Academic Publishers, pp 633–672.

Björkman, L. 1996. *The late holocene history of beech Fagus sylvatica and Norway spruce Picea abies at stand-scale in southern Sweden*. Lund: LUNDQUA Thesis 39, 44 pp.

Copus, A., Hall,C., Barnes, A., Dalton, G., Cook, P., Weingarten, P., Baum, S., Stange, H., Lindner, C., Hill, A., Eiden, G., McQuaid, R., Grieg, M. and Johansson, M. 2006. Study on Employment in Rural Areas (SERA) – Report prepared for the European Commission, DG Agriculture. Brussels: European Commission pp. 203. http://ec.europa.eu/agriculture/publi/reports/ruralemployment/sera_report.pdf (retrieved 20120903).

Cosgrove, D.E. 1998. *Social formation and symbolic landscape*. Madison, WI: University of Wisconsin Press, 293 p.

Cvetkov, M.A. 1957. *Izmenenije lesisosti Evropeiskoi Rossii s konca XVII stoletija po 1914 god* (in Russian), 213 pp.

Estonian Ministry of Agriculture. 2005. http://www.agri.ee/public/juurkataloog/STAT_2005.XLS (retrieved 20120903).

European Landscape Convention, 2000. European Treaty Series - No. 176, 8 pp.

Forman, R.T.T. and Godron, M. 1986. *Landscape ecology*. New York: John Wiley and Sons, 619 pp.

Frey, W. 1983. The influence of snow on growth and survival of planted trees. In: *Arctic and Alpine Research*, 15, 241–251.

Goldammer, J.G. 1998. History of fire in land-use systems of the Baltic region: Implications on the use of prescribed fire in forestry, nature conservation and landscape management. In: *Proceedings, First Baltic Conference on Forest Fires, Radom-Katowice, Poland, 5-9 May 1998*, 59-76 (in Polish with English summary).

Granö, J.G. 1929. *Reine Geographie. Eine methodologische Studie beleuchtet mit Beispielen aus Finnland und Estland*, Acta Geographica, 2, 2.

HELCOM, 2004. *The fourth Baltic sea pollution load compilation (PLC-4)*. Balt. Sea Environ. Proc. No 93, 188 pp.

Isakar, M. Läänemeri jääajajärgsel ajal. 2003 http://www.ut.ee/BGGM/eestigeol/l_m_parastj.html (retrieved 20120903).

Juske, A., Sepp, M. and Sihver, Ü. 1991. Maaparandustööd kahe ilmasõja vahel. In: Juske, A. (ed.) *Maaparandus. Eesti põllumajanduse infokeskus*, Tallinn,10-17.

Karavayeva, N.A., Nefedova, T.G. and Targulian, V.O. 1991. Historical landuse changes and soil degradation on the Russian plain. In: Brouwer, F.M.A., Thomas, J. and Chadwick, M.J. (eds.) *Land use changes in Europe: processes of change environmental transformation and future patterns*, Dordrecht: Kluwer, pp 351-377.

Kriiska, A. 2002. Lääne-Eesti saarte asustamine ja püsielanikkonna kujunemine. In: *Keskus–tagamaa–ääreala*. Muinasaja teadus, 11. Tallinn, pp 29–60.

Kriiska, A. 2003. From hunter-fisher-gatherer to farmer – changes in the neolithic economy and settlement on Estonian territory,. In: *Archaeologia Lithuana*, Vol. 4, pp 11-26.

Larsson, L. 1997. Coastal settlement during the Mesolithic and Neolithic periods in the southernmost part of Sweden. In: Król, D. (ed.). *The built environment of coastal areas during the Stone age*. Gdañsk, pp 12–22.

Laul, S. and Tõnisson, E. 1991. Muistsete sirpide ja vikatite kujunemisloost Eestis. In: *Arheoloogiline kogumik*. Muinasaja teadus, 1. Tallinn, pp 75–91.

Lõugas, V. 1980. Põllumajandusmaastiku ajaloost Eestis. In: Aasalo, L. (ed.) *Põllumajandusmaastik Eestis*, pp 50-84.

Messerli, B. and Messerli, P. 1978. MAB Schweitz. In: *Geographica Helvetica*. No 4.

Orrman, E. 2003. Rural conditions. In: Helle, K. (ed.). *The Cambridge history of Scandinavia*, Vol. 1, pp 250-311.

Palang, H. 1994. *Eesti maastike mitmekesisuse ja maakasutuse dünaamika XX sajandil*. Master Thesis at Tartu University, 59 p.

Palang, H., Rydén, L., Haber, Z., Elias, P., Elvisto, T., Emmanuelsson, U. and Migula, P. 2003. Society and landscape – space intrution and habitat destruction. In: Rydén, L., Migula, P. and Andersson, M. (Eds). *Environmental Science*. Ch 7. pp187-221.

Pitkänen, A., Huttunen, P., Jungner, H., Meriläinen, J. and Tolonen, K. 2003. Holocene fire history of middle boreal pine forest sites in eastern Finland. In: *Ann. Bot. Fennici*: 40, pp 15-33.

Rabbinge, R. and van Diepen, C.A. 2000. Changes in agriculture and land use in Europe. In: *European Journal of Agronomy*, Volume 13, Issues 2-3, pp 85-99.

Ratt, A. 1985. *Mõnda maaviljeluse arengust Eestis läbi aegade*, Tallinn: Valgus (in Estonian), 267 p.

Sauer, C. 1925. *The Morphology of Landscape*. University of California Publications in Geography. No. 22, pp 19-53.

Rydin, H, Snoeijs, P. and Diekmann, M. (Eds.) 1999. *Swedish plant geography*. Acta Phytogeographica Suecia 84, pp. 1-248.

Sporrong, U. 2003. The Scandinavian landscape and its resources. In: Helle, K. (ed.). *The Cambridge history of Scandinavia*, Vol. 1, pp 15-42.

Sporrong, U., Ekstam, U. and Samuelsson, K. 1995. *Swedish landscapes*. Swedish Environmental Protection Agency, 184 p.

State of Europe's Forests 2007. The MCPFE (Ministerial Conference on the Protection of Forests in Europe) Report on Sustainable Forest Management in Europe. MCPFE Liaison Unit Warsaw, UNECE and FAO, Warsaw, Poland, 247 p.

Troll, C. 1939. Luftbildplan und ökologische Bodenforschung (Aerial photography and ecological studies of the earth). In: *Zeitschrift der Gesellschaft für Erdkunde*, Berlin, pp 241-298.

Turner, M.G., Gardner, R.H. and O'Neill, R.V. 2001. *Landscape ecology in theory and practice: Pattern and process*. New York: Springer, 401 p.

UNEP/GRID-Arendal. http://maps.grida.no/go/graphic/arable_land_in_the_baltic_sea_region (retrieved 20120903).

Vervloet, A. 1986: *Inleiding tot de historische geografie van de Nederlandse cultuurlandschappen*. Wageningen.

Chapter 2

Ackerman, S. and Knox, J.A. 2006. *Meteorology: Understanding the atmosphere.* Pacific Grove, Ca.: Brooks Cole.

Alcamo, J. et al. 2003. *Ecosystems and human well-being: A framework for assessment*. Washington, D. C.: Island Press.

Babcock, B.A., Lichtenberg, E. and Zilberman, D. 1992. Impact of damage control and quality of output: Estimating pest control effectiveness. In: *American Journal of Agricultural Economics* 74, pp 163–172.

Balmford, A., Bruner, A., Cooper, P., Costanza, R., Farber, S., Green, R., Jenkins, M., Fefferiss, P., Jessamay, V., Madden, J., Munro, K., Myers, N., Naeem, S., Paavola, J., Rayment, M., Rosendo, S., Rouhgarden, J., Trumper, K. and Turner, R.K. 2002. Economic reasons for conserving wild nature. In: *Science*, 297, pp 950–953.

Bonnieux and Rainelli, 1996. Landscape and nature conservation: French country report. In: Umstaetter, J. and Dabbert, S. (Eds.) *Policies for landscape and nature conservation in Europe*: workshop 16-29 September 1996 at University of Hohenheim, Germany.

Brown, T.C., Bergstrom, J.C. and Loomis, J.B. 2006. *Ecosystem goods and services: Definition, valuation and provision*. RMRS-RWU-4851 Discussion Paper.

Costanza, R. et al. 1997. The value of the world's ecosystem services and natural capital. In: *Nature* 387, pp 253–260.

Daily, G.C. (ed) 1997. *Nature's services: Societal dependence on natural ecosystems*. Washington, DC: Island Press.

Dale, V.H. and Polasky, S. 2007. Measures of the effects of agricultural practices on ecosystem services. In: *Ecological Economics*, 64, pp 286–296.

de Groot, R.S. and Hein, L. 2007. Concept and valuation of landscape functions at different scales. In: Mander, Ü., Wiggering, H. and Helming, K. *Multifunctional land use*. Berlin Heidelberg: Springer Verlag pp 15–36.

de Groot, R.S., Wilson, M. and Boumans, R. 2002. A typology for the description, classification and valuation of ecosystem functions, goods and services. In: *Ecological Economics* Vol. 41 (3), pp 393–408.

de Groot, R.S. 1992. *Functions of nature, evaluation of nature in environmental planning, management and decision making*. Groningen: Wolters-Noordhoff.

European Union, *The Sixth Environmental Action Plan* (EAP) 2002-12.

EU Regulation 2078/92

FAOSTAT, 1999. http://faostat.fao.org/?alias=faostat1999. (retrieved 20120903).

Free, J.B. 1993. *Insect pollination of crops*. London: Academic Press.

Guo, Z., Xiao, X. and Li, D. 2000. An assessment of ecosystem services: water flow regulation and hydroelectric power production. In: *Ecological Applications* 10, pp 925–936.

Houlahan, J. and Findlay, C.S. 2004. Estimating the 'critical' distance at which adjacent land-use degrades wetland water and sediment quality. In: *Landscape Ecology* 19, pp 677– 690.

Jackson, J., Kirby, M., Berger,W., Bjorndal, K., Botsford, L., Bourque, B., Bradbury, R., Cooke, R., Erlandson, J., Estes, J., Hughes, T., Kidwell, S., Lange, C., Lenihan, H., Pandolfi, J., Peterson, C., Steneck, R., Tegner, M. and Warner, R. 2001. Historical over fishing and the recent collapse of coastal ecosystems. In: *Science* 293, pp 629–638.

Klein, A., Steffan-Dewenter, I. and Tscharntke, T. 2003. Fruit set of highland coffee increases with the diversity of pollinating bees. Proceedings of the Royal Society of London. Series B 270, pp 955–961.

Klein,A., Vaissière, B.E., Cane, J.H., Steffan-Dewenter, I., Cunningham, S.A., Kremen, C. and Tscharntke, T. 2007. Importance of pollinators in changing landscapes for world crops. In: *Proceedings of the Royal Society of London. B, Biological Sciences* 274 (1608), pp 303–313.

Losey, J.E. and Vaughan, M. 2006. The economic value of ecological services provided by insects. In: *Bioscience* 56 (4), pp 331–323.

Millennium Ecosystem Assessment (MA), 2005. *Ecosystems and human well-being: Synthesis*. Washington, DC: Island Press.

Myers, R.A. and Worm, B. 2003. Rapid worldwide depletion of predatory fish communities. In: *Nature* 423, pp 280–283.

Naylor, R. and Ehrlich, P. 1997. Natural pest control services and agriculture. In: Daily, G. (ed.) *Nature's services: Societal dependence on natural ecosystems*, pp. 151–174. Washington DC.

Paul, E.A. and Clark, F.E. 1996. *Soil microbiology and biochemistry*. New York: Academic Press.

Ratcliffe, B.C. 1970. Scarab beetles: Dung feeders, jeweled pollinations, and horned giants. In: *University of Nebraska News*, vol. 59. pp. 1– 4.

Roka, F.M. and Palmquist, R.B. 1997. Examining the use of national databases in a hedonic analysis of regional farmland values. In: *American Journal of Agricultural Economics* 79, 1651–1656.

Robertson, G.P., Burger, L.W., Kling, C.L., Lowrance, R. and Mulla, D.J. 2007. New approaches to environmental management research at landscape and watershed scales. In: Schnepf, M. and Cox, C. (eds.), *Managing agricultural landscapes for environmental quality. Soil and water conservation society*. Ankeny, IA, pp. 27–50.

Stoller, E.W., Harrison, S.K., Wax, L.M., Regnier, E.E. and Nafziger, E.D. 1987. Weed interference in soybeans (Glycine max). In: *Reviews of Weed Science* 3, pp 155–181.

Swinton, S.M, Lupi, F., Robertson, G.P. and Hamilton, S.K., 2007. Ecosystem services and agriculture: Cultivating agricultural ecosystems for diverse benefits. In: *Ecological Economics*, 64, 245–252.

Thies, C. and Tscharntke, T. 1999. Landscape structure and biological control in agroecosystems. In: *Science* 285 (5429), pp 893–895.

Tilman, D., Cassman K.G., Matson P.A. and Naylor R.L. 2002. Agricultural sustainability and intensive production practices. In: *Nature*, 418, pp 671–77.

USDA, 2007. *Agriculture Secretary Mike Johanns addressed the problem of honeybee colony collapse disorder*. USDA Satellite News Feed July 5, 2007.

Vitousek, P.M., Cassman, K., Cleveland, C., Crews, T., Field, C.B., Grimm, N.B., Howarth, R.W., Marino, R., Martinelli, L., Rastetter, E.B. and Sprent, J.I. 2002. Towards an ecological understanding of biological nitrogen fixation. In: *Biogeochemistry* 57/58 (1), pp 1– 45.

Wandén, S. and Schaber, P. 1998. Understanding Biodiversity. In: Catizzone, M., Larsson, T.B. and Svensson, L. (eds) *European Commission, Ecosystem Research Report No. 25*.

Weibull, A., Ostman, O. and Granqvist, A. 2003. Species richness in agroecosystems: the effect of landscape, habitat and farm management. In: *Biodiversity and Conservation* 12, pp 1335–1355.

Welbank, P.J. 1963. A comparison of competitive effects of some common weed species. In: *Annals of Applied Biology* 51, pp 107–125.

Whitmire, S.L. and Hamilton, S.K. 2005. Rapid removal of nitrate and sulfate by freshwater wetland sediments. In: *Journal of Environmental Quality*, 34, pp 2062–2071.

Wilby, A. and Thomas, M.B. 2002. Natural enemy diversity and pest control: Patterns of pest emergence with agricultural intensification. In: *Ecology Letters* 5, pp 353–360.

Wilkinson, T.K. and Landis, D.A. 2005. Habitat diversification in biological control: The role of plant resources. In: Wackers, F.L., van Rijn, P.C.J. and Bruin, J. (eds.), *Plant provided food and plant-carnivore mutualism*. Cambridge, U.K: Cambridge University Press.

Zhang, W., Ricketts, T.H., Kremen, C., Carney, K., Scott M. and Swinton, S.M. 2007. Ecosystem services and dis-services to agriculture. In: *Ecological Economics*, 64 , pp 253–260.

Chapter 3

Pikulik, M.M. and Kozulin, A.V. 2000. Recent State and significance of vertebrate animal populations of Belarusian Polesie. In: *The ecological and lowlands mires in the Polesie region*. Minsk P. 120-123.

Romanova, T.A. and Yatsukhno, V.M. 2001, Optimal proportion of grounds as a key to sustainable utilization and conservation of agrolandscapes of Polesye. In.: *Belarusian Polesye*. Belarusian Polesye Foundation, Pinsk, p. 38-42. (in Russian).

The scheme of rational distribution of nature protected areas of national importance before January 1, 2015. Minsk, 2007. 17 p.

Yatsukhno, V.M. 2006. Biological and landscape diversity conservationas a key sustainable agricultural development of Belarus of Belarusian Polesie. In: *Environment of Polesie: particularities and perspectives of development*. Vol. 1. Academia. Brest, 2006/ H/ 4-10.

Yatsukhno, V.M. 1995. *Formation of agrolandscapes and environment protection*. Institute of Geology, Minsk, 120 p. (in Russian).

Yatsukhno, V.M., Bambalov, N.N. and Davydik, E.E. 1998. On the necessity of the landscape approach to realization of measures aimed at the conservation of biological diversity in Belarus. In: *Natural resorses*. No. 3. 1998. P. 59-65. (in Russian).

Chapter 4

BALTEX (the Baltic Sea Experiment) a Regional Hydroclimate Project (RHP) of the Coordinated Energy and Water Cycle Observations Project (CEOP) within the Global Energy and Water Cycle Experiment (GEWEX) of the World Climate Research Programme (WCRP). http://www.baltex-research.eu/ (retrieved 20120917)

Baltic Environmental Atlas (including rivers, lakes, drainage basin), Baltic on-line interactive geographical and environmental information service (BOING). http://maps.grida.no/baltic/description.htm. (retrieved 20120917)

Bergström S. and Carlsson B. 1994. River runoff to the Baltic Sea 1950-1990. In: *Ambio* 23 280-287.

Bergström, S., Filatov, N., Pozdnjakov, D., Magnuszewski, A. and Bergström, H. 2000. The Baltic Basin – rivers, lakes and climate. In: Lundin, L-C. *The Waterscape*. Sustainable Water Management, Volume I. pp. 207. Uppsala: Baltic University Press.

Blomqvist P. and Brunberg A.K. 1998. *Environmental Protection and Management*, Socrates teaching material.

Blomqvist, P. and Brunberg , A-K. 2000. Lakes – origin, ontogeny and natural functions. In: Lundin, L-C. *The Waterscape*. Sustainable Water Management, Volume I. pp. 207. Uppsala: Baltic University Press.

The BUP course on Sustainable Water Management in the Baltic Sea Basin. http://www.balticuniv.uu.se/swm/ (retrieved 20120917)

Chave, P.A. 2001. *The EU Water Framework Directive: An Introduction*. IWA Publishing: Cornwall.

European Commission. 2003. *Monitoring under the Water Framework Directive*; Luxembourg.

European Commission, 2007. *Water Framework Directive – Facts, figures and maps*. http://ec.europa.eu/environment/water/water-framework/facts_figures/index_en.htm (retrieved 20120903).

Hordoir, R. H. and Meier, E. M. 2010 Freshwater fluxes in the Baltic Sea – a model study. In: *Journal of Geophysical Research*, Vol 115, August 2010

Integrated Water Resources Management (IWRM). http://www.un.org/waterforlifedecade/iwrm.shtml (retrieved 20120917)

International Decade for action 'Water for Life' 2005-2015. http://www.un.org/waterforlifedecade/ (retrieved 20120917)

Lundin, L. 2000. Wetands in the Baltic Sea region. In: Lundin, L-C. *The Waterscape*. Sustainable Water Management, Volume I. pp. 207. Uppsala: Baltic University Press.

Magnuszewski, A. 2000. Hydrology and water quality of European rivers. In: Lundin, L-C. *The Waterscape*. Sustainable Water Management, Volume I. pp. 207. Uppsala: Baltic University Press.

Raab and Vedin. 1995- Klimat sjöar och vattendrag. In: *Sveriges Nationalatlas*. Bra Böcker Höganäs, 176 pp (in Swedish).

Reckermann, M., Brander, K., MacKenzie, B.R. and Omstedt, A. (Eds.). 2012. *Climate Impacts on the Baltic Se*a. From Science to Policy Series: Springer Earth System Sciences. Springer Verlag, Heidelberg. 216 p.

Rydén, L., Migula, P. and Andersson, M. (Editors). 2003. *Environmental Science – understanding, protecting, and managing the environment in the Baltic Sea region*. pp. 823. Uppsala: Baltic University Press.

Wohl, E., Angermeier, P.L., Bledsoe, B., Kondolf, G.M., MacDonnell, L., Merritt, D.M., Palmer, M.A., Poff, N.L. and Tarboton, D. 2005. River restoration. In: *Water Resources Research*, 41, W10301.

Chapter 5

Fredman, P. 2002. *Forskning kring svensk fjällturism* – Fler turister i söder, ökad motorisering och konflikter mellan snöskoteråkare och turskidåkare http://www.utmark.org/utgivelser/pub/2002-3/art/fredman-utmark-3-2002.htm (retrieved 20120903).

Fredman, P. and Heberlein, T. A. 2003. Trender i Svensk fjällturism 1980-2000. In: *Svensk turismforskning - en tvärvetenskaplig antologi om turister, turistdestinationer och turismorganisationer*. ETOUR, Östersund, vetenskapliga bokserien, V 2003:13 (in Swedish)

Fredman, P. and Heberlein, T. A. 2005. In: *Mountain Tourism in Nothern Europe: Current Patterns and Recent Trends. Mountains of Northern Europe*. Conservation, management, People and Nature. Scottish Natural Heritage, Edinburgh

Fredman, P. 2008. Determinants of visitor expenditures in mountain tourism. In: *Tourism Economics*, 2008, 14 (2), 297–311

Meet Poland: Winter sports – Skiing in Poland. http://www.meetpoland.com/leisure/skiing.html (retrieved 20120903).

The *Sami People in Sweden* – Factsheet, 1999. Published by the Swedish Institute. February 1999.

Wikipedia: Carpathian Mountains. http://en.wikipedia.org/wiki/Carpathian_Mountains

UNEP-WCMC, Nordregio (kartan)

Chapter 6

Bogue, M. 1951. The Swamp Land Act and wet land utilization in Illinois, 1850-1890. In *Agricultural History* 25, pp 169-180.

Bogue, A. 1963. *From Prairie to Corn Belt: Farming on the Illinois and Iowa Prairies in the Nineteenth Century*. Chicago: University of Chicago Press.

Bogue, M. 2000. *Fishing the Great Lakes: An Environmental History 1783-1933*. Madison: University of Wisconsin Press.

Cochrane, W. 1993. *The Development of American Agriculture: A Historical Analysis (Second Edition)*. Minneapolis: University of Minnesota Press.

Cromartie, and S Bucholtz. 2007. Rural Definitions. US Department of Agriculture Economic Research Service. http://www.ers.usda.gov/data-products/rural-definitions.aspx (retrieved 20120917)

Cronon, W. 1991. *Nature's Metropolis: Chicago and the Great West*. New York: W. W. Norton & Co.

Davis M, C Douglas, R Calcote, K Cole, M Winkler and R Flakne. 2000. Holocene climate in western Great Lakes National Parks and Lakeshores: Implications for future climate change. In: *Conservation Biology* 14, pp 968-983.

Edwards, W. 1994. Agriculture and Wildlife in the Midwest. In McIsaac, G and W Edwards (Eds.). Sustainable Agriculture in the American Midwest, Urbana: University of Illinois Press.

Faith J, and T Surovell. 2009. Synchronous extinction of North America's Pleistocene mammals. In *Proceedings of the National Academy of Sciences USA* 106, pp 20641–20645.

Holder, P. 1970. *The Hoe and the Horse on the Plains: A Study of Cultural Development among North American Indians*. Lincoln: University of Nebraska Press.

Iverson, L. 1988. Land-use Changes in Illinois, USA: The Influence of Landscape Attributes on Current and Historic Land Use. In *Landscape Ecology* 2:1, pp 45-61.

Johnson, K. 1999. The rural rebound. In *Population Reference Bureau Reports on America* 1:3, pp 1-21.

Kellog, R, G TeSelle and J Goebel. 1994. Highlights from the National Resources Inventory. In *Journal of Soil and Water Conservation* 49:6, pp 521-27.

Mann, C. 2005. *1491: New Revelations of the Americas before Columbus*. New York: Alfred A. Knopf.

National Research Council, Committee on Conservation Needs and Opportunities. 1986. *Soil Conservation: Assessing the National Resources Inventory Volume 1*. Washington: National Academy Press.

Ostrom E. 2009. A general framework for analyzing sustainability of social-ecological systems. In *Science* 325, pp 419–422.

Perlin, J. 2005. *A Forest Journey: The Role of Wood in the Development of Civilization* (2nd ed). New York: W.W. Norton & Company.

Rasmussen, W. 1960. *Readings in the History of American Agriculture*. Urbana: University of Illinois Press.

Roe, J. 1916. *English and American Tool Builders*. New Haven: Yale University Press.

Salamon, S. 1992. *Prairie Patrimony: Family, Farming and Community in the Midwest*. Chapel Hill: University of North Carolina Press.

Salamon, S. 2003. *Newcomers to Old Towns: Suburbanization of the Heartland*. Chicago: University of Chicago Press.

Sawyer, J. 1954. The social basis for the American system of manufacturing. In *Journal of Economic History*. 14:4, pp 361-379.

Schwab, G.O., Fangmeier, D.D. Elliot, W.J., Fevert, R.K. 1993. *Soil and Water Conservation Engineering*. New York: John Wiley and Sons, Inc.

Smith, B. 1989. Origins of agriculture in eastern North America. In: *Science* 246, pp 1566-1571.

Smith, B. 1992. Prehistoric Plant Husbandry in Eastern North America. In: Cowan, C and P Watson. (Editors), *The Origins of Agriculture: an International Perspective*. Washington: Smithsonian Institution Press.

Strange, M. 1988. *Family Farming A New Economic Vision*. Lincoln: University of Nebraska Press, and Institute for Food and Development Policy.

Tanner, H, A Hast, J Peterson, R Surtees, and M Pinther. 1987. *Atlas of Great Lakes Indian History*. University of Oklahoma Press.

Trimble S and S Lund. 1982. Soil conservation, erosion and sedimentation, Coon Creek, Wisconsin. US Geological Survey Professional Paper 1234.

US. Environmental Protection Agency, US EPA. Land use, fisheries & erosion. http://www.epa.gov/greatlakes/atlas/images/big07.gif (retrieved 20120903).

U.S. Department of Agriculture. 2009. National Resources Inventory - 2007 NRI. http://www.nrcs.usda.gov/wps/portal/nrcs/main/national/technical/nra/nri (retrieved 20120903).

Walters, M and T Stafford. 2007. Redefining the Age of Clovis: Implications for the Peopling of the Americas. *Science* 315, pp 1122-6.

Warren, D. M. 1994. Indigenous Agricultural Knowledge, Technology and Social Change. In: McIsaac, G. and W. Edwards (eds). *Sustainable Agriculture in the American Midwest: Lessons from the Past, Prospects for the Future*. Urbana: University of Illinois Press. Pp 35-53.

Wik, R. 1953. *Steam Power on the American Farm*. Philadelphia: University of Pennsylvania Press.

Williams, J. 2000. Book Review: Bonnicksen, T. M. 2000. America's ancient forests: from the Ice Age to the Age of Discovery. Wiley, New York. In *Conservation Ecology* 4:2, articles 2. http://www.consecol.org/vol4/iss2/art2/ (retrieved 20120903)

Worster, D. 1979. *The Dust Bowl: The Southern Plains in the 1930's*. Oxford University Press.

Chapter 7

Bennett, J. 1988. "History that Stands Still": Women's Work in the European Past. In: *Feminist Studies*. 14: 2, pp. 269-283.

Bumblauskas, A. 2005. *Senosios Lietuvos Istorija 1009-1795*. (Lith: A History of Lithuania 1009-1795). Vilnius: R. Paknys Publishing House.

Christiansen, P.O. 1995. Culture and Contrasts in a Northern European Village: Lifestyles among Manorial Peasants in 18th-Century Denmark. In: *Journal of Social History*. 29:2, pp. *275-294*.

Conquest, R. 1986. *The Harvest of Sorrow: Soviet Collectivization and the Terror-Famine*. New York: Oxford University Press.

Davies, N. 1979. *God's Playground: A History of Poland, Vol. 1: The Origins to 1795*. New York: Columbia University Press.

Derry, T.K. 1979. *A History of Scandinavia: Norway, Sweden, Denmark, Finland and Iceland*. Minneapolis: University of Minnesota Press.

Fitzpatrick, S. 1994. *Stalin's Peasants: Resistance and Survival in the Russian Village after Collectivization*. Oxford: Oxford University Press.

Gimbutas, M. 1991. *The Civilization of the Goddess: The World of Old Europe*. San Francisco: Harper.

Harnesk, B. 2009. Everyday Resistance and the Hidden Transcript in Seventeenth-Century Sweden. In: Karonen,P., Eilola, J., Hakanen, M., Lamberg, M. and Matikainen, O. (eds.). *Hopes and Fears for the Future in Early Modern Sweden, 1500-1800*. Helsinki: Finnish Literature Society Publishing. Pp. 250-262.

Helle, K. 2003. *The Cambridge History of Scandinavia, Volume 1: Prehistory to 1520*. Cambridge: Cambridge University Press.

Hudson, B. 2005. *Viking Pirates and Christian Princes: Dynasty, Religion, and Empire in North America*. Oxford: Oxford University Press.

Jespersen, L. 2002. Court and Nobility in Early Modern Denmark. In: *Scandinavian Journal of History*. 27: 3, pp 129-142.

Johansen, H. C. 2002. *Danish Population History, 1600-1939*. Odense: University Press of Southern Denmark.

Jörgensen, H. 2006. The Inter-War Land Reforms in Estonia, Finland and Bulgaria: A Comparative Study. In: *Scandinavian Economic History Review*, 54: 1, pp 64-97.

Jussila, O., Hentila, S. and Nevakivi, J. 1999. *From Grand Duchy to a Modern State: A Political History of Finland Since 1809*. London: Hurst & Co. Publishers.

Kahk, J. 1990. The Mechanization of Agriculture in Estonia from 1860 to 1880. In: *Journal of Baltic Studies*. 21: 4, pp. 335-346.

Kjaergaard, T. 1995. *The Danish Revolution, 1500-1800: An Ecohistorical Interpretation*. Cambridge: Cambridge University Press.

Kujala, A. 2003. *The Crown, the Nobility and the Peasants 1630-1713: Tax, Rent and Relations of Power.* Helsinki: Suomalaisen Kirjallisuuden Seura.

Kujala, A. 2000. The Breakdown of a Society: Finland in the Great Northern War 1700-1714. In: *Scandinavian Journal of History*. 25: 1-2, pp. 69-86.

Lageras, P. 2007. *The Ecology of Expansion and Abandonment: Medieval and Post-medieval Agriculture and Settlement in a Landscape Perspective*. Stockholm: Riksantikvarieambetet.

L'Hereux, M.-A. 2010. Modernizing the Estonian Farmhouse, Redefining the Family, 1880s–1930s. In: *Journal of Baltic Studies*. 41: 4, pp. 473-506.

Löfgren, O. 1980. Historical Perspectives on Scandinavian Peasantries," In: *Annual Review of Anthropology*. 9, pp. 187-215.

Markkola, P. 2000. Promoting Faith and Welfare: The Deaconess Movement in Finland and Sweden, 1850–1930. In: *Scandinavian Journal of History*. 25: 1-2, pp. 101-118.

Meinander, H. 2011. *A History of Finland*. New York: Columbia University Press.

Mincyte, D. 2009. Everyday Environmentalism: The Practice, Politics, and Nature of Subsidiary Farming in Stalin's Lithuania. In: *Slavic Review*. 68: 1, pp. 31-49.

Munck, T. 1979. *The Peasantry and the Early Absolute Monarchy in Denmark, 1660-1708*. Copenhagen: Landbohistorisk Selskab.

O'Connor, K. J. 2003. *The History of the Baltic States*. Westport: Greenwood Press

Olden-Jørgensen, S. 2002. State Ceremonial, Court Culture and Political Power in Early Modern Denmark, 1536-1746. In: *Scandinavian Journal of History*. 27: 21, pp. 65-76.

Olwig, K. 2006. *The Nature of Cultural Heritage, and the Culture of Natural Heritage – Northern Perspectives on a Contested Patrimony*. London and New York: Routledge.

Paasivirta, J. 1981. *Finland and Europe: The Period of Autonomy and the International Crises, 1808-1914*. Minneapolis: University of Minnesota Press.

Pallot, J. 1979. Rural Settlement Planning in the USSR. In: *Soviet Studies*. 31:2, pp. 214-230.

Viola, L. 1996. *Peasant Rebels under Stalin: Collectivization and the Culture of Peasant Resistance*. Oxford: University of Oxford Press.

Wandycz, P. S. 1974. *The Lands of Partitioned Poland, 1795-1918*, Seattle: University of Washington Press.

Ågren, M. 2011. Families and States in Scandinavia. In: Skinner, Q. (ed.). *Families and States in Western Europe*. Cambridge: Cambridge University Press. Pp. 146-166.

Ågren, M. 2009. *Domestic Secrets: Women and Property in Sweden 1600-1857*. Chapel Hill: University of North Carolina Press.

Ågren, M. and Erickson, A.L. (eds.). 2005. *The Marital Economy in Scandinavia and Britain 1400-1900*. Burlington: Ashgate.

Østergård, U. 1997. The Geopolitics of Nordic Identity – From Composite States to Nation States. In: Sørensen, Ø. and Stråth, B. (eds.), *The Cultural Construction of Norden*. Oslo: Scandinavian University Press. Pp. 25-71.

Chapter 8

Applebaum, A. 2003. *Gulag. A history.* New York: Doubleday.

Atlas till världshistorien (Atlas to world history) 1958. Svenska Bokförlaget.

Bengtsson, A. 2007. *Bronssoldatens hämnd. Baltiska betraktelser*, (The revenge of the cast iron soldier. Baltic reflections). Vimmerby: Scandbook.

Blum, A. and Troitskaya, I. 1997. Mortality in Russia during the 18th and 19th century: Local assessments based on the Revizii. In: *Population*: An English Selection. 9:123-146

Burns, K. 2007. Russia's HIV/AIDS epidemic. In: *Problems of Post-Communism*, January/February

Central Intelligence Agency, CIA. Various years. *The world fact book.*

Central Statistical Office. CSO. 2008. *Polish statistical yearbook.* Warsaw.

Central Statistical Office. CSO. 2009. *Poland in figures.* Warsaw

Chawla, M., Betcherman, G. and Banerji, A. 2007. *From red to grey. The 'third transition' of aging populations in eastern Europe and the former Soviet Union.* Washington D.C.: World Bank.

Courtois, S. and Werth, N. et al. 1999. *Kommunismens svarta bok*, (The Black Book of Communism). Chap. pp. 7-15.

Danmarks statistik, 2008, 2009 Statistics Denmark (Central statistical office) Denmark.

DaVanzo, J. (ed.).1996. *Russia's demographic crises*, RAND, CR-124-CRES.

Da Vanzo, J. and Adamsson, D. 1997. *Russia's demographic 'crises'. How real is it?* Issue Paper, RAND. July 1997.

DaVanzo, J., Oliker, O. and Grammich, C. 2003. Too few good men. The security implications of Russian demographics. In: *Georgetown Journal of International Affairs*, Summer/Fall, 2003:(17).

Dempsey, J. 2007. Eastern Europe faces generation crisis. In: *International Herald Tribune*. 2007.08.30.

Dinkel, R.H. 1985. The seeming paradox of increasing mortality in a highly industrialized nation. The example of the Soviet Union. In: *Population Studies*, 39, pp. 87 ff.

The Economist. 2007.06.16. P.38.

European Bank for Reconstruction and Development, EBRD. 2002. *Transition Report Update*. May.

European Commission, Directorate General for Employment, Social Affairs and Equal Opportunities, UnitE.1 2006. *The Demographic future of Europe – From challenge to opportunity.* October.

Eurostat: *Country profiles: Poland.* 2009 See Statistical Office of the European Communities.

Federal Statistical Office. 2006. *Abortions in Germany 2002-2005*. September 8th.

Kingkade. W. 1997. *Population trends: Russia.* Washington, DC: U.S. Bureau of the Census.

Kingkade, W.W. and Dunlop, J.E. 1999. *Demographic developments in eastern Europe and the former Soviet Union. Present and future.* Washington D.C.:U.S. Census Bureau.

Kucera, T. 2007. *Transition and demographic development. Demographic changes in Eastern Europe.* Prague: Charles University of Prague, Dept of Demography.

Kuodote, D. and Traceskis, R. (eds.). 2005. *Siberia mass deportations from Lithuania to the USSR.* Vilnius: Genocide and Resistance Research Centre of Lithuania.

Magnusson, L. 1996. *Sveriges ekonomiska historia,* (The economic history of Sweden) Falun: ScandBook AB. pp. 414- 444.

Martinsson, Ö. 2010. *Historical atlas population of Russia.* At http://www.tacitus.nu/historical-atlas/population/russia.htm (retrieved 20120903)

Myrdal, A. and Myrdal, G., 1934. *Kris i befolkningsfrågan,* (The population crisis). Stockholm: Bonniers.

OECD,2007.10.07. *Social Statistics.*

Official Statistics of Denmark. 2008.

Official Statistics of Finland. 2007-10-4. Abortions.

O´Grady, S. Polish migrants heading home from UK. In: *BusinessWeek,* 2009 May 21.

Palm Andersson L. 2001. *Livet, kärleken och döden: fyra uppsatser om svensk befolkningsutveckling 1300-1850.* (Life, love , and death: four papers on Swedish population development 1300-1850). Göteborg.

RAND. 2001. *Russia's mortality crisis.* Population Matters, Policy Brief, RB-5056

Robine, J.-M., Le Roy, S., Jagger, C. and EHMU-team. *Changes in life expectancy in the EU since 1995.*

Russian Federal State Statistical Service, 2009. March

State Statistics Committee, Ukraine. 2008. Total Population.

Statistiska centralbyrån, 2007, 2009.Statistics Finland (Central statistical office) Finland.

Statistiska centralbyrån, SCB, (Central statistical office) Statistics Sweden.2008, 2009. Sweden

Thorborg, M (ed.) 1993. *Women around the Baltic Sea, part I. Women in the Baltic states Estonia, Latvia, and Lithuania.* Lund: Lund University, Institute of Education, 190 pp.

Thorborg, M. 1996 a. 1996. *Kompendium om kvinner i Sovjet og Russland,* (Collection on Women in the Soviet Union and Russia) Oslo: Likestillingsrådet, (Equality Council). April, 142 pp.

Thorborg, M. 1997. Women in the Baltic states since 1991. An economic overview. In: Thorborg, M. (ed.) *Women actors around the Baltic Sea.* Karlskrona: The Baltic Institute, pp. 11-22.

Thorborg, M. 2000. Latvian Women in a Comparative Framework. In: Thorborg, M. and Zarinna, I.B. (eds.) *Gender equality in Latvia at the threshold of the new millennium.* Riga: Latvian Academy of Sciences, pp.10-23.

Thorborg, M . 2002 a. Populations around the Baltic Sea. In: Maciejewski, W. (ed.). *The Baltic Sea region. Culture, politics, societies.* Uppsala: The Baltic University Programme.

Thorborg, M. 2002 b. (Section-ed.) Social Conditions. In:troduction. In: Maciejewski, W. (ed.). *The Baltic Sea region. Culture, politics, societies.* Uppsala: The Baltic University Programme.

Thorborg, M. 2002 c. La condition feminine in eastern Europe with special reference to the Baltic states. In: Christensen, B. (ed.). *Wissen, Macht, Geschlecht Philosophie und die Zukunft der "Condition feminine",* (Knowledge Power Gender, Philosophy and the Future of the "Condition Féminine"). Zürich: Chronos, pp. 530-537.

Thorton, A. and Philipov, D. 2007. *Developmental idealism and demographic change in central and eastern Europe.* Paper at Institute for Social Research and Department of Sociology. Ann Arbor and Vienna: The University of Michigan and Vienna Institute of Demography, Austrian Academy of Sciences.

Tikhomirov, V. 2000. *The political economy of post-soviet Russia.* Melbourne: University of Melbourne.

UNAIDS. 2008. *Eastern Europe 2008 Report.* September.

United Nations Development Program, UNDP/HDR. 2002. *Human Development Report, Russia.* The Russian Federation.

UNDP. 2006/2007. *Russia's regions:Facts and figures.*

UNDP. 2009. *Living with HIV in eastern Europe and the CIS.*

UNDY, United Nations Demographic yearbook. 2005. *Legally induced abortions 1996-2005.*

UN Department of Economic and Social Affairs. 2007. Table 13. Induced abortions 2006- preliminary data.

UN/ECE. 2000. *Economic survey of Europe 2000.* No.1 Chap.6.

UN Human Development Report, UNHDR. Various years.

United Nations, UN. 2005. *Population, development and HIV/AIDS with particular emphasis on poverty, economic & social affairs.* June.

UN. 2006. *International migration and development.* Population Division, Department of Economic and Social Affairs.

USAID. 2005 and 2007. *Divergence and convergence.* No.8.

USA TODAY. 2008.04.05. *After years of shrinking population, Russia eperiences baby boom.*

US Bureau of the Census. 2009.

Vidal-Naquet, P. and Bertin, J. (Eds). (1987/89).1991. *Atlas över mänsklighetens histroria.* (Atlas Historique) Bonnier Fakta Bokförlag.

Wheatcroft, S. 2000. The scale and the nature of the Stalinist repression and its demographic significance: On comments by Keep and Conquest. In: *Europe-Asia Studies* 52 (6): pp. 1143-1159.

Yang, D.T. 2008. China's agricultural crisis and famine of 1959-1961. A survey and comparison to Soviet famines. In: *Comparative Economic Studies*, Vol. 50, No.1.

Chapter 9

Agri-info EU. http://www.agri-info.eu/english/t_employment.php (retrieved 20120917)

Allard, C. and Annett, A. 2008. *Republic of Poland, selected issues,* IMF, EUR, 25th March.

Applebaum, A. 2003. *Gulag. A history.* New York: Doubleday

Baltic rim economies, BRE. 2009. Economic Reviews Bimonthly Review. Turko School of Economics. Finland Issue Nr 2, 29 April.

Barthelemy, P.A. 2009. *Changes in agricultural employment.* Eurostat ec.europa.eu/agriculture/envir/report/en/emplo_en/report_en.htm (retrieved 20120917)

Bengtsson, A. 2007. *Bronssoldatens hämnd. Baltiska betraktelser*, (The revenge of the cast iron soldier Baltic reflections). Vimmerby: Scandbook.

Burawoy, M. 1996. The state and economic involution. Russia through a China lens. In: Evans, P. (ed.). *State society – synergy. Government and social capital in developmen*. University of California Press, Vol.94.

Casula, P. 2008. *Authoritarian modernization or no modernization at all? Sources of stability in contemporary Russia*. Paper at 12ème Conference Générale de l´EADI – Gouvernance Globale pour un Développement Durable. 24-28 juin. Genéve, Switzerland.

Central Intelligence Agency, CIA. Various years. *The world fact book*.

Collier, P. 2007. *The bottom billion. Why the poorest countries are failing and what can be done about it*. Oxford: Oxford University Press.

Conquest, R. 1971. *Den stora terrorn. Stalins skräckvälde under 30-talet*. (The Great Terror, Stalin´s Purge during the Thirties, 1968), Halmstad.

Copus, A., Hall,C., Barnes, A., Dalton, G., Cook, P., Weingarten, P., Baum, S., Stange, H., Lindner, C., Hill, A., Eiden, G., McQuaid, R., Grieg, M. and Johansson, M. 2006. Study on Employment in Rural Areas (SERA) – Report prepared for the European Commission, DG Agriculture,. Brussels: European Commission pp. 203. http://ec.europa.eu/agriculture/publi/reports/ruralemployment/sera_report.pdf (retrieved 20120917)

Courtois, S. and Werth, N. et al. 1997. *Kommunismens svarta bok*, (The Black Book of Communism). Chap.s 7-15.

Fainsod, M. 1965. *How Russia is ruled*. Harvard: Harvard University press.

Geertz, C. 1963. *Agricultural involution. The process of ecological change in Indonesia*. University of California Press.

Griffin, K., Khan, A.R. and Ickowitz, A. 2002. Poverty and the distribution of land. In: *Journal of Agrarian Change*. Vol.2, No.3, July, pp 279-330.

Grundberg, S. 2009a. Euroskulder kan knaecka Baltikum, (Euro debts can break the Baltics). In: *Fokus*, 24-30 April.

Grundberg, S. 2009b. Vi vill ansluta oss till Euron (We want to link to the Euro). In: *Fokus*, 24-30 April.

IFAD. 2007. Rural poverty in Europe. In: *Rural Poverty Portal*. December. At http://www.ruralpovertyportal.org/web/rural-poverty-portal/region/home/tags/europe (retrieved 20120917)

International Labour Organization ILO, 2002. Statistics.

Kucera, T. 2007. *Transition and demographic development: Demographic changes in Eastern Europe*. Prague: Charles University of Prague, Dept of Demography.

Kuodote, D. and Traceskis, R. (eds.). 2005. *Siberia mass deportations from Lithuania to the USSR*. Vilnius: Genocide and Resistance Research Centre of Lithuania..

Leijonhielm, J. 2008. Medvedev´s economic plan. A liberal economist in the making? In: Jonsson, A., Blanck, S., Sherr, J. and Pallin, C. Vl. *Russia after Putin. Implications for Russia´s politics and neighbours*. Stockholm: Institute for Security & Development Policy. March.

Maddison, A. 2001. *The world economy. A millennial perspective*. OECD. Table B-21

Maddison, A. 2007. *Contours of the world economy, 1-2030 A. D. Essays in macro-economic history*". Oxford: Oxford University Press.

Magnusson, L. 1996. *Sveriges ekonomiska historia,* (The economic history of Sweden) Falun: ScandBook AB. pp. 414- 444

McKay, J.P., Hill, B.D. and Buckler, J. 1996. *A history of world societies*. Boston: Houghton Mifflin company, pp.1130-1131.

Matthews, O. 2008. Softer russian power. In: *Newsweek*, 2008.06.09.

O´Brien, S., Wegren, K. and Patsoirsky, V. 2007. Income stratification in Russian villages. In: *Problems of Post-Communism*, Vol.54, No.1, Jan.- Feb.

Official Statistics of Sweden. 2009. Agricultural Board, Jordbruksverket.

Porter, M.E. 1990. *The competitive advange of nations*. New York: The Free Press, pp. 331-355.

Prokopijevic, M. 2002. *Does growth further improve economic freedom*. March. At: http://www.freetheworld.com/papers/Miroslav_Prokopijevic.pdf. (retrieved 20120917)

Smee, J.O. 2001. *Belarus. Recent experience and challenges ahead*. IMF. Kiev: Speech at Belorussian Academy of Management.

Statistical Office of the European Communities, SOEC, 2009. Eurostat: *Country profiles. Poland*. 2009. at http://epp.eurostat.ec.europa.eu/guip/introAction.do?profile=cpro&theme=eurind&lang=en (retrieved 20120917)

Svenska Dagbladet,(Swedish Daily). 2009. p.8, "Fortsatt kräftgång i Baltikum", (Still going backwards in the Baltics), 25/3 2009, p.8, and 27/3 2009, "Börskollaps i Baltikum", (Collaps of the stock market in the Baltics)

Thorborg, M. (ed.). 1993. *Women around the Baltic Sea. Part I. Women in the Baltic states Estonia, Latvia, and Lithuania*. Lund: Lund University, Institute of Education, 190 pp.

Thorborg, M. 1996 a. 1996. *Kompendium om kvinner i Sovjet og Russland*, (Collection on Women in the Soviet Union and Russia) Oslo: Likestillingsrådet, (Equality Council). April, 142 pp.

Thorborg, M. 1996 b. Kvinnor i det tidiga Ryssland, (Women in early Russia). In: *Likt & Ulikt*, Likestillingsrådets Kvartalsmagasin, (Equal & Unequal Quarterly Magazine by the Equality Council) Oslo, No 19, June.

Thorborg, M. 1997. Women in the Baltic states since 1991. An economic overview. In: Thorborg, M. (ed.) *Women actors around the Baltic sea*. Karlskrona: The Baltic Institute, pp. 11-22

Thorborg, M. 1999. *En analys av genomförda insatser med inriktning på jämställdhet i Ryssland,* (Analysis of completed activities focusing on gender equality in Russia). Stockholm: Sida-Öst, (The Swedish International Development Authority-East), 60 pp.

Thorborg, M. 2000. Latvian Women in a Comparative Framework. In: Thorborg, M. and Zarinna, I.B. (eds.) *Gender equality in Latvia at the threshold of the new millennium*. Riga: Latvian Academy of Sciences, pp.10-23.

Thorborg, M. 2002 a. Populations around the Baltic Sea. In: Maciejewski, W. (ed.). *The Baltic Sea region. Culture, politics, societies*. Uppsala: The Baltic University Programme.

Thorborg, M. 2002 b. (Section-ed.) Social conditions. Introduction. In: Maciejewski, W. (ed.). *The Baltic Sea region. Culture, politics, societies*. Uppsala: The Baltic University Programme.

Thorborg, M. 2002 c. La condition feminine in Eastern Europe with special reference to the Baltic states. In: Christensen, B. (ed.). *Wissen, Macht, Geschlecht Philosophie und die Zukunft der "Condition feminine"*, (Knowledge power gender, philosophy and the future of the "Condition Féminine"). Zürich: Chronos, pp. 530-537.

Thorborg, M. 2003 a. Gendered notes on economic development and transition with special reference to the east of the Baltic Sea. In: Knopf, K., Putensen, D. and Schneikart, M. (eds.) *Frauen im Ostseeraum,* (Women around the Baltic Sea), Germany: Centaurus, 20 pp.

Thorborg, M. 2003 b. Labour Market Developments in Eastern Europe Particularly EU application Countries in a Global Perspective since Independence. In: Landuyt, A., Horga, I. and de Brosse, R. (eds.) *The contribution of mass media to the enlargement of the European Union*. Bruxelles International Institute of Administrative Studies, 2003, pp. 377-391

United Nations Development Program, UNDP 2003. Human Development Report Office. Occasional Paper. Background paper for HDR 2003. Russia.

UN/ECE. 2000. *Economic survey of Europe 2000*. No.1 Chap.6.

United Nations, UN. 2005. *Population, development and HIV/AIDS with particular emphasis on poverty, economic & social affairs*. June

USAID. 2005 and 2007. *Divergence and convergence.* No.8.

Wegren, S.K. 2007. Russian agriculture and the WTO. In: *Problems of post-communism*, July/August.

Wibberley, J. 2007. *CEEC Agri policy.* UK, Centre for Rural Research, University of Exeter. At http://www.euroqualityfiles.net/cecap/Report%203/Section%202%20country%20report/CEECAP%20report%203%20section%202%20CYPRUS.pdf. (retrieved 20120917)

World Economic Outlook, WEO 2010. IMF projected change July.

Yang, D.T. 2008. China's agricultural crisis and famine of 1959-1961: A survey and comparison to Soviet famines. In: *Comparative Economic Studies*, Vol. 50, No.1.

Chapter 10

Analiz sostoyaniya selskogo turizma 25.04.08. Biblioteka turizma, retrieved 25 March 2010, http://www.turbooks.ru/stati/vidy-turizma/350-analiz-sovremennogo-sostojanija.html

Analiz sovremennogo sostoyaniya. Vidy turisma. http://www.turbooks.ru/stati/vidy-turizma/350-analiz-sovremennogo-sostojanija.html (access 10.04.2010)

Augulyaviche, I.B. 2000. *Perspektivy razvitiya turizma na territrii Mariyampolskogo uezda Litvy* (monografiya.)

Birzhakov, M.B. 1999 *Vvedenie v turizm*. SPb: Izdat. Togov. dom «Gerda», 192s.

Blumental, M. *Turbiznes vytyanet latviyskoe selo?*

Bundesarbeitsgemeinschaft für Urlaub auf dem Bauernhof und Landtourismus in Deutschland. http://www.landsichten.de/ueber_uns/bundesarbeitsgemeinschaft/ (retrieved 20120917)

Eidukeviciene, M. 2001. *Ecological farming and rural tourism as alternative activity of rural population in West Lithuania*. Klaipeda.

A European Charter for Rural Areas, http://assembly.coe.int/Mainf.asp?link=/Documents/WorkingDocs/Doc96/EDOC7516.htm (retrieved 20120917)

Fennel, D.A. 1999. *Ecotourism. An introduction*. London and New York: Routledge, Taylor & Francis Group, p. 26-27

Fennel, D.A. 2003. *Ecotourism.* Second edition. London and New York: Routledge, Taylor & Francis Group

Fennell, D.A. and Dowling Ross, K. 2003 *Ecotourism Policy and Planning*. CABI Publishing, p. 207

Hall, C.M. and Page, S.J. 1999. *The geography of tourism and recreation: environment, place, and space*. London and New York: Routledge, p. 4

Here is my village! 2009. Travel catalogue / Commission for tourism and regional contacts of Administration of the Kaliningrad region. Kaliningrad, 2000, "New taste"/ "Svezij vkus", Travel catalogue, Administration of the Kaliningrad region, Kaliningrad.

Katalog selskih gostevyh domov. Project «A way home – tourism in the countryside of Leningrad region», 2009, http://www.lentravel.ru (retrieved 1 October 2012)

Kottedgy. Otdyh v Finlyandii,

Lopata, J. *Ecological tourism to organic farms as a tool to help small farmers make a sometimes difficult transition from conventional agriculture to ecological agriculture*

Makarenko, A. 2007. *Dollary s gektara. Selskiy turism – nastoyaschaya zolotaya zhila*, http://www.point.ru/news/stories/11402/4.html#story (retrieved 20120917)

Oleszek, W., Terelak, H., Maliszewska-Kordybach, B. and Kukuła, S. *Soil, Food and Agroproduct Contamination Monitoring in Poland*, http://6csnfn.pjoes.com/pdf/12.3/261-268.pdf (retrieved 20120917)

Otdel turizma Ministerstva promyshlnnosti Pravitelstva Kaliningradskoy oblasti. http://www.tourism-kaliningrad.ru (retrieved 20120917)

Platonova, U.V. *Selskoe gostepriimstvo – dopolnitelniy dohod v selskoy mesnosti*.

Roberts, L. and Hall, D. 2003. *Rural tourism and recreation*: Principles to practice. CABI Publishing

Rural tourism, 2000. Blekinge, Sweden, 62 p.

Turisticheskiy katalog: Krai Turku – massa vpechatleniy. 2001. Turku.

Turisticheskoe osvoenie Skandinavii prodolzhaetsya. 1998. In: *Turisticheskiy biznes*, №6, s. 34-35

Chapter 11

Ahlberg, N. 2005. *Stadsgrundningar och planförändringar*. Doctoral diss. Dept. of Landscape Planning, Ultuna, SLU. Acta Universitatis agriculturae Sueciae vol. 2005:94.

Aleklett, K. 2008. *Peak oil and the evolving strategies of oil importing and exporting countries – facing the hard truth about an import decline for the OECD countries*. Discussion paper 17. Joint Transport Research Centre (Paris).

Alexander, C., Ishikawa, S. and Silverstein, M. 1977. *A Pattern Language,Towns, buildings, construction.* Oxford Univ Press

Andersson, R. 1998. *Attraktiva städer – en samhällsekonomisk analys*. Byggforskningsrådet (Stockholm).

Bach, B. 2006. *Urban Design and Traffic – a selection from Bach's Toolbox*. C.R.O.W. (National Information and Technology platform for Infrastructure, Traffic, Transport and Public Space) – report 221. (Ede Netherlands)

Berg, P.G. 2010. *Timeless Cityland – an Interdisciplinary Approach to finding the Sustainable Human Habitat.* Baltic University Press and Department of Urban and Rural Development, SLU University (Uppsala) 250pp

Berg, P.G. 2007. Urban-rural connection. In: Berg, P.G. (ed) *Urban-rural cooperation.* Uppsala: Baltic University Press. Available online at: http://www.balticuniv.uu.se/buuf/ (retrieved 20120917)

Berg, P.G. 2006. Factor five flow city – the need for radical revision of cities in the Baltic Sea Region. In: Rydén, L. (ed) *Realising a common Baltic sea eco-region.* Proceedings from a seminar in Kaliningrad 2005 on Sustainable Regional Development in the BSR. Uppsala: Baltic University Press. Available online at: http://www.balticuniv.uu.se/index.php/other-publications/74-realizing-acommon-vision-for-a-baltic-sea-eco-region (retrieved 20120917)

Berg, P.G. 1993. *Biologi och Bosättning – Naturanpassning i Samhällsbyggandet* (Biology and Settlement – Nature adaptation in Community Construction – in Swedish). Natur och Kultur (Stockholm)

Berg, P.G. 1990. *Omsorg om vår planet* – Ekoteknik. Natur och Kultur och Institutet för framtidsstudier (Stockholm)

Berg, P.G., Eriksson, T.E. and Granvik, M. 2012. Functional Density – A Theoretical framework and development of Concepts in an Urban Townscape Areas Context. *Submitted to Nordic Journal of Architectural Resarch.*

Bokalders, V. and Block, M. 2010. *The Whole Building Handbook.* Earthscan and RIBA (London) 450 pp

Bolunda, P. and Hunhammar, S. 1999. Ecosystem services in urban areas. In: *Ecological Economics* Volume 29, Issue 2, May, p 293-301

Carstensson, R. (Ed.) 1992. *Infrastrukturen* (The Infrastructure – in Swedish), Sveriges Nationalatlas. Bra Böcker (Malmö)

Cooper Marcus, C. 1997. Nature as Healer: Therapeutic Benefits in Outdoor Places. In: *Nordisk arkitekturforskning* 1997;10(1):8–20.

Day, C. 2002. Spirit & Place. Gray Publishing (Tunbridge Wells, Kent)

Ebbersten, S. and Bodin, B. 1997. A sustainable Baltic Sea Region. Booklet 4 Food and fibres – sustainable agriculture, forestry and fishery – Baltic University Press, Uppsala University. http://www.balticuniv.uu.se/index.php/teaching-materials#a-sustainable-baltic-region (retrieved 20120917)

Edman, S. 2005. *Bilen, Biffen, Bostaden – Hållbara laster, smartare konsumtion.* Slutbetänkande av utredningen om en handlingsplan för hållbar konsumtion för hushållet. SOU 2005:51.

Egnor, T. 2009. *Ett grönt Paris – Om den hållbara staden och förändringar i stadslandskapet* (A green Paris? In Swedish with English Summary) Master Thesis at the Department of Urban and Rural Development – Unit of Landscape Architecture. SLU Uppsala.

Ericson, G. and Ingmar, T. 1989. *Nära till naturen.* Byggforskningsrådet Rapport R:102

Florgård, C. 2004. *Stockholm's blue-green infrastructure.* Case study in Working group 2 of COST ACTION 8 – Sustainable Urban Infrastructure. See Welsh School of Architecture on http://www.cardiff.ac.uk/archi/programmes/cost8/ (retrieved 20120917)

Frame B., Gordon R. & Mortimer C (eds.) 2009. *Hatched – The Capacity for Sustainable Development.* Landcare Research New Zealand Ltd (Lincoln)

Gaffron, P., Huismans, G. and Skala, F. (eds) 2008. *Ecocity. Book II – How to make it happen.* EU Commission project Urban development towards Appropriate Structures for Sustainable Transport. Hamburg University of Technology, SenterNovem, Dutch Agency for Sustainability and Innovation and Department of Ecological Economics and Management, Vienna University of Economics and Business Administration

Gaffron, P., Huismans, G. and Skala, F. (Eds.), 2005. *Ecocity. Book I – A better place to live.* EU Commission project Urban development towards Appropriate Structures for Sustainable Transport. Hamburg of Technology, SenterNovem, Dutch Agency for Sustainability and Innovation and Department of Ecological Economics and Management, Vienna University of Economics and Business Administration.

Garreau, J. 1992. *Edge city - Life on the new frontier.* Anchor Books (New York)

Helmfrid, S. (Ed.) 1994. *Kulturlandskapet och Bebyggelsen* (The Cultural Landscape and Settlement – in Swedish), Sveriges Nationalatlas, Bra Böcker (Malmö)

Geddes, P. 1904. *City development – a study of Parks, Gardens and Culture Institutions.* A Carnegie Trust report, London

Hanell, T. and Tornberg, P. 2007. Regional development trends in the Baltic Sea Region at the turn of the millennium. In: Berg, P.G. (ed) *Urban-rural cooperation.* Uppsala: Baltic University Press. Available online at: http://www.balticuniv.uu.se/buuf (retrieved 20120917)

Global Footprint Network. http://www.footprintnetwork.org. (retrieved 20120917)

Granvik, M. 2012. Localisation of food systems – a coming issue in Swedish municipal authorities. Accepted for publication in *International Planning Studies.*

Granvik, M., Lindberg, G., Stigzelius, K-A., Fahlbeck, E. and Surry, Y. 2012. Prospects of multifunctional agriculture as a facilitator of sustainable Rural Development. Swedish experience of Pillar Two of the CAP. Accepted for publication in *Norwegian Journal of Geography*

Gullberg, A., Höjer, M. and Pettersson, R. 2007. *Bilder av framtidsstaden. Tid och rum för hållbar utveckling.* Brutus Östlings Bokförlag Symposium, Stockholm/Stehag

Hall, P. 1998. *Cities in Civilization.* New York: Pantheon Books.

Howard, E. 1902. *Garden Cities of Tomorrow.* Faber & Faber (London)

Hyams E. 1976. *Soil and Civilisation.* John Murray (London)

IGBP, 2004. In: Steffen et al. (eds) *Global Change – a Planet under Pressure International Geosphere Biosphere Program,* The Royal Science Academy (Stockholm)

Jacobs, J. 1961. *The Death and Life of Great American Cities.* Blackwell – Wiley (New York)

Jordbruksdepartementet, 1989. *En ny livsmedelspolitik (A new policy for food production – in Swedish)* Departementserien 1989:63 (Stockholm)

Kahiluoto, H., Berg, P.G., Granstedt, A., Thomsson, O. and Fischer, H. 2006. *The Power of Local – sustainable food systems around the Baltic Sea.* Interdisciplinary synthesis of the Interreg III B project

Baltic Ecological Recycling Agriculture and Society (BERAS) *Report No 7*.

Kaplan, R, and Kaplan, S. 1989. *The experience of nature*. Cambridge, MA: Cambridge University Press

Kronenberg, J. and Bergier, T. (Eds). 2010. *Challenges of Sustainable Development in Poland* . Krakow:

Lisberg Jensen, E. 2008. *Gå ut min själ – forskningsöversikt om hälsoeffekter av utevistelser i närnatur*. Rapport Folkhälsoinstitutet.

Stigsdotter, U. and Grahn, P. 2003. Experiencing a Garden: A Healing Garden for People Suffering from Burnout Diseases. In: *Journal of Therapeutic Horticulture*. 14: 38-48.

Leader Regions 2000. http://ec.europa.eu/agriculture/rur/leaderplus/index_en.htm (retrieved 20120917)

Lundgren Alm, E. 2001. *Stadslandskapets obrukade resurs*. Akademisk avhandling. Chalmers (Göteborg)

Lynch, K. 1981. *A Theory of Good City Form*. MIT Press (Cambridge MA and London)

Maciejewski, W. (ed.) 2002. *The Baltic Sea Region – Cultures, Politics, Societies*. The Baltic University press. Uppsala University.

Mitchell, R. and Popham, F. 2008. Effect of Exposure to Natural Environment on Health Inequalities: an Observational Population Study. In: *The Lancet* vol 372 (9650) 1655-1660.

Moffat, S. 2003. CitiesPLUS In: Itoh, S. (ed) 2003. *Proposals for the International Competition of Sustainable Urban Systems Design – Report of the International Gas Union Special Project*. The Institute of Behavioural Science (Tokyo)

Mumford, L. 1961. *The City in History*. Hardcourt Inc. (San Diego)

Nilsson, K. 2003. *Planning in a sustainable direction – The art of conscious choices*. Trita Infra 03-58 Dissertation KTH (Stockholm)

Oberndorfer, E., Lundholm, J., BASS, B. and Coffman, R.R. 2007. Green Roofs as Urban Ecosystems: Ecological Structures, Functions, and Services, In: *BioScienc* Vol. 57 No. 10 November 2007 / p.823 http://www.aibs.org/bioscience-press-releases/resources/11-07.pdf (retrieved 20120917)

Persson, G. and Bro, A. 2002. Studying sustainability in municipal transformation. Strategies for managing economic decline, Managning housing policy during and economic decline, Culture in Municipal transformation (Chapter 7-10) The Hällefors Studies. In: Granvik, M. (ed) *Basic Patterns of Sustainability. Sustainable Urban Patterns around the Baltic Sea*. Case studies vol I. Reports from the Baltic University program Superbs project. Baltic University Press.(Uppsala) p. 57-80.

Rydén, L., Migula, P. and Andersson, M. (ed.) 2003. *Environmental Science*. The Baltic University press. Uppsala University.

Rådberg, J. 1988. *Doktrin och täthet i svenskt stadsbyggande 1875-1975* (Doctrine and density in Swedish City

Piracha, A.L. and Marcotullio, P.J. 2003. *Urban Ecosystems Analysis - Identifying Tools and Methods* United Nations University Institute of Advanced Studies 2003 report. Planning (in Swedish) Statens Råd för Byggnadsforskning. Rapport 1988:11 (Stockholm) http://www.ias.unu.edu/binaries/UNUIAS_UrbanReport2.pdf (retrieved 20120917)

Rees, W.E. 1996. Revisiting Carrying Capacity – Area-Based Indicators of Sustainability. In: *Population and Environment*: A Journal of Interdisciplinary Studies Volume 17, Number 3, January 1996 @ 1996 Human Sciences Press, Inc. The University of British Columbia http://dieoff.org/page110.htm (retrieved 20120917)

Roseland, M. 2005. *Toward Sustainable Communities – Resources for Citizens and their Governments*. New Socity Publishers (Vancouver BC)

Saifi, B. and Drake, L. 2007. A co-evolutionary model for promoting agricultural sustainability. In: *Ecol. Econ*. 65: 24-34.

Schorske, C. 1963. The Idea of the City in European Thought: Voltaire to Spengler. In: Handlin, O. & Burchard, J. *The Historian and the City* (Cambridge, Mass.)

SLL. 2009. *Regional Utvecklingsplan för Stor-Stockholm* (RUFS, 2010) Stockholms Läns Landsting. Spring.

SOU. 2005. *En Hållbar landsbygdsutveckling – Delbetänkande av Landsbygdskommittén* (A sustainable rural development – in Swedish – Swedish Public Investigation) (Stockholm)

Svensson, R. 1993. Periferin – centrum för ekologisk planering. I: Berg P.G. *Biologi och bosättning – naturanpassning i samhällsbyggandet*. Natur och Kultur (Stockholm)

Thompson, I. 1999. Ecology, *Community and Delight – Sources of value in Landscape Architecture* Spon Press (London)

UNCHS, 1996. *The Habitat Agenda and the Istanbul Declaration*. United Nations Conference on Human Settlements. UNHabitat (Nairobi)

UNHabitat. 2007. *State of the World Cities 2006/2007*. UNHabitat (Nairobi)

UNICEF. 1989. *Children Convention*.

Uppsala Kommun, 2002. *Uppsala Kommuns parkprogram*.

Chapter 12

Adolfsson, E., Holmberg, C. and Brena, B. 2000. Fishing and aquaculture. In: Lundin, L-C. (Ed.) *River Basin Management*. Sustainable Water Management, Volume III. pp. 243. Uppsala: Baltic University Press.

Adolfsson, E., Holmberg, C. and Brena, B. 2000. Tourism and recreation. In: Lundin, L-C. (Ed.) *River Basin Management*. Sustainable Water Management, Volume III. pp. 243. Uppsala: Baltic University Press.

Bergström, S., Filatov, N., Pozdnjakov, D., Magnuszewski, A. and Bergström, H. 2000. The Baltic Basin – rivers, lakes and climate. In: Lundin, L-C. (Ed.) *The Waterscape*. Sustainable Water Management, Volume I. pp. 207. Uppsala: Baltic University Press.

Blomqvist, P. and Brunberg , A-K. 2000. Lakes – origin, ontogeny and natural functions. In: Lundin, L-C. (Ed.) *The Waterscape*. Sustainable Water Management, Volume I. pp. 207. Uppsala: Baltic University Press.

Fishery statistics in the EU. http://epp.eurostat.ec.europa.eu/statistics_explained/index.php/Fishery_statistics (retrieved 20120917)

Helcom (Helsinki Commission) website on shipping. http://www.helcom.fi/shipping/en_GB/main/ (retrieved 20120917)

Lundin, L. 1999. Wetands in the Baltic Sea region. In: Lundin, L-C. The Waterscape. Sustainable Water Management, Volume I. pp. 207. Uppsala: Baltic University Press.

Maritime transport statistics - short sea shipping of goods in the EU. http://epp.eurostat.ec.europa.eu/statistics_explained/index.php/Maritime_transport_statistics_-_short_sea_shipping_of_goods (retrieved 20120917)

Norberg, P., Nilsson, A., Westfjord, P., Malmquist, Y. and Rydén, L. 2000. Shipping – boats, harbours and people. In: Lundin, L-C. River Basin Management. Sustainable Water Management, Volume III. pp. 243. Uppsala: Baltic University Press.

Rydén, L., Brinkman, I. and Malmquist, YB. 2000. *Water regulation and water infrastructure*. In: Lundin, L-C. (Ed.) River Basin Management. Sustainable Water Management, Volume III. pp. 243. Uppsala: Baltic University Press.

Rydén, L., Migula, P. and Andersson, M. (Editors). 2003. *Environmental Science – understanding, protecting, and managing the environment in the Baltic Sea region*. pp. 823. Uppsala: Baltic University Press.

Chapter 13

Baltic 21. 2005. *Action plan for the Baltic 21 forest sector 2005-2008*. Baltic 21 Publication Series 1/2005. http://www.baltic21.org/?sasp,6#action (retrieved 20120917).

European Forest Institute (EFI). 2009. *Report of the Mid-term evaluation of the implementation of the EU Forest Action Plan*. Service Contract No. 30-CE-0227729/00-59. Joensuu, Finland. http://ec.europa.eu/agriculture/eval/reports/euforest/synthetic_sum_en.pdf (retrieved 20120917)

Diamond, J. 2005. *Collapse – How societies choose to fail or to succeed*, Viking Penguin, USA.

Food and Agricultural Organisation (FAO). 2005. *Global forest resources assessment 2005. Progress towards sustainable forest management*. FAO Forestry Paper 147. ftp://ftp.fao.org/docrep/fao/008/A0400E/A0400E00.pdf (retrieved 20120917)

Food and Agricultural Organisation (FAO). 2009. *State of the World's forests 2009*. FAO, Rome.

Forest.fi. 2009. *Finnish forests owned by Finns*. http://www.forest.fi/smyforest/foresteng.nsf/allbyid/438DBC6361C9EB75C2256F34004154D8?Opendocument (retrieved 20120917)

Forest.fi. 2006. Forest sector produces and employs. http://www.forest.fi/smyforest/foresteng.nsf/allbyid/197B4F3FC67881E2C225783300415716?OpenDocument (retrieved 20120917)

Grober, U. 1990. *Deep roots: a brief conceptual history of sustainable development* – nachhaltigkeit http://skylla.wzb.eu/pdf/2007/p07-002.pdf (retrieved 20120917)

Lazdinis, M., Carver, A.D., Lazdinis, I. and Paulikas, V.K. 2009. From union to union: forest governance in a post-Soviet political system. In. *Env. Sci. & Policy 12 (2009),* pp. 309-320.

The Ministerial Conference on the Protection of Forests (MCPFE). 2010. *The MCPFE press kit*. http://5th.mcpfe.org/foresteurope.org/filestore/foresteurope/Press_material/FOREST_EUROPE_Press_Kit.pdf (retrieved 20120917)

Olmos et al. 1999. Non-wood forest products: utililzation and income generation in the Czech Republic, Finland and Lithuania. In: Dembner, S.A. and Perlis, A. *Non-wood forest products and income generation*. Unasylva – No. 198. FAO Corporate Document Repository. www.fao.org/DOCREP/X2450E/x2450e07.htm (retrieved 20120917)

Paul, K.I., Polglase, P.J., Nyakuengama, J.G. and Khanna, P.K. 2002. Changes in soil carbon following afforestation. In: *Forest Ecology and Management* 168:241-257.

United Nations (UN). 2007. *Non-legally binding instrument on all types of forests adopted by the UN General Assembly on 22 October 2007*. http://www.un.org/esa/forests/pdf/ERes2007_40E.pdf (retrieved 20120917)

United Nations Economic Commission for Europe (UNECE) and Food and Agricultural Organization of the UN (FAO). 2007. *State of Europe's forests 2007. The MCPFE report on sustainable forest management in Europe*. http://timber.unece.org/fileadmin/DAM/publications/State_of_europes_forests_2007.pdf (retrieved 20120917)

United Nations REDD Programme, http://www.un-redd.org (retrieved 20120917)

Chapter 14

Borealforest. 2009. *Management & Sustainability – Scandinavia*. www.borealforest.org/world/scan_mgmt.htm (retrieved 20120917)

Food and Agricultural Organisation (FAO). 2009. *State of the World's forests 2009*. FAO, Rome.

Lazdinis, M., Carver, A.D., Lazdinis, I. and Paulikas, V.K. 2009. From union to union: forest governance in a post-Soviet political system. In. *Env. Sci. & Policy 12 (2009),* pp. 309-320.

Ministry of Environment (MoE), Poland. 2009. *Fourth national report on the implementation of the Convention on Biological Diversity*. Warsaw, Poland. http://www.cbd.int/doc/world/pl/pl-nr-04-p1-en.pdf (retrieved 20120917)

Perlinge, A. (ed.). 1992. *Skogsbrukets tekniska utveckling under 100 år*. Stockholm: Nordiska museets förlag 119 pp (in Swedish)

Royal Swedish Academy of Agriculture and Forestry (KSLA). 2009. *The Swedish forestry model*. 15 pp. Stockholm

Saastamoinen, O. 1999. Forest policies, access rights and non-wood forest products in northern Europe. In: Dembner, S.A. and Perlis, A. *Non-wood forest products and income generation*. Unasylva – No. 198 . FAO Corporate Document Repository http://www.fao.org/DOCREP/X2450E/x2450e06.htm (retrieved 20120917)

The Swedish Forest Agency, 2009.

The Swedish Forest Industries. 2008. *The Swedish forest industries. Fact and figures 2008*.

UPM Forest AS. 2006. *Baltic states. Strict government regulation allows traceability of all timber*.

United Nations Economic Commission for Europe (UNECE) and Food and Agricultural Organization of the UN (FAO). 2007. *State of Europe's forests 2007. The MCPFE report on sustainable forest management in Europe*. Warsaw.

Chapter 15

Angelstam, P., Kapylova, E., Korn, H., Lazdinis, M., Sayer, J.A., Teplyakov, V. and Törnblom, J. 2005. Changing forest values in Europe. In: Sayer, J.A. and Maginnis, S. (eds.), *Forests in land-*

scapes. Ecosystem approaches to sustainability. Washington D.C.: Earthscan, pp. 59–74.

Angelstam, P., Dönz-Breuss, M., Roberge, J.-M. (eds) 2004. *Targets and tools for the maintenance of forest biodiversity*. Ecological Bulletins 51. 2004

Angelstam, P. and Törnblom, J. 2004. Maintaining forest biodiversity in actual landscapes – European gradients in history and governance systems as a 'landscape lab'. In: Marchetti, M. (eds.), *Monitoring and indicators of forest biodiversity in Europe – from ideas to operationality*. EFI symposium 51, pp. 299–313.

Anon. 2010. *Annual Review of state and usage of Republic Belarus forests in 2010*. Ministry of forestry Republic of Belarus.

Bihun, Yu. 2005. Principles of Sustainable Forest Management in the Framework of Regional Economic Development. In: *Vistnyk Lvivs'kogo unviversytetu. Seria geografichna* 32. pp.19–32.

Bobko, A. 2003. *O neporodoksalnyh putyah putayh sovershenstvovaniya Lesnogo kodeksa Ukrayny*. (in Russian).

Boreyko, V. 1995. *Istoriya zapovednogo dela v Ukraine*. Kiev.

Buksha, Ig. 2004. *Forestry sector of Ukraine in transition to market economy*. Kharkiv: Ukrainian Research Institute of Forestry and Forest Melioration.

Carlsson, L., Lundgren, N.-G. and Olsson, M.-O. 2001. The Russian detour: real transition in a virtual economy. In: *Europe-Asia Studies* 53(6). pp. 841–867.

Davies, N. 1996 . Europe: a history. Oxford: Oxford University Press.

Elbakidze, M. and Angelstam, P. 2007. Implementing sustainable forest management in Ukraine's Carpathian Mountains: The role of traditional village systems. In: *For Ecol Man* 249: 28–38

Elbakidze, M., Angelstam, P., Axelsson, R. 2007. Sustainable forest management as an approach to regional development in the Russian Federation: state and trends in Kovdozersky Model Forest in the Barents region. In: *Scandinavian Journal of Forest Research* 22: 568-581.

Essmann, H.-F. and Pettenella, D. (eds.) 2001. *Forestry in Ukraine at the crossroads. Problems and perspectives for a sustainable development*. Lviv: Afisha. 226 pp.

Hansen, M., Stehman, S. and Potapov, P. 2010. *Quantification of global gross forest cover loss* PNAS 107 (19): 8650-8655.

Hensiruk, S. 1964. *Lisy Ukrajinskykh Karpat ta jikh vykorystannia*. Kyiv: Naukova dumka. (in Ukrainian).

Hensiruk, S. 1992. *Lisy*. Kyiv: Naukova dumka. (in Ukrainian).

Hensiruk, S., Furduchko, O., Bondar, V. 1995. *Istoriya lisivnytstva v Ukrayni*. Svit, Lviv (in Ukrainian)

Holubetst, M. and Odynak, Ya. 1983. Korennoy biogeotsenotsicheskyy pokrov i ego antropogennye ismeneniya. In: Holubetst, M. (Eds.), *Biogeonotstycheskyy pokrov Beskyd i ego dimanicheskie tendentsii*. Kiev: Haykova dumka. pp. 179–182. (in Russian)

Holubetst, M. et al. 1988. *Ukrayns'ky Karpaty*. Kiev: Naukova dumka (in Ukrainian).

Hrushevsky, M., 1995. *Istorija Ukrajiny – Rusi*. Zhyttia ekonomichne, kulturne, natsionalne XIV–XVII vikiv. Kyiv (in Ukrainian).

Knize, A., Romaniuk, B. 2005. *O dvuch tochkakh zreniya na Rossiyskiy les i lesnoye khozyaystvo*. WWF (in Russian).

Krott, M., Tikkanen, I., Petrov, A., Tunytsya, Y., Zheliba, Y., Sasse, V., Rykowina, I. and Tunytsya, T. 2000. *Policies for sustainable forestry in Belarus, Russia and Ukraine*. Leiden: Koninlijke Brill NV.

Kubiyovych, V. 1938 . *Geografiya Ukrainskyh i symizhnyh zemel.* Volume 1. Lviv, Ukrainian Publishing House (in Ukrainian).

Levintanous, A. 2002. Russia – forest policy development and related institutional changes in the transition period. In: *Forests and forestry in Central and Eastern European countries. The transition process and challenges ahead.* Vienna: Ministerial Conference for the Protection of Forests in Europe (MCPFE), Liaison Unit

Listopad, O. 2000. *Lesnoe pravo na Ukraine i vozmozhnosti obzsestvennosti v ohrane lesa*. On: www.forest.ru. (in Russian).

Mellor Smith, A. 1979 . *Europe: a geographical survey of the continent.* Columbia University Press, New York.

Mongabay.com. http://rainforests.mongabay.com/deforestation/2000/Russian_Federation.htm

Nijnik M, van Kooten C.G. 2006. Forestry in the Ukraine: the road ahead? Reply. Forest Policy and Economics 8(1):6–9

Nilsson, S. and Shvidenko, A. 1999. *The Ukrainian forest sector in a global perspective. Interim Report IR-99-011*. Laxenburg: International Institute for Applied Systems Analysis.

Pipponen, M. 1999 . *Transition in the Forest Sector of the Republic of Karelia*. IIASA Interim Report IR-99-070. Laxenburg, Austria: International Institute for Applied Systems Analysis, forthcoming, December.

Polyakov, M. and Sydor. T. 2006. Forestry in the Ukraine: the road ahead? Comment. In: *Forest Policy and Economics* 8(1):1–5

Polyakova, L., Kyryluk, S., Storozhuk, V. and Popkov, M. 2001. Strategiya lisokorystuvannya ta potentsiyni mozhlyvosti. In: *Lisovyy i myslyvskyy zhurnal*. 1. pp. 13–27. (in Ukrainian).

Shorohova, E. and Tetioukhin, S. 2004 Natural disturbances and the amount of large trees, deciduous trees and coarse woody debris in the forests of Novgorod Region, Russia. In: *Ecological Bulletins* 51: 137–147.

Shvidenko, A. and Andrusishin, V. 1998. *Ukraine: the conditions and prospects of the forest sector*. Unpublished manuscript, IIASA, Austria.

Solberg, B. and Rykowski, K. 2000. *Institutional and legal framework for forest policies in the ECA region and selected OECD countries – a comparative analysis*. Forest policy review and strategy development: analytical studies/issues paper. Washington DC: The World Bank.

Synyakevych, Ih. 2004. *Ecologichna i lisova polityka*. Lviv: ZUKTS (in Ukrainian).

Synyakevych, Ih. 2005. *Lisova polityka*. Lviv: ZUKTS (in Ukrainian).

Teplyakov V., Kuzmichev E., Baumgartner D., and R.Everett. 1998. *A History of Russian Forestry and its Leaders*. Washington State University in cooperation with the Federal Forest Service of Russia and the Pacific Northwest Station of the U.S.D.A. Forest Service

Trokhimchuk, S. 1968. *Zmina landshaftiv Stryjsko-Sanskoji Verkhovyny v Ukrajinskykh Karpatakh za istorychnyj chas*. Lviv: Rukopys dysertatsiji. (in Ukrainian).

Volkov, A. and Gromtsev, A. 2004. *Antropogenic transformation of taiga ecosystems in Europe: environmental, resource and economic implications: Proceedings of International Conference*. Petrozavodsk.

World Bank, 2004. *Key challenges of the Russian forest policy reforms*. World Bank Discussion Paper. Washington DC: The World Bank.

Zibtsev, S., Kaletnik, M. and Savuschik, M. 2004. Forests and forestry of Ukraine in the transition period. In: *Proceedings of the FAO/Austria expert meeting on environmentally sound forest operations for country*. On: www.fao.org.

Chapter 16

Jørgensen, P.J. 2009. Biogas – green energy Process • Design • Energy supply • Environment. PlanEnergi and Researcher for a Day – Faculty of Agricultural Sciences, Aarhus University, Lemvig Biogas. http://lemvigbiogas.com/, (retrieved 20120925)

How to plan a micro hydropower plant. http://en.howtopedia.org/wiki/How_to_Plan_a_Micro_Hydro-power_Plant

Landsbygd.fi. http://www.rural.fi/sv/index/kommunikation/nyheter_och_meddelande/finlandarvarldsledandeifragaomanvandningav-bioenergi.html (retrieved 20120925)

Wikipedia. 2012. *Vattenkraft*. http://sv.wikipedia.org/wiki/Vattenkraft#cite_note-1

WorldWatch Blogs. 2011. http://blogs.worldwatch.org

Ziegler, H. 2011. New Ideas For Small Hydropower Plants. In: *The Energy collective*. March 22, 2011. http://theenergycollective.com/amelia-timbers/54211/new-ideas-small-hydropower-plants (retrieved 20120925)

Chapter 17

Boyden, B.H. and Rababah, A.A. 1995. Recycling nutrients from municipal wastewater. In: *Desalination* 106, pp. 241-246.

Börjesson, P. and Berndes, G. 2006. The prospects for willow plantations for wastewater treatment in Sweden. In: *Biomass & Bioenergy* 30, pp. 428-438.

Calfapietra, C., Gielen, B., Karnosky, D., Ceulemans, R. and Scarascia Mugnozza, G. 2020. Response and potential of agroforestry crops under global change. In: *Environmental Pollution* 158, pp. 1095-1104

Czart, K. 2005. *Growing willow for energy manual*. in polish. http://www.lasprywatny.pl/poradnik.

Dimitriou, I. And Rosenqvist, H. 2011. Sewage sludge and wastewater fertilization of Short Rotation Coppice (SRC) for increased bioenergy production – Biological and economic potential. In: *Biomass & Bioenergy* 35, pp. 835-842.

Fischer, G., Prieler, S. and van Velthuizen, H. 2005. Biomass potentials of miscanthus, willow and poplar:results and policy implications for Eastern Europe,Northern and Central Asia. In: *Biomass & Bioenergy* 28: 119–132.

Gonzáles-García, S., Mola-Yudego, B., Dimitriou, I., Aronsson, P. and Murphy, R. 2012. Environmental assessment of energy production based on long term commercial willow plantations in Sweden. In: *Science of the Total Environment* 421-422, pp. 210-219.

Karczmarczyk, A. and Mosiej, J. 2007. Aspects of wastewater treatment on short rotation plantations (SRP) in Poland. In: *Journal of Environmental Engineering and Landscape Management*, vol. XV, no 3, pp. 182a-187a.

Labrecque, M. and Teodorescu, T.I. 2001. Influence of plantation site and wastewater sludge fertilization on the performance and foliar status two willow species grown under SRIC in soutern Quebec (Canada). In: *Forest Ecology and Management* 150, pp. 223-239.

Mant, C., Peterkin, J., May, E. and Butler, J. 2003. A feasibility study of a Salix viminalis gravel hydroponic system to renovate primary settled wastewater. In: *Bioresource Technology* 90, pp. 19–25.

Mosiej, J. and Karczmarczyk, A. 2006. Closing the nutrient loop between urban and rural area – wastewater and sludge utilization in Ner River Valley. In: *Ecohydrology & Hydrobiology* vol 6, No 1-4, pp. 197-203.

Pertu, K. 1993. SRP – production of energy and utilization of wastewater and sewage sludge. in polish. In: *Aura*, no 3 , pp. 10-11.

Pulfold, I.D. and Watson, C. 2003. Phytoremediation of heavy metal-contaminated land by trees-a review. In: *Environmnet International* 29, pp. 529-540

Rodzkin, A., Ivanyukovich, V., Pronko, S. and Kresova, E. 2010. Willow wood production on radionuclide polluted areas. In: *Proc. Natural Science*, Matica Sprska 119. pp. 105–113.

Rosenquist, H., Aronsson, P., Hasselgren, K. and Perttu, K. 1997. Economics of using municipal wastewater for irrigation of eillow coppice crops. In: *Biomass & Bioenergy* 12 (1), pp. 1-8.

Styles, D. and Jones M. 2007. Energy crops in Ireland:quantifying the potential life-cycle greenhouse gas reductions of energy-crop electricity. In: *Biomass & Bioenergy* 31(11-12), pp. 759-772

Stolarski, M., Szczukowski, S., Tworkowski, J. and Klasa A. 2008. Productivity of seven clones of willow coppice In annual and quadrennial cycles. In: *Biomass & Bioenergy* 32, pp. 1227-1234

Vande Walle, I., Van Camp, N., Van de Casteele, L., Verheyen K. and Lemeur, R. 2007. Short-rotation forestry of birch, maple, poplar and willow in Flanders (Belgium) II. Energy production and CO2 emission reduction potential. *Biomass & Bioenergy* 31, pp. 276-283

Venturi, P., Gigler, JK. and Huisman, W. 1999. Economical and technical comparision between herbaceous (Miscanthus X Giganteous) and woody energy crops (Salix Viminalis). In: *Renew Energy* 16, pp. 1023-1026.

Further Reading

CAP. 2004. The common agricultural policy explained. European Commission Directorate General for Agriculture.

EEC/1986/278. 1986. Council Directive of 12 June 1986 on the protec tion of the environment, and in particular of the soil, when sewage sludge is used in agriculture (86/278/EEC) (OJ L 181, 4.7.1986, p. 6).

EUBIA (Editor) (n.y.): Short Rotation Plantations. Opportunities for efficient biomass production with the safe application of waste water and sewage sludge. Brussels: European Biomass Industry Association (EUBIA).

SUSANA (Editor). 2009. Links between Sanitation, Climate Change and Renewable Energies. Eschborn. Sustainable Sanitation Alliance (SuSanA) .

Chapter 18

AtKisson, A. 2008. *The ISIS agreement – How Sustainability Can Improve Organizational Performance and Transform the World.*

Backström, J. & Larsson, M. 2003. *Att söka framtiden – scenariometodik i praktiken.* Solna: Global Print (in Swedish, *To look for the future – scenario methodologies in practice*)

Boverket & Naturvårdsverket (National Board of Housing and Planning in Sweden & Swedish Environmental Protection Agency) (2000).

Planning with environmental objectives – a guide. Karlskrona and Stockholm, Boverket & Naturvårdsverket.

COMMIN The Baltic Spatial conceptshare, 2009. Available at: http://www.commin.org/ (retrieved 20120925)

ESPON, 2009. Available at: http://www.espon.eu/ (retrieved 20120925)

European Commission, 2008. Rural Development policy 2007-2013. http://ec.europa.eu/agriculture/rurdev/index_en.htm (retrieved 20120925)

European Landscape Convention http://conventions.coe.int/Treaty/en/Treaties/Html/176.htm (retrieved 20120925)

European Sustainable Cities and Towns Campaign, 2009. Available at: http://www.sustainable-cities.eu/ (retrieved 20120925)

Faludi, A. 1987. *A decision-Centred View of Environmental Planning*. Oxford: Pergamon Press.

Habitat Agenda 2009. Available at: http://www.unhabitat.org/downloads/docs/1176_6455_The_Habitat_Agenda.pdf (retrieved 20120925)

Healey, P. (1997a). *Collaborative Planning – Shaping Places in Fragmented Societies*. Hampshire, Macmillan Press LTD.

Leipzig Charter, 2009. Available at: http://www.eukn.org/E_library/Urban_Policy/Leipzig_Charter_on_Sustainable_European_Cities (retrieved 20120928)

Nilsson, K.L. 2003. *Planning in a Sustainable Direction – the art of Conscious Choices*. PhD thesis. TRITA-INFRA 03-58. Stockholm: Royal Institute of Technology, Department of Urban Studies.

Nilsson, K.L 2007. *Multilevel Sustainability Policies in Sweden*. Presentation at Cost action 27 meeting in Prague, Czech Republic, Sept. 2007.

Rydén, L. 2009. *Tools for Integrated Sustainability Mangement in Cities and Towns*, Uppsala: BUP Press.

Rydén, L. 2006. Urban Sustainability strategies – is there a common structure? In: Filho, W.L., Ubelis, A. and Berzina, D. (eds). *Sustainable development in the Baltic and beyon*d. Frankfurt am Main: Peter Lang, pp. 177-193.

UNCHS, 2001a

UNESCO world heritage 2009. Available at: http://whc.unesco.org/ (retrieved 20120925)

Chapter 19

A Typology of Rural Areas in Europe. 1999. In: *Towards a new urban rural partnership in Europe*. Strategic Study. Study Programme of the European Spatial Planning of the European Commission. http://www.mcrit.com/SPESP/SPESP_REPORT/2.3.final.pdf (retrieved 20121001)

Aleksa, J. 1999. *Ūkio, mokslo ir valstybės baruose*. Lietuvos ūkininkai ir Lietuvos valstybė // Agronomas. Sudarė prof. Mečislovas Treinys. Nirmedas, Vilnius. (in Lithuanian)

Grant, W. 1997. *The common agriculture policy*. Basingstoke: Macmillan.

Iwaskiw, W. R. (ed.) 1995. Structure of the Economy. In: *Lithuania. A country study*. Washington: GPO for the Library of Congress. http://countrystudies.us/lithuania/16.htm (retrieved 20120925).

Jasaitis, J. 2005. Lietuvos kaimiškųjų vietovių ekonominės ir socialinės situacijos pokyčiai.' *Socialiniai tyrimai*, Nr. 2 (6): p. 31–42. Šiaulių universiteto leidykla, Šiauliai. (in Lithuanian).

Jasaitis, J. 2006a. Kaimo raidos pokyčių tyrimo integralumo problema. Lietuvos ūkio transformacija 1990-2005 metais. *Ekonominės ir socialinės politikos studijos. Mokslinių straipsnių rinkinys (II)*. – Vilnius: Vilniaus pedagoginis universitetas. – 392 p. – ISBN 9955-20-105-3, p. 218-235. (in Lithuanian).

Jasaitis, J. 2006b. Diversification of Economical Activity and Changes in Structure of Rural Inhabitants as Main Indicators for Regional Development Planning. The Regional Economical Policy. *Materials of the international scientific conference, May 4-5, 2006, Grodno State University, 374 p. ISBN 985-417-761-0, Grodno (Belarus). p. 90-96.*

Jasaitis, J. 2006c. Kaimo raidos tyrimų kompleksiškumo problema. *Ekonomika ir vadyba: aktualijos ir perspektyvos, 1(6). Mokslo straipsnių rinkinys.* – Šiauliai: Šiaulių universitetas. – 203 p. – ISSN 1648-9098, p. 87-95. (in Lithuanian).

Jasaitis, J. and Šurkuvienė, S. 2006. Neurbanizuotų vietovių šiuolaikinių funkcijų sistemos kūrimas. // *Ekonomika ir vadyba: aktualijos ir perspektyvos, 2 (7). Mokslo straipsnių rinkinys.* Šiaulių universiteto leidykla, Šiauliai.p. 85-93. (in Lithuanian).

Lietuvos namų ūkio tyrimas. Lietuvos laisvosios rinkos institutas. V. Kaimo plėtra ir inovacijos. 2002. *Europos LEADER observatorija.* Brussels: - 1997. (in Lithuanian).

Rural Development – 2005. *The 2nd International Scientific Conference.* Lithuanian University of Agriculture.

Statistikos departamento prie LRV duomenys. 2007. *Prieiga per internetą:* (Žr. 2007 02 15). (in Lithuanian).

Treinys, M. 2005. Daugiafunkcinio kaimo plėtra. *Lietuvos kaimo raida.* LAEI, Vilnius: 2005. (in Lithuanian).

Treinys, M. 2006. Pogamybinis kaimas: mitas ar ateities realybė? *Mano ūkis,* Nr. 8, 2006. (in Lithuanian).

Wheelen, T.L. and Hunger, J.D. 2006. *Strategic management and business policy* – 10th ed. New Jersey: Pearson Education, Inc.

Vietos partnerystės organizavimas. "Inovacijos kaimo vietovėse". Sasiuvinis Nr. 2. Europos LEADER Observatorija.

Chapter 20

Dobkowski, A. and Skopiec, B. 2003. *Podstawowe zasady realizacji inwestycji w zakresie ochrony środowiska w rolnictwie i zagospodarowania odchodów zwierzęcych.* Warszawa: NFOŚiGW

EEA (European Environment Agency), 2006. *Integration of environment into EU agriculture policy* – the IRENA indicator-based assessment report.

Kędziora, A. 2005. Management of the water balance in catchment. In: Ryszkowski, L., Kedziora, A., van Es, H. [Eds]. *Management and protection on water resources in rural areas*. Research Centre for Agricultural and Forest Environment PAS, Poznań, pp. 16-20.

Kędziora, A., Ryszkowski, L. and Przybyła, C. 2005. *Ochrona i kształtowanie zasobów wodnych i ich jakości w krajobrazie rolniczym*. W: Gospodarowanie wodą w Wielkopolsce. Wyd. ABRYS, 16-25

Kopiński, J., Tujaka, A. and Igras, J. 2006. Nitrogen and phosphorus budgets in Poland as a tool for sustainable nutrients management, In: *Acta agriculturae Slovenica*. No. 1, pp. 173-181

Kowalik, P. 2003. Dyrektywa wodna Unii Europejskiej a rolnictwo. In: *Wiadomości Melioracyjne i Łąkarskie*. No. 1, pp. 3-7.

Manteuffel Szoege, H. and Sobolewska, A. 2003. Wpływ modernizacji gospodarki odchodami zwierzęcymi na zmiany emisji azotu do wód powierzchniowych i podziemnych. In: *Zeszyty Naukowe Politechniki Białostockiej - Inżynieria Środowiska*, No. 16, pp. 176-183.

Maruszczak, 1988. *Zmiany środowiska przyrodniczego kraju w czasach historycznych*. [W:] Przemiany środowiska geograficznego Polski. Zakł. Nar. im. Ossolińskich. Wrocław- -Warszawa, 109–135 (in Polish).

Mosiej, J. and Wyporska, K. 2004. Uwarunkowania i możliwości realizacji wymogów w zakresie ochrony środowiska na obszarach wiejskich. In: *Polska w Unii Europejskiej – nowy wymiar współpracy międzynarodowej w ochronie środowiska*, Radom, pp. 183 – 203.

Pierzgalski, E. 2002. Ograniczenia w gospodarowaniu wodą na obszarach dolinowych wynikające z konwencji i programów ochrony przyrody. In: *Wiadomości Melioracyjne i Łąkarskie*, No 3, pp.128-131.

Pijanowski, Z. 2006. *Rozwój obszarów wiejskich w Polsce a dyscyplina naukowa „kształtowanie środowiska". Przegląd naukowy „Inżynieria i Kształtowanie Środowiska", Roczn. XV, nr 2(34), 5-18.*

Rajda, W. 2005. *Woda w zagospodarowaniu przestrzennym obszarów wiejskich*. Post. Nauk Roln., nr 3, 33-42.

Ryszkowski, L. and Kędziora, A. 2007. *Sustainability and multifunctionality of agricultural landscapes*. Materialien der Interdisziplinären Arbeitsgruppe, Zukunftsorientierte Nutzung ländlicher Räume - LandInnovation, Materialen 15, Berlin-Brandenburgischen Akademie der Wissenschaften, Berlin, pp. 3-23.

Ryszkowski, L. and Kędziora, A. 2008. The influence of plant cover structures on water fluxes in agricultural landscapes. In: Bossio, D., Geheb, K. [Eds] *Conserving land, protecting water*. Comprehensive Assesment of Water Management in Agriculture Series 6, Centre for Agricultural Bioscience International, Wallingford, UK, pp. 163-177.

Sadurski, A. 2001. Polskie zmagania z wodą. In: *Jak wygrać bitwę o wodę?*, Świat Nauki, Kwiecień, pp. 41

Somorowski, C. 1996. *Współczesne problemy melioracji*. Wyd. SGGW (in Polish).

Steyaert, P., and Ollivier, G. 2007. The European Water Framework Directive: how ecological assumptions frame technical and social change. In: *Ecology and Society* 12(1): 25. Available online: http://www.ecologyandsociety.org/vol12/iss1/art25/ES-2007-2018.pdf

Swatoń, J. and Rogowski R.J. 2002. Informacja o projekcie 'Ochrona Środowiska na Terenach Wiejskich' - doświadczenia i nauki płynące z Polski. In: *Materiały z seminarium „Ograniczenia zanieczyszczeń pochodzenia rolniczego – wzorcowa praktyka'*, Przysiek k/ Torunia.

Wierzbicki, K. and Krajewski, K. 2003. Infrastruktura techniczna obszarów wiejskich warunkiem ich poprawnego rozwoju. In: *Wiadomości Melioracyjne i Łąkarskie*, 3: 108 -112.

WWF Polska GWP Polska, 2005. *Zasady gospodarowania na obszarach NATURA 2000 w dolinach rzek*. Warszawa

Chapter 21

Baelermanes, A. M., B. 1988. A critical evaluation of environmental assessment tools for sustainable foerst management Proceedings of the International Conference of Life Cycle Assessment in Agriculture, Agro- Industry and Forestry. D. Ceuterick. Brussels: 65-75.

Bell, S. and Morse, S. 2000. *Sustainability indicators. Measuring the immeasurable?* London: Earthscan Publications Ltd.

Benites, J.R. and Tschirley, J.B. 1997. Land quality indicators and their use in sustainable agriculture and rural development. In: *FAO Land and Water Bulletin,* 12:5, pp 2–6.

Bossel, H. 2001. Assessing viability and sustainability: a systems-based approach for deriving comprehensive indicator sets. Conservation Ecology 5(12): URL: http://www.consecol.org/vol5/iss2/art12/ (retrieved 20120925)

Büchs, W. (ed.) 2003. *Biotic indicators for biodiversity and sustainable agriculture*. Amsterdam: Elsevier

Commission of the European Communities. 2000. *Indicators for the integration of environmental concerns into the Common Agricultural Policy*. Brussels: CEC, 26 pp.

Commission of the European Communities. 2001. *Biodiversity Action Plan for Biodiversity*. Comunication from the Commission o the Council and the European Parliament. Brussels: CEC, 52 pp.

Cox, C. 2008. Beyond T: Standards and Tools for Sustainable Soil Management. A Report of Expert Consultation. Report summarizes outcome of consult held May 22-23, 2007. Nebraska City, Nebraska. IA, Soil and Water Conservation Society.

Dilly, O. and Blume, H.P. 1998. Indicators to assess sustainable land use with reference to soil microbiology. In Blume, H.P. et al. (eds.). *Towards sustainable land use. Furthering cooperation between people and institutions*. Reiskirchen: Catena Verlag, pp. 29-36.

Doherty, S. and Rydberg, T. 2002. *Ecosystem properties and principles of living systems as foundation for sustainable agriculture – critical reviews of environmental assessment tools, key findings and questions from a course process*. Ekologiskt Lantbruk no 32, Uppsala: SLU.

Eiden, G., Bryden, J. and Piorr. H.-P. (eds.) 2001: *Proposal on agri-environmenal indicators. Final report of the PAIS project.* Luxembourg: EUROSTAT.

European Commission. 2001. *A framework for indicators for the economic and social dimensions of sustainable agriculture and rural development*. Brussels: CEC.

European Environment Agency. 2004. *An inventory of biodiversity indicators in Europe*. Technical report no 92. Office for Official Publications of the European Communities. Luxembourg: European Communities.

Fehér, A. and Končeková, L. 2005. An analysis of indicators for sustainable land use based on research in agricultural landscape. In Filho, W.L. (ed.) *Handbook of sustainability research*. Frankfurt am Main: Peter Lang Europäischer Verlag der Wissenschaften, pp. 48-67.

Heinz, John H. III Center for Science, Economics and the Environment, 2002. The State of the National Ecosystems. Measuring the Lands, Waters, and Living Resources of the United States Cambrige University Press, New York NY.pp.269.

Heinz, John H. III Center for Science, Economics and the Environment, 2008. The State of the National Ecosystems. Measuring the Lands, Waters, and Living Resources of the United States Island Press, New York NY. Pp. 368. Washington, DC.

Hietala-Koivu, R. 2002. *Landscape indicators bridging nature and man – structure, function and value of an agricultural landscape*. Paper at the NIJOS/OECD Expert Meeting on Agricultural Landscape. 7-9 October 2002, Oslo, pp. 1-9.

Hill, S.B. and Ramsay, J. 1997. *Weeds as indicators of soil conditions*. EAP Publications no 67. Ecological Agriculture Projects. McGill University, http://www.eap.mcgill.ca/publications/EAP67.htm

Jesinghaus, J. 1999. *A European system of environmental pressure indices*. First Volume of the environmental pressure indices handbook: The indicators. http://esl.jrc.it/envind/theory/handb_.htm (retrieved 20120925)

Karlen, D. L., Stott, D. E., 1994. A framework for evaluating physical and chemical indicators of soil quality. In: Doran, J.W., Coleman, D.C., Bezdicek, D.F., Stewart, B.A. (Eds.), Defining Soil Quality for a Sustainable Environment. Soil Science Society of America (SSSA) Special Publication No. 35. SSSA, Madison, WI. pp. 53-72.

Liebig, MA., JW. Doran and JC. Gardner. "Evaluation of a field test kit for measuring selected soil quality indicators." Agronomy journal 88.4 (1996):683-686.

Lopez-Riduara, S., van Keulen, H., van Ittersum. M., Leffalaar, P. 2005. "Evaluating the sustainability." A MESMIS framework. Ecol Indicators (2).

McRae, T., Smith, C.A.S. and Gregorich, L.J. (eds.) 2000. *Environmental sustainability of Canadian agriculture*. Report of the agri-environmental indicator project of Canada, Ottawa: Agriculture and Agri-Food.

Meyer, J.R. 1992. Indicators of the ecological status of agroecosystems. In: McKenzie, D.H. et al. (eds.). *Ecological Indicators*. Essex: Elsevier Science Publ, pp. 629–658.

National Research Council, 2000. Ecological indicators for the nation. Washington DC: National Academy Press. 180 pages. Available online at: http://www.nap.edu/catalog.php?record_id=9720 (retrieved 20120925)

Organisation for Economic Co-operation and Development. 2001. *Environmental indicators for agriculture*. Methods and Results, Executive summary 2001 etc. Paris: Organisation for Economic Co-operation and Development, www.oecd.org.

Parris, K. 2002. *Agricultural landscape indicators in the context of the OECD work on agri-environemntal indicators*. Paper at the NIJOS/OECD Expert Meeting on Agricultural Landscape. 7-9 October 2002, Oslo, pp. 1-9.

Piorr, H-P. 2003. Environmental Policy, agri-environmental indicators and landcape indicators. In: *Agriculture, Ecosystems and Environment* 98, pp. 17-33.

Reid, W.J., McNeely, J.A. and Tunstall, D.B. et al. 1993: *Biodiversity indicators for policy-makers*. World Resources Institute and IUCN. Washington: World Conservation Union.

Ritcher, D.D. 2007. Humanity's transformation of Earth's soil: Pedology's new frontier. In: SOIL SCIENCE, 172: 957-967.

Schjonning, P. Elmholt S., and Christinsen, B. (eds). Managing Soil Quality: Challenges in Modern Agriculture. pp 386. CABI Press. Wallingford, Oxfordshire.

Shaxson, T.F. 1998. Concepts and indicators for assessment of sustainable land use. In: Blume, H. P. et al. (eds.). *Towards sustainable land use. Furthering cooperation between people and institutions.* Reiskirchen: Catena Verlag, pp. 11–19.

Stenberg, B. 1999. Monitoring soil quality of arable land. Microbiological indicators. In: *Acta Agriculturae Scandinavica* 49:1, pp. 1–24.

Tugel AJ, Herrick JE, Brown JR, Mausbach MJ, Puckett W, Hipple K. 2005. Soil change, soil survey, and natural resources decision making: A blueprint for action. SSSAJ 69: 738-747.

USDA Natural Resource Conservation Service. 1996. *Indicators for Soil Quality Evaluation*. Soil Quality Information Sheet. Washington: USDA NRCS.

Wander MM, Walter GL, Nissen TM, Bollero GA, Andrews SS. 2002. Soil quality: Science and process. Agronomy journal 94(1):23-32.

Van Cauwenbergh, N. , K. Biala, Bielders, B., Brouckaert, V., Franchois, L., Garcia Cidad, V., Hermy, M., Mathias, F., Muys, B., Reijnders,J., Sauvenier, X., Vlackx, J., Vanclooster, M., Van der Veken, B., Wauters, E., and A. Peeters. 2007. "SAFE- A heirarchical framework for assessing the sustainability of agricultural systems.". In: Agriculture, Ecosystems and Environment 120: 229-242.

Wander, M.M. 2009. Agroecosystem integrity and the internal cycling of nutrients. In: Agricultural Ecosystems; Unifying Concepts II. Bohlen, P. and G. House. (eds). Taylor and Francis, NY. pp. 137-166.In: Agricultural Ecosystems; Unifying Concepts II. Bohlen, P. and G. House. (eds). Taylor and Francis, NY. Pp. 137-166.

Washer, D.M. (ed.) 2000. *Agri-environmental indicators for sustainable agriculture in Europe*. ECNC Technical Report Series. Tillburg: European Centre for Natural Conservation ECNC.

Chapter 22

Andersson, M., Hagberg, J., Weidner, H., Jänicke, M., Rydén, L. and Seminene, D. Making and implementing environmental policy. In: Rydén, L., Andersson, M. and Migula, P. (Eds). 2003. *Environmental Science*. Uppsala: BU Press. pp 662-690.

Baltic Sea Foundation, 2012. (http://www.baltic-sea-foundation.de

Convention on the Protection of the Marine Environment of the Baltic Sea Area, 1992 (Helsinki Convention) at: http://www.helcom.fi/stc/files/Convention/Conv0704.pdf (retrieved 20120925)

Derkzen, P. and Bock, B.B. 2007. "The Construction of Professional Identity: Symbolic Power in rural Partnerships in The Netherlands" In: *Sociologia Ruralis*, vol. 47; no. 3 pp. 189-204.

Dimitrova, A. 2010. "The New Member States of the EU in the Aftermath of Enlargement: Do New European Rules Remain Empty Shells?" In: *Journal of European Public Policy* vol. 17, no. 1, pp. 137-148

EEA, 2010. EEA Viewer.

Easton, D. 1967. *A Systems Analysis of Political Life*, New York: John Wiley & Sons, Inc.

Eurobarometer 67, 2007 http://ec.europa.eu/public_opinion/archives/eb/eb67/eb67_en.htm (retrieved 20120925)

Eurobarometer 300, 2009 European's attitudes towards climate change. At http://www.ec.europa.eu/public_opinion/archives/ebs/ebs_300_full_en.pdf. (accessed July 2012).

Falkner, G., Hartlapp, M., Leiber, S., and Treib, O. 2004. "Non-Compliance with EU Directives in the Member States: Opposition through the Backdoor?" In: *West European Politics*, vol. 27, no. 3, pp. 452-473

Hardin, G. 1968. "The Tragedy of the Commons", In: *Science*, vol. 62, pp. 1243-1248.
Inglehart, R. 1990. *Culture Shift in Advanced Industrial Society*, Princeton.
Lipset, S.M. 1959. *Political Man*, London: Heinemann.
Maier, J., 1990. *The green parties in Western Europe – a brief history, their successes and their problems*. at: http://www.globalgreens.org/literature/maier/westerneurope (retrieved 20120925).
Müller-Rommel, F. 2002. "The Lifespan and Political performance of Green Parties in Western Europe" In: *Environmental Politics*, vol. 11. no1. pp. 1-16.
Norgaard, O. and Pedersen, K.H. 1994 "Political and administrative preconditions for environmental policies in the Baltic States" in Katarina Eckerberg et al. Comparing Nordic and Baltic Countries-environmental problems and policies in agriculture and forestry, In: *TemaNord*:572, pp. 98-122.
Olsen, S.B., Sutinen, J.G. Juda, L., Hennessey, T.M. and Grigalunas, T.A. 2006. *A Handbook on Governance and Socioeconomics of large marine Ecosystems*, University of Rhode Island. http://www.iwlearn.net/abt_iwlearn/pns/learning/lme-gov-handbook.pdf (retrieved 20120925)
Olson, M. 1965. *The Logic of Collective Action*, Cambridge, Mass: Harvard university Press.
Ostrom, E. 1990. *Governing the Commons: The Evolution of Institutions of Collective Action*, Cambridge: Cambridge University Press.
Pedersen, Karin Hilmer and Gert Tinggard Svendsen 2011. "Farmers as climate heroes?" (in Danish) In: *Politica*, vol. 43; 4. pp. 459-477.
Pedersen, Karin Hilmer and Gert Tinggard Svendsen work in process.
Semeniene and Zylicz, 1997
Svendsen, Gert Tinggard 2003. *The Political Economy of the European Union. Institutions, Policy and Economic Growth*, Cheltenham, Edward Elgar.
Truman, D. 1951. *The Process of Government*, New Your: Knopf Press.
Weale, A. 1992. *The New Politics of Pollution*. Manchester/New York: Manchester University Press.
World Commission on Environment and Development, 1987
World Development Indicators 2012 at: http://data.worldbank.org/data-catalog/world-development-indicators (accessed october 2012).
World Justice Project Index 2011. http://worldjusticeproject.org/sites/default/files/WJP_Rule_of_Law_Index_2011_Report.pdf

Chapter 23

Ministry of Agriculture and Rural Development, 2005. *Rural development plan for Poland 2004-2006*.
Ministry of Agriculture and Rural Development, 2006a. *Rural development programme for 2007-2013*.
Ministry of Agriculture and Rural Development, 2006b. *National strategic plan 2007-2013*.
Motyka K., 2007: *The EUruralis is approaching, what do we do? Policy-science interface in rural development practice in Poland.* MSc thesis, Warsaw University of Life Sciences, Interfaculty Department of Environmental Protection, p.132
Poland Central Statistical Office, 2007 http://www.stat.gov.pl (retrieved 20120925)

Chapter 25

Andersen, T.M. and Pedersen, L.H. 2005. Demography, prosperity dilemmas and macro-economic strategies (in Danish). In: *Nationaløkonomisk Tidsskrift* 143 (November 2005, No. 2):189-229.
Arrow, K., Bolin, B., Costanza, R., Dasgupta, P., Folke, C., Holling, C.S., Jansson, B.-O., Levin, S., Mäler, K.-G., Perrings, C. and Pimentel, D. 1995. Economic growth, carrying capacity, and the environment. In: *Ecological Economics* 15 (November 1995, No. 2):91-95. Reprinted from *Science* 268 (1995):520-521.
Arrow, K., Dasgupta, P., Goulder, L., Daily, G., Ehrlich, P., Heal, G., Levin, S., Mäler, K.-G., Scheider, S., Starrett, D. and Walker, B. 2004. Are we consuming too much?. In: *Journal of Economic Perspectives* 18 (Summer 2004, No. 3):147-172.
Burda, M. and Wyplosz, C. 1993. *Macroeconomics. A european text*. Oxford: Oxford University Press.
Cekanavicius, L., Semeniene, D., Oosterhuis, F. and Ierland, E.V. The cost of pollution. In: Rydén et al. 2003. Chap. 19, pp 566-597
Danish Ministry of Finance ; Finansministeriet. 1999. Manual for social and economic cost-benefit analysis (in Danish). Copenhagen: Ministry of Finance.
Economic Council. 2004: *The Danish Economy, Autumn 2004*. København: Det Økonomiske Råd.
The *Economist*, 16 June 2007, p 78
Hanley, N., Shogren, J.F. and White, B. 2001. *Introduction to environmental economics*. Oxford: Oxford University Press.
Hansen, A.C. Denmark: Energy Efficiency, Water Purification, and Policy Instruments 1998. In: Aage, H. (ed.) 1998. *Environmental transition in Nordic and Baltic countries*. Chap. 7, pp. 94-108
Hansen, A.S., Furu, A., Kjellingbro, P.M., Skotte, M. and Vigsø, D. 2003. *Knowledge, values and choice. Action plan for the aquatic environment III* (in Danish). København: Institut for Miljøvurdering.
Hansen, L.G. and Hasler, B. 2007. Is regulation of the nitrogen loss to the aquatic environment cost efficient? (in Danish). In: Halsnæs, K, Andersen, P. and Larsen, A. (eds.): *Miljøvurdering på økonomisk vis*. København: Jurist- og Økonomforbundets Forlag. Chap. 3, pp 51-68
Jacobsen, B.H. 2004. *Final Economic Evaluation of the Action Plan for the Aquatic Environment II* (in Danish with an English summary). Rapport nr. 169. Copenhagen: Fødevareøkonomisk Institut.
Jacobsen, B.H., Abildtrup, J., Andersen, M., Christensen, T., Hasler, B., Hussain, Z.B., Huusom, H., Jensen, J.D., Schou, J.S. and Ørum, J. E. 2004. *Costs of reducing nutrient losses from agriculture. Analysis prior to the danish aquatic programme III* (in Danish with an English summary). Rapport nr. 167. Copenhagen: Fødevareøkonomisk Institut.
Layard, P.R.G. and Walters, A.A. 1978. *Microeconomic Theory*. New York: McGraw-Hill.
Lomborg, B. 1998. Article. In: the Danish newspaper *Politiken*, 19 January 1998.
Lomborg, B. 2001. *The skeptical environmentalist: Measuring the real state of the world*. Cambridge: Cambridge University Press.
Maddison, A. 1991. *Dynamic forces in capitalist development. A long-run comparative view*. Oxford: Oxford University Press.

Maddison, A. 2003. *The world economy. Historical statistics*. Paris: OECD.
Mankiw, N.G. 1997. *Principles of macroeconomics*. Fort Worth: The Dryden Press.
Mankiw, N.G. 2000. *Macroeconomics* (4th ed.). New York: Worth.
McNeill, J. 2001. *Something new under the sun. An environmental history of the twentieth century.* London: Penguin.
Nordhaus, W.D. 1994. *Managing the global commons: The economics of climate change*. Cambridge, Mass: The IMT Press.
Nordhaus, W.D. A review of the Stern review on the economics of climate change . In: *Journal of Economic Literature* 45 (September 2007, No. 3): pp. 686-702.
Pearce, D.W. and Turner, R.K. 1990. *Economics of natural resources and the environment*. London: Harvester Wheatsheaf.
Plenty of gloom. In: The *Economist*, 18 Dec 1997 http://www.economist.com/node/455855 (retrieved 20120925)
Ponting, C.A 1991. *Green history of the world*. Harmondsworth: Penguin.
Rydén, L., Migula, P. and Andersson, M. (eds.) 2003. *Environmental science*. Uppsala: Baltic University Press.
Solow, R. 1974. The Economics of Resources and the Resources of Economics . In: *American Economic Review* 64 (No. 2, May 1974):1-14.
Solow, R. 1992. *An almost practical step towards sustainability*. Washington D.C. Resources for the Future.
Stern, N. (ed.) 2007. *The economics of climate change*. (The Stern Review, HM Treasury Independent Review). Cambridge: Cambridge University Press.
Stiglitz, J.E. 2000. *Economics of the public sector*. 3rd ed. New York: Norton.
Weitzman, M.L. 2007. A review of the Stern Review on the economics of climate change . In: *Journal of Economic Literature* 45 (September 2007, No. 3):703-724.
World Bank. 2003. *Sustainable development in a dynamic world. World development report 2003*. New York: Oxford University Press.
Aage, H. 1984. Economic arguments on the sufficiency of natural resources . In: *Cambridge Journal of Economics* 8 (March 1984, No. 1): 105-113.
Aage, H. (ed.) 1998. *Environmental transition in Nordic and Baltic countries*. Cheltenham: Edward Elgar.
Aage, H. 2002. The environment . In: W. Maciejewski (ed.): *The Baltic sea region. Cultures, policies, societies*. Uppsala: The Baltic University Press. Chap. 51, pp 639-650
Aage, H. 2008. Economic ideology on the environment - from Adam Smith to Bjørn Lomborg . In: *Global Environment* 2008 1 (November 2008, No 2): 8-45.
Åslund, A. 2002. *Building capitalism. The transformation of the former Soviet bloc*. Cambridge: Cambridge University Press.

Chapter 26

Autio, M. and Heinonen, V. 2004. To Consume or not to Consume? Young People's Environmentalism in the Affluent Finnish. In: *Young – Nordic Journal of Youth Research*, Vol. 12 (2): 137-153.
Bauman, Z. 1992. *Intimation of Postmodernity*. Chatham: Routledge.
Bourdieu, P. 1984. *Distinction – A Social Critic of the Judgement of Taste* (translated by R. Nice). London, Routledge & Kegan Paul.
Brower, M. and Leon, W. 1999. *The Consumer's Guide to Effective Environmental Choices*. Three Rivers Press, New York.
Callenbach, E. 2000. *Living Cheaply with Style – Spend Less Live Better*. Ronin Books.
Consumer International. http://consumersinternational.org
Cutter, S.L., Mitchell, J.T., Hill, A. Harrington, L., Katkins, S., Muraco,W., DeHart, J., Reynolds, A. and Shudak, R. 2002. Attitudes toward reducing greenhouse gas emissions from local places. In: *Global change and local places: Estimating, understanding, and reducing greenhouse gases*. Association of American Geographers. Global Change in Local Places (GCLP) Working Group. Cambridge, England: Cambridge University Press. Pp. 171-191
Dominguez, J. and Robin, V. 1996. *Your Money or Your Life*. Penguin Books.
Durning, A.T. 1992. *How Much is Enough? – The Consumer Society and the Future of the Earth*. Norton, New York.
Eurostat, 2012a. Motorisation rate: Passenger cars per 1000 inhabitants. http://epp.eurostat.ec.europa.eu/tgm/table.do?tab=table&init=1&plugin=1&language=en&pcode=tsdpc340 (retrieved 20120925)
Eurostat, 2012b Greenhouse gas emissions (http://epp.eurostat.ec.europa.eu/tgm/refreshTableAction.do?tab=table&plugin=1&pcode=tsdcc100&language=en)
Eurostat 2007c. Eco-labelling. http://epp.eurostat.ec.europa.eu/tgm/graphToolClosed.do?tab=graph&init=1&plugin=1&language=en&pcode=tsdpc420&toolbox=legend (accessed 9 February 2008)
The UK government gateway to Corporate Social Responsibility http://www.csr.gov.uk/ (accessed 6 March 2008)
Finnish National Commission on Sustainable Development (FNCSD). 2007. http://www.environment.fi/default.asp?contentid=245442&lan=EN (retrieved 20120925)
Fischer, F. and Hajer, M.A. (eds.) 1999. *Living with Nature – Environmental Politics as Cultural Discourse*. Oxford University Press.
Gabriel, Y. and Lang, T. 1995. *The Unmanageable Consumer – Contemporary consumption and its Fragmentations*. London: Sage.
Gabriel, Y. and Lang, T. 2006. *The Unmanageable Consumer* 2nd ed. London and Thousand Oaks, Sage.
Greenpeace. 2006. The cod fishery in the Baltic Sea: unsustainable and illegal. http://www.greenpeace.org/international/press/reports/cod-fishery-baltic-sea (retrieved 20120925).
Interactive Research Group. 2005. *Russian Economic Overview 2005.*
Libert, B. 1995. *The environmental heritage of Soviet agriculture.* CAB International, Sustainable Rural Development Series No. 2. Oxon, UK. 228 pp.
Michaelis, L. and Lorek, S. 2004. *Consumption and the Environment in Europe – Trends and Futures*. Danish Environmental Protection Agency, Environment Project No. 904, Copenhagen, Denmark
National Research Council. 2005. *Decision making for the environment: Social and behavioural science research priorities.* Panel on Social and Behavioural Science Research Priorities for Environmental Decision Making. G.D. Brewer and P.C. Stern, editors. Committee on the Human Dimensions of Global Change, Division of Behavioural and Social Sciences and Education. Washington, DC: The National Academic Press. 137 pp, 6 appendices.

National Sustainable Agriculture Coalition. http://www.sustainableagriculture.net/ (retrieved 20120925)

Robbins, J. 1998. *Diet for a New America*. H J Kramer, Tiburon, CA.

Rosenblatt, R. (eds) 1999. *Consuming Desires – Consumption, Culture, and the Pursuit of Happiness*. Island Press.

Shi, D. E. 1985. *The Simple Life – Plain Living and High Thinking in American Culture*. Oxford University Press.

Sierra Club. The True Cost of Food – Guide for Discussion Leaders. http://www.sierraclub.org/truecostoffood/ (retrieved 20120925)

Stern, P.C. 2002. Changing behaviour in households and communities. What have we learned? In: National Research Council. 2005. *Decision making for the environment. Social and behavioural science research priorities.* Panel on Social and Behavioural Science Research Priorities for Environmental Decision Making. G.D. Brewer and P.C. Stern, editors. Committee on the Human Dimensions of Global Change, Division of Behavioural and Social Sciences and Education. Washington, DC: The National Academic Press. Pp. 201-211.

Swedish Dairy Association: http://www.svenskmjolk.se/ (retrieved 20120925)

Symposium on Sustainable Consumption. Instruments for change – Definitions & Concepts. Oslo, Norway; 19-20 January 1994. http://www.iisd.org/susprod/principles.htm (retrieved 20120925)

UNECE, 2012. Final consumption. http://w3.unece.org/pxweb/quickstatistics/readtable.asp?qs_id=5 (retrieved 20120925)

United Nations Economic Commission for Europe (UNECE). 2008. Country data.

UNEP and CI. 2002. *Implementing Sustainable Consumption and Production Policies. North-South, South-South and East-West Partnerships – Meeting Report of Informal Expert Meeting*. Paris, France.

Wier, M., Munksgaard, J. Christoffersen, L.B. Jensen, T.S. Pedersen, O. G. Keiding, H. and Lenzen, M. 2003. Environmental performance indices, family types and consumption patterns. In: *Transactions on Ecology and the Environment* Vol. 63, pp. 657-667. London: WTT Press.

Wilbanks, T.J., and Stern, P.C. 2002. New tools for environmental protection. What we know and need to know. In: National Research Council; Dietz, T. and Stern, P. C. (eds) *New tools for environmental protection: Education, information, and voluntary measures.* Committee on the Human Dimensions of Global Change. Division of Behavioral and Social Sciences and Education. Washington, DC: National Academy Press. Pp. 337-348.

Further Reading

General

Baltic Sea Secretariat for Youth Affairs http://www.balticsea-youth.org/

Recycling Guide Org: http://www.recycling-guide.org.uk/ (accessed May 2012)

International Human Dimensions Programme on Global Environmental Change http://www.ihdp.unu.edu/ (accessed May 2012)

Worldwatch Institute http://www.worldwatch.org/ (accessed May 2012)

Research Foundations

Open Society Institute and Soros Foundation Network http://www.soros.org/ (accessed May 2012)

NGOs

Coalition Clean Baltic for Protection of the Baltic Sea Environment – a network of major national grassroots environmental organisations representing in total around half a million members: http://www.ccb.se/ (accessed May 2012)

Keep Baltic Tidy: http://www.keepbaltictidy.org/ (accessed May 2012)

World Wildlife Fund: http://www.wwf.org/ (accessed May 2012)

Greenpeace: http://www.greenpeace.org/ (accessed May 2012)

Corporate Social Responsibility

Wikipedia http://en.wikipedia.org/wiki/Corporate_social_responsibility (accessed May 2012)

The UK government gateway to Corporate Social Responsibility http://www.csr.gov.uk/ (accessed May 2012)

Management Systems and Certification

Certifiering.nu http://www.certifiering.nu/ecomedia/info/content.aspx?pid=32&TAB=home (accessed May 2012)

Images and Figure Sources

Cover Photograph: Family outside the village Pyzowka in southern Poland. Photo: Gary Scott. Source: http://www.flickr.com/photos/kingary/4728491888

Figure 1. The Baltic Sea region. The Baltic basin, i.e. the drainage area of the Baltic sea including Kattegatt, is marked by the bold line. In this region all water flows towards the Baltic sea. (Source: UNEP, Grid Arendal. http://maps.grida.no/baltic/.)

Figure 2. Ecological footprint in relation to United Nations Human Development Index, 2007. (Source: Ecological Footprint Atlas, 2010. http://issuu.com/globalfootprintnetwork/docs/ecological-footprint-atlas-2010).

Figure 3. Classification of rural areas based on the OECD NUTS3 definition. NUTS= Nomenclature of territorial units for statistics. Source: Eurostat, SIRE Database, IRPUD, 2001. http://ec.europa.eu/agriculture/publi/reports/ruralemployment/sera_report.pdf

Figure 1.1. Open wooded meadow in Matsalu National Park near Penijõe in western Estonia. The canopy contains much Ash (Fraxinus excelsior). Photo: Stuart Roberts. Source: http://www.flickr.com/photos/87532379@N00/2547322291.

Figure 1.2. Expansion and contraction of cultivated area in Europe during the last millennium (Rabbinge & van Diepen, 2000).

Figure 1.3. The vegetation zones in the Baltic region, with the four typical vegetation belts. Shaded areas are alpine zone, and subalpine and subarctic birch forest. (Adapted from Sjörs, in Rydin et al., 1999.)

Figure 1.4. Karums Alvar is a small area of semi-natural grassland in the middle part of Öland, Sweden. Photo: Bengt Olsson.

Figure 1.5. The main post-glacial stages of the Baltic Sea. From upper to lower right: The Baltic Ice Lake up to 10,000 years BP. : The Yoldia Sea 10,000-9,400 years BP. : The Ancylus Lake 9,400-8,000 years BP. : The Littorina Sea from 8,000 years BP, which gradually changed into the Baltic Sea. Source: Isakar, 2003. Mare Isakar, University of Tartu (http://www.ut.ee/BGGM/eestigeol/l_m_parastj.html)

Figure 1.6. Icetracks on coastal landscape. Photo: Ingrid Karlsson.

Figure 1.7. Stone wall in the province of Småland, Southern Sweden. All through the landscape farmers have removed stones from the fields to make way for arable land. Photo: Lars Rydén.

Figure 1.8. Farming in Sweden during the 18th century. Painting by Jan Eric Rehn, Petrus Strandberg, 1749. Source: Uppsala University Library.

Figure 1.9. Drained field. Photo: Ingrid Karlsson.

Figure 1.10. Mean annual area (thousand ha) of drained agricultural land in Estonia. Source: Estonian Ministry of Agriculture.

Figure 1.11. Arable land in the Baltic Sea region. Ratio of arable land out of total land use in the Baltic Sea drainage basin. The map displays the situation at approximately 1990. Cartographer: Hugo Ahlenius, UNEP/GRID-Arendal. Source: http://maps.grida.no/go/graphic/arable_land_in_the_baltic_sea_region.

Figure 1.12. Aerial patchwork landscape in Kåseberga, Sweden. Photo: Christopher Line. Source: http://www.flickr.com/photos/topherous/187692015.

Figure 1.13. Different time layers shine through in the same spot. Source: after Vervloet, 1986.

Figure 2.1. Possibility to pick mushroms and berries and enjoy wildlife and outdoor life are important ecosystem services provided by the forest. Photo: Ingrid Karlsson.

Figure 2.2. Provision of renewable energy from wind, water and sun are also ecosystem services. Photo: Lars Rydén.

Figure 2.3. The support provided by ecosystems services to human well-being. Source: Millennium Ecosystem Assessment, 2005.

Figure 2.4. Ecosystem services and dis-services to and from agriculture. Solid arrows indicate services, whereas dashed arrows indicate dis-services Source: Zhang et al., 2007.

Figure 2.5. Pollination is one of the most threatened ecosystem services. Photo: Marcin Bajer. Source: http://www.flickr.com/photos/rrrodrigo/4734344094

Figure 2.6. Camping at Abisko, Sweden. Photo: Tomas Hellberg. Source: http://www.flickr.com/photos/tomhe/40406129

Figure 2.7. View of the lower basin of the Biebrza National Park, Poland. Photo: Frank Vassen. http://www.flickr.com/photos/42244964@N03/4664144695/

Figure 2.8. Forest trail in Bialowieza National Park, Poland. Photo: Chad Chatterton. http://www.flickr.com/photos/oslochad/4559600253/

Figure 2.9. Sheep managing the landscape. Photo: Ingrid Karlsson.

Figure 3.1. Polesie is the largest natural wetland ecosystem in Central and Eastern Europe covering parts of Northern Ukraine, Western Poland and a large part of Southern Belarus. Source: Author..

Figure 3.2. The river Ubort. Not far from Chernobyl. Gomel. Of Belarus. Pool Pripyat River. Belarusian Polesie. Photo: Oleg Gritskevich (Belarus). http://www.flickr.com/photos/amnimaken/4815026144

Figure 3.3. Bug wetland in Pribuzhskoye-Polesie, Belarus which is a UNESCO biosphere reserve. Photo: Ivan Prakapiuk. Source: http://static.panoramio.com/photos/original/27743761.jpg

Figure 4.1. National and international river basin districts. Modified from larger map. Source: European Commission.
http://ec.europa.eu/environment/water/water-framework/facts_figures/index_en.htm

Figure 4.2. River Dvina (in Latvia Daugava) near Polotsk, Belarus demonstrate a mature river landscape. Photo: Lars Rydén.

Figure 4.3. As a whole the Baltic Sea basin receives 450 km3 precipitationper year. The amount of precipitation ranges from very wet areas in the Norwegian mountains with 3,000 mm annually, to drier areas on the north-eastern rim and southern agricultural regions with below 300 mm annually (data compiled by Lars Hedlund. Source: Rydén et al., 2003)

Figure 4.4. Lake Ladoga in Karelia, Russia is the largest lake in Europe. Draining into the Gulf of Finland through river Neva it provide freshwater for St Petersburg. Ladoga has also many environmental problems including eutrophication and pollution from industry. Photo: Jussi Huotari. http://www.flickr.com/photos/jussihuotari/2563259223

Figure 4.5. The Djurholma bog in southwestern Sweden i 70 ha large and is a nature protected area. From the bird tower it is possible to sometimes see grouse playing. Much larger bogs of this kind is to be found in the northern parts of the Baltic Sea region. Photo: Guillaime Baviere. Source: http://www.flickr.com/photos/84554176@N00/6567996965

Figure 4.6. Akkats Hydro power plant by Lule Älv river outside the small city Jokkmokk in Northern Sweden. The mural paitings entitled Uvssat davás in the Sami language (Doors to the West) are made by Bengt Lindström och Lars Pirak. Photo: Hans Blomberg/Vattenfall.

Figure 4.7. A sandy beach at Curzon Spit outside Kaliningrad. Photo: Lars Rydén.

Figure 5.1. Tatra mountain landscape in Southern Poland bordering the Slovak Republic. Photo: Lars Rydén.

Figure 5.2. Mountain ranges in Europe. Source: UNEP-WCMC, Nordregio. European Commission, 2004. Mountain Areas in Europe: Analysis of mountain areas in EU member states, acceding and other European countries. 271 p.

Figure 3.9 sid 39 http://ec.europa.eu/regional_policy/sources/docgener/studies/study_en.htm

Figure 5.3. During the winter the reindeer gather at the farm and the reindeer herdsmen feed them on pellets and hay. Photo: Rukakuusamu (Heather) http://www.flickr.com/photos/rukakuusamo/5725026813

Figure 5.4. Gruvberget, close to Svappavaara, Sweden. Photo: Fredrik Alm. http://www.lkab.com/Press/Bildarkiv/Bild/

Figure 6.1. Native American Encampment on Lake Huron. Oil on canvas by Paul Kane, c. 1845.The Granger Collection, New York Source: http://media-3.web.britannica.com/eb-media/78/132278-050-BD73EA64.jpg

Figure 6.2. View of Erie Canal by John William Hill, 1829. Source: http://www.history.rochester.edu

Figure 6.3. Clearing of land. Source: Perlin, 2005

Figure 6.4. The John Deere self-scoulding steel plow from 1837 made in much easier to till the thick clay soils of the midwest. http://www.augustana.edu/SpecialCollections/FarmLife/farm38.gif

Figure 6.5. Man and woman using a double-handled saw to clear trees from their land in Wisconsin 1905. Credit: Wisconsin Historical Society. http://www.wisconsinhistory.org/whi/permission/

Figure 6.6. Dredge boat. To dig dredge ditches to drain farm land for drainage district. A slip scraper was used to dig hole in middle of field till there was enough water to float this boat. It was prefabricated and had a steam shovel in front to dig it's way toward the river. Taken into the field by wagons and put together on site. Building on back is crew quarters. Photo from Moultrie county in Illinois around 1900. Source: Illinois Digital Archives, made available by the Arthur Public Library.

Figure 6.7. Buried machinery in barn lot in Dallas, South Dakota, United States during the Dust Bowl, an agricultural, ecological, and economic disaster in the Great Plains region of North America in 1936. Source: United States Department of Agriculture; Image Number: 00di0971

Figure 6.8. Maize being transferred from a combine to a truck for hauling during harvest near Champaign IL, circa 2008. Photo: T.P. Martins. http://www.flickr.com/photos/tjmartins/3995582085

Figure 6.9. Land use, fisheries & erosion in the Great Lakes region. Source: US. Environmental Protection Agency, US EPA. http://www.epa.gov/greatlakes/atlas/images/big07.gif

Figure 7.1. Iron age village at Lejre in Denmark with log canoes and a thatch roof building. This is one of several reconstructed villages to be found in the Baltic Sea region, such as Eketorp in Öland in southern Sweden and Hedeby in northern Germany. Photo: Kristian Mollenborg. Source: http://www.flickr.com/photos/mollenborg/4650109499

Figure 7.2. Reenactment of iron age farmers tilling the land with a wooden ard (plow) in Lejre, Denmark. © Lejre experimental Centre. http://www.tollundman.dk/tollundmandens-tid.asp

Figure 7.3. 15th century fresco from Rinkaby church by Albertus Pictor, Sweden portraing Adam (Old Testament, the Bible) plowing. Photo: Lennart Karlsson. National historical museum of Sweden in Stockholm. http://www.formonline.se/kyrkor/rinkaby/rink_valv2ost.jpg

Figure 7.4. Before the 18th Century Sweden was a country of villages. Farmers lived close to each other in settlements, while their fields were inter-mixed as a way of compensating each other for the good and less productive portions of the land. Despite of its advantages, it was a less productive system than individual-based farms because tilling, sowing and harvesting required a lot of coordination on the part of the farmers and new technologies and techniques were difficult to implement. In the 18th Century authorities introduced a reform designed to improve agricultural productivity. The new law required that the number of fields in each farm was decreased and larger fields were formed. The above map represents farms in the Orleka village in west Sweden in 1645 before the reforms were implemented. Each of the six farms is marked with different colours, showing to the distribution of the land around the village. Note how small the patches of the land are, and how widely dispersed each farm is. Given the complexity of the rural landholding structure before the reform, it is not surprising that it often led to conflicts among farmers and affected rural communities, especially when individual farmers moved out from the village closer to their newly formed fields. But is should also be noted that the reform brought an extensive expansion of agricultural land and the incorporation of previously unused land. The reform was particularly successful in the fertile plains of southern Sweden, while in the regions where more diverse soil productivity patterns, as it was in the north, it stalled. Today's rural landscape in Sweden, with individual farms sited separately from the village in the landscape, is very much a consequence of the 18th Century land reforms. Source: Friden-Fröjered-Korsberga hembygdsförening.

http://ffk-hembygd.se/A/Orleka/Studisirklar/LagaSkifte1850/Efter%20och%20foer%20skiftrena.htm#F%C3%B6re_1779_

structures in different scales for primary production, ecosystem services and recreation. This community has also developed a high diversity of small enterprises in the area. Photo: Courtesy of Varis Bokalders.

Figure 11.9. Pfaffenhofen experimental area 45 km north of München is planned as an eco-settlement with sustainable residential areas, farms, recycling units and recreational areas. The plans are to be net producers of electricity and soil – produced from waste water sludge, compost waste and charcoal. Illustration: Rolf Messerschmidt at Eble Architects in Tübingen.

Figure 11.10. Houten bicycle town. This little suburb to Utrecht has been optimized for bicycles, which has lead to that 80% of all (person-kilometer) internal mobility is with bikes and the cars are lead around the community. A remarkable feature of the little town is its nuanced soundscape, few accidents and a high air quality. Photo: Varis Bokalders.

Figure 11.11. The seminar park in Uppsala. This park with its seminar buildings is the only remaining complete seminar environment in Sweden. It is a strategic and exclusive area for developing a district park from a mature park structure including pedagogic gardening, ecosystems services for north-West Uppsala and recreation for its inhabitants. Still the Conservative party and the Social democrats are determined to exploit the area for new apartment buildings. Illustration of a city park: Tim Andreaheim Landscape Architect student, 3rd year.

Figure 11.12. Farmers market in Katarina Bangata in Stockholm. Stockholm greater region farmers directly meet with the city consumers, representing a small-scale food market. Resilient cityland markets will also be medium-scale markets in the boundary zone between town and country and large-scale regional and global markets. From an illustration to a EU-financed SLU report (2006) about local food production by Hans Månsson, Bild & Mening

Figure 11.13. Cultivation in the new fringe zone. In many suburban areas in Baltic Sea region Cities there is a direct contact with forests, fields and water and yet there is very little attempts to make use of the production values and other values related to urban farming. In this example large green areas have been transformed into productive land.

Figure 12.1. Containership. Photo: Niklas Liljegren. Courtesy of Sjöfartsverket. http://www.sjofartsverket.se.

Figure 12.2. Discovering the waterscape by paddling a canoe along the small Ljustorp river in northern Sweden. Photo: Leonard Broman. Source: http://www.flickr.com/photos/leendeleo/3690808501

Figure 12.3. Since the beginning of the 19th century about 3 million hectares of wetland has disappeared in Sweden mainly because of drainage to create farmland. In recent years however some wetlands have been recreated such as this one in Dalarna, Southern Sweden. The photos show Ansta before (left) and after restauration (right). Photo: Peter Sennblad(left) and Kajsa Andersson (right). Courtesy of Länsstyrelsen in Dalarna.

Figure 13.1. A planted forest in mid-Poland. plantation of forest monoculture have been a state priority since the 18th century. Today for example only 10% of forests in Sweden are so-called natural. Photo: Krzysztof Ciesielski.

Figure 13.2. The forestry carbon cycle. Source: http://www.bcclimatechange.ca/media/documents/Sustainable-Forestry-Carbon-Cycle.pdf

Figure 13.3. Forest area as % of total land area. Source: FAO, 2005; Appendix 3, Table 3.

Figure 14.1. Spruce forest. Photo: M. Gerentz. Source: Swedish University of Agricultural Sciences.

Figure 14.2. Planting of tree seedlings on clear-felled area. Photo: M. Gerentz. Source: Swedish University of Agricultural Sciences.

Figure 14.3. Land cover in the Baltic Sea region. Source: GRID/Arendal. http://www.grida.no/baltic/htmls/maps.htm

Figure 14.4. Decidious forest in Poland. Photo: Lars Rydén.

Figure 15.1. Graph showing the annual harvest of wood in the Komi Republic in the Russian Federation during the past 100 years. Source: Compilation of official forest statistics in the Komi Republic.

Figure 15.2. Naturally dynamic pine forest in a remote area of the Murmansk Region in north-west Russia (2007). Photo: Marine Elbakidze.

Figure 15.3. The area of main tree species in the Kovdozersky state forest management unit in the Murmansk region of north-west Russia Source: Archives of the Kovdozersky leshoz. Zelenoborskyy, Murmansk oblast.

Figure 15.4. The Carpathian Mountains in the Western Ukraine are one of the most forested regions. Photo: Marine Elbakidze.

Figure 15.5. Productive beech forests (Fagus silvatica) remain in the Ukrainian Carpathians. The height of these beech trees is more than 45 metres. Photo by Marine Elbakidze.

Figure 15.6. Bark-beetles (Ips spp.) are one of the main 'destroyers' of introduced Norway spruce forests in the Ukrainian Carpathians. Tracks of bark-beetle larvae in the bark of Norway spruce. Photo by Marine Elbakidze.

Figure 15.7. Logging operations on steep slopes without any ecological considerations are still being conducted in the Ukrainian Carpathians. Photo: Marine Elbakidze.

Figure 15.8. The traditional village system found in Europe's forest and woodland landscapes is characterised by a centre-periphery zoning from houses, gardens, fields, mowed and grazed grasslands to forests (i.e. the ancient system with domus, hortus, ager, saltus and silva). This view of the village Volosyanka in the Skole district of Ukraine's west Carpathian Mountains illustrates this. Beginning in the left part of the picture, the church in the very village centre is surrounded by houses that are located in the bottom of the shallow valley. The private gardens have many fruit trees and shrubs. Further to the right there is a fine-grained mixture of grasslands, some individual fields of which has been mowed and have hay-stacks and some not yet, and fields, like the potato field in the foreground. To the right there is forest, which is grazed by cattle moving in and out along specially designed fenced trails from the farm houses in the valley bottom. In addition, above the tree line on the top of the mountains, there are open grazed pasture commons. Photo: Per Angelstam.

Figurte 16.1. Energy independence growing on a regional level in Austria. The map depict regions indepenent of electricity, heat and/or transportation (red), regions with growing energy independence (yellow) and regions with high energy efficiency standards (green). Source: http://blogs.worldwatch.org/the-model-region-of-gussing-

%E2%80%93-an-example-of-the-austrian-grassroots-strategy-for-energy-independence/

Figure 16.2 Streaming water electricity. Electric energy may be extracted from the rural landscape in many ways. To the established hydropower, wind power, and solar electricity we may add this new method of generating electricity from streaming water. The technology is similar to the one used in wind power. A main difference is that water has a density 800 times larger than that of air. The energy density of a water stream of 1 m/sec thus corresponds to the energy density in air at 9 m/sec. Streaming water electricity is predicted to be mostly useable for ocean currents at coasts, but it can also be used in rivers. An advantage is that it does not require any large constructions, such as water reservoirs, and it is not visible from the outside making it much less provoking in the landscape. Streaming water electricity is studied at Uppsala University to develop new ways of renewable energy production. Illustration by Karin Thomas.

Figure 16.3. Solar plant farm in Sala Heby, Southern Sweden. Photo: Heby Municipality. Sala Heby Energy AB, SHE.

Figure 16.4. Biogas-production on the farm. This pig farm in mid Sweden, with an average occupancy of 3,000 pigs, use all manure for biogas production. The gas is used in a combined heat and power equipment, which provides all electricity and heat needed for the farm and a surplus sold to the electricity grid. To the right the anaerobic digester, also called fermentation tank. Photo: Lars Rydén.

Figure 16.5. Rapeseed field near Eslöv in Southern Sweden. The fatty acids from the oil in rapeseeds can be used for bio-diesel after methylation. Photo: Håkan Dahlström. http://www.flickr.com/photos/dahlstroms/4672519202/

Figure 16.6. Bio-dieselbus in Cambridge, UK. Photo: Hamster. Source: http://www.flickr.com/photos/33672038@N05/5481890327/

Figure 17.1. Willow plant plantation near the combined heating power station in Enköping, Sweden. The plantation is fertilized with affluents from the nearby waste water treatment plant and produces 10% of the input of biomass to the power station. Photo: Lars Rydén.

Figure 17.2. Willow plants on site (2), with a low degree of peat decomposition and peat depth > 50 cm. Four month after willow plantation". August 2010

Figure 17.3. Willow plants on site (1), with a high degree of peat decomposition and peat depth > 50 cm Four month after willow plantation". August 2010

Figure 18.1. In Latgale, the most eastern part of Latvia, several local authorities have formed Latgale Planning region as an established legal entity for cooperation in spatial planning. Latgale Planning Region is a derived public person established in accordance with the Regional Development Law on June 2006 under the supervision of the Ministry of Regional Development and Local Governments. Its activity has been financed from the state principal budget. (http://www.latgale.lv/en/padome). Latgale is not so modernised as the western part of Latvia and has a beautiful landscape and rich wildlife. http://www.flickr.com/photos/45360423@N05/5807670576 Photo: Päwels Cacivkins

Private photo and very similar to another photo perhaps we should take another one

Figure 18.2. Gaming as way to do planning. In 2009 a group of farmers and other stakeholders in western Poland took part in a game organised by teachers and students of AGH University in Krakow as an innovative way to evaluate different way to develop the watershed. Photo: Piotr Magnuszewski.

Figure 18.3. The small town Reszel in north-eastern Poland illustrate how urban and rural space is integrated and contribute to each other for the benefit of both.. Photo: Johan Anglemark. Source: http://www.flickr.com/photos/jophan/2856699968/

Figure 18.4. Planned route (red) of Via Baltica with alternative and later realised route (grey) through Rospuda valley.

Figure 18.5. View of Rospuda river valley. Photo: Mariusz Chilmon. Source: http://www.flickr.com/photos/vmario/388964824

Figure 18.6. A vision for Gotland. Gotland, the largest island in the Baltic Sea, published its vision for a sustainable society for 2025. The Vision covers a number of areas as illustrated on the cover of the 28 pages document (http://www.gotland.se/imcms/38064).

Figure 18.7. Alan AtKisson discussing sustainability indicators at a workshop on management of sustainable development using the pyramid model. Photo: Krysztof Cielinski.

Figure 18.8. The MUE25 cycle is a variant of the classical Deming cycle (Plan-Do-Check-Act) It was used in the Managing Urban Europe project (MUE25) for Sustainable Urban Development. The model is equally useful for managing sustainble rural development.

Figure 19.1. The Plokštine missile base is located near lake Plateliai, in the centre of Žemaitija National Park It was built in 1962 and housed R-12U intermediate range ballistic missiles, tipped with 2 megaton nuclear warheads. The base was closed in 1978 as the Americans had learnt of the location of the base through satellite photography and the place was looted and vandalised by the local population. After the collapse of the USSR the base was turned over to the national park administration who have made it an 'Exposition of Militarism' and run guided tours on request. Photo: Andrius Vangas. Source: http://www.flickr.com/photos/banditaz/215343308/

Figure 19.2. View of the small village Medingenai, in western Lithuania in 2005. Photo: Patrick Wilken/ www.radiant-flux.net

Figure 20.1. Vistula river in Poland, north of Warsaw illustrating the tight contact between the rural landscape and water. Photo: Sebastian Kruk. http://www.flickr.com/photos/skruk/3713862867

Figure 20.2. Fertilising fields with manure very often leads to excesss nutrients reaching surface water and groundwater with run-off from fields causing eutrophication, the most serious environmental problem in the whole Baltic Sea region. Photo: Karolina Kabat. Source: http://www.flickr.com/photos/barteko/5619493817

Figure 21.1. Example of an information iceberg: hierarchy of information and indication levels (according to Jesinghaus, xx)

Figure 21.2. Basic framework scheme of the PSR indication model.

Figure 21.3. Basic framework scheme of the DPSIR indication model.

Figure 21.4. Soil organic matter quality (a radar diagram). Conventional tillage for maize-soybean systems = solid line; no-till for maize-soybean = hatched; undisturbed or minimally disturbed grass-covered areas = light dashed area that is the benchmark for local region.

Figure 21.5. Two pathways of biodiversity indication. A. Habitat conditions indicate which species can occur there. B. Occurrence of a certain species in a habitat indicates the character or soil-climate conditions and intensity or frequency of the environment degradation (e.g. unwanted neophytes indicate potential environmental and/or economic losses in the system) (Fehér and Končeková, 2005).
Figure 21.6. Statistical restriction of expansive weeds occurring in synanthropic communities and invasive plant species preferring natural and semi-natural communities in the Žitný Ostrov Region (Slovakia) by canonical correspondence analysis according to the bond with a certain type of preferred habitat (Fehér and Končeková, 2005). Abbreviation of species: Abth – Abutilon theophrasti, Amar – Ambrosia artemisiifolia, Ampo – Amaranthus powelli, Aran – Artemisia annua, Asla – Aster lanceolatus, Asno – Aster novi-belgii, Bifr – Bidens frondosa, Caru – Cannabis ruderalis, Erca – Conyza canadensis, Faja/Fabo – Fallopia japonica and F. x bohemica (evaluated together), Hean – Helianthus annus, Imgl/Impa – Impatiens glandulifera and I. parviflora (same position), Ivxa – Iva xanthiifolia, Lyba – Lycium barbarum, Pami – Panicum miliaceum and other invasive Panicum species, Rupa – Rumex patientia, Soca – Solidago canadensis, Sogi – S. gigantea, Soha – Sorghum halepense, Stan – Stenactis annua.
Figure 22.1. A model for studying political life (Easton, 1967).
Figure 22.2. The World Justice Project (WJP) 2011 Index reports from 66 countries in the world, including several in the BSR, using nine dimensions of the Rule of Law, monitored by more than 50 different parameters. Here 9 parameters used to measure Accountable Government in Estonia are shown as an example. 1.0 means fully implemented and 0 absence. Estonia's values are 0.73 to 0.84, makes it the best country in its group of 12 in CEE and Central Asia. The corruption value is 0.86 making Estonia the most successful of the former Soviet Republics to reduce corruption. Source: http://worldjusticeproject.org/sites/default/files/WJP_Rule_of_Law_Index_2011_Report.pdf

Figure 23.1. Old combine harvester on the Lubartow Plateau, to the north of Lublin in Poland. Photo: Trevor Butcher. Source: http://www.flickr.com/photos/27888428@N00/2759013779/
Figure 23.2. Countryside fields near the village of Barniewice in northern Poland. Photo: Andrzej Otrebski. Source: http://www.flickr.com/photos/iks_berto/1343276418/

Figure 24.1. Composition of agricultural lands.
Figure 24.2. Basic duties of land users.
Figure 24.3. Land planning.
Figure 24.4. Basic provisions of the State Land Cadastre.
Figure 24.5. Methods of paying for land.

Figure 25.1. Distribution of pollution reduction costs between two enterprises by means of taxation and tradeable pollution permits.
Figure 25.2. Fishing activity and sustainable yield with and without government regulation.

Figure 26.1. Motorisation rate (private car ownership per 1,000 inhabitants) (data for 1995, 2004 and 2009). Source: Eurostat, 2012a (http://epp.eurostat.ec.europa.eu/tgm/table.do?tab=table&init=1&plugin=1&language=en&pcode=tsdpc340).
Figure 26.2. Greenhouse gas emissions and targets set by the Kyoto protocol. For US and Japan 2009-figures are from 2008. Source: Eurostat, 2012b. (http://epp.eurostat.ec.europa.eu/tgm/refreshTableAction.do?tab=table&plugin=1&pcode=tsdcc100&language=en)
Figure 26.3. Final consumption per capita in USD adjusted by purchasing power parities*, year 2010. Data from UNECE, 2012. (http://w3.unece.org/pxweb/quickstatistics/readtable.asp?qs_id=5)
Figure 26.4. Factors affecting individual choice.
Figure 26.5. Main geographical areas of different religious confessions Source: Eupedia.

List of Authors

Name of author	Position/Title	University/Affiliation	Email address
Hans Aage	Professor,	Roskilde University, Denmark	hansaa@ruc.dk
Per Angelstam	Professor	Swedish University of Agricultural Sciences, Skinnskatteberg, Sweden	per.angelstam@slu.se
Per G. Berg	Professor	Swedish University of Agricultural Sciences, Uppsala, Sweden	per.berg@slu.se
Marine Elbakidze	Professor	Ivan Franko National University, Lviv, Ukraine Swedish University of Agricultural Sciences, Skinnskatteberg, Sweden	Marine.Elbakidze@slu.se
Alexander Feher	Associate Professor	Slovak University of Agriculture, Nitra, Slovakia	alexander.feher@uniag.sk
Karin Hilmer Pedersen	Professor	Aahus University, Denmark	khp@ps.au.dk
Motaher Hossain	Associate Professor	University of Helsinki, Finland Jahangirnagar University, Dhaka, Bangladesh	motaher.hossain@helsinki.fi
Arvo Iital	Associate Professor	Tallinn University of Technology, Tallinn, Estonia	arvo.iital@ttu.ee
Jonas Jasaitis	Associate Professor	Siauliai University, Lithuania	kptc@smf.su.lt
Agnieszka Karczmarczyk	PhD	Agricultural University, Poland	agnieszka_karczmarczyk@sggw.pl
Ingrid Karlsson	PhD, Project leader	Uddevalla municipality, Sweden	ingrid.karlsson@uddevalla.se
Eugene Krasnov	Professor	Immanuel Kant Baltic Federal University, Kaliningrad, Russia	ecogeography@rambler.ru
Elena Kropinova	Associate Professor	Immanuel Kant Baltic Federal University, Kaliningrad, Russia	kropinova@mail.ru
Gregory McIsaac	Associate Professor	University of Illinois at Urbana-Champaign, USA	gmcisaac@illinois.edu>
Diana Mincyte	Associate Professor	University of Illinois, USA and Vytautas Magnus University, Kaunas, Lithuania	mincyte@uiuc.edu
Marja Molchanova		Immanuel Kant Baltic Federal University, Kaliningrad, Russia	
Józef Mosiej	Professor	Warsaw University of Life Sciences, Poland	jozef_mosiej@sggw.pl
Motaher Hussain	Associate Professor	University of Helsinki, Finland Jahangirnagar University, Dhaka, Bangladesh	motaher.hossain@helsinki.fi
Kristina L. Nilsson	Professor	Luleå University of Technology	kristina.l.nilsson@ltu.se
Aleh Rodzkin	Professor	International Sakharov Environmental University, Minsk, Belarus	aleh.rodzkin@rambler.ru
Lars Rydén	Professor Emeritus	Uppsala University, Sweden	lars.ryden@csduppsala.uu.se
Kalev Sepp	Professor	Estonian University of Life Sciences, Tartu, Estonia	kalev.sepp@emu.ee
Marina Thorborg	Professor	Södertörn University, Huddinge, Sweden	marina.thorborg@sh.se
Valery Tikhomirov		Belarusian State University, Minsk, Belarus	
Michelle Wander	Professor	University of Illinois, USA	mwander@uiuc.edu
Katarzyna Wyporska	PhD	Agricultural University, Poland	wyporska@yahoo.com
Isa Zeinalov		Immanuel Kant Baltic Federal University, Kaliningrad, Russia	
Valentin Yatsukhno		Belarusian State University, Minsk, Belarus	yatsukhno@bsu.by